THE
ENTREPRENEURIAL
VENTURE

The Practice of Management Series
HARVARD BUSINESS SCHOOL PRESS

The Craft of General Management
Readings selected by Joseph L. Bower

Managing People and Organizations
Readings selected by John J. Garbarro

Strategic Marketing Management
Readings selected by Robert J. Dolan

The Entrepreneurial Venture, Second Edition
Readings selected by William A. Sahlman, Howard H. Stevenson,
Michael J. Roberts, and Amar Bhidé

THE ENTREPRENEURIAL VENTURE

SECOND EDITION

READINGS SELECTED BY

William A. Sahlman,
Howard H. Stevenson,
Michael J. Roberts, and
Amar Bhidé

Harvard Business School Press

HARVARD BUSINESS SCHOOL PRESS
Boston, Massachusetts

Printed in the United States of America

03 02   5 4

Library of Congress Cataloging-in-Publication Data

The entrepreneurial venture : readings selected / by William A. Sahlman . . . [et al.]. — 2nd ed.
    p. cm. — (The practice of management series)
  Includes bibliographical references and index.
  ISBN 0-87584-892-3 (alk. paper)
  1. New business enterprises. 2. Entrepreneurship. I. Sahlman, William Andrews. II. Series.
  HD62.5 .E56 1999
  658.4'21—ddc21   98-56545
                                              CIP

The paper used in this publication meets the requirements of the American National Standard for Permanence of Paper for Printed Library Materials Z39.49-1984

ABOUT THE EDITORS

WILLIAM A. SAHLMAN is the Dimiti V. D'Arbeloff–Class of 1955 Professor of Business Administration at Harvard Business School. His research focuses on the investment and financing decisions made in entrepreneurial ventures at all stages of their development. Related lines of research concern the role of financial institutions in providing risk capital and the role of government policy in influencing capital formation in the entrepreneurial sector of the economy. Mr. Sahlman is the Senior Associate Dean, Director of Publishing Activities at Harvard Business School. He serves as chairman of the board for Harvard Business School Publishing Corporation, which is responsible for all external publishing activities, including *Harvard Business Review,* case studies, Management Productions, Harvard Business School Press, and interactive media. He is also a member of the board of directors of several private companies.

HOWARD H. STEVENSON is the Sarofim-Rock Professor of Business Administration at Harvard Business School. He serves as doctoral program coordinator in General Management. He is also faculty chair of the Owner/President Management Program in the Executive Education program and the chair of the Publications Review Board for Harvard Business School Press. Mr. Stevenson has authored, edited, or coauthored five books—including *Do Lunch or Be Lunch: The Power of Predictability in Creating Your Future* (HBS Press, 1997)—and 41 articles that have appeared in *Harvard Business Review, Sloan Management Review, Strategic Management Journal,* and elsewhere. He has also authored, coauthored, or supervised more than 150 cases. Currently he is a director of Bessemer Securities Corporation, Camp Dresser & McKee Inc., Landmark Communications, Sheffield Steel, Gulf States Steel, and The Baupost Group, Inc., as well as a trustee for several private trusts and foundations.

MICHAEL J. ROBERTS is the executive director of entrepreneurial studies and a lecturer at Harvard Business School, where he teaches the Entrepreneurial Management course and developed and taught the Managing the Growing Enterprise course. Mr. Roberts is responsible for helping to coordinate research and course-development efforts around entrepreneurial studies for the MBA and Executive Education programs. He is also the coordinator of activities at the new HBS California Research Center. Mr. Roberts is the author of more than 70 case studies on starting and managing entrepreneurial companies and, with Howard H. Stevenson and H. Irving Grousbeck, a coauthor of *New Business Ventures and the Entrepreneur.*

AMAR V. BHIDÉ, an associate professor at Harvard Business School, is currently a visiting faculty member at the University of Chicago. A former senior engagement manager at McKinsey & Company, vice president at E.F. Hutton, and associate fellow at Harvard Business School, Bhidé served on the staff of the Brady Commission, which investigated the stock market crash of 1987. Bhidé has published several articles on entrepreneurship, strategy, contracting, and firm governance that have appeared in the *Harvard Business Review, Wall Street Journal, New York Times,* and *L.A. Times.* His book *The Origin and Evolution of New Business* is scheduled for publication by Oxford University Press in November 1999.

CONTENTS

Introduction   1

William A. Sahlman, Howard H. Stevenson, Michael J. Roberts, and Amar Bhidé

PART ONE
ENTREPRENEURSHIP—WHAT IS IT?

1   **A Perspective on Entrepreneurship**   7

Howard H. Stevenson

2   **Entrepreneurship Reconsidered: The Team as Hero**   23

Robert B. Reich

3   **Capital Market Myopia**   35

William A. Sahlman and Howard H. Stevenson

4   **The Questions Every Entrepreneur Must Answer**   65

Amar Bhidé

5   **Why Be Honest If Honesty Doesn't Pay**   80

Amar Bhidé and Howard H. Stevenson

6   The Road Well Traveled   94
    Amar Bhidé

7   Making Business Sense of the Internet   101
    Shikhar Ghosh

PART TWO
STRATEGIES AND TACTICS FOR STARTING, ACQUIRING, AND GROWING
    THE VENTURE

SECTION A
EVALUATING NEW VENTURE OPPORTUNITIES

8   Developing Start-up Strategies   121
    Amar Bhidé

9   Some Thoughts on Business Plans   138
    William A. Sahlman

10 How to Write a Winning Business Plan   177
    Stanley R. Rich and David E. Gumpert

11 Purchasing a Business: The Search Process   189
    Michael J. Roberts and Ennis J. Walton

SECTION B
MARSHALING REQUIRED RESOURCES

12 Attracting Stakeholders   211
    Amar Bhidé and Howard H. Stevenson

13 Bootstrap Finance: The Art of Start-ups   223
    Amar Bhidé

14 The Financial Perspective: What Should Entrepreneurs Know?   238
    William A. Sahlman

CONTENTS

PART THREE
INNOVATION AND ENTREPRENEURSHIP IN THE LARGER COMPANY

27 **Tough-Minded Ways to Get Innovative**   481
    Andrall E. Pearson

28 **Discovery-Driven Planning**   493
    Rita Gunther McGrath and Ian C. MacMillan

29 **Disruptive Technologies: Catching the Wave**   506
    Joseph L. Bower and Clayton M. Christensen

30 **Managing for Creativity**   521
    Teresa M. Amabile

31 **The Business of Innovation: An Interview with Paul Cook** 537
    William Taylor

PART FOUR
ENTREPRENEURSHIP IN THE NONPROFIT SECTOR

32 **Virtuous Capital: What Foundations Can Learn from Venture 555
    Capitalists**
    Christine W. Letts, William Ryan, and Allen Grossman

33 **Starting a Nonprofit Venture**   566
    Alice Oberfield and J. Gregory Dees

34 **Surviving Success: An Interview with the Nature   580
    Conservancy's John Sawhill**
    Alice Howard and Joan Magretta

    Index   595

15   **Venture Capital**
      Constance Bagley and Craig Dauchy

16   **Aspects of Financial Contracting in Venture Capital**
      William A. Sahlman

17   **The Legal Protection of Intellectual Property**
      Michael J. Roberts

18   **The Horse Race Between Capital and Opportunity**   33.
      William A. Sahlman

19   **Strategy vs. Tactics from a Venture Capitalist**   351
      Arthur Rock

SECTION C
MANAGING THE GROWING ENTERPRISE

20   **The Challenge of Growth**   361
      Michael J. Roberts

21   **Managing Transitions in the Growing Enterprise**   377
      Michael J. Roberts

22   **Building the Self-Sustaining Firm**   392
      Amar Bhidé

23   **Going Public**   404
      Constance Bagley and Craig Dauchy

24   **Why Sane People Shouldn't Serve on Public Boards**   441
      William A. Sahlman

25   **How Small Companies Should Handle Advisers**   450
      Howard H. Stevenson and William A. Sahlman

26   **Bankruptcy: A Debtor's Perspective**   459
      Howard H. Stevenson and Michael J. Roberts

INTRODUCTION

Entrepreneurship is a management style that involves pursuing opportunity without regard to the resources currently controlled. Entrepreneurs identify opportunity, assemble required resources, implement a practical action plan, and harvest the rewards in a timely, flexible way. In the rapidly shifting and highly uncertain environment of the late 1990s, thinking entrepreneurially is an essential part of any manager's role.

There was a time when entrepreneurship was seen not as an end in itself, but as a stage that organizations passed through on the way to professional management. This view has changed. Entrepreneurial activity has flourished in unexpected ways, often generating more efficient and effective new technologies and more competitive products than large, traditionally managed corporations. By any measure, the rate of business start-up has soared. During the past 35 years, the number of new businesses created annually in the United States has risen from 93,000 to more than 1,000,000. The surge of interest in entrepreneurship in the past decade—from new publications to university courses to new venture programs in some of our largest, most well known corporations—testifies to the critical role that entrepreneurship now plays and is expected to play in shaping and strengthening our economy.

This collection of readings is designed to serve as a handbook that offers friendly advice for those considering or engaging in the entrepreneurial process. It contains different voices, different perspectives, different insights, and sometimes even contradictory advice—a variety that captures the reality of entrepreneurship.

Advice inevitably reflects the training, experience, and biases of the person giving it. While taking advice literally is almost always dangerous, so too is assuming that your opportunity, situation, and concerns are unique. Too often the entrepreneur wastes energy, time, and resources by failing to learn inexpensive lessons provided by the experiences of other people. Tuition in the school of hard knocks is costly, especially to entrepreneurs.

These readings explore common problems and opportunities found in entrepreneurship. They come from a variety of sources and serve a variety of purposes. Some are intended to inspire; others provide technical information; still others are designed to help the reader master important skills. As you consider the various perspectives offered, ask yourself how the logic applies to you and your current or prospective business.

Each reading can stand alone or be studied as part of a thematic unit. Taken together, the readings demonstrate that the entrepreneur is the ultimate general manager, responsible for orchestrating relationships among all parts of the enterprise. They underscore the versatility that entrepreneurs must cultivate to make their ventures succeed. They will also help you determine the key questions to ask as you plan and build each stage of your venture, suggest milestones by which you can measure your progress, and warn of the traps that have ensnared earlier explorers of the territory. The variety of readings offered here will also help you think about a new business venture from the perspective of its many stakeholders—the entrepreneur, the investors, the managers and employees, the suppliers, and the customers.

This collection can be used as both a travel guide and a reference source. Part One, "Entrepreneurship—What Is It?" can help you think about the concept of being an entrepreneur. The term itself was coined in the eighteenth century by economist Richard Cantillion, who believed that the primary role of the entrepreneur was to bear risk. Since then, the definition has evolved in different and occasionally contradictory ways. Some people have focused on risk seeking and risk bearing, while others, notably economist Joseph Schumpeter in the early part of this century, have associated entrepreneurship with innovation. More recently, psychological profiles detailing the entrepreneur's distinctive character traits have been developed. The popular press often portrays the entrepreneur as a high-tech genius or a flamboyant promoter.

The readings in this book ask you to challenge the stereotypes, to consider entrepreneurship as a *way* of managing rather than as an economic function or a set of personal characteristics. Indeed, as the numerous examples in this book—as well as your own experience—will demonstrate, many entrepreneurs break the mold. Some, for example, bear risk grudgingly. (As a highly successful entrepreneur once put it, "My idea of risk and reward is for me to get the reward and others to take the risk.") Others owe their success not to having a creative gift but to extending ideas originated by others or to finding better ways to deliver products and services to customers. The first reading in the book, Howard Stevenson's "A Perspective on Entrepreneurship," introduces and illuminates this concept by contrasting entrepreneurial behavior with administrative behavior. The selections that follow, including

Robert Reich's "Entrepreneurship Reconsidered: The Team as Hero," develop the concept of entrepreneurship further by depicting different entrepreneurial management styles in a range of settings.

In Part Two, "Strategies and Tactics for Starting, Acquiring, and Growing the Venture," the selected readings focus on each of the stages involved in taking a business from initial concept through to harvest. The first section in Part Two deals with techniques for evaluating new venture opportunities. Most ideas are just that—ideas, and not opportunities. This section describes how to develop start-up strategies and how to ensure that each opportunity is worth the investment of your time, money, and reputation. This section also focuses on the process of writing a business plan—not only as a means to explain ideas to others and enlist support, but as a vehicle for thinking through the complex array of issues involved in starting a new venture. Finally, this section also describes a process for purchasing an existing business as a route to an entrepreneurial career.

The second section in Part Two reviews the process of marshaling resources required to pursue an opportunity once it's been defined. One trick, of course, is minimizing the amount of capital needed; this is the subject of "Bootstrap Finance: The Art of Start-Ups." Other topics covered in this section include venture capital, intellectual property, and the process of attracting other stakeholders—like employees and customers—to the venture.

The final section in Part Two focuses on managing the growing enterprise. Topics covered include techniques for managing the challenges of growth and building the self-sustaining firm to going public and bankruptcy.

In Part Three, "Innovation and Entrepreneurship in the Larger Company," selected readings address the challenges of retaining an entrepreneurial spirit as size and scale make this more difficult. Authors address the tools and techniques that larger enterprises can use to remain creative, entrepreneurial, and on the cutting edge of technology.

Finally, Part Four examines "Entrepreneurship in the Nonprofit Sector." This sector of our economy is teeming with creative and motivated people who bring their own entrepreneurial passion to social issues and problems. In this section, readings address the topic of what foundations can learn from venture capitalists, as well as the challenges of starting a nonprofit venture.

The readings assembled here attempt to cover the spectrum of the entrepreneurial experience, from idea generation to harvest. Certain readings will be more relevant than others at any particular stage, but a notable recurring theme in this collection, however, is anticipation. Becoming an entrepreneur means that you are willing to accept the prospect of complexity, contradiction, and change. Indeed, successfully adapting to what you learn as you proceed is often more important than the specific qualities of the initial business concept.

By understanding and preparing for the realities that lie ahead, the entrepreneur can greet the future with enthusiasm. Perhaps the greatest challenge, once the entrepreneur has leaped the hurdles and mastered the important skills, is to continue to pursue opportunity rather than simply to consolidate past victories. We hope you will find excitement in the entrepreneurial challenge and in the lifelong learning that is required to achieve success in entrepreneurial management.

WILLIAM A. SAHLMAN
HOWARD H. STEVENSON
MICHAEL J. ROBERTS
AMAR BHIDÉ

PART ONE

ENTREPRENEURSHIP— WHAT IS IT?

A Perspective on Entrepreneurship 1

HOWARD H. STEVENSON

The term entrepreneurship *calls to mind so many varied images that a precise definition can be elusive. Popular views of the entrepreneur as do-it-yourself personality abound: the lone inventor working from a garage, the gourmet cook turning a home-based business into a restaurant, the experienced manager leaving the corporation to open a consulting practice. Such company founders are often protrayed as risk takers and mavericks. Politicians and editorial writers have seized on entrepreneurial spirit as the way to make companies—and the nation—more productive, innovative, and competitive. Looking to the entrepreneurial ideal, managers in companies large and small have responded by striving to foster creativity and flexibility in their organizations.*

In this reading, Stevenson seeks to interpret the concept by focusing on entrepreneurial thinking and behavior. Rejecting the notion that entrepreneurship is an all-or-nothing character trait of certain individuals or groups, the author looks specifically at how entrepreneurs capitalize on change, identify opportunity, and marshal resources. By highlighting the differences between the entrepreneur (the seeker of opportunity) and the administrator (the guardian of existing resources), the author develops an anatomy of entrepreneurship for both start-up and established companies.

——— INCREASING INTEREST IN ENTREPRENEURSHIP

It would be difficult to overstate the degree to which there has been an increase in the level of interest in entrepreneurship. A strong indicator of such interest is provided by the unprecedented rise in the rate of new business formation. The number of annual new business incorporations has doubled in the last ten years, from annual rates of about 300,000 to over 600,000.

These trends are mirrored in the capital markets that fund these start-ups. The decade 1975–1984 saw explosive growth in the amount of capital committed to venture capital firms in the United States. There was a

Professor Howard H. Stevenson prepared this case as the basis for class discussion. Copyright © 1983 by the President and Fellows of Harvard College. Harvard Business School case 384-131.

concurrent dramatic increase in the amount of money raised in the public capital markets by young companies.

In addition to interest on the part of individuals who wish to become entrepreneurs and investors who wish to back them, there has been a wave of interest in what some refer to as "Intrepreneurship," or entrepreneurship in the context of the larger corporation. In addition to the wealth of books and articles on the subject, some large firms seem to have recognized their shortcomings on certain critical dimensions of performance, and have structured themselves in an attempt to be more innovative.

Indeed, we believe that the strengthening of entrepreneurship is a critically important goal of American society. The first thirty years of the postwar period in the United States were characterized by an abundance of opportunity, brought about by expanding markets, high investment in the national infrastructure, mushrooming debt. In this environment, it was relatively easy to achieve business success, but this is no longer true. Access to international resources is not as easy as it once was; government regulation has brought a recognition of the full costs of doing business, many of which had previously been hidden; competition from overseas has put an end to American dominance in numerous industries; technological change has reduced product life in other industries; and so forth. In short, a successful firm is one that is either capable of rapid response to changes that are beyond its control, or, is so innovative that it contributes to change in the environment. Entrepreneurship is an approach to management that offers these benefits.

——— DEFINING ENTREPRENEURSHIP

As we have discussed, there has been a striking increase in the level of attention paid to the subject of entrepreneurship. However, we've not yet defined what the term means.

As a starting point, it may be helpful to review some of the definitions scholars have historically applied to entrepreneurship. There are several schools of thought regarding entrepreneurship, which may roughly be divided into those that define the term as an economic function and those that identify entrepreneurship with individual traits.

The functional approach focuses upon the role of entrepreneurship within the economy. In the 18th century, for instance, Richard Cantillon argued that entrepreneurship entailed bearing the risk of buying at certain prices and selling at uncertain prices. Jean Baptiste Say broadened the definition to include the concept of bringing together the factors of production. Schumpeter's work in 1911 added the concept of innovation to the definition of entrepreneurship. He allowed for many kinds of innovation including process innovation, market innovation, product innovation, factor innovation, and even organizational innovation. His seminal work emphasized the role of the entrepreneur in creating and responding to economic discontinuities.

While some analysts have focused on the economic function of entrepreneurship, still others have turned their attention to research on the personal characteristics of entrepreneurs. Considerable effort has gone into understanding the psychological and sociological sources of entrepreneurship—as Kent refers to it, "supply-side entrepreneurship." These studies have noted some common characteristics among entrepreneurs with respect to need for achievement, perceived locus of control, and risk-taking propensity. In addition, many have commented upon the common—but not universal—thread of childhood deprivation and early adolescent experiences as typifying the entrepreneur. These studies—when taken as a whole—are inconclusive and often in conflict.

We believe, however, that neither of these approaches is sound. Consider, for example, the degree to which entrepreneurship is synonymous with "bearing risk," "innovation," or even founding a company. Each of these terms focuses upon *some* aspect of *some* entrepreneurs. But, if one has to be the founder to be an entrepreneur, then neither Thomas Watson of IBM nor Ray Kroc of McDonald's will qualify; yet, few would seriously argue that both these individuals were not entrepreneurs. And, while risk bearing is an important element of entrepreneurial behavior, it is clear that many entrepreneurs bear risk grudgingly and only after they have made valiant attempts to get the capital sources and resource providers to bear the risk. As one extremely successful entrepreneur said: "My idea of risk and reward is for me to get the reward and others to take the risks." With respect to the "supply side" school of entrepreneurship, many questions can be raised. At the heart of the matter is whether the psychological and social traits are either necessary or sufficient for the development of entrepreneurship.

Finally, the search for a single psychological profile of the entrepreneur is bound to fail. For each of the traditional definitions of the entrepreneurial type, there are numerous counter-examples that disprove the theory. We simply are not dealing with one kind of individual or behavior pattern, as even a cursory review of well-known entrepreneurs will demonstrate. Nor has the search for a psychological model proven useful in teaching or encouraging entrepreneurship.

ENTREPRENEURSHIP AS A BEHAVIORAL PHENOMENON

Thus, it does not seem useful to delimit the entrepreneur by defining those economic functions that are "entrepreneurial" and those that are not. Nor does it appear particularly helpful to describe the traits that seem to engender entrepreneurship in certain individuals. From our perspective, entrepreneurship is an approach to management that we define as follows: the pursuit of opportunity without regard to resources currently controlled.

This summary description of entrepreneurial behavior can be further refined by examining six critical dimensions of business practice. These six dimensions are the following: strategic orientation, the commitment to opportunity, the resource commitment process, the concept of control over resources, the concept of management, and compensation policy.

We shall define these dimensions by examining a range of behavior between two extremes. At one extreme is the *"promoter"* who feels confident of his or her ability to seize opportunity regardless of the resources under current control. At the opposite extreme is the *"trustee"* who emphasizes the efficient utilization of existing resources. While the promoter and trustee define the end points of this spectrum, there is a spectrum of managerial behavior that lies between these end-points, and we define (overlapping) portions of this spectrum as entrepreneurial and administrative behavior. Thus, entrepreneurial management is not an extreme example, but rather a range of behavior that consistently falls at the end of the spectrum.

The remainder of this chapter defines these key business dimensions in more detail, discusses how entrepreneurial differs from administrative behavior, and describes the factors that pull individuals and firms towards particular types of behavior.

STRATEGIC ORIENTATION

Strategic orientation is the business dimension that describes the factors that drive the firm's formulation of strategy. A promoter is truly opportunity-driven. His or her orientation is to say, "As I define a strategy, I am going to be driven only by my perception of the opportunities that exist in my environment, and I will not be constrained by the resources at hand." A trustee, on the other hand, is resource-driven and tends to say, "How do I utilize the resources that I control?"

Within these two poles, the administrator's approach recognizes the need to examine the environment for opportunities, but is still constrained by a trustee-like focus on resources: "I will prune my opportunity tree based on the resources I control. I will not try to leap very far beyond my current situation." An entrepreneurial orientation places the emphasis on opportunity: "I will search for opportunity, and my fundamental task is to acquire the resources to pursue that opportunity." These perspectives are represented on *Exhibit 1*.

It is this dimension that has led to one of the traditional definitions of the entrepreneur as opportunistic or—more favorably—creative and innovative. But the entrepreneur is not necessarily concerned with breaking new ground; opportunity can also be found in a new mix of old ideas or in the

EXHIBIT 1
Strategic Orientation

PROMOTER		TRUSTEE
Driven by perception of opportunity	*Entrepreneurial Domain* ←——————→ ←——————→ *Administrative Domain*	Driven by resources currently controlled

Pressures toward this side	*Pressures toward this side*

• Diminishing opportunity streams
• Rapidly changing:
  Technology
  Consumer economics
  Social values
  Political rules
	• Social contracts
	• Performance measurement criteria
	• Planning systems and cycles

creative application of traditional approaches. We do observe, however, that firms tend to look for opportunities where their resources are. Even those firms that start as entrepreneurial by recognizing opportunities often become resource-driven as more and more resources are acquired by the organization.

The pressures that pull a firm towards the entrepreneurial range of behavior include the following:

· Diminishing opportunity streams: old opportunity streams have been largely played out. It is no longer possible to succeed merely by adding new options to old products.
· Rapid changes in:
  · Technology: creates new opportunities at the same time it obsoletes old ones.
  · Consumer economics: changes both ability and willingness to pay for new products and services.
  · Social values: defines new styles and standards and standards of living.
  · Political roles: affects competition through deregulation, product safety and new standards.

Pressures which pull a firm to become more "administrative" than entrepreneurial include the following:

· The "social contract": the responsibility of managers to use and employ people, plant, technology and financial resources once they have been acquired.
· Performance criteria: how many executives are fired for not pursuing an opportunity, compared with the number that are punished for not meeting return on investment targets? Capacity

utilization and sales growth are the typical measures of business success.
- Planning systems and cycles: opportunities do not arrive at the start of a planning cycle and last for the duration of a three- or five-year plan.

COMMITMENT TO OPPORTUNITY

As we move on to the second dimension, it becomes clear that the definition of the entrepreneur as creative or innovative is not sufficient. There are innovative thinkers who never get anything done; it is necessary to move beyond the identification of opportunity to its pursuit.

The promoter is a person willing to act in a very short time frame and to chase an opportunity quickly. Promoters may be more or less effective, but they are able to engage in commitment in a rather revolutionary fashion. The duration of their commitment, not the ability to act, is all that is in doubt. Commitment for the trustee is time-consuming, and once made, of long duration. Trustees move so slowly that it sometimes appears they are stationary; once there, they seem frozen. This spectrum of behavior is shown on *Exhibit 2*.

It is the willingness to get in and out quickly that has led to the entrepreneur's reputation as a gambler. However, the simple act of taking a risk does not lead to success. More critical to the success of the entrepreneurs is knowledge of the territory they operate in. Because of familiarity with their chosen field, they have the ability to recognize patterns as they develop, and the confidence to assume the missing elements of the pattern will take shape as they foresee. This early recognition enables them to get a jump on others in commitment to action.

Pressures which pull a business towards this entrepreneurial end of the spectrum include:

- Action orientation: enables a firm to make first claim to customers, employees and financial resources.
- Short decision windows: due to the high costs of late entry, including lack of competitive costs and technology.
- Risk management: involves managing the firm's revenues in such a way that they can be rapidly committed to or withdrawn from new projects. As George Bernard Shaw put it, "Any fool can start a love affair, but it takes a genius to end one successfully."
- Limited decision constituencies: requires a smaller number of responsibilities and permits greater flexibility.

In contrast, administrative behavior is a function of other pressures:

- Multiple decision constituencies: a great number of responsibilities, necessitating a more complex, lengthier decision process.

EXHIBIT 2
Commitment to Opportunity

PROMOTER		TRUSTEE
Revolutionary with short duration	*Entrepreneurial Domain* ←——————→ ←——————→ *Administrative Domain*	Evolutionary of long duration

Pressures toward this side	Pressures toward this side
• Action orientation • Short decision windows • Risk management • Limited decision constituencies	• Acknowledgment of multiple constituencies • Negotiation of strategy • Risk reduction • Management of fit

- Negotiation of strategy: compromise in order to reach consensus and resultant evolutionary rather than revolutionary commitment.
- Risk reduction: study and analysis to reduce risk slows the decision-making process.
- Management of fit: to assure the continuity and participation of existing players, only those projects which "fit" existing corporate resources are acceptable.

COMMITMENT OF RESOURCES

Another characteristic we observe in good entrepreneurs is a multi-staged commitment of resources with a minimum commitment at each stage or decision point. The promoters, those wonderful people with blue shoes and diamond pinky rings on their left hands, say, "I don't need any resources to commence the pursuit of a given opportunity. I will bootstrap it." The trustee says, "Since my object is to use my resources, once I finally commit I will go in very heavily at the front end."

The issue for the entrepreneur is: what resources are necessary to pursue a given opportunity? There is a constant tension between the amount of resources committed and the potential return. The entrepreneur attempts to maximize value creation by minimizing the resource set, and must, of course, accept more risk in the process. On the other hand, the trustee side deals with this challenge by careful analysis and large-scale commitment of resources after the decision to act. Entrepreneurial management requires that you learn to do a little more with a little less. *Exhibit 3* addresses this concept.

On this dimension we have the traditional stereotype of the entrepreneur as tentative, uncommitted, or temporarily dedicated—an image of unreliability. In times of rapid change, however, this characteristic of stepped,

EXHIBIT 3
Commitment of Resources

PROMOTER		TRUSTEE
Multistaged with minimal exposure at each stage	*Entrepreneurial Domain* ⟷ ⟷ *Administrative Domain*	Single-staged with complete commitment upon decision

Pressures toward this side		*Pressures toward this side*
• Lack of predictable resource needs • Lack of long-term control • Social needs for more opportunity per resource unit • International pressure for more efficient resource use		• Personal risk reduction • Incentive compensation • Managerial turnover • Capital allocation systems • Formal planning systems

multistaged commitment of resources is a definite advantage in responding to changes in competition, the market, and technology.

The process of committing resources is pushed towards the entrepreneurial domain by several factors:

· Lack of predictable resource needs: forces the entrepreneurs to commit less up front so that more will be available later on, if required.

· Lack of long-term control: requires that commitment match exposure. If control over resources can be removed by environmental, political or technological forces, resource exposure should also be reduced.

· Social needs: multistaged commitment of resources brings us closer to the "small is beautiful" formulation of E. F. Shumacher, by allowing for the appropriate level of resource intensity for the task.

· International demands: pressures that we use no more than our "fair share" of the world's resources, e.g., not the 35% of the world's energy that the United States was using in the early 1970s.

The pressures within the large corporation, however, are in the other direction—towards resource intensity. This is due to:

· Personal risk reduction: any individual's risk is reduced by having excess resources available.

· Incentive compensation: excess resources increase short-term returns and minimize the period of cash and profit drains—typically the objects of incentive compensation systems.

· Managerial turnover: creates pressures for steady cash and profit gains, which encourages short-term, visible success.

· Capital allocation systems: generally designed for one-time decision making, these techniques assume that a single decision point is appropriate.

- Formal planning systems: once a project has begun, a request for additional resources returns the managers to the morass of analysis and bureaucratic delays; managers are inclined to avoid this by committing the maximum amount of resources up front.

CONTROL OF RESOURCES

When it comes to the control of resources, the promoter mentality says, "All I need from a resource is the ability to use it." These are the people who describe the ideal business as the post office box to which people send money. For them, all additional overhead is a compromise of a basic value. On the other hand, we all know companies that believe they do not adequately control a resource unless they own it or have it on their permanent payroll.

Entrepreneurs learn to use other people's resources well; they learn to decide, over time, what resources they need to bring in-house. They view this as a time-phased sequence of decisions. Good managers also learn that there are certain resources you should never own or employ. For instance, very few good real estate firms employ an architect. They may need the best, but they do not want to employ him or her, because the need for that resource, although critical to the success of the business, is temporary. The same is true of good lawyers. They are useful to have when you need them, but most firms cannot possibly afford to have the necessary depth of specialization of legal professionals constantly at their beck and call. *Exhibit 4* illustrates this dimension.

The stereotype of the entrepreneur as exploitative derives from this

EXHIBIT 4
Control of Resource

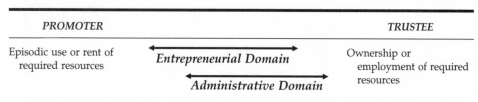

PROMOTER		TRUSTEE
Episodic use or rent of required resources	*Entrepreneurial Domain* / *Administrative Domain*	Ownership or employment of required resources

Pressures toward this side	*Pressures toward this side*
• Increased resource specialization	• Power, status, and financial rewards
• Long resource life compared to need	• Coordination
• Risk of obsolescence	• Efficiency measures
• Risk inherent in any new venture	• Inertia and cost of change
• Inflexibility of permanent commitment to resources	• Industry structures

dimension: the entrepreneur is adept at using the skills, talents, and ideas of others. Viewed positively, this ability has become increasingly valuable in the changed business environment; it need not be parasitic in the context of a mutually satisfying relationship. Pressures towards this entrepreneurial side come from:

- Increased resource specialization: an organization may have a need for a specialized resource like a VLSI design engineer, hi-tech patent attorney or state-of-the-art circuit test equipment, but only for a short time. By using, rather than owning, a firm reduces its risk and its fixed costs.
- Risk of obsolescence: reduced by merely using, rather than owning, an expensive resource.
- Increased flexibility: the cost of exercising the option to quit is reduced by using, not owning, a resource.

Administrative practices are the product of pressures in the other direction, such as:

- Power, status and financial rewards: determined by the extent of resource ownership and control in many corporations.
- Coordination: the speed of execution is increased because the executive has the right to request certain action without negotiation.
- Efficiency: enables the firm to capture, at least in the short run, all of the profits associated with an operation.
- Inertia and cost of change: it is commonly believed that it is good management to isolate the technical core of production from external shocks. This requires buffer inventories, control of raw materials, and control of distribution channels. Ownership also

EXHIBIT 5
Management Structure

PROMOTER		*TRUSTEE*
Flat with multiple informal networks	←→ *Entrepreneurial Domain* ←→ *Administrative Domain*	Formalized hierarchy

Pressures toward this side	*Pressures toward this side*
• Coordination of key noncontrolled resources • Challenge to legitimacy of owner's control • Employees' desire for independence	• Need for clearly defined authority and responsibility • Organizational culture • Reward systems • Management theory

creates familiarity and an identifiable chain of command, which become stabilized with time.
- Industry structures: encourage ownership to prevent being preempted by the competition.

MANAGEMENT STRUCTURE

The promoter wants knowledge of his/her progress via direct contact with all of the principal actors. The trustee views relationships more formally, with specific rights and responsibilities assigned through the delegation of authority. The decision to use and rent resources and not to own or employ them will require the development of an informal information network. Only in systems where the relationship with resources is based on ownership or employment can resources be organized in a hierarchy. Informal networks arise when the critical success elements cannot be contained within the bounds of the formal organization. *Exhibit 5* illustrates this range of behavior.

Many people have attempted to distinguish between the entrepreneur and the administrator by suggesting that being a good entrepreneur precludes being a good manager. The entrepreneur is stereotyped as egocentric and idiosyncratic and thus unable to manage. However, though the managerial task is substantially different for the entrepreneur, management skill is nonetheless essential. The variation lies in the choice of appropriate tools.

More entrepreneurial management is a function of several pressures:

- Need for coordination of key noncontrolled resources results in need to communicate with, motivate, control and plan for resources *outside* the firm.
- Flexibility: maximized with a flat and informal organization.
- Challenge to owner's control: classic questions about the rights of ownership as well as governmental environmental, health and safety restrictions, undermine the legitimacy of control.
- Employees' desire for independence: creates an environment where employees are unwilling to accept hierarchical authority in place of authority based on competence and persuasion.

On the other side of the spectrum, pressures push the firm towards more administrative behavior. These include:

- Need for clearly defined authority and responsibility: to perform the increasingly complex planning, organizing, coordinating, communicating and controlling required in a business.
- Organizational culture: which often demands that events be routinized.
- Reward systems: which encourage and reward breadth and span of control.

EXHIBIT 6
Reward Philosophy

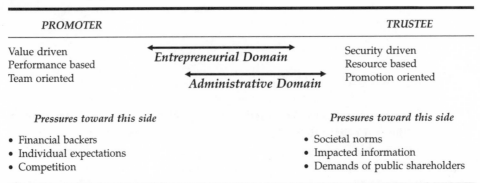

PROMOTER		*TRUSTEE*
Value driven	*Entrepreneurial Domain*	Security driven
Performance based		Resource based
Team oriented	*Administrative Domain*	Promotion oriented

Pressures toward this side	*Pressures toward this side*
• Financial backers	• Societal norms
• Individual expectations	• Impacted information
• Competition	• Demands of public shareholders

REWARD PHILOSOPHY

Finally, entrepreneurial firms differ from administratively managed organizations in their philosophy regarding reward and compensation. First, entrepreneurial firms are more explicitly focused on the creation and harvesting of value. In start-up situations, the financial backers of the organization—as well as the founders themselves—have invested cash, and want cash out. As a corollary of this value-driven philosophy, entrepreneurial firms tend to base compensation on performance (where performance is closely related to value creation). Entrepreneurial firms are also more comfortable rewarding teams.

As a recent spate of take-overs suggests, more administratively managed firms are less often focused on maximizing and distributing value. They are more often guided in their decision making by the desire to protect their own positions and security. Compensation is often based on individual responsibility (assets or resources under control) and on performance relative to short-term profit targets. Reward in such firms is often heavily oriented towards promotion to increasing responsibility levels. *Exhibit 6* describes this dimension.

The pressures that pull firms towards the promoter end of the spectrum include:

- Individual expectations: increasingly, individuals expect to be compensated in proportion to their contribution, rather than merely as a function of their performance relative to an arbitrary peer group. In addition, individuals seemingly have higher levels of aspiration for personal wealth.
- Investor demands: financial backers invest cash and expect cash back, and the sooner the better. Increasingly, shareholders in publicly held firms are starting to press with a similar orientation.
- Competition: increased people competition for talent creates pres-

sure for firms to reward these individuals in proportion to their contributions.

On the other side, a variety of pressures pull firms towards more trustee-like behavior:

- Societal norms: we still value loyalty to the organization, and find it difficult to openly discuss compensation.
- Impacted information: it is often difficult to judge the value of an individual's contributions, particularly within the frame of the annual compensation cycle performance review that most firms use.
- Demands of public shareholders: many public shareholders are simply uncomfortable with compensation that is absolutely high, even if it is in proportion to contribution.

─── SUMMARY

These characteristics have been gathered onto one summary chart (see *Exhibit 7*). In developing a behavioral theory of entrepreneurship, it becomes clear that entrepreneurship is defined by more than a set of individual traits and is different from an economic function. It is a cohesive pattern of managerial behavior.

This perspective on entrepreneurship highlights what we see as a false dichotomy: the distinction drawn between entrepreneurship and intrapreneurship. Entrepreneurship is an approach to management that can be applied in start-up situations as well as within more established businesses. As our definition suggests, the accumulation of resources that occurs as a firm grows is a powerful force that makes entrepreneurial behavior more difficult in a larger firm. But the fundamentals of the behavior required remain the same.

Still, our primary focus will be on the start-up. The situational factors that define a start-up situation do much to encourage entrepreneurship. As we look at the start-up process, however, it is worth keeping in mind that many of these lessons can be applied equally well in the large corporate setting.

─── DISCUSSION QUESTIONS

1. Do the behavioral dimensions of entrepreneurship described by the author capture what you believe to be the defining characteristics of entrepreneurship?
2. Are there situations when "administrative behavior" is more appropriate than "entrepreneurial behavior"?

EXHIBIT 7
A Perspective on Entrepreneurship Summary

PRESSURES TOWARD THIS SIDE	PROMOTER	KEY BUSINESS DIMENSION	TRUSTEE	PRESSURES TOWARD THIS SIDE
Diminishing opportunity streams Rapidly changing: Technology Consumer economics Social values	Driven by perception of opportunity	*Entrepreneurial Domain* ↔ *Administrative Domain* *STRATEGIC ORIENTATION*	Driven by resources currently controlled	Social contracts Performance measurement criteria Planning systems and cycles
Action orientation Short decision windows Risk management Limited decision constituencies	Revolutionary with short duration	*Entrepreneurial Domain* ↔ *Administrative Domain* *COMMITMENT TO OPPORTUNITY*	Evolutionary of long duration	Acknowledgment of multiple constituencies Negotiation of strategy Risk reduction Management of fit
Lack of predictable resource needs Lack of long-term control Social needs for more opportunity per resource unit Interpersonal pressure for more efficient resource use	Multistaged with minimal exposure at each stage	*Entrepreneurial Domain* ↔ *Administrative Domain* *COMMITMENT OF RESOURCES*	Single-staged with complete commitment upon decision	Personal risk reduction Incentive compensation Managerial turnover Capital allocation systems Formal planning systems

Pressures toward this side:

Increased resource specialization
Long resource life compared to need
Risk of obsolescence
Risk inherent in any new venture
Inflexibility of permanent commitment to resources

⟷ *Entrepreneurial Domain*
Administrative Domain
CONTROL OF RESOURCES

Episodic use or rent of required resources → Ownership or employment of required resources

Power, status, and financial rewards
Coordination
Efficiency measures
Inertia and cost of change
Industry structures

Coordination of key noncontrolled resources
Challenge to legitimacy of owner's control
Employees' desire for independence

⟷ *Entrepreneurial Domain*
Administrative Domain
MANAGEMENT STRUCTURE

Flat with multiple informal networks → Formalized hierarchy

Need for clearly defined authority and responsibility
Organizational culture
Reward systems
Management theory

Individual expectations
Competition
Increased perception of personal wealth creation possibilities

⟷ *Entrepreneurial Domain*
Administrative Domain
COMPENSATION/REWARD POLICY

Value based
Team based
Unlimited
→
Resource-based
Driven by short-term data
Promotion
Limited amount

Societal norms
IRS regulations
Impacted information
Search for simple solutions for complex problems
Demands of public shareholders

3. The author argues that entrepreneurship involves the pursuit of opportunity beyond resources currently controlled. How do large companies—with virtually unlimited resources—remain entrepreneurial?

Entrepreneurship Reconsidered: The Team as Hero

ROBERT B. REICH

In novel after novel, nineteenth-century author Horatio Alger celebrated the virtues of the lone entrepreneur—the plucky individual who relies on wits, energy, and daring to rise in the world. A century after Alger produced his bestsellers, Americans continue to admire the rugged individualist, the inspired maverick. Yet, argues Robert Reich, in a world of global competition, this model of entrepreneurship offers little hope for our economy. If America is to compete effectively and enjoy a rising standard of living, it must uphold a new and different ideal—companies that draw on the talents and creativity of employees at all levels of organization.

Emphasizing the power of images to shape our attitutdes and mobilize us to action, Reich contrasts individual and collective entrepreneurship and explains how new competitive realities require us to discard long-held values and aspirations. By delineating the features of entrepreneurial organization and using product histories to demonstrate the benefits of collaborative innovation, Reich sets forth an alternative ideal to guide the ways people work together to meet the challenge of global competition.

"Wake up there, youngster," said a rough voice.

Ragged Dick opened his eyes slowly and stared stupidly in the face of the speaker, but did not offer to get up.

"Wake up, you young vagabond!" said the man a little impatiently; "I suppose you'd lay there all day, if I hadn't called you."

So begins the story of *Ragged Dick, or Street Life in New York,* Horatio Alger's first book—the first of 135 tales written in the late 1800s that together sold close to 20 million copies. Like all the books that followed, *Ragged Dick* told the story of a young man who, by pluck and luck, rises from his lowly station to earn a respectable job and the promise of a better life.

Nearly a century later, another best-selling American business story offered a different concept of heroism and a different description of the route to success. This story begins:

"All the way to the horizon in the last light, the sea was just degrees of gray, rolling and frothy on the surface. From the cockpit of a small white sloop—she was 35 feet long—the waves looked like hills coming up from behind, and most of the crew preferred not to glance at them. . . . Running under shortened sails in front of the northeaster, the boat rocked one way, gave a thump, and then it rolled the other. The pots and pans in the galley clanged. A six-pack of beer, which someone had forgotten to stow away, slid back and forth across the cabin floor, over and over again. Sometime late that night, one of the crew raised a voice against the wind and asked, "What are we trying to prove?"

The book is Tracy Kidder's *The Soul of a New Machine,* a 1981 tale of how a team—a crew—of hardworking inventors built a computer by pooling efforts. The opening scene is a metaphor for their treacherous journey.

Separated by 100 years, totally different in their explanations of what propels the American economy, these two stories symbolize the choice that Americans will face in the 1990s; each celebrates a fundamentally different version of American entrepreneurship. Which version we choose to embrace will help determine how quickly and how well the United States adapts to the challenge of global competition.

Horatio Alger's notion of success is the traditional one: the familiar tale of triumphant individuals, of enterprising heroes who win riches and rewards through a combination of Dale Carnegie-esque self-improvement, Norman Vincent Peale-esque faith, Sylvester Stallone-esque assertiveness, and plain old-fashioned good luck. Tracy Kidder's story, by contrast, teaches that economic success comes through the talent, energy, and commitment of a team—through *collective* entrepreneurship.

Stories like these do more than merely entertain or divert us. Like ancient myths that captured and contained an essential truth, they shape how we see and understand our lives, how we make sense of our experience. Stories can mobilize us to action and affect our behavior—more powerfully than simple and straightforward information ever can.

To the extent that we continue to celebrate the traditional myth of the entrepreneurial hero, we will slow the progress of change and adaptation that is essential to our economic success. If we are to compete effectively in today's world, we must begin to celebrate collective entrepreneurship, endeavors in which the whole of the effort is greater than the sum of individual contributions. We need to honor our teams more, our aggressive leaders and maverick geniuses less.

▬▬ HEROES AND DRONES

The older and still dominant American myth involves two kinds of actors: entrepreneurial heroes and industrial drones—the inspired and the perspired.

In this myth, entrepreneurial heroes personify freedom and creativity. They come up with the Big Ideas and build the organizations—the Big Machines—that turn them into reality. They take the initiative, come up with technological and organizational innovations, devise new solutions to old problems. They are the men and women who start vibrant new companies, turn around failing companies, and shake up staid ones. To all endeavors they apply daring and imagination.

The myth of the entrepreneurial hero is as old as America and has served us well in a number of ways. We like to see ourselves as born mavericks and fixers. Our entrepreneurial drive has long been our distinguishing trait. Generations of inventors and investors have kept us on the technological frontier. In a world of naysayers and traditionalists, the American character has always stood out—cheerfully optimistic, willing to run risks, ready to try anything. During World War II, it was the rough-and-ready American GI who could fix the stalled jeep in Normandy while the French regiment only looked on.

Horatio Alger captured this spirit in hundreds of stories. With titles like *Bound to Rise, Luck and Pluck,* and *Sink or Swim,* they inspired millions of readers with a gloriously simple message: in America you can go from rags to riches. The plots were essentially the same; like any successful entrepreneur, Alger knew when he was onto a good thing. A fatherless, penniless boy—possessed of great determination, faith, and courage—seeks his fortune. All manner of villain tries to tempt him, divert him, or separate him from his small savings. But in the end, our hero prevails—not just through pluck; luck plays a part too—and by the end of the story he is launched on his way to fame and fortune.

At the turn of the century, Americans saw fiction and reality sometimes converging. Edward Harriman began as a $5-a-week office boy and came to head a mighty railroad empire. John D. Rockefeller rose from a clerk in a commission merchant's house to become one of the world's richest men. Andrew Carnegie started as a $1.20-a-week bobbin boy in a Pittsburgh cotton mill and became the nation's foremost steel magnate. In the early 1900s, when boys were still reading the Alger tales, Henry Ford made his fortune mass-producing the Model T, and in the process became both a national folk hero and a potential presidential candidate.

Alger's stories gave the country a noble ideal—a society in which imagination and effort summoned their just reward. The key virtue was self-reliance; the admirable man was the self-made man; the goal was to be your own boss. Andrew Carnegie articulated the prevailing view: "Is any would-be businessman . . . content in forecasting his future, to figure himself as labouring all his life for a fixed salary? Not one, I am sure. In this you have the dividing line between business and non-business; the one is master and depends on profits, the other is servant and depends on salary."[1]

The entrepreneurial hero still captures the American imagination.

---

1. Andrew Carnegie, *The Business of Empire* (New York: Doubleday, Page, 1902), 192.

Inspired by the words of his immigrant father, who told him, "You could be anything you want to be, if you wanted it bad enough and were willing to work for it," Lido Iacocca worked his way up to the presidency of Ford Motor Company, from which he was abruptly fired by Henry Ford II, only to go on to rescue Chrysler from bankruptcy, thumb his nose at Ford in a best-selling autobiography, renovate the Statue of Liberty, and gain mention as a possible presidential candidate.[2] Could Horatio Alger's heroes have done any better?

Peter Ueberroth, son of a traveling aluminum salesman, worked his way through college, single-handedly built a $300-million business, went on to organize the 1984 Olympics, became *Time* magazine's Man of the Year and the commissioner of baseball. Steven Jobs built his own computer company from scratch and became a multimillionaire before his thirtieth birthday. Stories of entrepreneurial heroism come from across the economy and across the country: professors who create whole new industries and become instant millionaires when their inventions go from the laboratory to the marketplace; youthful engineers who quit their jobs, strike out on their own, and strike it rich.

In the American economic mythology, these heroes occupy center stage: "Fighters, fanatics, men with a lust for contest, a gleam of creation, and a drive to justify their break from the mother company."[3] Prosperity for all depends on the entrepreneurial vision of a few rugged individuals.

If the entrepreneurial heroes hold center stage in this drama, the rest of the vast work force plays a supporting role—supporting and unheralded. Average workers in this myth are drones—cogs in the Big Machines, so many interchangeable parts, unable to perform without direction from above. They are put to work for their hands, not for their minds or imaginations. Their jobs typically appear by the dozens in the help-wanted sections of daily newspapers. Their routines are unvaried. They have little opportunity to use judgment or creativity. To the entrepreneurial hero belongs all the inspiration; the drones are governed by the rules and valued for their reliability and pliability.

These average workers are no villains—but they are certainly no heroes. Uninteresting and uninterested, goes the myth, they lack creative spark and entrepreneurial vision. These are, for example, the nameless and faceless workers who lined up for work in response to Henry Ford's visionary offer of a $5-per-day paycheck. At best, they put in a decent effort in executing the entrepreneurial hero's grand design. At worst, they demand more wages and benefits for less work, do the minimum expected of them, or function as bland bureaucrats mired in standard operating procedures.

The entrepreneurial hero and the worker drone together personify the

---

2. See Lee Iacocca and William Novak, *Iacocca: An Autobiography* (New York: Bantam Books, 1984).

3. George Gilder, *The Spirit of Enterprise* (New York: Simon and Schuster, 1984), 213.

mythic version of how the American economic system works. The system needs both types. But rewards and treatment for the two are as different as the roles themselves: the entrepreneurs should be rewarded with fame and fortune; drones should be disciplined through clear rules and punishments. Considering the overwhelming importance attached to the entrepreneur in this paradigm, the difference seems appropriate. For, as George Gilder has written, "All of us are dependent for our livelihood and progress not on a vast and predictable machine, but on the creativity and courage of the particular men who accept the risks which generate our riches."[4]

WHY HORATIO ALGER CAN'T HELP US ANYMORE

There is just one fatal problem with this dominant myth: it is obsolete. The economy that it describes no longer exists. By clinging to the myth, we subscribe to an outmoded view of how to win economic success—a view that, on a number of counts, endangers our economic future:

- In today's global economy, the Big Ideas pioneered by American entrepreneurs travel quickly to foreign lands. In the hands of global competitors, these ideas can undergo continuous adaptation and improvement and reemerge as new Big Ideas or as a series of incrementally improved small ideas.
- The machines that American entrepreneurs have always set up so efficiently to execute their Big Ideas are equally footloose. Process technology moves around the globe to find the cheapest labor and the friendliest markets. As ideas migrate overseas, the economic and technological resources needed to implement the ideas migrate too.
- Workers in other parts of the world are apt to be cheaper or more productive—or both—than workers in the United States. Around the globe, millions of potential workers are ready to under-bid American labor.
- Some competitor nations—Japan, in particular—have created relationships among engineers, managers, production workers, and marketing and sales people that do away with the old distinction between entrepreneurs and drones. The dynamic result is yet another basis for challenging American assumptions about what leads to competitive success.

Because of these global changes, the United States is now susceptible to competitive challenge on two grounds. First, by borrowing the Big Ideas and process technology that come from the United States and providing the hardworking, low-paid workers, developing nations can achieve competitive advantage. Second, by embracing collective entrepreneurship, the Japanese

---

4. Ibid., 147.

especially have found a different way to achieve competitive advantage while maintaining high real wages.

Americans continue to lead the world in breakthroughs and cutting-edge scientific discoveries. But the Big Ideas that start in this country now quickly travel abroad, where they not only get produced at high speed, at low cost, and with great efficiency, but also undergo continuous development and improvement. And all too often, American companies get bogged down somewhere between invention and production.

Several product histories make the point. Americans invented the solid-state transistor in 1947. Then in 1953, Western Electric licensed the technology to Sony for $25,000—and the rest is history. A few years later, RCA licensed several Japanese companies to make color televisions—and that was the beginning of the end of color-television production in the United States. Routine assembly of color televisions eventually shifted to Taiwan and Mexico. At the same time, Sony and other Japanese companies pushed the technology in new directions, continuously refining it into a stream of consumer products.

In 1968, Unimation licensed Kawasaki Heavy Industries to make industrial robots. The Japanese took the initial technology and kept moving it forward. The pattern has been the same for one Big Idea after another. Americans came up with the Big Ideas for videocassette recorders, basic oxygen furnaces, continuous casters for making steel, microwave ovens, automobile stamping machines, computerized machine tools, integrated circuits. But these Big Ideas—and many, many others—quickly found their way into production in foreign countries: routine, standardized production in developing nations or continuous refinement and complex applications in Japan. Either way, the United States has lost ground.

Older industrial economies, like our own, have two options: they can try to match the low wages and discipline under which workers elsewhere in the world are willing to labor, or they can compete on the basis of how quickly and how well they transform ideas into incrementally better products. The second option is, in fact, the only one that offers the possibility of high real incomes in America. But here's the catch: a handful of lone entrepreneurs producing a few industry-making Big Ideas can't execute this second option. Innovation must become both continuous and collective. And that requires embracing a new ideal: collective entrepreneurship.

—— THE NEW ECONOMIC PARADIGM

If America is to win in the new global competition, we need to begin telling one another a new story in which companies compete by drawing on the talent and creativity of all their employees, not just a few maverick inventors and dynamic CEOs. Competitive advantage today comes from continuous, incremental innovation and refinement of a variety of ideas that spread throughout the organization. The entrepreneurial organization is both experience-based and decentralized, so that every advance builds on every previous advance, and everyone in the company has the opportunity and capacity to participate.

While this story represents a departure from tradition, it already exists, in fact, to a greater or lesser extent in every well-run American and Japanese corporation. The difference is that we don't recognize and celebrate this story—and the Japanese do.

Consider just a few of the evolutionary paths that collective entrepreneurship can take: vacuum-tube radios become transistorized radios, then stereo pocket radios audible through earphones, then compact discs and compact disc players, and then optical disc computer memories. Color televisions evolve into digital televisions capable of showing several pictures simultaneously; videocassette recorders into camcorders. A single strand of technological evolution connects electronic sewing machines, electronic typewriters, and flexible electronic workstations. Basic steel gives way to high-strength and corrosion-resistant steels, then to new materials composed of steel mixed with silicon and custom-made polymers. Basic chemicals evolve into high-performance ceramics, to single-crystal silicon and high-grade crystal glass. Copper wire gives way to copper cables, then to fiber-optic cables.

These patterns reveal no clear life cycles with beginnings, middles, and ends. Unlike Big Ideas that beget standardized commodities, these products undergo a continuous process of incremental change and adaptation. Workers at all levels add value not solely or even mostly by tending machines and carrying out routines, but by continuously discovering opportunities for improvement in product and process.

In this context, it makes no sense to speak of an "industry" like steel or automobiles or televisions or even banking. There are no clear borders around any of these clusters of goods or services. When products and processes are so protean, companies grow or decline not with the market for some specific good, but with the creative and adaptive capacity of their workers.

Workers in such organizations constantly reinvent the company; one idea leads to another. Producing the latest generation of automobiles involves making electronic circuits that govern fuel consumption and monitor engine performance; developments in these devices lead to improved sensing equipment and software for monitoring heartbeats and moisture in the air. Producing cars also involves making flexible robots for assembling parts and linking them by computer; steady improvements in these technologies, in turn, lead to expert production systems that can be applied anywhere. What is considered the "automobile industry" thus becomes a wide variety of technologies evolving toward all sorts of applications that flow from the same strand of technological development toward different markets.

In this paradigm, entrepreneurship isn't the sole province of the company's founder or its top managers. Rather, it is a capability and attitude that is diffused throughout the company. Experimentation and development go on all the time as the company searches for new ways to capture and build on the knowledge already accumulated by its workers.

Distinctions between innovation and production, between top managers and production workers blur. Because production is a continuous process of reinvention, entrepreneurial efforts are focused on many thousands of small ideas rather than on just a few big ones. And because valuable information and expertise are dispersed throughout the organization, top management does not solve problems; it creates an environment in which people can identify and solve problems themselves.

Most of the training for working in this fashion takes place on the job. Formal education may prepare people to absorb and integrate experience, but it does not supply the experience. No one can anticipate the precise skills that workers will need to succeed on the job when information processing, know-how, and creativity are the value added. Any job that could be fully prepared for in advance is, by definition, a job that could be exported to a low-wage country or programmed into robots and computers; a routine job is a job destined to disappear.

In collective entrepreneurship, individual skills are integrated into a group; this collective capacity to innovate becomes something greater than the sum of its parts. Over time, as group members work through various problems and approaches, they learn about each others' abilities. They learn how they can help one another perform better, what each can contribute to a particular project, how they can best take advantage of one another's experience. Each participant is constantly on the lookout for small adjustments that will speed and smooth the evolution of the whole. The net result of many such small-scale adaptations, effected throughout the organization, is to propel the enterprise forward.

Collective entrepreneurship thus entails close working relationships among people at all stages of the process. If customers' needs are to be recognized and met, designers and engineers must be familiar with sales and marketing. Salespeople must also have a complete understanding of the enterprise's capacity to design and deliver specialized products. The company's ability to adapt to new opportunities and capitalize on them depends on its capacity to share information and involve everyone in the organization in a systemwide search for ways to improve, adjust, adapt, and upgrade.

Collective entrepreneurship also entails a different organizational structure. Under the old paradigm, companies are organized into a series of hierarchical tiers so that supervisors at each level can make sure that subordinates act according to plan. It is a structure designed to control. But enterprises designed for continuous innovation and incremental improvement use a structure designed to spur innovation at all levels. Gaining insight into improvement of products and processes is more important than rigidly following rules. Coordination and communication replace command and control. Consequently, there are few middle-level managers and only modest differences in the status and income of senior managers and junior employees.

Simple accounting systems are no longer adequate or appropriate for monitoring and evaluating job performance: tasks are intertwined and interdependent, and the quality of work is often more important than the quantity of work. In a system where each worker depends on many others—and where the success of the company depends on all—the only appropriate measurement of accomplishment is a collective one. At the same time, the reward system reflects this new approach: profit sharing, gain sharing, and performance bonuses all demonstrate that the success of the company comes from the broadest contribution of all the company's employees, not just those at the top.

Finally, under collective entrepreneurship, workers do not fear technology and automation as a threat to their jobs. When workers add value through judgment and knowledge, computers become tools that expand their discretion. Computer-generated information can give workers rich feedback about their own efforts, how they affect others in the production process, and how the entire process can be improved. One of the key lessons to come out of the General Motors–Toyota joint venture in California is that the Japanese automaker does not rely on automation and technology to replace workers in the plant. In fact, human workers still occupy the most critical jobs—those where judgment and evaluation are essential. Instead, Toyota uses technology to allow workers to focus on those important tasks where choices have to be made. Under this approach, technology gives workers the chance to use their imagination and their insight on behalf of the company.

THE TEAM AS HERO

In 1986, one of America's largest and oldest enterprises announced that it was changing the way it assigned its personnel: the U.S. Army discarded a system that assigned soldiers to their units individually in favor of a system that keeps teams of soldiers together for their entire tours of duty. An Army spokesperson explained, "We discovered that individuals perform better when they are part of a stable group. They are more reliable. They also take responsibility for the success of the overall operation."

In one of its recent advertisements, BellSouth captures the new story. "BellSouth is not a bunch of individuals out for themselves," the ad proclaimed. "We're a team."

Collective entrepreneurship is already here. It shows up in the way our best-run companies now organize their work, regard their workers, design their enterprises. Yet the old myth of the entrepreneurial hero remains powerful. Many Americans would prefer to think that Lee Iacocca singlehandedly saved Chrysler from bankruptcy than to accept the real story: a large team of people with diverse backgrounds and interests joined together to rescue the ailing company.

Bookstores bulge with new volumes paying homage to American

CEOs. It is a familiar story; it is an engaging story. And no doubt, when seen through the eyes of the CEO, it accurately portrays how that individual experienced the company's success. But what gets left out time after time are the experiences of the rest of the team—the men and women at every level of the company whose contributions to the company created the success that the CEO so eagerly claims. Where are the books that celebrate their stories?

You can also find inspirational management texts designed to tell top executives how to be kinder to employees, treat them with respect, listen to them, and make them feel appreciated. By reading these books, executives can learn how to search for excellence, create excellence, achieve excellence, or become impassioned about excellence—preferably within one minute. Managers are supposed to walk around, touch employees, get directly involved, effervesce with praise and encouragement, stage celebrations, and indulge in hoopla.

Some of this is sound; some of it is hogwash. But most of it, even the best, is superficial. Lacking any real context, unattached to any larger understanding of why relationships between managers and workers matter, the prescriptions often remain shallow and are treated as such. The effervescent executive is likely to be gone in a few years, many of the employees will be gone, and the owners may be different as well. Too often the company is assumed to be a collection of assets, available to the highest bidder. When times require it, employees will be sacked. Everybody responds accordingly. Underneath the veneer of participatory management, it is business as usual—and business as usual represents a threat to America's long-term capacity to compete.

If the United States is to compete effectively in the world in a way designed to enhance the real incomes of Americans, we must bring collective entrepreneurship to the forefront of the economy. That will require us to change our attitudes, to downplay the myth of the entrepreneurial hero, and to celebrate our creative teams.

First, we will need to look for and promote new kinds of stories. In modern-day America, stories of collective entrepreneurship typically appear in the sports pages of the daily newspaper; time after time, in accounts of winning efforts we learn that the team with the best blend of talent won—the team that emphasized teamwork—not the team with the best individual athlete. The cultural challenge is to move these stories from the sports page to the business page. We need to shift the limelight from maverick founders and shake-'em-up CEOs to groups of engineers, production workers, and marketers who successfully innovate new products and services. We need to look for opportunities to tell stories about American business from the perspective of all the workers who make up the team, rather than solely from the perspective of top managers. The stories are there—we need only change our focus, alter our frame of reference, in order to find them.

Second, we will need to understand that the most powerful stories get told, not in books and newspapers, but in the everyday world of work.

Whether managers know it or not, every decision they make suggests a story to the rest of the enterprise. Decisions to award generous executive bonuses or to provide plush executive dining rooms and executive parking places tell the old story of entrepreneurial heroism. A decision to lay off 10% of the work force tells the old story of the drone worker. Several years ago, when General Motors reached agreement on a contract with the United Auto Workers that called for a new relationship based on cooperation and shared sacrifice, and then, on the same day, announced a new formula for generous executive bonuses, long-time union members simply nodded to themselves. The actions told the whole story. It is not enough to acknowledge the importance of collective entrepreneurship; clear and consistent signals must reinforce the new story.

Collective entrepreneurship represents the path toward an economic future that is promising for both managers and workers. For managers, this path means continually retraining employees for more complex tasks; automating in ways that cut routine tasks and enhance worker flexibility and creativity; diffusing responsibility for innovation; taking seriously labor's concern for job security; and giving workers a stake in improved productivity through profit-linked bonuses and stock plans.

For workers, this path means accepting flexible job classifications and work rules; agreeing to wage rates linked to profits and productivity improvements; and generally taking greater responsibility for the soundness and efficiency of the enterprise. This path also involves a closer and more permanent relationship with other parties that have a stake in the company's performance—suppliers, dealers, creditors, even the towns and cities in which the company resides.

Under collective entrepreneurship, all those associated with the company become partners in its future. The distinction between entrepreneurs and drones breaks down. Each member of the enterprise participates in its evolution. All have a commitment to the company's continued success. It is the one approach that can maintain and improve America's competitive performance—and America's standard of living—over the long haul.

⸻ DISCUSSION QUESTIONS

1. Name some people—from business, sports, fiction, movies, politics, or your own personal experience—who have inspired you and shaped your professional ambitions. In considering the qualities you admire in these people, do you agree with Reich's assertion that we celebrate the virtues of individual heroes at the expense of team players?

2. Reich points out that foreign competitors quickly capitalize on American technological breakthroughs. "All too often," he observes, "American companies get bogged down somewhere

between invention and production." What conditions in the U.S. companies—structural, mangerial, financial, technological, or otherwise—account for our failure to reap the full benefits of our own ideas?

3. According to the reading, heroes are admired for their boldness and creativity, and drones are valued for their "reliability and pliability." What are the qualities of an effective team player? What incentives can an organization create to foster these qualities?

4. To compete effectively, says Reich, we need a new kind of workplace and new kinds of work relationships. Does Reich's vision strike you as a realistic blueprint or an unworkable ideal? What assumptions, attitudes, and practices have to change for this vision to be realized?

5. Given the magnitude of the changes needed, can the current generation of American managers and workers learn to think and behave in new ways? What other social institutions might need to change in order to foster the attitudes and behavior that Reich advocates?

Capital Market Myopia   3

WILLIAM A. SAHLMAN and HOWARD H. STEVENSON

In the late 70s and early 80s, private and public investors supplied large sums of money to manufacturers of Winchester disk drives. At its peak, the industry included well over 100 competitors, over 40 of which had been backed by professional venture capitalists. Competition was fierce. Eventually, a significant number of companies failed or were merged into other firms, and many investors in the industry were disappointed. This article describes how and why so many players in the same industry were financed and what the inevitable consequences were. Capital market myopia is a phenomenon where individual players in a market ignore the logical implications of their individual moves: as a result, wealth is created and destroyed. The basic premise of the article is that this destructive, myopic behavior can be avoided.

──── INTRODUCTION

From 1977 to 1984, professional venture capital firms invested almost $400 million in 43 different manufacturers of Winchester disk drives. The majority of that capital was invested during the last two years, 1983 and 1984, when $270 million was invested in approximately 51 distinct financing rounds, including 21 start-up or early stage investments. The pattern of these investments is shown in *Exhibit 1.*[1]

During this same period, the public capital markets were also a large supplier of funds to the disk drive industry. The total amount of money raised in public offerings of common stocks for participants in the industry was over $800 million. During the middle part of 1983, the capital markets assigned a value in excess of $5 billion to 12 publicly traded, venture capital backed hard

Associate Professor William A. Sahlman and Professor Howard H. Stevenson prepared this case as a basis for class discussion. Copyright © 1987 by the President and Fellows of Harvard College. Harvard Business School case 288-005.

While DISK/TREND, Inc. and Venture Economics graciously supplied data for this paper, responsibility resides with the authors for the analysis and conclusions.

1. Data on venture capital investment in the disk drive industry were provided by Venture Economics, publisher of the *Venture Capital Journal* (Wellesley, Massachusetts).

EXHIBIT 1
Number of Company Financing Rounds and Estimated Amount Invested ($000) by Disk Drive Technology and by Stage

		1977	1978	1979	1980	1981	1982	1983	1984	TOTAL ('77–'84)
All disk drive companies:										
Floppy disks	#	1	6	3	7	9	8	7	5	46
(17 companies)	$	200	5,955	8,250	19,766	23,414	30,862	29,125	16,915	134,487
Winchester disks	#	2	3	6	5	12	19	22	20	89
(43 companies)*	$	780	6,383	5,220	11,100	33,254	67,540	184,356	83,480	392,113
Optical disks	#	0	0	0	0	0	1	2	5	8
(7 companies)	$	0	0	0	0	0	150	9,326	15,162	24,638
Other disk related	#	0	0	0	0	0	1	2	5	8
(6 companies)	$	0	0	0	0	0	4,000	11,000	21,938	36,938
TOTALS	#	3	9	9	12	21	29	32	36	151
	$	980	12,338	13,470	30,866	56,668	102,552	233,807	137,495	588,176
Winchester disk drives only, by stages:										
Startup		0	1	1	2	7	8	4	6	29
Other early		0	1	3	1	2	1	9	2	19
Expansion		2	0	2	2	4	10	14	13	47
Other and unknown		0	1	0	0	0	2	3	0	6
TOTALS		2	3	6	5	13	21	30	21	101

Source: These data were supplied by Venture Economics of Wellesley, Massachusetts.

*43 separate Winchester disk drive companies received 89 rounds of venture capital financing.

disk drive manufacturers. The strong market valuation of these companies paralleled the boom in other high technology stocks and rising valuation levels in the stock market in general. *Exhibit 2* contains data on stock prices and valuation levels for some disk drive manufacturers, and *Exhibit 3* provides general data on the economy and capital markets.

The industry served by these companies was experiencing explosive growth by any measure. In 1978, total sales of hard disk drives to the Original Equipment Manufacturer (OEM) market were only $27 million. By 1983, total sales were approximately $1.3 billion. Projected sales in 1984 were almost $2.4 billion, an 84% increase. By 1987, sales were expected to reach $4.5 billion. Industry data are provided in *Exhibit 4.*[2]

Given these sanguine projections for the industry, the exuberance in the venture capital community and stock market seems somewhat plausible. However, by the end of 1984, the value assigned to those same 12 manufacturers of disk drives had declined from a high of $5.4 billion to only $1.4 billion. Further, the fundamentals for almost every participant had deteriorated badly, particularly in late 1984. Losses began to appear, and sales even declined for some companies. One company, Seagate, had revenues in each of the first two quarters of 1984 of approximately $100 million only to have total revenues in the third quarter fall to the $50 million level. (See *Exhibit 5*, column 10). For all 12 companies, aggregate net income in the quarter ended September 30, 1984 was only $2.3 million, down from an average of $24.2 million in the previous three quarters.

The purpose in writing this article is to focus attention on a phenomenon we call capital market myopia, a situation in which participants in the capital markets ignore the logical implications of their individual investment decisions. Viewed in isolation, each decision seems to make sense. When taken together, however, they are a prescription for disaster.

Capital market myopia leads to over-funding of industries and unsustainable levels of valuation in the stock market. While we will use the Winchester disk drive industry to elucidate the phenomenon, capital market myopia has arisen in many other industries at many points in the past. No doubt, it will occur in the future.

We will argue that capital market participants should have seen the problem coming. They should have known that valuation levels were absurd, based in large part on the greater fool theory. The data necessary to anticipate the problem were readily available before the troubles began. We will try to offer some simple lessons to help investors and entrepreneurs avoid charter membership in the greater fool club.

---

2. Data on the disk drive industry were provided by James N. Porter of DISK/TREND, Inc. (Mountain View, California).

EXHIBIT 2
Stock Market Valuations and Return Data

COMPANY	5 YEAR HIGH		LAST PO		8/1/83		12/30/83		12/30/84	
	PRICE	VALUE	PRICE	VALUE	PRICE	VALUE	PRICE	VALUE	PRICE	VALUE
Miniscribe*	$14.00	$214,284	$11.50	$202,469	$1.00	$15,306	$11.00	$190,366	$3.00	$51,720
Masstor	$30.25	396,033	$16.00	207,840	$17.75	232,383	$8.25	108,950	$3.88	51,786
Rodime	$28.75	174,426	$13.75	107,071	$22.50	136,508	$21.25	128,924	$7.00	53,095
Iomega	$10.13	128,881	$10.00	130,690	$10.13	128,881	$5.63	73,316	$7.88	106,068
Cipher Data	$27.50	352,880	$21.38	278,559	$19.00	243,808	$19.75	259,811	$22.00	298,056
Computer Memories	$30.00	279,000	$18.75	209,625	$26.00	241,800	$8.00	87,840	$3.25	35,685
Onyx + IMI	$22.25	230,822	$13.00	128,882	$12.88	133,565	$9.50	98,553	$1.38	14,399
Seagate	$22.13	967,261	$12.44	543,743	$17.75	775,995	$13.88	606,587	$5.00	220,795
Quantum	$34.25	313,833	$20.50	187,452	$23.25	213,040	$18.75	172,406	$21.00	199,836
Micropolis	$25.00	224,750	$17.00	156,842	$19.50	175,305	$10.75	96,643	$4.88	43,826
Priam	$23.25	343,961	$17.00	258,043	$19.25	284,785	$10.75	165,539	$4.75	77,682
Tandon	$34.25	1,739,112	$15.50	788,702	$30.50	1,548,699	$20.00	1,015,540	$6.00	304,710
TOTAL		$5,365,242		$3,199,918		$4,130,073		$3,004,475		$1,457,658

Stock Market Returns (% change in value)

Percentage change from period:

BEGINNING ENDING	HIGH 12/31/84	LAST PO 8/31/83	LAST PO 12/31/83	8/31/83 12/31/83	8/31/83 12/31/84	12/31/83 12/31/84	LAST PO 12/31/84
Miniscribe	−78.6%	1050.0%	4.5%	1000.0%	200.0%	−72.7%	−73.9%
Masstor	−87.2%	−9.9%	93.9%	−53.5%	−78.2%	−53.0%	−75.8%
Rodime	−75.7%	−38.9%	−35.3%	−5.6%	−68.9%	−67.1%	−49.1%
Iomega	−22.2%	−1.2%	77.8%	−44.4%	−22.2%	40.0%	−21.3%
Cipher Data	−20.0%	12.5%	8.2%	3.9%	15.8%	11.4%	2.9%
Computer Memories	−89.2%	−27.9%	134.4%	−69.2%	−87.5%	−59.4%	−82.7%
Onyx + IMI	−93.8%	1.0%	36.8%	−26.2%	−89.3%	−85.5%	−89.4%
Seagate	−77.4%	−29.9%	−10.4%	−21.8%	−71.8%	−64.0%	−59.8%
Quantum	−38.7%	−11.8%	9.3%	−19.4%	−9.7%	12.0%	2.4%
Micropolis	−80.5%	−12.8%	58.1%	−44.9%	−75.0%	−54.7%	−71.3%
Priam	−79.6%	−11.7%	58.1%	−44.2%	−75.3%	−55.8%	−72.1%
Tandon	−82.5%	−49.2%	−22.5%	−34.4%	−80.3%	−70.0%	−61.3%
ALL COMPANIES	*−72.8%*	*−22.5%*	*6.5%*	*−27.3%*	*−64.7%*	*−51.5%*	*−54.4%*

Notes:

PO—Public offering of common stock.

These twelve companies were active in manufacturing Winchester disk drives (or tape backups) for the OEM market.

*Miniscribe went public on November 3, 1983. The $1.00 per share valuation listed for 8/1/83 was the last price paid per share by venture capital investors prior to the public offering.

EXHIBIT 3
Selected Data on the Economy, Public Capital Markets and Venture Capital Activity

ROW	1973	1974	1975	1976	1977	1978	1979	1980	1981	1982	1983	1984
Macroeconomic data												
1 Nominal gross national product	1,359	1,473	1,598	1,783	1,991	2,250	2,508	2,732	3,053	3,166	3,406	3,765
2 Percent change in GNP deflator	6.5	9.1	9.8	6.4	6.7	7.3	8.9	9.0	9.7	6.4	3.9	3.8
3 Percent change in real GNP	5.2	-0.5	-1.3	4.9	4.7	5.3	2.5	-0.2	1.9	-2.5	3.6	6.4
4 Consumer price inflation	8.8	12.2	7.0	4.8	6.8	9.0	13.3	12.4	8.9	3.9	3.8	4.0
5 Unemployment rate	4.8	5.5	8.3	7.6	6.9	6.0	5.8	7.0	7.5	9.5	9.5	7.4
6 Industrial product index (mfg)	94.0	92.6	83.4	91.9	100.0	107.1	111.5	108.2	110.5	102.2	110.2	123.4
7 Net business formation index	119.1	113.2	109.9	120.4	130.8	138.1	138.3	129.9	124.8	116.4	117.5	121.3
8 New business incorporations	329	319	326	376	436	478	525	534	581	567	600	635
9 Business failure rate (per 10,000)	36.4	38.4	42.6	34.8	28.4	23.9	27.8	42.1	61.3	89.0	110.0	107.0
Financial market data												
10 3-month U.S. treasury bills	7.0	7.9	5.8	5.0	5.3	7.2	10.0	11.5	14.1	10.7	8.6	9.6
11 Long-term government bonds	6.8	7.6	8.0	7.6	7.4	8.4	9.4	11.5	13.9	13.0	11.1	12.4
12 Corporate Aaa bonds	7.4	8.6	8.8	8.4	8.0	8.7	9.6	11.9	14.2	13.8	12.0	12.7
13 Prime interest rate	8.0	10.8	7.9	6.8	6.8	9.1	12.7	15.3	18.9	14.9	10.8	12.0
14 Standard & Poors 500 Index (EOY)	97.6	68.6	90.2	107.5	95.1	96.1	107.9	135.8	122.6	140.6	164.9	167.2
15 NASDAQ Composite Index (EOY)	92.2	59.8	77.6	97.9	105.1	139.3	152.3	208.2	223.5	340.7	328.9	258.9
16 Venture 100 Index (EOY)	58.5	30.9	72.4	116.0	164.0	261.5	369.7	655.7	569.8	715.7	842.6	536.3

ROW	1973	1974	1975	1976	1977	1978	1979	1980	1981	1982	1983	1984
Venture capital and IPO activity												
17 Net new commitments to the venture capital industry ($mil)	56	57	10	50	39	600	300	700	1,300	1,800	4,500	4,200
18 Estimated disbursements to portfolio companies ($mil)	450	350	250	300	400	550	1,000	1,100	1,400	1,800	2,800	3,250
19 Public underwritings of companies with net worth less than $5 MM (#)	69	9	4	29	22	21	46	135	306	113	477	224
20 Amount raised ($mil)	160	16	16	145	75	129	183	822	1,760	619	3,671	1,190
All IPOs												
21 Number of offerings	100	15	15	34	40	45	81	237	448	222	884	548
22 Amount raised ($mil)	330	51	265	234	153	249	506	1,397	3,215	1,446	12,619	3,832

Notes:
Most of the data in Rows 1 through 13 represent averages for the relevant time period.
EOY—End of year data
IPO—Initial public offerings

Sources:
Economic Report of the President
Venture Economics, Wellesley, Massachusetts (Rows 16 to 20)
Going Public: The IPO Reporter, Howard & Company, Philadelphia, PA (Rows 21 and 22)

EXHIBIT 4
Disk Drive Industry Forecasts vs. Actual

	YEAR OF FORECAST	1978	1979	1980	1981	1982	1983	1984	1985	1986	1987	CAGR
Total world wide	1979	3,457.4	3,885.4	4,502.2	5,434.9	6,337.0	16.4%					
	1980		3,816.7	4,805.7	6,018.7	7,684.3	8,988.4	23.9%				
($000)	1981			5,181.2	7,037.7	9,443.6	11,914.0	14,147.7	28.5%			
	1982				6,370.6	7,925.3	10,300.8	13,122.0	15,415.0	24.7%		
	1983					7,403.4	9,331.1	12,072.5	14,557.8	16,943.0	23.0%	
	1984						9,112.4	12,922.7	15,623.6	19,088.4	22,608.0	25.5%
Total WW Disk Storage		3,457.4	3,816.7	5,181.2	6,370.6	7,403.4	9,112.4	12,922.7	15,623.6	19,088.4	22,608.0	23.2%
Total OEM-WW	1979	473.3	686.0	806.9	917.5	1,008.5	20.8%					
	1980		643.6	968.3	1,242.0	1,494.9	1,693.9	27.4%				
($000)	1981			835.4	1,212.0	1,746.2	2,201.8	2,603.4	32.9%			
	1982				1,110.9	1,472.1	1,950.6	2,402.8	2,803.3	26.0%		
	1983					1,312.6	2,038.0	2,694.6	3,269.2	3,728.9	29.8%	
	1984						1,940.5	3,031.1	3,688.7	4,377.7	5,041.0	27.0%
Total OEM world wide		473.3	643.6	835.4	1,110.9	1,312.6	1,940.5	3,031.1	3,688.7	4,377.7	5,041.0	30.1%

Total hard disk OEM

($000)	Actual	Actual	Actual	Actual	Actual	Forecast	Forecast	Forecast	Forecast	Forecast	CAGR
1979	27.1	77.4	167.3	245.1	295.2						81.7%
1980		62.0	149.0	327.7	522.5	693.2					82.9%
1981			99.8	339.3	734.5	1,120.6	1,480.8				96.3%
1982				341.6	770.3	1,265.7	1,763.2	2,175.2			58.9%
1983					599.2	1,381.6	2,097.4	2,703.5	3,193.1		51.9%
1984						1,285.0	2,358.1	3,032.8	3,795.7	4,493.4	36.7%

Total Hard Disk OEM	Actual	Actual	Actual	Actual	Actual	Forecast	Forecast	Forecast	Forecast	Forecast	CAGR
	27.1	62.0	99.8	341.6	599.2	1,285.0	2,358.1	3,032.8	3,795.7	4,493.4	76.5%

Summary ($000):	Actual	Actual	Actual	Actual	Actual	Forecast	Forecast	Forecast	Forecast	Forecast	CAGR
Total WW disk storage	3,457.4	3,816.7	5,181.2	6,370.6	7,403.4	9,112.4	12,922.7	15,623.6	19,088.4	22,608.0	23.2%
Total OEM world wide	473.3	643.6	835.4	1,110.9	1,312.6	1,940.5	3,031.1	3,688.7	4,377.7	5,041.0	30.1%
Total hard disk OEM	27.1	62.0	99.8	341.6	599.2	1,285.0	2,358.1	3,032.8	3,795.7	4,493.4	76.5%

Notes:
WW—World wide
OEM—Original equipment manufacturer
CAGR—Compound annual growth rate
The figures at the end of each row represent compound annual rates of growth for the forecast period.
Each row represents a forecast made in a different year.

Source: James N. Porter, DISK/TREND, Inc., from various issues of DISK/TREND Report (Mountain View, California).

EXHIBIT 5
Sales, Profits, and Margins Data on Disk Drive Companies

COLUMN	1	2	3	4	5	6	7	8	9	10	11
YEAR	1977	1978	1979	1980	1981	1982	1983	PERIOD ENDED	3 QUARTERS ENDED 9/30/84	QUARTER ENDED 9/30/84	CUMULATIVE 1977 TO 1983
Sales ($000):											
Miniscribe	0	0	0	0	81	5,043	76,591	12/31/83	95,490	26,101	81,715
Masstor	0	5	10	721	2,949	19,238	20,170	12/31/83	17,260	6,200	43,093
Rodime	0	0	0	0	217	10,871	42,794	9/30/83	47,332	19,300	53,882
Iomega	0	0	0	162	665	1,240	7,080	12/31/83	32,277	15,700	9,147
Cipher Data	9,090	14,425	21,572	22,815	55,164	76,429	116,064	6/30/84	103,994	38,894	315,559
Computer Memories	0	0	0	0	2,445	16,027	47,428	3/31/84	61,921	30,210	65,900
Onyx + IMI	0	0	1,370	14,478	40,940	58,674	74,218	9/30/83	75,208	26,482	189,680
Seagate	0	0	0	9,792	40,445	110,411	343,903	6/30/84	252,158	50,600	504,551
Quantum	0	0	0	0	13,656	41,779	67,069	3/31/84	77,400	30,085	122,504
Micropolis	0	3,174	8,300	11,500	23,900	33,000	51,600	12/31/83	41,338	15,400	131,474
Priam	0	0	0	5,997	30,003	63,400	94,300	6/30/84	64,685	20,609	193,700
Tandon	0	1,362	3,206	6,565	22,761	150,500	303,400	9/30/83	311,929	100,000	487,794
Total	9,090	18,966	34,458	72,030	233,226	586,612	1,244,617		1,180,992	379,581	2,198,999
Net income ($000):											
Miniscribe	0	0	0	(64)	(1,040)	(3,247)	4,788	12/31/83	1,161	(2,505)	437
Masstor	(750)	(560)	(1,390)	(3,369)	(8,123)	1,513	(9,377)	12/31/83	(14,800)	(3,725)	(22,056)
Rodime	0	0	0	0	(115)	2,567	7,206	9/30/83	5,900	2,800	9,658
Iomega	0	0	0	(745)	(3,780)	(6,063)	(9,190)	12/31/83	12	1,519	(19,778)
Cipher Data	258	745	975	75	2,236	5,161	11,459	6/30/84	10,454	3,764	20,909
Computer Memories	0	0	(9)	(28)	(369)	1,211	1,402	3/31/84	2,853	1,475	2,207

Onyx + IMI	0	(865)	(1,647)	473	4,455	5,186	3,661	9/30/83	(4,225)	(5,871)	11,263
Seagate	0	0	(248%)	1,801	6,949	13,089	42,019	6/30/84	23,586	577	63,610
Quantum	0	0		(1,769)	186	7,838	10,673	3/31/84	12,187	4,687	16,928
Micropolis	0	29	698	(512)	246	83	3,536	12/31/83	1,192	102	4,080
Priam	0	(1,097)	(2,887)	(3,747)	1,450	4,790	9,905	6/30/84	3,801	624	8,414
Tandon	89	163	161%	1,507	4,505	15,735	23,700	9/30/83	30,583	(1,100)	45,860
Total	(403)	(1,585)	(4,347)	(6,378)	6,600	47,863	99,782		72,704	2,347	141,532

Net margin:

Miniscribe	0.0%	0.0%	0.0%	-1284.0%	-64.4%	6.3%		12/31/83	1.2%	-9.6%	0.5%
Masstor	-11200.0%	-13900.0%	-467.3%	-275.4%	7.9%	-46.5%		12/31/83	-85.7%	-60.1%	-51.2%
Rodime	0.0%	0.0%	0.0%	-53.0%	23.6%	16.8%		9/30/83	12.5%	14.5%	17.9%
Iomega	0.0%	0.0%	-459.9%	-568.4%	-489.0%	-129.8%		12/31/83	0.0%	9.7%	-216.2%
Cipher Data	2.8%	5.2%	4.5%	0.3%	4.1%	6.8%	9.9%	6/30/84	10.1%	9.7%	6.6%
Computer Memories	0.0%	0.0%	0.0%	0.0%	-15.1%	7.6%	3.0%	3/31/84	4.6%	4.9%	3.3%
Onyx + IMI	0.0%	0.0%	-120.2%	10.9%	8.8%	4.9%		9/30/83	-5.6%	-22.2%	5.9%
Seagate	0.0%	0.0%	18.4%	17.2%	11.9%	12.2%		6/30/84	9.4%	1.1%	12.6%
Quantum	0.0%	0.0%	0.0%	1.4%	18.8%	15.9%		3/31/84	15.7%	15.6%	13.8%
Micropolis	0.0%	0.9%	8.4%	-4.5%	1.0%	0.3%	6.9%	12/31/83	2.9%	0.7%	3.1%
Priam	0.0%	0.0%	0.0%	-62.5%	4.8%	7.6%	10.5%	6/30/84	5.9%	3.0%	4.3%
Tandon	0.0%	12.0%	5.0%	23.0%	19.8%	10.5%	7.8%	9/30/83	9.8%	-1.1%	9.4%
For all companies	-4.4%	-8.4%	-12.6%	-8.9%	2.8%	8.2%	8.0%		6.2%	0.6%	6.4%

The remainder of the paper will be divided into six sections:

- The Winchester Disk Drive Industry (1973 to 1983)
- What happened?
- Could the problems have been predicted?
- What are the implications?
- What are the lessons?

────── THE WINCHESTER DISK DRIVE INDUSTRY (1973 TO 1983)

Winchester disk drives are high-speed data storage devices for computers. The technology was first introduced in 1973 by IBM. After IBM, a number of independent firms introduced competitive products based on the same basic technology. New entrants included Memorex, Control Data, and Storage Technology.

For the most part, these disk drives were designed for use with mainframe computer systems and later minicomputers. The drives were expensive relative to alternative data storage technologies like magnetic tape or floppy disk drives. However, performance of Winchester disk drives was also far superior to these less expensive media.

The mid to late 1970s were characterized by very rapid technological change in the computer and related peripherals industries. Briefly told, all sectors of the computer industry experienced rapid growth. However, the most rapidly growing sectors were in the mini- and microcomputer industries.

As had always been the case in the computer industry, there was an inexorable increase in the performance of machines combined with a decline in cost. This statement was true of the computers; it was also true of peripherals such as disk drives. The cost of 10-megabytes of hard disk capacity in 1973 was almost $40,000; by 1983, the same 10-megabytes cost one-tenth as much. Equally importantly, as mini- and microcomputers increased in power, so too did data storage requirements. Hard disk drives were tailor made to meet these needs.

By the late 1970s, many analysts predicted an especially bright future for suppliers of hard disk drives to the OEM marketplace. One prominent analyst, Jim Porter of *DISK/TREND Reports,* predicted in 1979 that total sales of hard disk drives to the OEM market would be almost $700 million by 1983, up from only $27 million for all of 1978. The following year, Porter was forced to revise upward his forecast: total 1983 sales were expected to be $1.1 billion, followed by $1.5 billion in 1984. The pattern of rising expectations is shown in *Exhibit 4.*

These projections did not go unnoticed in the industry. A number of executives in firms active in the data storage industry decided to go after a share of the OEM market. Typical were some executives at Memorex, one of the early entrants into the Winchester disk drive industry after IBM. William Schroeder, a product planning manager, and Al Wilson, a disk drive project manager at Memorex with 27 years of disk drive engineering experience, left Memorex in 1978 to form Priam Corporation to produce high-performance 14-inch disk drives for the small business computer market. Priam's drives would incorporate the same basic technology as had been used by IBM in its initial product in the area, but would be much less expensive to manufacture.

Priam was able to garner capital funding from some of the leading venture capital firms. The venture capital community was attracted to the industry because of the explosive growth prospects. Moreover, the quality of the entrepreneurial team at a start-up like Priam was very high.

Early entrants into the OEM disk drive industry focused on bringing the high end disk drive technology to the mini- and microcomputer market. These firms were confronted with many difficult issues. Basically, they were shooting at a moving target. They had to make a myriad of decisions about technology, production and manufacturing, marketing and finance.

Priam, to illustrate, started essentially from scratch in 1978. Early work centered on designing a 14-inch 34-megabyte Winchester drive for sale to OEMs. Before production could begin, however, competing firms announced plans to introduce competitive 8-inch products. Priam was forced to start a parallel development effort for an 8-inch line of drives. Finally, Priam, like other start-ups, had to design a complete manufacturing system in an industry in which quality control was absolutely essential.

Many other start-ups joined Priam in entering the market. Each new entrant learned something from previous entrants in terms of how to attack particular industry problems such as manufacturing. Each used the best available technology. Each later entrant also benefited from new information about the nature of the market, and could thus tailor its own plans to match the needs of the OEM industry.

Many of the new entrants were started by seasoned executives from the disk drive industry. Memorex, an early producer of disk drives, was an especially fertile supplier of start-up management talent. The founders of Priam came from Memorex. So too did the founders of Seagate, Tandon, Miniscribe, and International Memories (the "IMI" in Onyx-IMI), some of the more successful disk drive manufacturers.

As the industry evolved, there were many dramatic shifts in the marketplace. One of the most important was the move towards smaller dimension disk drives, first from 14-inch to 8-inch and later to the 5.25-inch size. Projections called for the 5.25-inch segment to grow at the fastest rate.

The first product announcement of a 5.25-inch product was by Seagate, a company which had been founded in 1979 by Alan Shugart. Shugart had been an executive at IBM, then Memorex, and had launched another company called Shugart Associates in 1973 to produce high capacity floppy disk drives. Shugart Associates had been sold to Xerox in the mid 1970s. Seagate first began shipping a 5.25-inch 6.38-megabyte drive in July 1980, slightly less than two years after the company had been founded. During the first year of operations (ended June 30, 1981), Seagate reported sales of almost

$10 million and a net profit of $1.8 million. The company had been financed by professional venture capital, and by Dysan Corporation, a manufacturer of high quality floppy diskettes.

Finding equity capital to fund start-ups in the industry was relatively easy. The industry growth prospects were excellent. The entrepreneurs were extremely well-qualified. Some, like Alan Shugart, had already been involved with successful ventures. Others, like Vertex Peripherals, a late 1981 start-up focusing on the 5.25-inch disk drive segment, had top executives who cumulatively had over 100 years of disk drive industry experience.

Equally important, the late 1970s and early 1980s were characterized by a sharp increase in the level of funds available for venture capital investment. From an almost imperceptible $10 million in new capital committed to the venture capital industry in 1975, $1.3 billion was committed in 1981. Key factors underlying the explosion in venture capital activity included the 1978 and 1981 decreases in capital gains tax rates, the 1979 liberalization of pension fund investment regulations under E.R.I.S.A., and the wealth of opportunities to create new companies triggered by factors ranging from technology (e.g., the microprocessor chip) to deregulation of industries from airlines to financial services.

The period from the mid 1970s to the early 1980s was also a period of robust stock market performance. The stocks of smaller companies, including many high technology companies, had been stellar performers from 1975 to 1981. Higher prices for stocks and greater venture capital activity also was a contributing factor in the reemergence of the new issue market. From a low in 1975, in which 4 companies with a net worth of under $5 million raised $16 million, 306 small companies raised $1.7 billion in 1981 alone. These trends were reflected in the market as a whole as shown in *Exhibit 3*.

With respect to the disk drive industry *per se*, the ebullience of the initial public offering (IPO) markets was an important factor in the development of the industry. First, a number of firms began to raise capital through the public market rather than continued reliance on venture capital funding. Seagate, for example, raised $26 million net in September 1981, having only introduced its first product in July 1980. The value assigned to Seagate after that offering was $185 million, over 18 times trailing twelve months sales. Tandon, Cipher Data and Onyx + IMI (then called Dorado Systems) also raised money in the IPO market on favorable terms during 1981. In fact, Tandon actually raised money twice in 1981, $17 million in February and $53 million in November of the same year. Data on all public stock offerings by some of the disk drive companies are provided in *Exhibit 6*.

The fact that the IPO market was receptive to disk drive companies was very important in several dimensions. First, the IPOs revealed how intensely profitable investments in disk drive companies could be. The venture capitalists in Seagate had paid $1 million for 17% of the company. Their share of Seagate's total post-IPO market value was worth almost $32 million.

The second reason why an attractive IPO market was important was that the venture capitalists were able to see a way in which they could convert illiquid letter stock holdings into liquid holdings of registered common stock. During the mid 1970s, harvesting of venture investments had been very difficult because there was no IPO market. Many investments were liquefied through mergers. The existence of an IPO market with high valuations was a very important factor in attracting venture capital investment in the disk drive industry as well as many other high potential industries at the time.

The final and obvious reason why the hot IPO market was important in shaping the industry was that the participants in the industry were able to raise large amounts of equity capital on attractive terms. *Exhibit 6* also shows the percentage of the total equity capital provided by public stock offerings and the percentage of total shares outstanding attributable to the public owners of the company as a result of their cash investment.

The events described above in the 1980 to 1981 period set the stage for even more impressive venture capital and IPO activity in 1982 and particularly 1983. In 1982, $1.8 billion was infused into the venture capital industry. This was followed in 1983 by $4.5 billion. These figures should be contrasted with the $10 million in new capital committed in 1975. The $4.5 billion in 1983 was approximately equal to the entire amount invested over the preceding five years. Not only did existing firms raise record amounts, many new venture capital partnerships were formed in 1982 and 1983.

Beginning in 1981, venture capital began to pour into the Winchester disk drive industry. In 1981, 12 different companies were funded. The following year, 19 companies were funded, and in 1983, 22 Winchester disk drive companies received venture capital investments. In total, slightly over $300 million was invested by venture capitalists from 1977 to 1983. This figure in turn represented just under 4% of the total capital invested by the venture capital industry over the same period. (See *Exhibits 1* and *3*.)

With respect to the IPO market, in 1982, 113 small companies raised $619 million, down significantly from 1981. However, during 1983, 477 companies with a net worth less than $5 million raised $3.7 billion in the new issue market. 1983 was a remarkable year for all new issues: a staggering 884 companies raised over $12 billion, shattering all previous records. (See *Exhibit 3*.)

During 1982 and 1983, a number of disk drive companies went public or raised new money in the stock market. A sample of 12 of the major industry participants sold stock worth over $600 million in 1982 and 1983. Of that amount, over $50 million was raised by selling shareholders. As of the public offerings, the median total market value assigned to those companies going public was approximately 6 times trailing twelve months sales. For the subset of companies going public in the seven months ended July 1983, every IPO was characterized by an increase of at least 10% in shares being offered and 20% in price, when compared to initial estimates in the preliminary prospectuses filed with the SEC. Investors clamored for new issues in disk drive companies. (See *Exhibit 6*.)

EXHIBIT 6
Summary of All Public Offerings of Common Stock

COLUMN	1	2	3	4	5	6	7	8
COMPANY	OFFERING DATE	TOTAL SHARES (000)	PRICE PER SHARE	GROSS AMOUNT ($000)	IMPLIED VALUE ($000)	ACTUAL NET TO CO. ($000)	VALUE/TTM SALES	PO OWNERSHIP (%)
Miniscribe	Nov '83	2,300	$11.50	26,450	202,469	24,130	7.3	13.1%
Masstor	Mar '83	3,000	$16.00	48,000	207,833	39,565	10.8	18.4%
Rodime	Sep '82	1,100	$8.00	8,800	40,477	8,078	404.8	21.7%
	Mar '83	1,375	$19.00	26,125	117,644	17,616	13.4	18.2%
	Apr '84	1,725	$13.75	23,719	107,069	21,000	3.0	22.2%
Iomega	Jul '83	2,420	$10.00	24,200	130,690	20,909	163.4	18.5%
Cipher Data	Oct '81	2,420	$4.75	11,495	37,339	10,291	1.6	30.8%
	Oct '82	2,882	$8.88	25,578	93,232	22,129	1.3	24.6%
	May '83	2,200	$21.38	47,025	278,559	45,412	3.9	16.9%
Computer Memories	Jan '82	660	$7.00	4,620	21,595	5,220	108.0	21.4%
	Dec '82	930	$16.25	15,115	100,389	13,717	12.0	11.1%
	Aug '83	2,200	$18.75	41,250	209,629	30,656	8.9	16.8%
Onyx + IMI	Apr '81	1,300	$13.00	16,900	128,883	17,525	8.9	13.1%
Seagate	Sep '81	6,600	$5.00	33,000	185,237	25,865	18.9	15.1%
	Feb '83	6,600	$12.44	82,088	543,735	71,987	9.5	15.1%
Quantum	Dec '82	2,750	$20.50	56,375	187,460	31,477	6.3	18.3%
Micropolis	Jun '83	2,599	$17.00	44,183	156,837	39,180	4.2	26.9%
Priam	Jun '83	4,235	$17.00	71,995	258,036	66,594	5.0	27.9%
Tandon	Feb '81	2,173	$16.00	34,767	138,642	17,533	4.8	13.8%
	Nov '81	1,980	$29.50	58,410	322,748	53,007	6.0	18.1%
	Nov '82	3,300	$31.00	102,300	788,689	88,755	5.2	13.0%
Total		44,398		802,393	4,257,192	670,647		17.6%

COMPANY	BALANCE SHEET DATE	TOTAL SHARE EQUITY ($000)	RETAINED EARNINGS ($000)	NET $ FROM ALL POS ($000)	RE/SE (3)/(2)	IPO/SE (4)/(2)	CUMULATIVE PO OWN (%)
Miniscribe	12/31/83	41,829	437	24,130	1.0%	57.7%	13.1%
Masstor	12/31/83	47,842	(21,960)	39,565	−45.9%	82.7%	18.4%
Rodime	6/30/84	53,258	7,286	46,694	13.7%	87.7%	50.7%
Iomega	12/31/83	17,932	(19,873)	20,909	−110.8%	116.6%	18.5%
Cipher Data	6/30/84	104,834	20,795	77,832	19.8%	74.2%	55.3%
Computer Memories	3/31/84	51,809	2,206	49,593	4.3%	95.7%	28.8%
Onyx + IMI	9/30/83	31,779	10,969	17,525	34.5%	55.1%	13.1%
Seagate	6/30/84	165,026	63,610	97,852	38.5%	59.3%	27.9%
Quantum	3/31/84	60,311	16,928	31,477	28.1%	52.2%	18.3%
Micropolis	12/31/83	59,780	4,352	39,180	7.3%	65.5%	26.9%
Priam	6/30/84	91,020	8,171	66,594	9.0%	73.2%	27.9%
Tandon	9/30/83	212,030	45,835	159,295	21.6%	75.1%	25.5%
Total		937,451	138,756	670,647	14.8%	71.5%	

Sources: Securities Data Corporation (New York, New York) and company documents.
Notes:
PO—Public offerings, including initial public offerings (IPOs).
TTM Sales—Trailing twelve month sales
RE—Retained earnings
SE—Shareholders equity
PO Ownership or PO Own represents the share of the company's stock owned by buyers in public offerings.
Net to Co—Proceeds after underwriters' fees and net of any secondary offering proceeds.

——— WHAT HAPPENED?

To summarize, the period from 1977 to 1983 was one in which a number of factors combined which resulted in a massive infusion of capital—from venture capitalists and from the capital markets—into the Winchester disk drive industry. First, the product market was perceived to be very attractive. There was an ample supply of management talent. There was also an ample supply of risk capital on very attractive terms, particularly from the public capital market.

The outcome of the confluence of these factors was a remarkable chapter in American business history. A company like Seagate went from a standing start in 1979 to attain revenues in the year ended 12/31/83 of $223 million with net income of over $30 million. A number of the other participants showed similarly striking records through 1983. The sales and net income records of the public companies are shown in *Exhibit 5*.

The total industry grew at a remarkable rate during the period from 1979 to 1983. To illustrate, total disk storage industry revenues rose from $3.5 billion in 1978 to slightly over $9 billion in 1983. The OEM segment of the industry increased from $473 million to $1.9 billion over the same period. And, the hard disk drive segment of the OEM disk drive industry experienced a sales increase from $27 million in 1978 to $1.3 billion in 1983. Projections called for 1987 revenues of $22.6 billion for the entire disk drive industry, $5.0 billion for the OEM segment, and $4.5 billion for the hard disk drive portion of the OEM market. (See *Exhibit 4*.)

The spectacular performance of the industry and of the companies was reflected in valuation levels in the stock market. The highest valuations were attained in mid-1983. The aggregate market value of the twelve public companies during 1983, measuring each at the high for the year, was $5.4 billion.[3] This figure can be compared to total sales for the year for these companies of $1.2 billion, and total net income of $100 million. Sales and net income for the previous year were $587 and $48 million, respectively.

To put the valuation figures in perspective, the mid 1983 total market value of Burroughs, Control Data, Honeywell, NCR and Sperry was only $12.8 billion on 1983 sales and net income of $22.2 and $1.1 billion, respectively. (See *Exhibits* 2 and 5.)

Equally revealing is a comparison of the lofty valuation figures for the disk drive companies with those accorded a broad mix of companies at about the same time. To illustrate, at the end of 1982, for $5.5 billion an investor could have purchased a portfolio comprised of the following 10 companies: Commerce Clearing House, Paine Webber, SCOA Industries, Tuscon Electric, Cray Research, Potlatch, Emhart, ALCO Standard, Belco and Norton Simon.

---

3. The highs for each of the companies were recorded in a relatively short time frame from May to July 1983. An exception was Miniscribe which did not go public until November 1983.

In 1982 these companies generated $11.8 billion in sales and $546 million in net income.

Similarly, at the end of 1983, for $5.5 billion an investor could have purchased a portfolio comprised of the following companies: Clorox, Coastal States, Wachovia Bank, MAPCO, MGM United Artists, Payless Cashway, NCNB and Premier Industries. The total sales and net income for these 8 companies in 1983 were $12.4 billion and $504 million, respectively.

Finally, when making these valuation comparisons, it is important to note that a large percentage of the income generated by the hard disk drive companies came from interest income on excess cash raised in the IPO market. Specifically, in 1983 (see Column 7 of *Exhibit 5*), the 12 disk drive companies had $25 million in net interest income. Only 2 of the companies actually had net interest expense in that year.

To summarize, the industry had benefited substantially from the chain of success:

    →Projected Growth
        ↓
    Valuation Increase
        ↓
    Access to Capital
        ↓
    New Technical and Human Resources available
        ↓
    Technological and Manufacturing Innovation
        ↓
    Price Reductions
        ↓
    New Uses of Disk Drives
        ↓
    Projected Growth

However, while the industry as a whole and individual companies made tremendous strides in fundamental operating performance during this period, many companies ran into difficulties. The sources of problems were many, but fell into a few broad categories: technology, manufacturing, market development, customer base, competitive and financial.

In the technology area, the fundamental fact of life in the hard disk drive industry was that disk drives were complicated products to design and manufacture. Moreover, there were many different possible ways to design drives. As new firms entered the market, more ambitious standards were set for all the competitors in terms of product performance traits. However, in order to accomplish these ambitious goals, new related technology in areas such as platter media would have to be made. Some companies, such as Evotek, were never able to create the product envisioned in their business plans because media suppliers were never able to supply them.

Even when a product could be created in test quantities (essentially by hand), the transition to volume manufacturing was fraught with difficulty. The quality control standards for hard disk drives were exceptionally high, and the manufacturing requirements exacting. Some companies were able to produce sufficient acceptable quality drives at low levels of production, but experienced disastrous quality control problems when operating at higher rates.

Further, the OEM marketplace to which the disk drives were directed was not an easy market to sell. Several issues arose. First, while the total industry was experiencing explosive growth, it was not always clear who the winners would be. Many of the customers of the disk drive manufacturers were not very solid in terms of financial health or market penetration. For some of these customers, betting on a new supplier of better, cheaper disk drives was easy. But, these customers were not always the best kind of customers. When the computer industry began a shake out in late 1983 and 1984, many of these companies folded, including Eagle, Franklin, Osborne and others.

Even the "good" customers like IBM or Hewlett-Packard did not always turn out to be very good. IBM was a notoriously tough buyer. For a small company to have IBM as its largest customer was akin to playing Russian roulette. Customers like Digital Equipment or Hewlett-Packard were less cutthroat, but did not always achieve the market penetration they had forecast when signing up disk drive suppliers.

The other characteristic of the OEM marketplace was that some industry pundits and participants seem to have fallen into the log-linear extrapolation trap. That is, projections called for continued very high growth rates. However, in 1983 there was a significant downturn in the rate of growth of computer sales when compared to projections. Companies whose plans were based on the more optimistic projections experienced great difficulty. They were caught on the horns of the classic growth industry dilemma. If they did not staff, build and finance for growth, they could never achieve it. If they prepared for growth and it did not arrive on schedule, they were faced with the painful and often permanently damaging need to scale back people and plant *and* give great disappointment to the financial backers.

The greatest single industry wide problem that arose in 1983 and 1984 was the increased intensity of competition. Any industry with over 70 companies vying for a share of the market is an industry in which margins are difficult to sustain. Price cutting to get "designed-in" was rampant. Prices fell more rapidly than anyone had predicted. Given high fixed costs, including R&D, margins fell sharply.

The competitive battle took place on dimensions other than price as well. As noted earlier, each new entrant came equipped with a better or less expensive technology. Firms already in the marketplace were buffeted with demands from OEMs for better products. There was essentially no customer loyalty in this kind of market, except that enforced by the nature of the product and the "design-in" phenomenon.

The competitive battles made continued expenditures on R&D a necessity. But continued R&D increased the rate at which cash was consumed (the "burn rate") without any necessary return. Often, companies had geared up to meet high growth rates but then had to scale back when the company's market did not develop as fast as thought. Managing hyper-growth is hard; managing vacillating hyper-growth is near impossible.

All of these factors combined to put intense pressure on the financial resources of the companies in the industry. For the public companies, many had raised capital in the markets which made them better able to weather the storm. For the private companies, the problem was more serious. These companies were dependent on the venture capital and banking industries to supply necessary capital.

However, few problems are tougher for venture capitalists or bankers than to be confronted with deciding whether or not to put more money into a situation which develops slower than anticipated. It always seems that the next $1 million is all the company needs, but history shows this is a fallacy.

In this regard, the marked slowdown in the IPO market in late 1983 and the tremendous decline in the prices of some of the leading disk drive firms from mid-1983 to late 1984 caused especially troublesome problems. Basically, the public capital markets were no longer a viable source of funds for the disk drive industry. (See *Exhibit 3*.) One firm, Miniscribe, which went public in November of 1983 had to scale back the number of shares being offered from 3 to 2 million and the price from $15.00 to $11.50. Nor were the public capital markets available to some of the firms which supplied the drive manufacturers or firms which used their products.

The venture capital market also experienced a significant decline in available funds in 1984. First, the amount of new capital committed declined to $4.2 billion from $4.5 billion in 1983. Second, more money had to be set aside for investment in expansion stage financing for portfolio companies, given slow progress of those companies and the less attractive IPO market. By mid 1984, valuations in the venture capital market were down by over 40%. This decline in valuation levels mirrored a decline in the level of the Venture 100 Index of 43% from June 1983 to June 1984 and 24% from December 1983 to June 1984.

▬ COULD THE PROBLEMS HAVE BEEN PREDICTED?

It is always tempting to rely upon *ex post facto* analysis in order to demonstrate one's brilliance. In the case of the hard disk drive industry, however, much of what has happened was imminently predictable. The year 1982 was critical in the industry. Almost two-thirds of the venture capital investments were made in 1982–1984. Twenty-one out of twenty-six issues of common stock associated with disk drive companies occurred in that same period. The question for *a priori* prediction is what could have been known and what should have been known. In order to address these questions we have looked at the critical bets which were being placed and at the sources of information which were readily available at the time.

IDENTIFICATION OF CRITICAL BETS

In studying this industry in 1982, five critical bets were identifiable as determining economic success in the business. These five bets were in disk drive technology, customer development, market maturation, manufacturing technology and in the future requirements for research and development. In order to have a successful company, as distinguished from a profitable short-term investment, all five bets had to have favorable outcomes. The questions raised in the analysis were relatively simple. We shall examine the bets in turn.

Technology   Two issues were clearly important in the technological evolution: Would other computer systems components be developed which could utilize the projected power of the new hard disks being designed? Would the parts which make up the disk drive be available on a basis of timeliness, cost and technical performance which would allow assembly of the finished product? These two bets were in many ways independent. The first depended upon accurate assessment of the state of the progression toward standards in the OEM marketplace. By that time (ca. 1982) apparent standards did exist for controllers, data transfer protocols, etc. Innovative high performance disk drive designs not conforming to industry standards often met OEM resistance rendering many of the performance improvements un-attainable. Some non-conformist designs were rejected outright.

The second technological issue meant that the manufacturers of the hard drives themselves were basing their economic future on the emergence of qualified, reliable suppliers of critical components, including heads, plat-ters, motors and controls. In many cases these supplier firms were also new and untested and their specifications were elements of their own ambitious business plans. Thus the emerging company had to bet both that others saw the same technical solutions and that these suppliers would deliver on time and on budget. Many contemporary comments were made regarding the lack of judgment on the part of competitors in such reliance. Unfortunately, the name of the money raising game became having the "highest spec" product, so that for the latest disk drive entrant, the basis of initial competition became integrating all possible state of the art advancements. Such products were based on yet to be introduced supplier technologies and were intended for use with yet to be designed computer systems components (e.g., controllers) in yet to be designed computers.

Customer Development   As noted previously, two types of customers were emerging: the conservatives and the adventuresome. In many cases, the conservatives were the customers who had established markets, marketing and production facilities. Their primary concern became on-time delivery without the thirty percent "dead on arrival" factor which characterized many drive manufacturers. The other players in the computer systems market soon emerged as the major market for "the innovators." These customers were in a specifications war themselves and wished to be armed with the most advanced weapons. They were quick with the purchase order since that often guaranteed a place at the front of the delivery line if shortages materialized. Unfortunately, these same firms were often slow with payments for any other than evaluation samples. They too were dependent on the disk drive manufacturers. They often had other dependencies as well including their own in house development processes. It made no sense to have many drives on hand if there were no way to assemble them into a final deliverable package.

Ultimately, then, success for drive manufacturers hinged either on breaking into the credibility circle to become a supplier to a major (e.g., Digital Equipment or Hewlett-Packard) or else making the right bet on which of the hundreds of houses which had hung out the systems integrator shingle were going to survive. Market credibility and financial strength had to be the *sine qua non* of customer selection. Unfortunately for the newly emerging firm, breaking into the credibility circle was time consuming, costly and did not necessarily take advantage of the technological breakthroughs which had motivated formation of the venture in the first place. Basing a strategy on the emerging new computer firms exposed them to the risks associated with being a link in a chain of new ventures. At best, they could be a part of the success. At worst, they could be exposed to one of three critical sources of failure—financial default of a major customer such as Otrona, Osborne, Eagle, et cetera; technological usurpation by another emerging supplier with better, faster or cheaper specifications; or missing a critical deadline for a customer within the "credibility circle."

Market Maturation   The new venture in the disk drive industry was subject to the normal forces of market maturity. The computer industry had exhibited the same pattern repeatedly: technological based competition evolved into service based competition evolved into price competition. The rapidity of new product development in the field left some with the hope that the competition would remain technological based. However, it soon became clear that OEM customers looked to the disk drive suppliers as unenthusiastic allies in price based battles. Even worse, the possibility was present from the start that the competitive battles would take place on both a technological *and* a price basis, particularly given the intense competitive war being waged in the OEM computer market.

A second feature was also present regarding the pattern of industry structure. Many of the drive customers were knowledgeable in both the technology and manufacturing arenas. There was a significant threat of forward integration on the part of the major OEM accounts. The product had many characteristics which would encourage such integration: it was expensive, critical to long term performance, shared many operations in scope with other manufacturing steps and could be sold to others without impinging on the proprietary technology at the core of the business. Furthermore, the industry was faced with certain knowledge that many of the critical steps in the manufacturing process were of interest to formidable competitors offshore in Japan, Korea and Singapore. The *only* barrier to vertical integration and to massive foreign entry was the fact that a large, standardized market had not yet been proved to exist. Thus, normal patterns of market maturation in the computer industry would indicate rapid drops in margins which could only be arrested through dramatic increases in sales volume. In this regard, it is interesting to note that in mid 1983 there were 63 active suppliers of disk drives to the OEM market. Of these, 17 had both OEM sales *and* captive sales; and there were 21 Japanese and European companies active in the OEM market already.

Manufacturing Technology   The most critical assumption in many cases was that the product could be produced at a price which would yield profits. In many cases, manufacturing cost assumptions were based on straight line projection of rapid cost decreases. Such projections were based upon experience with the storage media which heretofore had large electronic components. The question was: could such experience be translated to the highly significant electromechanical component in the hard disk drives? Many of the significant technologies: plating, motor control and positioning were more dependent on mechanical than electronic developments. The pricing decisions for some entrants seemed predicated on learning curve effects which seemed unlikely to pan out.

Future Research and Development   The final critical bet as to the success of the companies being funded was with respect to research and development activities. In many cases, companies were founded around a basic technological idea which had its origins at previous employers. For many of the companies, the first two or three years were devoted to perfecting the application of the idea and to "ramping up the manufacturing." Few companies could afford the luxury of pursuing a second generation product while the first generation was as yet unproduced. However, it was clear from the continuing stream of product announcements and new company formations that the rate of progress of the technology would continue unabated. The successful company, at a minimum, would have to be prepared for a sequence of technological breakthroughs, not just the initial launch. Even more complex was the self-evident requirement for increased integration. The components of the hard drives—heads, platters, motor controls, arms and electronics— were coming from outside suppliers, many of which had uncertain futures. The controllers and data channels were coming from other producers. It seemed obvious that many competitors would be either integrating forward from the components to the manufacture of whole drives, or backward to the components. These changes in industry structure would require careful strategic planning. Furthermore, they would tax the already strained research and development capacities of the non-integrated players.

In sum, there were five key areas of uncertainty confronting entrants into the disk drive industry and their financial backers. A truly successful venture would only result from simultaneous positive outcomes on all five bets.

WHAT COULD BE KNOWN?

The above analysis was based on data available in the public domain. Information was readily available on the market, the technology and competition. The manner of new entrants arrival made data readily accessible. Finally, the financial data available made a count of new competitors and their prospective capabilities relatively easy to assess.

Information Available   The fact of rapid growth in the hard disk industry had made this an industry of interest to the providers of data. Market data were collected by such organizations as Dataquest, IDC, Venture Development Corporation and DISK TREND, Inc. These organizations provided extensive analysis of the market and the technology, including lists of existing and potential competitors. Technological data were readily available through a variety of industry and non-industry sources with magazines for general readership such as *High Technology* providing extensive overviews. *Computer Systems News* and *Mini-Micro Systems* provided entire issues profiling the markets, technology and competitors.

New Entrant Announcements   Almost every issue of the major trade publications provided announcements of new products and new companies. The battle for financing became a battle of public relations experts as new firms announced product capabilities as a preemptive strategy and as a device to gain financial market recognition. These announcements often included technical specifications, estimated development dates, customer letters of intent and other data of great use in analysis of the bets outlined previously.

Financial Data   By December, 1982, at least seven firms in the industry had made 12 public offerings of securities. Thus, considerable financial data were available directly from the public record. Even more valuable were the data collected by *Venture Economics*. This firm tracks all investments by venture capital firms. Thus it was possible to identify the 89 placements in 43 different companies which had been made. The amount of money available and the number of independent technological new ventures was readily apparent. Data such as those collected by Venture Economics are interesting from an historical perspective: they are critical in assessing the future course of an industry.

It is also interesting to note that venture capitalists had a potentially invaluable source of data—the torrent of business plans for entrants or participants in the disk drive and related (supplier, OEM) markets. Venture capitalists also often had simultaneous investments in one or more participants in the technological chain ranging from suppliers to drive manufacturers to computer systems builders.

Valuation Economics   Some simple calculations in mid-1983 would have revealed the absurdity of valuation levels attained by the industry participants. To illustrate, if one assumes that Jim Porter's OEM sales forecasts for 1983 to 1987 are correct, that industry sales grow at 15% per year for the next five years (1988 to 1992) and 10% per year for the following 20 years, that net margins are 10%, and that net fixed assets are 80% of sales, then the free cash flows generated by the industry can be calculated. In turn, these cash flows can be discounted to the present and compared with the valuation levels assigned in the public markets. Assuming a terminal value in year 30 equal to net book value, the present values of the projected cash flows at different discount rates are listed below:

Discount Rate	Present Value
10%	$5.3 billion
12%	$2.5 billion
18%	$0

The reader can assess the reasonableness of these assumptions but should keep in mind two factors: (1) the profitability assumption is very generous considering the existence of over 70 competitors; and (2) the values calculated above pertain to the entire OEM disk drive industry, not just the 12 companies assigned a value of $5.4 billion in mid 1983.

These data, taken as a whole, indicated the extreme risk in the bets being placed. The data suggested that while the individual bets might have reasonable probability of paying off, rational analysis clearly revealed that there was an extremely low probability for any individual firm succeeding considering that favorable outcomes on all bets was a prerequisite for success. A profitable strategy would have been to sell short a portfolio comprised of the stocks of *all* public disk drive companies knowing full well that a few companies would prosper, while most valuations would collapse under the weight of ruinous competition.

Yet, as late as the Fall of 1983, venture capitalists and stock market investors continued to pour money into the disk drive industry.

── IMPLICATIONS

Instead of the chain of success identified previously, there was a chain of failure:

┌→ Risks in Innovation Materialize
│   ↓
│   Customer Disappointments Foster Conservative Stance or
│   ↓
│   Expose Customer Financial Weaknesses or
│   ↓
│   Expose Supplier Financial Weaknesses
│   ↓
│   Which Increased Competitive Pressure to Find the Winners
│   ↓
│   Which Changes Basis of Competition to Price
│   ↓
│   Which Lowers Margins
│   ↓
│   Which Affects Capital Availability and Reduces Expenditures
│   on Future Development
│   ↓
└── Which Causes More Risk of Innovation to Materialize

The implications for the industry of this chain are obvious. It is interesting to note the important role of the capital markets in the chain. The availability of external capital served as one of the major precipitating elements both for the growth and for the downward spiral. Moreover, problems in the supply of capital affected disk drive users (OEMs) and disk drive suppliers, exacerbating the financial woes of the disk drive manufacturers themselves.

When the data shown in the exhibits are examined, it seems clear that those in the private and public capital markets had the best vantage point to anticipate:

- the emergence of numerous well financed competitors;
- the existence of multiple competing technologies;
- the absolute requirement for continuing R&D expenditures; and
- the need for external capital to fund working capital, plant and equipment which could not be generated internally during periods of rapid growth.[4]

---

4. For every $1.00 of sales, disk drive companies needed approximately $0.80 in fixed assets and working capital. To sustain high rates of growth with normal profitability levels necessitates heavy reliance on outside capital. Low profits or losses combined with rapid growth creates an untenable situation.

The professional investors did not serve the function of policing the capital markets. In fact, they continued to pour money into the industry well after the game should have been finished.

This capital market myopia may prove to be costly for both early and later players. From a national policy point of view it may prove costly as well. Initiatives may well be abandoned which might have provided the basis for improved national competitiveness. The industry has been sufficiently decimated to open the doors to foreign competition without credible threat of competitive retaliation. Moreover, the havoc wreaked in the capital markets may make it far harder for companies to raise money on acceptable terms in the future.

It is clear that massive industry restructuring will occur. Some major mergers have already been announced. Failures are being announced weekly. The returns to investors will be positive if and only if they can avoid becoming as myopically pessimistic as they were myopically optimistic. In late 1984, some of the public disk drive companies were trading at prices below net working capital per share.

▬ LESSONS TO BE LEARNED

There are several lessons which we believe can be learned by careful examination of the disk drive experience in the period under study. These include:

Taking the Broad View of the Industry Is the Key to Profitable Investment
The investment mania visited on the hard disk industry contained inherent assumptions about long-run industry size and profitability and about the future growth, profitability and access to capital for each individual company. These assumptions, had they been stated explicitly, would not have been acceptable to the rational investor. Certainly there are valuations which arise which cannot be justified under any circumstance. These are the times for the manager to raise money from the public capital markets. Those managers who took advantage of unsustainable valuation levels now have a chance to survive the shakeout.

Growth Is Not Equivalent to Profitability   The high growth rate in the industry made it the focus of considerable managerial, investor and technological attention. The industry attracted so many resources that the growth had high probability of being unprofitable. Excesses in the capital market turned an opportunity into a disaster.

Profits for Some Are Not Equivalent to a Good Business   Many players made high profits by investing in the hard disk drive business, including the investment bankers and certain of the venture capital groups which invested early enough to "catch the wave" of euphoria in the stock market and still sell under Rule 144. Many others rode the cycle up and down without liquidity. For many buyers of disk drive stocks in 1983, losses were massive. Short-term successes of some gave the illusion of long-term profitability for all. Investors should not be fooled by such inevitably ephemeral successes.

Market Instability Can Be All Bad News Very rapid change often creates entrepreneurial opportunity: it also creates risk. Analysis of the hard disk drive industry reveals the dark side of rapid technological evolution and of customer instability. Early players are often preempted by changes in technology and in customer needs. Early birds are not always winners in product markets, but late comers are almost always losers.

Recognizing the Chain One of the more important lessons to be learned from the tale of the disk drive industry is that all players—entrepreneurs, venture capitalists, investment bankers, industry analysts and investors—must recognize the chains involved in such a process. First, there was a technological chain, a series of bets on technological advances in disk drive components, disk drive designs and end-user designs. Then, there was a financial chain, a series of related bets on the internal financial health of each player in the technological chain and on the nature of access to capital in the private and public markets. The likelihood that *any* player in the disk drive industry would prosper without a serious setback due to a weak link was effectively zero. Indeed weaknesses in the chain were created *by exactly the same people whose* financial success depended on an unbroken series of favorable outcomes.

—— SUMMARY

The process of industry analysis described in this paper can be applied in many settings. All industry participants must focus first on the prospects for the industry. How large will it be? How profitable will it be? What will the path to maturity look like? Then, analysis of the prospects for individual players can be assessed. Ultimately, the effects of decisions at the individual company level *must be reconciled* with the aggregate industry view. Had this process been applied in the Winchester disk drive industry, the carnage would have been far less severe.

The lessons from the disk drive industry appear to have broad applicability in other industries ranging from biotechnology to integrated software to pizza parlor theaters. Investors who invest both their money and their sweat can benefit substantially from the kind of financial, strategic and competitive analysis which has been outlined here.

In this information age, a great deal of timely, relevant data are available. Wise investors accept consensus conclusion at their peril. Good decision making requires independent judgment. In essence, capital market myopia is a treatable disease.

—— BIBLIOGRAPHY

Going Public: The IPO Reporter, Howard & Company, Philadelphia, PA, various issues.

Porter, James N., *DISK/TREND Report,* 1979 to 1984 Editions, DISK/TREND, Inc., Mountain View, CA.

Securities Data Company, New York, NY.

Venture Capital Journal, Venture Economics, Wellesley, MA, various editions.

Venture Economics, Wellesley, MA.

—— DISCUSSION QUESTIONS

1. Why did so many smart people assume that the disk drive company in which they invested would succeed?
2. What information could be gathered to help investors place more sensible bets in rapidly growing industries?
3. Who were the winners and who were the losers in the disk drive story?
4. What are the implications of such an investment frenzy for society and national competitiveness?

The Questions Every Entrepreneur Must Answer

4

AMAR BHIDÉ

There are almost as many flavors of entrepreneurial ventures as there are entrepreneurs. The folklore regarding the risk inherent in the entrepreneurial venture is based on the fact that most ventures don't succeed and that each failure arises from a mismatch between the entrepreneur and the venture or between the venture and its context.

Amar Bhidé poses an important series of questions for the entrepreneur. These questions frame the decision process for analysis of both the fit of the entrepreneur to the venture and of the venture to its context. Complete, honest answers to the tough questions provide a go/no-go framework for the aspiring entrepreneur.

Of the hundreds of thousands of business ventures that entrepreneurs launch every year, many never get off the ground. Others fizzle after spectacular rocket starts.

A six-year-old condiment company has attracted loyal customers but has achieved less than $500,000 in sales. The company's gross margins can't cover its overhead or provide adequate incomes for the founder and the family members who participate in the business. Additional growth will require a huge capital infusion, but investors and potential buyers aren't keen on small, marginally profitable ventures, and the family has exhausted its resources.

Another young company, profitable and growing rapidly, imports novelty products from the Far East and sells them to large U.S. chain stores. The founder, who has a paper net worth of several million dollars, has been nominated for entrepreneur-of-the-year awards. But the company's spectacular growth has forced him to reinvest most of his profits to finance the business's growing inventories and receivables. Furthermore, the company's profitability has attracted competitors and tempted customers to deal directly with the Asian suppliers. If the founder doesn't do something soon, the business will evaporate.

Like most entrepreneurs, the condiment maker and the novelty importer get plenty of confusing counsel: Diversify your product line. Stick to your knitting. Raise capital by selling equity. Don't risk losing control just because things are bad. Delegate. Act decisively. Hire a professional manager. Watch your fixed costs.

Why all the conflicting advice? Because the range of options—and problems—that founders of young businesses confront is vast. The manager of a mature company might ask, What business are we in? or How can we exploit our core competencies? Entrepreneurs must continually ask themselves what business they *want* to be in and what capabilities they would *like* to develop. Similarly, the organizational weaknesses and imperfections that entrepreneurs confront every day would cause the managers of a mature company to panic. Many young enterprises simultaneously lack coherent strategies, competitive strengths, talented employees, adequate controls, and clear reporting relationships.

The entrepreneur can tackle only one or two opportunities and problems at a time. Therefore, just as a parent should focus more on a toddler's motor skills than on his or her social skills, the entrepreneur must distinguish critical issues from normal growing pains.

Entrepreneurs cannot expect the sort of guidance and comfort that an authoritative child-rearing book can offer parents. Human beings pass through physiological and psychological stages in a more or less predetermined order, but companies do not share a developmental path. Microsoft,

EXHIBIT 1
An Entrepreneur's Guide to the Big Issues

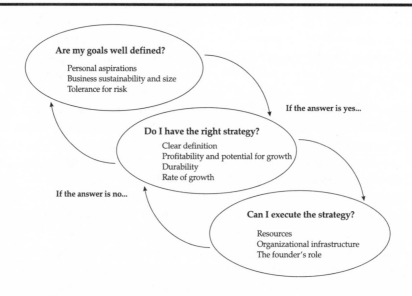

Are my goals well defined?

Personal aspirations
Business sustainability and size
Tolerance for risk

If the answer is yes...

Do I have the right strategy?

Clear definition
Profitability and potential for growth
Durability
Rate of growth

If the answer is no...

Can I execute the strategy?

Resources
Organizational infrastructure
The founder's role

Lotus, WordPerfect, and Intuit, although competing in the same industry, did not evolve in the same way. Each of those companies has its own story to tell about the development of strategy and organizational structures and about the evolution of the founder's role in the enterprise.

The options that are appropriate for one entrepreneurial venture may be completely inappropriate for another. Entrepreneurs must make a bewildering number of decisions, and they must make the decisions that are right for them. The framework I present here and the accompanying rules of thumb will help entrepreneurs analyze the situations in which they find themselves, establish priorities among the opportunities and problems they face, and make rational decisions about the future. This framework, which is based on my observation of several hundred start-up ventures over eight years, doesn't prescribe answers. Instead, it helps entrepreneurs pose useful questions, identify important issues, and evaluate solutions. The framework applies whether the enterprise is a small printing shop trying to stay in business or a catalog retailer seeking hundreds of millions of dollars in sales. And it works at almost any point in a venture's evolution. Entrepreneurs should use the framework to evaluate their companies' position and trajectory often—not just when problems appear.

The framework consists of a three-step sequence of questions. The first step clarifies entrepreneurs' current goals, the second evaluates their strategies for attaining those goals, and the third helps them assess their capacity to execute their strategies. The hierarchical organization of the questions requires entrepreneurs to confront the basic, big-picture issues before they think about refinements and details. (See *Exhibit 1*, "An Entrepreneur's Guide to the Big Issues.") This approach does not assume that all companies—or all entrepreneurs—develop in the same way, so it does not prescribe a one-size-fits-all methodology for success.

—— CLARIFYING GOALS: WHERE DO I WANT TO GO?

An entrepreneur's personal and business goals are inextricably linked. Whereas the manager of a public company has a fiduciary responsibility to maximize value for shareholders, entrepreneurs build their businesses to fulfill personal goals and, if necessary, seek investors with similar goals.

Before they can set goals for a business, entrepreneurs must be explicit about their personal goals. And they must periodically ask themselves if those goals have changed. Many entrepreneurs say that they are launching their businesses to achieve independence and control their destiny, but those goals are too vague. If they stop and think about it, most entrepreneurs can identify goals that are more specific. For example, they may want an outlet for artistic talent, a chance to experiment with new technology, a flexible lifestyle, the rush that comes from rapid growth, or the immortality of building an institution that embodies their deeply held values. Financially, some entrepreneurs are looking for quick profits, some want to generate a satisfactory cash flow, and others seek capital gains from building and selling a company. Some entrepreneurs who want to build sustainable institutions do not consider personal financial returns a high priority. They may refuse acquisition proposals regardless of the price or sell equity cheaply to employees to secure their loyalty to the institution.

Only when entrepreneurs can say what they want personally from their businesses does it make sense for them to ask the following three questions:

What Kind of Enterprise Do I Need to Build?   Long-term sustainability does not concern entrepreneurs looking for quick profits from in-and-out deals. Similarly, so-called lifestyle entrepreneurs, who are interested only in generating enough of a cash flow to maintain a certain way of life, do not need to build businesses that could survive without them. But sustainability—or the perception thereof—matters greatly to entrepreneurs who hope to sell their businesses eventually. Sustainability is even more important for entrepreneurs who want to build an institution that is capable of renewing itself through changing generations of technology, employees, and customers.

Entrepreneurs' personal goals should also determine the target size of the businesses they launch. A lifestyle entrepreneur's venture needn't grow very large. In fact, a business that becomes too big might prevent the founder from enjoying life or remaining personally involved in all aspects of the work. In contrast, entrepreneurs seeking capital gains must build companies large enough to support an infrastructure that will not require their day-to-day intervention.

What Risks and Sacrifices Does Such an Enterprise Demand?   Building a sustainable business—that is, one whose principal productive asset is not just the founder's skills, contacts, and efforts—often entails making risky long-term bets. Unlike a solo consulting practice—which generates cash from the start—durable ventures, such as companies that produce branded consumer goods, need continued investment to build sustainable advantages. For instance, entrepreneurs may have to advertise to build a brand name. To pay for ad campaigns, they may have to reinvest profits, accept equity partners, or personally guarantee debt. To build depth in their organizations, entrepreneurs may have to trust inexperienced employees to make crucial decisions. Furthermore, many years may pass before any payoff materializes—if it materializes at all. Sustained risk taking can be stressful. As one entrepreneur observes, "When you start, you just do it, like the Nike ad says. You are naïve because you haven't made your mistakes yet. Then you learn about all the things that can go wrong. And because your equity now has value, you feel you have a lot more to lose."

Entrepreneurs who operate small-scale, or lifestyle, ventures face different risks and stresses. Talented people usually avoid companies that offer no stock options and only limited opportunities for personal growth, so the entrepreneur's long hours may never end. Because personal franchises are difficult to sell and often require the owner's daily presence, founders may become locked into their businesses. They may face financial distress if they become sick or just burn out. "I'm always running, running, running," complains one entrepreneur, whose business earns him half a million dollars per year. "I work 14-hour days, and I can't remember the last time I took a vacation. I would like to sell the business, but who wants to buy a company with no infrastructure or employees?"

Can I Accept Those Risks and Sacrifices? Entrepreneurs must reconcile what they want with what they are willing to risk. Consider Joseph Alsop, cofounder and president of Progress Software Corporation. When Alsop launched the company in 1981, he was in his mid-thirties, with a wife and three children. With that responsibility, he says, he didn't want to take the risks necessary to build a multi-billion-dollar corporation like Microsoft, but he and his partners were willing to assume the risks required to build something more than a personal service business. Consequently, they picked a market niche that was large enough to let them build a sustainable company but not so large that it would attract the industry's giants. They worked for two years without salaries and invested their personal savings. In ten years, they had built Progress into a $200 million publicly held company.

Entrepreneurs would do well to follow Alsop's example by thinking explicitly about what they are and are not willing to risk. If entrepreneurs find that their businesses—even if very successful—won't satisfy them personally, or if they discover that achieving their personal goals requires them to take more risks and make more sacrifices than they are willing to, they need to reset their goals. When entrepreneurs have aligned their personal and their business goals, they must then make sure that they have the right strategy.

—— SETTING STRATEGY: HOW WILL I GET THERE?

Many entrepreneurs start businesses to seize short-term opportunities without thinking about long-term strategy. Successful entrepreneurs, however, soon make the transition from a tactical to a strategic orientation so that they can begin to build crucial capabilities and resources.

Formulating a sound strategy is more basic to a young company than resolving hiring issues, designing control systems, setting reporting relationships, or defining the founder's role. Ventures based on a good strategy can survive confusion and poor leadership, but sophisticated control systems and organizational structures cannot compensate for an unsound strategy. Entrepreneurs should periodically put their strategies to the following four tests:

Is the Strategy Well Defined?   A company's strategy will fail all other tests if it doesn't provide a clear direction for the enterprise. Even solo entrepreneurs can benefit from a defined strategy. For example, deal makers who specialize in particular industries or types of transactions often have better access to potential deals than generalists do. Similarly, independent consultants can charge higher fees if they have a reputation for expertise in a particular area.

An entrepreneur who wants to build a sustainable company must formulate a bolder and more explicit strategy. The strategy should integrate the entrepreneur's aspirations with specific long-term policies about the needs the company will serve, its geographic reach, its technological capabilities, and other strategic considerations. To help attract people and resources, the strategy must embody the entrepreneur's vision of where the company is going instead of where it is. The strategy must also provide a framework for making the decisions and setting the policies that will take the company there.

The strategy articulated by the founders of Sun Microsystems, for instance, helped them make smart decisions as they developed the company. From the outset, they decided that Sun would forgo the niche-market strategy commonly used by Silicon Valley start-ups. Instead, they elected to compete with industry leaders IBM and Digital by building and marketing a general-purpose workstation. That strategy, recalls cofounder and former president Vinod Khosla, made Sun's product-development choices obvious. "We wouldn't develop any applications software," he explains. This strategy also dictated that Sun assume the risk of building a direct sales force and providing its own field support—just like its much larger competitors. "The Moon or Bust was our motto," Khosla says. The founders' bold vision helped attract premier venture-capital firms and gave Sun extraordinary visibility within its industry.

To be useful, strategy statements should be concise and easily understood by key constituents such as employees, investors, and customers. They must also preclude activities and investments that, although they seem attractive, would deplete the company's resources. A strategy that is so broadly stated that it permits a company to do anything is tantamount to no strategy at all. For instance, claiming to be in the leisure and entertainment business does not preclude a tent manufacturer from operating casinos or making films. Defining the venture as a high-performance outdoor-gear company provides a much more useful focus.

Can the Strategy Generate Sufficient Profits and Growth?   Once entrepreneurs have formulated clear strategies, they must determine whether those strategies will allow the ventures to be profitable and to grow to a desirable size. The failure to earn satisfactory returns should prompt entrepreneurs to ask tough questions: What's the source, if any, of our competitive edge? Are our offerings really better than our competitors'? If they are, does the premium we can charge justify the additional costs we incur, and can we move enough volume at higher prices to cover our fixed costs? If we are in a commodity business, are our costs lower than our competitors'? Disappointing growth should also raise concerns: Is the market large enough? Do diseconomies of scale make profitable growth impossible?

No amount of hard work can turn a kitten into a lion. When a new venture is faltering, entrepreneurs must address basic economic issues. For instance, many people are attracted to personal service businesses, such as laundries and tax-preparation services, because they can start and operate those businesses just by working hard. They don't have to worry about confronting large competitors, raising a lot of capital, or developing proprietary technology. But the factors that make it easy for entrepreneurs to launch such businesses often prevent them from attaining their long-term goals. Businesses based on an entrepreneur's willingness to work hard usually confront other equally determined competitors. Furthermore, it is difficult to make such companies large enough to support employees and infrastructure. Besides, if employees can do what the founder does, they have little incentive to stay with the venture. Founders of such companies often cannot have the lifestyle they want, no matter how talented they are. With no way to leverage their skills, they can eat only what they kill.

Entrepreneurs who are stuck in ventures that are unprofitable and cannot grow satisfactorily must take radical action. They must find a new industry or develop innovative economies of scale or scope in their existing fields. Rebecca Matthias, for example, started Mothers Work in 1982 to sell maternity clothing to professional women by mail order. Mail-order businesses are easy to start, but with tens of thousands of catalogs vying for consumers' attention, low response rates usually lead to low profitability—a reality that Matthias confronted after three years in the business. In 1985, she borrowed $150,000 to open the first retail store specializing in maternity clothes for working women. By 1994, Mothers Work was operating 175 stores generating about $59 million in revenues.

One alternative to radical action is to stick with the failing venture and hope for the big order that's just around the corner or the greater fool who will buy the business. Both hopes are usually futile. It's best to walk away.

Is the Strategy Sustainable?   The next issue entrepreneurs must confront is whether their strategies can serve the enterprise over the long term. The issue of sustainability is especially significant for entrepreneurs who have been riding the wave of a new technology, a regulatory change, or any other change—exogenous to the business—that creates situations in which supply cannot keep up with demand. Entrepreneurs who catch a wave can prosper at the outset just because the trend is on their side; they are competing not with one another but with outmoded players. But what happens when the wave crests? As market imbalances disappear, so do many of the erstwhile high fliers who had never developed distinctive capabilities or established defensible competitive positions. Wave riders must anticipate market saturation, intensifying competition, and the next wave. They have to abandon the me-too approach in favor of a new, more durable business model. Or they may be able to sell their high-growth businesses for handsome prices in spite of the dubious long-term prospects.

Consider Edward Rosen, who cofounded Vydec in 1972. The company developed one of the first stand-alone word processors, and as the market for the machines exploded, Vydec rocketed to $90 million in revenues in its sixth year, with nearly 1,000 employees in the United States and Europe. But Rosen and his partner could see that the days of stand-alone word processors were numbered. They happily accepted an offer from Exxon to buy the company for more than $100 million.

Such forward thinking is an exception. Entrepreneurs in rapidly growing companies often don't consider exit strategies seriously. Encouraged by short-term success, they continue to reinvest profits in unsustainable businesses until all they have left is memories of better days.

Entrepreneurs who start ventures not by catching a wave but by creating their own wave face a different set of challenges in crafting a sustainable strategy. They must build on their initial strength by developing multiple strengths. Brand-new ventures usually cannot afford to innovate on every front. Few start-ups, for example, can expect to attract the resources needed to market a revolutionary product that requires radical advances in technology, a new manufacturing process, and new distribution channels. Cash-strapped entrepreneurs usually focus first on building and exploiting a few sources of uniqueness and use standard, readily available elements in the rest of the business. Michael Dell, the founder of Dell Computer, for example, made low price an option for personal computer buyers by assembling standard components in a college dormitory room and selling by mail order without frills or much sales support.

Strategies for taking the hill, however, won't necessarily hold it. A model based on one or two strengths becomes obsolete as success begets imitation. For instance, competitors can easily knock off an entrepreneur's innovative product. But they will find it much more difficult to replicate *systems* that incorporate many distinct and complementary capabilities. A business with an attractive product line, well-integrated manufacturing and logistics, close relationships with distributors, a culture of responsiveness to customers, and the capability to produce a continuing stream of product innovations is not easy to copy.

Entrepreneurs who build desirable franchises must quickly find ways to broaden their competitive capabilities. For example, software start-up Intuit's first product, Quicken, had more attractive features and was easier to use than other personal-finance software programs. Intuit realized, however, that competitors could also make their products easy to use, so the company took advantage of its early lead to invest in a variety of strengths. Intuit enhanced its position with distributors by introducing a family of products

EXHIBIT 2
Finding the Right Growth Rate

Finding the optimal growth rate for a new enterprise is a difficult and critical task. To set the right pace, entrepreneurs must consider many factors, including the following:

Economies of scale, scope, or customer network. The greater the returns to a company's scale, scope, or the size of its customer network, the stronger the case for pursuing rapid growth. When scale causes profitability to increase considerably, growth soon pays for itself. And in industries in which economies of scale or scope limit the number of viable competitors, establishing a favorable economic position first can help deter rivals.

The ability to lock in customers or scarce resources. Rapid growth also makes sense if consumers are inclined to stick with the companies with which they initially do business, either because of an aversion to change or because of the expense of switching to another company. Similarly, in retail, growing rapidly can allow a company to secure the most favorable locations or dominate a geographic area that can support only one large store, even if national economies of scale are limited.

Competitors' growth. If rivals are expanding quickly, a company may be forced to do the same. In markets in which one company generally sets the industry's standard, such as the market for personal-computer operating-system software, growing quickly enough to stay ahead of the pack may be a young company's only hope.

Resource constraints. A new venture will not be able to grow rapidly if there is a shortage of skilled employees or if investors and lenders are unwilling to fund an expansion that they consider reckless. A venture that is growing quickly, however, will be able to attract capital as well as the employees and customers who want to go with a winner.

Internal financing capability. When a new venture is not able to attract investors or borrow at reasonable terms, its internal financing capability will determine the pace at which it can grow. Businesses that have high profit margins and low assets-to-sales ratios can fund high growth rates. A self-funded business, according to the well-known sustainable growth formula, cannot expand its revenues at a rate faster than its return on equity.

Tolerant customers. When a company is young and growing rapidly, its products and services often contain some flaws. In some markets, such as certain segments of the high-tech industry, customers are accustomed to imperfect offerings and may even derive some pleasure from complaining about them. Companies in such markets can expand quickly. But in markets in which buyers will not stand for breakdowns and bugs, such as the market for luxury goods and mission-critical process-control systems, growth should be much more cautious.

Personal temperament and goals. Some entrepreneurs thrive on rapid growth; others are uncomfortable with the crises and fire fighting that usually accompany it. One of the limits on a new venture's growth should be the entrepreneur's tolerance for stress and discomfort.

for small businesses, including QuickBooks, an accounting program. It brought sophisticated marketing techniques to an industry that "viewed customer calls as interruptions to the sacred art of programming," according to the company's founder and chairman, Scott Cook. It established a superior product-design process with multifunctional teams that included marketing and technical support. And Intuit invested heavily to provide customers with outstanding technical support for free.

Are My Goals for Growth Too Conservative or Too Aggressive? After defining or redefining the business and verifying its basic soundness, an entrepreneur should determine whether plans for its growth are appropriate. Different enterprises can and should grow at different rates. Setting the right pace is as important to a young business as it is to a novice bicyclist. For either one, too fast or too slow can lead to a fall. The optimal growth rate for a fledgling enterprise is a function of many interdependent factors. (See *Exhibit 2*, "Finding the Right Growth Rate.")

━━━ EXECUTING THE STRATEGY: CAN I DO IT?

The third question entrepreneurs must ask themselves may be the hardest to answer because it requires the most candid self-examination: Can I execute the strategy? Great ideas don't guarantee great performance. Many young companies fail because the entrepreneur can't execute the strategy; for instance, the venture may run out of cash, or the entrepreneur may be unable to generate sales or fill orders. Entrepreneurs must examine three areas—resources, organizational capabilities, and their personal roles—to evaluate their ability to carry out their strategies.

Do I Have the Right Resources and Relationships?   The lack of talented employees is often the first obstacle to the successful implementation of a strategy. During the start-up phase, many ventures cannot attract top-notch employees, so the founders perform most of the crucial tasks themselves and recruit whomever they can to help out. After that initial period, entrepreneurs can and should be ambitious in seeking new talent, especially if they want their businesses to grow quickly. Entrepreneurs who hope that they can turn underqualified and inexperienced employees into star performers eventually reach the conclusion, along with Intuit founder Cook, that "you can't coach height." Moreover, after a venture establishes even a short track record, it can attract a much higher caliber of employee.

In determining how to upgrade the workforce, entrepreneurs must address many complex and sensitive issues: Should I recruit individuals for specific slots or, as is commonly the case in talent-starved organizations, should I create positions for promising candidates? Are the recruits going to manage or replace existing employees? How extensive should the replacements be? Should the replacement process be gradual or quick? Should I, with my personal attachment to the business, make termination decisions myself or should I bring in outsiders?

A young venture needs more than internal resources. Entrepreneurs must also consider their customers and sources of capital. Ventures often start with the customers they can attract the most quickly, which may not be the customers the company eventually needs. Similarly, entrepreneurs who begin by bootstrapping, using money from friends and family or loans from local banks, must often find richer sources of capital to build sustainable businesses.

For a new venture to survive, some resources that initially are external may have to become internal. Many start-ups operate at first as virtual enterprises because the founders cannot afford to produce in-house and hire employees, and because they value flexibility. But the flexibility that comes from owning few resources is a double-edged sword. Just as a young company is free to stop placing orders, suppliers can stop filling them. Furthermore, a company with no assets signals to customers and potential investors that the entrepreneur may not be committed for the long haul. A business with no employees and hard assets may also be difficult to sell, because potential buyers will probably worry that the company will vanish when the founder departs. To build a durable company, an entrepreneur may have to consider integrating vertically or replacing subcontractors with full-time employees.

How Strong Is the Organization? An organization's capacity to execute its strategy depends on its "hard" infrastructure—its organizational structure and systems—and on its "soft" infrastructure—its culture and norms.

The hard infrastructure an entrepreneurial company needs depends on its goals and strategies. (See *Exhibit 3*, "Investing in Organizational Infrastructure.") Some entrepreneurs want to build geographically dispersed businesses, realize synergies by sharing resources across business units, establish first-mover advantages through rapid growth, and eventually go public. They must invest more in organizational infrastructure than their counterparts who want to build simple, single-location businesses at a cautious pace.

A venture's growth rate provides an important clue to whether the entrepreneur has invested too much or too little in the company's structure and systems. If performance is sluggish—if, for example, growth lags behind expectations and new products are late—excessive rules and controls may be stifling employees. If, in contrast, the business is growing rapidly and gaining share, inadequate reporting mechanisms and controls are a more likely concern. When a new venture is growing at a fast pace, entrepreneurs must simultaneously give new employees considerable responsibility and monitor their finances very closely. Companies like Blockbuster Video cope by giving frontline employees all the operating autonomy they can handle while maintaining tight, centralized financial controls.

EXHIBIT 3
Investing in Organizational Infrastructure

Few entrepreneurs start out with both a well-defined strategy and a plan for developing an organization that can achieve that strategy. In fact, many start-ups, which don't have formal control systems, decision-making processes, or clear roles for employees, can hardly be called organizations. The founders of such ventures improvise. They perform most of the important functions themselves and make decisions as they go along.

Informality is fine as long as entrepreneurs aren't interested in building a large, sustainable business. Once that becomes their goal, however, they must start developing formal systems and processes. Such organizational infrastructure allows a venture to grow, but at the same time, it increases overhead and may slow down decision making. How much infrastructure is enough and how much is too much? To match investments in infrastructure to the requirements of a venture's strategy, entrepreneurs must consider the degree to which their strategy depends on the following:

Delegating tasks. As a young venture grows, its founders will probably need to delegate many of the tasks that they used to perform. To get employees to perform those tasks competently and diligently, the founders may need to establish mechanisms to monitor employees and standard operating procedures and policies. Consider an extreme example. Randy and Debbi Fields pass along their skills and knowledge through software that tells employees in every Mrs. Fields Cookies shop exactly how to make cookies and operate the business. The software analyzes data such as local weather conditions and the day of the week to generate hourly instructions about such matters as which cookies to bake, when to offer free samples, and when to reorder chocolate chips.

Telling employees how to do their jobs, however, can stifle initiative. Companies that require frontline employees to act quickly and resourcefully might decide to focus more on outcomes than on behavior, using control systems that set performance targets for employees, compare results against objectives, and provide appropriate incentives.

Specializing tasks. In a small-scale startup, everyone does a little bit of everything, but as a business grows and tries to achieve economies of scale and scope, employees must be assigned clearly defined roles and grouped into appropriate organizational units. An all-purpose workshop employee, for example, might become a machine tool operator, who is part of a manufacturing unit. Specialized activities need to be integrated by, for example, creating the position of a general manager, who coordinates the manufacturing and marketing functions, or through systems that are designed to measure and reward employees for cross-functional cooperation. Poor integrative mechanisms are why geographic expansion, vertical integration, broadening of product lines, and other strategies to achieve economies of scale and scope often fail.

Mobilizing funds for growth. Cash-strapped businesses that are trying to grow need good systems to forecast and monitor the availability of funds. Outside sources of capital such as banks often refuse to advance funds to companies with weak controls and organizational infrastructure.

Creating a track record. If entrepreneurs hope to build a company that they can sell, they must start preparing early. Public markets and potential acquirers like to see an extended history of well-kept financial records and controls to reassure them of the soundness of the business.

An evolving organization's culture also has a profound influence on how well it can execute its strategy. Culture determines the personalities and temperaments of the workforce; lone wolves are unlikely to want to work in a consensual organization, whereas shy introverts may avoid rowdy outfits. Culture fills in the gaps that an organization's written rules do not anticipate. Culture determines the degree to which individual employees and organizational units compete and cooperate, and how they treat customers. More than any other factor, culture determines whether an organization can cope with the crises and discontinuities of growth.

Unlike organizational structures and systems, which entrepreneurs often copy from other companies, culture must be custom built. As many software makers have found, for instance, a laid-back organization can't compete well against Microsoft. The rambunctiousness of a start-up trading operation may scare away the conservative clients the venture wants to attract. A culture that fits a company's strategy, however, can lead to spectacular performance. Physician Sales & Service (PSS), a medical-products distribution company, has grown from $13 million in sales in 1987 to nearly $500 million in 1995, from 5 branches in Florida to 56 branches covering every state in the continental United States, and from 120 employees to 1,800. Like other rapidly growing companies, PSS has tight financial controls. But, venture capitalist Thomas Dickerson says, "PSS would be just another efficiently managed distribution company if it didn't have a corporate culture that is obsessed with meeting customers' needs and maintaining a meritocracy. PSS employees are motivated by the culture to provide unmatched customer service."

When entrepreneurs neglect to articulate organizational norms and instead hire employees mainly for their technical skills and credentials, their organizations develop a culture by chance rather than by design. The personalities and values of the first wave of employees shape a culture that may not serve the founders' goals and strategies. Once a culture is established, it is difficult to change.

Can I Play My Role?   Entrepreneurs who aspire to operate small enterprises in which they perform all crucial tasks never have to change their roles. In personal service companies, for instance, the founding partners often perform client work from the time they start the company until they retire. Transforming a fledgling enterprise into an entity capable of an independent existence, however, requires founders to undertake new roles.

Founders cannot build self-sustaining organizations simply by "letting go." Before entrepreneurs have the option of doing less, they first must do much more. If the business model is not sustainable, they must create a new one. To secure the resources demanded by an ambitious strategy, they must manage the perceptions of the resource providers: potential customers, employees, and investors. To build an enterprise that will be able to function without them, entrepreneurs must design the organization's structure and systems and mold its culture and character.

While they are sketching out an expansive view of the future, entrepreneurs also have to manage as if the company were on the verge of going under, keeping a firm grip on expenses and monitoring performance. They have to inspire and coach employees while dealing with the unpleasantness of firing those who will not be able to grow with the company. Bill Nussey, cofounder of the software maker Da Vinci Systems Corporation, recalls that firing employees who had "struggled and cried and sacrificed with the company" was the hardest thing he ever had to do.

Few successful entrepreneurs ever come to play a purely visionary role in their organizations. They remain deeply engaged in what Abraham Zaleznik, the Konosuke Matsushita Professor of Leadership Emeritus at the Harvard Business School, calls the "real work" of their enterprises. Marvin Bower, the founding partner of McKinsey & Company, continued to negotiate and direct studies for clients while leading the firm through a considerable expansion of its size and geographic reach. Bill Gates, cofounder and CEO of multibillion-dollar software powerhouse Microsoft, reportedly still reviews the code that programmers write.

But founders' roles must change. Gates no longer *writes* programs. Michael Roberts, an expert on entrepreneurship, suggests that an entrepreneur's role should evolve from doing the work, to teaching others how to do it, to prescribing desired results, and eventually to managing the overall context in which the work is done. One entrepreneur speaks of changing from quarterback to coach. Whatever the metaphor, the idea is that leaders seek ever increasing impact from what they do. They achieve this by, for example, focusing more on formulating marketing strategies than on selling; negotiating and reviewing budgets rather than directly supervising work; designing incentive plans rather than setting the compensation of individual employees; negotiating the acquisitions of companies instead of the cost of office supplies; and developing a common purpose and organizational norms rather than moving a product out the door.

In evaluating their personal roles, therefore, entrepreneurs should ask themselves whether they continually experiment with new jobs and responsibilities. Founders who simply spend more hours performing the same tasks and making the same decisions as the business grows end up hindering growth. They should ask themselves whether they have acquired any new skills recently. An entrepreneur who is an engineer, for example, might master financial analysis. If founders can't point to new skills, they are probably in a rut and their roles aren't evolving.

Entrepreneurs must ask themselves whether they actually want to change and learn. People who enjoy taking on new challenges and acquiring new skills—Bill Gates, again—can lead a venture from the start-up stage to market dominance. But some people, such as H. Wayne Huizenga, the moving spirit behind Waste Management and Blockbuster Video, are much happier moving on to get other ventures off the ground. Entrepreneurs have a responsibility to themselves and to the people who depend on them to understand what fulfills and frustrates them personally.

Many great enterprises spring from modest, improvised beginnings. William Hewlett and David Packard tried to craft a bowling alley foot-fault indicator and a harmonica tuner before developing their first successful product, an audio oscillator. Wal-Mart Stores' founder, Sam Walton, started by buying what he called a "real dog" of a franchised variety store in Newport, Arkansas, because his wife wanted to live in a small town. Speedy response and trial and error were more important to those companies at the start-up stage than foresight and planning. But pure improvisation—or luck—rarely yields long-term success. Hewlett-Packard might still be an obscure outfit if its founders had not eventually made conscious decisions about product lines, technological capabilities, debt policies, and organizational norms.

Entrepreneurs, with their powerful bias for action, often avoid thinking about the big issues of goals, strategies, and capabilities. They must, sooner or later, consciously structure such inquiry into their companies and their lives. Lasting success requires entrepreneurs to keep asking tough questions about where they want to go and whether the track they are on will take them there.

—— DISCUSSION QUESTIONS

1. How do you evaluate the match between the appropriate goals for the business and the nature of the entrepreneur's ambition and willingness to take risks?
2. How can entrepreneurs decide what business they want to be in?
3. What new skills and attitudes must an entrepreneur have or develop to transform a fledgling business into a long-lived institution?

5   Why Be Honest If Honesty Doesn't Pay

AMAR BHIDÉ and HOWARD H. STEVENSON

One of the compelling reasons to become an entrepreneur is the opportunity to shape the culture of your company. Many people who start or acquire a company are escaping a situation where a conflict of values exists with their boss or other significant parties with whom they deal.

Bhidé and Stevenson argue that the entrepreneur must make some critical choices up front. Contrary to the arguments made by both ethicists and economists that "ethical behavior pays off," they find that there is little penalty for "bad" behavior. They argue that the fundamental reason for acting properly is the individual's sense of self. The wheels of society are greased by forgiveness, forgetfulness, and tolerance.

We bet on the rational case for trust. Economists, ethicists, and business sages had persuaded us that honesty is the best policy, but their evidence seemed weak. Through extensive interviews we hoped to find data that would support their theories and thus, perhaps, encourage higher standards of business behavior.

To our surprise, our pet theories failed to stand up. Treachery, we found, can pay. There is no compelling economic reason to tell the truth or keep one's word—punishment for the treacherous in the real world is neither swift nor sure.

Honesty is, in fact, primarily a moral choice. Businesspeople do tell themselves that, in the long run, they will do well by doing good. But there is little factual or logical basis for this conviction. Without values, without a basic preference for right over wrong, trust based on such self-delusion would crumble in the face of temptation.

Most of us choose virtue because we want to believe in ourselves and have others respect and believe in us. When push comes to shove, hard-headed businessfolk usually ignore (or fudge) their dollars-and-cents calculations in order to keep their word.

And for this, we should be happy. We can be proud of a system in which people are honest because they want to be, not because they have to be. Materially, too, trust based on morality provides great advantages. It allows us to join in great and exciting enterprises that we could never undertake if we relied on economic incentives alone.

Economists and game theorists tell us that trust is enforced in the marketplace through retaliation and reputation. If you violate a trust, your victim is apt to seek revenge and others are likely to stop doing business with you, at least under favorable terms. A man or woman with a reputation for fair dealing will prosper. Therefore, profit maximizers are honest.

This sounds plausible enough until you look for concrete examples. Cases that apparently demonstrate the awful consequences of abusing trust turn out to be few and weak, while evidence that treachery can pay seems compelling.

The moralists' standard tale recounts how E.F. Hutton was brought down by its check-kiting fraud.[1] Hutton, once the second largest broker in the nation, never recovered from the blow to its reputation and finances and was forced to sell out to Shearson.

Exxon's *Valdez* disaster is another celebrated example. Exxon and seven other oil companies persuaded the town of Valdez to accept a tanker terminal by claiming that a major spill was "highly unlikely." Their 1,800-page contingency plan ensured that any spill would be controlled within hours. In fact, when Exxon's supertanker spewed forth over 240,000 barrels of oil, the equipment promised in the cleanup plan was not available. The cost? According to recent (and still rising) estimates, Exxon's costs could exceed $2 billion, and the industry faces severe restrictions on its operations in Alaska.

But what do these fables prove? Check-kiting was only one manifestation of the widespread mismanagement that plagued Hutton and ultimately caused its demise. Incompetently run companies going under is not news. Exxon's underpreparedness was expensive, but many decisions turn out badly. Considering the low probability of a spill, was skimping on the promised cleanup equipment really a bad business decision at the time it was taken?

More damaging to the moralists' position is the wealth of evidence against trust. Compared with the few ambiguous tales of treachery punished, we can find numerous stories in which deceit was unquestionably rewarded.

Philippe Kahn, in an interview with *Inc.* magazine, described with apparent relish how his company, Borland International, got its start by deceiving an ad salesman for *BYTE* magazine.

---

1. The HBR Collection *Ethics in Practice* has six citations (Boston: Harvard Business School Press, 1989).

Inc.: *The story goes that Borland was launched by a single ad, without which we wouldn't be sitting here talking about the company. How much of that is apocryphal?*

Kahn: It's true: one full-page ad in the November 1983 issue of *BYTE* magazine got the company running. If it had failed, I would have had no-where else to go.

Inc.: *If you were so broke, how did you pay for the ad?*

Kahn: Let's put it that we convinced the salesman to give us terms. We wanted to appear only in *BYTE*—not any of the other microcomputer magazines—because *BYTE* is for programmers, and that's who we wanted to reach. But we couldn't afford it. We figured the only way was somehow to convince them to extend us credit terms.

Inc.: *And they did?*

Kahn: Well, they didn't *offer*. What we did was, before the ad salesman came in—we existed in two small rooms, but I had hired extra people so we would look like a busy, venture-backed company—we prepared a chart with what we pretended was our media plan for the computer magazines. On the chart we had *BYTE* crossed out. When the salesman arrived, we made sure the phones were ringing and the extras were scurrying around. Here was this chart he thought he wasn't supposed to see, so I pushed it out of the way. He said, "Hold on, can we get you in *BYTE*?" I said, "We don't really want to be in your book, it's not the right audience for us." "You've got to try," he pleaded. I said, "Frankly, our media plan is done, and we can't afford it." So he offered good terms, if only we'd let him run it just once. We expected we'd sell maybe $20,000 worth of software and at least pay for the ad. We sold $150,000 worth. Looking back now, it's a funny story; then it was a big risk.[2]

Further evidence comes from professional sports. In our study, one respondent cited the case of Rick Pitino, who had recently announced his decision to leave as coach of the New York Knicks basketball team with over three years left on his contract. Pitino left, the respondent wrote, "to coach the University of Kentucky (a school of higher learning, that like many others, is a party in breaking contracts). Pitino was quoted in the *New York Times* the week before as saying that he never broke a contract. But he's 32 years old and has had five jobs. What he neglected to say is that he's never completed a contract. The schools always let him run out, as they don't want an unhappy coach.

"The same thing is done by professional athletes every year. They sign a long-term contract and after one good year, they threaten to quit unless the contract's renegotiated. The stupidity of it all is that they get their way."

---

2. "Management by Necessity." *Inc.*, March 1989, p. 33. Reprinted with permission. Copyright © 1989 by Goldhirsh Group, Inc., 38 Commercial Wharf, Boston, Mass. 02110.

Compared with the ambiguity of the Hutton and Exxon cases, the clear causality in the Kahn and Pitino cases is striking. Deceiving the *BYTE* salesman was crucial to Kahn's success. Without subterfuge, Borland International would almost certainly have folded. And there is a hard dollar number (with lots of zeros in it) that professional athletes and coaches gain when they shed a contract.

What of the long term? Does treachery eventually get punished? Nothing in the record suggests it does. Many of today's blue chip companies were put together at the turn of the century under circumstances approaching securities fraud. The robber barons who promoted them enjoyed great material rewards at the time—and their fortunes survived several generations. The Industrial Revolution did not make entirely obsolete Machiavelli's observation, "Men seldom rise from low condition to high rank without employing either force or fraud."[3]

Power can be an effective substitute for trust. In theory, Kahn and Coach Pitino should suffer the consequences of their deceits and incomplete contracts: scorned by its victims and a just society, Borland shouldn't be able to place an ad. Pitino shouldn't be able to blow a whistle. But they continue to prosper. Why do reputation and retaliation fail as mechanisms for enforcing trust?

Power—the ability to do others great harm or great good—can induce widespread amnesia, it appears. Borland International's large ad budget commands due respect. Its early deceit is remembered, if at all, as an amusing prank. Pitino's record for winning basketball games wipes out his record for abandoning teams in midstream.

Prestigious New York department stores, several of our respondents told us, cavalierly break promises to suppliers.

"You send the department store an invoice for $55,000 and they send you $38,000. If you question it they say, 'Here is an $11,000 penalty for being two days late; here is the transportation tax and a dockage fee . . . you didn't follow our shipping instructions, Clause 42, Section 3C. You used the wrong carrier.' And half the time they call the order in and send the 600-page confirming document later, and they say you didn't follow our order."

"Department stores are horrible! Financial types have taken control, the merchants are out. The guy who keeps beating you down goes to his boss at the end of the year and says 'Look at the kind of rebates I got on freight reduction—$482,000. I delayed payments an average of 22 days from my predecessor at this kind of amount, and this is what I saved.'"

Nevertheless, suppliers still court their tormentors' orders.

"Don't tell me that department stores will go out of business because

_____

3. *The Discourses*, Chapter XIII, Book 2, Modern Library Edition, 1950.

they treat their suppliers like that! I don't believe that at all. They have too much power—they screw one guy, and guys are waiting in line to take a shot at them again."

Heroic resistance to an oppressive power is the province of the students at Tiananmen Square, not the businessfolk in the capitalist societies the students risk their lives to emulate. Businesspeople do not stand on principle when it comes to dealing with abusers of power and trust. You have to adjust, we were told. If we dealt only with customers who share our ethical values, we would be out of business.

A real estate developer we interviewed was blunt:

"People are really whores. They will do business with someone they know they can't trust if it suits their convenience. They may tell their lawyers: 'Be careful, he's dishonest; he's not reliable and he will try to get out of the contract if something happens.' But those two do business with each other. . . . I've done transactions with people knowing that they were horrible and knowing that I'd never talk to them. But the deal was so good, I just accepted it, did the best I could, and had the lawyers make triply sure that everything was covered."

Sometimes the powerful leave others no choice. The auto parts supplier has to play ball with the Big Three, no matter how badly he or she has been treated in the past or expects to be treated in the future. Suppliers of fashion goods believe they absolutely have to take a chance on abusive department stores. Power here totally replaces trust.

Usually, though, power isn't quite that absolute, and some degree of trust is a necessary ingredient in business relationships. Pitino has demonstrated remarkable abilities in turning around basketball programs, but he isn't the only coach available for hire. Borland International's business is nice to have, but it can't make or break a computer magazine. Nevertheless, even those with limited power can live down a poor record of trustworthiness. Cognitive inertia—the tendency to search for data that confirm one's beliefs and to avoid facts that might refute them—is one reason why.

To illustrate, consider the angry letters the mail fraud unit of the U.S. Post Office gets every year from the victims of the fake charities it exposes. Apparently donors are annoyed that they can't keep sending contributions to a cause they believed in. They want to avoid information that says they have trusted a fraud.

When the expected reward is substantial and avoidance becomes really strong, reference checking goes out the window. In the eyes of people blinded by greed, the most tarnished reputations shine brightly.

Many a commodity broker's yacht has been financed by cleaning out one customer after another. Each new doctor or dentist who is promised the moon is unaware of and uninterested in his or her predecessor's fate. Such investors want to believe in the fabulous returns the broker has promised.

3

They don't want references or other reality checks that would disturb the dreams they have built on sand. Thus can the retail commodity brokerage business flourish, even though knowledgeable sources maintain that it wipes out the capital of 70% of its customers every year.

The search for data that confirm wishful thinking is not restricted to naïve medical practitioners dabbling in pork bellies. The *Wall Street Journal* recently detailed how a 32-year-old conglomerateur perpetrated a gigantic fraud on sophisticated financial institutions such as Citibank, the Bank of New England, and a host of Wall Street firms. A Salomon Brothers team that conducted due diligence on the wunderkind pronounced him highly moral and ethical. A few months later. . . .

Even with a fully disclosed public record of bad faith, hard-nosed businesspeople will still try to find reasons to trust. Like the proverbial "other woman," they'll reason, "It's not his fault." And so it comes to pass that Oscar Wyatt's Coastal Corporation can walk away from its gas-supply contracts;[4] then, with the consequent lawsuits not yet settled, issue billions of dollars of junk bonds. Lured by high yields, junk bond investors choose to believe that their relationship will be different: Wyatt *had* to break his contracts when energy prices rose; and a junk bond is so much more, well, *binding* than a mere supply contract.

Similarly, we can imagine, every new Pitino employer believes the last has done Pitino wrong. Their relationship will last forever.

Ambiguity and complexity can also take the edge off reputational enforcement. When we trust others to keep their word, we simultaneously rely on their integrity, native ability, and favorable external circumstances. So when a trust appears to be breached, there can be so much ambiguity that even the aggrieved parties cannot apprehend what happened. Was the breach due to bad faith, incompetence, or circumstances that made it impossible to perform as promised? No one knows. Yet without such knowledge, we cannot determine in what respect someone has proved untrustworthy: basic integrity, susceptibility to temptation, or realism in making promises.

The following example, in which we hear the buyer of a company who was taken in by the seller's representations, is instructive:

"The seller said: 'We have a technology that is going to be here for a long time. We own the market.' We liked this guy so much, it was funny. He's in the local area, he knew my father. He's a great guy to talk to, with all sorts of stories.

"He managed to fool us, our banks, and a mezzanine lender, and he

---

4. "In the early 1970s," reports Forbes (Toni Mack, "Profitable if Not Popular," May 30, 1988, p. 34), "Wyatt found himself, squeezed between rising natural gas prices and low-priced contracts to supply gas to cities like San Antonio and Austin. His solution? Renege. He simply refused to honor the contract."

ended up doing quite well on the deal. Then the company went on the skids. The funny thing is, afterwards he bought the business back from us, put a substantial amount of his own capital in, and still has not turned it around. I'm just not sure what was going on.

"I guess he believed his own story and believed it so much that he bought the business back. He was independently wealthy from another sale anyway, and I think he wanted to prove that he was a great businessman and that we just screwed the business up. If he was a charlatan, why would he have cared?"

Where even victims have difficulty assessing whether and to what extent someone has broken a trust, it is not surprising that it can be practically impossible for a third party to judge.

That difficulty is compounded by the ambiguity of communication. Aggrieved parties may underplay or hide past unpleasantnesses out of embarrassment or fear of lawsuits. Or they may exaggerate others' villainies and their own blamelessness. So unless the victims themselves can be trusted to be utterly honest and objective, judgments based on their experiences become unreliable and the accuracy of the alleged transgressor's reputation unknowable.

A final factor protecting the treacherous from their reputations is that it usually pays to take people at face value. Businesspeople learn over time that "innocent until proven guilty" is a good working rule and that it is really not worth getting hung up about other people's pasts.

Assuming that others are trustworthy, at least in their initial intentions, *is* a sensible policy. The average borrower does not plan million-dollar scams, most coaches do try to complete their contracts, and most buyers don't "forget" about their suppliers' bills or make up reasons for imposing penalties.

Even our cynical real estate developer told us:

"By and large, most people are intrinsically honest. It's just the tails, the ends of the bell-shaped curve, that are dishonest in any industry, in any area. So it's just a question of tolerating them."

Another respondent concurred:

"I tend to take people at face value until proven otherwise, and more often than not, that works. It doesn't work with a blackguard and a scoundrel, but how many total blackguards and scoundrels are there?"

Mistrust can be a self-fulfilling prophecy. People aren't exclusively saints or sinners; few adhere to an absolute moral code. Most respond to circumstances, and their integrity and trustworthiness can depend as much on how they are treated as on their basic character. Initiating a relationship assuming that the other party is going to try to get you may induce him or her to do exactly that.

Overlooking past lapses can make good business sense too. People and companies do change. It is more than likely that once Borland International got off the ground, Kahn never pulled a fast one on an ad salesman again. Today's model citizen may be yesterday's sharp trader or robber baron.

Trust breakers are not only unhindered by bad reputations, they are also usually spared retaliation by parties they injure. Many of the same factors apply. Power, for example: attacking a more powerful transgressor is considered foolhardy.

"It depends on the scale of the pecking order," we were told. "If you are a seller and your customer breaks promises, by and large you don't retaliate. And if you are an employee and your employer breaks promises, you usually don't retaliate either."

Where power doesn't protect against retaliation, convenience and cognitive inertia often do. Getting even can be expensive; even thinking about broken trusts can be debilitating. "Forget and move on" seems to be the motto of the business world.

Businesspeople consider retaliation a wasteful distraction because they have a lot of projects in hand and constantly expect to find new opportunities to pursue. The loss suffered through any individual breach of trust is therefore relatively small, and revenge is regarded as a distraction from other, more promising activities.

Retaliation is a luxury you can't afford, respondents told us.

"You can't get obsessed with getting even. It will take away from everything else. You will take it out on the kids at home, and you will take it out on your wife. You will do lousy business."

"It's a realization that comes with age: retaliation is a double loss. First you lose your money; now you're losing time."

"Bite me once, it is your fault; bite me twice, my fault. . . . But bite me twice, and I won't have anything to do with you, and I'm not going to bite back because I have better things to do with my life. I'm not going to litigate just for the pleasure of getting even with you."

Only those who have their best years behind them and see their life's work threatened actively seek to retaliate. In general, our interviews suggested, businesspeople would rather switch than fight. An employee caught cheating on expenses is quietly let go. Customers who are always cutting corners on payments are, if practicable, dropped. No fuss, no muss.

Our interviewees also seemed remarkably willing to forget injuries and to repair broken relationships. A supplier is dropped, an employee or sales rep is let go. Then months or years later the parties try again, invoking some real or imaginary change of circumstances or heart. "The employee was under great personal strain." "The company's salesman exceeded his brief." "The company is under new management." Convenience and cognitive inertia seem to foster many second chances.

What about the supposed benefits of retaliation? Game theorists argue that retaliation sends a signal that you are not to be toyed with. This signal,

we believe, has some value when harm is suffered outside a trusting relationship: in cases of patent infringement or software piracy, for example. But when
a close trusting relationship exists, as it does, say, with an employee, the
inevitable ambiguity about who was at fault often distorts the signal retaliation sends. Without convincing proof of one-sided fault, the retaliator may
get a reputation for vindictiveness and scare even honorable men and women
away from establishing close relationships.

Even the cathartic satisfaction of getting even seems limited. Avenging
lost honor is passé, at least in business dealings. Unlike Shakespeare's Vene-
tian merchant, the modern businessperson isn't interested in exacting revenge
for its own sake and, in fact, considers thirsting for retribution unprofessional
and irresponsible.

"There is such a complete identification in my mind between my
company's best interests and what I want to do that I am not going to permit
anything official out of spite. If I can't rationalize (retaliation) and run it
through my computer brain, it will be relegated to my diary and won't be a
company action."

We would be guilty of gross exaggeration if we claimed that honesty
has no value or that treachery is never punished. Trustworthy behavior does
provide protection against the loss of power and against invisible sniping. But
these protections are intangible, and their dollars-and-cents value does not
make a compelling case for trustworthiness.

A good track record can protect against the loss of power. What if you
stop being a winning coach or your software doesn't sell anymore? Long-
suppressed memories of past abuses may then come to the fore, past victims
may gang up to get you. A deal maker cited the fate of an investment bank
that was once the only source of financing for certain kinds of transactions.

"They always had a reputation for being people who would outline
the terms of the deal and then change them when it got down to the closing.
The industry knew that this is what you had to expect; our people had no
choice. Now that the bank has run into legal problems and there are other
sources of funds, people are flocking elsewhere. At the first opportunity to
desert, people did—and with a certain amount of glee. They are getting no
goodwill benefit from their client base because when they were holding all
the cards they screwed everybody."

Another entrepreneur ascribed his longevity to his reputation for
trustworthiness:

"The most important reason for our success is the quality of my
(product) line. But we wouldn't have survived without my integrity because
our lines weren't always very successful. There are parabola curves in all
businesses, and people still supported me, even though we had a low, because
they believed in me."

Trustworthiness may also provide immediate protection against invisible sniping. When the abuse of power banishes trust, the victims often try to get their own back in ways that are not visible to the abuser: "I'm not in business just to make a profit. If a client tries to jerk me around, I mark up my fees." "The way to get even with a large company is to sell more to them."

On occasion, sniping can threaten the power it rebels against. The high-handedness of department stores, for example, has created a new class of competitors, the deep discounter of designer apparel.

"Ordinarily, manufacturers don't like to sell their goods at throwaway prices to people like us," says one such discounter. "But our business has thrived because the department stores have been systematically screwing their suppliers, especially after all those leveraged buyouts. At the same time, the manufacturers have learned that we treat them right. We scrupulously keep our promises. We pay when we say we'll pay. If they ask us not to advertise a certain item in a certain area, we don't. If they make an honest mistake in a shipment, we won't penalize them.

"The department stores have tried to start subsidiaries to compete with us, but they don't understand the discount business. Anyone can set up an outlet. What really matters is the trust of the suppliers."

Neither of these benefits can be factored easily into a rational business analysis of whether to lie or keep a promise. Sniping is invisible; the sniper will only take shots that you cannot measure or see. How could you possibly quantify the financial repercussions when suppliers you have abused refuse your telephone orders or ship hot items to your competitors first?

Assessing the value of protection against the loss of power is even more incalculable. It is almost as difficult to anticipate the nature of divine retribution as it is to assess the possibility that at some unknown time in the future your fortunes *may* turn, whereupon others *may* seek to cause you some unspecified harm. With all these unknowns and unknowables, surely the murky future costs don't stand a chance against the certain and immediate financial benefits from breaking an inconvenient promise. The net present values, at any reasonable discount rate, must work against honoring obligations.

Given all this, we might expect breaches of trust to be rampant. In fact, although most businesspeople are not so principled as to boycott powerful trust breakers, they do try to keep their own word most of the time. Even allowing for convenient forgetfulness, we cannot help being swayed by comments like this:

"I've been in this business for 40 years. I've sold two companies; I've gone public myself and have done all kinds of dealings, so I'm not a babe in the woods, OK? But I can't think of one situation where people took advantage of me. I think that when I was young and naïve about many things, I may have been underpaid for what my work was, but that was a learning experience."

One reason treachery doesn't swamp us is that people rationalize constancy by exaggerating its economic value.

"Costs have been going up, and it will cost me a million dollars to complete this job. But if I don't, my name will be mud and no one will do business with me again."

"If I sell this chemical at an extortionate price when there is a shortage, I will make a killing. But if I charge my customers the list price, they will do the right thing by me when there is a glut."

Just as those who trust find reasons for the risks they want to run, those who are called on to keep a difficult promise cast around for justification even when the hard numbers point the other way. Trustworthiness has attained the status of "strategic focus" and "sustainable competitive advantage" in business folklore—a plausible (if undocumented) touchstone of long-term economic value.

But why has it taken root? Why do business men and women want to believe that trustworthiness pays, disregarding considerable evidence to the contrary? The answer lies firmly in the realm of social and moral behavior, not in finance.

The businesspeople we interviewed set great store on the regard of their family, friends, and the community at large. They valued their reputations, not for some nebulous financial gain but because they took pride in their good names. Even more important, since outsiders cannot easily judge trustworthiness, businesspeople seem guided by their inner voices, by their consciences. When we cited examples to our interviewees in which treachery had apparently paid, we heard responses like:

"It doesn't matter how much money they made. Right is right and wrong is wrong."

"Is that important? They may be rich in dollars and very poor in their own sense of values and what life is about. I cannot judge anybody by the dollars; I judge them by their deeds and how they react."

"I can only really speak for myself, and to me, my word is the most important thing in my life and my credibility as an individual is paramount. All the other success we have had is secondary."

The importance of moral and social motives in business cannot be overemphasized. A selective memory, a careful screening of the facts may help sustain the fiction of profitable virtue, but the fundamental basis of trust is moral. We keep promises because we believe it is right to do so, not because it is good business. Cynics may dismiss the sentiments we heard as posturing, and it is true that performance often falls short of aspiration. But we can find no other way than conscience to explain why trust is the basis for so many relationships.

At first, these findings distressed us. A world in which treachery pays because the average businessperson won't fight abusive power and tolerates dishonesty? Surely that wasn't right or efficient, and the system needed to be fixed! On further reflection, however, we concluded that this system was fine, both from a moral and a material point of view.

The moral advantages are simple. Concepts of trust and, more broadly, of virtue would be empty if bad faith and wickedness were not financially rewarding. If wealth naturally followed straight dealing, we would only need to speak about conflicts between the long term and the short, stupidity and wisdom, high discount rates and low. We would worry only about others' good sense, not about their integrity. It is the very absence of predictable financial reward that makes honesty a moral quality we hold dear.

Trust based on morality rather than self-interest also provides a great economic benefit. Consider the alternative, where trust is maintained by fear.

A world in which the untrustworthy face certain retribution is a small world where everyone knows (and keeps a close eye on!) everyone else. A village, really, deeply suspicious not only of commodities brokers but also of all strangers, immigrants, and innovators.

No shades or ambiguities exist here. The inhabitants trust each other only in transactions in which responsibilities are fully specified—"deliver the diamonds to Point A, bring back cash"—and breaches of trust are clear. They do not take chances on schemes that might fail through the tangled strands of bad faith, incompetence, overoptimism, or plain bad luck.

A dark pessimism pervades this world. Opportunities look scarce and setbacks final. "You can't afford to be taken in even once" is the operating principle. "So when in doubt, don't."

In this world, there are no second chances either. A convicted felon like Thomas Watson, Sr. would never be permitted to create an IBM. A Federal Express would never again be extended credit after an early default on its loan agreements. The rules are clear: an eye for an eye and a tooth for a tooth. Kill or be killed.

Little, closed, tit-for-tat worlds do exist. Trust is self-reinforcing because punishment for broken promises is swift—in price-fixing rings, loan-sharking operations, legislative log rolling, and the mutually assured destruction of nuclear deterrence. Exceed your quota and suffer a price war. Don't pay on time and your arm gets broken. Block my pork barrel project and I'll kill yours. Attack our cities and we'll obliterate yours.

At best such a world is stable and predictable. Contracts are honored and a man's word really does become his bond. In outcome, if not intent, moral standards are high, since no one enters into relationships of convenience with the untrustworthy. On the other hand, such a world resists all change, new ideas, and innovations. It is utterly inimical to entrepreneurship.

Fortunately, the larger world in which we live is less rigid. It is populated with trusting optimists who readily do business with strangers and innovators. A 26-year-old Steve Jobs with no track record to speak of or a

52-year-old Ray Kroc with nearly ten failures behind him can get support to start an Apple or a McDonald's. People are allowed to move from Maine to Montana or from plastics to baked goods without a lot of whys and wherefores.

Projects that require the integrity and ability of a large team and are subject to many market and technological risks can nonetheless attract enthusiastic support. Optimists focus more on the pot of gold at the end of the rainbow than on their ability to find and punish the guilty in case a failure occurs.

Our tolerance for broken promises encourages risk taking. Absent the fear of debtors' prison and the stigma of bankruptcy, entrepreneurs readily borrow the funds they need to grow.

Tolerance also allows resources to move out of enterprises that have outlived their functions. When the buggy whip manufacturer is forced out of business, we understand that some promises will have to be broken— promises that perhaps ought not to have been made. But adjustments to the automobile age are more easily accomplished if we don't demand full retribution for every breach of implicit and explicit contract.

Even unreconstructed scoundrels are tolerated in our world as long as they have something else to offer. The genius inventors, the visionary organizers, and the intrepid pioneers are not cast away merely because they cannot be trusted on all dimensions. We "adjust"—and allow great talent to offset moral frailty—because we know deep down that knaves and blackguards have contributed much to our progress. And this, perhaps unprincipled, tolerance facilitates a dynamic entrepreneurial economy.

Since ancient times, philosophers have contrasted a barbaric "state of nature" with a perfect, well-ordered society that has somehow tamed humankind's propensity toward force and fraud. Fortunately, we have created something that is neither Beirut nor Bucharest. We don't require honesty, but we honor and celebrate it. Like a kaleidoscope, we have order and change. We make beautiful, well-fitting relationships that we break and reform at every turn.

We should remember, however, that this third way works only as long as most of us live by an honorable moral compass. Since our trust isn't grounded in self-interest, it is fragile. And, indeed, we all know of organizations, industries, and even whole societies in which trust has given way either to a destructive free-for-all or to inflexible rules and bureaucracy. Only our individual wills, our determination to do what is right, whether or not it is profitable, save us from choosing between chaos and stagnation.

—— DISCUSSION QUESTIONS

1. How do you distinguish between behavior that is simply not nice and behavior that is immoral?

2. When confronted with an explicit or implicit breach of faith, how do you decide whether it is worth trying to "punish" the transgressor?
3. When do you accept or try to change "common practices" in your industry that you think may be unethical?

6   The Road Well Traveled

AMAR BHIDÉ

Although entrepreneurship has been studied extensively in the last decade, it remains the subject of much myth and speculation. Comments like "it's risky," "if you haven't done it by the time you're 40, it's too late," and "you need a truly innovative and creative idea to be successful" abound.

In this piece, Bhidé reports on a survey of several groups of entrepreneurs, including Harvard Business School graduates and 100 of the Inc. *"500." The results suggest that entrepreneurship is a career option that is available to many. Common sense suggestions focus on where opportunities are most likely to be found, as well as how the prospective entrepreneur can prepare to take advantage of them.*

▬▬ ALMOST EVERYONE CAN

It doesn't take an exceptional MBA graduate to start his or her own business. This survey reveals that many MBA's have been doing so for a great many years. The trend clearly predates the current popularity of the entrepreneurial folk heroes. The entrepreneurs surveyed don't appear obviously less capable of holding down a job than the rest of their classmates. They do work for several years for someone else; they don't switch jobs particularly frequently; and they don't start their businesses because they had a disagreement or have been fired by their employers. The "self-employed" do regard themselves as being greater risk takers than their classmates, but this may simply be an ex-post facto assessment: because they are more on their own, they suppose that they must have taken more risk.

Many individuals in the population at large may lack the basic drive to start a business, but such individuals are unlikely to apply to business school or secure admission if they do. Moreover, the wide range of potential

---

Amar Bhidé prepared this note as the basis for classroom discussion rather than to illustrate effective or ineffective handling of an administrative situation. It is a rewrite based on a previous case by the same author titled "The Road Well Traveled" HBS note No. 396-277. Copyright © 1998 by the President and Fellows of Harvard College. Harvard Business School case 898-205.

opportunities that entrepreneurs can pursue allows many different types of individuals to succeed. For instance, the person who would flop as film producer may have just the right personality to start a money management firm for conservative clients. Given a baseline of ambition and business skills, therefore, becoming an entrepreneur is more a matter of finding the right fit between the individual and the opportunity than it is of conforming to an idealized entrepreneurial type.

The *Inc.* "500" interviews and this survey should also reassure those who lack self-confidence in their creative abilities and prescience. Entrepreneurs seldom invent and market unique products; rather, they build their ventures around incremental innovations and modifications. They usually take advantage of industry changes that others initiate rather than lead or force change themselves. They don't even appear to get an especially early start in capitalizing on new trends—they tend to enter industries in their growth phase, not in their infancy.

THE REWARDS APPEAR WORTHWHILE

Albeit at the cost of somewhat greater stress, almost all entrepreneurs appear to find fulfillment in their work. Many also report significant financial rewards, turning modest initial net worth into millions a decade or so after graduation. Of course, not everyone did so, but starting their own businesses put the entrepreneurs in a position where a combination of luck and talent could lead to great wealth in a relatively short period of time. Few jobs in established firms offer as much potential, except for very senior executives.

AND WHAT'S THE ALTERNATIVE?

Working in a large corporation is unlikely to offer enough long-term security or opportunity for advancement to compensate for the more limited financial opportunities. The data suggest that large companies, with their numerous entry level positions, are a magnet for graduating MBAs. As the years pass, however, the typically ambitious and hard-driving MBAs find that the supply of the positions they seek is small compared to the demand. Let's assume (generously) that each of the 500 largest companies in the United States has 10 positions that an MBA would be satisfied with, 20 years after graduation. If the net retirement rate in these positions is of the order of 10% annually, then there are only 500 positions that the tens of thousands of MBAs who graduate every year can compete for.

Before large corporations got lean and mean, folklore held that managers who didn't climb to the top of the corporate ladder could rest on middle management rungs. Much data, however, suggests that even in the bygone era of corporate benevolence, "up-or-out" was the norm for many MBAs.

Those in large companies who weren't promoted either left or were pushed out to make way for younger, cheaper, and hungrier replacements. This migratory process is likely to accelerate in the future for several reasons:

- The huge growth in the supply of MBAs (more than 60,000 degrees are now granted in the United States every year).
- The thinning of middle management ranks.
- The adoption of up-or-out, which has long been the de facto reality in many large firms, as an explicit general rule.

——— DON'T RUSH—OR WAIT FOREVER

Only a handful of MBA graduates start their businesses right out of school. The peak period for starting a business appears to be five to ten years after graduation for alumni starting "traditional" ventures and somewhat longer for professional service entrepreneurs. The advantages of waiting seem to include:

- Exposure to opportunities. The data suggest that most entrepreneurs exploit opportunities they perceive in the course of their jobs rather than through top-down research. Besides, the passage of time increases the number of ideas that prospective entrepreneurs encounter (or that are brought to their attention) and therefore the likelihood of finding a good one.
- Time to accumulate personal capital to seed the venture.
- Building of credibility and relationships with potential clients, especially for professional service entrepreneurs.

At the same time, waiting too long may not be optimal. There is little evidence that very deep experience matters, except perhaps in starting professional service firms. This survey also suggests that the longer graduates put off self-employment, the more likely they are to start personal consulting practices rather than launch larger-scale traditional ventures. Although some individuals may want to operate solo, casual observation suggests that many are forced into independent consulting because they lost their jobs, don't have the idea or the energy to start any other kind of business, and need to generate income quickly. Therefore, while it is inadvisable to jump on the first opportunity that comes by, it probably helps to start looking early, begin thinking about start-up ideas, and cultivate the networks that might provide leads, rather than have to scramble in the face of an involuntary job transition.

——— KNOW WHERE THE FISH ARE

Entrepreneurially inclined individuals will tend to generate lots of ideas for a business, but they will have limited time to evaluate them, especially while holding down a full-time job. Evaluating potential opportunities is also challenging because reliable information can be difficult to obtain in the turbulent markets that often hold the most potential. The aspiring entrepreneur therefore needs to develop the capacity to weed out the obviously unusable ideas quickly and focus on the opportunities that are more likely to work. The experienced entrepreneurs surveyed suggest several rules of thumb for evaluating opportunities rapidly. For example, the typical entrepreneur who starts off without a proprietary, blockbuster idea should look for:

- Markets in flux rather than stable or mature markets. Entrepreneurs should ask themselves "Why wouldn't this concept have worked five years ago?" and be suspicious of situations where there has been no recent external change that has created the opportunity.
- Industries with low capital requirements and flat or declining returns to scale so that the start-up does not confront large incumbents.
- Markets where customers will pay a significant premium for customization and personalized service.
- Products or services where the unit sale is large enough to support a direct sales effort.

PREPARE TO TRAVEL STEERAGE CLASS

Business school graduates enjoy some advantages in raising capital but can raise significant amounts only if they have a powerful concept for establishing sustainable advantages in a large market. Entrepreneurs usually do not often have this kind of compelling vision and must therefore rely on personal resources or relatively small amounts of capital raised from others. This lack of initial capital also forces entrepreneurs to operate in quite a different mode than they may have been used to as employees of established companies. For instance, they have to do without administrative support and infrastructures and perform many mundane or menial tasks themselves. They can't afford to advertise widely or implement the marketing approaches that are routine in large companies. They may have to live with marginal or unqualified employees and the lack of stimulation and feedback that talented colleagues can provide. Because they lack standby lines of credit and trained financial staff, cash flow is a constant concern.

Besides setting the appropriate expectations, the aspiring entrepreneur can prepare for the transition from employee to business owner by observing how others successfully make do with less. One suggestion is to build a "play book" of ways to generate free publicity, project a big company image, find employees who are "diamonds in the rough" and make the most of them, collect receivables early and stretch the payables, negotiate bank loans, and so on.

MAINTAIN LOW PERSONAL OVERHEAD

After having lived on student budgets, MBAs naturally feel the urge to enjoy a better lifestyle after they graduate. But high personal spending patterns can impair your chances of succeeding in an entrepreneurial career. As we have seen, the majority of MBA graduates cannot rely on starting businesses with other people's money and need personal savings to finance their ventures. Even those few who do have a venture that others are willing to fund can enhance their credibility and negotiating position if they commit personal funds to get the enterprise rolling. Moreover, whether or not a venture is self funded, the entrepreneur can more easily nurture it through its start-up phase if he or she has low personal overhead and does not need to draw down funds to support a luxurious lifestyle.

LEARN TO SELL

The data suggest that face-to-face selling is a crucial skill: for most ventures to have any chance of success the entrepreneur has to be able to call on a customer and secure an order for a product or service that usually performs the same functions as rival offerings. Such selling skills are often not well developed among MBAs. Although they all "sell" themselves to colleges, graduate schools, and employers and some may even have worked in a sales function, they will rarely have faced the special sales challenges confronted by entrepreneurs. These challenges include:

- The lack of a name or track record. Entrepreneurs don't have the entree that graduating MBAs have with recruiters or that IBM sales representatives have with MIS departments. Also, when they do get through a prospect's door, they are likely to face the "How do we know you are going to be around?" question.
- Extreme asymmetry of power. Graduating MBAs and IBM sales representatives have some leverage with recruiters and computer buyers who are predisposed to see the talent or product offered as necessary, valuable, and distinctive. Entrepreneurs, we have seen, are generally in a much weaker position—their products or services often represent a discretionary purchase, and their offerings lack inherent distinctiveness.
- The real-time integration of selling with marketing and strategy formulation. The data suggest that entrepreneurs often differentiate their offering by customizing features or ancillary services. And, to the extent that access to prospects is limited, the entre-

preneurs have to make on-the-spot decisions about what features to offer, what to charge, and so on—which may have long-term implications for a firm's marketing and other strategies. The IBM salesperson, in contrast, operates off product and pricing policies that others have previously made and generally does not have to formulate strategy on the fly.

Developing the appropriate selling skills therefore requires work not only on the basics (such as eliciting information, objection handling, and closing) but also on attitudes. Entrepreneurs must learn, my interviews with the *Inc.* "500" founders suggest, to utterly subjugate their egos. They have to deal with frequent rejection, suppress the desire to show how smart they are by scoring debating points, be willing to capitulate to unreasonable demands, and sometimes, as one founder put it, to beg for the order. These are typically not the reflexes MBAs develop in classrooms or in large companies.

EXPECT MAJOR COURSE CHANGES

Only a few entrepreneurial voyages resemble those of spaceships launched with all the fuel they need to attain stable orbit after liftoff. Most begin, we have seen, with ideas and resources that cannot take them very far. They have little cash and weak personnel. Their profits derive more from the entrepreneur's hustle or temporary market dislocations than from durable competitive advantages. Moreover, approaches that help an entrepreneur get started with minimal resources often do not lead to a self-sustaining enterprise. The personal drive and attention that win over early customers, for instance, are not enough to sustain a durable franchise. If an entrepreneur wishes to build a business for the long haul, he or she has to consider making major changes. The personnel may have to be upgraded and new controls and systems introduced. Similarly, an underlying business concept may have to be restructured to establish sustainable advantages and realize economies of scale and scope.

KNOW WHAT YOU WANT

But why should an entrepreneur want a durable enterprise in the first place? There are some obvious tradeoffs: Building a self-sustaining enterprise frees entrepreneurs from the constant effort of keeping their ventures going and gives them the option of harvesting the fruits of their past labors. At the same time, building such an enterprise often entails making long-term bets. That is, it involves risk. Unlike a solo consulting practice, which generates cash from the start but cannot outlive the entrepreneur, the venture needs continued investment in working capital to build sustainable advantages. And many years may pass before the entrepreneur sees any payoff.

This survey of entrepreneurs shows that individuals find attractive financial and psychological rewards from both large and small ventures, those that rely on the entrepreneur's personal capabilities as well as those with independent structural advantages. Apparently, decisions about what business to start and whether and how to grow it, are to a considerable degree matters of personal preference. Possibly the greatest luxury an entrepreneurial career affords lies in the freedom it gives the entrepreneur to pursue his or her own goals—provided, of course, that those goals have been well thought out in the first place. You have to know what you want.

—— DISCUSSION QUESTIONS

1. What kind of work experience seems most likely to provide the benefits the author describes in "Don't rush—or wait forever"?
2. Can you provide a rationale for each of the points articulated in "Know where the fish are"? Can you describe examples of industries that seem to meet these criteria?
3. What barriers or hurdles do you see as you contemplate your own entrepreneurial career?

Making Business Sense of the Internet 7

SHIKHAR GHOSH

Shikar Ghosh is chairman and cofounder of Open Market, an Internet-commerce-software company. In this piece, Ghosh offers an enlightening perspective on entrepreneurial thinking. The Internet represents an exciting set of new business opportunities, as firms like Amazon.com and Netscape have demonstrated. Additionally, Internet commerce is both a threat and an opportunity to many established businesses. Ghosh provides a well-reasoned example of entrepreneurial thinking as it applies to these opportunities. He describes various Web-based business models, the assumptions upon which they are based, and the strategies required to succeed with each of these models.

This piece is an excellent example of the kind of disciplined, opportunity-oriented thinking that is the hallmark of entrepreneurial behavior.

The Internet is fast becoming an important new channel for commerce in a range of businesses—much faster than anyone would have predicted two years ago. But determining how to take advantage of the opportunities this new channel is creating will not be easy for most executives, especially those in large, well-established companies.

Three years after emerging into the spotlight, the Internet poses a difficult challenge for established businesses. The opportunities presented by the channel seem to be readily apparent: by allowing for direct, ubiquitous links to anyone anywhere, the Internet lets companies build interactive relationships with customers and suppliers, and deliver new products and services at very low cost. But the companies that seem to have taken advantage of these opportunities are start-ups like Yahoo! and Amazon.com. Established businesses that over decades have carefully built brands and physical distribution relationships risk damaging all they have created when they pursue commerce in cyberspace. What's more, Internet commerce is such a new phenomenon—and so much about it is uncertain and confusing—that it is difficult for executives at most companies, new or old, to decide the best way to use the channel. And it is even more difficult for them to estimate accurately the returns on any Internet investment they may make.

Nonetheless, managers can't afford to avoid thinking about the impact of Internet commerce on their businesses. At the very least, they need to understand the opportunities available to them and recognize how their companies may be vulnerable if rivals seize those opportunities first. To determine what opportunities and threats the Internet poses, managers should focus in a systematic way on what the Internet can allow their particular organization to do. Broadly speaking, the Internet presents four distinct types of opportunities.

First, through the Internet companies can establish a direct link to customers (or to others with whom they have important relationships, such as critical suppliers or distributors) to complete transactions or trade information more easily. Second, the technology lets companies bypass others in the value chain. For instance, a book publisher could bypass retailers or distributors and sell directly to readers. Third, companies can use the Internet to develop and deliver new products and services for new customers. And, fourth, a company could conceivably use the Internet to become the dominant player in the electronic channel of a specific industry or segment, controlling access to customers and setting new business rules.

By exploring the opportunities and threats they face in each of these four domains, executives can realistically assess what, if any, investments they should begin to make in Internet commerce and determine what risks they will need to plan for. A sound Internet-commerce strategy begins by articulating what is possible.

━━━ ESTABLISHING THE INTERNET CHANNEL

To deliver new services or bypass intermediaries, companies first need to build direct connections to customers. That means more than just designing a Web site to market a company's offerings. The behavior of customers who are already buying goods and services on-line clearly indicates that companies can build momentum in their digital channels by using Internet technology to deliver three forms of service to customers.

First, companies are giving customers just about the same level of service through the Internet that they can currently get directly from a salesperson. For instance, Marshall Industries, a distributor of electronic components, makes it very convenient for customers to search for and order parts on-line. Visitors to the company's Web site can hunt for a part by its number, by a description, or by its manufacturer. They can place an order for parts, pay for them electronically, track the status of previous orders, and even speed delivery time by connecting directly from Marshall Industries' Web site to the shipping company's site.

Second, companies are using new Internet technologies to personalize

EXHIBIT 1
At What Point Should You Master Your Internet Channel?

Not all companies will want to conduct business over the Web yet. Ask these questions to see if you can reduce costs and increase service levels by establishing an Internet channel.

1. How much does it cost me to provide services that customers could get for themselves over the Internet?
2. How can I use the information I have about individual customers to make it easier for them to do business with me?
3. What help can I give customers by using the experience of other customers or the expertise of my employees?
4. Will I be at a significant disadvantage if my competitors provide these capabilities to customers before I do?

interactions with their customers and build customer loyalty. One way is to tailor the information and options customers see at a site to just what they want. For example, when visitors arrive at Time Warner's Pathfinder Internet site—which contains articles and graphics from more than 25 of the company's publications—they can register, identifying the topics that interest them. Then the Pathfinder site recognizes the visitors whenever they return and tailors the content delivered to their screens.

Similarly, Staples is using personalization to reduce the cost large companies incur when ordering its office supplies electronically. Staples is creating customized supply catalogs that can run on its customers' intranets. These catalogs contain only those items and prices negotiated in contracts with each company. The Staples system can maintain lists of previously ordered items, saving customers time when reordering. By searching and ordering electronically, Staples' customers can reduce their purchase-order processing costs—which through traditional channels can sometimes amount to more than the cost of the goods purchased. And over time, Staples could learn a great deal about its customers' preferences and use that information to offer other customized services that competitors, especially in the physical world, would find difficult to duplicate. For example, Staples could recommend new items to customers to complement what they have previously purchased or offer price discounts for items that customers have looked at in their on-line catalogs but have not yet bought.

Third, companies can provide valuable new services inexpensively. A company could, for example, draw on data from its entire customer base to make available wide-ranging knowledge of some topic. For instance, if a customer has a problem with a product, he or she might consult a site's directory of frequently asked questions to see how others have solved it. Or the customer might benefit from knowing how others have used a particular product. Amazon.com, the on-line bookstore, encourages customers to post reviews of books they have read for other visitors to see, making it possible for customers to scan reviews by peers—in addition to those from publications such as the *New York Times*—before deciding to order a book.

The combination of these three levels of service could make the Internet channel very compelling for customers. And because these services are basically just electronic exchanges, they can be delivered at very low cost. Investments in the electronic channel displace traditional sales, marketing, and service costs; moreover, the technology allows companies to offer increasingly higher levels of service without incurring incremental costs for each transaction. For example, Cisco Systems conducts 40% of its sales—$9 million per business day—over the Internet. The company expects the volume to increase from its current level of more than $2 billion per year to $5 billion by July. By selling through the Internet, the company has reduced its annual operating expenses by nearly $270 million. But Cisco's managers say the real value of the electronic channel is that it allows the company to provide buyers with a range of advantages—convenience, information, personalization, and interactivity—that competitors cannot.

The opportunity for those companies that move first to establish electronic channels is a threat to those that do not. When customers choose to do business through an Internet channel, they make an investment of their time and attention. It takes time to figure out how to use a site and become comfortable with it. If a site involves personalization, customers have to fill out profiles and, perhaps, update or otherwise adjust them over time. They may also modify their own systems to make better use of electronic connections: for instance, ten of Cisco's largest customers are installing new software in their own computers to tie their inventory and procurement systems to Cisco's systems. Finally, customers must offer sensitive information, such as credit card numbers, and trust that the seller will manage that information discretely. For these reasons, the average customer, once he or she has established a relationship with one electronic seller, is unlikely to go through the effort again with many suppliers.

This all-too-human reluctance to abandon what works is a formidable obstacle to companies that do not move aggressively enough. Followers in this new channel risk being stuck with the unenviable task of getting customers to abandon investments they have already made in a competitor—and this will be a barrier that increases over time as the relationship between customer and competitor deepens.

The emergence of the direct connection could have another consequence that managers need to anticipate. Companies that currently do not want to participate in Internet commerce may be forced to by competitors or customers. Consider how Internet commerce could affect Dell and Compaq as potential suppliers of computer equipment to General Electric. Several major divisions of GE are completing plans to put parts and equipment up for bid on the Internet. They intend to deal directly with suppliers over the Net and to receive multiple bids for every part. Based on early trials, GE estimates that it will shave $500 million to $700 million off its purchasing costs over three years and cut purchasing cycle times by as much as 50%. The company expects that in five years it will purchase the majority of everything it buys through this Web-based bidding system.

Dell sells computer equipment directly to its customers, sometimes over the Internet, but Compaq sells through distributors. That could put Compaq at a disadvantage for GE's business. Its distribution costs are higher, its pricing and information systems are designed for conducting business through distributors, and any move Compaq makes toward accepting orders over the Internet could threaten those distributors.

What's worse from Compaq's point of view, Dell could gain internal efficiencies through the Internet channel, as Cisco has discovered, and learn a great deal more about customers. Dell is currently selling almost $3 million worth of computers a day through its Web site. By the year 2000, the company expects to handle half of all its business—ranging from customer inquiries to orders to follow-up service—through the Internet. Such developments are forcing Dell's rivals in the computer industry to develop Internet channels of their own. And first movers like Dell, both established companies and start-ups, are already beginning to emerge in other industries, such as auto retailing (General Motors and Auto-By-Tel), financial services (Merrill Lynch and E*Trade), and trade publishing (Cahners and VerticalNet).

As pioneering companies in an industry begin to build electronic channels, rivals will need to reexamine their value chains. New companies have no existing value chains to protect, of course, and so can set up their businesses in ways that take advantage of the Internet. But companies that deal through others to reach end customers (such as Compaq and IBM in the computer industry) will need to weigh the importance of protecting existing relationships with the distributors and partners that account for most of their current revenue against the advantages of establishing future strategic positions and revenue streams. This is one of the most difficult issues that large, established companies face in making decisions about engaging in Internet commerce. For instance, although a book publisher might be tempted to use the Internet to sell directly to bookstores or even to readers, it runs the risk of damaging long-standing relationships with distributors.

─── PIRATING THE VALUE CHAIN

Companies may find they have little choice but to risk damaging relationships in their physical chains to compete in the electronic channel. The ubiquity of the Internet—the fact that anyone can link to anyone else—makes it potentially possible for a participant in the value chain to usurp the role of any other participant. Not only could the book publisher bypass the distributor and sell directly to readers, but Barnes & Noble and Amazon.com could

EXHIBIT 2
Should You Pirate Your Value Chain?

When companies pirate the value chain of their industry, they are essentially eliminating layers of costs that are built into the current distribution system. Ask these questions to see if the distribution chain in your industry is likely to consolidate and if you should take the initiative to make that happen.

1. Can I realize significant margins by consolidating parts of the value chain to my customer?
2. Can I create significant value for customers by reducing the number of entities they have to deal with in the value chain?
3. What additional skills would I need to develop or acquire to take over the functions of others in my value chain?
4. Will I be at a competitive disadvantage if someone else moves first to consolidate the value chain?

decide to publish their own books—after all, they have very good information, gathered and collated electronically, about readers' interests.

Consider how various participants in the personal-computer value chain are already squaring off against one another to reach the end customer. Currently, computer manufacturers like Apple, Compaq, and IBM purchase the components that make up the computers from suppliers like Intel (which makes microprocessors), and Seagate Technology (which produces hard-disk drives). Manufacturers supply machines to distributors such as Ingram Micro and MicroAge, which in turn supply retailers like CompUSA. That is the physical value chain for much of the industry (excluding manufacturers that sell through direct mail, such as Dell and Gateway 2000). But Internet commerce is already blurring the boundaries in that chain. Ingram Micro and MicroAge are seeking to bypass the physical retailers by setting up Internet-based services that would allow anyone to become an on-line retailer of computers. MicroAge lets physical or virtual resellers choose from a selection of computer systems on-line whose availability and prices vary daily. Soon, on-line retailers will be able to relay orders directly from customers to Ingram Micro, which will acquire the computers from the manufacturer or if necessary assemble the components, ship the computers directly back to the customer, and provide subsequent support services.

At the same time, retailers like CompUSA are establishing their own brands of computers, which they intend to sell both in stores and over the Internet. They will order parts electronically from component suppliers. (The Internet makes the logistics of such a system easier to manage.) Finally, Apple and other computer makers have made the difficult choice to sell computers over the Internet, too.

Competition is even coming from outside the value chain. United Parcel Service has announced that it is setting up a service for virtual merchants. Using Internet commerce software, a merchant can create a product catalog and a storefront on the Web. UPS will then manage the operations. The merchant or its customers will be able to schedule deliveries, track packages, and coordinate complex schedules over the Web. Conceivably, an on-line PC vendor could let consumers create customized machines, made up of components drawn from several different manufacturers. UPS would then gather the parts overnight, deliver them to an assembly facility, pick up the assembled product, and deliver it to the customer.

On-line providers of information about computers, such as CNET, are already becoming resellers of software and hardware products. For instance, visitors to the CNET Web site can read reviews of software and then order a highly touted product from the CNET store without ever leaving the site. The Internet search-service Yahoo! also sells hardware and software through its site by linking seamlessly to partners' sites. Even ancillary players in the industry's value chain—including banks like Barclays and First Union, and telecommunications providers, such as AT&T—have established shopping services on their sites and could sell computers (or anything else) to their customers. In other words, once companies establish an electronic channel, they could choose to become pirates in the value chain, capturing margins from other participants up or down the chain.

Pirates will probably emerge from the ranks of those innovative companies that can recognize where core value will be most effectively delivered to customers over a network. Consider how RoweCom, an electronic subscription agent on the Internet, has captured margins from intermediaries in the value chain for periodicals by using the network to change the industry's business model. Publishers traditionally have sold periodicals to libraries through subscription agents. Agents typically consolidate orders from many libraries and forward them to publishers, charging 3% to 5% of the list price for their services. RoweCom allows libraries to order periodicals directly from publishers over the Internet and make payments electronically through Banc One. RoweCom also provides a new level of service. For instance, libraries can place orders at any time and can easily use the site to track their budgets. Most important, however, RoweCom charges $5 per transaction, not the 3% to 5% of the list price. As a result, libraries have been moving their expensive orders to RoweCom. In the past 18 months, more than 75 libraries—including some of the largest in the nation—have subscribed to RoweCom's Internet service.

Individual publishers are also linking directly to end users. For example, Academic Press has established an Internet channel to deliver content electronically to libraries. Other academic and professional publishers have also done this, but Academic Press has changed the business model for electronic-content delivery. Rather than issuing licenses to individual libraries, the company has begun selling site licenses for all the libraries in an entire country. For instance, any library in Finland can now access all of Academic Press's publications under a single countrywide license—eliminating the need for a distributor or an agent. Competing publishers will now need to reconsider their distribution chain in any nation where libraries have signed up for Academic Press's broader license.

Value chain pirates are in a position to define new business rules and introduce new business models. But pirates will also need to develop new capabilities. Those companies that stand to lose margins to pirates currently provide very real value to customers—such as merchandising skills (which Ingram Micro does not have but CompUSA does), logistics expertise (which CompUSA does not have but UPS does), and information management (which CNET can do better than Apple). To succeed, pirates must be able to provide that value, either by building the skills in house or by allying with others.

IBM discovered this to be the case when in 1996 it launched Infomart, an electronic-content delivery initiative, and World Avenue, a cyberspace mall. IBM had believed that it could use its computer network to become a new intermediary, pirating margins from physical distributors. Infomart would have challenged the physical distribution chain for publications by making it possible for customers to go to a single site to have material from several different publishers delivered to them electronically. World Avenue was to be a single site from which consumers could access a number of different electronic stores. But IBM soon recognized that being a superpublisher required more than just making content available, and on-line merchandising meant more than just being a storefront. IBM lacked the editorial and magazine-circulation skills of publishers and the merchandising and advertising skills of retailers. The computer company had the direct connection to customers, but that was not enough to make the initiatives succeed. IBM halted both initiatives the following year.

DIGITAL VALUE CREATION

Instead of (or perhaps in addition to) pirating value from others in the value chain, companies that establish Internet channels can choose to introduce new products and services. Not only is the Internet channel a direct connection to customers or to any participant in the value chain, it is also a platform for innovation. It is a way to produce and distribute new combinations of digital information—or to create new transaction models and services—without incurring the traditional costs of complexity that exist in the physical world. And clearly, innovation will heighten competition if companies choose to create new value through the Internet by providing something that had previously been furnished by someone else.

For instance, a broker that has established an Internet channel to offer securities transaction services might begin to provide customers with access to research reports for free, which, of course, will harm businesses that offer such reports for a fee. Each time a company, large or small, succeeds in taking away a small piece of someone else's business, it undermines the economics of that business—like termites eating away at the support beams of a house.

The Internet presents three opportunities for creating new value by taking away bits of someone else's business. First, a company can use its direct access to customers; each time a customer visits a company's Web site is an opportunity to deliver additional services or provide a path for other businesses that want to reach that customer. Snap-on Tools Corporation, a manufacturer of professional-grade tools for automobile repair businesses, adds new value for its customers by supplying them with regulatory information about such subjects as waste disposal at no fee. This strengthens Snap-on Tools' relationship with its customers, but it weakens the business of commercial publishers that provide such information for a fee. Netscape Communications Corporation, a company that develops and sells Internet software, receives significant additional revenue at very little marginal cost by selling advertising space on its site. Netscape effectively draws revenue away from sites that derive the bulk of their revenue from advertising.

Second, a company can mine its own digital assets to serve new customer segments. Standard & Poor's Corporation, a company that has traditionally provided financial information to institutional customers, is using the information it has stored digitally to provide financial planning services to individuals over the Internet. For a small fee, customers will be able to evaluate the risk of their individual securities portfolios, make portfolio allocation decisions based on the advice of market experts. They can even be alerted electronically to changes in analysts' recommendations that affect their portfolios. Standard & Poor's could never afford to target individuals with

EXHIBIT 3
Can You Create New Digital Value?

Companies that seek to create digital value using their Internet channels could do so in a number of ways. Ask these questions to see how your company could best leverage its existing digital assets or leverage the digital assets of other companies that are on the Internet.

1. Can I offer additional information or transaction services to my existing customer base?
2. Can I address the needs of new customer segments by repackaging my current information assets or by creating new business propositions using the Internet?
3. Can I use my ability to attract customers to generate new sources of revenue, such as advertising or sales of complementary products?
4. Will my current business be significantly harmed by other companies providing some of the value I currently offer on an à la carte basis?

this service through a sales force or other traditional sales channels. But by offering the service at low cost over the Internet, the company will be able to compete with brokers and financial analysts.

Finally, a company can take advantage of its ability to conduct transactions over the Internet to take away value from others. For example, a major bank that has traditionally provided check-clearing services is planning to use the Internet to offer complete bill-payment services for universities and order-management services for retailers. The new, targeted services should help strengthen the bank's core transaction-processing business, and it will also eat away at the business of companies that currently provide these services, such as those that furnish electronic data interchange (EDI) services.

In all three cases, each addition of digital value by one company weakens the business proposition of another company in a small way. Ultimately, the risk for established businesses is not from digital tornadoes but from digital termites.

———— CREATING A CUSTOMER MAGNET

Companies that can establish direct links to their customers, pirate their industry's value chain, and take away bits of value digitally from other companies may put themselves in a position to become powerful new forces in electronic commerce. They may become the on-line versions of today's category-killer stores—such as Toys "R" Us and Wal-Mart—and become *category destinations.*

Certainly, there are economies of scale inherent in concentration on the Internet. Traditional reasons for having numerous suppliers in an industry are not valid on the Internet. First, the Internet makes physical distance between consumers and suppliers largely irrelevant: any store is equally accessible to any customer. Second, stores that establish a strong position or dominant brand on the Internet can grow rapidly, relatively unhampered by the costs and delays common when expanding in the physical world. Third, single stores can differentiate services for many customer segments, customizing offerings and tailoring the way visitors enter and move around the site to address regional or individual differences. As a result, a small number of companies can meet the diverse needs of large segments of the global market.

But more important, if customers are not willing to learn how to navigate hundreds of different sites, each with its own unique layout, then the Web will turn out to be a naturally concentrating medium. People feel comfortable returning to the stores they know, virtual or physical, because they can easily navigate the familiar aisles and find what they are looking for. They will gravitate toward sites that can meet all their needs in specific categories. And customers will head for the places many other customers frequent if they can interact with one another and derive some value from the interaction.

Consider how this might work. A customer magnet for music compact discs might offer visitors a choice of practically any CD available by connecting to all major distributors. The site might also offer a rich selection of CD reviews from public and specialized sources—everything from the most popular music magazines to the electronic bulletin boards of major music schools. It could enable customers to interact with one another, sharing experiences and opinions. It could also offer several transaction options: customers might choose to participate in for-fee membership programs or benefit from affinity or loyalty programs. The site might be structured to appear differently to customers from different countries or to those with varying levels of technical skills. It might also co-opt other sites aimed at the same customer base by offering commissions for every visitor a customer sends along. Finally, the site could create marketing programs in the physical world to ensure that its brand became synonymous with music CDs. The customer magnet would own the connection, the access, and the direct interface to the customer. Industry participants, such as the CD distributors and music magazines, would have to operate through the magnet.

The steps a company could take to become a customer magnet are remarkably similar in very different industries. A solid-waste company, too, could develop the ability to provide its customers with an electronic place for gathering information, for interacting with other customers, and for conducting transactions, and then invest in creating critical mass and momentum. In this instance, industry participants might include government agencies in different countries and various suppliers of pumps and valves.

In any case, it is conceivable that some companies will attempt to control the electronic channel by becoming the site that can provide customers

EXHIBIT 4
Should I Become a Customer Magnet?

Becoming a customer magnet involves a substantial investment in marketing and infrastructure. Ask these questions to see if you should make the investment to become a magnet or how you should work with other companies to influence the type of customer magnet that develops in your industry.

1. Can my industry be divided into logical product, customer, or business-model segments that could evolve into customer magnets?
2. What services could an industry magnet offer my customers that would make it efficient for them to select and purchase products or services?
3. What partnerships or alliances could I create to establish the critical mass needed to become an industry magnet?
4. Will the emergence of a competing industry magnet hurt my relationships with customers or my margins?

with everything they could want. Customer magnets could organize them-selves around a specific type of product or service, a particular segment of customers, an entire industry, or a unique business model. A given industry may have room for only five, or even fewer, such magnets. Being few in number, they will have a tremendous influence on the shape of their industry. They will not own all the assets for delivering service—such as CD distribu-tion or solid-waste pumps—but they could control access to suppliers and subtly sway customers' choices by promoting or ignoring individual brands. Over time, a customer magnet could become the electronic gateway to an entire industry.

PRODUCT MAGNETS

Amazon.com has quickly established itself as a product magnet and today is synonymous with book retailing on the Web. Amazon offers custom-ers virtually every book available, provides access to reviews, to book discus-sion groups, and even to authors themselves. It also offers a number of other services, such as notifying readers by E-mail when a new book is available and recommending books based on patterns perceived in customers' past purchases.

Consider the implications of Amazon's success. Today, only Barnes & Noble rivals Amazon in the electronic channel. Customers will probably need no more than four or five of these companies. As on-line revenues increase for these two electronic merchants, what role will there be in the channel for the thousands of book retailers that have physical operations? Moreover, could Amazon use its infrastructure to move into music or professional peri-odicals? The tendency toward concentration in the electronic channel, which is unfolding in book sales, is likely to occur in a variety of other product categories as well.

SERVICE MAGNETS

Companies like Yahoo!, Excite, and Lycos are becoming magnets in information services about the Internet. In less than two years, the field of competitors in this category has been reduced from more than 20 to fewer than 5 companies, and none of the established yellow-page companies or other paper-based search providers, such as the *Thomas Register*, is on the list. Today, new search services targeted at ever narrower subsegments—such as those for locating people or telephone numbers—find it more efficient to market themselves under the Yahoo! umbrella rather than go it alone. The cost of attracting a critical mass of customers on the Web is too high for companies that are not magnets. The fact that smaller companies are willing to offer their services through Yahoo! suggests that Yahoo! has already achieved the critical mass it needs to be a service magnet.

CUSTOMER SEGMENT MAGNETS

New companies are targeting well-defined segments of customers and becoming their premier electronic channel. Tripod, for example, bills itself as an "electronic community" that targets Generation Xers—18 to 35 year olds. The service provides information on such issues as careers, health, and money, and facilitates commerce by linking directly to the sites of other companies directed at this segment. Visitors to Tripod's Web site can find jobs through Classifieds2000, for instance, or establish bank accounts through Security First Network Bank. In less than two years, Tripod's community has grown to more than 300,000 members.

INDUSTRY MAGNETS

Companies such as Auto-By-Tel and Microsoft CarPoint (which sell cars, trucks, and other vehicles over the Internet); Imx Mortgage Exchange; the FastParts Trading Exchange (which distributes electronic components); and InsWeb Corporation (which offers insurance) could become customer magnets for entire industries. These companies bring hundreds of suppliers together under one virtual roof, providing customers with an easy, convenient way to compare and purchase offerings.

InsWeb, for example, allows customers to compare prices for several different products, including health, life, and automobile insurance. The site also contains consumer information about insurance products, lists available agents, gives visitors access to Standard & Poor's ratings of insurance companies, and offers on-line simulation tools to help customers estimate the amount of coverage they may need for certain lines of insurance. If a customer likes a quote for, say, a ten-year term-life insurance policy from a highly rated company, he or she can click on a button to obtain an on-line application form and begin the application process.

The insurance companies that market themselves and sell policies through InsWeb will face challenges similar to those other established companies are likely to encounter when more industry magnets begin to appear in Internet channels: How can a company differentiate its products when the rules are determined by other parties? In side-by-side comparisons, how can a company emphasize its unique value? How can it differentiate itself through marketing when the magnet can standardize the information or determine which differentiating features will be emphasized? For a while, insurance providers could refuse to join InsWeb's listings. They might even sell policies through their own individual sites. But customers will prefer the convenience of shopping in one location. If InsWeb can get enough providers and build significant traffic to its site, laggard insurers will have little choice but to participate.

BUSINESS MODEL MAGNETS

Companies could become magnets by introducing new business models that take advantage of the interactive capabilities of the Internet. For instance, Onsale is an on-line auction house for consumer electronic products, computer equipment, and sporting goods. Customers can visit the site any time, day or night, to learn about various goods and make a bid. Similarly, NECX is establishing a spot market for computer parts. And Altra Energy Technologies is an Internet-based marketplace for natural gas that had revenues of more than $1 billion in 1997. Other companies are trying to establish similar marketplaces for advertising space, airline seats, ship-cargo space, and other perishable goods. In each case, an entire industry really only needs one magnet to manage the interactions between suppliers and customers.

Clearly, few companies can justify the investment that will be needed to become a customer magnet. Managers can't yet quantify the financial rewards from such an initiative, and the risks are daunting. It is difficult and expensive for companies to integrate their existing business applications with the Internet technologies they will need to conduct commerce on-line. It will also be difficult to integrate electronic processes for commerce with existing physical processes that often involve numerous functions and many business units within an organization. And companies that create customer magnets will likely need to work with competitors—and their systems and processes—to offer customers everything they could want.

But if companies decide that Internet commerce is too important to ignore, it may be possible for them to adopt less risky approaches to protect their positions in the electronic channel. For instance, more than ten of the nation's largest banks, including Banc One, Citicorp, and First Union, have formed a joint venture with IBM to create a common industry interface for retail banking over the Internet. The banks recognize that owning direct access to the customer is critical. They do not want to cede that access to an industry outsider, such as a home-banking software provider like Intuit or Microsoft, or to a single enterprising bank. Instead, the partners in the joint venture are sharing the costs of building a technological base for electronic banking, and in the process they are attempting to protect their industry's existing relationships with its customers.

Established companies might also stake out competitive positions in the electronic channel by allying with others to create cascading value chains. That is, companies that furnish complementary services to a common customer base could band together to establish an exclusive bundle of services in the electronic channel. For instance, hotels, travel agents, guidebook publishers, and car rental agencies could create an exclusive network that would provide customers with everything they need when traveling.

Finally, established companies could find ways to embed their products or services in customer magnets. For instance, Amazon has become a book provider to Yahoo!'s customers. When someone visits Yahoo!'s site to search for, say, furniture repair, a button pops up asking the visitor if he or she wants a book on the topic.

For managers in established businesses, the Internet is a tough nut to crack. It is very simple to set up a Web presence but quite difficult to create a Web-based business model. One thing is certain: the changes made possible by the Internet are strategic and fundamental. However these changes play out in individual industries, they will unquestionably affect every company's relationship with its customers and the value propositions for many companies in the foreseeable future.

——— DISCUSSION QUESTIONS

1. What factors determine whether a company is well served by establishing an Internet channel?
2. What kind of businesses are best positioned to do business over the Internet?
3. What factors influence the type of Internet business model most appropriate for a particular enterprise?

PART TWO

STRATEGIES AND TACTICS FOR STARTING, ACQUIRING, AND GROWING THE VENTURE

EVALUATING NEW VENTURE OPPORTUNITIES

Developing Start-up Strategies   8

AMAR BHIDÉ

A great deal of attention is often focused on the business plan for a start-up venture. Yet, very few business plans actually portend the future of the venture. Unexpected situations arise affecting the capacity of the entrepreneur and the organization to take advantage of change.

Bhidé's analysis of entrepreneurial ventures points to the important role of action, *choosing the right niche for a base, and then moving decisively in response to change. He gives guidance for integrating action and analysis that has helped many successful entrepreneurs convert small ideas into world-class opportunities.*

Seize the day or look before you leap? Apparently, many entrepreneurs act before they analyze. Of the hundreds of thousands who "just do it" every year, only a few earn an attractive return. The great majority of start-ups fold or drag along in what one entrepreneur calls the land of the living dead. And although bad luck plays an important role, many failures are predestined and predictable. Then too, we find a great many individuals whose endless research precludes action: By the time they can fully investigate an opportunity, it no longer exists. Entrepreneurs may also lose their enthusiasm, as continued analysis engenders a corrosive pessimism.

     Entrepreneurs don't need, however, a better manual for evaluating opportunities. The strategic and financial analytical frameworks used in large corporations require more time, money and data than entrepreneurs can muster. Finding an effective middle ground between planning paralysis and none at all requires a more fluid, ad-hoc approach. To minimize the time and effort spent, the astute entrepreneur screens out obvious losers quickly. Ideas that do pass the screen are analyzed parsimoniously, focusing on just those issues which matter. And, action is so closely integrated with analysis that, on the surface, we may not even see any formal planning.

Professor Amar Bhidé prepared this note as the basis for class discussion. Copyright © 1993 by the President and Fellows of Harvard College. Harvard Business School case 394-067.

——— SO MUCH TO DO . . .

The decision to launch a new venture rests on an assessment of its *viability*—whether it can earn a profit—and its *attractiveness,* as compared to other opportunities that could be pursued.

Assessing viability requires analyzing a venture's ability to profitably compete for customers, capital, employees and other resources. Entrepreneurs often focus on whether customers will buy their goods and services, but not on why sales will lead to profits. Of course a start-up must attract customers; a viable enterprise must also enjoy higher prices or lower costs than its rivals so that its revenues exceed expenses.

Analyzing a start-up's competitive prospects, though, is daunting. A complete analysis must take a great many industry participants into account: as Porter and other strategy gurus have pointed out, a start-up faces competition not only from rivals offering the same goods but also potentially from substitutes, suppliers, buyers, and other new entrants. In bidding for employees and capital, a start-up even competes with firms totally outside its industry. Complementing the external analysis of competitors, internal core competencies and weaknesses should be probed. Entrepreneurs must analyze their costs and access to capital, technology, distribution channels and so on.

Experts recommend dynamic analyses because the when of competitive advantage is as important as the what. The development of a new technology may be sufficient to overcome competitive barriers if it is completed by January, but worthless if delayed till December. And, the compleat strategist deals in hard numbers: What are the dollars-and-cents cost advantages of the incumbent's scale? What R&D expenditures are likely to be needed to invent around the incumbent's patents and the advertising costs required to gain a point of market share? If the industry suffers from excessive rivalry, how much higher must our margins have to rise to be profitable?

Well-reasoned, deeply footnoted tomes which document these tasks, have found a goodly following in the corporate world. For start-ups however, meticulous analyses are rarely feasible or particularly useful even. Entrepreneurs typically lack the time and money to interview a representative cross-section of potential customers, analyze substitutes, re-construct competitors' cost structures, project alterative technology scenarios and so on. The few individuals who do have the resources lack the imagination and gumption to start a business. Opportunities are short-lived and often, we find an inverse relationship between the data available to analyze an opportunity and its attractiveness. The more thoroughly the prospects of a start-up can be researched, the more intense the competition it is likely to face.

Not surprisingly, the evidence shows little relationship between planning and success. A National Federation of Independent Business study of 2,994 start-ups showed that founders who spent a long time in study, reflection, and planning were no more likely to survive their first three years than founders who seized opportunities that came by without much planning.[1] In corporations where systematic analysis is taken seriously, we often find a refined incapacity for seizing opportunities. The demand for hard data on market size and industry profitability delays entry until the business is proven, popular, and hence unprofitable. Or, diligent analysis generates many obvious objections ("customers are tied to their existing suppliers") which are used to kill the idea.

Comparing the attractiveness of a venture to alternatives that could be pursued can also prove perplexing.

Many large corporations use the discounted cash flow (DCF) they expect from a project as the standard measure of its attractiveness. DCF apparently eliminates the biases inherent in other methods. Evaluating projects by their expected payback period, for example, will favor ventures that are expected to generate high but short-lived profits over those that promise sustainable profits after a long gestation period. DCF provides for a more reasonable trade-off between longevity and a quick return of capital.

Entrepreneurs, however, can't just use DCF. Cash flows from a new venture are highly unpredictable as compared to those from, say, expanding the capacity of an existing plant. Small changes in (largely unverifiable) assumptions lead to huge differences in projected value.[2] And, unlike a large corporation with relatively easy access to capital, entrepreneurs cannot back several projects simultaneously. Indeed, they can't count on obtaining resources at an acceptable price for a single venture. An unexpected need for cash (because, say, one large customer is unable to make timely payment or raw materials have to be bought to meet an unexpected surge of orders) may shut down a venture or force the entrepreneur to give away an unreasonably large share of the equity to the one investor who is willing to provide the funds.

Therefore, a wealth-constrained, one-venture-at-a-time entrepreneur must use multiple criteria, favoring ventures with:

- Low capital requirements—ventures that can be launched with little external capital and have the profit margins to sustain high growth with internally generated funds.
- High margin for error—ventures with simple operations and low fixed costs which are less likely to face a cash crunch because of technical delays, cost over-runs and slow build-up of sales.
- Significant payoffs—ventures whose rewards are substantial enough to compensate for the future opportunities the entrepre-

---

1. *Inc.*, July 1992, p. 49.
2. Some theorists may question whether the DCF of a new venture is at all meaningful. For example, Frank Knight in his 1921 classic *Risk, Uncertainty, and Profit,* argued that entrepreneurs can expect a profit only to the extent that they bear unmeasurable and unquantifiable risk, which he called uncertainty; if the magnitude and volatility of a venture's cash flows can be reasonably estimated, it cannot be expected to yield a true profit.

neur can't pursue because of a commitment to see this one
through.

- Low exit costs—ventures that can be shut down without a significant loss of time, money, or reputation. Thus, for example,
ventures whose failure is known quickly are better than projects
that are not expected to make a profit for a long period and
therefore cannot be reasonably abandoned in the interim. Similarly, short payback periods have value because the entrepreneur's
loss of self-esteem, reputation, and, of course, personal wealth due
to the closing of a venture are lower if it has already returned the
investment made in it.

- Options for cashing in—ventures that can be sold or taken public.
An entrepreneur locked into an illiquid business cannot easily
pursue other more attractive opportunities and faces problems of
fatigue and burn-out. Therefore, entrepreneurs should prefer businesses with a sustainable competitive advantage, such as a proprietary technology or brand name, which others would be willing to buy.

Evaluating the attractiveness of a start-up by these many criteria is
much harder than applying a corporate rule of backing all projects with
positive DCFs. Several criteria, for instance the opportunities for cashing in
or the costs of exit, cannot be quantified. And, ventures that shine by one
measure are often questionable on another. For example, businesses with
sustainable advantages that can be sold easily may entail more investment
and complexity than ventures with quick payback.

Inevitably, therefore, assessing an opportunity and developing a strategy to exploit it requires a number of judgments; entrepreneurs cannot rely
on a mechanistic flow chart or template. The entrepreneur has to judge which
issues need careful analysis and what should be taken for granted. Judgement
is required to determine whether the start-up can overcome critical obstacles.
Can the capabilities of the established competitors' direct sales force be topped
by a creative plan to use distributors? Can customers' loyalty to their current
suppliers be overcome with a new ergonomic product design? There is no
common unit of measurement to weigh the pros against the inevitable cons;
and equally experienced and astute entrepreneurs can easily disagree. And,
the entrepreneur must make subjective assessments of attractiveness—
whether, for instance, a quick payback provides adequate compensation for
low sustainability.

——— ARMCHAIR REFLECTION: SCREENING OUT LOSERS

The first issue an individual with an idea for a business confronts is
whether it's worth researching. Timely judgments about the viability and
attractiveness of a venture can save a great deal of wasted effort. Successful

EXHIBIT 1
How Start-ups Overcome Competitive Barriers

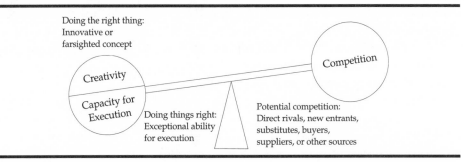

entrepreneurs, too, have many crazy ideas; but they discard or reformulate them quickly before drawing up financial projections, consulting experts, or interviewing potential customers.

What quick check for viability can an entrepreneur apply? A start-up's ability to compete depends on the *creativity* of the underlying concept and the entrepreneur's *capacity* to execute. (See *Exhibit 1*.) Creativity involves innovation or special foresight. Innovations change the existing order; entrepreneurs who would make waves in a mature industry must invent a new product or process to wrest business from established competitors. Foresight leverages external change. Entrepreneurs who want to ride a new wave must have a special insight about the direction, longevity, or consequences of the changes they expect to capitalize on. The gold rush made paupers of the thousands caught in the frenzy—Levi Strauss started a legend by recognizing the opportunity to supply rugged jeans to the prospectors.

But entrepreneurs can't just rely on inventing a new product or anticipating a trend; entrepreneurs must also have the capacity to execute well. Through their zeal, knowledge, contacts, personal commitment, and skill, entrepreneurs must persuade customers, investors, employees, and suppliers to support an uncertain enterprise and then manage competently what resources they can rustle up. Execution is especially critical when concepts can be easily copied. For example, if an innovation cannot be patented or kept secret, entrepreneurs must acquire and manage the resources needed to build a brand name or other barrier that will deter imitators. Superior execution can also compensate for a "me-too" concept in emerging or rapidly growing industries where doing it quickly and doing it right is more important than a brilliant strategy.

Many ventures obviously lack an innovative or far-sighted concept as well as any special capacity to execute. These can be discarded quickly, without much research or data collection. The entrepreneur should already be familiar with the basic facts about competitors' channels, customer behavior, technologies, and so on needed to judge whether a venture has *prima facie* merit. Lack of such knowledge constitutes a red flag. My research suggests that good ideas generally arise out of prior experience. Successful ventures solve problems their founders have personally grappled with as customers, employees, or bankers. Ventures like Federal Express which reputedly grew out of founder Fred Smith's senior thesis in college are rare.

Start-ups need not, however, possess an edge on every front. The creativity of successful entrepreneurs varies considerably. Some implement a radical idea, some modify, and some show no originality. Their capacity for execution varies as well. Selling an industrial niche product doesn't call for the charisma required to pitch trinkets through infomercials. There is no ideal entrepreneurial profile: successful individuals may be gregarious or taciturn; analytical or intuitive; good or terrible with details; risk-averse or thrill seeking; delegators or control freaks; pillars of the community or outsiders and outcasts. The necessary creativity and capacity to execute depends on what the entrepreneur hopes to accomplish and how.

Ventures that seek to effect a *revolution* demand great creativity and exceptional capacity to execute. Launching a Xerox or Federal Express requires a blockbuster new product or service rather than a marginal tinkering with carbon paper or existing delivery services. Revolutionary offerings usually require new processes or manufacturing techniques; competitive markets rarely fail to provide valuable products or services unless there are serious technological problems involved in providing them. For example, Federal Express founder Fred Smith may not have been the first to think of the need for reliable overnight package delivery, but he did pioneer the hub-and-spoke logistics needed to get the job done.[3]

Requirements for execution are also stiff. Revolutionary ventures consume vast resources. They require, for example, significant capital to develop new technology; build new facilities—Federal Express, for example, had to acquire its own fleet of aircraft; market a totally new product; and sustain losses during a long ramp-up period. Entrepreneurs therefore require exceptional charisma and evangelical ability to attract and retain the support of investors, customers, employees, and suppliers for a seemingly outlandish vision.

Entrepreneurs require unusual competence in managing the resources. Often forced to make rather than buy, the entrepreneur must have the organizational and leadership skills to build a large, complex firm quickly. In addition, the entrepreneur may require considerable technical skills in deal making, strategic planning, managing overhead, and so on. The revolutionary entrepreneur, in other words, would appear to require almost superhuman qualities: Ordinary mortals need not apply.

Entrepreneurs who seek to build a *niche* business require less radical concepts. They do require some ingenuity to design a product that will draw

---

3. Revolutionary concepts do not, however, involve much foresight regarding external change. The revolutionary start-up generally throws a stagnant, mature industry into tumult instead of riding external changes. In fact, with great external uncertainty, customers and investors may be hesitant to back a radical product and technology until the environment settles down.

customers away from more mainstream offerings and overcome the cost penalty of serving a small market. But, too novel features can be a hindrance; a niche market will rarely justify the investment required to educate customers and distributors of the benefits of a radically new product. Similarly, a niche venture cannot support too much production or distribution innovation; unlike Federal Express, the specialty food manufacturer cannot afford its own fleet of trucks.

Moreover, a creative view of changing markets or technologies can compensate for the lack of independent innovation. For example, the personal computer revolution created opportunities to provide a variety of complementary goods and services such as add-on boards, math co-processors, and software training videos and books. Entrepreneurs who recognized these opportunities quickly could build profitable businesses without an original technological breakthrough.

Entrepreneurs do not require exceptional ability to raise funds because the investment that can be justified by a niche market is limited. Nor do they require the revolutionary's ability to build and lead complex organizations. Rather the entrepreneur must have the capacity to make do with less—for example, to negotiate favorable terms with suppliers or use guerilla marketing and word-of-mouth instead of national advertising to build brand awareness.

Creative concepts play an even smaller role in the success of *propagators* of an emerging technology or product who race to dominate a new market. For example, a new generation of microprocessors can spark a race in new downstream products, such as personal computers. Or a new downstream market, such as laptop computers, creates a race to produce new components, such as long-lived batteries. Successful ventures in these hot markets don't rely on an innovative concept: target customers and their needs are common industry knowledge. Choices about components, technologies, and distribution channels are limited, and the advantages and disadvantages of the alternatives are well known. Adopting an unconventional approach—for example, by departing from industry standards—can actually scare off investors and potential customers.

Success depends mainly on superior execution—the ability to design and produce a quality product on time and on budget and then sell it effectively. Losers usually fold because they lack a product that works, not because they have pursued a poor strategy. Investment requirements, though substantial, merely represent the entry fee for the race; more money rarely provides a competitive advantage. Correspondingly, entrepreneurs need superior skills in managing engineering, production, and marketing experts, and adequate competence in fund raising and deal making.

Ventures based on "*hustle*"[4] in fragmented service businesses such as investment management, investment banking, head-hunting, or consulting

---

4. For a detailed discussion, see Bhidé, Amar (1986), "Hustle as Strategy," *Harvard Business Review,* September–October.

also rely mainly on execution. Innovative strategies count for little in fields where imitation is easy and the perceived quality of the service provided is more critical than a unique technology, installed base, or captive distribution channel. The nature of superior execution is however different: engineering, production, industrial marketing, and fund-raising are of little import. Rather, the entrepreneur's personal selling skills, network of contacts, reputation for expertise, and ability to convince clients of the value of services rendered are crucial. A capacity for institution-building—recruiting and motivating stellar professionals, articulating and reinforcing firm values, and so on—is also invaluable. With few natural economies of scale, the entrepreneur cannot create a going concern out of a one-man band or ad hoc ensemble without excellence in organization development.

Entrepreneurs who *speculate* in, for example, oil and gas properties when the energy market has collapsed or in office buildings in a real estate slump, require foresight about the out-of-favor asset. The entrepreneur merely anticipates that the confusion or panic will pass; the concept does not entail significant innovation.

To execute, entrepreneurs must have the ability to raise funds for a contrarian bet; the entrepreneur's willingness to risk personal capital, connections with investors, and deal-making skills can be crucial. Successful execution does not however require exceptional managerial capacity. Organizational development, engineering or marketing abilities add little value when an entrepreneur buys assets at a low price, expecting to sell them at a high price.

GAUGING ATTRACTIVENESS

Entrepreneurs should also reflect on the attractiveness of their ventures from a personal point of view—does the venture fit what they want to do as well as what they can do? Surviving the inevitable disappointments and near-disasters requires passion for the enterprise; ability and desire are inseparable. And, projects that enthuse one individual may well leave another cold, depending on their personalities, age, wealth, and so on.

Therefore, entrepreneurs should know what they're looking for and the sacrifices they're willing to make. Do I want to make a fortune, or will a small profit suffice? Do I seek public recognition? The stimulation of working with exciting technologies, customers, and colleagues? Am I prepared to devote my life to a venture, or do I want to cash out quickly? Can I tolerate working in an industry with questionable ethical standards? High uncertainty? What financial and career risks am I prepared to take and for how long?

These deeply personal preferences determine the type of ventures that will enthuse and fortify an entrepreneur. For example, *revolutionary* ventures fit entrepreneurs who want to win or lose on a grand scale. Success can create dynastic fortunes and turn the entrepreneur into a near-cult figure. But the risks also are substantial. Revolutions may fail for any number of reasons: the product is flawed, cannot be made or distributed cost-effectively, serves no compelling need, or requires customers to incur unacceptable switching cost. Worse, the failure may not be apparent for several years, locking the entrepreneur into an extended period of frustrating endeavor. Even revolutions that are successful may not be financially rewarding for their founders, especially if they encounter delays en route. Investors may dump the visionary founders or demand a high share of the equity for additional financing.

The founder of a revolutionary venture must therefore anticipate recurring disappointments and a high probability that years of toil may come to naught. Unless entrepreneurs have a burning desire to change the world, they should not undertake revolutions.

Niche ventures often hold greater financial promise. Although, compared to a successful revolutionary venture, the niche venture may create less total wealth, the entrepreneur can often keep a higher share. Niche ventures require less capital and can achieve financial self-sufficiency faster; therefore, the entrepreneur's equity interest is less likely to be diluted through multiple rounds of financings. But, entrepreneurs must be willing to prosper in a backwater; dominating an obscure niche can be more profitable than intellectually stimulating or glamorous. Niche enterprises can also enter the "land of the living dead" because their market is too small for the business to thrive, but the entrepreneur has invested too much effort to be willing to quit.

Ventures that *propagate* a new technology can provide considerable thrill from racing against determined rivals in a hot field. The entrepreneur's downside is cushioned by the sometimes irrational willingness of investors to bear most of the risk. And, ventures that don't work out get put out of their misery quickly, freeing the entrepreneur to move on. The odds of winning big, however, are also low. Controlling investors may oust the founder in a panic. Competition is fierce and the winner of the current race may be overtaken when a new upstream component or downstream product sparks a fresh contest. Exit options are subject to the vagaries of the IPO (Initial Public Offering) market: When the venture is hot, the IPO market might not be.

Hustle ventures also provide the satisfaction of working with talented colleagues in a fast-moving market. Capital requirements are low and investments can be staged as the business grows. Entrepreneurs can therefore avoid significant personal risk and meddling by outside investors. But, although a hustle business can provide attractive current income, great wealth is elusive: hustle businesses, which lack a sustainable franchise, cannot be easily sold or taken public at a high multiple of earnings. The entrepreneur must therefore savor the venture enough to make a long-term career of it rather than enjoy the fruits of its quick harvest.

The *speculators'* enjoyment lies in outwitting the market rather than building a firm or introducing an innovation to the world. The financial risks and returns depend on "the terms of the deal"—the capital the entrepreneur puts at risk, the conditions and amount of borrowing, and, of course, the price of the asset acquired. Risks are generally not staged—the entrepreneur is fully exposed when the asset is acquired. Liquidity or exit options often turn on the success of the speculation: if, as expected, prices rise, the speculator can expect many buyers for the asset owned, but if prices decline or stay depressed, market liquidity for the asset will be generally poor. All told, such ventures appeal most to entrepreneurs who enjoy deal-making and rolling the dice.

PITFALLS AVOIDED

Timely reflection should force entrepreneurs to confront a basic flaw in many start-ups: the lack of any special idea or capacity to execute that could provide a competitive edge. In their enthusiasm many entrepreneurs dilute the much-better-than-your-rivals imperative to an as-good-as standard. Perhaps they have been conditioned to believe that failure is the consequence of a pathological hubris or ineptitude. Just as we expect every healthy newborn to survive infancy, entrepreneurs assume that their ventures will naturally succeed. But, in fact, competition makes the demise of start-ups normal, to-be-expected events; expectations of profitable survival must be predicated on a superior idea or capacity for execution.

Entrepreneurs may also find a poor fit between what they have and what a particular venture takes. Common problems thus flagged include:

- Relying on hustle or a minor idea against entrenched competitors. High levels of operational excellence won't sustain a new hamburger chain against competition from rivals who enjoy national purchasing economies, brand names and high-traffic locations. Good management—listening to customers, maintaining quality, paying attention to costs, and so on—which can improve the profits of a going business, can't propel a start-up over "structural" barriers. A creative new process or product is a must.
- Launching revolutionary products in niche markets. Steve Jobs introduced truly user-friendly personal computing through the Lisa in 1983. Positioned as a high-end $10,000 product, it couldn't attract the critical mass of software writers, value-added resellers, distribution channels and users it needed to survive. When the same technology was reintroduced for a broader market as the Macintosh however, the product was a smash hit.

Entrepreneurs should, however, use the initial screen to drop only truly dead-ended projects, not to kill all ideas by identifying their every short-coming. And, with the right attitude, reflecting on entrepreneur-venture fit can in fact, give courage to the waverers. Except perhaps in revolutionary ventures, success does *not* usually require extraordinary ideas, resumes or talent. For example:

- The advent of a new distribution option (such as home shopping channels) or a new regime (as in Eastern Europe) creates great opportunities for the determined novice. Entrepreneurs who are willing to act quickly can create profitable niche or hustle businesses with just a little ingenuity because they don't face entrenched competitors and customers tolerate imperfections and inexperience. Even buttoned-down IBM turned to a college dropout, Bill Gates, to source the operating system for their first personal computer.
- In some service businesses dominated by fly-by-night or unreliable operators, modest professionalism can provide a meaningful edge. For instance, superior execution in providing transportation services for rock bands may simply require showing up on time.
- In a new technology race, native talent can prevail over qualifications and experience. In the workstation market, for example, Sun Microsystems beat over a dozen start-ups including Apollo, a textbook venture launched by industry stars. Sun's four 27-year old founders, who had virtually no business or industry experience, simply out-engineered and outsold their rivals.[5]

───── PARSIMONIOUS PLANNING AND ANALYSIS

To conserve time and money, entrepreneurs must minimize the resources they devote to researching the ideas that pass their initial screen. Unlike the corporate world, where foil-mastery and completed staff work can make a career, the entrepreneur only does as much planning and analysis as seems necessary and useful.

How much effort should an entrepreneur devote? The appropriate analytical "budget" that a start-up merits depends on several factors: Ventures that require significant capital have to be better researched and documented than ventures which can be self-financed. Professional investors usually require a written business plan because it provides clues about the entrepreneur's seriousness of purpose, concern for investors, and competence; and it can be conveniently evaluated on airplanes. So entrepreneurs must cobble together a plausible book, even if they are skeptical about its relationship to subsequent outcomes. The degree of innovation attempted also affects the utility of analysis. For example, focus groups and surveys have little value in predicting demand for products which closely resemble existing offerings or products which are so novel that customers can't express a useful opinion. Market research helps most with intermediate levels of innovation.

Businesses with more complex operations or development tasks require more analysis and planning. Complexity increases the costs of poor

---

5. See "Vinod Khosla and Sun Microsystems," HBS Case no. 390-049.

coordination or timing; besides, the process of jointly thrashing out a plan can help build cohesion in the multifunctional teams that such ventures require.

Changing technologies, customer preferences, regulations and so on militate against extensive analysis. Entrepreneurs cannot rely on research conducted under conditions of such turbulence; and besides, if they expect to take advantage of the external changes, they can't spend time dotting i's and crossing t's. This is not to imply, however, that start-ups in a stable environment merit leisurely investigation. Entrepreneurs can't allow the availability of time and other resources to stimulate more analysis. With spreadsheet software, for example, it is easy to churn out detailed but not particularly insightful analyses of a project's breakeven point, capital requirements, payback period, or DCF.

Given a limited budget, how should entrepreneurs set their analytical priorities? The entrepreneur may be tempted to touch lightly all of the innumerable issues that might be analyzed or to spend a lot of effort in areas where data is most readily available. Parsimonious analysis, however, entails a triage: With issues where the impossibility of obtaining data precludes analysis, entrepreneurs simply have to take their chances. Other issues deserve only passing attention, because although lots of data can be collected, the analyses can't be acted on. Entrepreneurs should concentrate on issues which they can reasonably expect to resolve *and* which determine whether and how they will proceed. Resolving a few big questions—understanding what *must* go right and anticipating the venture-destroying pitfalls, for instance—is more important than investigating many nice-to-know matters.

An entrepreneur cannot use a standard checklist or a one-size-fits-all approach to analysis; issues most worthy of analysis will depend on the type of venture undertaken.[6] To illustrate:

In *revolutionary* ventures, market size and growth is notoriously difficult to predict. At best, entrepreneurs may satisfy themselves that their novel product or service delivers considerably greater value than current offerings; how quickly it catches on is a blind guess. Leverage may be obtained, however, from analyzing how customers might buy and use the product or service. Understanding the purchase process can help identify the right decision makers for the new offering—in the case of Federal Express, for instance, it was important to go beyond the mail-room managers who traditionally bought delivery services. Similarly, understanding how products

---

6. The types of ventures I have described are not intended to be mutually exclusive or collectively exhaustive. Nor do I suggest that entrepreneurs should maintain purity of style and avoid hybrids. For example, there is nothing intrinsically flawed about a venture to establish a network that provides a revolutionary service to participants. I offer the typology merely as an aid to pruning the analytical task efficiently. If a venture straddles two types, entrepreneurs should construct an analytical approach that combines the relevant features of both or think of another analogy that is more appropriate. What should be avoided is a laundry-list approach, in which all possible issues are halfheartedly analyzed, as well as a blind just-do-it attitude.

are used can reveal obstacles that must be overcome before customers can realize the benefit from the revolutionary offering.

Another important issue for revolutionaries lies in the appropriability of returns from their innovation. Many concepts are difficult to prove, but once proven, easy to imitate. Unless the pioneer is protected by sustainable barriers to entry, the benefits of the hard-fought revolution become a public good rather than the source of entrepreneurial profit. Given the magnitude of the organizational building task in a revolutionary venture, entrepreneurs may also address issues such as the values members of the firm will uphold, how they will communicate with each other and how they will resolve disputes. Resolving these corporate culture issues early can protect the organization from the subsequent stress of rapid growth.

Niche start-ups often fail because the costs of serving a specialized niche exceed the benefits to customers. Entrepreneurs should therefore analyze carefully the incremental costs of serving a niche, taking into account their lack of scale and the difficulty of marketing to a small diffused segment. And, especially if the cost disadvantage is significant, entrepreneurs should determine whether their offering provides a significant price or performance benefit. Established companies may vie for share through line extensions or marginal tailoring of their products and services; the start-up must really wow its target customers. A marginally tastier cereal won't knock Kellogg's corn flakes off supermarket shelves.

Another significant risk with niche ventures is that their payoffs are too small. For example, a niche venture which can't support a direct sales force may not generate enough commissions to attract an independent broker or manufacturers' rep. Entrepreneurs too will eventually lose interest if the rewards aren't commensurate with their efforts. Therefore the entrepreneur should verify that everyone who contributes may reasonably expect a high, quick or sustainable return even if the total profits of the venture are small.

The most critical issue for the *propagators* of a new technology—their ability to outpace rivals—cannot be easily analyzed. Who could have forecast, for example, that the inexperienced founders of Sun Microsystems would beat out Apollo's veterans? Entering a race basically requires faith in one's ability to finish ahead of the pack. Analyzing whether the rewards for winning are commensurate with the risks, however, can be more feasible and worthwhile. In some technology races, success is predictably short-lived. In the disk drive industry, for example, firms that succeed with one generation of products are often leap-frogged when the next generation arrives. In engineering workstations however, Sun was able to realize relatively long-term gains from its early success because it established a durable "architectural" standard.

Operational analysis and planning usually deserves more attention than strategic planning, because getting a product that works out quickly is crucial. For example, Sun's business plan, one founder recalls, was mainly an operating plan, containing specific timetables for product development, opening sales and service offices, hiring engineers and so on.

In ventures based on *hustle,* a detailed analysis of competitors and industry structure is rarely of much value. The ability to seize short-lived opportunities and execute them brilliantly is of far more importance than a long-term competitive strategy. Analysis of specific clients and relationships dominates general market surveys. Partnership agreements, terms for offering equity to later employees, performance measurement criteria, and bonus plans are important determinants of firm success and are best thought through before launch rather than hastily improvised later on. And, although projections of long-term cash flows are not meaningful, back of the envelope, short-term cash forecasts and analyses of break-evens can keep the entrepreneur out of trouble. Overall, though, the analytical preparation required for such ventures is modest.

With *speculative* ventures, two sets of analysis are crucial. One relates to the market dynamics for the asset being acquired, or, more specifically, why the prices of the asset may be expected to rise. Entrepreneurs should try to determine whether prices are temporarily low (due to, say, an irrational panic or a temporary surge in supply), in secular decline because of permanent changes in supply or demand, or merely correcting after an irrational prior surge. The other analysis is of the entrepreneur's ability to hold or carry the asset till it can be sold at a profit, because it is difficult to predict when temporarily depressed prices will return to normal. Carrying capacity depends on the extent of borrowing used to purchase the asset, the conditions under which financing may be revoked, and the income produced by the asset. Rental properties or a producing well that provides ongoing income, for example, can be carried more easily than raw land or drilling rights. For certain kinds of assets—for example, mines and urban rental properties—the entrepreneur should also consider the risks of expropriation and windfall taxation.

—— INTEGRATING ACTION AND ANALYSIS

Standard operating procedure in large corporations usually entails a clear distinction between analysis and execution. In contemplating a new venture, established firms face issues about its "fit" with ongoing activities: Does the proposed venture leverage corporate strengths? Will the resources and attention it requires reduce our ability to build customer loyalty and improve quality in our core markets? These concerns dictate a deliberate, "trustee"[7] approach: before they can launch a venture, managers must investigate an opportunity extensively, seek the counsel of Higher-Ups, submit a

7. See Howard Stevenson and David Gumpert (1985), "The Heart of Entrepreneurship," *Harvard Business Review,* March–April.

formal plan, respond to criticisms by bosses and corporate staff, and secure a head-count and capital allocation.

Entrepreneurs who start with a clean slate, however, don't have to obtain all the answers before they act. In fact, they often can't easily separate action and analysis. The attractiveness of a new restaurant, for example, may depend on the terms of the lease—low rents can turn the venture from a mediocre proposition to a money machine. But an entrepreneur's ability to negotiate a good lease cannot easily be determined from a general prior analysis; he or she must enter into a serious negotiation with a specific landlord for a specific property. And, performing a lot of other analyses without first testing the ability to get a good lease can be a serious waste of time and money.

Acting before an opportunity is fully analyzed has other benefits. Doing something concrete builds confidence in oneself and in others. Key employees and investors will often follow the individual who has committed to action by, for instance, quitting a job, incorporating, or signing a lease. By taking a personal risk, the entrepreneur convinces others that the venture *will* proceed and, if they don't sign up, they could be left behind.

Early action can generate more robust, better informed strategies. Extensive surveys and focus group research about a concept can produce misleading evidence: Slippage can arise between research and reality because the potential customers interviewed are not representative of the market, their enthusiasm for the concept wanes when they see the actual product, or they may lack the authority to sign purchase orders. More robust strategies may be developed by first building a working prototype and asking customers to use it before conducting extensive market research.

The entrepreneur's ability to undertake execution quickly will naturally vary. Trial and error is less feasible with large-scale capital intensive ventures like Federal Express than with a consulting firm start-up. Nevertheless, we can find some common characteristics of an approach which integrates action and analysis.

Staging Analytical Tasks   Given the uncertainties of a new venture, the returns from more fact gathering, interviews, or cash flow projections diminish rapidly. Therefore, rather than resolve all issues at once, the entrepreneur does only enough research to justify the next action or investment. For example, an individual who has developed a new medical technology may first obtain crude estimates of market demand to determine whether it is worth seeing a patent lawyer. If the crude estimates and lawyer are encouraging, the individual may do some more analysis to establish the wisdom of spending the money to obtain a patent. Several more iterations of analysis and action will follow before a formal business plan is prepared and circulated to venture capitalists.

Plugging Holes Quickly   As soon as analysis reveals problems and risks, the entrepreneur moves to find solutions. For example, suppose that an entrepreneur finds that it will be difficult to raise capital for a venture. Rather than kill the idea, the entrepreneur thinks creatively about solving the problem. Perhaps the investment in a fixed plant can be reduced by modifying the technology to use more standard equipment that can be rented. Or, under the right terms, a customer might underwrite the risk by providing a large initial order. Or, expectations and goals for growth might be scaled down, and a niche market could be tackled first. Except with obviously unviable ideas that can be easily ruled out through elementary logic, the purpose of analysis is not to find fault with new ventures or find reason for abandoning them. Analysis should be considered as an exercise in what to do next more than what not to do.

Evangelical Investigation   Entrepreneurs often blur the line between research and selling. As one individual recalls: "My market research consisted of taking a prototype to a trade show and see if I could write orders." "Beta-sites" in the software industry provide another example of simultaneous research and selling; customers actually pay to help the vendor test early versions of software and will often place larger orders if they are satisfied.

From the beginning, entrepreneurs don't just seek opinions and information, they also seek to gain others' commitment. Entrepreneurs treat everyone they talk to as a potential customer, investor, employee, or supplier or at least as a potential source of leads. Even if they don't actually "ask for the order" they take the time to build enough interest and rapport so that they can come back later. This simultaneous listening and selling approach may not produce truly objective market research and statistically significant results. But the resource-constrained entrepreneur doesn't have much choice. Besides, in the initial stages, the deep knowledge and support of a few is often more valuable than broad, impersonal data.

Flexible Perseverance   Entrepreneurs who act on sketchy information and back of the envelope plans must stand ready to change their strategies as events unfold. Successful ventures don't always proceed in the direction that they initially set out along. A significant proportion develop entirely new markets and products and sources of competitive advantage. Therefore, although perseverance and tenacity represent valuable entrepreneurial traits, they must be complemented with flexibility and willingness to learn. If customers who should be placing orders don't, the entrepreneur should consider reworking the concept. Similarly, the entrepreneur should also be prepared to exploit opportunities that didn't figure in the initial plan.

The apparently sketchy planning and haphazard evolution of many successful ventures doesn't mean that entrepreneurs should follow a ready-fire-aim approach. In spite of appearances, astute entrepreneurs do analyze and strategize extensively. They realize, however, that businesses cannot be launched like space shuttles, with every detail of the mission planned in advance. In fact, to paraphrase Cardinal Newman, the quest for the perfect start-up plan is often the enemy of the good. Initial analyses only provide plausible hypotheses, which must be tested and modified. Entrepreneurs should play with and explore ideas, letting their strategies evolve through a seamless process of guesswork, analysis, and action.

──── DISCUSSION QUESTIONS

1. Formulate ten short rules of thumb to identify attractive opportunities.
2. What are the risks and rewards of trying to exploit truly innovative ideas? Can an idea be *too* innovative?
3. How do the different types of opportunities map to the personal traits and skills an entrepreneur must have?

9 Some Thoughts on Business Plans

WILLIAM A. SAHLMAN

Most would-be entrepreneurs believe that the key to a successful new business is a well-crafted business plan. This note suggests that the key to a successful new business is assembling a competent team, marshaling the appropriate resources, and executing its strategy in an environment that demands constant reassessment of the opportunity and realignment of the resources. This is why professional investors like venture capitalists often read a business plan that begins with resumés and ends with a detailed description of the specific business being launched. These investors know that the critical ingredient in any business is the quality of the people involved.

At the same time, writing a business plan can be an extremely useful process for launching a new venture, even within the context of an existing enterprise. Writing the plan entails asking and then addressing some questions that are common to all businesses. For example, Who is the customer? How does the customer make decisions? What is the business model for the venture? Is it attractive? How could the business model be improved?

Finally, the business plan should address the potential good and bad news that confronts all ventures. What can go wrong? What can go right? What decisions can management make today that improve the odds of success? What decisions can management make as new information arrives to tilt the risk/reward ratio in favor of the venture? These are the issues a well-crafted business plan must address.

─── INTERNET WICKED ALE

Bill Sahlman, Dimitri V. D'Arbeloff Professor of Business Administration, smiled as he was handed the business plan for Internet Wicked Ale, Inc. (IWA), an interactive, on-line marketing company being formed to sell pre-

Professor William A. Sahlman prepared this note as the basis for class discussion rather than to illustrate either effective or ineffective handling of an administrative situation. Copyright © 1996 by the President and Fellows of Harvard College. Harvard Business School case 897-101.

mium beers made by microbreweries over the Internet. According to the president of the company—a soon-to-graduate MBA candidate at a well-known eastern business school—a prototype Web site had already been developed using the now ubiquitous Java programming language. Literally thousands were visiting the site each day: an early review had described the Web site as "way cool." Participating in the meeting were two other MBA candidates. Prior to jointly founding IWA, the three had worked in management consulting and investment banking: each, however, did have substantial experience with beer.

Sahlman glanced over the shoulder of the IWA team—he took note of his ever growing stack of Internet based business plans, each proposing to "revolutionize" an industry, each "conservatively" projecting at least $50 million in revenues within five years based on a modest market share of under 10%, and each containing a projection of likely investor returns of over 100% per annum. He quickly averted his stare from the business plans in the corner of his less than tidy office so as not to offend his eager audience. They looked so young—they were so enthusiastic—their business plan was so meticulously printed on the new color laser printers in the technology lab. . . . Sahlman wondered what to say next.

——— INTRODUCTION

This note is about entrepreneurial ventures and the role of business plans. Few areas of new venture creation receive as much attention. There are MBA and undergraduate courses on business plan writing. There are countless books describing how to write a business plan. There is even software that will help create a business plan, complete with integrated financial projections. All across the U.S., and increasingly in other countries, there are contests designed to pick the "best business plan."

Judging by the amount of attention paid to business plans in graduate business schools and the popular press, you would think that the only thing standing between a would-be entrepreneur and spectacular success is a well-crafted and highly regarded business plan. Yet, in my experience, nothing could be further from the truth: on a scale from 1 to 10, business plans rank no higher than 2 as a predictor of likely success. There are many other factors that dominate the business plan, per se.

The disparity between my view and that implicit in the business plan feeding frenzy is rooted in over fifteen years of field research and personal experience in the world of entrepreneurship. The rest of this note develops a conceptual framework for understanding entrepreneurial venture creation and management, which is based on studying hundreds of successful and unsuccessful companies. The goal is to give the reader insights into sensible entrepreneurial management, and, by implication, into the business plan used to describe a venture.

In my framework, there are four dynamic components of any entrepreneurial process or venture:

- the **people,**
- the **opportunity,**
- the **external context,** and
- the **deal.**

By people, I mean those individuals or groups who perform services or provide resources for the venture, whether or not they are directly employed by the venture. This category encompasses managers, employees, lawyers, accountants, capital providers, and parts suppliers, among others. By opportunity, I mean any activity requiring the investment of scarce resources in hopes of future return. By context, I mean all those factors that affect the outcome of the opportunity but that are generally outside the direct control of management. Examples of contextual factors include the level of interest rates, regulations (rules of the game), macroeconomic activity, and some industry variables like threat of substitutes. Finally, by deal, I mean the complete set of implicit and explicit contractual relationships between the entity and all resource providers. Examples of deals range from contracts with capital suppliers to the terms of employment for managers.

The fundamental insight gained from studying hundreds of successful and unsuccessful ventures is the concept of integration, referred to as "fit," which is defined as the degree to which the people, the opportunity, the deal, and the context together influence the potential for success. Phrased differently, the degree of fit is the answer to the following questions:

- To what degree do the people have the right experience, skills and attitudes, given the nature of the opportunity, the context and the deals struck?
- To what degree does the opportunity make sense, given the people involved, the context and the deals struck?
- To what degree is the context favorable for the venture, given the people involved, the nature of the opportunity and the deals struck?
- To what degree do the deals involved in the venture make sense, given the people involved, the nature of the opportunity, and the context?

These questions focus attention on the fact that excellence in any single dimension is not sufficient: the proper perspective from which to make an evaluation takes into account all of the elements simultaneously. An appropriate analogy might be that of a sports team. It is not sufficient to have the best individual players at each position; rather, success will be a function of how they play together, how the team is managed, what deals have been struck inside and outside the team, and what else goes on in the league. A diagram of the basic framework is provided in Appendix 1.

Nor is it sufficient to focus on these elements and their relationship from a static perspective. The people, opportunity, context and deal (and the relationship among them) are all likely to change over time as a company goes from identification of opportunity to harvest. To focus attention on the dynamic aspects of the entrepreneurial process, three related questions can be asked to guide the analysis of any business venture:

- What can go wrong?
- What can go right?
- What decisions can management make today and in the future to ensure that "what can go right" does go right, and "what can go wrong" is avoided, or failing that, is prevented from critically damaging the enterprise? Phrased another way, what decisions can be made to tilt the reward to risk ratio in favor of the venture?

This framework and set of questions are extremely powerful in understanding how ventures evolve over time and how managers can affect outcomes. The balanced emphasis on anticipating (as opposed to predicting) good and bad news is a distinctive feature of the framework. Most students (and practitioners) are adept at identifying risks, far fewer are practiced at foretelling the good news, and even fewer have thought systematically about how they can manage the reward to risk ratio. Yet, there are some recurrent themes in the world of venturing. That projects often take more time and money than originally estimated should not surprise people. Indeed, part of the goal in a course like the one I teach on Entrepreneurial Finance is to provide people with a rich sense of the patterns that underlie real-world entrepreneurship.

These questions described above concerning potential good and bad news also shed light on the fact that current decisions affect future decisions: some decisions open up or preserve options for future action while others destroy options. Managers must be cognizant of this relationship between current and future decisions.

According to this framework, great businesses have some easily identifiable (but hard to assemble) attributes. They have a world class managerial team in all dimensions, from the top to the bottom, and across all relevant functions. The teams have directly relevant skills and experiences for the opportunity they are pursuing. Ideally, the team has worked successfully together in the past. The opportunity has an attractive, sustainable business model: it is possible to create a competitive edge and to defend it. There are multiple options for expanding the scale and scope of the business and these options are unique to the enterprise and its team. There are a number of ways to extract value from the business either in a positive harvest event or in a scale down or liquidation mode. The context is favorable both with respect to the regulatory environment and the macroeconomic situation. The deals binding the people to the opportunity are sensible and robust: they provide the right incentives under a wide range of scenarios. The venture is financed by individuals or firms who add value in addition to their capital, thereby increasing the likelihood of success. The financing terms provide the right incentives for the provider and the recipient. There is access to additional capital on an as-warranted basis. In short, the venture is characterized by a high degree of dynamic **fit** (see Appendix 2 for a diagram of the expanded fit management framework).

A great business may or may not have currently, or have ever had for that matter, a great business plan. In the beginning, moreover, a great business may not even have demonstrated a high degree of **fit:** the important issue is whether the deficiencies are recognized and fixable. Phrased differently, the role of management is to continuously adapt a business to improve the degree of **fit:** doing so does not guarantee success, but it does increase the odds.

This assessment raises the obvious issue of what role a business plan plays in entrepreneurship. I believe that a useful business plan is one that addresses the elements of the venture—people, opportunity, context, and deal—in the proper dynamic context. In the end, the business plan must provide reasonable answers to the following questions:

- Who are the people involved? What have they done in the past that would lead one to believe that they will be successful in the future? Who is missing from the team and how will they be attracted?
- What is the nature of the opportunity? How will the company make money? How is the opportunity likely to evolve? Can entry barriers be built and maintained?
- What contextual factors will affect the venture? What contextual changes are likely to occur, and how can management respond to those changes?
- What deals have been or are likely to be struck inside and outside the venture? Do the deals struck increase the likelihood of success? How will those deals and the implicit incentives evolve over time?
- What decisions have been made (or can be made) to increase the ratio of reward to risk?

Each of these areas will be addressed in the sections that follow.

—— **PEOPLE**

When reading any business plan, or assessing any business, for that matter, I start with the resume section, not with the description of the business. I ask a series of structured questions, some of which are listed below:

- Who are the founders?
- What have they accomplished in the past?

- What directly relevant experience do they have for the opportunity they are pursuing?
- What skills do they have?
- Whom do they know and who knows them?
- What is their reputation?
- How realistic are they?
- Can they adapt as circumstances warrant?
- Who else needs to be on the team? Are the founders prepared to recruit high-quality people?
- How will the team respond to adversity?
- Can they make the inevitable hard choices that have to be made?
- What are their motivations?
- How committed are they to this venture?
- How can I gain objective information about each member of the team including how they will work together?
- What are the possible consequences if one or more of the team members leaves?

We can now come full circle and begin to evaluate the Internet Wicked Ale proposal and the team of MBA founders. Starting first with the people lens, I am not sanguine about IWA's prospects. The founding team has experience drinking, not starting an on-line business or a beer distribution business. Typically, the business plan for such a team talks about the need to recruit experienced people, but it's rather like trying to draw 4 cards to complete a 5-card straight in poker: a low-probability event. Moreover, having a founding team without tremendous experience but large equity ownership often makes it extremely difficult to attract high-quality people on "acceptable" terms.

I should note that the framework described above and the pessimistic assessment of the prospects for IWA are not foolproof. Lots of inexperienced teams succeed, occasionally because they are not weighted down by conventional wisdom. This is particularly true in new markets, the Internet representing a very important current illustration. In such markets, commercial innovation is often driven by relatively inexperienced entrants, teams that are repeatedly told they are unlikely to succeed. At the same time, starting a new enterprise with little or no management experience is a little like crossing the Mass Turnpike blindfolded: yes, you can make it to the other side, but having done so, you shouldn't assume the trip was riskless.

Reading a business plan from the resume section first also illustrates a truism of professional venture capital investing. A typical venture capital firm receives approximately 2,000 business plans per year. A non-scientific survey of several prominent firms reveals that they only invest in plans that come in with a specific letter of referral from someone well known by the partners of the firm. That is, they do not invest in, nor do they even investigate fully, plans that are unsolicited.

My colleague Myra Hart has a useful way of describing the process of attracting financial and other resources to a venture. Her research suggests that successful venture founders have two characteristics: they are "known" and they "know." Tackling the latter first, the founders know the industry for which they propose to raise capital and launch a venture—they know the key suppliers, the customers, and the competitors. They also know who the talented individuals are who can contribute to the team. At the same time, they are known in the industry: people can comment on their capabilities and can provide objective referrals to resource suppliers like professional venture capitalists. Suppliers, customers, and employees are willing to work with them in spite of the obvious risks of dealing with a new company.

Thus, the model in venture capital is to back teams with great (directly relevant) track records who are pursuing attractive opportunities. The old adage in venture capital circles is: "I'd rather back an 'A' team with a 'B' idea than a 'B' team with an 'A' idea." Of course, the goal is to only back high-quality teams with high-quality opportunities, but that is not always feasible.

In sum, the IWA business plan doesn't pass the threshold for consideration by professional investors even if the idea is a pretty good one. Again, a truism from the world of venture capital is that ideas are a dime-a-dozen: only execution skills count. Arthur Rock, a venture capital legend associated with the formation of such companies as Intel, Apple, and Teledyne, stated bluntly, "I invest in people, not ideas."[1]

——— OPPORTUNITY

Rather than rejecting the IWA plan out of hand, however, let's assume that the team is acceptable or that there are indications that an appropriate team can be built. What is the next step? What other questions do investors or entrepreneurs ask to evaluate prospective ventures?

In my experience, the next major issue is the nature of the opportunity, starting first with an assessment of the overall market potential and its characteristics. Two key initial questions are:

- Is the total market for the venture's product or service large and/or rapidly growing?
- Is the industry one that is now or can become structurally attractive?

Entrepreneurs and investors look for large or rapidly growing markets for a variety of reasons. First, it is often easier to obtain a share of a growing market than to fight with entrenched competitors for a share of a mature or stagnant market. Professional investors like venture capitalists try to identify high growth potential markets early in their evolution: examples range from

---

1. Michael W. Miller, "How One Man Helps High-Tech Prospects Get to the Big Leagues," *Wall Street Journal*, December 31, 1985, page 1.

integrated circuits to biotechnology. Indeed, they will not invest in a company that cannot reach a significant scale (e.g., $50 million in annual revenues) within five years.

Obviously, all markets are not created equal: some are more attractive than others. Consider, to illustrate, the independent computer disk drive business as it has evolved over the past twenty years. Disk drives were first developed by IBM in the late 1960s and early 1970s. Some of the original engineering team members ultimately left IBM to form independent companies to develop products based on the same technology. Indeed, over the next two decades, scores of new companies were formed to exploit the rapidly growing market for data storage. Examples include Memorex, Seagate, Priam, Quantum, Conner Peripherals, and EMC.

The problem with disk storage, however, is that the industry is not structurally attractive, nor is it ever likely to be. Disk drive manufacturers must design their products to meet the perceived needs of OEMs (original equipment manufacturers) and end-users. Selling a product to OEMs is complicated and often has low margins. The customers are large relative to the supplier. There are lots of competitors, each with high-quality offerings in the same market segment. Because there are so many competitors, product life cycles are short and ongoing technology investments high. The industry is subject to major shifts in technology and customer base (e.g., the shift in form factors or storage medium and the shift from minicomputers to microcomputers). Rivalry also leads to lower prices and hence, lower margins. In the end, it is extremely difficult to build and sustain a profitable business.

In this regard, the disk drive business looks suspiciously like the tire industry. When the tire industry developed, there were many competitors, each trying to sell their tires to the automobile manufacturers and to end-users. Rivalry was intense. The customers got larger and larger, squeezing the profitability of the tire suppliers. Ultimately, the industry evolved to the point where there were a handful of competitors, each with modest margins and highly cyclical results.

Compare the situation described for disk drives to that confronting biotechnology companies. If a biotech company creates a new product, intellectual property laws grant a certain amount of protection from competitive forces. Competitors must invent new approaches to the same underlying problem or they must license the product from the inventor. The extended duration of patent protection makes it possible as well to build a brand image that provides a certain amount of economic protection even after patent coverage expires. In the end, a model for a successful biotechnology company is a pharmaceutical company. On average, the latter companies are far more profitable than most precisely because of the structural attractiveness of their industry.

This extended discussion of growth and industry illustrates another important factor in venture formation and investing. What are the appropriate analogies? If a venture is successful, what will it look like? Identifying opportunities is a complex game of pattern recognition which is aided by experience and by honest assessment of business history. Knowing that the disk drive business is like the tire industry and that biotech is like the pharmaceutical industry is helpful in determining where to invest capital or human resources. Tom Stemberg once described what he was trying to accomplish in founding Staples, "I said I wanted to build the Toys "R" Us of office supplies." He picked a successful model, one that spoke volumes about what he intended to do and the consequences if he were successful.[2]

To reiterate, the goal is to pick industries that have lots of potential to create and protect value. Growth in sales is not equivalent to growth in value. Also, marrying great management to such markets is the primary tool for increasing the likelihood of success. Consider, to illustrate, the story of the formation of Compaq Computer. The founders were senior executives at Texas Instruments. Their original business plan described a plan to enter the disk drive business. They sent the plan to L. J. Sevin and Ben Rosen, venture capitalists with extensive experience in the electronics industry. Sevin and Rosen rejected the plan but liked the team. Ultimately, on a place mat in a local diner in Texas, a plan was sketched out to design, manufacture and market a portable personal computer. The rest, as they say, is history.[3]

I am also reminded of what the immensely successful venture capitalist, Don Valentine, says about venture investing. Most in the venture industry focus on the three determinants of venture success—people, people, and people. Valentine insists that the real trick is to find markets with explosive potential, to back great technology, and to put management in place as needed. He wants to invest in industries where growth can overcome the shortcomings of management. Valentine cites as Exhibit A his $2.0 million investment in Cisco, a networking company, that seven years later was worth over $6 billion.[4] In like vein, Peter Lynch, the famous manager of Fidelity's Magellan Fund, tried to invest in companies whose fundamental industry factors were so favorable that even incompetent management couldn't cause the stock to go down.

What is most important in new venture formation—the market being served, the specific product or service, or the quality of the people involved? I suspect that the correct answer is "yes." In the final analysis, the issues are not unrelated. Great people are those who can identify attractive markets and build compelling strategies. As General Doriot, one of the early pioneers in the venture capital industry once stated, "The problem is to judge ideas and men and the value of the possible combination—a very difficult task."[5]

---

2. For information on the launch of Staples, see Thomas G. Stemberg, *Staples for Success,* KEX Press, 1996.

3. Benjamin Rosen, "Rosen's Ten Rules," in *Raising Money,* Amacom Press, 1990, pp. ix–xxv.

4. Valentine's perspective is described in "Rise of the Silicon Patriots," *Worth Magazine,* December/January, 1996, pp. 86–92, 137–146.

5. *Georges F. Doriot: Manufacturing Class Notes, Harvard Business School, 1927–1966,* The French Library, 1993, page 85.

The next major issue in evaluating a venture is the specific plan for building and launching a product or service. I will not dwell on this topic in spite of its obvious importance but will instead focus on some very simple questions that can help sort out good ideas from potential disasters. I can also quote Arthur Rock to remind the reader of the proper perspective for evaluating business proposals, "If you can find good people, if they're wrong about the product they'll make a switch, so what good is it to understand the product that they're talking about in the first place?"[6] Rock's admonition notwithstanding, there are a few issues that a business plan must address, including the following:

- Who is the customer?
- How does the customer make decisions?
- To what degree is the product or service a compelling purchase for the customer?
- How will the product or service be priced?
- How will the venture reach the identified customer segments?
- How much does it cost (time and resources) to acquire a customer?
- How much does it cost to produce and deliver the product or service?
- How much does it cost to support a customer?
- How easy is it to retain a customer?

Often, asking and answering these kinds of questions will reveal a fatal flaw in a plan. For example, it may be too costly to find the customers and convince them to buy the product. Economically viable access to customers is the key to business, yet many entrepreneurs take the Hollywood approach to this area—"Build it and they will come." That strategy is great in the movies but not very sensible in the real world.

I should note that it is not always easy to answer questions about possible customer response to new products or services. One entrepreneur I know proposed to introduce an electronic news clipping service. He made his pitch to a prospective venture capital investor who rejected the plan, stating, "I just don't think the dogs will eat the dogfood." Later, when the entrepreneur's company went public, he sent the venture capitalist an anonymous package comprised of an empty can of dogfood and a copy of his prospectus. If it were easy, there wouldn't be any opportunities.

The issue of pricing is particularly important in analyzing a business proposal. Sometimes the "dogs will eat the dogfood," but only at a price less than cost. Investors always look for opportunities that entail value pricing in which the price the customer is willing to pay is high. A good example is Sandra Kurtzig's description of how she set prices in the early days of ASK Computer Systems. ASK developed programs to help users monitor and evaluate their manufacturing process (scheduling, cost analysis, etc.). The

---

6. *op. cit.,* page 1.

software was extremely valuable to a user and there were few competitors or alternatives: Kurtzig called her pricing model the "flinch method." When asked how much the software was, she would respond, "$50,000." If the buyer didn't flinch, she would add, "per module." Again, if there were no visible choking, she would add, "per year." And so on, and so on. Kurtzig was ultimately able to build a very profitable multi-hundred million dollar business using this kind of "street smart" pricing.

The list of questions above focuses on the top and bottom line of a business—the direct revenues and the costs of producing and marketing a product. That's fine, as far as it goes. Sensible analysis of a proposal, however, involves also assessing the business model from a different perspective that takes into account the investment required (i.e., the balance sheet side of the equation). Consider the following questions that I use to assess the cash flow implications of pursuing an opportunity:

- When do you have to buy resources (supplies, people, etc.)?
- When do you have to pay for them?
- How long does it take to acquire a customer?
- How long before the customer sends you a check?
- How much capital equipment is required to support a dollar of sales?

Underlying these questions on the balance sheet is a simple yet powerful maxim in business:

Buy low, sell high, collect early, and pay late.[7]

The best businesses are those in which you have large profit margins, you get paid by your customers before you have to deliver the product, and the fixed asset requirements are modest. It goes without saying, in addition, that such a business should also be characterized by insuperable entry barriers.

Consider, to illustrate, the magazine publishing business. Once up and running, a successful magazine has remarkably attractive cash flow characteristics. Subscribers pay in advance of receiving the magazine. Often, magazines can even get subscribers to pay for several years' in advance. I once discovered that I had nine years' worth of service coming on a magazine because I diligently paid the bill each time they sent it to me, taking advantage of multi-year discounts. If the magazine can maintain compelling content, then current subscribers tend to re-subscribe on a regular basis with low incremental marketing cost. It is always easier to retain a customer than to acquire a new one. If the demographic profile of the readers is attractive, then advertisers use the magazine to reach a target audience, a successful example

---

7. This is the title of a useful book—Richard Levin, *Buy Low, Sell High, Collect Early and Pay Late: The Manager's Guide to Financial Survival*, Prentice-Hall, 1983.

of "if you build it, they will come." It takes very little plant and equipment to run a magazine: printing and fulfillment are often farmed out to vendors who specialize and deliver high-quality service at low cost. The editorial costs of a magazine are typically low. In essence, magazine publishing has all the attractive characteristics listed above.

Of course, the fact that a magazine property is valuable once it is up and running has not escaped people's attention. Each year, hundreds of new magazines are launched: most, to quote test pilot Chuck Yeager, "auger in." The Achilles heal in publishing is the cost of acquiring a customer in a world where most niches have already been recognized and served.

There are some other attractive business models that warrant mention. When I assess a business, I look for ways in which a company can expand the range of products or services being offered to the same customer base. Often, companies are able to create virtual "pipelines" which support the economically viable creation of new revenue streams. In the magazine business, for example, it is possible to create other lines of products or services that are attractive to subscribers. *Inc.* Magazine, to illustrate, has expanded beyond the basic magazine business to offer seminars, books, and videos for the *Inc.* subscriber (and others). In this example, a virtuous cycle is established in which success in the basic magazine leads to new related business opportunities that might not exist in the absence of the magazine.

A similarly attractive business model is illustrated by Intuit, which is best known for its personal financial program Quicken. The latter program helps users organize their checkbook. After the initial success of Quicken, Intuit was able to offer a wide range of additional services, including electronic banking, personal printing supplies, tax preparation software, and on-line information services. Because some of these ancillary services are so profitable, Intuit is able to give away the software program in hopes of creating a lifelong customer who buys additional services and products from the company. Intuit also discovered that many users of its personal finance program Quicken were small businesses: they soon introduced a variant of the program, called QuickBooks, that is designed to meet the specific accounting needs of small businesses. The QuickBooks division is now more profitable than the original consumer focused one, demonstrating how success in one business can lead to success in another that is closely related.[8]

Not all businesses are created equal in terms of the kind of growth opportunities described above. In some businesses, success in one product or service does not necessarily create additional opportunities with the same customer base. Again, the disk drive business is informative because competitors have historically been unable to replicate success in one part of the

---

8. Interestingly, the original Intuit business plan was sent to quite a few venture capitalists, including two members of Scott Cook's HBS class. The plan was rejected by one and all. Only later did the two classmates get an opportunity to invest in Intuit while it was still private. The potential small business accounting opportunity was specifically mentioned in the original Intuit plan.

industry in another. For example, those firms that were successful in producing 5.25" drives were not, for the most part, successful in producing 3.5" drives. Catching one technology wave does not always imply an ability to catch the next one. As colleagues Clayton Christensen and Joseph Bower have observed, the old axiom about staying close to the customer works if and only if you choose the right customer.[9]

An obvious extension of the pipeline model relates to geographic expansion possibilities. Some businesses are attractive because a successful model in one region can be rolled out to other regions. Such is the case in the theme restaurant business. If Hard Rock Café works in Paris and London, then it will probably work in New York and Chicago. This kind of business is rich in growth options that result from success.

There are many other successful business models that entrepreneurs and investors look for when making resource commitments to opportunities. I try, for example, to find companies that "sell ammunition to all sides of the war without end" rather than engage in direct combat. An illustration is A. C. Nielson, which measures marketing response for companies selling products or services but does not have to try to compete in the actual markets (e.g., Coke versus Pepsi, or ABC versus NBC). A similar company called Internet Profiles exists in the Internet world: it measures activity at Web sites rather than trying to compete with other Web site purveyors.

Another illustration of the "ammunition" strategy is a company called Abacus Direct. This company was founded to help catalog merchants improve the effectiveness of their customer acquisition strategies. Briefly, the co-founders convinced a large number of catalog companies (e.g., Lands' End and Orvis) to give them a data file comprised of the purchasing histories of each catalog's customers. The data on customers of many different catalogs was then pooled and analyzed. Using proprietary software, Abacus Direct was able to help the catalog companies identify high potential customers to whom new catalogs could be mailed and eliminate low potential customers from their lists.

Six years after starting, Abacus Direct was able to achieve a 75% share of the domestic catalog business. The company was extremely profitable early in its development, with net margins in the 30% range. Three contextual factors helped Abacus Direct enormously. First, competition among catalog companies was fierce and Abacus Direct benefited by helping competitors be more effective. Second, postage cost increases changed the business model for catalog merchants, making it imperative that direct mail effectiveness be improved. Finally, the cost of managing and analyzing a massive database, one containing purchase histories on almost 90 million people, fell dramatically. What used to take a mainframe computer many hours to analyze now

---

9. Clayton Christensen and Joseph Bower, "Disruptive Technologies: Catching the Wave," *Harvard Business Review* (January/February, 1995), pp. 43–53.

takes minutes on a powerful workstation. The founders of Abacus Direct had previously founded a company that handled warranty card registrations for major appliance manufacturers. Again, that company had sold mailing lists based on purchase histories: the company was successful and was sold to a larger company some five years after it was founded. To use the terminology introduced in the section on "people," the founders "knew" the industry and they were "known," dramatically increasing the likelihood of their success.

Another simple example of an oft-repeated successful business model involves the old "razors and razor blades" strategy made famous by Gillette. The razors are sold at cost, and all the money is made on the blades. There are many companies pursuing a variation of this strategy, Gillette being the best known. The recently introduced data storage device called the Zip Drive by Iomega illustrates a policy of giving away the device at cost or a small profit and making all of the money on the proprietary disks that go with the drive. Nintendo makes most of its money on software, not on the game players it sells.

There are some opportunity traps that warrant mention. Some businesses have distinctly unattractive economic prospects, defined as high capital costs (front-loaded), low margins, and high risk. The disk drive business probably fits this description well. So too does the airline business. In such industries, however, the business plans that are written do not really address the problems. They describe instead the opportunity in glowing terms. They state that the market is large and growing, and that all the new entrant needs to do is to attain a 10% market share to achieve great success. Unfortunately, if hundreds of capable teams all enter a market looking for a 10% share, I don't think the math quite works out. In some industries, even great teams can't overcome poor industry business models, as the great investor Warren Buffett discovered when he bought part of US Air.

I have also come to believe that the world of "invention" is fraught with danger. Over the past fifteen years, I have seen scores of individuals who have invented a "better mousetrap." They have developed tools or systems in areas that range from bicycle pumps to inflatable pillows for use on airlines to automated car parking systems. Their technology is patented and seems on the surface to be a "no-brainer" to potential adopters. In spite of the seeming attractiveness of the innovation, however, I have seen very few examples of successful commercialization. It turns out that idea-driven companies typically undervalue commercialization capabilities. The inventor frequently refuses to spend the money required or refuses to share the rewards with the business side of the company, the inevitable consequence of which is that the technology never gets implemented regardless of how compelling it seems to be.

My views of the importance of commercialization skills were influenced by one of the first technology based companies I ever visited. In the early 1980s, a group of Harvard undergraduates acquired the rights to a technology that would help improve the combustion characteristics of certain grades of fuel oil. Essentially, the process would enable fuel burners to use much cheaper oil to accomplish a given task. I was intrigued by the process and admired the dogged determination of the young entrepreneurs.

Ultimately, this company, Fuel Tech, raised $75 million from private investors around the globe. The technology I described never proved to be commercially viable. The company founders scrambled to find an alternative path to business success for Fuel Tech. To my utter amazement, they were able to acquire some operating companies at attractive prices. The company was eventually sold at a price that netted handsome returns for the investors and the founders. Later, the lead entrepreneur, William Haney, acquired the rights to some environmental technology developed at MIT. He founded, and currently is chairman of, a company called Molten Metals, which has a current market capitalization of almost $500 million. During his Fuel Tech days, he learned how to make money, a far more valuable skill, I submit, than the ability to invent.[10]

One final comment on opportunities involves what I call "arbitrage" businesses. Basically, these businesses exist to take advantage of some pricing disparity in the marketplace. The classic entrepreneurial example was MCI Telecommunications which was formed to offer long distance service at a lower price than AT&T. Similar current examples of arbitrage exist in the health care business in which entrepreneurs are finding ways to offer comparable services to hospitals at much lower costs. Or, some of the industry consolidations going on today reflect a different kind of arbitrage—the ability to buy small businesses at a "wholesale" price, roll them up into a larger package, and take them public at a "retail" price, all without necessarily adding true value in the process.

Taking advantage of arbitrage opportunities is a viable and potentially profitable way to enter a business. In the final analysis, however, all arbitrage opportunities go away. It is not a question of whether, only when. The trick in these businesses is to use the arbitrage profits to build a more enduring business model.

COMPETITION

The notion that all arbitrage opportunities go away reflects a more general belief that all opportunities go away. For any given opportunity, there are a myriad of potential competitors. In 1995, to illustrate, almost $30 billion was invested in private equity funds, of which perhaps 20% was in traditional venture capital. In 1995, over 1 million new businesses were incorporated in

---

10. Actually, Molten Metals is not yet profitable, and, given the inevitable difficulties confronting any company scaling up a new technology, success is certainly not guaranteed.

the U.S. The situation outside the U.S. is similar in the sense that many investors are seeking to back competent entrepreneurial ventures around the world. Moreover, all large companies have become more attuned to opportunity, suggesting a more rapid and competent attempt to identify and exploit them.

A business plan must address the current competitors and the potential competitors in a sensible way. Among the specific issues a plan should cover are the following:

- Who are the current competitors?
- What resources do they control? What are their strengths and weaknesses?
- How will they respond to our decision to enter the business?
- How can we respond to their response?
- Who else might be able to observe and exploit the same opportunity?
- Are there ways to co-opt potential or actual competitors by forming alliances?

Business is like chess: to be successful, you must anticipate several moves in advance in order to have any chance. A business plan that describes an insuperable lead or a proprietary position is by definition written by naïve people.

——— GRAPHICAL ANALYSIS TOOLS FOR ASSESSING OPPORTUNITIES (OR, HAROLD AND THE PURPLE CRAYON MEETS ENTREPRENEURIAL FINANCE)

I like to think of business opportunities in terms of their risk/reward profiles. I have two graphical tools that I apply to understand a business model. The first entails drawing a simple cash flow diagram for the business and the second entails assigning probabilities to certain outcomes. Starting first with the cash flow diagram, consider, to illustrate, a proposal to start a new airline. The cash flow pattern depicted in the business plan looks something like *Exhibit 1*.

Essentially, starting an airline involves a very large capital commitment up front followed by some unknown returns in the future. When I look at this pattern, I focus first and foremost on the likelihood of achieving positive cash flow, when that event might occur, and the potential payoff structure if I am successful. In my view, the airline business is a bad business because the payoffs are too low and risky and too far in the future, given the upfront capital required. The business has high fixed costs of operation, which is often associated with vicious pricing cycles in which prices are driven down to the level of marginal costs. It's rather like the Harvard freshmen football

EXHIBIT 1
Cash Flow Diagram for an Airline

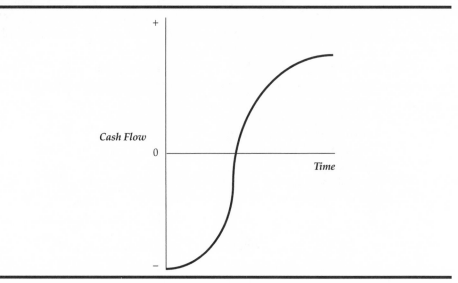

coach said when describing his team, "They're not big, but they're slow." Airlines aren't very profitable, but they require a huge amount of capital.[11]

Compare an airline with an electronically delivered newsletter for which subscribers pay in advance. As noted earlier, the capital requirements in publishing are modest and the potential margins high. If such a plan had a compelling editorial position and could attract subscribers at acceptable costs, then the cash flow pattern might be as depicted in *Exhibit 2*.

Returning to the discussion earlier of business models, it turns out that successful companies typically have more than one relevant cash flow S-curve. In such companies, there are growth opportunities, defined as opportunities to profitably invest additional funds because of success in the first project. For example, a magazine that is launched and attracts an audience might be able to introduce a related product or service (e.g., seminars or conferences, additional magazines targeted at a segment of the overall leadership). Similarly, a single successful restaurant may form the foundation for a chain of restaurants in different areas. Or, a successful software company might have international expansion possibilities that are as attractive (or more so) than the domestic one. The goal in investing or in identifying opportunities from the perspective of the entrepreneur is to identify businesses that have many such growth options and to preserve the right to exploit them.

---

11. Far better than entering the airline business itself is starting a service for all of the companies in the airline business. Prominent successful examples include Flight Safety, which builds flight simulators, and Sabre Corporation, which was originally started by American Airlines to automate flight scheduling and reservations.

EXHIBIT 2
Cash Flow Diagram for a Newsletter

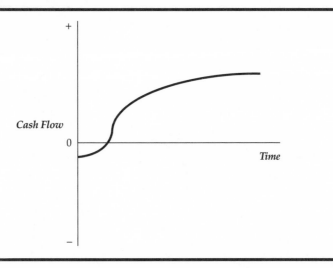

EXHIBIT 3
Cash Flow Diagram for a Magazine or a Restaurant

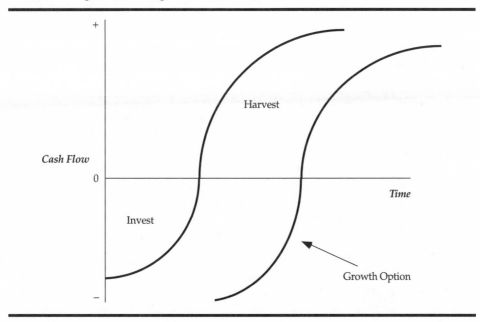

Exhibit 3 depicts a favorable growth option pattern, one like a magazine or a restaurant.

Finding opportunities with ample growth options is a goal: many industries, however, have a pattern that looks attractive but is not. In the disk drive business, for example, success in one investment category does not

EXHIBIT 4
Cash Flow Diagram for the Disk Drive Business

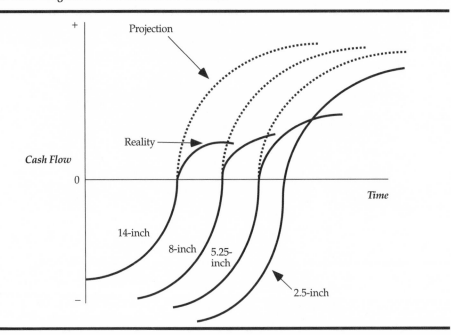

necessarily lead to success in another: indeed, there is some evidence that success leads to disaster. In such industries, which might be called "wave" industries, it is very hard if not impossible to catch successive waves without crashing and burning. The disk drive industry is portrayed in *Exhibit 4*.

A question that leaps out of the cash flow diagrams depicted above is: how do I make decisions that involve tradeoffs between the present and the future? How do I decide whether the potential future cash is big enough to justify the initial investment? To answer these questions, it is clear that you have to assess the riskiness of the bet you are making.

There are two ways to portray the riskiness of a project such as a new airline or an on-line publication. One is to draw the same diagrams as above but to depict reasonable scenarios as well as the expected values. *Exhibit 5* shows three scenarios: the original business plan model, a success scenario in which the company achieved its goals but only after investing more time and money (a frequent event for companies that succeed), and a third scenario in which the company failed after a considerable investment and time period.

The other way to shed light on the riskiness of a project is to assign probabilities to different outcomes for returns on investment. *Exhibit 6* shows the payoff structure for an investment in a new software company.

If I make an investment in a new software company, there is some considerable risk that I will lose all of my money. At the same time, I might

EXHIBIT 5
Cash Flow Scenarios

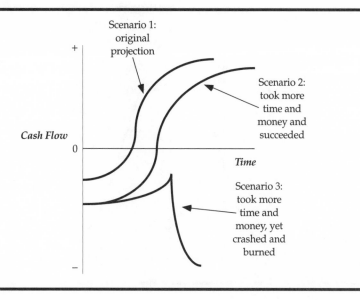

Scenario 1: original projection

Scenario 2: took more time and money and succeeded

Cash Flow

0

Time

Scenario 3: took more time and money, yet crashed and burned

EXHIBIT 6
Probability Distribution for a High Risk/High Reward Software Company

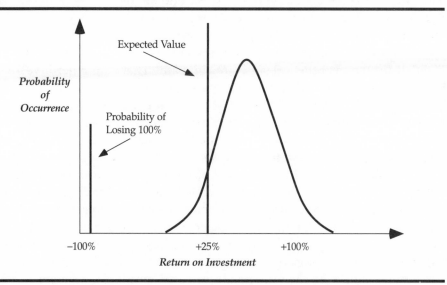

Expected Value

Probability of Occurrence

Probability of Losing 100%

−100%   +25%   +100%

Return on Investment

well invest in the next Microsoft or Netscape, in which case I will have very high returns, perhaps in excess of 100% per year. *Exhibit 6* suggests that there is a small, perhaps even negligible probability of earning a small rate of return on an investment in a software company. The rationale is that most small

EXHIBIT 7
Payoff Structure for a Mature Company

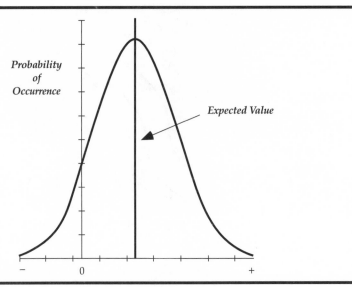

software companies are not very profitable and are therefore not worth much very much. Unless the venture reaches escape velocity, it probably won't succeed.

There is a broad class of investments whose payoff structures look like that for the hypothetical software company. There are other investments where the risk reward pattern looks quite different. Consider an investment in a franchise of a well-established fast food company. In such an investment, there is an extended history of profitable operations. The company has a solid business plan and reasonably predictable results. In this case, the payoff structure might be as depicted in *Exhibit 7*.

In this example, the likelihood of losing all of your money is modest but so too is the upside potential. Of course, return on investment depends on who is asking the question and on the price paid to invest. If you have to pay a high franchise fee, then you lower your potential return and increase the likelihood of a loss. Or, if you are a venture capital investor who strikes a deal with the entrepreneur that is generous to the entrepreneur (e.g., if you pay a high valuation), then the risk/reward pattern looks different.

In general, these graphical tools can be used to describe investment opportunities. Investments involve different combinations of capital requirements and payoffs. They involve differing degrees of uncertainty. To reiterate the obvious, you want opportunities that offer the prospect of high, safe returns on modest investment, with lots of attractive and proprietary growth options—a simple rule to describe, but one that is almost impossible to follow in the real world.

CONTEXT

Opportunities exist in a context. At one level, there is the macroeconomic environment, including the level of economic activity, inflation, exchange rates, and interest rates. There are also a wide range of rules and regulations that affect opportunity and how resources are marshaled to exploit it. Examples range from tax policy to the rules concerning raising capital for a private or public company. Then, there are factors like technology, which affect what a business or its competitors can accomplish.

I will not dwell on context here except to remark that context often has a tremendous impact on every aspect of the entrepreneurial process, from identification of opportunity to harvest. In some cases, changes in some contextual factor create opportunity. For example, when the airline industry was deregulated in the late 1970s, over one hundred new airlines were formed. The context for financing was also favorable, enabling new entrants like People Express to go to the public market for capital even before starting operations.

Conversely, there are periods when the context makes it hard to start new enterprises. In the early 1990s, to illustrate, there was a difficult recession, combined with a difficult financing environment for new companies: venture capital disbursements were low as was the amount of capital raised in the public markets. Paradoxically, these relatively tight conditions, which made it harder for new entrants to get going, were associated with very high investment returns later in the 1990s as the capital market environment heated up.

Sometimes, a shift in context turns an unattractive business into an attractive one, and vice versa. A colleague was on the board of a struggling packaging company some years ago. The board had decided to sell the business. Within weeks of that decision, however, there was an incident in which bottles of Tylenol were tampered with, resulting in multiple deaths. The particular company happened to have an efficient mechanism for putting tamper-proof seals on Tylenol bottles. What had been a poorly performing business quickly turned into a spectacular one, all in a matter of weeks. Conversely, for companies in the real estate business, the tax reforms enacted in 1986 in the U.S. created havoc: almost every positive incentive to invest in real estate was reversed. Many previously successful firms in the real estate industry went out of business soon after the new rules were put in place.

When I read a business plan, I look for two pieces of evidence related to context. First, I want to see that the entrepreneurial team is aware of the context and how it helps or hinders their specific proposal. Second, and more importantly, I look for sensitivity to the fact that the context will inevitably change. If so, how might the changes affect the business? And, what can management do in the event the context worsens? Finally, are there ways in which management can affect context in a positive way? For example, can management have an impact on regulation or on setting industry standards?

We will address the issue of dealing with contextual factors in more detail shortly.

—— DEALS

Most people think of valuation and terms when considering deals. What share of the company will they have to give to the investors to raise capital? What are the terms of the financing? These are the prominent questions. In this section, I will address these issues, but only after considering the sources of capital and the amount raised. The rationale for this sequencing will become apparent shortly.

When I talk to young (and old) entrepreneurs looking to finance their ventures, they obsess about valuation. Their explicit goal seems to be to minimize the dilution they will suffer in raising capital. Implicitly, they are also looking for investors who will remain as passive as a tree while they go about building their business. On the food chain of investors, it seems, doctors and dentists are best and venture capitalists worst because of the degree to which the latter group demands a large share of the returns and demands control rights.

I confess to a bias on the subject of financing ventures. My rule is the following:

From whom you raise capital is often more important than the terms.

Let me explain. Ventures are inherently risky. Murphy often is a member of the management team—what can go wrong will. Most ventures end up taking more time and more money than the entrepreneur ever imagined. The name of the game, then, is not to minimize dilution at each stage of a company's existence but rather to maximize the value of your share at the end of the process.

I have seen quite a few examples of entrepreneurs raising money from unsophisticated investors at high prices. When the inevitable bad news arrives, the investors panic and get angry. They refuse to advance the company more money. They are surprised that results are disappointing. In such situations, it is often difficult to recruit new investors. The new investor has to worry about the old investor group—if they're not putting up more money, what's wrong? The old investors are also reticent to accept the valuation proposed by the new investor.

I view the financing decision as having two fundamental elements: a capital raising decision and a hiring decision. Consider, to illustrate, raising capital from a professional venture capitalist. The investor typically seeks to earn high returns, perhaps 50% per year or greater. This seems on the surface like very high cost money, almost loan-shark like. Suppose, however, that the venture capitalist is the leading expert in the world in the business being financed. Suppose as well that the venture capitalist can increase the potential reward and decrease the potential risk by being involved in the business. In this case, the value of the entrepreneur's share of the company assuming the venture capitalist invests may be higher than it would have been if the company had raised money from less competent investors. Phrased differently, the total pie is increased in size so much that the value of the entrepreneur's smaller slice of the pie is larger.

There are many examples of venture capitalists whose presence in a deal helps enormously. John Doerr, for example, is a partner of the highly successful firm Kleiner, Perkins. Mr. Doerr was a top-ranked salesman at semiconductor powerhouse Intel in the mid 1970s. Doerr has invested in such companies as Sun Microsystems, Intuit and Netscape. He knows the process of building large and successful companies. He has a world-class rolodex, which helps his portfolio companies form valuable connections. I would want John Doerr on my team and I would be prepared to pay a high price to get him. The same is true of other similarly skilled and experienced investors like Arthur Rock or L. J. Sevin. I should also note that if these individuals work with my company, they won't work with my competitor.

I believe that every high-potential venture needs an investor who is "process literate." By this, I mean that they have been through the game many times. They are very good at helping companies grow. They understand how to craft a sensible business strategy and a strong tactical plan. They help recruit, compensate, and motivate great team members. They are coaches and cheerleaders, and they understand the distinction between being an investor and being the entrepreneur. I believe as well that good investors do not panic when bad news arrives. They roll up their sleeves and help the company solve its problems.

There are many decisions in a venture that entrepreneurs will have to face only once or twice in their careers. An example is the decision to go public. The entrepreneur is pitted against highly experienced but not necessarily disinterested service providers like investment bankers, lawyers, and accountants. It is extremely useful in such a situation to have advisors who have "been there and done that." The same is true about other process decisions, such as introducing a new product, dealing with a lawsuit, recruiting a VP of Marketing, or selling a business.

There are other areas in which the choice of a financial partner can help a company. For example, sometimes it is advantageous to raise money from customers. Those customers can help sell the product or service. The best form of customer money is a prepaid order, but it might also make sense to have the customer own equity. The same might be true of suppliers. Even potential competitors are on the list of possible investors, if by investing they forgo the option of entering the business directly. Raising money from these non-traditional sources might seem to create conflicts of interest. As Howard Stevenson says, however, "without conflict, there is no interest."

Though I have started this discussion of "deals" by focusing on who invests, an issue of great importance is how much money to raise and in what stages. Most ventures need more money than they are initially able to raise. Investors are loath to hand over large sums of capital up front to an eager team of business founders. If a company believes it ultimately will need $10 million to develop and introduce a software product, they are likely to find that no investor will invest the full $10 million. Rather, the investor will stage the commitment of capital over time, preserving the right to invest more money and preserving the right to abandon the project in the event the team or the business idea doesn't work out. The investor might offer to invest $1 million while the software is finished. If the software looks attractive, the investor will put in $4 million for the launch of the product. If the launch is promising, then the investor will put up more money, perhaps the remaining $5 million or more, to support expansion of the company.

The issue of how much money to invest in a company is exceedingly difficult and the perspective of the players often differs. Entrepreneurs want all the money up front, while investors want to stage the capital over time in order to "buy" more information. There is no right answer in this ancient debate. There are, however, some useful ways to think about the issues inherent in financing new ventures.

An old saying is "time is money." In entrepreneurial finance, the expression gets turned around: "money is time." By this I mean that money buys time for a venture to find the right combination of people, strategy, and tactics to succeed. Each chunk of money buys an additional chunk of time.

I think of ventures as complicated options such as one finds in financial markets. In this regard, raising money is like extending the expiration date of the option. If the company runs out of money, investors will have to decide whether or not it makes sense to buy more time and, if so, on what terms.

There is also another way in which money is time. Often, a company is pursuing an opportunity for which time to market is critical: the first mover gets the largest share, and the second place finisher is far less attractive. Money can help a company accelerate its entry plan. Some aspects of the business can be done in parallel rather than in sequence. From one perspective, the decision to accelerate spending would seem risky: just the opposite may be true. To go slow is to risk everything. Consider, to illustrate, the famous case on Science Technology used at Harvard Business School. The case mentions that the company invented the oscilloscope after World War II. The case also mentions a sign on the factory floor that stated, "We don't want to grow too large." Unfortunately, they succeeded beyond their wildest dreams: another company pursued the oscilloscope opportunity faster and captured the market leaving Science Technology as small as it apparently aspired to be.

There are other paradoxes in the world of raising money. Sometimes having too much money dooms a company. The founders (and employees) don't view money as a scarce resource: this often occurs in large companies, which have managers who rely on the deep pockets of the parent organization. At other times, a company starves an opportunity.

There are some useful questions that speak to the issue of how time and money should relate to each other in a specific venture, including the following:

- What new information would dramatically change your perception of the likelihood of success for a given venture?
- How much time and money are required to "buy" that information?
- To what degree does the company have control over the rate at which it exploits an opportunity?
- Who else might be pursuing the same opportunity and what are the consequences of losing the race?

The final issue to be covered in this section on deals relates specifically to their structure. There are two important aspects of deal structure that preoccupy entrepreneurs, judging by the number of phone calls I get asking for advice: valuation and terms (i.e., other aspects of the deal, such as employment contracts, etc.).

Unfortunately, there are very few definitive rules when it comes to structuring deals. On the one hand, I believe in the golden rule: "He who has the gold rules." On the other hand, I believe that deals that are too tough on either side generally don't work.

Over the years, I have developed a set of principles to guide deal making. First, deals fundamentally allocate risk and reward and therefore value. Whenever risk and reward are allocated, the deal maker has to be concerned with the three issues:

- What are the incentive effects of the allocation?
- Who will be attracted by the terms offered?
- What are the logical implications if the parties to a deal behave in their own perceived best interest?

Consider, to illustrate, a typical deal between a venture capital firm and a venture. During the past twenty years, the structure of such deals has evolved to a recognizable standard. First, venture capitalists invest in stages: they do not give all the money to the entrepreneurial team that will be required to exploit the opportunity. They almost always invest in the form of a convertible preferred. The preferred has liquidation preference: if the company is liquidated, the principal of the preferred must be paid back before the equityholders receive any of the liquidation proceeds. The preferred has a dividend that is payable at the discretion of the board of directors but adds to the liquidation principle if not paid before liquidation. The preferred is convertible into common stock at some stated price: conversion is typically mandatory if the company goes public. The investors preserve the right to invest additional money by having preemptive rights or rights of first refusal on subsequent financing. The investors have some protection against dilution such as might occur if the company raises additional capital at a lower price. Often, the investors have the right to force the company to repurchase the preferred at some point in the future on some prearranged terms. The investors have certain information rights, enabling them to receive timely (and credible) financial reports and to be notified before major events at the company. The investors also have certain governance rights such as the right to appoint directors or the right to replace the founder or founders. The management team, including the founders typically receive common stock (or stock options) and are subject to vesting requirements: if they leave the company, they lose the unvested portion of their options or stock.

Implicit in each element of the standard venture capital deal is a notion of how the incentives ought to be set. Any time an investor gives money to someone else, he/she has to concern him/herself with possible conflicts of interest. The entrepreneur might, for example, pay him/herself a large salary, depleting the funds of the venture. The entrepreneur might decide to keep the company private, never enabling the investor to get a return on investment.

The deal structure described above is designed to protect the investor and provide appropriate incentives to the entrepreneurial venture. Consider, to illustrate, the rationale for staging the commitment of capital—investing less than might ultimately be needed to exploit an opportunity. Suppose a venture needs $20 million to go from concept to commercialization. Why don't investors just give the full $20 million up front? Well, it's not hard to figure out, when you think about it. I have previously noted that there is often a discrepancy between outcomes and plans. In this hypothetical $20 million venture, it is highly likely that there will be some bad news early in its evolution.

Suppose that, six months after the team receives the $20 million, they discover a fatal flaw in their engineering. Will they call the investors, admit to their discovery, and send back the unspent funds? Not on this planet, they won't. Never in the history of entrepreneurship has an entrepreneur announced defeat. They always believe that the problem can be fixed—all they need is a little more time and a little more money. By the way, sometimes they are right. Federal Express approached bankruptcy three times before it gained escape velocity.

The point here is that investors need to have the right to decide whether or not to continue to back the team and the project: they should not cede decision rights to the team because the team will almost always make a self-interested choice. Indeed, if the entrepreneurial team were to insist that the entire $20 million be invested up-front, they would likely find no (rational) investors willing to make the bet, regardless of the share of the company they would acquire. Also, because the entrepreneurs are likely to have to agree to a staged infusion of capital—with each additional investment based on new information and a price reflecting that information—the entrepreneurs signal their belief in their ability to bring the project to fruition.

The incentive effects of deal structuring could occupy a book and I will not attempt to describe this topic in detail in this note.[12] Rather, the important lesson for entrepreneurs writing business plans is that they have to structure deals that reflect their incentives and those of investors. There is an implicit balancing act. The specific deal will be tailored to the characteristics of the individuals involved, the nature of the opportunity, and the contextual setting.

One caution is appropriate about deal structuring: there is an old expression—"too clever by half"—which is directly relevant. Often, deal makers get creative in structuring deals. For example, they design complex valuation schemes that involve conditional pricing of a deal. If the company does as well as management thinks, then management gets some extra options. If the venture only does as well as the venture capitalist thinks, then the terms are more onerously tilted in favor of the investors. Through painful experience, I have come to believe that simple is better than complex. Trying to structure such complex deals often ends up turning partners into adversaries. In the deal described above, perhaps the venture capitalist will be better off if the company does poorly (but not too poorly) for some period and then takes off. Does the venture capitalist really want to be conflicted in this way? I think not.

In my experience, sensible deals have the following characteristics:

- They are simple.
- They are fair.
- They reflect trust rather than legalese.
- They are robust—they do not blow apart if actual differs slightly from plan.
- They do not provide perverse incentives that will cause one or both parties to behave in destructive ways.
- They do not foreclose valuable options.
- The papers used to describe the deal are no greater than one-quarter inch.

No discussion of deals would be complete without a section on valuation. How are ventures valued, particularly ones for which there is massive uncertainty? The short (and flip) answer is: "aerial extraction." A less curt answer is that venture valuation is an art not a science. Every entrepreneur I have met says something like the following: "Based on my projections, you (the investor) should be willing to value my company at $10 million. If you

---

12. For more information on deals and incentives, see William A. Sahlman, "Note on Financial Contracting: 'Deals,'" Harvard Business School Case # 288-014. See also William A. Sahlman, "The Structure and Governance of Venture Capital Organizations," *Journal of Financial Economics*, October 1990.

do, you will earn a 78% percent internal rate of return, based on our going public in five years." The response is: "I'll value your company at $3 million—your numbers aren't worth the paper they're written on. . . ."

Only if you had omniscience would it be easy to value companies early in their life. The venture investor knows from hard-earned experience that few if any ventures come anywhere close to meeting their projections. Only 10% to 20% of the deals in which they invest will do really well. Some 30% will actually result in losses, in some cases complete loss. What seasoned investors do, therefore, is base their valuations on the overall experience they have had. The reasoning goes something like the following: "If I value early stage software companies at $5 million or less, then I will be able—after it is all said and done—to earn a rate of return on my portfolio that is acceptable to me and my limited partners."

My students are always disappointed that there are not formulae for calculating the value of a venture. They do not like the fact that there are a wide range of possible valuations that are OK or "in the ballpark." They do not like the fact that their negotiating skill and assets (i.e., the degree to which the team and the opportunity are outstanding and proprietary) will determine what happens. I too wish it were easier to come up with answers, or at least narrow ranges: it would certainly make my job less stressful![13]

In closing, this section on deals has been implicitly based on a simple set of structured questions, which are listed below:

- From whom should the money be raised?
- How much money is needed and for what purpose?
- What deal terms are fair and provide the appropriate incentives for each side under a wide range of scenarios?

——— RISK/REWARD MANAGEMENT

One fascinating aspect of business is the degree to which the future is hard to predict. It is certainly possible to write down a detailed description of a bright future, but hard to make it happen. The notion above that there is a known probability distribution for outcomes is useful but slightly misleading. There are no immutable distributions of outcomes. It is ultimately the responsibility of management to change the distribution, to increase the likelihood and consequences of success and decrease the likelihood and implications of problems.

One of the great myths about entrepreneurs is that they are risk seekers. My sense is that all sane people want to avoid risk. As colleague

---

13. For more than you ever wanted to know about valuing venture deals, see Daniel R. Scherlis and William A. Sahlman, "A Method for Valuing High-Risk, Long-Term Investments," Harvard Business School Case # 288-006.

Howard Stevenson says, true entrepreneurs want to capture all of the reward and give all of the risk to others. The best business is a post office box to which people send cashiers checks. Yet, risk is unavoidable. So what is a rational person to do?

My answer to this question is that you must assess the risks and find mechanisms to manage them. Consider, to illustrate, a risk inherent in the context, the set of factors outside the control of the entrepreneur. There might be an increase in interest rates: if a venture is highly leveraged, then an increase in interest cost might sink it. To manage this risk, it might make sense to hedge the exposure in the financial futures market so that a contract is purchased that does well when interest rates go up. This is equivalent to buying insurance: you pay a premium to do so, but you can preserve a company's business model by doing so.

In general, there are a myriad of things that can go wrong or right in a venture. Though it is impossible to predict the future, it is possible to change the odds or manage the consequences of adverse events. For example, suppose you write a great novel. You go to an agent. The agent sells the rights to the book to a publisher. What should you worry about?

Clearly, a successful novel has a number of attractive follow-on possibilities/growth options, including a potential movie based on the book. You can insist that the contract you sign enables you—rather than the publisher—to reap the bulk of the rewards from a movie. I promise, however, that the initial contract you receive will grant to the publisher all ancillary rights associated with the book, from software to video. I also promise that the contract will be tilted in favor of the publisher in other ways. To illustrate, the contract will spell out possible royalty rates: you must not become so preoccupied with getting a high royalty rate that you ignore what that rate is applied to. Many naïve authors have signed movie deals where they get a share of the net income generated in the movie: lo and behold, the movie grosses $500 million, but the author receives no royalties. She is told the movie was unprofitable. . . .

In this example, you cannot predict the success or failure of the book in the marketplace, but you can preserve the option to benefit if it is a success. You can retain certain rights and you can pay attention to the nature of those rights, including the incentives of the other party. Or, you can cross the Mass Turnpike blindfolded. The basic model of risk/reward management is depicted in *Exhibit 8*.

One specific area of importance in the realm of risk/reward management relates to harvesting. Earlier, I suggested that opportunities differed in terms of the implicit growth options defined as opportunities that companies have by dint of their entering a market (e.g., to sell additional products or services to the same customers). Businesses also differ in terms of their harvest potential by which I mean the ability to reap the rewards of the investment process.

For example, venture capitalists often ask if a company is "IPOable,"

EXHIBIT 8
Risk/Reward Management

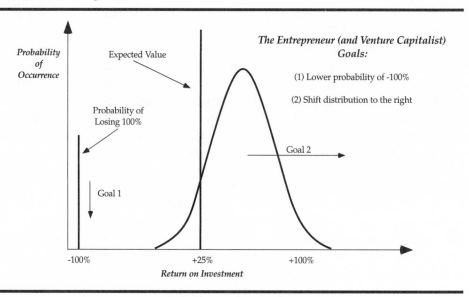

by which they mean: can the company be taken public at some point in the future? Some businesses are inherently difficult to take public, sometimes because doing so would reveal information that might harm the competitive position of the firm (e.g., reveal profitability, thereby encouraging entry or angering customers or suppliers). Some businesses are not companies, but rather products—they are not sustainable as an independent business.

One important task for entrepreneur and investor alike is to think hard at the beginning about the end of the process. Specifically, how will you get money out of the business, assuming it is successful, or even if it is only marginally successful? Some businesses are rife with harvest potential: they involve products or services that are worth a great deal to many potential buyers. If you are currently in the telecommunications software industry today, for example, you are witnessing one of the greatest industry consolidations ever. Companies like Cisco, 3Com, and Bay Networks are on acquisition binges. If you have created a successful niche product or service, there is a strong possibility that one of those three companies will try to buy you. Moreover, because each of the three must compete with the other two, the sellers might well get additional (even unwarranted) benefits from playing one firm off against another.

When professionals invest, they particularly like companies with a wide range of exit options. They work hard to preserve and enhance those options along the way. For example, they avoid forming a strategic relationship with a major company early in the process because doing so often forecloses the exit option of having multiple large firms bid against each other for the right to buy the company. There is an old saying: "If you don't know where you are going, any road will get you there." In crafting sensible entrepreneurial strategies, just the opposite is true: you had better know where you might end up and have a plan for getting there.

FINANCIAL PROJECTIONS

No discussion of business plans would be complete without addressing the ubiquitous proformas that populate them. Most business plan writers spend countless hours on detailed financial projections. They imagine that a potential investor will pore over the numbers asking a myriad of questions. They also imagine that the investor will propose a deal based on the numbers in the plan.

When I first started to study entrepreneurial ventures, I too turned first to the numbers. Of late, I have gotten to the point where I hardly even look at them. Indeed, if I receive a plan that has five years of monthly projections, I immediately and enthusiastically throw the plan in the circular file next to my desk.

Every business plan contains the following phrase: "we conservatively project." Only about 1 in 20 plans are conservative in the sense that the company comes even close to meeting its plan. If you observe one hundred companies and only five come close to their original projections, then you begin to pick up a pattern.

I have come to believe that spreadsheets have an innate virus that infects the projections made in business plans. The virus turns what might be sensible people into wildly optimistic, nonsensical maniacs.

There are two or three possible explanations for why the virus is so widespread. First, in every business, there is what I call the "horse race between fear and greed." Entrepreneurs want to preserve the largest possible ownership stake when raising capital. At the same time, they are afraid of running out of capital. Very few if any entrepreneurs correctly anticipate how much capital and time will be required to accomplish their objectives. Venture capitalists automatically discount what is in a plan to reflect the consistency and predictability of the optimism.

Of course, if the entrepreneurs know that the venture capitalist will discount his or her projections, then they pad the projections to offset the likely haircut to be applied. This sounds to me like a vicious cycle in which reality becomes hard to find.

It's rather like the distinction between "buying proformas" and "selling proformas." It all depends on your perspective. Indeed, I always ask a simple question when looking at projections: Who wrote the proforma and why?

When I read a proforma projection, I look first and foremost for evidence of a business model that makes sense and an appreciation of the fact that the specific numbers proffered are almost certain to be wrong. I like to see that the entrepreneurial team has thought through the key drivers that will determine success or failure. In a traditional magazine business, to illustrate, among the key business drivers are: total possible subscribers in the target audience; gross response rate (how many respond to a mailing that they are interested in subscribing?); net response (how many who say they will try the magazine actually pay?); and renewal rate (how many who subscribe actually renew their subscription when it lapses?). These factors help determine the profitability of a magazine because they affect the cost of acquiring and retaining a subscriber. Also important would be the advertising attractiveness of the audience and the costs of creating (editorial), printing and fulfilling the magazine.

In a software business, the economic drivers differ. Of critical importance are the cost and time schedule for creating the software. Then, the economics of the various distribution channels are at the top of the list. What margins will the retail or OEM channel require? What are the economics of a direct sales force model? How much territory can a salesperson cover? What compensation is required to attract, retain and motivate a talented sales force and a software development team?

Common to all business models is the issue of break-even: at what level does the business begin to make a profit? Even more important, at what level does the company turn cash flow positive?

In addition to a clear appreciation of the factors that will affect the economics of the business, I look for sensible sensitivity analysis. What would happen, for example, if net response rates were 20% lower for the magazine? What would happen if the software project took 20% longer than estimated? These are the kinds of questions that I believe the team should address in presenting their model to prospective resource providers.

Many successful companies find that their basic business model was too optimistic. Though ultimately the business model works, more time and capital are required. I was a director of two companies that started out predicting that they would each need less than $2 million to reach escape velocity. One, Avid Technology, went through $25 million before it reached positive cash flow. Avid sells digital video editing software and went from startup in 1988 to over $400 million in 1995. Another company in the information business went through $10 million as compared to its initial guess of $1.5 million. We had a saying at that company when I was a director: "We never wrote a business plan we couldn't miss." This company now does $160 million in revenue, with $60 million in operating profits. This company also came perilously close to bankruptcy before figuring out its business model.

One final note about proformas in business plans for high potential ventures—they all look the same. Over the past decade, hundreds of books on entrepreneurship and venture capital have been published. Most of these volumes comment that venture capitalists will not consider making an investment in a company that cannot reasonably project $50 million in annual revenues within five years. It is not surprising that almost every plan I receive shows year five sales of $55 million, representing a 10% cushion over the presumed minimum. They also need only a 10% share, and they all show at least a 10% net margin . . . and they are all conservative (see Appendix 3 for a glossary of terms found in business plans and an explanation of what they really mean).

——— DUE DILIGENCE

A business plan is often used as a blueprint for asking questions. Professional investors conduct due diligence in order to assess the people and the opportunity described in a plan. They will call references including people not suggested by the entrepreneurs. They will call actual or potential customers, suppliers, and other resource providers. They will talk to competitors, both actual and potential. And, they will grill the team based on the questions they believe must be answered before they will invest.

I recently participated in a meeting at which an entrepreneurial team tried to convince a group of individuals to invest. The team leader had a well-practiced pitch, complete with color slides and attractive props. At several points in the meeting, the presenter noted that "the business model was proved," by which he meant that there was substantial evidence that the company knew how the opportunity would play out. Unfortunately, the individuals to whom the presentation was being made had done some homework. One had called a potential advertiser, and another had called someone in the retail channel. Each gave a sharply divergent story about the company, its business model, and the likely evolution of the relationship with the company. If the presenter had only hedged his bets by describing the process by which he intended to convert promises (or hints) to reality, his pitch would have been successful. It was not.

The process of investigating a potential investment is driven by experience. After investing in a few companies, you begin to build up a sense of what can go right and what can go wrong. You learn to ask questions that you wish you had asked in the last unsuccessful deal you did. You develop a repertoire of tools to ferret out what is really going on in a venture. One friend always asks the same question when he visits a company seeking investment: "Why are sales so bad?" In some cases, the entrepreneur launches into a discussion of the failings of the sales force or the manufacturing problems confronted by the company. In other cases, the entrepreneur takes offense and describes why sales are going great. In either case, my friend has the information he needs to assess the business and its management team.

One final comment about due diligence is appropriate: it is not infallible. Before Bain Capital invested in Staples, it commissioned a survey of small businesses on their use of supplies. The results of the survey were not consonant with the assumptions made in the Staples business plan. The founder, Tom Stemberg, insisted that Bain Capital revisit the issue and check how much small businesses actually spent on supplies as compared with what they thought they spent. As it turned out, Stemberg was right, and Staples is now a multi-billion dollar business. Bain Capital did invest, which turned out to be a wise decision.

——— SUMMARY AND CONCLUSION

In summary, a business plan is neither necessary nor sufficient. Many successful businesses never had a formal plan and many unsuccessful ventures had a beautifully crafted but irrelevant plan.

A business plan must provide reasonable answers to the following questions:

- Who are the people involved? What have they done in the past that would lead one to believe that they will be successful in the future? Who is missing from the team and how will they be attracted?
- What is the nature of the opportunity? How will the company make money? How is the opportunity likely to evolve? Can entry barriers be built and maintained?
- What contextual factors will affect the venture? What contextual changes are likely to occur, and how can management respond to those changes?
- What deals have been or are likely to be struck inside and outside the venture? Do the deals struck increase the likelihood of success? How will those deals and the implicit incentives evolve over time?
- What decisions have been made (or can be made) to increase the ratio of reward to risk?

Among the many sins committed by business plan writers is arrogance—believing they have a completely proprietary idea or an insuperable lead. In today's economy, few ideas are truly proprietary. Moreover, there has never been a time in recorded history when the supply of capital did not outrace the supply of opportunity. The true half-life of opportunity is decreasing with the passage of time.

A plan must not be an albatross, something that is cast in concrete, hangs around the neck of the entrepreneurial team, and drags them into oblivion. As Steinbeck said, "the best laid plans of mice and men. . . ."; the world changes, and the team must change accordingly.

A plan must be a dynamic call for action, one that recognizes that the responsibility of management is to fix what is broken prospectively and in real time. Risk is inevitable, avoiding risk impossible. Risk management is the key, always tilting the venture in favor of reward and away from risk.

A plan must demonstrate mastery of the entire entrepreneurial process, from identification of opportunity to harvest. To paraphrase George

Bernard Shaw on the subject of love affairs, "Any fool can start a business—it takes a genius to harvest one."

A plan is not a means for separating unsuspecting investors from their money by hiding the fatal flaw. In the final analysis, the only one being fooled is the entrepreneur.

The ultimate tools in business are people, the leaders of the venture, the people who work at the venture, and all of the suppliers, including the financiers. Picking the A-team is the only way to manage reward and risk in the long term.

PERSONALIZING

Writing a business plan can be a terrific educational experience. It is an integrative exercise, requiring the venture team to bring to bear a wide range of skills and experiences. It is human *and* it is analytical. Working on a plan can be a useful tool for gaining commitment and consensus among team members, even if the plan turns out to be impractical.

The real purpose of this note is to get MBAs and others to think about their careers using the entrepreneurship lens. To what degree do they know what an opportunity is and how to marshal the required resources? What is missing, and how can the gaps be addressed?

We live in a golden age, one characterized by tremendous opportunity and a myriad of examples of successful entrepreneurship. A young dropout from college, Bill Gates of Microsoft fame, ends up as the wealthiest individual in America. Three young graduates from Harvard Business School, David Thompson, Bruce Ferguson, and Scott Webster, built Orbital Sciences Corporation into a multi-hundred million dollar, publicly-traded company whose mission is to commercialize space.

Writing a business plan is useful as part of a lifelong educational experience. If and only if the writer has the skills, experience, contacts, and attitude that are required for the business, then, by all means, the Nike model should be invoked—

Just Do It!
If not,
Just Say No!

DISCUSSION QUESTIONS

1. Using the people-opportunity-context-deal framework, analyze a new venture opportunity with which you are familiar. What issues are illuminated?

2. What are the cash flow characteristics of this business? How do you evaluate whether this is attractive or not?
3. What tools are available for the entrepreneur for managing risk and reward?

APPENDIX 1
The Concept of Fit

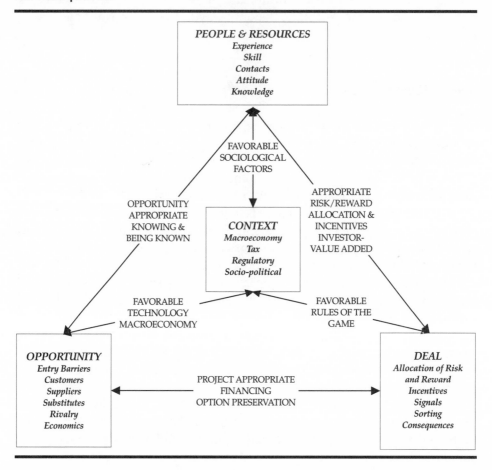

APPENDIX 2
Dynamic Fit Management

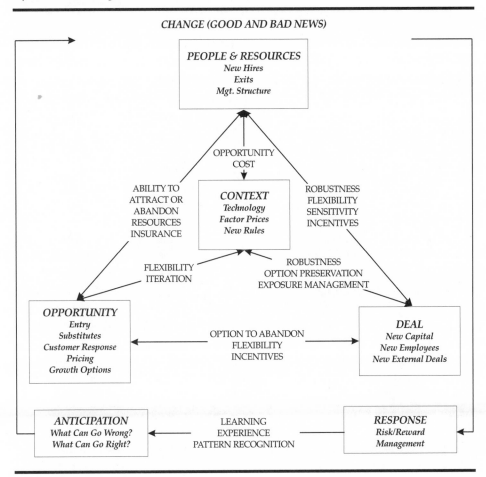

CHANGE (GOOD AND BAD NEWS)

PEOPLE & RESOURCES
New Hires
Exits
Mgt. Structure

OPPORTUNITY
COST

ABILITY TO
ATTRACT OR
ABANDON
RESOURCES
INSURANCE

CONTEXT
Technology
Factor Prices
New Rules

ROBUSTNESS
FLEXIBILITY
SENSITIVITY
INCENTIVES

FLEXIBILITY
ITERATION

ROBUSTNESS
OPTION PRESERVATION
EXPOSURE MANAGEMENT

OPPORTUNITY
Entry
Substitutes
Customer Response
Pricing
Growth Options

OPTION TO ABANDON
FLEXIBILITY
INCENTIVES

DEAL
New Capital
New Employees
New External Deals

ANTICIPATION
What Can Go Wrong?
What Can Go Right?

LEARNING
EXPERIENCE
PATTERN RECOGNITION

RESPONSE
Risk/Reward
Management

Appendix 3
Translation Glossary for Business Plans

Business Plan Phrase	*What It Really Means*
We conservatively project . . .	We read a book that said we had to have sales of $50 million in 5 years, and we reverse engineered the numbers . . .
We took our best guess and divided by 2 . . .	We accidentally divided by .5 . . .
We project a 10% margin . . .	We did not modify any of the assumptions in the business plan template we downloaded from the Internet . . .
The project is 98% complete . . .	To complete the remaining 2% will take as long as to create the initial 98%, but will cost twice as much . . .
Our business model is proved . . .	If you take the evidence from the past week for the best of our fifty locations and extrapolate it for all of the others . . .
We have a six-month lead . . .	We have not tried to find out how many other people also have a six month lead . . .
We only need a 10% market share . . .	So too do all the other 50 entrants getting funded . . .
Customers are clamoring for our product . . .	We have not yet broached the issue of them paying for it. Also, all of our current customers are relatives . . .
We are the low-cost producer . . .	We have not produced anything yet, but we are confident that we will be able to . . .
We have no competition . . .	Only Microsoft, Netscape, IBM, and Sun have announced plans to enter the business . . .
Our management team has a great deal of experience . . .	. . . consuming the product or service . . .
A select group of investors is considering the plan . . .	We mailed a copy of the plan to everyone in Pratt's Guide . . .
We seek a value-added investor . . .	We are looking for a passive, dumb-as-rocks investor . . .
If you invest on our terms, you will earn a 68% IRR . . .	If everything that could conceivably ever go right does go right, you might get your money back . . .

How to Write a Winning Business Plan 10

STANLEY R. RICH and DAVID E. GUMPERT

Many entrepreneurs continue to believe that if they build a better mouse-trap, the world will beat a path to their door. A good product or service is important, but it is only part of the challenge. Equally important is writing a business plan that will address the concerns of the constituencies that give the venture its financial viability—marketers and investors. Marketers want to see evidence of strong customer interest in the product or service. Investors want to know how good the financial projections are and when they can realize a return. Pointing out that creating a business plan is more an art than science, Rich and Gumpert provide valuable guidelines for writing a plan that looks outward to key constituencies, demonstrates what is unique about the enterprise, and wins the necessary investment and support.

A comprehensive, carefully thought-out business plan is essential to the success of entrepreneurs and corporate managers. Whether you are starting up a new business, seeking additional capital for existing product lines, or proposing a new activity in a corporate division, you will never face a more challenging writing assignment than the preparation of a business plan.

Only a well-conceived and well-packaged plan can win the necessary investment and support for your idea. It must describe the company or proposed project accurately and attractively. Even though its subject is a moving target, the plan must detail the company's or the project's present status, current needs, and expected future. You must present and justify ongoing and changing resource requirements, marketing decisions, financial projections, production demands, and personnel needs in logical and convincing fashion.

Because they struggle so hard to assemble, organize, describe, and document so much, it is not surprising that managers sometimes overlook the fundamentals. We have found that the most important one is the accurate reflection of the viewpoints of three constituencies.

1. The market, including both existing and prospective clients, customers, and users of the planned product or service.

2. The investors, whether of financial or other resources.
3. The producer, whether the entrepreneur or the inventor.

Too many business plans are written solely from the viewpoint of the third constituency—the producer. They describe the underlying technology or creativity of the proposed product or service in glowing terms and at great length. They neglect the constituencies that give the venture its financial viability—the market and the investor.

Take the case of five executives seeking financing to establish their own engineering consulting firm. In their business plan, they listed a dozen types of specialized engineering services and estimated their annual sales and profit growth at 20%. But the executives did not determine which of the proposed dozen services their potential clients really needed and which would be most profitable. By neglecting to examine these issues closely, they ignored the possibility that the marketplace might want some services not among the dozen listed.

Moreover, they failed to indicate the price of new shares or the percentage available to investors. Dealing with the investor's perspective was important because—for a new venture, at least—backers seek a return of 40% to 60% on their capital, compounded annually. The expected sales and profit growth rates of 20% could not provide the necessary return unless the founders gave up a substantial share of the company.

In fact, the executives had only considered their own perspective—including the new company's services, organization, and projected results. Because they had not convincingly demonstrated why potential customers would buy the services or how investors would make an adequate return (or when and how they could cash out), their business plan lacked the credibility necessary for raising the investment funds needed.

We have had experience in both evaluating business plans and organizing and observing presentations and investor responses at sessions of the MIT Enterprise Forum. We believe that business plans must deal convincingly with marketing and investor considerations. This reading identifies and evaluates those considerations and explains how business plans can be written to satisfy them.

——— EMPHASIZE THE MARKET

Investors want to put their money into market-driven rather than technology-driven or service-driven companies. The potential of the product's markets, sales, and profit is far more important than its attractiveness or technical features.

You can make a convincing case for the existence of a good market by demonstrating user benefit, identifying marketplace interest, and documenting market claims.

SHOW THE USER'S BENEFIT

It's easy even for experts to overlook this basic notion. At an MIT Enterprise Forum session an entrepreneur spent the bulk of his 20-minute presentation period extolling the virtues of his company's product—an instrument to control certain aspects of the production process in the textile industry.[1] He concluded with some financial projections looking five years down the road.

The first panelist to react to the business plan—a partner in a venture capital firm—was completely negative about the company's prospects for obtaining investment funds because, he stated, its market was in a depressed industry.

Another panelist asked, "How long does it take your product to pay for itself in decreased production costs?" The presenter immediately responded, "Six months." The second panelist replied, "That's the most important thing you've said tonight."

The venture capitalist quickly reversed his original opinion. He said he would back a company in almost any industry if it could prove such an important user benefit—and emphasize it in its sales approach. After all, if it paid back the customer's cost in six months, the product would after that time essentially "print money."

The venture capitalist knew that instruments, machinery, and services that pay for themselves in less than one year are mandatory purchases for

---

1. The MIT Enterprise Forum—Organized under the auspices of the Massachusetts Institute of Technology Alumni Association in 1978, the MIT Enterprise Forum offers businesses at a critical stage of development an opportunity to obtain counsel from a panel of experts on steps to take to achieve their goals.

In monthly evening sessions the forum evaluates the business plans of companies accepted for presentation during 60- to 90-minute segments in which no holds are barred. The format allows each presenter 20 minutes to summarize a business plan orally. Each panelist reviews the written business plan in advance of the sessions. Then each of four panelists—who are venture capitalists, bankers, marketing specialists, successful entrepreneurs, MIT professors, or other experts—spends five to ten minutes assessing the strengths and weaknesses of the plan and the enterprise and suggesting improvements.

In some cases, the panelists suggest a completely new direction. In others, they advise more effective implementation of existing policies. Their comments range over the spectrum of business issues.

Sessions are open to the public and usually draw about 300 people, most of them financiers, business executives, accountants, lawyers, consultants, and others with special interest in emerging companies. Following the panelists' evaluations, audience members can ask questions and offer comments.

Presenters have the opportunity to respond to the evaluations and suggestions offered. They also receive written evaluations of the oral presentation from audience members. (The entrepreneur doesn't make the written plan available to the audience.) These monthly sessions are held primarily for companies that have advanced beyond the start-up stage. They tend to be from one to ten years old and in need of expansion capital.

The MIT Enterprise Forum's success at its home base in Cambridge, Massachusetts has led MIT alumni to establish forums in New York, Washington, Houston, Chicago, and Amsterdam, among other cities.

many potential customers. If this payback period is less than two years, it is a probable purchase; beyond three years, they do not back the product.

The MIT panel advised the entrepreneur to recast his business plan so that it emphasized the short payback period and played down the self-serving discussion about product innovation. The executive took the advice and rewrote the plan in easily understandable terms. His company is doing very well and has made the transition from a technology-driven to a market-driven company.

FIND OUT THE MARKET'S INTEREST

Calculating the user's benefit is only the first step. An entrepreneur must also give evidence that customers are intrigued with the user's benefit claims and that they like the product or service. The business plan must reflect clear positive responses of customer prospects to the question "Having heard our pitch, will you buy?" Without them, an investment usually won't be made.

How can start-up businesses—some of which may have only a prototype product or an idea for a service—appropriately gauge market reaction? One executive of a smaller company had put together a prototype of a device that enables personal computers to handle telephone messages. He needed to demonstrate that customers would buy the product, but the company had exhausted its cash resources and was thus unable to build and sell the item in quantity.

The executives wondered how to get around the problem. The MIT panel offered two possible responses. First, the founders might allow a few customers to use the prototype and obtain written evaluations of the product and the extent of their interest when it became available.

Second, the founders might offer the product to a few potential customers at a substantial price discount if they paid part of the cost—say one-third—up front so that the company could build it. The company could not only find out whether potential buyers existed but also demonstrate the product to potential investors in real-life installations.

In the same way, an entrepreneur might offer a proposed new service at a discount to initial customers as a prototype if the customers agreed to serve as references in marketing the service to others.

For a new product, nothing succeeds as well as letters of support and appreciation from some significant potential customers, along with "reference installations." You can use such third-party statements—from would-be customers to whom you have demonstrated the product, initial users, sales representatives, or distributors—to show that you have indeed discovered a sound market that needs your product or service.

You can obtain letters from users even if the product is only in prototype form. You can install it experimentally with a potential user to whom you will sell it at or below cost in return for information on its benefits and an agreement to talk to sales prospects or investors. In an appendix to the business plan or in a separate volume, you can include letters attesting to the value of the product from experimental customers.

DOCUMENT YOUR CLAIMS

Having established a market interest, you must use carefully analyzed data to support your assertions about the market and the growth rate of sales and profits. Too often, executives think "If we're smart, we'll be able to get about 10% of the market" and "Even if we only get 1% of such a huge market, we'll be in good shape."

Investors know that there's no guarantee a new company will get any business, regardless of market size. Even if the company makes such claims based on fact—as borne out, for example, by evidence of customer interest—they can quickly crumble if the company does not carefully gather and analyze supporting data.

One example of this danger surfaced in a business plan that came before the MIT Enterprise Forum. An entrepreneur wanted to sell a service to small businesses. He reasoned that he could have 170,000 customers if he penetrated even 1% of the market of 17 million small enterprises in the United States. The panel pointed out that anywhere from 11 million to 14 million of such so-called small businesses were really sole proprietorships or part-time businesses. The total number of full-time small businesses with employees was actually between 3 million and 6 million and represented a real potential market far beneath the company's original projections—and prospects.

Similarly, in a business plan relating to the sale of certain equipment to apple growers, you must have U.S. Department of Agriculture statistics to discover the number of growers who could use the equipment. If your equipment is useful only to growers with 50 acres or more, then you need to determine how many growers have farms of that size, that is, how many are minor producers with only an acre or two of apple trees.

A realistic business plan needs to specify the number of potential customers, the size of their businesses, and which size is most appropriate to the offered products or services. Sometimes bigger is not better. For example, a saving of $10,000 per year in chemical use may be significant to a modest company but unimportant to a Du Pont or a Monsanto.

Such marketing research should also show the nature of the industry. Few industries are more conservative than banking and public utilities. The number of potential customers is relatively small, and industry acceptance of new products or services is painfully slow, no matter how good the products and services have proven to be. Even so, most of the customers are well known and while they may act slowly, they have the buying power that makes the wait worthwhile.

At the other end of the industrial spectrum are extremely fast-growing and fast-changing operations such as franchised weight-loss clinics and computer software companies. Here the problem is reversed. While some companies have achieved multi-million-dollar sales in just a few years, they are vulnerable to declines of similar proportions from competitors. These companies must innovate constantly so that potential competitors will be discouraged from entering the marketplace.

You must convincingly project the rate of acceptance for the product or service—and the rate at which it is likely to be sold. From this marketing research data, you can begin assembling a credible sales plan and projecting your plant and staff needs.

ADDRESS INVESTORS' NEEDS

The marketing issues are tied to the satisfaction of investors. Once executives make a convincing case for their market penetration, they can make the financial projections that help determine whether investors will be interested in evaluating the venture and how much they will commit and at what price.

Before considering investors' concerns in evaluating business plans, you will find it worth your while to gauge who your potential investors might be. Most of us know that for new and growing private companies, investors may be professional venture capitalists and wealthy individuals. For corporate ventures, they are the corporation itself. When a company offers shares to the public, individuals of all means become investors along with various institutions.

But one part of the investor constituency is often overlooked in the planning process—the founders of new and growing enterprises. By deciding to start and manage a business, they are committed to years of hard work and personal sacrifice. They must try to stand back and evaluate their own businesses in order to decide whether the opportunity for reward some years down the road truly justifies the risk early on.

When an entrepreneur looks at an idea objectively rather than through rose-colored glasses, the decision whether to invest may change. One entrepreneur who believed in the promise of his scientific-instruments company faced difficult marketing problems because the product was highly specialized and had, at best, few customers. Because of the entrepreneur's heavy debt, the venture's chance of eventual success and financial return was quite slim.

The panelists concluded that the entrepreneur would earn only as much financial return as he would have had holding a job during the next three to seven years. On the downside, he might wind up with much less in exchange for larger headaches. When he viewed the project in such dispassionate terms, the entrepreneur finally agreed and gave it up.

CASHING OUT

Entrepreneurs frequently do not understand why investors have a short attention span. Many who see their ventures in terms of a lifetime commitment expect that anyone else who gets involved will feel the same. When investors evaluate a business plan, they consider not only whether to get in but also how and when to get out.

Because small, fast-growing companies have little cash available for dividends, the main way investors can profit is from the sale of their holdings, either when the company goes public or is sold to another business. (Large corporations that invest in new enterprises may not sell their holdings if they're committed to integrating the venture into their organizations and realizing long-term gains from income.)

Venture capital firms usually wish to liquidate their investments in small companies in three to seven years so as to pay gains while they generate funds for investment in new ventures. The professional investor wants to cash out with a large capital appreciation.

Investors want to know that entrepreneurs have thought about how to comply with this desire. Do they expect to go public, sell the company, or buy the investors out in three to seven years? Will the proceeds provide investors with a return on invested capital commensurate with the investment risk—in the range of 35% to 60%, compounded and adjusted for inflation?

Business plans often do not show when and how investors may liquidate their holdings. For example, one entrepreneur's software company sought $1.5 million to expand. But a panelist calculated that, to satisfy their goals, the investors "would need to own the entire company and then some."

MAKING SOUND PROJECTIONS

Five-year forecasts of profitability help lay the groundwork for negotiating the amount investors will receive in return for their money. Investors see such financial forecasts as yardsticks against which to judge future performance.

Too often, entrepreneurs go to extremes with their numbers. In some cases, they don't do enough work on their financials and rely on figures that are so skimpy or overoptimistic that anyone who has read more than a dozen business plans quickly sees through them.

In one MIT Enterprise Forum presentation, a management team proposing to manufacture and market scientific instruments forecast a net income after taxes of 25% of sales during the fourth and fifth years following investment. While a few industries such as computer software average such high profits, the scientific instruments business is so competitive, panelists noted, that expecting such margins is unrealistic.

In fact, the managers had grossly—and carelessly—understated some important costs. The panelists advised them to take their financial estimates back to the drawing board and before approaching investors to consult financial professionals.

Some entrepreneurs think that the financials are the business plan. They may cover the plan with a smog of numbers. Such "spreadsheet merchants," with their pages of computer printouts covering every business variation possible and analyzing product sensitivity, completely turn off many investors.

Investors are wary even when financial projections are solidly based on realistic marketing data because fledgling companies nearly always fail to achieve their rosy profit forecasts. Officials of five major venture capital firms we surveyed said they are satisfied when new ventures reach 50% of their financial goals. They agreed that the negotiations that determine the percentage of the company purchased by the investment dollars are affected by this "projection discount factor."

THE DEVELOPMENT STAGE

All investors wish to reduce their risk. In evaluating the risk of a new and growing venture, they assess the status of the product and the management team. The farther along an enterprise is in each area, the lower the risk.

At one extreme is a single entrepreneur with an unproven idea. Unless the founder has a magnificent track record, such a venture has little chance of obtaining investment funds.

At the more desirable extreme is a venture that has an accepted product in a proven market and a competent and fully staffed management team. This business is most likely to win investment funds at the lowest costs.

Entrepreneurs who become aware of their status with investors and think it inadequate can improve it. Take the case of a young MIT engineering graduate who appeared at an MIT Enterprise Forum session with written schematics for the improvement of semiconductor-equipment production. He had documented interest by several producers and was looking for money to complete development and begin production.

The panelists advised him to concentrate first on making a prototype and assembling a management team with marketing and financial know-how to complement his product-development expertise. They explained that because he had never before started a company, he needed to show a great deal of visible progress in building his venture to allay investors' concern about his inexperience.

THE PRICE

Once investors understand a company qualitatively, they can begin to do some quantitative analysis. One customary way is to calculate the company's value on the basis of the results expected in the fifth year following investment. Because risk and reward are closely related, investors believe companies with fully developed products and proven management teams should yield between 35% and 40% on their investment, while those with incomplete products and management teams are expected to bring in 60% annual compounded returns.

Investors calculate the potential worth of a company after five years to determine what percentage they must own to realize their return. Take the hypothetical case of a well-developed company expected to yield 35% annually. Investors would want to earn 4.5 times their original investment, before inflation, over a five-year period.

After allowing for the projection discount factor, investors may postulate that a company will have $20 million annual revenues after five years and a net profit of $1.5 million. Based on a conventional multiple for acquisitions of ten times earnings, the company would be worth $15 million in five years.

If the company wants $1 million of financing, it should grow to $4.5 million after five years to satisfy investors. To realize that return from a company worth $15 million, the investors would need to own a bit less than one-third. If inflation is expected to average 7.5% a year during the five-year period, however, investors would look for a value of $6.46 million as a reasonable return over five years, or 43% of the company.

For a less mature venture—from which investors would be seeking 60% annually, net of inflation—a $1 million investment would have to bring in close to $15 million in five years, with inflation figured at 7.5% annually. But few businesses can make a convincing case for such a rich return if they do not already have a product in the hands of some representative customers.

The final percentage of the company acquired by the investors is, of course, subject to some negotiation, depending on projected earnings and expected inflation.

▬▬ MAKE IT HAPPEN

The only way to tend to your needs is to satisfy those of the market and the investors—unless you are wealthy enough to furnish your own capital to finance the venture and test out the pet product or service.

Of course, you must confront other issues before you can convince investors that the enterprise will succeed. For example, what proprietary aspects are there to the product or service? How will you provide quality

EXHIBIT
Packaging Is Important

A business plan gives financiers their first impressions of a company and its principals.

Potential investors expect the plan to look good, but not too good; to be the right length; to clearly and concisely explain early on all aspects of the company's business; and not to contain bad grammar and typographical or spelling errors.

Investors are looking for evidence that the principals treat their own property with care—and will likewise treat the investment carefully. In other words, form as well as content is important, and investors know that good form reflects good content and vice versa.

Among the format issues we think most important are the following:

Appearance The binding and printing must not be sloppy; neither should the presentation be too lavish. A stapled compilation of photocopied pages usually looks amateurish, while bookbinding with typeset pages may arouse concern about excessive and inappropriate spending. A plastic spiral binding holding together a pair of cover sheets of a single color provides both a neat appearance and sufficient strength to withstand the handling of a number of people without damage.

Length A business plan should be no more than 40 pages long. The first draft will likely exceed that, but editing should produce a final version that fits within the 40-page ideal. Adherence to this length forces entrepreneurs to sharpen their ideas and results in a document likely to hold investors' attention.

Background details can be included in an additional volume. Entrepreneurs can make this material available to investors during the investigative period after the initial expression of interest.

The Cover and Title Page The cover should bear the name of the company, its address and phone number, and the month and year in which the plan is issued. Surprisingly, a large number of business plans are submitted to potential investors without return addresses or phone numbers. An interested investor wants to be able to contact a company easily and to request further information or express an interest, either in the company or in some aspect of the plan.

Inside the front cover should be a well-designed title page on which the cover information is repeated and, in an upper or a lower corner, the legend "Copy number ____" provided. Besides helping entrepreneurs keep track of plans in circulation, holding down the number of copies outstanding—usually to no more than 20—has a psychological advantage. After all, no investor likes to think that the prospective investment is shopworn.

The Executive Summary The two pages immediately following the title page should concisely explain the company's current status, its products or services, the benefits to customers, the financial forecasts, the venture's objectives in three to seven years, the amount of financing needed, and how investors will benefit.

This is a tall order for a two-page summary, but it will either sell investors on reading the rest of the plan or convince them to forget the whole thing.

The Table of Contents After the executive summary include a well-designed table of contents. List each of the business plan's sections and mark the pages for each section.

control? Have you focused the venture toward a particular market segment, or are you trying to do too much? If this is answered in the context of the market and investors, the result will be more effective than if you deal with them in terms of your own wishes.

An example helps illustrate the potential conflicts. An entrepreneur at an MIT Enterprise Forum session projected R&D spending of about half of gross sales revenues for his specialty chemical venture. A panelist who had analyzed comparable organic chemical suppliers asked why the company's R&D spending was so much higher than the industry average of 5% of gross revenues.

The entrepreneur explained that he wanted to continually develop new products in his field. While admitting his purpose was admirable, the panel unanimously advised him to bring his spending into line with the industry's. The presenter ignored the advice; he failed to obtain the needed financing and eventually went out of business.

Once you accept the idea that you should satisfy the market and the investors, you face the challenge of organizing your data into a convincing document so that you can sell your venture to investors and customers. We have provided some presentation guidelines in the *Exhibit* "Packaging Is Important."

Even though we might wish it were not so, writing effective business plans is as much an art as it is a science. The idea of a master document whose blanks executives can merely fill in—much in the way lawyers use sample wills or real estate agreements—is appealing but unrealistic.

Businesses differ in key marketing, production, and financial issues. Their plans must reflect such differences and must emphasize appropriate areas and deemphasize minor issues. Remember that investors view a plan as a distillation of the objectives and character of the business and its executives. A cookie-cutter, fill-in-the-blanks plan or, worse yet, a computer-generated package, will turn them off.

Write your business plans by looking outward to your key constituencies rather than by looking inward at what suits you best. You will save valuable time and energy this way and improve your chances of winning investors and customers.

—— DISCUSSION QUESTIONS

1. "Too many business plans are written from the viewpoint of the third constituency—the producer," state the authors. How can entrepreneurs or producers leave their imprint on the business plan while addressing the concerns of the market and of the investors?

2. To write a persuasive business plan, an entrepreneur must be able to look at the product or service from the customer's point of view.

Think of a product or service that you value and purchase regularly. If you were writing a business plan for this product or service, how would you describe its benefits?

3. Consider some of the important topics covered in a business plan—the product or service itself, resource requirements, user benefit and market interest, financial projections, management team, and so on. What aspects of these topics would be of particular concern to the following constituencies—bankers, venture capitalists, customers, suppliers, employees?

4. The main purpose of a business plan is to win investment and support for a new enterprise. In what other ways can writing a business plan benefit an entrepreneur?

5. Can you think of any additional features not mentioned in the reading that would enhance effectiveness of a business plan?

Purchasing a Business: 11
The Search Process

MICHAEL J. ROBERTS and ENNIS J. WALTON

*There are several advantages to purchasing an existing company. The buyer
need not create a new product or service; all that is needed is sufficient
operation capital. Even when the purchase price exceeds start-up costs, a
buyer typically incurs a lower risk than the founder of the business. Moreover, once the deal is closed, the new owner can focus more quickly than
the founder on building and adding value to the business. However, difficulties exist as well. Few written rules govern the search for an existing
business to purchase, and there is no established marketplace. The buyer
must be prepared to assume responsibility for an enterprise that bears
another's imprint.*

*This reading provides a framework for negotiating an inevitably predictable
process. It covers such essentials as assessing your own personal motives
and expectations, establishing selection criteria, locating deal sources, gathering resources, planning and negotiating the deal, and adding new value
to the enterprise. The authors stress that although ideal acquisition candidates are rare, a realistic personal assessment combined with sound search
and negotiation techniques can significantly improve the buyer's chance for
success.*

—— INTRODUCTION

Purchasing an existing business is an excellent alternative for individuals interested in running a small- to medium-sized company. While not
usually considered as "entrepreneurial" as developing the next generation of
personal computers in a tiny garage, purchasing a company demands making
many of the same difficult decisions required of a successful entrepreneur. In

This note was prepared by Research Associate Ennis J. Walton, under the supervision of
Assistant Professor Michael J. Roberts, as the basis for class discussion. It is based on "Buying an
Existing Business" (#385-330) by Lynn Radlauer and Ned Lubell, and on "Note on Buying a Business"
by David Hull, Byron Snider, Robert Stevenson, and Robert Winter. Copyright © 1987 by the President
and Fellows of Harvard College. Harvard Business School case 388-044.

addition, it provides an opportunity for the purchaser to leverage his/her financial resources and concentrate sooner on "value adding" issues that are traditionally taught in business school management courses.

Buying a business is an informal process. No one has yet written a book that successfully defines the correct steps and best alternatives for every situation. Hence, there is no substitute for personal commitment, good business sense, and a cautiously optimistic exploration of every opportunity. Success in this process may occur randomly, and can often depend on serendipity—being the right person in the right place at the right time. It is a mistake, however, to depend on good luck rather than good work.

This note will provide a framework that outlines many of the steps necessary to identify, evaluate and negotiate a successful buyout. It is important to note, however, that this framework is not exhaustive. Rather, it provides a starting point that can be tailored to suit the particular nature of your search.

The areas discussed in this note are as follows:

- *Self-Assessment:* understanding your motives, expectations, risk profile, and financial and professional resources; and, determining the seriousness of your search process.
- *Deal Criteria:* clarifying the dimensions of the project and characteristics that you find attractive.
- *Deal Sources:* learning how to differentiate between the various deal sources in order to find a source that best fits your personal needs and established criteria.
- *Resources:* evaluating and garnering the additional cash, credibility, personal and professional contacts, and information necessary to begin the deal process.
- *The Deal Process:* recognizing the sequential, often random, search process; establishing a deal timing schedule and work plan that allows you to evaluate deals that do not occur in parallel; understanding how to start the process, keep it moving, and establish initial contact with prospective sellers; and, assessing the sellers' motives, weaknesses, strengths and special nonfinancial requirements.
- *The Evaluation Process:* understanding the various analytical methods used by sellers; requesting or obtaining the key financial indicators; and, analyzing the important financial dimensions of the deal.
- *Negotiating the Deal:* identifying potential deal killers; learning from the collapsed deal; and, pursuing attractive deals.
- *Adding Value:* Applying your managerial skills to add new value to the enterprise; and, understanding important harvesting options for the new enterprise.

━━━━ SELF-ASSESSMENT

The first step in buying an existing business is a personal assessment. This step is crucial because it will help you identify, articulate and evaluate your hidden motives, expectations, risk profile and ultimately, the seriousness of your search. Without a good sense of these personal values, the search process can become unfocused and unrewarding, causing you to waste time, resources, and energy.

The problems that could materialize in the absence of a thorough self-evaluation are intensified if you are attempting to purchase a company with another individual. In such cases, it is absolutely essential that all parties understand and agree upon their motives and goals. Proceeding with a false sense of those aspirations will more than likely lead to problems—disagreements which impact on the efficiency and effectiveness of the group during the later stages of the process when clear vision and communication are important to make important decisions.

A good self-assessment will probably place you in one of three broad categories:

SERIOUS The serious and realistic search involves:
- a high level of commitment to the search;
- an ambitious set of expectations consistent with the degree of effort and commitment; and,
- a willingness to:
    - risk at least some personal wealth/security
    - deeply research the target industry
    - be patient and wait for the "right" opportunity
    - move quickly and decisively as needed
    - pursue the search full-time, if needed.

CASUAL The casual and realistic search involves:
- a set of expectations that is consistent with this lessened degree of commitment and effort;
- less willingness to move quickly or decisively on opportunities;
- no specified time horizon for search; and,
- not being overly hungry to control one's own firm.

UNREALISTIC The unrealistic search involves:
- objectives that are inconsistent with level of commitment;
- waiting for a "great deal" to fall in place; and,
- looking for bargains and short-cuts.

While there is nothing wrong with either of the second two categories, the number and quality of opportunities discovered is proportional to the intensity of the search. This is not to say, however, that one cannot find excellent deals by "shopping" the market casually, but only that the process may take quite a while.

Another aspect of the self-assessment process that many people deal too lightly with is the listing of any and all business or personal relationships that can be called upon to add credibility or offer advice. Since the search process is lengthy and filled with important decision points, it is of great value to have others whose opinion you trust to call upon for advice.

The most important reason for the self-assessment, however, is tactical. Throughout the search process, you will have to deal with sellers or their intermediaries to get a sense of the deal. Because these individuals are often reluctant to invest their time with individuals unless they sense a degree of rational forethought and commitment, it's important to have a clear and convincing sense of what it is you're looking for. Thus, the better you have assessed yourself, the easier it will be to persuade others to take you seriously or work productively on your behalf.

——— DEAL CRITERIA

A consistent and thorough screening method is essential for the successful completion of the acquisition process. Consistency is required so that analyses performed on one company are more readily comparable with those of other candidates. Thoroughness is required because all relevant aspects of a potential acquisition must be identified and analyzed. While thoroughness is critical, the screening method should have a clear focus and be kept fairly simple.

There are numerous ways to define the desired target company profile. At a minimum, one should think along such dimensions as:

- size of deal (purchase price) desired;
- preferred industry;
- key factors for success: logistics, marketing, technology, etc.;
- type of customer base (i.e., industrial vs. consumer, national vs. regional, etc.);
- geographic preference; and,
- profile of current ownership (i.e., how many, willingness to sell, reputation)

The mechanical dimensions highlighted above establish a preliminary framework for identifying deals that are appropriate for the particular search being undertaken. The screening process must then tackle the issue of distinguishing "good" deals from "bad" deals. Though there are several intangible and intuitive issues involved in this process, as a rule of thumb, an ideal buyout target should include:

- potential for improving earnings and sales;
- predictable cash flow;
- minimum existing debt; and,
- an asset base to support substantial new borrowings.

EXHIBIT 1
Deal Sources by Size (Purchase Price)

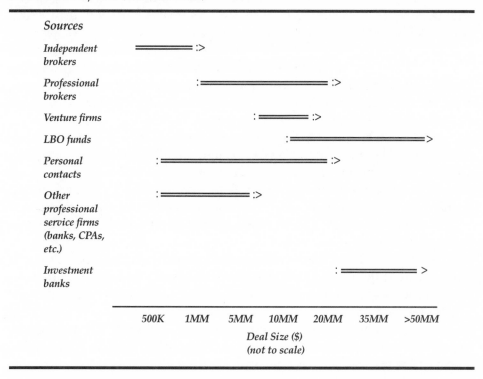

Sources							
Independent brokers							
Professional brokers							
Venture firms							
LBO funds							
Personal contacts							
Other professional service firms (banks, CPAs, etc.)							
Investment banks							
	500K	1MM	5MM	10MM	20MM	35MM	>50MM

Deal Size ($)
(not to scale)

When searching for a business, the buyout candidate will most likely not fit in a "nice, neat, little box," so flexibility is important. One must constantly rethink and reassess the criteria developed. Do they fit? Are they appropriate? Is this the best way to examine this company? Will the criteria help to achieve the objective in mind?

—— DEAL SOURCES

Initiating and sustaining the deal flow is one of the most challenging tasks in buying a business. In general, expect to look at dozens of deals for every one that might appear worth pursuing; there are simply a lot of poor deals out there. A seemingly endless amount of groundwork is often necessary to initiate a deal, and a targeted effort is far more likely to result in a high percentage of attractive candidates. Thus, one of the first orders of business when starting out to locate a company is to know where to look.

Depending on what size deal is sought, there are a number of potential deal sources, and each has its own approach to acquisitions. *Exhibit 1* is a subjective assessment of the various sources of deals and the territory they cover. The number of deals in the lower ranges—particularly in the $1 million to $50 million category—is on the rise. Geneva Business Services, Inc., a leading national broker of small businesses, estimates that more than 15,000 deals involving companies valued in this range will close in 1987. Mainstream investment banks, on the other hand, are rarely interested in any deal valued less than $10–20 million. Recognizing the particular niches these players inhabit will help to minimize lost time and unnecessary frustration chasing deals where they are not likely to be found. The paragraphs below will help identify sources according to the size of deal handled.

Business brokers—independent and professional alike—are the most readily available resource; they are listed individually in the Yellow Pages of most phone directories and advertise in the business sections of many newspapers. The broker's primary function is to work on behalf of sellers to find appropriate buyers for their clients' businesses, and he/she is compensated by the seller for closing a deal based on a percentage of the price basis. Occasionally, a broker will work for a buyer to search for a business in return for a retainer fee and/or a percentage of the ultimate purchase price. It should be emphasized though that the broker's motivation is to close each transaction; he/she should not necessarily be considered a business consultant in the search process.

Business brokers obtain listings through cold calls and advertising. Because these listings are actively marketed, it is safe to assume that you are probably not the first prospective buyer to see the business. More reputable brokers tend to regulate how "shopped" a business becomes in order to preserve its value and may not even list properties which the seller himself has already tried to market.

At your initial meeting with the broker, you should be prepared to describe your financial constraints and industry preference. It is also valuable to indicate that you have a well-defined time horizon for a search and some knowledge of the target industry. You might want to touch base occasionally with each broker whom you meet, but it is a safe bet that you will be notified if there is an interesting opportunity and if you are a qualified buyer.

Some attention should be focused on the role of independent brokers since they are often the first place people turn for deal flow. Independent brokers are almost entirely unregulated. Because no license is required, and anyone can claim to be one, it is essential to check references (should the broker not supply them) and reputation with other intermediaries and past clients. Fourteen states require brokers to have a real estate broker's license, but, for the most part, anyone with a telephone can call themselves a business broker. The largest network of independent brokers is VR Business Brokers, headquartered in Boston, Mass. VR has 10 franchised brokerages operating offices in 500 cities. VR claims to close up to 7,500 deals per annum, 80% of which are companies with sales below $800,000. On the other end of the spectrum, one can find a seemingly endless supply of one-person brokerage services in most any city. As such, one must be exceedingly cautious when trying to land a deal via this route. First of all, the deals are going to be small, less than $500,000 in sales. Second, they are most likely to be owned by entrepreneurs who have an unrealistic impression of the value of their businesses, an impression often fueled by the brokers themselves.

Professional brokers are business firms—rather than simply individuals—who specialize in the sale of companies; a few prominent ones are worth noting here:

- Geneva Business Services in Costa Mesa, California;
- W.T. Grimm & Co. in Chicago, Illinois;
- First Main Capital Corp. in Plano, Texas; and,
- Nation-List Network of Business Brokers, Inc. in Denver, Colorado is a cooperative exchange of some 50 independent brokers.

These organizations tend to operate on a far more professional basis than the independents, but they still represent the seller. Their interest is in obtaining a high price for the company, thereby ensuring high commission fees (usually around 10% to 12% at closing). However, most brokers are more interested in closing the deal than in squeezing out the last dollar in purchase price. Also, note that deals coming via professional brokers are very likely to be highly "shopped." The deals' legitimacies are often prescreened, but count on paying a premium for businesses carried by professional brokers.

Venture capital firms will most likely be looking for liquidity on investments they made three to five years earlier. Venture-backed companies that have reached this stage are generally beyond many of the risks associated with start-ups and may pose a solid acquisition opportunity. Several points should be noted, however. First, venture capitalists are highly sophisticated investors and will likely extract the highest possible price for the company. Second, they want liquidity for their investment, and will be less interested in earn-outs and other creative financing than a deal that is primarily financed with cash. In addition, existing management will likely be highly entrepreneurial and will be wary of the control issues introduced by new owners in the company. Finally, venture firms are often motivated to sell their "problem" companies; be sure to understand what type of situation you are walking into.

Leveraged buyout funds in some sense pose competition to the buyout effort. As a potential deal source, however, there may be opportunity to pick up on deals that are of no interest to the LBO fund. Such deals may still be attractive candidates if they were passed over simply because the deal did not match the particular focus of the LBO fund. Or, LBO firms may be selling portions of some acquired businesses to generate cash to pay back debt. These, too, can be attractive deals.

Personal contacts, although often overlooked, may be helpful. Self-initiated contacts with people who have successfully completed the search process for their own businesses may be a good source of both information and moral support. Depending on your specific situation and their area of expertise, they may be able to suggest specific contacts and strategies or allow you to tap their network. Additionally, you may be able to learn some of the common pitfalls they encountered and some rules of thumb they use. These resources may be located through your network or by tracking recently completed deals.

On occasion, combing prominent business periodicals will identify opportunities. Indications that a company will be spinning off subsidiary operations are frequently mentioned in articles in some level of detail. Nationally, the *Wall Street Journal* and publications such as *Inc.* and *Venture* routinely list business opportunities. On the local or regional level, there are business journals, franchise fairs, classified ads, and notices of bankruptcies and deaths. Newspapers, and the offices of the county clerk and court clerks are good sources, as are computer databases, available on a time-sharing basis that provide lists of prospective buyers and sellers of businesses. Academic and commercial institutions in some communities sponsor industry forums or trade association meetings. Industry and phone directories (Yellow Pages, Dun & Bradstreet, *Million Dollar Directory,* Thomas' *Register of American Manufacturers,* etc.) may be useful for a cold call or letter writing campaign and as a possible screen for industry, size and location. You can run this process in reverse by placing your own advertisement in newspapers or journals stating your desire and criteria for purchasing a business.

Local banks represent a broad range of local businesses and have in-depth knowledge of their finances and managerial situations. Like business brokers, the M&A-type departments of banks are primarily interested in closing transactions. Their inventory of deals may include both banking clients that may be for sale or other firms that have engaged the bank to help them find a suitable buyer. A bank may also be amenable to helping you conduct a search on a success-fee basis. A good banker will also be instrumental in structuring the financial arrangements of the newly acquired business. As with lawyers and accountants, the bank may often expect to become the new firm's principal banker.

Trust departments of banks often are the executors of estate business. In cases where there is a need to dispose of such a business, a bank trust officer may serve the same role as an estate lawyer. While the trust officer has a fiduciary responsibility to seek the highest price for the business, an equally important consideration is keeping the transaction clean, fast and, to the extent possible, in cash.

Bank work-out departments are another potential source of "bargain" opportunities. While the bank certainly has a strong interest in not disclosing credit problems, it may be a confidential go-between for a potential buyer and the owners of a deeply troubled client if a mutually satisfactory offer were presented. However, bankers indicate that because of pressures within the bank to reschedule the debt and the willingness of owners to personally collateralize additional loans, most troubled loans are in fact worked out.

Traditional, main-line investment banks pose both a problem and an opportunity for buyers seeking a mid-sized deal. The problem is that investment banks are rarely interested in deals below, say, $20 million. Attracting their attention can be troublesome, and getting them to spend time moving on a relatively small deal requires patience and tenacity. The opportunity, for nearly the same grounds, exists because small deals carried by the investment banks are unlikely to have been widely shopped. Owners who rely exclusively on an investment bank to market their company will probably not receive extraordinary service. A buyer who works this route may find a fairly responsive seller on the other end of this inattentive deal pipeline.

No matter where the deal comes from, there will be a seller to contend with. Whether the seller is a single individual, a group of investors, or the shareholders of a small public company, one will have to evaluate their motivations. Issues of timing, types of financing, credibility, desire to remain with the company after acquisition, and the like, are all relevant points of thought when approaching the seller. Fairly early on, conversations should focus on the seller's motives for selling the business and their expectations as to the value and form of deal. A cautious investor will also use this opportunity to gauge the character and integrity of the seller, as such traits will likely have influenced how the business has been managed in the past.

RESOURCES

Aside from tireless energy and a wealth of patience, resources critical to the buyout project are cash, credibility, and contacts. These three factors, more than anything else, govern the success of the effort. How much will be required is simply a question of deal size. Purchasing a $300,000 business certainly requires fewer resources than putting together a $20 million buyout. As deals get larger, one is competing with a more sophisticated group of potential buyers. Larger deals are more complex, and sellers of larger companies will demand of the potential buyer those credentials they believe are necessary to put the deal together. Lacking the resources necessary to pull off the deal, the potential buyer may not even be successful in establishing an initial meeting with the seller. To get farther than the first phone call with larger deals, one should be prepared to satisfactorily respond to such inquiries as:

- How much cash do you have available?
- Who are your backers?
- What other deals have you done?
- What kind of management talent do you bring?
- What do you plan to do with the company?

Sellers value their time as much as the prospective buyer does. Neither wants to spend fruitless energy on meetings where there is an obvious mismatch between what the buyer brings to the table and what the target company will require. No amount of debt leverage will compensate for a lack of the equity capital and demonstrated personal background needed to purchase and operate the target company. Take stock of the resources available for the buyout project, and then target deals that can be reasonably snared with the resources at hand.

If a potential purchaser plans to employ the resources of backers, they must realize the extent to which they are dependent upon the backer and gauge how committed the backers are to the project. All the backers' cash and contacts are absolutely useless if they are unwilling to spend the time and energy needed to pursue the deal. Evaluate the backers' incentives. How important is the project to them? How much time have they agreed to set aside? Do their timing considerations match those of the group? Some backers are quite willing to employ the free efforts of a buyout group simply hoping they will luck into a treasure chest. Be cautious of working like a neglected employee, rather than a respected partner. Such characteristics may prove difficult to evaluate, particularly early on when enthusiasm runs high for the project. Make a critical and even skeptical assessment of the backers' sincerity, interest, and ability to follow through on their part of the bargain before relying on them for the resources critical to the effort's success.

In addition, an experienced lawyer is absolutely essential to the prudent buyer. An attorney's principal role in the search process is usually to review documents with the aim of protecting the client with adequate contractual conditions and to insure proper disclosure and legal and regulatory compliance. An attorney can also provide tax advice and may be able to identify potential risks and liabilities in a transaction. In many cases, more experienced lawyers turn out to be cheaper because they know the appropriate safeguards and can create good standard documents without extensive new research. In addition, as established members of the local professional community, attorneys may have access to a wider network of contacts than the buyer. For example, they sometimes sit on the boards of local businesses and may have a variety of contacts in the target industry. While tapping into this network might not generate a deal, it may provide you with opportunities to learn about the target industry and to gain credibility therein.

Occasionally, in larger law firms, there may also be an "inventory" of business acquisition opportunities. The buyer must usually compensate the lawyer for time and effort, and if the deal is successful, he/she generally expects to become the newly acquired firm's corporate counsel. As for selecting a business lawyer, there are issues to consider. For instance, you should determine whether or not the lawyer has a potential conflict of interest (e.g., if he is representing the seller). Although no reputable attorney would pursue an engagement while conflict exists without full disclosure, it is still up to you to determine the services she or he might provide. Another issue is the lawyer's reputation. It is wise to do some background or information checks of individual attorneys or their firms. Finally, your choice of lawyer should reflect your perceived legal and other professional needs at various stages of the search and deal process.[1]

THE DEAL PROCESS

Once you have specified the characteristics that you are looking for in a company, understood the best ways to generate deal flow, and have garnered the resources necessary to successfully purchase an existing company, you should prepare to enter the deal market. At this phase, it is important to recognize and prepare for the random nature of the process.

There are two important timing issues to be concerned with when you enter the deal market. First, the sequential nature of the search process makes it difficult to compare deals in parallel. Rarely will you be able to view two deals within a timeframe which allows you to evaluate them comparatively. Given that fact, it is important to realize that if you let one deal pass, you will probably encounter another one in the near future. An analytical framework to help you screen businesses (see *Exhibit 2*) will better equip you to track and compare various deals as you interface with sellers, deal sources and other active parties at different points throughout the deal process.

The second critical issue concerns the timing of the approach: before it hits the market, as soon as it hits the market, or after it has been "shopped." There are advantages and disadvantages to entering at each stage. In some cases, being the first person to see a deal (before it is on the market) may give you the inside track or first right to refuse. Yet, at this early stage, the seller will not have developed a realistic perspective on his/her demands (asking price, terms, inclination to provide desired information, willingness to actually part with the business, etc.). In such a case, discussions might be futile or you may end up paying a relatively high price. In a later stage, the seller may be more eager to sell, but you should be concerned about the health or the attractiveness of the business that has been on the market for a lengthy period.

Once you understand these basic timing issues, prepare a schedule and work plan, you should begin your search. Most of the search resources are amenable to a free introductory meeting even on the basis of a cold call. A persuasive presentation at this first meeting might include a demonstration of your industry research or experience, a well-thought-out preliminary business plan, a realistic assessment of your financial resources and suitable dress and demeanor. Academic credentials help your chances of getting in the door, as does the referral of a mutual acquaintance. This meeting should not nec-

---

1. For example, a lawyer with the technical knowledge to structure the deal from a tax perspective may not be the most skilled negotiator.

EXHIBIT 2
Business Screening Analyses

1. *General*
   Company, business strategy, age and history, trends
2. *Product*
   Description/technical specifications, function, volumes, prices, value added/commodity?, patents
3. *Management Team*
   Key employees—names, positions, education, track record, skills
   Organization chart
   Is management team complete? Efforts/ability to hire new management?
   Willingness to remain after purchase?
   Characterization of management team (i.e., aggressive/passive, young/old, etc.)
4. *Market Position*
   Market size ($, units)
   Market growth and growth drivers
   Segmentation of the market (geographic, functional)
   Who, how, and why does the buyer buy (id of buyer)?
   Relationship with customers (number, loyalty, concentration)
   Distribution channels (types, support/training required, advertisement strategy)
   Market share of major players
   Company's major differentiating factors (price, quality, service, features, brand identity)
5. *Competitive Analysis*
   Barriers to entry/exit—economies of scale, proprietary technology, switching cost, capital requirements, access to distribution, cost advantages, government policy, expected retaliation, brand identity, exit cost
   Competitive factors—number, strength, characterization, product differences, concentration, diversity, management, financials/ratio analysis, industry capacity, competitive advantages, corporate stakes
   Substitution threat—relative price/performance of substitutes, switching cost, buyer propensity to substitute
   Suppliers' power—relationship, concentration, manufacturing/marketing process, presence of substitute inputs, importance of volume to supplier, switching cost of supplier, cost relative to total purchases, impact of inputs on cost or differentiation, threat of forward integration, supplier profitability
   Buyers' power—bargaining leverage, buying patterns, concentration, volume, switching cost, ability to backward integrate, substitute products, price sensitivity, price/total purchases,

product differences, brand identity, impact on quality/performance, buyer profitability, decision-making units' incentives and complexity

Trends—Technology, economic, changes in tax law

6. *Operations*

Work force—seize, union/nonunion, work rules, contract expiration, age and skill level, match with developing technology, attrition, attitude, manufacturing engineering staff competence

Manufacturing flow and scheduling—job shop/batch continuous, systems, process flow, material handling, multiplant strategy/logistics, cost accounting, work discipline, work order tracking, % dead time

Capacity—% of total capacity, bottlenecks current and projected

Purchasing—opportunities for redesign, fewer parts, add/subtract vendors, larger discounts, incoming material sampling, out-sourcing policies

Quality control—attitude/priority, problem areas, methodology

Capital equipment—age/maintenance, sophistication, general v. special purpose, level of automation, trends

R&D—% of sales compared to industry, type, technical strengths/weaknesses, organization, importance, trends

Information systems—importance, competitive advantage, level of sophistication, systems under development

7. *Financials*

Sales/Profitability

Income statement

Historical and 2-, 3-, and 5-year pro formas

Growth—sales, costs, profits, EPS, sustainable growth rates

Quality of earnings—accounting, pension funding, depreciation, write-offs, earnings segments, earnings patterns, earnings sensitivity

Ratio analysis—compared to competitors and industry averages, gross margins, ROS, ROE, P/E comparables

Leverage and Liquidity

Balance sheet

Historical and pro formas

Examination of equity and debt composition

Ratio analysis—current and quick ratios, debt as percentage of total capitalization, assets/equity, days receivable, days payable, days inventory.

Funds flow

Statement of changes

Historical and pro formas

Analysis of sources and uses of cash

Assets

Composition and type, quality, bankability, book and market values, obsolescence, age

8. *Valuation*

Terminal value—FCF perpetuity/annuity, book value, liquidation value, P/E value.

Components of value (i.e., investment tax credits, depreciation, energy cost savings, etc.)

Sensitivity analysis

Expected returns analysis

9. *Risk/Reality Check*

Industry

Technology

Financial

Product/company liability

Employee/supplier/customer response

Seller's desire to do the deal

Is value appropriate?

Prohibitive terms?

Value to be added

This is by no means a complete list, but simply an overview of some key parts.

---

essarily result in a commitment; in fact, you might consider meeting with many attorneys, CPAs and bankers, or others you deem helpful before committing to work with anyone in particular. You might also schedule some "warm-up" sessions with some of these professionals before meeting with your highest priority contacts.

The preliminary meeting should serve several purposes: resources will be interested in qualifying you both as a realistic potential buyer and as someone they will want to work with. You should attempt to determine their expertise and willingness to help, along with any conditions on your relationship with them. With regard to establishing fees, practice ranges from hourly fees to contingent fees; the arrangement of one lawyer may be substantially different from another. This is another reason to meet with many professionals before committing to work exclusively with any one in particular.

In most of these preliminary discussions, the issue of exactly what cards to show arises. While this is a personal decision, a perspective on your financial resources and backing, level of commitment and objectives is probably best expressed frankly. You may want to be more vague if you are dealing with an intermediary who represents a potential seller or if you have reservations about the person with whom you are meeting. The fact that your backers may want their identities shielded will also push you to be somewhat guarded. Checking out the reputations of such individuals before divulging any private information is the only prudent course of action.

The average time required to find the right business runs about one year—significantly longer if your search is more casual or if your target is more elusive. Therefore, depending on your degree of commitment, your financial flexibility and your time schedule, you may elect to manage your own search by calling on the search resources periodically, or you may choose to retain a search resource to conduct the search for you.

An attorney, for instance, could make cold calls and write letters to industry sources on your behalf. While his personal and professional contacts may unearth your dream business, much of the research you pay him for could be easily done yourself from industry directories, Yellow Pages, etc. Thus, if time permits or your budget requires and you are sophisticated enough about basic business and legal issues, you may choose to undertake many of the basic research tasks yourself. This also provides first-hand contact with the marketplace.

The industry-specific knowledge you pick up may be invaluable to you later on, when you need to demonstrate expertise or commitment to financing sources or to a seller. In some industries, acquisition opportunities rarely reach the marketplace because the industry is essentially closed. Therefore, if you are interested in entering such an area, you must "network" your way in. This might include meeting owners or executives of any firms in that industry whether or not they are interested in selling their own businesses. Industry association meetings or trade meetings can be good places to meet people and become more of an insider.

You might consider periodically touching base with some of the individuals in your new network to see if they have any ideas for you and to reiterate your degree of interest. But be sensitive to the demands you are making: a short phone call every three or four weeks is appropriate—more frequent contact may be annoying. You might also update them on your progress, especially because they may be able to help you more at different phases in your search. Keep in mind that they would more likely readily share information or leads with you if you exchange any ideas or intelligence with them.

Once underway, you may come across a potential acquisition candidate. An inexpensive way to obtain financial and operating information on the company and biographical background on the owners or officers is through a Dun & Bradstreet report or by other background checks. Note that the D&B report is based upon information provided by the subject company and is not independently verified.

In addition to doing some preliminary investigative research, it is important to meet the owner(s) and visit the business. An aspect of this evaluation is to understand the "seller's psychology," for it is critical to appreciate the seller's needs—financial and psychological. There are cases in which the owner has no emotional attachment to the business, and he or she would willingly sell to the highest bidder. More likely, especially in small operations, much of the seller's life is tied up in the business, resulting in a high degree of emotional involvement. There may be other significant psychological considerations you could identify, such as the seller's age, marital situation, illness or family situation. Usually, a deal structure will need to reflect these factors in the form and terms of the consideration. In these cases you may need to "sell" the seller.

"Selling" the seller does not simply include a generous financial package (e.g., insurance, providing for his family, etc.), but may require demonstrating your commitment to preserve the character, quality, and spirit of the enterprise he worked long and hard to build. Occasionally, even when an owner indicates a willingness to sell, he or she may in fact be unwilling to part with the firm when it comes to closing the deal and transferring control. Reading the owner's psyche ahead of time may avoid such fruitless discussions or may provide insight into a more mutually satisfying deal structure.

In this respect, your professional resources may be able to provide a great deal of insight and advice because they may either know the seller or have dealt with similar situations previously. It also may be helpful to have your agent negotiate on your behalf for a variety of reasons: to preserve your rapport with the seller, to neutralize personality clashes, and to preserve and improve decision options.

───── THE EVALUATION PROCESS

After preliminary research and introductory meetings with the prospective seller, you may decide to pursue the opportunity, which would involve reviewing confidential operating and financial statements and interviewing key employees and customers.

"Getting the numbers" can be more easily said than done. Generally, small business owners are reluctant to share any operating and financial data with outsiders, often for tax and competitive reasons. Typically a buyer does not receive any meaningful financials until after signing a purchase agreement and putting down a deposit. Thus, a good understanding of the business and the industry may give you increased credibility and leverage with the seller. A seller with a distressed business may be more willing to provide numbers earlier in the process, and for bankrupt firms, the numbers may be part of the public domain. In most cases, confidentiality agreements must be signed before reviewing any financials.

While not necessary, you are well advised at this point to retain your own counsel to ensure that you are protected and are covering all bases, especially if you are signing any documents or agreements. An accountant might also be very useful depending on the complexity of the situation (financial reports, taxes, inventory, etc.). Other experts may help investigate leases and contracts. To the extent that these are people with whom you have already worked, you will be more comfortable dealing with them and trusting them.

It is often useful to collect a "thumb-nail" sketch of the deal's financial attractiveness prior to performing any detailed analysis. As some preliminary checks, one can screen against company size, profitability, and attractiveness of the balance sheet. Some deals may be thrown out on this basis, while others will merit a more thorough examination of "the numbers."

There are several ways to reasonably estimate the value of a company, and it is most often useful to employ more than one method when performing a valuation analysis. How much to pay, how much debt and from what source, and potential harvest values are going to be valued differently. Each plays an important role in the assessment of the opportunity at hand. *Exhibit 3* shows types of analysis that can prove useful in establishing an estimate of the deal's price.

Both cash flow analysis and multiples analysis estimate the opportunity's value based upon future events, either operating results or market reaction to public offering. When trying to place a value on a business in this manner, there are a multitude of assumptions that must be made. Some of the most prominent include:

- *level of risk:* how volatile are the company's cash flows?
- *competition:* how fiercely contested is the market for the company's products?
- *industry:* is this a growing or declining industry, and what profitability trends exist?
- *organizational stability:* how well established is this company in the intended line of business?
- *management:* is a competent and complete team in place?
- *company growth:* historically, has the company been growing or shrinking, and how fast?
- *general desirability:* to what degree does the marketplace find this line of business attractive?

A cautionary note on valuations: many deal proposals are put together with "recast financial statements." In theory, such a practice is legitimate and endeavors to reflect true operating results possible in the business. In reality, assumptions implicit in the recast are not always reasonably attainable and

EXHIBIT 3

METHOD USED	*WHAT THE RESULTS INDICATE*
Discounted Cash Flow	Underlying operating value of the business, and ability to service debt.
Asset Valuation	Liquidation value and/or adjusted book value of assets.
Multiples	Multiples of cash flow, P/E, sales, or EBIT are useful to establish some sense for market value relative to other firms in the same industry and offer some indication of harvest potential. Each type of multiple has its own merit; what is critical is that one be consistent in applying them.

can be downright misleading. Always ask whether or not the financials shown have been recast, and, if so, understand all adjustments that have been made to the statements. No assumption should be left unchallenged. This will be particularly true for smaller companies whose owners will often have previously operated with numerous adjustments to minimize their tax burden.

Once a general idea on price is established, the deal will have to be structured with attractive returns to one's equity investment. There are two fundamental considerations. First is the overall financeability of the deal, which includes:

- assets to secure bank financing;
- cash flow to support further debt instruments (i.e., company-issued debentures); and,
- personal collateral, if any.

Second, one must consider (possibly in conjunction with the above analysis) the actual structure of the financing. What is desired here is a structure which caters to the interest of all parties involved. The buyer might, for example, establish financing "strips" of debt and equity to provide both secured fixed income and participation in potential capital appreciation. Tax losses may be scrutinized and sold to investors who will find such items attractive.

──── NEGOTIATING THE DEAL

When you discover a company the purchase of which is financially feasible and meets your other criteria, it is important to negotiate carefully. The wave of enthusiasm over having finally found a company may cloud one's judgment. Often, during negotiations, new information will trickle out on a relatively constant basis—a lawsuit that isn't quite settled, a previous industrial accident, receivables that seem less collectible than they appeared. It is important to constantly reevaluate this information in an objective fashion.

The seller can get cold feet as well, or develop second thoughts about selling at a particular price. It is important to develop a sense of momentum by turning documents around quickly, and by dealing personally with the seller. Don't let lawyers become intermediaries in the transaction—manage the process.

Such obstacles do not necessarily have to get in the way, but one should be prepared to greet them if they do appear. Indeed, you may have to walk away from your share of deals. While having to walk away from a business you wanted can be disappointing, you should learn several important lessons. For example, you should become a better judge of character and business situations, knowledge that will be invaluable to you as you continue the deal process. Also, the first-hand experience and knowledge you gain about the industry in the collapsed deal may result in greater credibility in the future with sellers or their intermediaries.

ADDING VALUE

Before you purchase a company, you can begin to concentrate on ways to improve the firm's performance. Indeed, such plans are a vital component of understanding a business's potential and your willingness to pay. Adding value to a new firm can be accomplished in many ways:

- Making operational changes: You should give a good deal of thought up front as to what you plan to do with the company after the acquisition. You may recognize an opportunity to broaden distribution, open new markets, and otherwise make operational changes that boost sales and/or margins. In evaluating such possibilities, be realistic. Chances are the easy things have already been tried, so exercise some creative thought in defining positive operating improvements. This also requires an assessment of the management team and personnel in place. In short, are they reliable, competent, honest, and are they the right people for the challenge that lies ahead for the business?
- Changing the financial structure of the business: In many small businesses, the very essence of the company can be improved if the underlying financial structure is modified. For example, negotiating a longer payment schedule with your creditors, creating incentives for your customers to pay bills sooner, and obtaining lines of credit from commercial banks can help change the dynamics of the business and improve cash flow.

CONCLUSION

Searching for a small business to buy can be difficult; not only is there no established marketplace for these firms, but you are trying to purchase an entity created and cultivated by another individual, and you are attempting to meld it with your own style, character and interests. This process can be extremely time-consuming, expensive, and frustrating. And although available research indicates that good acquisition candidates are few and far between, sound search techniques and a realistic personal assessment can significantly improve your chances of success and allow you to achieve some measure of control over some of the more random elements of the process.

Finally, remember that this process is also an investment decision. Even a superb company is of little value to an investor if nobody is willing to pay for it. Identifying an appropriate "exit" strategy to make one's investment liquid will define the project's monetary returns. This can include running the company in perpetuity, getting out in a secondary public offering, liquidating the assets, or selling out to another organization.

——— DISCUSSION QUESTIONS

1. Suppose you have made a decision to purchase a business. In assessing your motives and goals, what questions would you ask yourself?
2. What are the advantages of purchasing rather than founding a business? What special skills and attributes should a purchaser bring to the enterprise?
3. What are the advantages and disadvantages of working with business brokers? With venture capitalists? With banks?
4. Think of a type of business you would be interested in purchasing and imagine yourself meeting for the first time with a prospective seller. What questions are you going to ask?
5. The authors mention two ways in which a buyer can add value to an existing business: making operational changes and changing the financial structure. Using your example from question 4, in what additional ways could you add value to your new company?

MARSHALING REQUIRED RESOURCES

Attracting Stakeholders 12

AMAR BHIDÉ and HOWARD H. STEVENSON

Every new enterprise needs employees, customers, suppliers, and financiers who are willing to risk time and money. Attracting stakeholders and inspiring their confidence in a new and untried venture is particularly challenging. This reading spells out tasks involved in enlisting stakeholder commitment: designing the enterprise to minimize stakeholder exposure, selecting stakeholders who are most willing and able to bear the risk, and convincing stakeholders to participate in the enterprise. Acquiring resources is a basic entrepreneurial task requiring preparation and skill; done carefully, it is the key to turning an opportunity into a business operation.

Acquiring resources—or to put it more broadly, attracting stakeholders—is a basic entrepreneurial task. While every enterprise needs employees, customers, suppliers and financiers who are willing to risk their time and money, attracting these "stakeholders" to an entrepreneurial venture is a particularly difficult challenge. This note first describes the importance of the challenge and then the set of tasks the entrepreneur must work on in order to overcome it: Designing the enterprise to minimize the stakeholder investment needed, selecting the right stakeholders and, then convincing them to participate in the enterprise. We will use the example of a hypothetical entrepreneur (like Steve Jobs) who wishes to launch a revolutionary computer but the principles we describe are generally applicable to any entrepreneurial venture.

——— THE CHALLENGE OF ATTRACTING STAKEHOLDERS

Many participants are at risk in any enterprise by virtue of the irreversible investment they make in it. The most obvious are the financial stakeholders—the venture capital firms, institutional and individual investors, bond holders, banks or factors who provide our entrepreneur with the

---

Assistant Professor Amar Bhidé and Professor Howard H. Stevenson prepared this note as the basis for class discussion. Copyright © 1989 by the President and Fellows of Harvard College. Harvard Business School case 389-139.

funds needed for R&D, machinery, new product promotion and growth in inventory and receivables. Much of this investment is irreversible—if the enterprise fails, liquidation of its tangible and intangible assets will rarely make the financial stakeholders whole, especially when their opportunity costs are properly taken into account.[1]

Employees, customers and suppliers have an equally important, if less obvious, stake in the success of the enterprise they participate in as well. The individual who leaves IBM to head up marketing for our hypothetical entrepreneur's new computer project may be as much at risk as the venture capitalists who fund it. If the enterprise fails, the marketing manager is unlikely to be made whole for the time and effort she invested; IBM will not have her back in her old position and she may have to eat into her savings while looking for a new job.

Failure of the enterprise may similarly wipe out suppliers' and customers' investments. Suppliers may not recover the costs of designing and producing special components for the new computer or collect on their receivables. Similarly, customers may find they have invested time and money on hardware that cannot be easily serviced and upgraded.

Moreover, attracting the stakeholders needed to launch a new computer is much more of a challenge for an individual entrepreneur than it is for a large corporation like IBM. Since IBM's managers effectively control the corporation, they can mandate the investment of shareholder funds for a new product. In addition, since IBM has a well-established, profitable franchise in mainframe computers as well as a long-standing reputation for fair dealing, employers, suppliers and customers have the confidence that they will not be left in the lurch if the new product fails.[2]

The individual entrepreneur who cannot inspire such confidence may therefore face employees, suppliers, customers and financiers whose perception of their downside risk causes them to demand conditions of exchange that cannot be met if the enterprise is to be viable. In the extreme, they may not participate at all. Suppliers may refuse to dedicate a production run without a cash advance that a fledgling enterprise cannot provide; demands by venture capitalists and key employees for ownership stakes may exceed the total equity pie; and worst of all, conservative purchasing agents may not touch an innovative computer even if it does offer outstanding price/performance.

---

1. This is true, the record shows, even for the lenders whose investment is supposedly secured by assets.

2. They may take heart from the example of the PC Jr. computer, which IBM kept alive for longer than might have been economically justified in order to protect the interests of the stakeholders. None of the employees who worked on the product were let go, as jobs were found for them elsewhere in the IBM organization.

——— MINIMIZING STAKEHOLDER EXPOSURE

The extent to which stakeholders are at risk in a venture depends upon the irreversibility of their investment. While entrepreneurs cannot make the investment required by their ventures fully reversible, they can hold the required "sunkenness" to a minimum and thus overcome stakeholders' reluctance to participate.

REUSABLE, OFF-THE-SHELF, INPUTS

Financiers', suppliers', and employees' risks may be reduced by using components, capital equipment and other factors of production that can be easily put to alternative uses, and preferably, are available off the shelf. Then, financiers, suppliers and employees do not have to commit substantial resources, and what resources they do commit can be easily recovered if the enterprise fails.

Using standard fungible inputs affect several strategic choices; for our computer start-up these might include:

- Hardware design that relies on off-the-shelf processors and subsystems.
- A product that is differentiated along easily comprehensible performance dimensions, or on price. Then salesmen (or distributors) do not have to acquire special skills or knowledge in order to sell it.
- Software based on an industry standard operating system such as UNIX or MS-DOS.
- An assembly line restricted to elementary capital goods such as a conveyor belt and screwdrivers. Where required, general-purpose machine tools, ovens and CAD-CAM tools can be used instead of special designs.
- A Silicon Valley, Route 128, or Research Triangle site so that key employees do not have to make an investment to relocate and can find alternative employment more easily.
- Modest volume or market share goals so that suppliers do not have to dedicate special production runs or build new capacity.
- A marketing plan that seeks product awareness through a few influential opinion makers in the industry rather than through advertising or missionary selling.

Even seemingly trivial decisions may matter. For example, using an industry standard accounting or word processing package reduces the training required for accounting and typing staff, enhances their marketability in the eyes of other employers, and thus reduces their risk in joining a new venture.

CUSTOMER INVESTMENT

Many of the product design decisions that help reduce other stake-holders' investment in an enterprise will often reduce customers' risks as well. For example, the use of industry standard components in a computer reduces the buyer's risk of being stuck without spare parts should the vendor go out of business. The adoption of an industry standard operating system likewise eliminates the investment a customer might otherwise have to make in adapting existing applications software to a new supplier's hardware. At the simplest level, products that can be easily purchased due to some simple cost or performance advantages do not require the customer to sink much time and money in the purchase decision and in employee education.

Other product decisions may be taken that directly reduce a customer's investment in learning, search and adaptation. For example, a new computer may be designed to slot easily into customers' existing hardware networks. In the software arena, "open system architecture," which allows the customer (or any other qualified firm) to easily modify or upgrade the product without the assistance of the original vendor may be adopted to reduce the customer's "stake" in the start-up.

TRADE-OFFS

Unfortunately, there is no free lunch. Securing the participation of stakeholders by reducing the "sunkenness" of their investment may reduce the profitability and long-run sustainability of the enterprise. For example, in the case of the computer start-up:

- Industry standard, off-the-shelf components may lead to higher variable costs and rapid knock-offs by competitors.
- Flexible capital equipment designed to have high salvage value may be more expensive.
- A Silicon Valley, Route 128, or Research Triangle location may entail high real estate and labor costs.
- A plug-compatible, "me too" product with low switching costs for the customer may be vulnerable to competitors offering marginally better prices or features.

The entrepreneur may thus be squeezed between being unable to get the enterprise off the ground at all because the risks to stakeholders are too high, or launching a marginally profitable, short-lived venture.

One key to resolving this dilemma lies in undertaking irreversible investment only where the greatest leverage is expected in terms of profitability or sustainability or where a stakeholder is most prepared to make the investment for idiosyncratic reasons. For example, a computer start-up may seek irreversible stakeholder investment in the one element, such as a proprietary microprocessor, unique architecture, a low-cost, out-of-the-way location, or new distribution channel, where stakeholder investment seems most readily available and/or where the investment will provide the greatest sustainable advantage. This same company will forcefully adhere to industry standards in all other areas. Asking the question: "Is this uniqueness really the key to a major competitive edge?" is often a good starting place.

Another resolution to the viability/sustainability dilemma can lie in phased investment. The enterprise may be launched with very low irreversible investment, gradually building to higher levels as stakeholder confidence is gained. Apple is a case in point. In its early years its products were based on an industry standard operating system (CP/M), were promoted virtually without any advertising and were manufactured in plants whose capital equipment consisted largely of conveyor belts and screwdrivers. As the company gained the confidence of stakeholders, however, its new products used a proprietary operating system, were assembled in highly automated state-of-the-art plants and launched with multimillion dollar advertising budgets.

SELECTING STAKEHOLDERS

Since irreversible investment required by an enterprise cannot be entirely eliminated, another entrepreneurial task is to select stakeholders who are the most willing to and capable of bearing the risk. All other things being equal, the most desirable stakeholders fit one or more of the following characteristics: they are diversified, experienced in the type of risks they are expected to bear, have excess capacity and are risk seekers. Let us consider these in turn.

DIVERSIFICATION

Diversified stakeholders are more capable of bearing the risk of investing in an enterprise than these undiversified stakeholders. Thus, for a computer start-up:

- The venture capitalist with a large diversified portfolio of investments can be expected to be more capable of providing risk capital than an individual with no other start-up investments.
- The distributor who handles the products of a number of vendors will probably be less concerned about dedicating 10% of the time of 10 salespersons to the new machine than any one salesman considering full-time employment with the start-up.[3]
- The buyer for a firm with an installed base of computers from a

---

3. In general we may note that employees in a single business start-up will not be able to diversify their risks to the same extent as "outside" subcontractors serving many businesses.

variety of manufacturers will likely be more comfortable trying out a new vendor than the buyer at a customer who has standardized on just one.

EXPERIENCE AND SPECIALIZATION

The risk that a particular individual or firm sees in investing in an enterprise can depend as much upon the investor's past experience and knowledge as upon the objective dangers. Therefore an entrepreneur should, when possible, seek the participation of stakeholders who are experienced in bearing the risks required of them. Our computer start-up may, for example, seek to establish relationships with:

- Customers who have bought (and, preferably, successfully used) computers from start-ups in the past rather than customers who have never strayed from "name" vendors.
- Law and accounting firms that specialize in new ventures and recognize that an up-front investment in helping a start-up can pay off handily in the long term.
- Employees who have worked for a start-up that failed before and know that being laid off is a setback, not the end of the world. People who have been employed, for example, at IBM for their entire working lives, may grossly overestimate the risks of not being able to find a new job.
- Lenders who have dealt with the industry and products often have a feeling of comfort about the downside and experience with the upside which makes them more adventurous.

Experienced and specialized participants may not only be easier to sign on, they can also help secure the participation of other stakeholders. Participants in a venture need reassurance about the competence and reliability of each other—the customer who orders a new computer has to be confident that the vendor's service staff is capable and the key software engineer needs reassurance that the venture capitalists backing the project are solid. Targeting an experienced "team" of stakeholders can thus go a long way towards building this necessary mutual confidence.

"Bell cows"—individuals or organizations which have established reputations as leaders and as savvy precursors of the future—are especially valuable. If our entrepreneur can get Arthur Rock, the doyen of high-tech venture capitalists, or Steve Wozniak, designer of the first Apple to sign on, a number of other investors, employees, suppliers and customers will participate too. If Rock or Wozniak are players, then the venture must be real!

Bell cows open doors and they often induce timely commitment for the entrepreneur. They are often the most important form of "reality check." Bell cows stand at the nexus of important networks. Entrepreneurs have two problems: finding them and convincing them.

Finding bell cows requires industry knowledge. The fledgling entrepreneur has to have it or access it. Having industry knowledge is a function of time, effort and having knowledge to exchange. It helps to know who is doing what. It helps to read the industry trade papers and it helps to have made friends.

Accessing industry knowledge beyond your own depends on building your team. Both insiders and service providers such as lawyers, accountants, advertising and P/R firms and consultants are critical. Even more critical is the entrepreneur's reputation for reciprocity and follow-through.

EXCESS CAPACITY

The risks of participation are lower for stakeholders with excess capacity who are not required to make any "new" investment or incur significant opportunity costs and may even be under pressure to utilize existing resources. Therefore our illustrative computer start-up may target:

- Customers with a well-staffed, technology evaluation department for whom the time required to assess a new product is "free" and who may also be under organizational pressure to make new product recommendations, rather than customers with a small, overworked purchasing department.
- Venture capitalists (or banks) with a large, unused "quota" of technology investments (or loans). Often newly raised venture funds or ones which have developed a bad reputation as being "slow off the mark" are likely targets.
- Writers of technical manuals and product literature who are not kept fully occupied by their employers or who may work part time for personal reasons.
- The young professionals in an accounting firm who are under pressure to "build a client base" in order to make partner.
- Distributors with a "hole" in their product line but good customer coverage.
- Board stuffers and other suppliers with unused capacity—especially note those who have recently undergone aggressive capacity expansion programs.

Obviously the stakeholders' unused capacity must be greater than the enterprise's needs for this criterion of selection to be useful; hence as mentioned in a previous section, staged growth and volume goals are a great help in attracting stakeholders. Capitalizing on "excess" capacity also requires the entrepreneur to carefully understand the cost structure and organizational dynamics of the target stakeholder.

RISK SEEKING

Rather than target those stakeholders whose participation in an enterprise involves the least risk to them, the entrepreneur may instead cultivate risk seekers—individuals or firms who because of their temperament or circumstance take on projects that have a negative expected value. For example, the entrepreneur in our computer start-up might seek:

- "Leading edge" customers for whom the publicity and thrill of being the first user of a new technology far outweighs the economic downside.
- Cultist programmers who derive satisfaction from working for a "Mission Impossible" type enterprise.
- Very wealthy individuals for whom an investment in the venture is like the casual purchase of a lottery ticket or a contribution made to support the local theater company.

There are, however, risks in seeking the participation of risk seekers. First, they may be fickle—the wealthy individual who invests with our entrepreneur on a lark may not be as prepared to invest in future rounds as a professional, level-headed venture capitalist. Secondly, the participation of risk seekers may scare away other more conservative players. The reputation of your stakeholders has potential for both a halo effect and a negative aura.

CONVINCING STAKEHOLDERS

Assume that our entrepreneur has formulated a plan that minimizes risk for stakeholders and has identified the most appropriate participants for the computer venture. The most formidable task—a challenging mix of analysis and action—remains. The project must be sold; expressions of interest and encouragement from the participants must be converted into firm commitments. This requires the entrepreneur to possess the necessary attitudes and reputation, go through a process of "ham and egging" and to master basic closing techniques.

ENTREPRENEURIAL ATTRIBUTES

A prerequisite for gaining stakeholder commitment is the entrepreneur's enthusiasm and belief in the project. The immediate payoff for stakeholders in an entrepreneurial project is almost always low—their decision to participate is based on expectations of substantial long-term reward. The entrepreneur cannot create this expectation without a strong inner conviction that the project can and will succeed.

Another requirement for the entrepreneur is a reputation for reliability. A track record for success is helpful—a Steve Jobs will have a tremendous edge in launching a new venture—but is not absolutely necessary. What participants will look for is evidence that in the past the entrepreneur has:

- Honored implicit as well as explicit promises and has fairly shared rewards with stakeholders.
- Has not abandoned ventures in midstream when things have gone badly.

HAM AND EGGING

Besides these attributes and reputation (which an entrepreneur either has or hasn't) there are a number of skills and techniques that can be adopted to secure commitment, one of the most important of which is "ham and egging."

The need for ham and egging arises from the desire of each participant to see the others commit first. Customers are reluctant to spend the time to evaluate, much less place an order for a new computer until the entrepreneur can actually deliver a product; employees are hesitant to sign on until the financing is in place; and investors are unwilling to step forward unless customers have shown a willingness to buy.

The ultimate ham and egging solution is for the entrepreneur to simultaneously convince each participant that everyone else is on board, or almost on board. Not all entrepreneurs have the ability to pull this off or can even feel comfortable trying to. The alternative is to ask for a small increment of commitment from a participant, parlay that commitment into another increment of commitment from the next participant and repeat the cycle for as many times as is necessary.

Our computer entrepreneur may for example:

- Get customers to spend a little time talking about the general attributes they would like to see in a new machine.
- Use these customer reactions to raise money to build a prototype.
- Persuade an engineer to work part time on the prototype for payment in cash and equity.
- Go back to the customer with the prototype asking for more detailed feedback.

This sequential ham and egging process works particularly well if one or more of the participants is a "bell cow."

BASIC SALES CLOSING SKILLS

Ham and egging is a process that is somewhat unique to launching new ventures. In addition, the entrepreneur needs to employ techniques that are basic to closing any kind of sale such as developing a schedule, knowing in depth what you are asking for, anticipating objections, managing advisors, and handling the problems after the close.

Developing a Schedule   Entrepreneurship is like driving fast on an icy road—it requires anticipation. Early in the selling process a schedule must be agreed upon so that the program can be checked and commitment tested. Intermediate points help you to know whether the stakeholder is stringing you along or is really going to participate. One of the greatest dangers in securing the commitment of stakeholders comes when one on whom you depend drops out. It destroys the ham and egging, it damages credibility and leaves a critical resource gap. A schedule, known to all induces social pressure and lets the entrepreneur maintain the appearance of control, since if others don't meet the schedule, the entrepreneur can initiate quickly a search for a replacement.

Knowing What You Need   It is always nice to have "more." Successful entrepreneurs know what degree of commitment is required at any given moment and ask only for that degree. Knowing the bottom line for both time and commitment is a great aid to effective negotiation.

Anticipating Objections   Stakeholders have both real and imaginary concerns. Getting to closing on a commitment requires addressing both. Real objections need be met with both acknowledgement and contingency plans. A prospective employee wants to know that you are aware of the real risks that she is taking. Acknowledging that risk and discussing the window of foresight which will be available before problems become serious, and even honestly discussing the "fume date" is often all the reassurance a prospective employee needs. A customer can be reassured about the risk of committing to your product by understanding how service could be handled even if your firm were gone.

Imaginary objections need be dealt with, too. Often, however, the important thing is to find out why the issue is being raised so that underlying uncertainty can be addressed with realistic answers and well thought through contingency plans.

Handling Advisors   Lawyers, accountants and staff have different motives than principals. They often get no credit when things go right, but bear the brunt of blame when things go wrong. Agreed schedules, anticipation of objections, and a sense of being a valued team member are often critical to getting the job done. Your advisors and the stakeholders' advisors often are the roadblocks on the road to commitment. As an entrepreneur, you have to manage them closely and create an expectation and incentives for getting the deal done. Often this means getting them to see the closing of an agreement as the beginning and not the end of the relationship.

Following Up   Many deals have been broken after a commitment is secured. In spite of the hectic pace of the entrepreneurial life, one of the most critical skills is maintaining the commitment. New objections arise as customers see the problems in implementation. New alternatives arise for employees when their old employer sees their departure and recognizes the potential loss. The details of covenants, warranties and representations become points of contention, then points of honor, then irreconcilable differences in the process of negotiation. The entrepreneurial task remains one of keeping the sale in place. That can only be done by constant attention and follow-up.

SUMMARY

Securing stakeholders is the critical process for an entrepreneur who seeks to pursue opportunity beyond the resources that he or she currently controls. It requires understanding who will provide the needed resources, what resources will be needed, when they will be needed and how the provider will benefit from his/her participation. The process is iteratively analytical and action oriented. It requires preparation and skill. It is, however, the key to leveraging an idea into opportunity and opportunity into a real business operation.

DISCUSSION QUESTIONS

1. Choose a hypothetical product and identify the major production factors needed. Which factors require an irreversible investment and why? In what ways can you minimize the resources committed to the others?

2. The authors of the reading emphasize the importance of securing the trust and confidence of stakeholders; entrepreneurs must sell themselves as much as their product or service. What personal qualities would financiers, customers, suppliers, and employees look for in an entrepreneur? In what ways, large and small, can entrepreneurs best demonstrate their credibility to potential stakeholders?

3. The entrepreneur must be a good judge of character. In addition to the criteria mentioned in the reading, by what standards would you assess the suitability of the financiers, customers, and employees you plan to approach?

4. As this piece suggests, the entrepreneur must, above all, be versatile; at different times he or she will assume the roles of product expert, market analyst, politician, salesperson, team builder, diplomat, negotiator, and so on. Which of these roles do you feel prepared to take on? How would you cultivate the skills needed to assume the other roles?

5. Suppose you are trying to persuade a marketing manager to quit a secure, prestigious, well-paying position to join your new venture. How would you convince the person that such a move would be worthwhile? What objections would he or she be likely to raise, and how would you respond to them?

Bootstrap Finance: The Art of Start-ups

13

AMAR BHIDÉ

Many entrepreneurs believe the illusion that a good idea will attract finan-cial backers. Venture capital, equity investors, and bankers are supposed to recognize the merits of the idea and provide the necessary capital. The reality of most ventures is very different.

Bhidé's research found that most ventures bootstrap themselves. Their growth capital comes from creative deals struck with vendors, customers, and employees. "Cheap" is a word with which many entrepreneurs can identify. They restrict spending, find inexpensive ways to build the required assets, and manage their growth to conserve cash.

Entrepreneurship is more celebrated, studied, and desirable than ever. Business school students flock to courses on entrepreneurship. Managers, fearful of losing their step on the corporate ladder, yearn to step off on their own. Policymakers pin their hopes for job creation and economic growth on start-ups rather than on the once-preeminent corporate giants.

Belief in a "big money" model of entrepreneurship often accompanies this enthusiasm. Books and courses on new ventures emphasize fund raising: how to approach investors, negotiate deals, and design optimal capital structures. The media focuses on companies like Immulogic, which raised over $20 million in venture capital years before it expected to ship any products. Executives-turned-entrepreneurs try to raise millions from venture capitalists before they have sold a dime's worth of goods to customers. Lawmakers who favor entrepreneurship focus on tax incentives for venture capital and loan guarantees for start-ups.

This big-money model has little in common with the traditional low-budget start-up. Raising big money requires careful market research, well thought-out business plans, top-notch founding teams, sagacious boards, quarterly performance reviews, and devilishly complex financial structures.

It is an environment in which analytical, buttoned-down professionals can make a seamless transition from the corporate world to the world of entrepreneurship. It is not the real world of the entrepreneur.

Without question, some start-ups powered by other people's money have rocketed to success. Mitch Kapor raised nearly $5 million of venture capital in 1982, enabling Lotus to launch 1–2–3 with the software industry's first serious advertising campaign. Significant initial capital is indeed a must in industries such as biotechnology or supercomputers where tens of millions of dollars have to be spent on R&D before any revenue is realized. But the fact is that the odds against raising big money are daunting. In 1987—a banner year—venture capitalists financed a grand total of 1,729 companies, of which 112 were seed financings and 232 were start-ups. In that same year, 631,000 new business incorporations were recorded.

Does this disparity mean that the United States needs more tax breaks, aggressive investors, and financially sophisticated entrepreneurs to channel venture capital to more start-up companies? Not at all. Over the past two years, my associates and I interviewed the founders of 100 companies on the 1989 *Inc.* "500" list of the fastest growing private companies in the United States (see the *Exhibit,* "The Study of Start-ups"). The companies—Software 2000, Symplex Communications, Gammalink, and Modular Instruments, to mention just a few—are not household names. But they are the mainstay of the entrepreneurial revolution that politicians want to sustain and that so many people, managers and business students alike, hanker to join.

These interviews attest to the value of bootstrapping: launching ventures with modest personal funds. From this perspective, Ross Perot, who started EDS with $1,000 and turned it into a multibillion-dollar enterprise (and a presidential campaign), remains the rule, not the exception. More than 80% of these companies were financed through the founders' personal savings, credit cards, second mortgages, and in one case, "a $50 check that bounced." The median start-up capital was about $10,000. Furthermore, fewer than one-fifth of the bootstrappers had raised equity for follow-on financing in the five or more years that they had been in business. They relied on debt or retained earnings to grow.

What, then, is the problem? To quote Michael Lutz, CEO of Gammalink, a high-flying Silicon Valley venture that provides PC-to-facsimile communications services, "Raising money has become a disease. Entrepreneurs are wasting lots of brainpower scheming to raise money."

Professionals with MBAs and corporate experience are attempting to strike out on their own as never before: Michael Lutz, for example, is a physicist and Stanford MBA who worked at Hughes Aircraft and Raychem for 15 years before he joined up with a Silicon Valley guru to launch a new venture. Unlike the scrappy dropouts and malcontents of yore, however, these new entrepreneurs are unwilling to pursue business opportunities without raising big money first. Following textbook formulas for snaring investors, they attempt to recruit experienced teams. They write business plans with

EXHIBIT
The Study of Start-ups

Lessons about entrepreneurship are often drawn from individual case studies, which provide rich but potentially idiosyncratic data, or from survey statistics that reveal little of the hows and whys of success. In pursuit of both depth and breadth, I recently completed a far-reaching field study of start-ups. With the help of Research Associates Kevin Hinton and Laura Pochop and Professor Howard Stevenson, I interviewed 100 company founders about how they overcame the daunting obstacles that confront start-ups.

The companies in the study came from the 1989 *Inc.* "500" list, a compilation of the fastest growing privately held companies in the United States that had sales of at least $100,000 in 1983. (The average company on this list had 1988 revenues of about $15 million, 135 employees, and a five-year sales growth record of 1,407%.) I narrowed my list of prospective interviewees to companies founded after 1982, on the grounds that the start-up history of older companies would be more difficult to obtain.

Finding a representative cross section of start-ups was a challenge. Since many incorporations are just attempts at self-employment or poorly conceived ventures that would say little about starting new businesses, I could not simply draw from the hundreds of thousands of new businesses incorporated every year. At the same time, I also wanted to avoid the few billion-dollar successes like Federal Express or Microsoft, which the typical entrepreneur cannot realistically hope to emulate. My sample provided a happy middle ground. The *Inc.* list's requirement of a five-year track record of rapid growth helped eliminate low-potential or "born to fail" ventures. And with 500 companies on the list, I avoided "outliers" that succeeded because of the unusual talent (or luck) of the founder.

To get the start-ups' stories in all their complexity, I chose to conduct face-to-face interviews rather than send out a mail survey. Start-ups are characterized by close relationships among financing, marketing strategies, hiring, and control systems that would be hard to capture through a structured survey. Since executives of successful companies are inundated with mail surveys, response rates are generally low. Although we had some difficulty in contacting entrepreneurs and scheduling appointments, only a few declined to be interviewed.

Each interview lasted from one to three hours. Usually two researchers took handwritten notes, which were then compiled into a single transcript and returned to the interviewees for review.

To my knowledge, this is one of the broadest, most in-depth studies of U.S. start-ups. Where other field studies have focused on limited geographic regions or industries, we visited over 20 cities and towns in a dozen states to interview entrepreneurs in a wide range of businesses. Researchers who have tackled similarly broad samples have relied on mail surveys.

Reflecting *Inc.*'s criteria, my sample *was* biased toward very high-growth companies. But the skew actually reinforces my findings about the importance of bootstrapping: start-ups that grow more slowly are even less likely to need or be able to attract outside risk capital.

crisp executive summaries describing their proprietary edge. If venture capitalists are unresponsive, they network with venture angels. Even today, they have heard there is more money than good ideas.

In fact, as Gammalink's founders learned, an entrepreneur's time is rarely well spent courting investors. Despite a well-written business plan and excellent contacts, Lutz and his partner failed to attract venture capital in a year of trying. Eventually, they contributed $12,500 each to launch Gammalink. Years later, after their company was a proven success, it attracted $800,000 in unsolicited venture capital.

For the great majority of would-be founders, the biggest challenge is not raising money but having the wits and hustle to do without it. To that end, it helps to understand what it takes to start a business—and why that is likely to conflict with what venture capitalists require.

──── A POOR FIT

Many an entrepreneur's hopes are dashed when a venture capitalist rejects a promising business plan. But would-be founders should not interpret lack of interest from the investor community as a pronouncement that the business is doomed. Often entrepreneurs fail to qualify for venture capital not because their proposals are poor but because they do not meet the exacting criteria that venture capitalists must use.

Venture capitalists (and other investors in start-ups) are neither greedy nor shortsighted, as some disappointed entrepreneurs believe; they are simply inappropriate for most start-ups. Their criteria are understandably exacting: venture capitalists incur significant costs in investigating, negotiating, and monitoring investments. They can back only a few of the many entrepreneurs who seek funding, and they must anticipate that several investments will yield disappointing returns. One study of venture capital portfolios by Venture Economics, Inc. indicates that about 7% of the investments account for more than 60% of the profits, while a full one-third result in a partial or total loss. Each project must therefore represent a potential home run.

Start-ups, however, typically lack all or most of the criteria investors use to identify big winners: scale, proprietary advantages, well-defined plans, and well-regarded founders.

Most start-ups begin by pursuing niche markets that are too small to interest large competitors—or venture capitalists. Venture capitalists are hesitant to pursue small opportunities where even high-percentage returns will not cover their investment overhead. They favor products or services that address hundred-million-dollar markets. Legendary investor Arthur Rock goes so far as to limit his investments to businesses that have "the potential to change the world."

Few entrepreneurs start with a truly original concept or a plan to achieve a sustainable competitive advantage through a proprietary technology or brand name. Instead, they tend to follow "me too" strategies and, particularly in service businesses, to rely on superior execution and energy to generate profits. But it is hard for outside investors to evaluate an entrepreneur's ability to execute. Nor can they count on cashing in their investments in companies whose success cannot be sustained without the founders' capabilities.

Many entrepreneurs thrive in rapidly changing industries and niches where established companies are deterred by uncertain prospects. Their ability to roll with the punches is far more important than planning and foresight. Investors, on the other hand, prefer ventures with plausible, carefully thought-out plans to address well-defined markets. A solid plan reassures them about the competence of the entrepreneur and provides an objective yardstick for measuring progress and testing initial assumptions.

Finally, many entrepreneurs are long on energy and enthusiasm but short on credentials. Michael Dell was a freshman at the University of Texas when he started selling computer parts by mail order. Others are refugees from declining or oligopolistic industries, seeking new fields that offer more opportunity but where they lack personal experience.

Investors who see hundreds of business plans and entrepreneurs, however, cannot gauge or rely on the intangibles of personality. Thus Mitch Kapor was a good bet for investors because he already had a successful software product, Visiplot, under his belt before he launched Lotus. Bill Gates, on the other hand, a teenage college dropout when he launched Microsoft with his high school friend, Paul Allen, probably was not.

THE HIDDEN COSTS OF OTHER PEOPLE'S MONEY

Entrepreneurs who try to get investors to bend their criteria or create the perception that they meet those criteria do so at their peril. Several entrepreneurs pointed to the pitfalls of rushing to raise external financing. Winning over investors too early, they said, can compromise your discipline and flexibility.

Bootstrapping in a start-up is like zero inventory in a just-in-time system: it reveals hidden problems and forces the company to solve them. "If we had had money," said Tom Davis of Modular Instruments, manufacturers of medical and research equipment, "we would have made more mistakes. This way, I wrote all the checks. I knew where the money was going."

There can also be problems with raising too much money. As one founder noted, "It is often easier to raise $5 million than $1 million because venture capitalists would rather not have to worry about a lot of tiny investments. But then you have $4 million you didn't need but spend anyhow."

George Brostoff, cofounder of Symplex Communications, which manufactures data communications equipment, agreed. "People in my industry think they need to be able to do x, y, and z at the outset. But the money gets burned up quickly, and it doesn't produce either profits or sales. Then they address the symptom—'we need more money'—instead of the underlying problems."

Diminished flexibility is often another consequence of premature funding. Start-ups entering new industries seldom get it right the first time. Success, especially in new and growing industries, follows many detours and unanticipated setbacks; strategies may have to be altered radically as events unfold. Failure to meet initial goals is a poor guide to future prospects. For example, Gammalink expected its first product, a high-speed modem, to be used to allow PCs to communicate with each other. Cofounder Lutz thought he had done his homework and was sure there was a market for the product. But, in fact, buyers never materialized. Gammalink next tried to sell its modem in volume to Dialog as part of a new database Dialog was developing for corporate attorneys. But the database never got off the ground, and Dialog bought a mere three modems.

Lutz and his partner had to rethink their strategy again. This time they targeted large companies with dispersed PCs. They sent out 5,000 mailers at $1 each and got only 25 responses. Twenty-four of them led nowhere but the twenty-fifth, from BMW of North America, said, "This is the product we've been waiting for." BMW bought a few, then placed a blanket order for $700,000.

Outside investors, however, can hinder entrepreneurs from following the try-it, fix-it approach required in the uncertain environments in which start-ups flourish. The prospect of a radical change in course presents outside investors with a quandary: "Was the original concept wrong or was it poorly executed?" The entrepreneur is sure the new strategy will work but was just as confident about the original plan. The investors wonder, "Are we being fooled twice?" Supporting the proposed new strategy rather than, say, changing management is an act of faith that requires investors to discard what seems like hard evidence of poor planning, bad judgment, or overselling.

For their part, entrepreneurs may develop the confidence to push back against investors once the business has taken shape. But in the early years, they tend to avoid direct challenges. Instead, they stick with their original plans even when they begin to lose faith in them because they fear that radical shifts will draw the wrong kind of scrutiny. The former CEO of an advanced materials company described the pressure to stick with untenable strategies that outside investors can create.

"When we started, well-defined markets for our materials did not exist. My first job as CEO was to figure out what product market we would go after, so I hit the road for about three months. I identified a product—aluminum oxide substrates—but by the time we got to market, the competition had improved and our substrates never really took off. I realized that, given our size, we should have been manufacturing to order rather than for the market at large. But by that time, we were already stumbling and I was losing credibility with the investors. They weren't interested in a new strategy. They just wanted the substrates to be profitable. I wish I had stood my ground and said, 'I'm turning off the furnace tomorrow.' But I didn't quite have the guts to do that."

Conflicts between investors in a business and its day-to-day managers are a fact of life. They are less debilitating, however, after the entrepreneur has the credibility to be a true partner. Entrepreneurs who are unsure of their markets or who don't have the experience to deal with investor pressure are better off without other people's capital, even if they can somehow get investors to overlook sketchy plans and limited credentials.

——— FLYING ON EMPTY

Starting a business with limited funds requires a different strategy and approach than launching a well-capitalized venture. Compaq Computer, for example, was a venture capitalist's dream. Rod Canion, Jim Harris, and Bill Murto had all been senior managers at Texas Instruments, and they had a well-formulated plan to take on IBM with a technologically superior product. Seasoned investor Ben Rosen helped Canion raise $20 million in start-up capital—funds that allowed the new business to behave like a big company from the start. Canion could attract experienced managers by offering them generous salaries and participation in a stock option plan. Compaq also had a national dealer network established within a year of exhibiting its first prototype. Sales totaled more than $100 million in the first year.

Bootstrappers need a different mind-set and approach. Principles and practices imported from the corporate world will not serve them as well as the following axioms drawn from successful entrepreneurs.

GET OPERATIONAL QUICKLY

Bootstrappers don't mind starting with a copycat idea targeted to a small market. Often that approach works well. Imitation saves the costs of market research, and the start-up entering a small market is unlikely to face competition from large, established companies.

Of course, entrepreneurs do not reap fame and fortune if their enterprises remain marginal. But once they are in the flow of business, opportunities often turn up that they would not have seen had they waited for the big idea.

Consider, for example, the evolution of Eaglebrook Plastics, now one of the largest high-density polyethylene recyclers in the United States. Eaglebrook was founded in 1983 by Andrew Stephens and Bob Thompson, who had been chemical engineering students at Purdue. At first, they bought plastic scrap, had it ground by someone else, then sold it, primarily to the pipe industry. One year later, they bought a used $700 grinder, which they operated at night so that they could sell during the day. Soon they moved up to a $25,000 grinder, but they only began to hire when they couldn't keep up with demand.

In 1985, the company developed an innovative process for purifying paper-contaminated plastic scrap—and began to make a name for itself in the industry. In 1987, with the profitability of scrap declining, the partners turned to recycling plastic bottles, a novel idea at the time. Next came plastic lumber made from recycled materials and then, most recently, a joint venture with the National Polyethylene Recycling Corporations to manage their styrofoam recycling operations. Few if any of these opportunities could have been foreseen at the outset.

LOOK FOR QUICK BREAK-EVEN, CASH-GENERATING PROJECTS

The rule in large companies and well-funded enterprises is to stick to the basic strategy. Not so with the bootstrapped start-up. Profit opportunities that might be regarded as distractions in a large company are immensely valuable to the entrepreneur. A business that is making money, elegantly or not, builds credibility in the eyes of suppliers, customers, and employees, as well as self-confidence in the entrepreneur.

For example, Raju Patel launched NAC with the ambitious goal of serving the Baby Bells created by the AT&T breakup. NAC's first offering, however, was a low-end auto-dialer targeted to the many start-ups that were reselling long-distance services from carriers like MCI. "We thought it would be appropriate to get a cash generator to make us known as a new entrant," Patel explained. Then at a conference, Patel happened to meet a reseller who mentioned his need for more accurate customer-billing capability. NAC stopped work on the auto-dialer and rapidly developed and shipped a billing system. The system was later phased out as the customers themselves began to fold. But its quick, albeit short-lived, success helped NAC attract the engineers it needed to grow because it enabled Patel to offer security as well as the excitement of a start-up. "We weren't seen as a revolving-door company. We were able to offer health plans and other benefits comparable to those of large companies." More ambitious products, aimed at the Bell companies, followed. Today NAC is well established as a small systems supplier to the Bell companies.

Robert Grosshandler's Softa group also used the cash flow from one business to develop another. "Our property management software was funded by selling hardware and peripherals to *Fortune* '500' companies. It was low-margin, but it had fast turnaround. Goods arrived in the morning and left in the evening. Our software, on the other hand, took nearly a year to develop."

Many entrepreneurs sustained themselves by part-time consulting. In the early days, says Robert Pemberton of Software 2000, which develops and distributes business applications software, consulting accounted for more than 50% of the revenue of the business.

OFFER HIGH-VALUE PRODUCTS OR SERVICES THAT CAN SUSTAIN DIRECT PERSONAL SELLING

Getting a customer to give up a familiar product or service for that of a shaky start-up is arguably the most important challenge an entrepreneur faces. "When we first started selling," Modular's Davis recalled, "people would ask, 'When are you going to go out of business?'"

Many entrepreneurs underestimate the marketing costs entailed in overcoming customer inertia and conservatism, especially with respect to low-value or impulse goods. Launching a new packaged food product without substantial financial resources, for example, is an oft-undertaken and futile endeavor. Creating a serious business means persuading hundreds of thousands of customers to try out a new $5 mustard or jam in place of their usual brand. Without millions of dollars of market research, advertising, and promotion, this can be a hopeless task.

Therefore, successful entrepreneurs often pick high-ticket products and services where their personal passion, salesmanship, and willingness to go the extra mile can substitute for a big marketing budget. As John Mineck, cofounder of Practice Management Systems said, "People buy a salesperson. They bought me and I had no sales experience. But I truly believed our systems and software for automating doctors' offices would work—so the customers did too. Also, we did an awful lot for our first clients; if they wanted something, we'd deliver. We were providing service and support long before that became a cliché."

Like Mineck, three-quarters of the founders we interviewed were also their company's chief or only salesperson. They sold directly, usually to other businesses. Only 10% used brokers or distributors, and only 14% offered consumer goods or services. The median unit sale was $5,000, an amount high enough to support direct personal selling and also, presumably, to get the attention of buyers. The few consumer items we encountered were also important purchases for buyers: a $20,000 recreational vehicle from Chariot Eagle or an SAT preparation course from the *Princeton Review*, rather than a $5 to $10 staple that consumers purchase without great thought.

Overcoming customer inertia is easier and cheaper if a product offers some tangible advantage over substitutes. Our successful entrepreneurs overcame reservations about their long-term viability by selling concrete performance characteristics—faster chips and fourth-generation language software, for instance—rather than intangible attributes like a tangier sauce or more evocative perfume. "We had no track record and no commercial office—I was running the company from my home," recalled Prabhu Goel, founder of

Gateway Design Automation, which supplies CAE software tools. "So we went after the most sophisticated users who had a problem that needed to be solved. The risk of dealing with us was small compared with the risk of not solving the problem."

Concrete product attributes also contribute to important serendipitous sales. With just a prototype, Brostoff of Symplex got an order for 100 units from Mead Data, his first significant customer. "We didn't call them, they called us," Brostoff told us. "A high-level manager read an article about us that suggested our product could offer customers like Mead dramatic cost savings—as much as $55,000 annually on a one-time investment of $10,000 to $20,000. Mead had an on-line database product and was looking to cut costs."

Intangibles like responsiveness and attention do provide greater leverage for entrepreneurial selling in service and distribution businesses. Clay Teramo, founder of Computer Media Technology, a computer supplies distributor, described the way he used service—and the customer's perception of service—to make up for the fact that early on his competitors had far more resources. When someone called with a next-day order that Computer Media couldn't handle, Teramo would tell them that he didn't have the whole order in stock and ask if he could fill part of it the next day and part later on. If the customer agreed, he'd follow up personally to make sure everything had gone smoothly and to say thanks. As Teramo pointed out, his competitors could probably have filled the whole order at once. But the customer wouldn't think he had received any special service.

Carol Russell of Russell Personnel Services took a similar approach. "Our business is done on the cult of personality," she said. "You roll up your sleeves and say to the customer, 'Hi, I'm Carol Russell, and I'm going to work overtime to get you employed or employees.' In a people business, being a young company and visible is an advantage. In the large services, you won't meet the Mr. Olstens or the Mr. Kellys."

FORGET ABOUT THE CRACK TEAM

It is not unusual for investor-backed start-ups to hire CFOs or marketing managers at $100,000 a year. Bootstrappers cannot afford this investment. Besides, if the entrepreneurs' credentials aren't strong enough to attract investors, they are even less likely to be able to attract a highly qualified team. Novices who are urged to recruit a well-rounded team rarely succeed. Steve Jobs had his pick of talent for NeXT; Apple, however, was built by youthful exuberance.

The start-ups that we studied attracted employees by providing them with opportunities to upgrade skills and build résumés, rather than by offering cash or options. Their challenge was to find and motivate diamonds in the rough.

"I never hired experienced people," said Bohdan Associates's founder

Peter Zacharkiw, "and there are very few college graduates here. My vice president of sales was the best curb painter around—but that's the secret. He'll always be the best at what he does. Personality and common sense are the most important things that people here have."

John Greenwood's first employee at Micron Separations was a 62-year-old machine shop worker who had just been laid off. His production manager was a Worcester Polytechnic Institute graduate who had been working as an accountant in a company he hated and was looking for another job. "We never attempted to lure anybody away from another company," Greenwood told us. "One, we were cheap. Two, we had moral reasons—if we went under and it didn't work out for them, we wouldn't feel so bad. We never felt that we had an inadequate pool, though. I believe the people in the 'unemployment market' are just as good if not better than the people in the employment market. And we have no prejudice against people who've been fired. My partner and I started Micron after we were fired! In large companies, people tend to get fired for lack of political skills."

Not all entrepreneurs were so fortunate, however. Some had to cope with employees who had neither the formal qualifications nor the right temperament and attitude for their jobs. "Large companies can hire by credentials and screen people carefully," said Robert Rodriguez of National Communications Sales Promotion, a Miami-based company that helps customers manage their sales promotion campaigns. "We needed to have things happen quickly and took people on the basis of their initial presentation. But many didn't do what they said they could."

KEEP GROWTH IN CHECK

Start-ups that failed because they could not fund their growth are legion. Successful bootstrappers take special care to expand only at the rate they can afford and control. For example, they tend to invest in people or capacity only when there is no alternative, not in advance of needs. "Our first product was done before the company was founded," said Warren Anderson, founder of Anderson Soft-Teach. "I produced it, paid for it, took it to a trade show, and we started taking orders before we hired people. It was like brick-laying. We added one layer at a time. We didn't have a venture capitalist putting up money for us—just $30,000 of our own money—and we were selling our tapes for $200 each."

Keeping growth in check is not only financially prudent but it also helps the entrepreneur develop management skills and iron out problems under less pressure. Even entrepreneurs who don't have to make radical changes in strategy may have to make adjustments as they learn about the nuances of their chosen industry. Learning the nuts and bolts of running a business is particularly important for first-time entrepreneurs. Stephanie Di-Marco and her partner encountered few major surprises when they started

Advent Software. Nevertheless, in the early years, DiMarco noted, they felt constrained by their lack of knowledge and held back on their growth. "Instead of trying to create an organization, I wanted to prove myself first. It was important for me to learn the business before I hired someone else. I had never managed anyone before." After the partners learned how to run a business, Advent enjoyed explosive growth.

In their rush to grow, some entrepreneurs told us, they took on customers who nearly put them under. "When you are new and cold-calling customers," observed Fred Zak of Venture Graphics, "the business that comes your way is usually from customers who can't pay their bills or shop only on price—the worst kind of customer base. About 40% of our early work came from deadbeats. I soon determined that I would have to call on them personally, and I'd show up unannounced. It was nerve-racking, but they would pay us off so that they wouldn't have to see me again!"

Some will argue that controlled growth and reactive investments allow competitors to preempt the market. In fact, there are few businesses that entrepreneurs can realistically expect to start in which grabbing dominant market share first is crucial. In mature service industries such as temporary services, advertising, or public relations (where many of our entrepreneurs found their niches), dominance, early or late, is out of the question. But even in high-tech fields, first-mover advantages are often short-lived. Compaq's early start in the IBM clone market did not thwart later bootstrapped entrants like Dell Computer and AST Research. Similarly, WordPerfect, today's dominant player in word processing software, was not among the first half-dozen entrants.

Frequent changes in technology allow entrepreneurs who miss one wave while getting organized to ride the next. Several computer distributors we interviewed missed getting in on the first generation of PCs and so could not obtain the all-important "IBM Authorized Dealer" medallion. But the growth of Novell and local area networks created new opportunities, which the established, first-generation competitors, engrossed in traditional products, couldn't easily take advantage of.

FOCUS ON CASH, NOT ON PROFITS, MARKET SHARE, OR ANYTHING ELSE

A well-funded start-up can afford to pursue several strategic goals; bootstrappers usually cannot. For example, cash-constrained start-ups cannot "buy business." In venture capital-backed or intrapreneurial ventures, it may be feasible for a start-up to sell at a loss in anticipation of scale economies or learning curve advantages. But the bootstrapper must earn healthy margins, practically from day one, not only to cover the company's costs but also to finance growth. "I learned early that it is better to have a low-profile, positive cash-flow job than a high-ego, negative cash-flow job," said Keith Kakacek, founder of the commercial insurance group, SIR Lloyds. "If the market doesn't pay for your business—and you can't develop positive cash flow—you probably don't have a good enough concept."

Getting terms from suppliers and timely payments from customers are critical in managing cash. Ron Norris of Automotive Caliper Exchange told us he started with and maintained positive cash flow from operations in spite of rapid growth. Building on contacts developed over 20 years, he went to six suppliers and asked for 90- to 120-day terms for one time only on his first order. All but one agreed. Now established, Norris gives modest discounts to customers who pay quickly. But he won't tolerate any "gray" whatever. If a customer doesn't pay in 30 days—and hasn't called to explain why—the company won't sell to him any longer.

Equally important is knowing when to spend and when to economize. Successful bootstrappers are generally cheap, except in one or two crucial areas. "We began in a modest room," recalled Brian Cornish of Oscor Medical Corporation, which makes instruments for microsurgery. "We licked stamps instead of buying a Pitney Bowes machine. We never had plush offices or any of the other trappings of some start-ups. But we made sure we got the very best microscopes."

CULTIVATE BANKS BEFORE THE BUSINESS BECOMES CREDITWORTHY

It is common wisdom that bank loans can be a cheap alternative to external equity and crucial for financing additional inventory or larger receivables. But bank financing is often unavailable for start-ups, as many entrepreneurs we interviewed discovered. Winning bankers over requires preparation and careful timing.

Consider, for example, how Phil Bookman of Silton-Bookman went about managing his company's bank relationship. Bookman did not even try to borrow until his software company was creditworthy. But he made sure that the company kept good books, that its records were immaculate, and that its balance sheets were sound. In addition, he opened accounts with a big bank's local branch and from time to time asked the branch manager's advice to familiarize him with Silton-Bookman's business. Then when the company had been in business for the requisite three years, Bookman went to the banker with the company's business plan. "He looked over the numbers," Bookman explained, "and said, 'It looks like you need a $50,000 term loan.' We knew that all along, but it was important that he suggested it. We got the loan and paid it back, then used the same method the next year to get a line of credit."

——— ABANDONING THE RULES

Growth and change create difficult transitions for all entrepreneurial companies. The challenges faced by a charismatic founder in letting go and designing an organization in which authority and responsibility are appropriately distributed are well-known. The bootstrapper's problem is particularly acute, however. To build a durable business—as opposed to a personal project or an alternative to employment—successful entrepreneurs not only have to modify their personal roles and organization, but they may also have to effect a U-turn and abandon the very policies that allowed them to get up and running with limited capital. As part of these changes, the start-up may have to:

- Emerge from its niche and compete with a large company. When *Princeton Review* was launched, it competed with private tutors of uneven quality in Manhattan. To become a nationally franchised operation, the company had to confront the well-established Stanley Kaplan chain.
- Offer more standard, less customized products. "We did a lot of things for our first clients that we wouldn't do today," said Practice Management Systems's Mineck. "The easiest thing for a salesperson to say is, 'we can do it,' and the hardest thing is, 'we can't do this for you.'"
- Bring critical services in-house. Automotive Caliper never hired an in-house controller because it didn't need the expertise. But it does have its own fleet of trucks. The smartly dressed drivers project the company's image, and they provide an important source of information because they can find out things the sales force cannot see.
- Change management's focus from cash flow to strategic goals. Phil Bookman, a self-confessed "cash management fanatic" in the early years, pointed out how important—and hard—it was to shift gears later on and remind people that they had to think more about the big picture and worry less about the little expenditures.
- Recruit higher priced talent, perhaps encouraging early employees to move on. Sometimes the need to turn over early employees and hire professionals in their place is an obvious business decision. At National Communications Sales Promotion, for example, all but two of Rodriguez's original employees left within a few years. A few had simply grown stale, but most were fired for unprofessional behavior or because their attitude was bad. To get people with the right attitude and experience, Rodriguez began to pay more and to look for different qualities: MBAs with family responsibilities replaced "swinging singles" who weren't above making side deals.

More often, however, replacing the start-up's early team presents the entrepreneur with one of the most difficult transitions he or she must confront.

At Rizzo Associates, an engineering and environmental services company, four of the first seven employees had to leave because they could not grow with the company. "We promised employees substantial opportunities in terms of personal growth and sold them a future," William Rizzo recalled. "But we did not tell them that they had to live up to that future. In time, we had to bring people in over them, and they felt their future was sealed off. Eventually they said, 'The hell with you.' Today I would be more candid about the fact that our promises are contingent on their performance."

Changes in strategy or personnel at more "professionally" designed and launched start-ups may be less dramatic or personally wrenching. But hard as making these changes may be, they are unavoidable for the entrepreneur who succeeds enough to turn a start-up venture into an ongoing business.

—— DISCUSSION QUESTIONS

1. What kinds of markets or industries are most hospitable to the undercapitalized entrepreneur?
2. How does the bootstrapper decide it is time to raise outside capital?
3. What personal traits or skills are required by individuals who want to follow the bootstrap approach?

14   The Financial Perspective: What Should Entrepreneurs Know?

WILLIAM A. SAHLMAN

Are concepts and tools from finance useful to entrepreneurial managers? Describing finance as a way to think about cash, risk, and value, this reading says that the answer is an unequivocal yes. Entrepreneurs start out with few resources; to survive and create value, they must consider the financial perspective as well as other perspectives when making decisions. This reading explores some fundamental concepts from finance that are particularly useful to entrepreneurs and points out their relationship to managerial decision making. It concludes with several observations on the benefits and limitations of the financial perspective.

Finance is the study of the allocation of scarce resources within the firm. It helps managers in companies of all sizes to ask the right questions: How should they make investment decisions, that is, decisions entailing current sacrifice for future gain? How should they arrange for the financing of investment decisions? What effect do the decisions managers make have on value for shareholders and other constituencies—management, labor, suppliers, customers, government, society?

This definition of finance relies on two important premises. First, finance is the study of how decisions *should* be made. Second, finance is not just the domain of the financial manager; properly considered, it is also a task for general managers.

Like any management tool, finance cannot stand alone. Managers who view decisions only from the finance perspective are not doing their jobs. They must remember that the numbers they manipulate are generated by real people selling real products in a competitive market. To ignore the human or the production perspective would be just as fatal as ignoring the finance perspective.

If finance is useful to general managers of large firms, it is especially useful to entrepreneurs, for they are the ultimate general managers, responsible for making many, if not most, of the decisions in their enterprises.

Professor William A. Sahlman prepared this case as the basis for class discussion rather than to illustrate either effective or ineffective handling of an administrative situation. Copyright © 1992 by the President and Fellows of Harvard College. Harvard Business School case 293-045.

Entrepreneurs are value creators, investing today in hopes of generating cash flows tomorrow. They must understand what cash flow will do; they must understand and manage risk; they must understand how value is determined. Indeed, the importance of thinking through problems from the finance perspective is probably even more important for entrepreneurial firms than it is for larger companies. A key goal of the entrepreneur must be to keep playing the game; ignoring finance risks being forced to stop playing.

In the following paragraphs, I identify certain concepts and tools of finance that are useful to general managers and critical to entrepreneurs. The list is divided into three sections—cash, risk, and value.

CASH

The first principle of all financial thinking is that cash is what is important. Because cash can be consumed—traded for other assets in the economy that have utility—all analysis of investment or financing decisions must focus on cash.

ACCOUNTING INCOME VERSUS FREE CASH FLOW

Cash income is not, however, the same as accounting income. Finance relates to financial accounting only in that the financial analyst must be able to infer from reported financial statements what cash is doing. Whereas the accountant tries to match revenues with expenses, the manager focuses on the difference between cash inflow and cash outflow. Accountants distinguish between *expenditures* and *expenses*; they define *net income* as the difference between revenues and expenses. Managers define economic income as the difference between cash income and the sum of all cash outlays required to produce the cash income, whether called expenses or expenditures. That difference, called *free cash flow*, is the amount of cash income that can be consumed in any period (or invested in new projects) without hurting the cash flow stream. Free cash flow is defined as net income plus depreciation, minus required investments in working capital, plant, and equipment. It takes into account both the benefits and the costs of investing.[1]

---

1. A more complete definition of free cash flow is as follows:
   Earnings Before Interest and Taxes (EBIT)
   Less Tax Rate × EBIT
   Plus Depreciation
   Less Change in Required Working Capital
   Less Change in Required Gross Fixed Assets

This definition does not reflect how the free cash flow stream has been financed. That is, interest expense, loan amortization requirements, and common stock dividends have not been taken into account. Free cash flow is a measure of the net cash generated by a decision, before considering how it should be financed.

MEASURING PROFITABILITY

The manager's measure of profitability differs from the accountant's. Managers measure profitability on the basis of *net present value:* the difference between the present value of the future free cash flows and the initial investment, given the assessed riskiness of the flows. The accountant's measure of profitability (e.g., book return on equity) is probably unrelated to the manager's measure. Book return reflects the concept of matching income and expenses and ignores the expenditures necessary to produce the income. Moreover, book value is not the same as market value.

PERFORMANCE EVALUATION AND INCENTIVE COMPENSATION

A basic tenet of finance is that individuals act to maximize their own wealth. A company's incentive compensation system will therefore have a strong effect on the actions of its managers. If the firm's objective is to maximize *value,* and value depends on *cash* and *risk,* then the incentive compensation system must focus on all three factors. If, instead, it focuses on the accountant's measure of performance, the results are likely to be counterproductive; acting in their own self-interest, managers will make decisions that maximize accounting income rather than value. When performance evaluation systems focus on accounting systems, managers usually consider sunk costs when making decisions and often refuse to make a decision that would ultimately enhance value because the result would be to lower accounting income.

TAXES AND CASH

An important determinant of cash flow is taxation. Four kinds of decisions affect taxes: legal (e.g., incorporation), investment, financing, and accounting. Managers must try to minimize the resources (corporate and personal) siphoned off to the government within the constraints of the law. To do otherwise would be to ignore one of the key responsibilities of management: to minimize costs in order to compete effectively. If one firm pays more taxes than an essentially identical competitor, the first firm will fail. The ultimate losers will be the firm's constituencies: management, shareholders, labor, consumers, and so on.

CASH AND GROWTH

Another important determinant of cash flow is the rate of sales growth. Growth in sales must be supported by growth in assets (working capital and fixed assets). In turn, growth in assets must be supported by increases in stockholders' equity through retained earnings, stock sales, or increases in external liabilities. High growth rates may require successful firms to rely heavily on external funding.

It is essential that managers distinguish between real growth and growth in prices—that is, inflation. High inflation rates can have a much more damaging effect on a company's long-term financial health than high rates of real growth, especially in view of the historical cost basis for tax accounting used in the United States.

PATTERN RECOGNITION

A critical skill for managers is the ability to recognize and respond to patterns. Many patterns affect cash: cyclical, seasonal, competitive, technological, regulatory, and tax. A hallmark of good managers is their ability to recognize an opportunity to create value *and* to act on it. Becoming proficient at pattern recognition enables them to commit resources quickly to a perceived opportunity. By recognizing and responding to patterns of cash flow behavior, and by using past and current information, successful managers seek to predict the future and to take action.

Pattern recognition helps managers make both defensive and offensive decisions. Consider the effects of a recession. Battening down the hatches when the recession has been recognized is an example of a defensive action. Deciding to accelerate an investment in capacity during a recession precisely because the competition is battening down the hatches is an example of an offensive decision. Recognizing the event—a recession—and anticipating how the competition will react to it drives the company's decisions.

Of course, managers cannot always identify the patterns that are affecting cash flows at a particular time. They may not know, for example, when a recession begins or even ends; their reactions will therefore be delayed. If, however, they have studied the issues before they arise and have come up with a plan of action, they will do a better job than if they had not thought about the problem in the first place.

SCENARIO PLANNING

Scenario planning can be a useful way to analyze cash flows. A scenario is a numerical depiction of a logically consistent set of events that are likely to occur in the future. The scenario reflects past and potential management decisions. It also considers the probable moves of competitors. It is a way to manage in an uncertain environment.

Scenario planning is not the same as worst case, expected values, and best-case forecasting. These simplistic depictions of future events are not particularly useful. The reason is simple. Consider the worst-case scenario. Rarely will all the elements of a worst case scenario occur simultaneously. Moreover, these scenarios often fail to account for an explicit change in management decisions. They assume that management will keep making the same decisions it would have made had the expected outcomes occurred; in reality, managers may go so far as to abandon a project altogether. Best-case scenarios have the same pitfalls.

Nor is scenario planning the same thing as linear extrapolation. Few trends persist without interruption. Many planning errors are made because the planners extrapolate from past data. During the 1970s, many banks lent to energy companies based on values that reflected a continuation of rapidly escalating oil and gas prices—at rates above the expected rise in general prices. When oil and gas prices fell, both in absolute terms and relative to other prices in the economy, the values on which loans had been made vanished. This example, which admittedly relies on hindsight, is nonetheless useful because the pattern has been and will be repeated time and time again.

An unwritten rule states that every forecast a manager makes will turn out with hindsight to be wrong. But by making internally consistent forecasts that reflect reasoned management decisions and that are economically significant (i.e., not so unlikely as to be irrelevant), managers can manage in an uncertain world.

One final note: there is a crucial distinction between evaluating the effects of a particular event occurring and being able to predict the occurrence of the event with certainty. A good example is interest rates. No evidence indicates that any individual or group of individuals can predict interest rates with any precision. Nevertheless managers must evaluate the consequences of interest rate changes.

CONSIDER ALL THE CASH FLOWS

Suppose I am considering an investment strategy that involves acquiring at least three companies in the hand tool business over the next few years.[2] I already own a hand tool division that sells a narrow product line, and I have chosen this acquisition strategy because adding the three companies will produce significant economies (cost savings) in distribution.

However, my financial vice president has come up with financial projections for the first acquisition candidate that do not justify making the investment. What should I do?

The first question to consider is: Does the analysis take into account

---

2. This example is drawn from "Cooper Industries, Inc." Harvard Business School Case No. 9-274-116.

all the cash flow effects of the investment? Does it include the potential savings to be realized by adding the new business to my existing business? Do the figures reflect any synergies (increased revenues) that might result from being able to offer the market a broader line of products? Finally, do they allow for the fact that the next acquisition will look even better because the division will already have two hand tool companies rather than one?

As this example suggests, any prediction of cash flows must take into account all the cash flow effects of the decision. The relevant question to ask is simple: If I make this investment, what cash flows will I get? If I don't make this investment, what cash flows will I get? Will I create opportunities to invest profitably in other new projects because I invest in the project under consideration? Considered in this light the acquisition strategy appears to be eminently sensible, and carrying it out will add measurably to the value of the company. Viewed individually, however, the investments do not look attractive. Focusing on the trees rather than the forest would be a serious error.

One element of successful pattern recognition is the ability to recognize how current investment or financing decisions affect cash flows from the firm's existing assets or from future investment and financing decisions. Attributing these effects (whether positive or negative) to the decision under consideration is an important element of financial thinking.

DON'T RUN OUT OF CASH

This is a fundamental rule of finance (and of business generally). Just as blood sustains living organisms, cash sustains a business. Most competitive moves can be thought of as investments; even the decision to cut prices temporarily is an investment decision. In a competitive economy, the inevitable result of being unable to invest due to a cash constraint is atrophy and death. Not only is the company unable to seize profitable investment opportunities, but financial weakness might encourage the competition to attack. By forecasting and planning for future cash flow patterns, managers can avoid jeopardizing their firms' survival.

Note that the definition of cash I use is very broad. What I really have in mind is the potential to raise cash from inside and outside the firm. To obtain cash from external sources, however, there must be value within the firm that can be sold off.

—— RISK

The riskiness of a particular cash flow stream determines its value. How is risk measured? How do managers deal with uncertainty?

HOW IS RISK MEASURED?

There are really two answers to this question. One way to define risk is as the total amount of uncertainty about future cash flows. A manager will never be able to predict future events with certainty. The managers of a rocket-launching company may have a good idea what cash flows will be if the rocket is successfully launched or if it dies on the launching pad; they cannot predict exactly which of these two events will occur. This first notion of risk focuses on that total uncertainty about future events.

Another notion of risk deals with only a portion of total risk: the portion of the total risk that cannot be diversified away. Suppose, for example, that an investor had the following choices: invest in a suntan lotion manufacturer on a small tropical island; invest in an umbrella manufacturer on the same island; or invest in both. The expected return from investing in either company is 10%. The actual return depends on whether the island has a sunny year, a normal year, or a rainy year. In the first case, the suntan lotion producer will do well and the return on investment will be 30%. The umbrella manufacturer, on the other hand, will do poorly in the sunny year and will report a negative 10% return. The opposite pattern will occur in a rainy year. During a normal year, the investor will earn a 10% return on an investment in either company. Unfortunately, no one on the island had developed a foolproof way to predict the weather for the forthcoming year. What should the investor do?[3]

The answer is obvious when you think about it. Investing in both companies rather than in just one eliminates the uncertainty about the investor's return. The investor is certain to get a 10% return on his or her money *regardless* of the weather during the next year. By combining the two companies, the investor gets the expected level of return while removing all risk.

A fundamental principle of finance is that investors will seek to maximize return for a given level of risk and minimize risk for a given level of expected return. In the preceding example, the only rational decision for an investor unable to forecast the weather is to invest in both the umbrella manufacturer and the suntan manufacturer. Investing in only one of the two would expose the investor to unnecessary risk. Investors will not be compensated for bearing any risk they can get rid of without cost; that is, they cannot expect higher returns for bearing diversifiable risk.

This example demonstrates a powerful principle: don't put all your eggs in one basket. Successful professional investors obey this rule. To the extent that they do, the price of risk in the capital markets depends on that part of total risk that cannot be diversified away, not on total risk. Phrased

---

3. This example is drawn from David W. Mullins, "Does the Capital Asset Pricing Model Work?" *Harvard Business Review* (January–February 1982): 105–14.

another way, the discount rate that will be applied to future cash flows to convert them to current dollars (present value) will depend principally on the systematic riskiness of the cash flows. *Systematic risk* is defined as the covariability of the return on the particular asset with the return on a portfolio comprised of all risky assets in the economy (the ultimate diversified portfolio).

Outside the world of academic finance, this is a controversial assertion. It shouldn't be. Still, the principle should not be carried to an illogical extreme. The statement that the price of risk depends solely on the undiversifiable (i.e., systematic) risk applies only to investors with diversified portfolios.

Many rational investors have undiversified portfolios. It is important, then, to distinguish between active and passive investors. Active investors have significant control over the returns they will receive on their investments. An example would be an owner-manager of a company. The owner-manager generally has an undiversified portfolio and must therefore be concerned with total risk, not just systematic risk. Passive investors exercise essentially no control over their investments. It would be irrational for these investors not to diversify their investments, and they will, therefore, measure risk as the systematic component.

For managers acting in the best interests of their diversified shareholders, the cash flows from investing should be discounted at a rate that reflects only the systematic riskiness of the project, not the total risk. This rule applies even to managers who are personally undiversified but are making decisions on behalf of diversified investors.[4] An important corollary is that diversified investors will pay no premium for diversification by companies because they can achieve such diversification on their own at no cost.

RISK, DISCOUNT RATES AND BENCHMARKS

Modern finance textbooks put great emphasis on determining the "right" discount rate or the "correct" cost of capital and often provide complicated formulas for calculating the discount rate. This preoccupation is misguided. The current state of finance theory and experience suggests that the search for exactitude will not be successful. We simply cannot be precise in our calculations.

The inability to be precise does not alleviate managers' responsibility

---

4. This statement is intended to be normative rather than descriptive. Inevitably, managers will take their own personal risk exposure into account in evaluating any decision. The point here is that the performance evaluation and incentive compensation systems should be set up to encourage managers to take risks, per se, and to make decisions using as a metric the effect of the decisions on the wealth of the shareholders.

for estimating the opportunity cost of investing. When making decisions based on value, managers must estimate discount rates, just as they estimate future cash flows.

What, then, is a reasonable discount rate? While a complete discussion of this issue is beyond the scope of this reading, some elementary principles can be outlined. First, it is most useful to think of the determinants of the discount rate as follows:

$$\text{discount rate} = \frac{\text{risk-free}}{\text{rate}} + \frac{\text{business-risk}}{\text{premium}} + \frac{\text{financial-risk}}{\text{premium}}$$

As this equation shows, the discount rate has three elements. The base level is the rate of return required on investments that have no business or financial risk. An example would be a government bond. A premium must be added to reflect business risk. The preceding discussion about what constitutes risk then becomes relevant: for diversified investors and for managers of companies acting on behalf of diversified investors, business risk is measured relative to all risky investments; for undiversified investors, total risk is what matters. Next, a premium for financial risk must be added. When a company or project is financed by using debt, the returns accruing to the equity owner are riskier. The interest must be paid before the shareholder gets any return. Therefore, equity investors will require higher returns (holding all other things constant) from debt-financed investments than they will from equity-financed projects.

This simple description of the determinants of the discount rate does not imply an equally simple way to estimate discount rates in the real world. However, there are some guiding principles. The first source of data must be the capital market's current risk free interest rate. This is the fundamental benchmark. Then, the appropriate premiums must be added, depending on the assessed degree of basic business risk and the financial strategy employed by the company. Once again, a useful, but not infallible, source of data on the riskiness of relevant cash flows and on the required premiums is the capital market.[5]

In estimating discount rates for most complex projects, the best managers can hope to do is decide whether a project is low, middle, or high risk. To expect an analysis to yield more exact estimates would be inappropriate and even dangerous.

---

5. One measure of risk from the capital markets is known as *beta*. Beta is a measure of how sensitive the returns on a given stock are relative to returns on the market. The process of estimating risk and an associated discount rate from capital markets data is fraught with pitfalls. But, these data, when combined with common sense, often offer reasonable guides to the appropriate discount rate. Moreover, there is usually a very close correspondence between virtually all measures of risk, including systematic and unsystematic.

RISK MANAGEMENT

The preceding discussion focused on how the capital markets charge for risk. An issue of greater importance is managing total risk. The basic tools have already been described: pattern recognition and scenario planning. What are the events that will affect the company? How likely are they to occur? How will we respond when and if they occur? What are the likely consequences of the event and the reaction to the event in terms of cash, risk, and value?

Another principle of risk management has already been discussed. Managers should try to get rid of risks if they can do so at relatively low cost. (For passive investors, getting rid of exposure to certain kinds of risk turns out to be simple and cost free: hold a diversified portfolio.) Managers should transfer risk to those most able and willing to bear it. Certain kinds of risks can be transferred to others at low cost. If a major risk confronting a company is the possible death of a top executive, then the company can purchase life insurance on that executive's life. This is an example of an event outside the control of management that can and should be guarded against. The insurance company charges a low premium for the policy, implying a favorable benefit-to-cost ratio. The policy premium is low because the contribution to the risk of the insurance company of adding one more insurance policy to its portfolio is negligible.

Another example of transferable risk is the technological risk inherent in buying a computer. Certain leasing firms specialize in bearing this risk. The larger leasing companies often hold widely diversified portfolios of assets, including many different kinds of computers. By virtue of their diversification and their expertise in managing technological risk, these firms are better able and more willing to bear the risks associated with purchasing a computer. A firm that only needs the services of the computer might be well advised to lease rather than buy one.

The underlying principle of risk management is that company officers should choose with deliberation the risks they are willing to bear.

RISK, TIME AND INVESTMENTS IN RISK REDUCTION

Risk is not constant over time; with the passage of time, uncertainty is usually resolved. A large R&D project may look quite risky at first, but preliminary results, whether good or bad, will gradually reduce the uncertainty.

A useful way to take likely changes in risk into account is to break down the elements of a project into modules, or stages. While the potential returns from such a strategy may be lower than if the project is undertaken all at once, the reduced risk may more than compensate for the lower return.

RISK, PERFORMANCE EVALUATION, AND INCENTIVE COMPENSATION

An important issue for top management is how to evaluate and reward managers operating in uncertain environments. Here are three useful guidelines:

· Measure performance in a relative rather than an absolute sense;
· Assess performance on the basis of value rather than single-period accounting data;
· Compensate managers accordingly

For example, the absolute performance of a manager's business unit may be poor; but this may not mean the manager has done a poor job if the reasons for the poor performance were beyond his or her control—say an economic recession or an unexpected change in the regulatory environment. To keep managers from avoiding all risky decisions, even those with positive net present values, it is essential to compensate them on the basis of how well they respond to actual opportunities. Identifying scenarios for future cash flows and managerial decisions will help top management assess and reward performance.

In assessing performance, top management must also focus on how decisions contribute to long-term value rather than short-term operating results.[6] Managers supervising major strategic investments can have poor current results—low profits or even losses—while doing an outstanding job of creating long-term value. Penalizing these managers could lead to missed investment opportunities and long-term competitive decline. An incentive compensation system that focuses on short-term accounting performance will discourage long-term value building.

RISK AND THE RULES OF THE GAME

Certain rules and regulations—for example, tax policies, antitrust regulations, health and safety regulations—govern every business decision. Naturally, these rules change over time, and the effects of change can be devastating. Planning for alterations in the rules of the game is an essential part of management thinking.

Suppose, for example, that the level of allowable depreciation changes. Depreciation is a noncash charge to pretax income. Increases in

---

6. A consistent theme of this reading has been that value is a useful metric for evaluating the consequences of decisions. This does not mean that managers of publicly traded companies should build corporate strategies based on current stock price. Rather, managers should focus on the long-term fundamental valuation implications of their decisions; in doing so they should not ignore current information from the capital market.

allowable depreciation expense would lead to increased cash flow from any given investment project. A company that has made a high capital expenditure under the prior rules will be at a cash flow disadvantage compared with a competitor that has delayed investing until the new rules were passed.

The point here is simple: ignoring the ways in which changes in the rules of the game can affect the absolute and relative position of the company is a serious mistake.

—— VALUE

Value is determined by the interaction of cash and risk and is affected by investment decisions that create future cash flows and by financing decisions that market the existing and future cash flow streams to shareholders and bondholders.

GETTING YOUR MONEY OUT

A simple rule of finance is that the present value of nothing is nothing. Professional managers and investors must ask a fundamental question before committing resources to any investment: How will I get my money out?

POSITIVE NET PRESENT VALUE DECISIONS

A decision has a positive net present value if the discounted present value of the expected cash flow exceeds the purchase price. If you buy a project and the expected rate of return exceeds the opportunity cost of capital for a project with the same level of risk, then the project has a positive net present value.

Managers who find a project that seems to have a very high expected return and a high net present value must ask and answer one simple question: How will the return be achieved? If this question cannot be answered, the project probably does not have a positive net present value. Investments only have positive net present values when there exists, or is likely to exist, a specific advantage for the company making the investment. These advantages may include superior management, controlled access to scarce resources, product differentiation, economies of scale, or other cost advantages unavailable to the competition.

Once again, a key component of successful pattern recognition is the ability to identify potential positive net present value decisions and to respond to them before the competitive advantage disappears.

SENSITIVITY ANALYSIS

All financial analysis seeks to identify critical assumptions and key managerial concerns. Sensitivity analysis accomplishes this goal through asking a series of simple questions, the answers to which are important because they affect both the initial decision and the way in which subsequent decisions are made.

The objective in sensitivity analysis is identification of the major determinants of value by creating an economic model of a decision. The first step is to break down an aggregate estimate of the cash flow effects of a given decision into major components. The value of each of the component streams can then be calculated, given the magnitude, timing, and estimated riskiness of the relevant cash flows. The values of the component cash flow streams add up to the value of the entire project.

The next step is identifying the key determinants of the project's ultimate value. Almost invariably, the value of the project is highly sensitive to changes in the major assumptions. In measuring the sensitivity of value to these changes, managers must consider not only changes in the level of certain variables but also changes in the timing of certain events.

Consider a typical investment project. Among the questions one might ask would be the following:

- What will happen to value if target market share is never attained?
- What will happen if the target share is attained one year later than projected?
- What will happen if there is a major cost overrun in construction?
- What will happen if inflation differs from the projected level?
- What will happen if interest rates differ from the projected level? (If inflation is different, interest rates are also likely to change.)
- What will be the effects of a typical economic recession? Of a typical economic boom?
- What will happen if unit variable costs are different?
- What will happen if fixed costs vary from those projected?
- What will happen if the competition responds to our moves by lowering price 10% below projections for a period of one year?
- What will happen if the competition's unit costs are lower than ours?
- How low could estimated terminal value fall before the net present value of the decision is zero?
- How high could the estimated discount rate rise before the net present value of the project falls to zero?
- Does making this investment create opportunities to invest later that would not otherwise exist? If so, how valuable are these growth options?

The particular set of questions to be addressed in sensitivity analysis depends on the nature and importance of the decision being analyzed. The skill described earlier as pattern recognition will guide the questioning process; past events that have had a strong impact on the success or failure of projects will be the focus of attention in evaluating future projects. The objective of sensitivity analysis is clear: to locate the crucial determinants of the success or failure of the current decision, taking uncertainty into account.

Like scenario planning, sensitivity analysis focuses on the effects of possible events that are economically important. The difference is that sensitivity analysis seeks to identify the critical assumptions by measuring the degree to which a change in each assumption affects value.

GENERAL EQUILIBRIUM VERSUS PARTIAL EQUILIBRIUM

Economists distinguish between two modes of analysis: partial and general equilibrium. In *partial equilibrium analysis,* the objective is to determine the implications of changing an assumption, holding all other related values constant. In *general equilibrium analysis,* the objective is to determine the effects of changing an assumption, while simultaneously allowing all other related variables to change.

For scenario planning or sensitivity analysis to have meaning, managers must have an understanding of the fundamental economic relationships among certain variables. Consider, for example, the relationship between the level of interest rates and the level of anticipated inflation. Loosely put, the nominal interest rate is equal to the sum of the real interest rate and the expected inflation rate. If a manager wishes to understand the effect of changing the assumed level of anticipated inflation on the value of a specific project, he or she must also consider the effects of changes in the level of interest rates: these two economic quantities are interdependent. Furthermore, the level of economic activity is almost always affected by the level of interest rates and inflation. In turn, the level of revenues (for a cyclical product) are likely to be affected by changes in the assumed level of inflation or interest rates.

The economic conditions in an industry are greatly affected by decisions made by the major participants. If management is studying a decision to cut prices, it must simultaneously consider the response of each of the actual and potential competitors, including indirect competitors that supply substitutable products. Management cannot make a reasonable decision by focusing solely on a partial equilibrium analysis of its own particular situation.

A requisite skill for successful pattern recognition is the ability to see the way in which certain economic variables are related. Some patterns occur time and time again. Analyzing decisions by making assumptions that ignore these fundamental economic relationships is a serious mistake.

VALUE CREATION POTENTIAL FROM FINANCING DECISIONS

Financing a company is the process of marketing claims on the company's current and future economic cash flows. That is, financial decisions entail selling the rights to the free cash flows the company generates. The way in which a company is financed can affect its value in three different ways.

1. By substituting debt for equity in the capital structure, a company can increase the amount of income that can be distributed to and retained by shareholders and bondholders, because interest is a tax-deductible expense. There are, of course, limits to the degree that debt can be added, for increasing debt raises the probability that the company will get into financial difficulty or go bankrupt.
2. At certain times, financial decisions result in value transfers among the various owners of the firm.
3. The method of financing can affect the incentives of the various players, especially management.

Even though employing debt capital to finance a business increases the risk to shareholders, most companies do use debt. The key reasons for concern in these decisions are usually taxes, financial distress, and bankruptcy. First, U.S. tax laws are biased toward debt financing. Interest is a tax-deductible cost; dividends are not. Offsetting this tax advantage is the fact that for the recipient interest income is generally taxed at higher rates than returns from owning common stocks (i.e., dividends and capital gains). On balance, a bias toward debt persists because the total amount of cash flow that can be paid out to and retained by owners (stockholders and bondholders) increases as debt is introduced to the capital structure.[7]

The second factor is financial distress. Companies that have debt outstanding are more likely to find themselves in a position in which they are financially weak and therefore vulnerable. Consider events at Chrysler Corporation in 1980. Many potential car buyers probably avoided buying Chrysler products because they thought the company would go bankrupt and be unable to fulfill warranty obligations. Some suppliers undoubtedly balked at giving credit to Chrysler for the same reason. General Motors, Ford, Toyota, and the other car manufacturers had an incentive to force Chrysler into bankruptcy. Because of its precarious financial position Chrysler would be unable to respond or even threaten to respond to competitors' actions.

Debt in the capital structure did not cause Chrysler's problems; the

---

7. For a more complete discussion of the capital structure decision, see Thomas R. Piper and Wolf A. Weinhold, "How Much Debt Is Right For Your Company?" *Harvard Business Review* (July–August 1982): 106–14.

existence of debt in the capital structure detracted significantly from the basic value of the company; it caused free cash flow and value to be lower than it would have been had the company been all equity financed.

The final factor in the capital structure decision is the risk and cost of bankruptcy. Filing for bankruptcy entails significant losses: management must spend most of its time negotiating with creditors; legal and administrative costs are high; bankrupt companies have great difficulty persuading suppliers and customers to continue to do business with them; companies in bankruptcy often lose the value of options to invest in profitable projects in the future, options that have been created and nurtured in the past. These potential costs of bankruptcy deter the use of debt capital.

In summary, substituting debt for equity in the capital structure increases the risk to which the shareholders are exposed while increasing the expected return. Because the U.S. tax code has a bias toward debt financing, the increase in expected return more than compensates for the increased risk. There are limits, however, to the amount of debt capital that can be employed. These limits result from possible adverse cash effects when a company faces financial difficulty and bankruptcy.

The process of debt financing I have described is one in which the total cash flows that a company can distribute, and hence its total market value, is affected by the capital structure decision. Another way in which financial decisions can affect value has more to do with value transfers than with value creation. The total size of the (value) pie is not changed by these decisions, but the size of the different slices is.

For example, some financial decisions entail selling or buying securities that are incorrectly priced. An example would be the decision to issue stock when the manager believes the stock is overvalued. If the stock is too high, given the firm's prospects, this decision results in a value transfer from new shareholders (they paid too high a price) to old shareholders and management, who benefit to the extent of the overvaluation.

Another example of value transfer is when a management decision changes the character of the cash flow stream in a way unanticipated by former capital suppliers. If management changes from a conservative to a risky company strategy, the suppliers of debt will suffer a capital loss, and their loss will accrue to the owners of the equity. An essential element of both these examples of value transfers is the ability of management to fool some group of suppliers of capital.

Finally, the way in which a company is financed can affect its value by changing managers' incentives in positive or negative ways. I will return to this point in the next section.

It is important to keep in mind the degree to which making financial decisions can add value to a company. The ability to create value by purely financial machinations pales in comparison to the potential to create value by making investment decisions. That is, opportunities to create value are more likely to reside on the lefthand than on the righthand side of the balance sheet.[8]

VALUE, CONTRACTS AND INCENTIVES

As we noted in the section on cash, a company's performance evaluation and incentive compensation systems can affect managerial behavior. Similarly, the nature of the contracts between the managers of the firm and the suppliers of capital will affect managerial behavior. The goal of the manager (and of the investor) should be to negotiate individual contracts that make sense in terms of cash, risk, and value, and to select a mix of contracts (e.g., debt and equity) that create rather than detract from value. Two problems may appear in connection with contracts. First, contract provisions may be counterproductive to increasing value. Consider bank loan covenants that often prescribe minimum levels of working capital or coverage ratios. Such covenants may be drafted in such a way as to cause managers seeking to avoid technical default to make decisions that lower value—either by increasing risk or decreasing cash potential. In such cases, the banker who wrote the covenant ends up detracting from what is, after all, the only possible source of repayment: the value of the company.

Second, the *mix* of contracts might affect behavior. Consider, for example, the existence of debt in the capital structure. A management acting in the best interests of shareholders may decide to forgo investing in a project that would increase net present value because all the gains would accrue to the owners of the debt and not to the shareholders. In this case, the existence of debt has caused management to make a decision that detracts from value. However, in situations in which a firm is near bankruptcy, there may be an incentive for management to invest in a very risky project, even if it has a negative net present value. The reason is simple: the shareholders have a worthless claim unless the firm strikes it rich.

On the other hand, having debt outstanding might have a positive effect on managerial decision making. Evidence suggests, for example, that managers perform better after leveraged buyouts than before; these managers often end up with a larger share of equity after the buyout than they had before and thus have strong incentives to perform well. In contrast to the destructive incentive effects described above, the effect in the case of issuing large amounts of debt in leveraged buyouts seems to be positive.

The nature of the contract between the managers and the suppliers of

---

8. One way in which financial decisions might affect value has been omitted from this list. In some cases, potential buyers of streams of free cash flows will disagree over value, even if they have exactly the same information. Reasons for disagreement might include different assessments of risk or different cash flow expectations. To the extent managers can identify the groups willing to pay the highest price for an equity or debt stake, value can be enhanced.

capital can also act as a mechanism for separating highly capable from less capable managers. Consider, for example, two possible contracts governing an infusion of capital into a venture. In the first, the entrepreneur demands 51% of the business. In the second, the entrepreneur expresses a goal of 51% ownership but is willing at the beginning to give 100% of the equity to the supplier of capital while earning the 51% on the basis of actual performance set forth in a plan. Such an entrepreneur is making a strong statement of faith in his or her own abilities to perform; willingness to accept capital on these terms signals commitment and may result in superior performance in the long run.

THE CONCEPT OF MARKET EFFICIENCY

One of the most pervasive notions in financial economics is that the capital markets are efficient. An efficient capital market is one in which prices accurately reflect all relevant information at each point in time. If prices reflect information in this way, then prices are said to be fair: investors cannot expect to achieve returns on their investments that exceed the opportunity cost of investing in the asset. Therefore, according to economists, there are no positive net present value investment opportunities in efficient capital markets: all decisions have a zero net present value. Capital markets are efficient simply because they are extremely competitive. There are lots of well-informed, rational, intelligent players trying to gain an advantage.

Many professional managers and investors, however, do not believe the capital market is efficient. They cite numerous examples of incorrect pricing or irrationality. It is not essential that managers accept the economist's view of capital market efficiency without question. The important point is that managers should, in fact, be skeptical. Assuming that every price observed in the capital markets is wrong is more dangerous than assuming the opposite. The road to bankruptcy is littered with companies whose executives acted on the belief that prices were wrong. Such dangerous beliefs may be reflected in statements that:

- We should defer raising the money needed for capital expenditures because interest rates are going to fall.
- We should borrow short term because short-term rates are a lot lower than long-term interest rates.
- We should issue debt rather than equity because our stock price is grossly undervalued.

Clearly, the level of interest rates or stock prices is of great importance to managers, and some projects do not make sense when the cost of capital is too high in an absolute sense. The question posed here, however, is whether managers are capable of identifying incorrect rates or prices. Basing strategic decisions on faith in such skills appears to be ill advised.

Managers should also be wary of basing decisions on the perception that certain kinds of financial decisions affect capital market valuations. For example, some analysts recommend that companies not enter into mergers when the effect of the merger would be to dilute earnings per share. Managers' assumption should be that the capital market can see through the short-term accounting effects of the merger to the real, long-term economic effects. Moreover, if some managers or investors can see the true economic effects of the merger, then they can profit at the expense of those who do not understand. It is exactly this phenomenon—the reaction of smart investors to profit potential from economic analysis—that suggests that markets do react to real effects, not solely to financial or accounting effects. Although many strictly financial decisions are benign (e.g., stock splits or stock dividends), others—such as a decision not to make an acquisition that would create true economic value because of earnings-per-share dilution—are not defensible in a reasonably competitive and efficient capital market.

In summary, when managers believe they have identified potential market inefficiency, they should be prepared to say why it exists and why they alone have been smart enough to identify the inefficiency. Generally, prolonged inefficiencies will only exist in situations in which there are few competitors or in which information necessary to value a security is not freely available.

OPTIONS AND VALUES

An option is defined as the right to do something at some future date under a predetermined set of conditions. In securities markets, for example, the owner of a call option has the right to purchase a common stock at a set price (the exercise price) at any point over a specified period of time (time to maturity). A put option gives someone the right to sell a stock at a fixed price during the relevant period.

For the entrepreneur and general manager, it is important to understand the characteristics of options and their valuation. It is not easy to value options correctly using traditional discounted cash flow techniques. But understanding the determinants of the value of options is essential because many of the decisions managers make are similar to the decision to exercise an option or have the effect of creating new options that can be exercised later. The option element in various decisions is described below.

- A decision to enter a new product market on a small scale may create options to invest more at a future date. Viewed in isolation, the entry decision may not make sense (i.e., has a negative net present value). But if the initial foray into the market enables the company to invest heavily and profitably once a position has been established, it should not be rejected without taking into account the value creation potential from subsequent decisions.

- Expenditures on research and development create options to invest in subsequent product development. That is, R&D spending creates value indirectly by providing a company with the ability to pursue (or abandon) commercial introduction of ideas that result from it.

- When considering any investment decision, managers should assess the option to abandon the project at an intermediate stage. In some cases, it will make sense to scrap the project (i.e., exercise the option) rather than to continue. The value associated with the option to abandon may make a marginal project economically attractive.

- Venture capitalists often insist on investing money in stages. This reflects their perception of the value of the option to abandon the venture at different points in time. Similarly, the demand of many venture capital investors for a right of first refusal constitutes an option to put in more money where warranted.

- Financial securities often involve options. For example, a convertible bond is a regular bond with an option that gives the holder the right to buy common stock at a fixed price over some specified period of time. A callable bond is one that grants the issuer the option to buy the bond back at a fixed price at some point in the future.

- A line of credit is equivalent to an option granted to a company to borrow at some point in the future under predetermined conditions.

- Incentive compensation schemes sometime involve options. Managers are often given options to purchase stock at a fixed price for some specified time period.

- A company pension plan has two separate option elements. First, beneficiaries of the plan have a call on the assets of the firm equal to the value of the liability. This liability is offset by the value of the existing assets invested in the pension fund. In addition, the company has the option to put the liability to the Pension Benefit Guarantee Corporation in the event of bankruptcy.

- At a more general level, owning stock in a company with debt outstanding is like having the option to buy the whole company at a fixed price—the value of the outstanding bonds. In some sense, the bondholders own the company but have issued the stockholders the right to buy the company back by paying off the bonds.

- Limited liability can be thought of as an option granted to the stockholders of a company to transfer ownership of the company to the bondholders by defaulting when the total value of the firm is less than the face value of the debt.

- A warranty contract provides the consumer with the option to put the equipment back to the producer to be fixed or replaced. This

option is valuable to the consumer and therefore represents a
liability to the company issuing the warranty.
· A loan guarantee is an option to transfer a liability to the guaran-
teeing party.

Options have value. Determining the value of particular options can
be tricky, but there are some fundamental principles. In assessing the value
of a simple call option on a publicly traded common stock, four factors are
important.

1. *Time to Maturity.* The longer the option exists, the more valuable
   it is.
2. *Level of Uncertainty.* The greater the uncertainty (as measured by
   the standard deviation of expected returns) about the value of the
   common stock, the more valuable the option.
3. *Level of Interest Rates.* The higher the interest rates, the higher
   the value of the option.
4. *Level of the Exercise Price.* The higher the exercise price relative
   to the value of the stock, the lower the value of the option.

An intuitive explanation can be provided for each of these factors. The
first is obvious: having a longer period of time in which to decide whether or
not to exercise an option increases the likelihood that the stock price will
exceed the exercise price.

With respect to uncertainty, consider the case in which the exercise
price exceeds the current price of the stock. If there were no uncertainty about
the future price of the stock (i.e., the price remains constant), the option would
be worthless. However, if the future price is unknown and might exceed the
exercise price, then the option has value. The higher the degree of uncertainty
about the future price, the more one should be willing to pay for the option.

The fact that a high degree of uncertainty is associated with a high
value for an option seems counterintuitive. Normally, one would expect a
lower value because of the high risk. In this case, however, because the value
of an option cannot be less than zero, increased uncertainty is associated only
with an increased probability that the value of the stock will be high relative
to the exercise price.

The level of interest rates affects the value of options because buying
an option to purchase a stock in the future at a fixed price is like getting a
free loan. The amount of the loan is the exercise price. The higher the level
of interest rates, the more valuable the loan.

Finally, if the exercise price is high relative to the current stock price,
the value of the option to buy the stock is not high, because it is unlikely that
the stock price will ever exceed the exercise price.

One element missing from the above list is the expected return on the
common stock. Investors can create a perfect hedge by buying a stock and
selling call options on the stock. A perfect hedge is one for which the expected
return is risk-free: there is no uncertainty about the income that will result

from the strategy. The return is the same whether the stock price increases or decreases. The value of an option is determined in relation to the stock price, given the expected volatility, interest rates, exercise price, and time to maturity. Whether the stock price is expected to increase or decrease does not change the value of the option.

However, expected return is absent from the list of determinants of an option's value only when a hedged position can be created. For many option-like decisions confronting managers, it is simply not feasible to find the publicly traded options necessary to create hedges. In these cases, the value of the underlying option will depend in part on the expected return or price of the underlying asset, as well as on the level of uncertainty about the expected return. The other factors in the list will also be important. The fact that both expected return and uncertainty enter the valuation equation suggests that a fundamental role of management is to manage the risk/reward trade-off. And even though high uncertainty is associated with high option values, managers must still manage risk in order to maximize return for a given level of risk.

The manager confronts many investment and financing decisions that have option-like characteristics. Understanding how to value the options is essential to making reasoned decisions. For entrepreneurial ventures in particular, a great deal of the firm's value lies in options to invest rather than in assets already in place. Knowing what constitutes a valuable option, knowing when to exercise the option, and understanding the factors that influence the valuation of the option are all skills required to be successful in new ventures.

THE VALUE OF FINANCIAL FLEXIBILITY

Opportunities to invest can arrive without warning. To survive in a competitive product market, firms must be able to invest when the time is right. Financial flexibility is defined as the ability to invest or threaten credibly to invest when needed. Maintaining financial flexibility is like owning an option to exercise the option to invest.

Financial flexibility has value. Maintaining financial flexibility, however, entails incurring costs. For example, a firm may decide to keep cash balances on hand that exceed the level required to meet transaction balances. The interest income on these balances may be taxed at the corporate level and at the individual level if the income is paid out in the form of dividends. Shareholders of companies with large cash balances would in some sense be better off if the cash were distributed to them and they invested in marketable securities on their own account. Then the income would be taxed only once at the individual level. Corporations are simply not tax-efficient banks.

Does this mean that companies should never hold excess cash balances? No, because having excess cash gives a company the ability to exercise valuable investment opportunities as need arises. And since the competition knows that the company can afford to respond to competitive thrusts by retaliatory investing, the competition may decide not to attack the firm's position in the product market in the first place.

Maintaining financial flexibility clearly has some benefits. However, because it is costly to keep financial reserves on hand, whether in the form of excess cash, unused debt capacity, or lines of credit, firms do not maintain unlimited flexibility.

Financial flexibility, per se, does not necessarily mean that a company can invest or threaten credibly to invest when the need arises. The organization must also be able to respond to changes in the economic environment. If, for example, a company has a rigid capital budgeting system, it may be difficult to exercise valuable investment options that arise outside the normal budgeting cycle. Some investment options decline precipitously in value if they are not acted upon quickly.

SUMMARY

Finance is a way of thinking about cash, risk, and value. Managers must be able to view problems from the financial perspective as well as from other perspectives. But finance does not answer questions; it does not make decisions. Finance can help identify the right questions to ask and narrow down the options. When viewed from the finance perspective, some decisions will turn out to be illogical or unfeasible. Deciding what should not or cannot be done is a valuable aid to general managers.

Finance also teaches skepticism. The number of profitable investment opportunities people think exists far exceeds the actual number. Figuring out how a particular decision will create value is a key responsibility of management and does not require elaborate systems. Financial analysis can be carried out in the mind as well as on paper. Finance is thinking hard about the future course of events and trying to chart a sensible path.

Finally, financial thinking is useful only to the extent it helps managers make better decisions. The emphasis must be on action. A recurrent danger in employing the financial perspective is that it can easily become an excuse for inaction.

—— DISCUSSION QUESTIONS

1. As the reading suggests, a finance perspective is both vital and risky. In what ways can a preoccupation with financial analysis jeopardize a firm's well-being? How can the finance perspective help the general manager make sound decisions in other functional areas—personnel, marketing, and production, for example?

2. How do the responsibilities and objectives of the accountant differ from those of the general manager with a financial perspective?

3. Choose a type of business that interests you—in retail, high technology, or service, for example. Identify important patterns that would affect cash flow.

4. Suppose you are an executive sketching scenarios in the business you chose in question 3. What kind of decisions could you or your managers make if your goal was to maximize accounting income? What kinds of decision could help build long-term value? What risks does the latter decision entail?

5. "If the firm's objective is to maximize value, and value depends on cash and risk, then the incentive compensation system must focus on all these factors." What kinds of compensation policies and practices in an organization will encourage managers to focus on opportunities to maximize value?

15   Venture Capital

CONSTANCE BAGLEY and CRAIG DAUCHY

In this chapter, Bagley (of Stanford Business School) and Dauchy (of Cooley Godward LLP) provide an overview of venture capital (VC) and the role it can play in financing new ventures. Although VC is a well-known form of financing, it is relatively uncommon: most new ventures are still funded by family and friends, or the entrepreneur's own capital. Yet, because VC is used to finance many high-profile start-ups, it receives a great deal of attention.

The authors explain what venture capitalists are looking for, and how they evaluate a business plan. They also offer an excellent overview of the language used by VCs and the typical terms governing their investment.

This chapter builds on discussions introduced in The Entrepreneur's Guide to Business Law *by Bagley and Dauchy, and develops them in the context of an entrepreneur seeking venture capital.*

The most common sources of capital for start-up enterprises are the entrepreneur and the entrepreneur's family and friends. For the most part, institutional investors have little interest in investing in start-up companies. One notable exception is the investment funds that comprise the venture capital industry. In the past forty years venture capitalists have grown some of the nation's leading companies, including Cisco, Netscape, Amgen, Genentech, Microsoft, and Sun Microsystems. Venture capitalists are making investments at a record pace. In 1996, the venture capital industry invested more than $10 billion in more than 1200 companies, according to VentureOne, a San Francisco firm that researches the industry. Venture funds raised $6.3 billion from investors in 1996, a new record. Venture capital money is available as never before to fund the dreams of entrepreneurs.

This chapter first discusses the pros and cons of seeking venture capital, then outlines strategies for finding it, and provides tips for preparing business plans to present to venture capitalists. It then highlights factors to consider when selecting a venture capitalist. Next follows a discussion of how the parties reach agreement on a valuation for the company, and thus the percentage of the equity the venture capitalists will receive in exchange for their investment. The chapter then analyzes the rights and protections normally given venture capitalists buying preferred stock. These include the liquidation preference, the dividend preference, redemption rights, conversion rights, antidilution provisions (including preemptive rights and price-protection provisions), voting rights, registration rights, information rights, and co-sale rights. The chapter concludes with a brief description of the vesting requirements normally imposed by venture capitalists, and their expectations with respect to the granting of employee stock options.

Certain aspects of the topics covered in this chapter were introduced [elsewhere]. This chapter will build on those discussions and further develop them in the context of an entrepreneur seeking venture capital.

DECIDING WHETHER TO SEEK VENTURE CAPITAL

The first question the entrepreneur should consider in deciding whether to pursue venture capital is whether the new venture will meet the criteria used by most venture capitalists (often referred to as *VCs*). Generally, a venture capitalist will want to invest a substantial amount of money, usually more than $500,000 and often more than $1,000,000. However, a few funds will do seed investing for a new start-up at a lower level. Venture capitalists are usually looking for an enterprise that has the potential to grow to a significant size quickly and to generate an annual return on investment in excess of 40%. Venture capitalists need to target that rate of return to realize the compounded returns of at least 20% per annum expected by their investors.

For the most part, venture capitalists have focused on the information-technology industry, which includes computer hardware and software, scientific instruments, telecommunications, multimedia, and, most recently, cyberspace. Venture-backed public companies include Netscape, Yahoo!, and Apple Computer. The second largest concentration of venture capital investing has been in life science companies, including those focusing on biotechnology, medical devices, diagnostics, and therapeutics. Genentech and Amgen were both venture-backed. Although venture capital investment remains most concentrated in these two fields, venture capitalists are financial investors seeking an optimal rate of return, and they have invested successfully in other areas such as retail, consumer products, new materials, health services, and environmental technology. For example, Odwalla, a fresh-juice producer based in Half Moon Bay, California, relied on venture capital to grow before going public in 1993.

Venture capital financing can be an attractive funding source for a number of reasons. Venture capital may allow the entrepreneur to raise all of the capital from one source, or from a lead investor who can attract other venture funds. Venture capitalists have experience with the challenges of start-ups and know how to grow a company to an initial public offering, sale of the business, or other liquidity event. Experienced venture capitalists have a large network of contacts who can help the company succeed. Venture capitalists are often able to provide valuable assistance in recruiting other members of the management team. Being venture-backed gives an enterprise a certain cachet, which can open doors to other financing and resources.

Most venture capitalists look for companies that can provide liquidity in three to five years. If an entrepreneur is looking for a longer time horizon—a factor that should be discussed with any investor—the enterprise may not be suitable for venture capital. Other reasons to avoid using venture capital funding include these: (1) Venture investors are more sophisticated and may drive a harder bargain on pricing their investment than friends or family; (2) venture investors may be more likely to assert their power in molding the enterprise than more passive investors; and (3) venture investors may be more interested than passive investors in taking control of the enterprise if the entrepreneur stumbles.

Most commonly, an entrepreneur's choice will be between raising the funds from family and friends and obtaining venture capital financing. Family and friends may be willing to invest at a lower price (i.e., to accept a higher valuation of the company at the time they invest) but often bring little else to the table. Venture capitalists may demand a lower valuation but will almost always bring many intangibles that can assist the company to grow faster and to be more successful. Often this decision is referred to as the choice between "dumb money" and "smart money."

——— FINDING VENTURE CAPITAL

Sending unsolicited business plans to a venture capital firm is almost certainly a formula for failure. Venture capitalists receive dozens of unsolicited plans each week. Very few of these plans are read thoroughly, if at all, and even fewer lead to financing.

A good way to get a venture capitalist's attention is to arrange an introduction by someone who knows the venture capitalist. If the entrepreneur has friends who have obtained venture capital financing, they may be able to provide the introduction. Similarly, personnel at universities, government labs, and other entities that license technology to venture-backed companies may have connections worth pursuing. Accountants and bankers who

---

From the Trenches

Three entrepreneurs—Dr. Arnold Kresch, Dr. George Savage, and Andrew Thompson—incorporated FemRx in November 1994. Dr. Kresch had an idea for a new resectoscope to treat abnormal uterine bleeding. Under visual guidance, the scope could be used to collect a pathology sample, resect (cut) the endometrial lining and automatically remove the excised tissue from the uterus, and coagulate the entire uterine cavity. The founders believed that they could build a significant company quickly based on the Kresch invention and possibly go public at an early stage, but only if they had the assistance and imprimatur of experienced venture capitalists. In April 1995, FemRx raised $6 million in a financing led by Sprout Capital and U.S. Venture Partners. The venture capitalists helped recruit key employees and directors, provided valuable direction on product development, and introduced the company to potential investment bankers. In March 1996, FemRx was taken public by Robertson Stephens & Company and Dillon, Read & Co. Inc. at a post-money valuation of $75 million.

---

do business with venture-backed companies also are good sources for introductions, as are money managers at pension funds, insurance companies, universities, and other institutions that invest in venture funds.

Perhaps the best way to find venture money is to engage a lawyer who works primarily in the venture capital field as a business attorney. Although many lawyers may have done a venture capital deal, fewer than a dozen law firms nationwide truly specialize in representing venture-backed companies. More than half of these law firms are located in or near northern California's Silicon Valley.

In choosing a law firm, an entrepreneur should ask for information about the venture funds that the law firm has formed, the number and identity of venture funds the firm has represented in investments, and the venture-backed companies the firm represents. A law firm that specializes in this area will have lists of these clients readily available. Less experienced firms may speak in generalities.

A firm that specializes in this area will also have lawyers with the experience to give information and advice, and to ensure that negotiations with the venture capitalists go smoothly. Although deal-making in the venture capital industry is not rocket science, it is a bit clubby, and it helps to have an attorney who knows the club rules.

Because it is a small club, it is likely that the entrepreneur's lawyer may have represented, or is currently representing, the venture capitalist. The legal code of ethics requires that the attorney disclose his or her involvement in other transactions to both parties and obtain appropriate consents. An entrepreneur may wish to explore with the attorney his or her relationships with the venture capitalists to whom the entrepreneur is being introduced.

Because attorneys in this industry work with a large number of venture capitalists, they should be able to introduce the entrepreneur to those venture capitalists who would be most interested in this particular deal. Most venture capitalists specialize in particular industries; thus, it does not make much sense to present an Internet deal to a venture capitalist who specializes in medical device companies. Venture capitalists also tend to prefer to invest at a particular stage of development: *seed* (raw start-up); *early stage* (product in beta testing or just being shipped); *later stage* (product is fully developed or is being sold and generating revenue); or *mezzanine* (the financing round before the anticipated initial public offering).

There are a number of sources of printed and electronic information on the venture industry. An entrepreneur may wish to consult published guides such as *Pratt's Guide to Venture Capital* and *West Coast Venture Capital*; magazines that cover the industry such as *Upside* and *The Red Herring*; and reports from information-gathering organizations such as VentureOne Corporation, Venture Economics, and Securities Data Corporation. An entrepreneur may also want to use Nexis or a similar on-line service to cull news articles on particular companies or venture capitalists. Some information also may be available on the World Wide Web.

——— SELECTING A VENTURE CAPITALIST

Generally, an entrepreneur begins the process of seeking venture capital by preparing a business plan, although many deals have been done without a plan. However, plans prepared for venture capitalists should be more concise and less legalistic than plans prepared for other investors. Venture capitalists are very sophisticated and do not need, or expect, the type of disclosure mandated by federal and state securities laws for sales to less experienced investors.

The business plan prepared for circulation to venture capitalists usually describes the product or service concept and the opportunity for investors. Typically, the plan includes sections describing the industry, the market, the means for producing the product or delivering the service, the competition, the superiority of this product or service over existing products or services, the marketing plan, the barriers to entry, and the strengths of the management team. Projections and the assumptions on which they are based are generally included. The entrepreneur should prepare an executive summary, keeping in mind that many venture capitalists will not read beyond the first paragraph of that summary. Therefore, the compelling reason to make the investment should appear at the top of the executive summary and should be borne out by the remainder of the plan. An experienced lawyer can assist in editing the business plan.

Most venture capitalists will focus on the viability of the concept, the size of the opportunity, and the quality of the management team. To the extent that there are holes in the team (e.g., the team has technicians but no experienced managers, or the team lacks a strong CFO or VP of Marketing), these weaknesses should be acknowledged in discussions with venture capitalists, and the venture capitalists should be asked for assistance in finding the right people. More than one venture capitalist has said that the three most important factors in making an investment are "people, people, and people." The right team can fix a flawed concept, but a flawed team cannot get a brilliant concept to market.

Venture capitalists comment that certain weaknesses appear again and again in the plans they review. The following are some common pitfalls:

- **The plan is too long.** Most venture capitalists will have little tolerance for reading more than fifteen to twenty pages. Details such as projections, financials, press clips, detailed biographies, detailed schematics, and detailed market analysis can be shortened, eliminated (for now, but presented later to those really interested), or moved into appendices for the most interested reader.
- **The executive summary is too long.** The executive summary should be one page and should concisely describe (1) the market; (2) the unmet need in the market; (3) the compelling solution offered by the entrepreneur; (4) the strategy for connecting the need, the solution, and the customers; (5) the technology or other proprietary aspects of the solution that will give this venture an edge over the competition; and (6) the experience of the team that demonstrates that the plan can be implemented.
- **The opportunity is too small.** There are many good business opportunities that are too small for venture investors because of their need to earn a high return on investment. Although other investors might be willing to put up $2 million to grow a company into a $25 million business with net income of 10% of sales in five years, these returns are too low to interest most venture capitalists.
- **The plan is poorly organized.** A poorly organized plan suggests that the team may be incapable of taking on the larger task of organizing a company. There is no set formula, but a plan should have a logical progression and should not be overly focused on one area at the expense of others. For example, many plans drafted by engineers devote substantial pages to explaining the technology in minute detail but fail to adequately describe the market, the competition, or the strategy for connecting customers and the product.
- **The plan lacks focus.** Many plans call for a company to pursue multiple opportunities simultaneously in multiple markets. The more complex the story, the harder it is to sell to venture capitalists. Great opportunities are conveyed in few words (e.g., remember "plastics" from the movie *The Graduate*). Focus on the greatest opportunity. The other opportunities can be discussed later or handled in a very brief section toward the back of the plan.

Once introductions are made, venture capitalists will follow up with meetings if they are interested in investing. This begins a courtship process that typically takes two to three months. For this reason, it is a good idea to engage a number of venture capitalists in discussions simultaneously, rather than serially. Generally, venture capitalists will be quick to let a company know if they are interested. Follow-up meetings are an expression of interest, and many venture capital funds hold weekly internal meetings to discuss the status of various prospects.

As a part of this courtship, the venture capitalists will perform due diligence. *Due diligence* is the process through which venture capitalists will examine a company's concept, product, potential market, financial health, and legal situation. Due diligence is typically conducted by venture capitalists or consultants with financial and technical expertise and by lawyers. This means they often will send in a technical or industry expert to meet with the entrepreneur and take a close look at the technology or concept. Also, the venture capitalist may talk with potential customers to help understand the size of the potential market for the product.

Similarly, as the courtship continues, the entrepreneur should perform due diligence on the venture capitalist. Much information can be gathered conversationally. Appropriate questions include these:

- What other companies within this industry has the venture fund invested in?
- What deals has this particular venture capitalist done?
- On what boards does the venture capitalist sit?
- How many more years are there to run in the fund that will be making the investment?
- Will the venture capitalist be willing and able to participate in the next round of financing?
- Are there other venture capital firms that the venture capitalist thinks should be invited into the deal?
- Would the venture capitalist be willing to work alongside other venture capitalists with whom the entrepreneur is in discussions?
- How has the venture capitalist handled management changes in the past?
- Are there any founders who were pushed aside or pushed out?
- What is the time horizon for this investment?
- What if there is no exit event providing liquidity by that date?
- What kind of return does the venture capitalist need to make on this investment?

The venture capitalist should be asked to provide introductions to other founders of companies in which he or she has invested, and those founders should be contacted to provide insight on the kind of partner the venture capitalist is likely to be.

If it is possible to attract and accommodate more than one venture capitalist in a round, it can be to the company's advantage to do so. Although it may be a bit more complicated to work with more than one venture investor, it does increase the network of resources available to the company. In addition, another venture capitalist may be able to serve as a counterbalance if the entrepreneur and the first venture capitalist end up at loggerheads on some issue. Such venture capitalists are often excellent partners. However, some venture capitalists will not participate in a deal unless they are the only investor or the only lead investor.

In raising money during the next round of venture capital, the company will want to be able to tell new investors that the prior-round investors are stepping up to invest more. Often the lead venture capitalist in the prior round will allow the new investor(s) to take the lead in negotiating with the company the price of the stock in the subsequent round. Once price is set, the lead investors from the prior round will indicate how much stock they will buy. If there is more than one venture capitalist in the initial round, the company will stand a better chance of having at least one of the existing investors invest in the next round. Also, if the company underperforms, the entrepreneur is more likely to have an ally who can coax further investment from the group if there are several venture investors in the initial round.

——— DETERMINING THE VALUATION

Eventually, a venture capitalist will indicate that he or she is ready to make the investment, and the discussion will turn to valuation. In essence, this is a discussion of price: How much will the venture capitalist pay for what percentage of the company?

The venture capitalist's offer is often communicated in an arcane shorthand that is unfathomable to the uninitiated. For example, a venture capitalist might say,

- "I'll put in $2 million based on three pre-money."
- "I'm thinking two-thirds based on three pre-; that will get you to five post."
- "I'm looking for two-fifths of the company post-money, and for that I'll put up the two."
- "It's worth $3 million pre-money, and I want to own 40% of it after we close."

What does all this mean? This is exactly the question the entrepreneur needs to ask to make sure that there is no misunderstanding about the price being offered.

Each of the above statements is a different way of expressing exactly the same proposal. The venture capitalist is willing to invest $2 million in the company. The terms *pre-money* and *post-money* refer to what valuation is put on the company before and after the investment. The venture capitalist is proposing that the company is worth $3 million before the investment of

---

From the Trenches

Polly President, the founder of a multimedia company, bootstrapped her company into a leader in its nascent industry. The company had been financed by family and friends, plus modest earnings. With the advent of cyberspace, Polly decided to raise $2.5 million in venture capital to move into the new medium. By chance, she was introduced to Joe Venture, a venture capitalist who had just set up a new fund for cyberspace investing. Polly had little time to devote to fund-raising, and because the discussions with Joe were going so well, she decided not to seek introductions to any other venture capitalists. After weeks of discussion, Joe and Polly agreed on a valuation, and Joe sent over a term sheet. Unbeknownst to Polly, Joe's prior employment had been in the banking industry, and he had only recently moved into the bank's venture fund, which did only mezzanine investing (the financing round before an anticipated public offering). The term sheet Joe presented looked more like a complex loan deal than a venture deal, due both to his background in banking and the focus of mezzanine-round investors on protecting against the downside (due to the limited upside of a mezzanine deal). It took more than five months to conclude a deal with Joe, and the ultimate deal contained highly unusual downside protection for Joe's fund. Although Joe had the right industry focus for Polly's company, an inquiry about his experience would have revealed that he was the wrong investor for this stage of investment.

Comment: Had Polly pursued multiple investors and selected a more appropriate venture capitalist, she would have saved time and been able to negotiate a less onerous deal.

$2 million and is therefore worth $5 million immediately after the investment. The amount of ownership being requested is an amount equivalent to $66\frac{2}{3}\%$ of the equity based on the pre-money number (i.e., $2 million/$3 million), which is 40% of the company measured immediately after the closing of the deal (i.e., $2 million/$5 million). It is a very good idea to ask what dollar amount is to be invested and what the percentages of the equity are that translate into pre- and post-money.

If the investor knows the number of shares the company has outstanding, he or she may give the entrepreneur a per-share price. It is relatively easy to translate valuations based on share prices into pre- and post-money company valuations, and vice versa. For example, if 6 million shares were outstanding, 4 million shares would need to be issued at $0.50 per share for a venture capitalist to invest $2 million and end up owning 40% of the company.

If one knows what percentage the investor wants to own after the deal closes, one can back into the number of shares that will need to be issued through the following two equations:

(1) Shares outstanding post-money = Shares outstanding pre-money divided by 1 minus the percentage to be owned by investor post-money

(2) Shares to be issued = Shares outstanding post-money minus shares
outstanding pre-money

Accordingly, if 6 million shares are outstanding pre-money and the venture capitalist wants to end up owning 40% of the company, then 6 million divided by 60% (i.e., 1 minus .40) tells us that 10 million shares need to be outstanding after the offering. Therefore, the company will need to issue 4 million new shares.

Often there is some negotiation during pricing discussions. A venture capitalist may ask what valuation the company is seeking or may volunteer a ballpark figure for pricing. Valuing a company is never easy. It is especially difficult with a start-up, which has no operating history. Venture capitalists will often base their valuations on management's own projections and on other deals done in the industry by other companies. Obtaining information on comparable companies that have received venture financing can help the entrepreneur establish the right valuation.

The entrepreneur should press the venture capitalist on how the reservation of shares for future stock issuances to employees will work or, alternatively, propose to the venture capitalist how it will work. For example, if the venture capitalist's offer of $2 million is for 40% of the company *including* the reservation of 1 million shares for options, then he or she is saying that there are in effect 7 million shares outstanding or reserved (not 6 million). Therefore, under the formulas set forth above, the venture capitalist would be entitled to 4.667 million shares (not 4 million) for the $2 million investment. Applying the formulas:

$$11.667 \text{ million} = \frac{7 \text{ million}}{60\%}$$

$$4.667 \text{ million} = 11.667 \text{ million} - 7 \text{ million}$$

If this is not what the entrepreneur has in mind, the company should propose that the 1 million reserved shares should *not* be taken into account in the valuation. If they are not, then the venture capitalist will be issued 4 million shares, as we saw above. In that case, the holders of the 6 million old shares and the venture capitalist holding the 4 million new shares will jointly bear the dilution for the 1 million reserved shares in a ratio of 60/40, rather than having the holders of the 6 million old shares bear all of the dilution.

When the entrepreneur is confident that an offer is about to be made, or immediately after an offer is made, he or she will want to inform the other potential venture capitalists and ask any that remain interested for their offers. Provided that they have had a chance to do some due diligence and to discuss the investment with their colleagues within the fund, other venture capitalists who are interested in the deal will generally put their valuation offers on the table fairly quickly. These valuations may differ sustantially, and the entrepreneur may attempt to use the higher offers to persuade others to pay a higher price.

The venture capitalist willing to pay the highest price is not necessarily the person whom the entrepreneur will want most in the deal. Another venture capitalist who is not willing to pay quite as much may be a better partner in growing the business. Due diligence in the form of reference checks should be undertaken by the entrepreneur to determine who the best partners might be. An entrepreneur who has more than one offer should be pleased and move quickly to choose the investors and finalize the deal. Indeed, if the entrepreneur is extremely comfortable with the venture capitalist with whom he or she has been primarily negotiating, the entrepreneur may decide not to shop the offer to other venture capitalists after reviewing the initial offer but may simply proceed to a closing.

Although it may seeem like a good idea just to get all the suitors into a room to negotiate the price, this approach should be resisted. There is little incentive for those offering the higher valuation to talk the lower offerors into offering more, and the lower offerors may convince those willing to pay a higher price that they are paying too much.

The final price will depend on whom the entrepreneur wants to have in the deal and how much money needs to be raised. For tax reasons and for fairness, generally there is just one price paid for the stock in a round. Once the valuation is agreed upon, it is unusual to revisit the issue, unless there is a material adverse change in the business before the closing, or material adverse information is discovered. Although most venture capitalists will not attempt to renegotiate the price absent those kinds of developments, there are always some who feel that all items are negotiable before the deal is closed. To avoid these types of partners, the entrepreneur should find out all he or she can about each venture capitalist.

By far the most important issue in these negotiations will be price. Nonetheless, some of the most time-consuming and difficult negotiations may still lie ahead—determining the other terms and conditions of the investment.

RIGHTS OF PREFERRED STOCK

For tax reasons, most venture funds are precluded by their pension-fund limited partners from investing in a tax pass-through vehicle such as an S corporation, a limited partnership, a general partnership, or a limited liability company. Therefore, when venture capitalists make an investment, it is almost always in preferred stock of a C corporation.

Traditional preferred stock issued by large, publicly traded companies carries a preference on liquidation, pays a higher dividend than common stock, and is often set up to be redeemed at a certain date. It is usually not convertible into common stock and is often nonvoting. In many ways, it functions like debt.

Venture capital preferred stock is a very different beast. It does have a preference on liquidation. It also has a dividend preference but typically only if and when the directors declare dividends; everyone's expectation is that none will be declared. If all goes well, the preferred stock will almost certainly be converted into common stock (upon an initial public offering or upon a successful sale of the company). The preferred stock is convertible at any time at the election of the holder and automatically converts on certain events. It votes on an as-if-converted-to-common basis and may have special voting rights with respect to certain events and the election of directors. It often has no mandated redemption provision, which would require the company to buy back the stock at a set price on a given date in the future. Even if it does have a redemption provision, the ability of a start-up company to make the redemption is far from certain.

Over the years a number of bells and whistles have been added to the preferred stock issued to venture capitalists. At first this was done to differentiate it from the common stock and to bolster the argument that it has a higher value for tax purposes. This allows the common stock to be sold to the founders and employees at a much lower price than the preferred stock. Later, many features were added to increase the rights and protections provided to the preferred investors in the event that the company ran into difficulty.

Many seasoned venture capitalists will tell you that no investor has ever made any significant money off of these downside protection features, and they receive far too much attention in the negotiation of a venture deal. Under this line of reasoning (which an entrepreneur should embrace in the negotiations), once the valuation is set, the preferred stock only needs to have a liquidation preference and a dividend preference (if declared); the preferred stock should otherwise function as common stock so that all investors are on essentially the same terms going forward. By having all shareholders aligned in this manner, the entrepreneur and the outside investors will focus only on what will create value for the company, rather than on special circumstances that may afford one or the other greater leverage or returns. If the preferred stock gets special rights and downside protection, the stock begins to look like debt rather than equity. If it functions like debt, the argument goes, it should have a fixed return (like a loan) rather than the unlimited upside of equity in a high-growth venture.

Other venture capitalists will argue that the special rights of preferred stock are necessary because the investors are putting up most of the cash for the enterprise and will not be managing company affairs on a day-to-day basis. They will argue that if there are difficulties down the road, the preferred investors may need to assert certain rights to protect their investment from mismanagement or abuse by the founders, who hold common stock. This debate over what rights the preferred stock requires and whether these rights will create misalignment in the shareholders' incentives as the company goes forward often arises as the various terms of the investment are discussed and negotiated.

Most of the terms of the deal will relate to rights that attach to the preferred stock. These rights will be spelled out in the company's certificate of incorporation. Certain other rights will not be contained in the company's charter but will be established in one or more contracts.

The next sections of this chapter review the typical rights sought by venture capitalists investing in preferred stock. The discussion begins with the simplest type of deal and then proceeds with an outline of the different bells and whistles that may be added and the reasons raised for and against such additions.

Entrepreneurs should bear in mind that most venture capitalists have completed far more venture investment deals than have the entrepreneurs with whom they negotiate. It helps to have an advisor who has seen dozens of these transactions from different perspectives. An entrepreneur should also be skeptical about any term that is described as "standard." What is "standard" for one venture fund may be unusual for another.

Another very important issue for entrepreneurs to remember is that there are likely to be subsequent rounds of financing for the company. In deciding what rights to give investors in the first round, the company must also consider the effect that giving rights to this group of investors will have on negotiations with investors in subsequent rounds. It is highly unusual for investors in a subsequent round to accept fewer rights than were granted in a prior round.

Each round of investors is likely to receive a slightly different type of preferred stock (usually differentiated at least by price). Each round typically receives what is called a different *series* of preferred stock. By convention, the first round purchases a security called "Series A Preferred Stock"; each subsequent series follows alphabetically: "Series B Preferred," "Series C Preferred," and so on.

LIQUIDATION PREFERENCE

Simply put, the *liquidation preference* provides that upon a liquidation or dissolution of the company, the preferred shareholders must be paid some amount of money before the common shareholders are paid anything. The definition of a liquidation is typically broad enough to include any sale of the business or sale of substantially all of the company's assets. In the simplest case, the preference amount typically is an amount equal to the amount initially paid for the stock.

For example, if the Series A Preferred is sold to the investors at a price of $.50 per share, it would be given a liquidation preference of $.50 per share. This means that if the preferred shareholders invested $2 million for 40% of the company, then the first $2 million to be distributed to shareholders would go to the preferred shareholders. The remainder would then go to the common shareholders. If the company were to be liquidated for more than $5 million, it would make sense for the holders of the preferred stock to convert to common stock immediately prior to the liquidation. For example, if the

---

From the Trenches

The first-round investor's rights in an investment in a telecommunications company included the right to put the stock back to the company if the company did not make its projections, the right to add directors and control the board if milestones were missed, a full-ratchet antidilution provision, and a right to buy all of any future issuance. Extending these rights to additional investors would have created misaligned incentives and created rivalry within the investor group.

When the company lined up its second-round investors, it went back to the first-round investor and explained that it had investors ready to put in $4 million. The company also explained that if these rights stayed in place, the new investors would either seek the same rights or would want a deep discount on the true value of the company. The first-round investor agreed to carve back its rights to those found in a conventional deal so that the company could have the greatest opportunity for success.

Comment: This entrepreneur was fortunate in being able to convince subsequent investors to take lesser rights and to restructure the rights of the earlier round to be less onerous. The better practice is to consider carefully the rights to be given to a round of investors on the assumption that investors in follow-up rounds will expect rights that are at least as great.

---

company is to be liquidated for $9 million, the preferred shareholders would be better off converting to common stock and abandoning their liquidation preference (since 40% of $9 million is $3.6 million as opposed to the $2 million liquidation preference).

Often the liquidation preference will add to the original purchase price any accrued and unpaid dividends. Because most venture-backed companies do not expect to pay dividends, this language normally has little effect. However, in some deals (as discussed below), there will be a mandatory annual dividend that, if not paid, will cumulate (a *cumulative dividend*). Usually, the sole purpose of this cumulation is to build up the liquidation preference over time. Everyone expects that the dividend will never be paid if the company does well and the preferred stock converts (on a public offering or a high-priced sale of the company), but it will be there to ensure that the preferred investors receive some rate of return on the investment ahead of the common shareholders if the company does not do well. Sometimes, rather than having dividends cumulate (which may require an accounting footnote of explanation), the same objective is achieved by having the liquidation preference increase annually by some rate (often 6%, 7%, or 8%, sometimes higher).

The venture capitalist who seeks either a cumulative dividend or an increasing liquidation preference will argue that the hard-money investors are entitled to receive at least a money market rate of return before the common shareholders are paid on their very cheaply priced common stock. The entrepreneur may want to resist this concept by pointing out that this transaction is not a loan deal with a guaranteed rate of return and no other upside. Instead, the entrepreneur will argue that each of the investors should be focused on what brings the greatest value for the company, rather than creating a situation in which some investors may push to sell the company because a particular deal provides a better return on their series of stock than available alternatives. The entrepreneur will also argue that while the common stock may have been sold cheaply, it is as "hard dollar" as the preferred stock when the value of the "sweat equity" of the entrepreneur is taken into account.

Another twist on the liquidation preference concept is called participating preferred. If an investor holds *participating preferred stock,* then after the preferred stock is paid its liquidation preference, it also, in addition, receives its pro rata share of what remains as though the preferred stock had converted to common stock. If the preferred shareholder is not participating, all proceeds in excess of the liquidation preference go to the common shareholders.

The investor's argument here is similar. If the founders have paid only pennies for their stock (as is typically the case) and the preferred investors have paid hard dollars, then there are prices for the company at which the preferred stock would sensibly convert to common stock but would still earn only a relatively modest internal rate of return on the investment. In contrast, the common shareholders who paid little for their stock would earn huge internal rates of return. For example, if the company is sold after five years for $8 million and the preferred stock converts into common stock to get its $3.2 million return (40% of $8 million) on its $2 million investment, the internal rate of return is only about 11%, which is a disappointment in a venture portfolio; the founder team, on the other hand, which may have paid less that $100,000 for its common stock, is able to split the remaining $4.8 million for a large return. So, the argument goes, the preferred shareholders should both receive their preference (commonly referred to as *getting the bait back*) and be allowed to participate in the common stock share. The entrepreneur can argue that the preferred shareholder is trying to double-dip and should either take its preference or convert. Founders can be quite emotional about the issue because holders of the common stock have invested not just their cash but also years of sweat equity in building the company. If the preferred shareholder is to participate, one could argue, then the founders should receive back pay at the market rate.

When a subsequent series of preferred stock is issued, one matter that will need to be addressed is whether one series comes before the other in a liquidation, or the series are all treated equally (in legal terms, *pari passu*) with a pro rata allocation based on what is available to satisfy the liquidation preferences of the preferred stock prior to any distribution to the common stock. The new money has the greatest negotiating leverage for being paid out first (otherwise it may not invest), but to maintain good relations among preferred investors (and to set the precedent for the next round), the new investors may consent to having payouts to the preferred be pari passu.

From the Trenches

An entrepreneur and a venture capitalist had agreed on a $10-million post-money valuation for a storage device company but were at loggerheads over the issue of whether the venture capitalist's preferred stock should be participating. The entrepreneur appreciated the venture capitalist's point that if the company were only modestly successful (often referred to as a *sideways deal*), the venture capitalist's return on its investment would be quite small. However, the entrepreneur could not understand why, in a successful deal, the venture capitalist ought not only to share in the upside enjoyed by the common shareholders, but also to receive a return of its capital. To solve the impasse, the venture capitalist proposed that the preferred stock be participating if, at exit, the company was worth less than $30 million; at any greater valuation, the participating feature would be inoperative. The entrepreneur agreed, and the deal was struck.

DIVIDEND PREFERENCE

Typically, the preferred stock is to earn a dividend at some modest rate (6% to 8%) when and if declared by the board of directors of the company. As noted above, the venture capitalist does not expect the dividend to be declared; this provision is included primarily to bolster the argument for tax purposes that the preferred stock is worth more than the common stock purchased by the founders at a lower price.

Also, as noted above, some deals provide for cumulative dividends, used primarily to push up the value of the liquidation preference over time.

REDEMPTION RIGHTS

Some venture investors will ask for the right to force the company to repurchase (i.e., *redeem*) its own stock at some point in the future (a *voluntary redemption right*). The investors may argue that they are minority shareholders and need some mechanism to ensure that they will have some exit from the investment in the future. In asking for a redemption right, the venture capitalist is concerned that if the company does not perform well enough to be a public offering or acquisition candidate, there may be no effective way to achieve any liquidity.

Although redemption requests seem reasonable on their face, and are increasingly granted, they can cause difficulties for companies both in raising future rounds of capital and in meeting redemption requirements. If a redemption right is granted, the next round of investors may be legitimately concerned that the money they are putting into the company may be used to redeem the earlier-round investors rather than to grow the company. Also, once a redemption right is granted, it is likely that future investors will want one as well.

The company can argue that no redemption rights should be given and that the investors should rely on the judgment of the board of directors on liquidity matters. The board will seek a liquidity opportunity for all investors but should not be forced into making a poorly timed decision because of a looming redemption deadline. Another strong argument against redemption rights is that they may turn out to be meaningless if the company has no money. Of course, a counterargument is that if they are so meaningless, there is no harm in granting them.

Another tactic in resisting redemption rights is to suggest that if the investor is to have what is in essence a *put* on the stock (i.e., the right to sell the stock back to the company at a set price by a given date in the future), then it is only fair that the company should have a right to *call* the stock (the right to force the investors to sell the stock back to the company at a set price by a given date in the future). However, this strategy is of little benefit to the company. In reality, a fast-growing company is probably not going to want to use its limited cash to exercise the call. In addition, the put-and-call approach could end up pitting different investor groups against one another, as their own interests are no longer aligned with what creates the most value for the company as a whole.

If redemption rights must be granted, they should be pushed as far into the future as possible. Redemption rights that are seven years out are not as threatening as those that kick in after five years. Similarly, it might be worthwhile to specify that the actual payment of the redemption price be

---

From the Trenches

One San Francisco Bay Area venture fund is particularly fond of redemption rights and insists on them in every deal. The fund does a fair amount of investing outside the technology industry, where it is less likely to run into companies with advisors who are knowledgeable about typical venture deals. In one such deal, the venture capitalists requested a redemption right that kicked in after three years at a price equal to twice the initial investment. The venture capitalists explained that, without the redemption right, they would receive less than a 25% internal rate of return, which would be deemed a bad investment in the venture industry. In addition, they argued that the company should be willing to honor their request because their management's own projections had shown a much higher rate of return. The management responded that it had no doubt that the company was a good long-term investment but that it could not accurately predict every bump in the road toward success. The company could not take the risk of being caught in a cash-short position if the venture capitalist exercised the redemption right at an inopportune time. After much haggling, the parties agreed to a redemption right at any point after the seventh year for the then fair-market value of the stock as determined by an appraiser.

---

spread over two or three years in order to have as little impact as possible on the company's cash flow. The period in which redemption can be requested should be quite limited so that the threat to cash flow is not an ongoing concern. Any redemption rights should terminate upon an initial public offering.

The redemption price is another matter for negotiation. Often, venture capitalists will want the stock redeemed at its liquidation preference plus any accumulated but unpaid dividends. However, if the sole purpose is to give the investor liquidity, an argument can be made that the redemption price should be based on the fair market value of the company's stock at the time (which may be less than the investment plus unpaid dividends). If not agreed upon by the company and the investors, the fair market value may be determined by an appraisal process that should apply appropriate discounts for any lack of liquidity of the stock and the lesser value of a minority interest.

CONVERSION RIGHTS

Right to Convert   Holders of preferred stock in venture deals normally have the right to convert their preferred stock into common stock at any time. The ratio at which preferred stock is converted into common stock is typically determined by dividing the initial purchase price of the preferred stock by a number called the *conversion price,* which is adjusted upon certain events. Initially, the conversion price is equal to the purchase price of the preferred stock, so the preferred stock converts into common stock on a one-to-one basis.

Automatic Conversion   The preferred stock usually is automatically converted into common stock upon certain events. Typically, these events are the vote of some specified percentage of the preferred stock or an initial public offering that meets certain criteria. The company would like the preferred stock to convert as soon as possible to eliminate its special rights and to clean up the balance sheet for the initial public offering.

Often an affirmative vote of a majority or a supermajority of the preferred stock is required to force an automatic conversion of all of the preferred stock. A high threshold requirement ensures that no one investor controls the preferred stock. The entrepreneur should favor a simple majority or as small a supermajority as possible, and should resist any language that gives one investor the right to block a conversion if the other investors believe it is in the company's best interest. If there are only a few investors in the deal, or if one investor holds a majority of the preferred stock, it may be difficult to avoid having an investor with a blocking right.

The criteria for automatic conversion on an initial public offering generally include the following: (1) The offering must be firmly underwritten (i.e., the underwriters must have committed to placing the entire offering, rather than adopting the best efforts approach common in penny stock offerings); (2) the offering must raise a certain amount of money for the company; and (3) (often) the offering price must be at a certain minimum (e.g., four times the conversion price of the preferred stock).

Upon any conversion of the preferred stock, the rights associated with it (i.e., liquidation preference, dividend preference, antidilution protection, special voting rights, and redemption provisions) cease to exist. Some contractual rights, such as *registration rights* (the right to force the company to register the holder's stock), usually survive, although other, such as *information rights* (the right to certain ongoing financial information about the company) and *preemptive rights* (the right to buy stock issued by the company), often will terminate upon an initial public offering.

ANTIDILUTION PROVISIONS

Structural Antidilution   Any equity issuance to another person can be considered a dilutive issuance to existing shareholders, because it reduces their percentage ownership stake. All shareholders are customarily entitled to protection against the dilution caused by certain issuances. For example, when common stock is issued as a stock dividend, a pro rata dividend is given to each common shareholder, not just to some of them.

Preferred stock is also customarily given antidilution protection against stock dividends, stock splits, reverse splits, and similar recapitalizations. The conversion price is adjusted to ensure that the number of shares of common stock issuable upon conversion of the preferred stock represents the same percentage of ownership (on a converted-to-common basis) as existed prior to the stock dividend, stock split, reverse split, or recapitalization. For example, if there is a five-to-one stock split, the conversion price would be reduced to one fifth of its prior amount. If the conversion price was $1.25 prior to the split, it would be $0.25 after the split. In this way, the number of shares of common stock issuable upon the conversion of the preferred stock would increase proportionately with the effect of the split.

This type of *structural antidilution protection* from stock dividends, stock splits, and reverse splits is the most basic kind of antidilution provision and is nearly always included in venture capital financings. When venture capitalists say they want protection against dilution, they may be referring to this basic type of protection, or they may have in mind some of the more complex provisions discussed below.

Preemptive Right and Right of First Refusal   Another type of antidilution provision is called a right of first refusal or preemptive right. A *right of first refusal* or *preemptive right* entitles any shareholder to purchase his or her pro rata share in any subsequent issuance to ensure that the shareholder maintains his or her percentage ownership. In venture deals, this type of provision, if adopted, usually is a contractual right that terminates upon an initial public offering. It can, however, be made a right attached to the preferred stock if it is included in the certificate of incorporation. In its most extreme form, a preemptive right can require the company to first offer all shares of subsequent offerings to the venture group, not merely sufficient shares to maintain their pro rata ownership interest.

Although a pro rata preemptive right appears reasonable on its face, there are many circumstances in which a company may want to sell stock to a particular investor without being required to first offer it to every current investor. For that reason, if this right is included, it usually exempts stock issued to employees, directors, consultants, strategic partners, those providing leases or loans to the company, and acquisition targets.

Waiting for a right-of-first-refusal time period to expire (or soliciting waivers of such rights) can be time-consuming and can interfere with consummating a deal. An entrepreneur may want to avoid giving up the company's flexibility to choose to whom it sells stock in the future. For example, the company may want to bring in a new venture capitalist or corporate investor but may find that, due to the exercise of preemptive rights, there is not enough stock to meet the new investor's minimum investment criteria. Also, if there is no such right, investors who want to be invited to buy in future rounds have an incentive to remain on good terms with the company. Finally, a preemptive right, if exercised by a large shareholder, may force other investors either to buy into the offering or to risk losing control of the company.

Price Protection   One could argue that the two types of antidilution provisions discussed above (protection from stock splits and the like, and the right to participate in future offerings) should be sufficient protection for an investor. However, most venture deals feature a third type of antidilution protection known as price protection. *Price protection* gives the venture capitalist some protection from subsequent financing rounds in which stock is issued at a lower share price than the investor paid.

The theory behind price protection is that the valuation of a company at the time a venture capitalist purchases stock is open to debate, and the investor is entitled to a price adjustment if it turns out that the company was overvalued. As it is impractical to give back a portion of the venture capitalist's money, more shares are issued to the investor to make the investor whole.

Full Ratchet   The simplest form of price protection (although by no means the fairest) is called full ratchet antidilution protection. If the venture capitalist has *full ratchet antidilution protection,* then if stock is sold at a lower price per share in a subsequent round, the ratio for converting preferred stock to common stock is adjusted so that an investor in a higher-priced earlier round gets the same deal as he or she would have gotten had the purchase been made in a later lower-priced round. The mechanics of the adjustment are straightforward: The conversion price of the prior round is adjusted to the purchase price of the new round.

Consider this example:

Acorn Enterprises issues Series A Preferred Stock based on a pre-money valuation of $9,000,000. Acorn issues shares resulting in a 25% ownership interest to investors for $3,000,000 (i.e., post-money valuation of $12,000,000). Assuming that there are 4,500,000 shares of common stock outstanding (which founders may have bought in the early days of the company for pennies a share or more recently for 20 cents a share), the Series A investors will purchase 1,500,000 shares at $2.00 per share. The shares convert into common stock based on the original price, so $3,000,000 of preferred stock at $2.00 per share will convert into 1,500,000 shares of common stock. It is said to initially convert on a one-to-one basis.

Business does not go according to plan, and when Acorn tries to raise another $2,000,000, it finds it can obtain a pre-money valuation of only $10,000,000. It may seem counterintuitive that the second round could have a valuation lower than the post-money valuation of the first round, but it does happen. Typically, this occurs either because the earlier round was overvalued or because the business has not met the projections in its plan.

The second-round Series B venture capitalists buy their preferred stock at $1.67 per share (i.e., the $10,000,000 pre-money valuation divided by the 6,000,000 total shares already outstanding). At this valuation, the second-round investors will receive 1,200,000 shares of Series B Preferred Stock for the $2,000,000 second-round investment. After the first and second rounds the capitalization would be as follows:

	No. of Shares	% of Company
FIRST ROUND		
Common	4,500,000	75.00
Series A	1,500,000	25.00
SECOND ROUND (with no adjustment for dilution)		
Common	4,500,000	62.50
Series A	1,500,000	20.83
Series B	1,200,000	16.67

The Series A venture capitalists will be none too pleased about overpaying for their Series A stock compared to the Series B investors. If the Series A investors have full ratchet antidilution protection, their conversion price will be reset to the lower sale price of the Series B stock. It is as though the Series A investors were able to purchase at the most recent price. The

$3,000,000 Series A investors would now be able to convert into 1,800,000 shares of common stock. As a result of the lower-priced dilutive issuance, additional stock would be issued to the Series A upon conversion of their preferred stock, and the capitalization would be as follows:

	No. of Shares	% of Company
SECOND ROUND (with full ratchet protection)		
Common	4,500,000	60.00
Series A	1,800,000	24.00
Series B	1,200,000	16.00

Full ratchet appears simple and fair on its face, but it is rarely used because it is widely viewed as unfair. Most of the dilution is pushed onto the common shareholders, and in an anomaly, the Series B ends up buying less of the company than it bargained for (which can push down its price even further). Perhaps most unfairly, all of the Series A stock is repriced regardless of the size of the issuance of Series B stock.

Although the ratchet formula is used much less often than the weighted average formula discussed next, a ratchet may be appropriate under some limited circumstances. For example, if a venture capitalist uncovers a fact in due diligence that suggests that the company is overvalued and may need a cash infusion sooner than was anticipated, a company might agree to a ratchet for six or twelve months to give the investors some assurance that there will not need to be a subsequent financing at a lower price per share than the price paid in the previous financing (a *down-priced financing*). Similarly, if some event may occur within the next year that will have a dramatic effect on valuation (such as the issuance of a patent), the venture capitalist may seek ratchet protection to protect him or her if the event does not occur and more money must be raised. Also, investors in a mezzanine round might be concerned about the company being overvalued and about a down-priced financing if the public market window closes. They too might seek a ratchet for a limited period. In such cases, typically when the ratchet period expires, the weighted average method becomes applicable.

Weighted Average Today almost all venture deals use a weighted average antidilution formula, which attempts to calibrate the repricing based on the size and price of the dilutive round. *Weighted average antidilution* sets the new conversion price of the outstanding preferred stock as the product of (a) the old conversion price multiplied by (b) a fraction in which (1) the numerator is the sum of (x) the number of shares outstanding before the issuance plus (y) the quotient of the amount of money invested in this round divided by the old conversion price, and (2) the denominator is the sum of (x) the shares outstanding before this round and (y) the shares issued in this round. Algebraically,

$$NCP = OCP \times \frac{OB + \dfrac{MI}{OCP}}{OB + SI}$$

where *NCP* is the new conversion price, *OCP* is the old conversion price, *OB* is the number of shares outstanding before the issuance, *MI* is the amount of money invested in the current round, and *SI* is the number of shares issued in the current round.

The weighted average formula provides a result that adjusts the conversion price based on the relative amount of the company that is being sold at the lower price.

Applying this formula to the example set forth above, one calculates the new conversion price as follows:

$$NCP = 2.00 \times \frac{6,000,000 + \dfrac{2,000,000}{2.00}}{6,000,000 + 1,200,000}$$

$$NCP = \$1.944$$

Under weighted average antidilution, the capitalization table would be as follows:

	No. of Shares	% of Company
SECOND ROUND (with weighted average protection)		
Common	4,500,000	62.13
Series A	1,542,860	21.30
Series B	1,200,000	16.57

No longer does the Series A stock convert on a one-to-one basis; each share of Series A stock now converts into 1.029 shares of common (\$2.00/1.944) based on the new conversion price.

The weighted average formula is fairly standard in venture capital financings, but there are some variations. The most common variation involves how options are counted—whether as issued or unissued common stock. Although counting the options would add the same amount to both the denominator and the numerator in the weighted average formula, the effect of including them is that the broader base absorbs more dilution and keeps the conversion price from falling as quickly. Often, shares reserved for options already granted are counted, but those reserved for future grants are not. This issue is a minor negotiating point, as it tends to have a negligible effect unless the option pool is unusually large.

Certain issuances will often be carved out from the price-protection antidilution provisions. For example, it is usually anticipated that additional members of the management team will have to be hired and that it will be necessary to offer those employees stock options or low-priced common stock.

Over time, other members of management may need to have their incentives revitalized (following dilutive venture rounds) with additional stock options. For this reason, options to be granted under stock option plans and other equity arrangements with employees are generally excluded from the price-protection formula. Often, there is a cap on the aggregate amount of stock that a board can allocate under this carve-out (typically between 10% and 30% of the stock for equity incentive programs) without obtaining the approval of the investors. Similarly, any outstanding rights to purchase shares at a lower price that were granted prior to the issuance of the preferred stock are usually excluded. Shares of common stock issued upon conversion of preferred stock into common stock are also excluded.

Pay to Play   Some venture capitalists like to add a pay-to-play provision. With a *pay-to-play provision,* a holder of preferred stock gets the benefit of price protection antidilution only if it buys its pro rata share of any subsequent down-priced round. An investor who does not participate at least pro rata in a down-priced round is automatically converted into a different series of preferred stock that is identical to the original series in all respects, except that there is no price protection. This provision is intended to encourage all investors to step up and help the company in difficult times, and is therefore generally favored by entrepreneurs as well as by some venture capitalists. Although prominent in discussions of types of antidilution provisions, in practice, pay-to-play provisions are atypical.

VOTING RIGHTS

The preferred stock issued to the venture capitalist votes on most matters on an as-converted-to-common basis (i.e., one vote for each common share into which the preferred can be converted). On most matters the preferred and common shareholders vote together.

Protective Provisions   There may be certain matters for which the company must obtain the approval of the preferred stock voting as a class. These matters generally include any change in the certificate of incorporation that would adversely affect the rights, preferences, and privileges of the preferred shareholders. For example, the liquidation preference cannot be changed without the consent of the preferred shareholders. There is often a separate prohibition on the issuance of any security senior to (or even on par with) the existing preferred stock, as well as separate provisions prohibiting changes in the liquidation preference, dividend rights, conversion rights, voting rights, or redemption rights of the preferred shareholders (even though all of these rights might be considered to fall within the general prohibition on adverse change to the preferred shareholders).

Some investors will want these *protective provisions* to require the approval of holders of each series of preferred stock, with each series voting separately, because these investors control a larger percentage of a particular series than of the preferred stock as a whole. It is in the company's best interest to avoid a series vote in order to give the company greater flexibility and to lessen the likelihood that any single investor will have blocking power. Even if some investors end up with blocking power, the fewer who have this power, the better for the company.

Another common protective provision is a prohibition on the redemption of stock, other than redemptions provided for in the certificate of incorporation and repurchases from departed employees, consultants, and directors pursuant to the contractual arrangements made when stock was sold to such persons (but often still subject to some cap on the number of shares that can be redeemed). There may be a prohibition on any sale of substantially all of the assets of the company or merger in which the surviving entity is not controlled by shareholders of the company prior to the merger. Any increase in the authorized number of shares of stock may be prohibited. If there is an agreement on how the board is to be elected, changes in the number of directors or the designation of who elects a stated number of directors may also require approval by the preferred shareholders.

Some preferred investors may try to expand the number of items requiring their approval to include the types of matters often found in bank loan covenants, such as (1) investing in any other enterprise; (2) establishing subsidiaries; (3) incurring certain levels of indebtedness; (4) making loans to others; and (5) exceeding certain levels for capital expenditures. Generally, such provisions should be vigorously resisted by the company. The investors should rely on the board of directors of the company to do what is prudent, rather than forcing such matters to be delayed by a shareholder vote.

Board Elections   The board of directors is charged with the management of the company's business affairs, and it appoints the officers to carry out board policies and handle day-to-day operations. In America's version of shareholder democracy, as reflected in the corporation laws of the fifty states, the shareholders elect the board to run the company; at the same time, the shareholders are permitted to vote on a limited number of matters (e.g., amendments to the certificate of incorporation, decisions about selling the business, certain merger transactions, and dissolution). Control of the company is determined by the persons with the power to elect the board of directors, along with the directors themselves.

Generally, the lead venture capitalist in a round will expect a board seat. Sometimes, each venture capitalist would like a board seat. As the number of venture investors increases over time, the board can become too large and may find itself completely dominated by financial investors.

At the time of the first venture round, it is likely that the founders will retain a majority of the company and will be permitted to elect a majority of the board. If there is only one venture fund in the round, it is not unusual for it to request two board seats.

Usually, the founders and the investors will enter into a voting agreement or will designate in the certificate of incorporation that a certain number of seats are to be elected by the common shareholders, another number of seats are to be elected by the preferred shareholders, and perhaps the balance elected by the shareholders at large. Keep in mind that control of the board is likely to shift over time as subsequent financings occur.

An entrepreneur may wish to establish from the outset that he or she wants to be able to look to the board as a repository of business experience and advice. To this end, the founder group may decide to limit itself to just two founders on the board, with one or two seats reserved for venture investors, and two or three seats reserved for industry leaders who are respected by the venture capitalists and founders. With this type of board composition, no one group controls the board, and the board can focus on what is in the best interest of the company rather than on what is in the best interest of any particular group.

MILESTONES

Sometimes venture capitalists will require the company to achieve certain goals (*milestones*) within a specified time. These milestones might include reaching certain points in product development, or attaining certain sales or profitability levels. The rationale for milestones is that they protect the venture capitalist from overvaluing the company to a greater degree than price antidilution provisions. Sometimes the achievement of milestones will trigger an obligation by the venture capitalist to make a follow-on investment in the company at a previously determined price per share. In some cases, failure to meet the milestones will permit the investor to purchase shares at a much lower price. In other cases, the conversion price of the venture capitalist's preferred stock may be adjusted downward, with the effect of increasing the venture capitalist's ownership of the company. In still other cases, an investor will suggest that control of the board should shift to the investors if the management team fails to achieve the milestones.

The company should resist any milestones that would result in a change of control. Business is filled with risks, and the unexpected can occur. When that happens, all shareholders in the company need to pull together, rather than splitting into groups of shareholders trying to use the company's difficulty to their own advantage. Although milestones associated with subsequent rounds of investment are not quite as onerous, they too may cause misalignment of incentives among shareholders. For example, some may want the company to fall short, in order to be relieved of a further investment obligation (or, more likely, to be in a position to purchase stock cheaply or to renegotiate the deal). Milestones that trigger ownership adjustments similarly put the venture capitalist and the founders on different sides of the table, which is hardly where the parties should or want to be. Finally, milestones of any kind in a deal may distort the behavior of the entrepreneur, whose focus may be too much on the milestone and not enough on what actions or expenditures are in the best interest of the business. For these reasons, many venture capitalists avoid using milestones.

REGISTRATION RIGHTS

The parties will devote a fair amount of discussion to the subject of registration rights. A *registration right* is the right to force the company to register the holder's stock with the Securities and Exchange Commission (SEC) so that it can be sold in the public markets. Often when a company goes public, the underwriters are unwilling to permit existing shareholders to sell in the offering, as such sales will adversely affect the marketing of the new issuance of stock being sold by the company to raise capital. If the shareholder has held the stock for more than one year and the company is public, the holder may be able to sell a limited amount of stock (up to the greater of 1% of the outstanding stock and the average weekly trading volume in the preceding four weeks) in any three-month period under rule 144. But if the holder wishes to sell more than that amount or is unable to sell under rule 144 (for example, because it has held the shares for less than one year or because it is an *affiliate* [officer, director, or owner of more than 5% to 10% of the outstanding shares] of a private company), it may need to register the shares to exit from the investment.

There are three types of registration rights that venture investors are likely to request: demand rights, S-3 rights, and piggyback rights.

A *demand right* is a right to demand that the company file a registration statement on form S-1 to sell the holder's stock. This is the form the company uses for an initial public offering (IPO); it requires a prospectus with extensive information about the company and the offering. A company generally will want to limit this right as it can be expensive and time-consuming, and can adversely affect the company's own capital-raising plans. Generally, the investor group will receive only one or two demand rights, with limits on when they can be exercised. The company will resist granting demand rights that can be used to force the company to go public. The argument is that one cannot force a management team to find underwriters, to do the road show required for the offering, and to make the offering successful if the company is not yet ready. (During the *road show*, the company's managers and investment bankers travel around the country and make presentations to potential investors.) The investors will seek such a right, arguing that an IPO may be their only path to liquidity.

An S-3 right is actually another type of demand right. An *S-3 right* allows the investor to force the company to register the investor's stock on form S-3. This form is part of a simpler procedure that can be used by most companies with a *public float* (market value of securities held by nonaffiliates) of at least $75 million twelve months after they have gone public. The S-3 form permits the registration statement to incorporate by reference information already on file with the SEC, so the preparation of the registration statement is simpler, less time-consuming, and cheaper than the preparation of a form S-1 registration statement. S-3 rights granted to venture capitalists tend to be unlimited in quantity but are available only once or twice per year and may expire at some point.

A *piggyback right* is the right to participate in an offering initiated by the company. Piggyback rights are generally subject to a cutback or elimination by the offering's underwriter, who may determine, based on market conditions, that a sale by shareholders will adversely affect the company's capital-raising effort. The venture capitalist will seek rights that may not be completely cut back except in connection with the company's initial public offering. Piggyback rights granted to venture capitalists are generally unlimited in number but often expire five to seven years after the company's initial public offering or after a certain percentage of the venture investors have sold their shares. Unless the rights expire, the company must notify all holders of rights every time the company has a public offering and perhaps include a portion of the holder's shares in the offering.

INFORMATION RIGHTS

Holders of significant blocks of preferred stock may be granted the rights to certain information, such as monthly financial statements, annual audited financial statements, and the annual budget approved by the board. These rights should expire upon an initial public offering, when the investors will be able to rely on SEC filings.

Some investors may seek more expanded rights, such as review of the auditor's letter to management concerning the audit of the financial state-

---

From the Trenches

One venture fund was quite thankful that it had obtained a demand registration right exercisable five years after it invested in a consumer products company that became very successful. The founder decided that he liked running a profitable private company and had no desire to take it public. He was also unwilling to sell the company or to find some other path to liquidity at a high enough valuation to satisfy the investor. The investor insisted on a public offering and threatened to exercise its demand right. Because the company had a well-known brand and was not a development-stage technology company, it appeared that a fairly successful offering could be consummated even without an enthusiastic management team. Faced with the investor's threat, the founder and management agreed that the company should go public and completed a successful offering, which gave the investors liquidity.

ments and any weaknesses in internal controls, prepared by the company's accountants; the right to make on-site inspections and inquiries of officers or employees; and the right to observe board meetings. Generally, these additional information rights should be resisted. They can be disruptive to the company's operation and conflict with the board's performance of its duties. Investors who maintain good relations with the company will be able to obtain sufficient information to monitor their investment without placing undue burdens on the start-up enterprise.

CO-SALE RIGHTS

Venture capitalists will often ask for a co-sale right. Typically, a *co-sale right* binds some of the key founders of the company and gives the investor a contractual right to sell some of the investor's stock alongside the founder's stock if the founder elects to sell stock to a third party. A co-sale right protects the investor from a situation in which the founder transfers control of the company by selling his or her stock to another person. In such a circumstance, the investor is looking for the opportunity to consider exiting as well. Mechanically, a co-sale right usually gives the investor the right to replace a portion of the stock the founder planned to sell with the investor's stock. The portion is usually the pro rata share of the investor's total holdings compared with the founder's total holdings.

It is reasonable for a founder to resist a co-sale right except in those circumstances in which a substantial portion of the stock held by all founders is being sold. Founders may insist on exceptions to permit a sale of some of their stock for liquidity purposes (e.g., to cover a house down payment or private-school tuition) and carve-outs for dispositions upon death or upon termination of employment. Founders may also ask for a reciprocal co-sale right so that they can obtain some liquidity if the venture capitalist seeks to sell its shares. This reciprocal right is not usually given.

—— OTHER PROTECTIVE ARRANGEMENTS

VESTING

The venture investors may request that the founders subject their stock, and all other common stock to be sold to employees, to a vesting schedule if they have not already done so. The vesting schedule is usually four years, with cliff vesting for the first year, then monthly vesting for the next three years. If the vesting schedule is not put in place until the venture round closes, the founders may want to commence the vesting period on an

---

From the Trenches

One venture fund learned the hard way the merits of a co-sale right. The fund led a $2 million financing of a toy-and-video-game distribution company. The key founder resisted any effort to put vesting on his shares, arguing that the company was more than two and a half years old and he had earned his shares. He also argued successfully that a co-sale right was not needed, because he had no reason to transfer his shares as the company could not make it without him and the shares represented most of his net worth. He also persuaded the venture capitalist that it was fundamentally unfair to put restrictions on his right to transfer his shares. Within twelve months of the closing, the entrepreneur transferred his shares to a competitor for more than $1 million and left the company. The company was unable to compete effectively without the entrepreneur, and the venture capitalist's investment became virtually worthless.

---

earlier date, such as the day founders first acquired stock or joined the company.

Employees whose stock is subject to repurchase will likely want to file a *section 83(b) election* with the IRS. This election allows the stock to be taxed at the time it is acquired (when there is no tax, assuming the employee paid fair market value) rather than on the date the vesting is complete (when it may have increased dramatically in value over the original purchase price). The 83(b) election must be filed within thirty days of the commencement of the vesting arrangement. It is extremely important that this filing be made on time; a missed or late filing can result in a very large tax bill at a time when the shareholder has no money because the stock is not liquid.

OPTIONS

Common stock is typically issued to founders at the earliest stages of a company. However, soon thereafter, many companies set up stock option plans as additional equity incentives for employees. The venture capitalist understands well the need for such programs and is a supporter of them as long as they are not excessively generous.

Options provide employees with an opportunity to share in the equity upside of the business without having to invest any of their own money until a future date. Incentive stock options (ISOs) are particularly popular because they permit an employee to purchase cheap common stock at a future date without triggering a taxable event. After a company goes public, ISOs become less important because there is liquidity in the stock, and an option holder can buy the stock and then sell enough to pay taxes on the gain within the same tax period.

An entrepreneur will want to reserve (at least mentally) a certain percentage of the company for future equity incentives to new and existing employees. Generally, somewhere between 10% and 30% of the stock post-venture financing is reserved for this purpose. A generous plan will dilute the holders of the common stock and the preferred stock alike, so such options should be granted with some care. Nonetheless, a healthy pool of options will likely be advisable so that the young company can attract the talent necessary for success. Options generally vest over four or five years (although credit is sometimes given in the initial grant for prior service to the company). Unlike stock, which vests by the repurchase right lapsing, options vest by the exercise right extending to a greater proportion of the grant over time.

The entrepreneur should reach agreement with the venture capitalist on the scope of any option plan prior to the closing of the financing. If the company later wishes to exceed this scope, the entrepreneur may be required to obtain the written approval of the investors. Alternatively, the investors may agree that the scope can be exceeded so long as their representatives on the board vote in favor of the option grants.

EXHIBIT 1
Putting It into Practice

Alexandra talked with Michael Woo about venture capital funding. Because WebRunner had successfully validated the technology and had modest overhead needs, Alexandra figured that WebRunner was worth about $1,200,000 and would need only about $600,000 in an initial round. This would result in one-third ownership by the venture capitalists. Michael suggested bumping that figure up to $800,000 to reflect unanticipated delays and expenses, and to allow a venture capitalist to buy 40% of the company. Alexandra agreed, particularly in light of her earlier miscalculation of cash needs. Also, she hoped some of the extra money could be used to buy out Kevin Jordan, who had become dissatisfied with his $50,000 investment during WebRunner's earlier financial crisis. Michael liked this idea, because it meant that the new investors would be able to purchase Series A Preferred Stock rather than a Series B, thus simplifying the capital structure.

Alexandra had already prepared a business plan for Michael's review. She worked with Josh Austin to pull together all of the company's material agreements and information on its technology, so that once an investor was selected, the investor could proceed quickly with its due diligence investigation.

Michael suggested approaching Centaur Partners, a venture capital group looking for Internet opportunities, which he thought would be a good investor. Michael told Alexandra that he was obligated to disclose that his firm had represented Centaur Partners in the past and would continue to do so in the future. He said that he personally always represented the issuer in venture capital financings and that his firm would not represent Centaur in any business relating to WebRunner. Michael told Alexandra, however, that he would understand if she wanted to seek other representation for the transaction. Alexandra said she was comfortable with Michael continuing to represent WebRunner, and asked Michael to contact Centaur on her behalf.

Michael set up an initial meeting between Alexandra and Centaur's managing partner. That meeting went well, and Alexandra used the opportunity to discuss her thoughts on valuation and to sound out Centaur on such issues as their vision for the company, their willingness and ability to step up for other rounds, their view on the company's weaknesses, and their capabilities in assisting the company in addressing those weaknesses. Alexandra also performed her own due diligence investigation of Centaur, keeping in mind that Centaur was not just a source of needed capital but was about to become her partner in one of the most important undertakings of her life.

After several more successful meetings, including meetings involving all three Centaur general partners and the Eagles, Centaur agreed to invest in WebRunner, pending a satisfactory due diligence review. Alexandra, along with Michael and Josh, met with Centaur and its counsel to hammer out a term sheet.

After much negotiation, the two parties agreed on a term sheet that reflected the $1,200,000 pre-money valuation that Alexandra was seeking. (A sample venture capital term sheet is set forth in *Exhibit 2*, "Getting It in Writing.") Centaur agreed to use $60,000 of its investment to purchase Kevin Jordan's 50,000 shares, which would then be folded into the new Series A Preferred Stock to be issued by WebRunner.

Michael negotiated a provision that would permit WebRunner to bring in another venture firm for up to $200,000 of the $800,000 financing, with Centaur's permission. After the meeting, Michael suggested gently to Alexandra that she might want to talk to a few other firms and to select one to be another voice in the investor group. However, Alexandra was comfortable with Centaur being the only investor because of the rapport she had established with the Centaur partners and the smoothness with which negotiations had occurred. Michael pointed out that other venture funds could be part of the next round, as Centaur had agreed to a limited preemptive right of 50% of future financings.

Alexandra instructed Michael to immediately draft and circulate documents for closing the transaction. Although the attorneys for Centaur, Michael, and the principals were able to reach agreement on the documents within three weeks, Centaur did not complete its due diligence until a month after the principals had agreed to the term sheet. As no problems were found, Centaur proceeded to invest $800,000.

Having locked up sufficient funding for at least the next year, Alexandra focused on forming a board that would provide her with sound business advice and expertise. She asked the Centaur partners for help in finding additional board members. She also began to work closely with Centaur's board representative to make sure he was kept in the loop on activities at the company. Alexandra planned to brief Centaur's representative prior to board meetings so that board discussions could be as thoughtful as possible and surprises could be kept to a minimum. Centaur would play a critical role in helping the company raise money in subsequent rounds, and her relationship with the Centaur board representative was central to the success of their partnership.

EXHIBIT 2
Getting It in Writing

SAMPLE VENTURE CAPITAL TERM SHEET

WEBRUNNER INC.
SALE OF SERIES A PREFERRED STOCK
SUMMARY OF TERMS

Issuer:

WebRunner Inc. (the "Company").

Amount of Financing:

$800,000.

Type of Security:

666,667 shares of Series A Convertible Preferred Stock (the "Series A Preferred"), initially convertible into an equal number of shares of the Company's Common Stock (the "Common Stock").

Price:

$1.20 per share (the "Original Purchase Price").

Resulting Capitalization:

The Original Purchase Price represents a post-financing valuation of $2 million, based on fully diluted outstanding common stock of 1,666,667 shares as of the Closing.

Purchaser(s):

Centaur Partners, L.P. as lead investor will purchase at least $600,000 and up to $800,000 of Series A Preferred. The Company may seek other investors (together with the lead investor, the "Investors") to invest up to $200,000, subject to the approval of the lead investor.

Anticipated Closing Date
(the "Closing"):

March 5, 1997.

TERMS OF SERIES A PREFERRED STOCK
Dividends:

The holders of the Series A Preferred shall be entitled to receive cumulative dividends in preference to any dividend on the Common Stock at the rate of 7% of the Original Purchase Price per annum, when and as declared by the Board of Directors. The Series A Preferred will participate pro rata in dividends paid on the Common Stock.

Liquidation Preference:

In the event of any liquidation or winding up of the Company, the holders of the Series A Preferred shall be entitled to receive in preference to the holders of the Common Stock an amount equal to the Original Purchase Price plus any unpaid cumulative dividends (the "Liquidation Preference"). After the payment of the Liquidation Preference to the holders of the Series A Preferred, the remaining assets shall be distributed ratably to the holders of the Common Stock and the Series A Preferred until the Series A Preferred holders have received three times their original investment. All remaining assets shall be distributed ratably to the Common Stock. A merger, acquisition, or sale of substantially all of the assets of the Company in which the shareholders of the Company do not own a majority of the outstanding shares of the surviving corporation shall be deemed to be a liquidation.

Conversion:

The holders of the Series A Preferred shall have the right to convert the Series A Preferred, at any time, into shares of Common Stock. The initial conversion rate shall be 1:1, subject to adjustment as provided below.

Automatic Conversion:

The Series A Preferred shall be automatically converted into Common Stock, at the then applicable conversion price, (i) in the event that

	the holders of at least 50% of the outstanding Series A Preferred consent to such conversion, or (ii) upon the closing of a firmly under-written public offering of shares of Common Stock of the Company at a per share price not less than $3.60 per share (as presently constituted) and for a total offering of not less than $10,000,000 (before deduction of underwriters' commissions and expenses).
Antidilution Provisions:	The conversion price of the Series A Preferred will be subject to a weighted average adjustment to reduce dilution in the event that the Company issues additional equity securities (other than employee, director, and consultant shares approved by the Board of Directors) at a purchase price less than the applicable conversion price. The conversion price will also be subject to proportional adjustment for stock splits, stock dividends, recapitalizations, and the like.
Redemption at Option of Investors:	Commencing on the fifth anniversary of the Closing, at the election of the holders of at least 50% of the Series A Preferred, the Company shall redeem the outstanding Series A Preferred in three equal annual installments. Such redemption shall be at the Original Purchase Price plus any unpaid cumulative dividends.
Voting Rights:	The Series A Preferred will vote together with the Common Stock and not as a separate class except as specifically provided herein or as otherwise required by law. Each share of Series A Preferred shall have a number of votes equal to the number of shares of Common Stock then

issuable upon conversion of such share of Series A Preferred.

Board of Directors:

The size of the Company's Board of Directors shall be changed to five. The holders of the Series A Preferred, voting as a separate class, shall be entitled to elect two members of the Company's Board of Directors. The holders of the Common Stock shall be entitled to elect two directors. The fifth director must be approved by both the Common Stock and Preferred Series A holders, voting separately.

Protective Provisions:

For so long as at least 300,000 shares of Series A Preferred remain outstanding, consent of the holders of at least 50% of the Series A Preferred shall be required for any action which (i) alters or changes the rights, preferences, or privileges of the Series A Preferred, (ii) increases or decreases the authorized number of shares of Series A Preferred, (iii) creates (by reclassification or otherwise) any new class or series of shares having rights, preferences, or privileges senior to or on a parity with the Series A Preferred, (iv) results in the redemption of any shares of Common Stock (other than pursuant to employee agreements), or (v) results in any merger, other corporate reorganization, sale of control, or any transaction in which all or substantially all of the assets of the Company are sold.

Information Rights:

So long as an Investor continues to hold shares of Series A Preferred or Common Stock issued upon conversion of the Series A Preferred, the Company shall deliver to the Investor audited annual and unaudited quarterly financial statements. So long as an Investor holds not less than 120,000 shares of Series A Preferred, the Company will furnish the Investor with monthly financial statements and will provide a copy of the Company's annual operating plan within thirty (30) days prior to the beginning of the fiscal year. Each Investor shall also be entitled to standard inspection and visitation rights. These provisions shall terminate upon a registered public offering of the Company's Common Stock.

Registration Rights:

Demand Rights: If Investors holding at least 50% of the outstanding shares of Series A Preferred, including Common Stock issued on conversion of Series A Preferred ("Registrable Securities"), request that the Company file a Registration Statement for at least 30% of the Registrable Securities having an aggregate offering price to the public of not less than $5,000,000, the Company will use its best efforts to cause such shares to be registered; provided, however, that the Company shall not be obligated to effect any such registration prior to the third anniversary of the Closing. The Company shall have the right to delay such registration under certain circumstances for two periods not in excess of ninety (90) days each in any twelve (12) month period.

The Company shall not be obligated to effect more than two (2) registrations under these demand right provisions, and shall not be obligated to effect a registration (i) during the ninety (90) day period commencing with the date of the

Company's initial public offering, or (ii) if it delivers notice to the holders of the Registrable Securities within thirty (30) days of any registration request of its intent to file a registration statement for such initial public offering within 90 days.

Company Registration: The Investors shall be entitled to "piggyback" registration rights on all registrations of the Company or on any demand registrations of any other investor subject to the right, however, of the Company and its underwriters to reduce the number of shares proposed to be registered pro rata in view of market conditions. If the Investors are so limited, however, no party shall sell shares in such registration other than the Company or the Investor, if any, invoking the demand registration. No shareholder of the Company shall be granted piggyback registration rights that would reduce the number of shares includable by the holders of the Registrable Securities in such registration without the consent of the holders of 50% of the Registrable Securities.

S-3 Rights: Investors shall be entitled to two (2) demand registrations on Form S-3 per year (if available to the Company) so long as such registered offerings are not less than $500,000.

Expenses: The Company shall bear registration expenses (exclusive of underwriting discounts and commissions) of all such demands, piggybacks, and S-3 registrations (including the expense of a single counsel to the selling shareholders, which counsel shall also be counsel to the Company unless there is a conflict of interest with respect to the representation of any selling shareholder or the underwriters otherwise object).

Transfer of Rights: The registration rights may be transferred to (i) any partner or retired partner of any holder that is a partnership, (ii) any family member or trust for the benefit of any individual holder, or (iii) any transferee who acquires at least 100,000 shares of Registrable Securities; provided the Company is given written notice thereof.

Termination of Rights: The registration rights shall terminate on the date five years after the Company's initial public offering.

Other Provisions: Other provisions shall be contained in the Stock Purchase Agreement with respect to registration rights as are reasonable, including cross-indemnification, the period of time in which the Registration Statement shall be kept effective, and underwriting arrangements.

Right of First Refusal: The investors shall have the right in the event the Company proposes to offer equity securities to any person (other than securities issued to employees, directors, or consultants, or pursuant to acquisitions, etc.) to purchase up to 50% of such shares (on a pro rata basis among the Investors). Such right of first refusal will terminate upon an underwritten public offering of shares of the Company.

Purchase Agreement:

The investment shall be made pursuant to a Stock Purchase Agreement reasonably acceptable to the Company and the Investors, which agreement shall contain, among other things, appropriate representations and warranties of the Company, covenants of the Company reflecting the provisions set forth herein, and appropriate conditions of closing, including an opinion of counsel for the Company. The Stock Purchase Agreement shall provide that it may only be amended and any waivers thereunder shall only be made with the approval of the holders of 50% of the Series A Preferred. Registration rights provisions may be amended or waived solely with the consent of the holders of 50% of the Registrable Securities.

EMPLOYEE MATTERS

Stock Vesting:

Unless otherwise determined by the Board of Directors, all stock and stock equivalents issued after the Closing to employees, directors, and consultants will be subject to vesting in accordance with the vesting provisions currently in place under the Company's stock option plan.

Proprietary Information and Inventions Agreements:

Each officer and employee of the Company shall enter into acceptable agreements governing nondisclosure of proprietary information and assignment of inventions to the Company.

Co-Sale Agreement:

The shares of the Company's securities held by Alexandra Scott, Paul Eagle, and Sheryl Eagle shall be made subject to a co-sale agreement (with certain reasonable exceptions) with the holders of the Series A Preferred such that they may not sell, transfer, or exchange their stock unless each holder of Series A Preferred has an opportunity to participate in the sale on a pro rata basis. This right of co-sale shall not apply to and shall terminate upon the Company's initial public offering. In addition, such co-sale agreement will contain a right of first refusal such that Scott, Eagle, and Eagle may not sell, transfer, or exchange their stock without first offering to the Company and then to each holder of Series A Preferred the opportunity to purchase such stock on the same terms and conditions as those of the proposed sale.

Key-Person Insurance:

As soon as reasonably possible after the Closing, the Company shall procure key-person life insurance policies for each of Alexandra Scott, Paul Eagle, and Sheryl Eagle in the amount of $1,000,000 each, naming the Company as beneficiary.

OTHER MATTERS

Finders:

The Company and the Investors shall each indemnify the other for any finder's fees for which either is responsible.

Legal Fees and Expenses:

The Company shall pay the reasonable fees, not to exceed $15,000, and expenses of one special counsel to the Investors.

DISCUSSION QUESTIONS

1. For what type of start-up might venture capital make sense?
2. What factors influence the valuation of a company that is being considered for an investment?
3. VCs often make investments on a staged or "milestone" basis. What are the advantages and disadvantages of this approach for the VC? For the entrepreneur?
4. As an entrepreneur, which of the rights of preferred stock articulated by Bagley and Dauchy make you most uncomfortable? What is the VC attempting to achieve with this provision? Can you propose an alternative that you think would satisfy the VC?

16   Aspects of Financial Contracting in Venture Capital

WILLIAM A. SAHLMAN

Once the entrepreneur has determined what resources the venture needs, identified the most likely avenues for pursuing them, and learned the ins and outs of fundraising, he or she must be prepared to enter negotiation with investors and make a deal.

All deals have certain elements in common. They take place in an uncertain environment. They require the resolution of several key issues: How are cash and risk allocated? What are the incentives for each of the partners in the deal? Beyond these basics, endless variations on a theme are possible. Through a series of examples illustrating transactions between an entrepreneur and a venture capitalist, the reading suggests the numerous possibilities for structuring deals and distinguishing between the characteristics of a sensible deal and a bad deal. As these examples demonstrate, financing terms can be crucial in determining the ultimate value of an investment— for both entrepreneur and venture capitalist.

The interaction of entrepreneur and venture capitalist has resulted in the evolution of a unique set of financial contracts. And in no other kind of transaction does the implied link between value and financial structure appear so strong and direct as in the typical venture capital deal. As I hope to show in this reading, an effective financial design may well be the difference between a flourishing and a failed (if not a still-born) enterprise.

FIRST PRINCIPLES

As is true of all financial transactions, structuring a venture capital deal involves the allocation of economic value. Value, in turn, is determined by the interaction of three major ingredients: cash, risk, and time.

My colleague Bill Fruhan argues that all financial transactions can be

Journal of Applied Corporate Finance, summer 1998. Copyright © Stern Stewart Management Services. Reprinted by permission.

classified into three categories: those that create value, those that destroy value, and those that transfer value between two or more parties.[1] This taxonomy can be readily transferred to venture capital because almost all venture capital deals either create, destroy, or transfer value. For example, a sound deal that provides appropriate incentives for an entrepreneur is likely to result in significantly higher value to be shared by entrepreneur and venture capitalist alike. The same deal, while increasing total value, may also have opposite effects on the value of two different claims on total value (for example, debt and equity), thus providing an example of a value transfer. Finally, a promising deal that is not well designed can result in a failed venture, the extreme case of value destruction.

A SIMPLE EXAMPLE

Before turning to the case of venture capital, let's begin by considering a very simple project with the following characteristics:

Investment required at time 0	$1000
Annual cash flow	$500
Total number of cash payments	5
Terminal value (end of year 5)	$1000

The resulting cash flows are put in *Exhibit 1*. Suppose also that the payment of these cash flows is guaranteed by the government and that the current appropriate risk-free discount rate is 10%.

In this case, the present value of the future cash flows is $2,516, and the net present value of the project is $1,516. If you owned the rights to this investment project, you would be indifferent between selling the rights to another person (with the same information) for $1,516 or keeping the project for yourself. Any offer above that value would induce you to sell. In this

EXHIBIT 1

PERIOD	0	1	2	3	4	5
Investment	(1,000)					
Cash inflow		500	500	500	500	500
Terminal value						1,000
Net cash flow	(1,000)	500	500	500	500	1,500

---

1. William E. Fruhan, Jr., *Financial Strategy: Studies in the Creation, Transfer, and Destruction of Shareholder Value* (Homewood, Ill.: Richard D. Irwin, Inc., 1979).

simple deal, the cash flows are known with certainty by both the buyer and the seller. Moreover, each agrees, or is likely to agree, on the appropriate discount rate to apply to convert future cash flows to the present. And, finally, the expected cash flows are not affected by any action by the buyer or the seller. Given these conditions, it is easy to describe the terms on which a deal such as this one will trade.

DEALMAKING IN THE REAL WORLD

If the world consisted principally of investment projects like this one, then the study of deals would not be very important, or very interesting. In the real world, however, the following conditions are far more likely to apply:

- The future cash flows are unknown (both in amount and timing);
- The appropriate discount rate is unknown;
- Any two parties analyzing the same deal will disagree about the future cash flows, the appropriate discount rate to apply, or both;
- The sources of potential disagreement are many and range from simple disagreement based on common knowledge to the fact that the parties may be governed by different rules (for example, tax treatment) to the possibility that one party knows more than the other;
- There will be conflicts of interest: one or more of the dealmakers may be in a position to influence the outcome of the project so as to benefit at the expense of the other participants; and
- The terms that govern the allocation of the cash flows will themselves affect the nature (amount, timing, and risk) of the cash flow stream.

Now, take the same basic expected cash inflows and outflows from the example above, but introduce uncertainty. That is, the annual cash flow is *expected* to be $500 per year, but the actual number will only be known over time. In this case, it may be appropriate to apply a higher discount rate than before (especially if the new risk includes a systematic, or market-related, component).

Suppose the appropriate discount rate were 20% instead of 10%. In this case, the present value of the cash flows would be $1,897 (instead of $2,516), and thus the net present value would be $897 (instead of $1,516). If someone offered you $1,000 today for the right to exercise the option to invest in this project, then you would gladly sign it over. If you were to offer to sell for $800, then any investor would gladly buy.

In the preceding paragraph, I assumed that buyers and sellers could agree on the expected cash flows and on the discount rate. Obviously, Pandora's box could be opened further, and the introduction of differences and disagreements between dealmakers will reveal many other grounds on which to trade.

If, for example, the parties to the deal disagree about the magnitude or the nature of the risk inherent in the cash flow, then they will apply different discount rates in their analysis. This sort of disagreement may render impossible an agreement on an appropriate price. Or, it may expand the set of possible deal terms. For example, if the potential seller used a discount rate of 20% and the buyer thought 10% to be the correct figure, then there would be a wide range of prices (in this case, between $897 and $1,516) at which the seller would gladly sell and the buyer willingly buy the right to make the investment. Or, if the buyer thought the cash flows would rise at an annual rate of 5%, then even if the buyer and seller used the same discount rate (of 20%), they would both be willing to accept a price between $897 (the seller's minimum) and $1,026 (the buyer's maximum).

ALLOCATING CASH FLOW

Now the fun starts. Suppose this generic deal is now called a start-up venture, and the two parties negotiating are identified as the entrepreneur and the venture capitalist. The venture capitalist uses a discount rate of 40% for projects like the one under consideration. The question is, what proportion of the equity will the venture capitalist demand in order to justify investing the $1,000 capital required to get the project off the ground?

To answer this question, you must determine what proportion of each future cash flow figure would provide a 40% annual rate of return to the venture capitalist, given an initial investment of $1,000. One way to attack this problem is to calculate the present value of the gross future cash flows, using the venture capitalist's 40% required return. In so doing, we find that the present value is equal to $1,204.

This is the total "value pie" to be split between entrepreneur and venture capitalist. If the venture capitalist only needs to invest $1,000 to receive all of these cash flows, then he would increase his net present value by $204. If the venture capitalist owned only 83% ($1,000/$1,204) of the deal, however, then the present value of his share of the future cash flows would be $1,000, exactly equal to the cost of the investment. Therefore, the venture capitalist would willingly pay $1,000 to buy 83% of the equity in this hypothetical venture because the anticipated return would be 40% per year. The entrepreneur would be left with the remaining 17% of the equity, corresponding to $204 divided by $1,204.

ALLOCATING RISKS

The analytics described above are straightforward and are based on some simplifying assumptions. Suppose, however, that the venture capitalist and the entrepreneur are in the process of negotiating a deal and that the

EXHIBIT 2

COMMON STOCK (PROPORTIONAL SHARING)	VENTURE CAPITALIST		ENTREPRENEUR		TOTAL	
Share of total stock	83%		17%		100%	
Annual cash received: Bad scenario	$ 373	83	$ 77	17	$ 450	100
Annual cash received: Good scenario	415	83	94	17	550	100
Expected annual cash received	415	83	85	17	500	100
PV of cash received (incl. TV)	1,000	83	204	17	1,204	100
Net PV (incl. investment)	0		204		204	100
Std. dev'n of PV (and of NPV)	85	83	18	17	102	100

PREFERRED STOCK	VENTURE CAPITALIST		ENTREPRENEUR		TOTAL	
Share of total stock	83%		17%		100%	
Annual cash received: Bad scenario	$ 415	93	$ 35	7	$ 450	100
Annual cash received: Good scenario	415	73	135	27	550	100
Expected annual cash received	415	83	85	17	500	100
PV of cash received (incl. TV)	1,000	83	204	17	1,204	100
Net PV (incl. investment)	0		204		204	100
Std. dev'n of PV (and of NPV)	0	0	102	100	102	100

forecasts are those included in the company's business plan. The venture capitalist, having seen hundreds of unfulfilled "conservative" projections in the past, is skeptical about the numbers. Partly, his skepticism is already reflected in the higher discount rate applied to the estimates, a discount rate that is higher than the true expected return on the venture capital portfolio. Other than buying simple common equity, and thus implicitly agreeing to a proportional risk-reward sharing scheme, how else could the venture capitalist structure a deal with the entrepreneur to assuage his skepticism? (See *Exhibit 2*).

One possibility would be to invest in the form of preferred (or, more commonly, convertible preferred) stock.[2] In this alternative, the venture capitalist would have a prior claim on the earnings of the company and may also have a prior claim on the liquidation value of the company. Suppose, for example, that the venture capitalist asks for a preferred stock that entitles him

---

2. Convertible preferred is the convention; we use straight preferred for purposes of simplicity in exposition.

to receive up to $415 in the form of dividends from the company each year before the entrepreneur receives anything. (Note that $415 is equal to 83% of the expected cash flow of $500.) Also assume that the two parties split the $1,000 return of capital in the final year according to the original 83%/17% rule. What has changed?

In this new situation, a great deal has changed; there has been a major shift in risk from the venture capitalist to the entrepreneur. This shift in risk occurs even though the expected return to each party remains the same. To explore this risk-shifting process, suppose there were really two different, but equally likely scenarios for future cash flows. In the first, the actual cash flows turn out to be $450 per year. In the other, the cash flows are $550 per year. The terminal value is the same under either scenario.

Obviously, under both the proportional sharing rule and the new preferred stock arrangement, the expected total annual cash flow is $500, the expected total present value is $1,204, and the expected total net present value is $204. The standard deviation of the total expected present value is $102.

Under the straight equity deal, the venture capitalist and entrepreneur share proportionately (83%/17%) both the risk and the reward. That is, the venture capitalist has an expected present value of $1,000, an expected net present value of $0, and a standard deviation of expected present value of $85; the entrepreneur has an expected present value of $204, an expected net present value of $204, and a standard deviation of expected present value of $18. Note that the total risk in the project, as measured by the standard deviation, is split according to the 83%/17% rule.

Under the new preferred stock deal, however, the venture capitalist has managed to shift all of the risk to the entrepreneur. That is, given the narrow range of possible cash flow outcomes, the venture capitalist will always receive his $415 per annum cash flow. The entrepreneur, however, will no longer receive 17% of the cash flows regardless of the actual cash flow; instead, he will receive $35 per year in the bad scenario (7% of the expected value) and $135 in the favorable scenario (27%). The standard deviation of the venture capitalist's return is now zero, while the standard deviation of the entrepreneur's present value is $102.

The reader should ignore the fact that the example is contrived and slightly silly. No investor would demand a 40% return for a riskless project. Also, the lower and upper bound of possible annual cash flows are purely arbitrary and meant only to simplify the example to show how risk is shifted from one party to the other. In the real world, the lower bound would almost always be significantly lower than the expected value of the venture capitalist's share, thus forcing the venture capitalist to bear enough risk to justify use of a 40%-return requirement. And if the lower bound were below the expected value of the venture capitalist's share, then the expected present value would be lower than in the previous scenarios unless the entrepreneur were required to meet the shortfall in preferred stock dividends out of his own pocket, or the venture capitalist were entitled to receive a bonus payment during the favorable scenario.

Why would the venture capitalist suggest using preferred stock rather than straight equity? The obvious reason would be to try to improve his reward-to-risk ratio. But simply transferring risk to the entrepreneur by gaining liquidation preferences is probably not the primary motive for structuring venture capital deals this way. Two other possibilities come to mind: (1) by increasing the entrepreneur's risk, the venture capitalist is trying to "smoke out" the entrepreneur and get the entrepreneur to signal whether he really does believe the forecasts in the business plan; and (2) the venture capitalist is trying to provide the strongest possible incentives for the entrepreneur to do at least as well as projected. If the business exceeds plan, then the entrepreneur will share disproportionately in the benefits of doing so. Given the entrepreneur's strong incentives to beat the plan, structuring the deal this way may actually increase the probability that a more favorable outcome will occur.

SUMMING UP

Let's stop here for a moment and briefly review our progress to this point.

The process of financial contracting in venture capital focuses on a few very simple questions:

- How is cash allocated?
- How is risk allocated?
- What are the incentives for both parties in the deal?

In the examples above, we looked at two simple versions of common arrangements for sharing risk and reward. In the first example, a proportional sharing scheme was employed. In the second, a nonproportional scheme was introduced in which the venture capitalist demanded a fixed dollar return, regardless of the actual outcomes.

There are of course a myriad of possible variations on this theme. It is possible to combine proportional sharing schemes with fixed hurdles. Or, the timing of the hurdles can be altered. There are also many other mechanisms for affecting the allocation of value and the implicit incentives in a given deal. What is important to note, at this point, is that investors can infer information about the abilities and convictions of entrepreneurs by offering different deal terms and gauging the response. The ability to signal intentions credibly may enable some entrepreneurs to obtain funding that would not have been available were there no means for communicating true abilities or convictions.

STAGED CAPITAL COMMITMENT

Suppose you present an investment proposal to a venture capitalist that calls for an expenditure of $20 million to build a semiconductor fabrication facility. The $20 million will be required over a three-year period. How will the venture capitalist respond to your offer to sell him 75% ownership of the venture for $20 million?

After picking himself up off the floor, the venture capitalist will begin a process of trying to educate you about the real world. And, if he has not been too offended by your proposal, he will make a counter-proposal. The terms of the counter-offer will likely call for staged infusions of capital over time. In the first round, for example, the venture capitalist might offer to invest $1 million for the purpose of assembling the managerial team, writing a business plan, completing engineering specifications, conducting market research, and testing the feasibility of the process.

The $1 million capital would be expected to last about nine months. At that point, the venture would be expected to raise additional capital for the purpose of building a prototype manufacturing plant. That process might require $4 million in capital. Finally, there would be plans for a third round of financing for the purpose of building a full-scale manufacturing facility and beginning to market. The investment required at that point might be $15 million.

With respect to valuation at each stage of the process, it is entirely possible that the entrepreneur will end up owning the 25% share that he demanded in the initial negotiation. But the process by which that ownership is attained will be very different. One plausible scenario is described in *Exhibit 3.*

In this plan, the company raises the total of $20 million over three rounds. At each point new capital is infused into the company, the valuation increases. In the first round, for example, the venture capitalist demands 50% of the company for only $1 million. In the last round, however, the venture capitalist is content to receive only 25% of the company in return for $15 million, thus implying a post-money evaluation of $60 million.[3]

Why does the venture capitalist demand that capital be staged over time rather than committed up-front? Why would any self-respecting entrepreneur accept such a process? Remember that the venture is scheduled to run out of capital periodically; if it cannot raise capital at the second or third rounds, then it goes out of business and the entrepreneur is out of a job.

---

3. Note that, although the venture capitalist purchases a third of the company in this round, he only increases his cumulative share by a sixth (to 66.7%). When a company issues new shares of stock to raise capital, the resulting dilution is essentially charged proportionately to each existing shareholder. Thus, the venture capitalist's share increases only by that portion of the new equity he does not already hold. To compute the cumulative shares: *Second Round:* 50.0% + (33.3% × (1 − 50.0%)) = 66.7%; *Third Round:* 66.7% + (25.0% × (1 − 66.7%)) = 75.0%.

EXHIBIT 3

| ROUND OF FINANCING | AMOUNT INVESTED THIS ROUND | % REC'D THIS ROUND | CUMULATIVE | | IMPLIED VALUATION (POST MONEY) |
			VC'S SHARE	FOUNDER'S SHARE	
First round	$ 1,000,000	50.0%	50.0%	50.0%	$ 2,000,000
Second round	4,000,000	33.3	66.7	33.3%	12,000,000
Third round	15,000,000	25.0	75.0	25.0%	60,000,000

To begin to understand the reasons underlying this seemingly peculiar process, it is important to think about how the venture under consideration will evolve over time. In particular, what new information will the venture capitalist and the entrepreneur have at each point that the company goes back to raise capital?

Consider the point at which the company needs to raise $4 million. At this point, the venture capitalist and entrepreneur will know how the company has performed relative to its initial business plan. What is the management team like? How do they work together? Does the new business plan make sense? Has the company developed complete engineering specs? How has the perceived opportunity changed? Does the market research reveal adequate demand? What new competition exists? How have valuations in the capital market changed since the previous financing round? These are the types of questions that can be answered at the end of the first nine months of operation. If all goes well, the major risks outstanding at the time of the first round of financing—the "people risk" due to the lack of a complete management team, the technical risk from the lack of product specification, and the market risk due to the lack of market research—will have been greatly reduced. If so, the venture capitalist will be willing to buy shares at a much higher price, thus in effect accepting a lower expected rate of return.

If the company continues to proceed as hoped while approaching the third round of financing, there should be a similar reduction in perceived risk to the investor. Whereas, at the second round, consulting engineers could evaluate the product specifications for the venture capitalist, now there will be an actual product. Market research and initial marketing should by now have produced verifiable interest in the product, if not a backlog of orders. At this stage, then, the venture capitalist is evaluating an investment in a real product, within a known competitive context, on the eve of full-scale production and marketing. The increase in valuation at the third round reflects the further reduction of risk of investing at this point.

Suppose, however, that all does not go according to plan. At the time the $4 million is required, the company has not done well, and there are new competitors not previously anticipated. At this point, the venture capitalist can either abandon ship and allow the company to fail, or can strike a new price with the entrepreneur that reflects the less sanguine outlook. For example, the venture capitalist might demand as much as 50% of the company for his $4 million, implying a total valuation of only $8 million.

The point here is simple: by staging the commitment of capital the venture capitalist gains the options to abandon and to revalue the project as new information arrives. These are extremely valuable options, as will be demonstrated later.

But does this process make sense from the standpoint of the entrepreneur? Go back to the original proposal. Remember that the entrepreneur asked for $20 million in return for 75% of the shares. It seems likely that, even if the venture capitalist had been willing to consider the offer, he would have demanded a much higher share of the company than 75%, given the enormous risk as of the first round. This would likely have created a situation in which neither side would have found it sensible to proceed. The entrepreneur would have had too little incentive to risk his career, and the venture capitalist would have been worried about this loss of motivation. (As a general rule, if there does not appear to be enough room to provide sufficient incentives to management, then the deal probably won't get done.)

THE VALUE OF THE OPTION TO ABANDON

Why do the venture capitalist and the entrepreneur seem to end up better off under the alternative of staged capital commitment? To explore this issue, it will make sense to return to our simple example at the beginning. For a $1,000 initial investment, the projected cash flows were $500 per year for each of five years, followed by a $1,000 return of capital at the end of the fifth year. Suppose that instead of a simple $1,000 investment up-front, the investment can be made in two stages of $500 each. Suppose also that there is great uncertainty about the future annual cash flows to be received. There is a 50% chance they will be $50 per year and a 50% chance they will turn out to be $950 per year; and the expected value thus remains $500 per year.

We will now explore two different sets of rules governing this investment project. In the first, the venture capitalist has no choice but to invest the second $500 in the second year; that is, even if the actual annual cash flows turn out to be $50, the $500 will be spent. Under the second set of rules, the venture capitalist has the right, or option, to decide whether or not to invest the second $500. He can make this decision at the end of the first year, just after he has learned what the actual annual cash flows will be. If he decides not to invest (that is, to abandon the project), then he forfeits the right to receive any of the annual cash flows and receives a reduced share, $750, of the terminal payment of $1,000. The different possible sets of cash flows are provided in *Exhibit 4*.

What is the present value of the investment project under the different sets of rules? Evaluating the first is easy; the expected present value of the

EXHIBIT 4

	0	1	2	3	4	5	PV @ 40%
Rule I: VC Must Invest in Both Years							
Good scenario		$950	$950	$950	$950	$950	$1,933
Bad scenario		50	50	50	50	50	$ 102
Expected Ann's cash		500	500	500	500	500	$1,018
Terminal value						1,000	$ 186
Expected cash in	($500)	500	500	500	500	1,500	$1,204
Investment		(500)					($ 857)
Expected net cash	($500)	$ 0	$500	$500	$500	$1,500	$ 346

	0	1	2	3	4	5	PV @ 40%
Rule II: VC Has Option to Abandon in Year One							
Good scenario							
Annual cash flow		$950	$950	$950	$950	$950	$1,933
Terminal value						1,000	$ 186
Investment	($500)	(500)					($ 857)
Net cash flow	($500)	$450	$950	$950	$950	$1,950	$1,262
Bad scenario							
Annual cash flow		$ 0				$ 0	
Terminal value						750	$ 139
Investment	($500)						($ 500)
Net cash flow	($500)	$ 0	$ 0	$ 0	$ 0	$750	($ 361)
Expected (or average) value of scenarios[1]							
Expected net cash	($500)	$225	$475	$475	$475	$1,225	$ 451

1. Expected value of option to abandon (Rule I – Rule II): $104

cash inflows and outflows is $846 and the expected net present value is $346. Note that the latter figure is higher than the $204 determined in the previous section because the venture capitalist is now allowed to defer investing $500 for one year.

Under the second set of rules, the venture capitalist must evaluate whether or not it makes sense to invest in the second year, after the actual cash flows are revealed. If the cash flows turn out to be $950 per year, then the venture capitalist would be crazy not to spend the $500 necessary to receive the annual cash flows. (An investment that required investing $500 to receive $950 immediately, not to mention $950 for four years and an additional $250 of terminal value, has an infinite internal rate of return.)

If, however, the cash flows turn out to be only $50 per year, then the venture capitalist has a tougher analysis. If he invests $500, he will receive

$50 immediately and $50 a year for 4 years, as well as an additional $250 in terminal value. If he chooses not to invest, he will forfeit the $50 payment stream and the additional terminal value.

Given a discount rate of 40%, it turns out that he is much better off deciding not to invest. The net present value of the incremental investment from that point forward is –$292. By not investing, the venture capitalist raises the net present value of the project as a whole, as of year 1, from –$97 to $195, thus "creating" $292 in value.

After determining the optimal decision, conditional on the arrival of new information, the venture capitalist can then evaluate the entire project looking forward. Because he can cut off the investment process if the cash flows turn out to be low, the venture capitalist has an expected present value of $951 and an expected net present value of $451.

The new expected net present value of $451 can be compared to the $346 determined when the venture capitalist had no choice. Somehow, an extra $104 of value has been created simply by changing the rules a little bit. This difference is the value of the option to abandon. To gain this option, the venture capitalist would be willing to invest up to an additional $104 at the outset for a given level of ownership.

In this regard, the process of estimating the value of the option to abandon is usually far more complex than that described above. This is so because the number of possible scenarios is effectively infinite, as is the number of points in time at which the value of continuing the project must be evaluated. Despite the obvious complexity of the real world, financial economists have devised promising techniques for valuing such operating options by using an offshoot of option pricing theory called "contingent claims analysis."[4]

This analysis reveals, among other things, that the value of the option to abandon is higher under the following conditions:

- The greater the uncertainty about the future value of the venture;
- The greater the amount of time before the actual decision to abandon must be made; and
- The higher the ratio of the value of the abandoned project (the liquidation value) to the value of the project if pursued (present value of additional free cash flow less additional investment).

It is important to note that the traditional process of calculating expected net present values does not give the same answer as the process described above, in which each decision is evaluated at each point in time and the decision tree folded back to the present assuming optimal decisions are made at each intermediate point in time. In our example, to be sure, the difference in approaches does not change the basic fact that the project looks

---

4. *See* Volume 5, Number 1 of the *Midlands Corporate Finance Journal*, which is devoted almost entirely to the applications of contingent claims analysis in capital budgeting.

good. But it is very easy to imagine situations in which the value of the option to abandon might be sufficiently high to change the net present value from negative to positive. Such might be the case when there is great uncertainty and the investor has the option to stage the capital investment over time. But, this is exactly the case in most venture capital investments; and this is why one almost always sees staged capital commitment in these investments.

APPLICATION TO DEALMAKING

From the above analysis, it seems clear that a driving force behind staged capital commitment is the preservation of the option to abandon. This option has great value to the venture capitalist. And, indeed, the option is exercised relatively frequently in the real world.

But let's return once more to the view of the entrepreneur. Because the option to abandon is valuable to the venture capitalist doesn't necessarily mean, after all, that it adds value for the entrepreneur. Wouldn't the entrepreneur almost always be better off if the venture capitalist committed all the required capital up-front?

While generalizations are dangerous, staged capital commitment probably makes as much sense for the entrepreneur as for the venture capitalist. The reason, as I suggested earlier, is that the entrepreneur has a chance to minimize the dilution he suffers by bringing in outside capital. Because there is more value initially (precisely because of the option to abandon), the share of value awarded to the venture capitalist is lower, holding all other things constant.

In addition, staged capital commitment not only provides the venture capitalist with the option to abandon, but also gives the entrepreneur the option to raise capital at a higher valuation. The entrepreneur is betting that there will be positive results on which to base higher and higher valuations as the company grows, thus necessitating less dilution at each stage that new capital is required. And the willingness of the entrepreneur to bet on himself, as we have seen, sends a positive signal to the venture capitalist.

The entrepreneur, then, faces a conflict of motives in raising capital. On the one hand, he is tempted to raise only the minimum necessary amount of capital to avoid selling too much stock in early rounds at low prices, thus suffering great dilution. At the same time, however, he is also tempted to raise excessive amounts of capital early to preserve the option to continue operations through tough times. Some have described this problem confronting the entrepreneur as "the horse race between fear and greed"—that is, between the fear of running out of capital and the desire to retain maximum possible ownership (and I will return to this later).

Finally, there is an additional and powerful reason why the deals should be structured in stages. There is no more powerful motivator than the knowledge that the enterprise is scheduled to run out of cash in the relatively near future. In the parlance of entrepreneurial finance, the rate at which a company consumes cash is called the "burn rate." Given any level of initial cash and a burn rate, it is possible to calculate the "fume date"—the date on which the company will have exhausted its cash and will be operating solely on fumes. The existence of periodic "fume dates" focuses the energies of management on creating value from limited resources; and this process can accrue to the benefit of both entrepreneur and venture capitalist.[5]

To summarize, then, a common technique used in financing new ventures is to infuse capital over time, retaining the option to abandon the venture at any point that the net present value, looking forward, is negative. This technique appeals to venture capitalist and entrepreneur alike. The venture capitalist preserves a valuable option and also creates the strongest possible incentives for management to create value and meet goals. The entrepreneur minimizes dilution and also benefits to the extent that his energies are appropriately focused on value creation.

But while the above example tends to suggest that the preservation of such financing options is an unequivocal boon, the reader should also always keep in mind the fact that the real world is more complicated and that providing such options to the venture capitalist may create its own problems. For example, having a periodic "fume date" will work in many situations as a motivating factor. In others, though, it may create incentives to aim for short-term success rather than long-term value creation. This may or may not be in the best interests of both parties. Also, the future cash flows will never be known with any degree of certainty. Because of the great uncertainty remaining at any stage of development, some ventures will be abandoned even though they actually have excellent prospects; and some will be funded when they should not be.

It is worth noting in passing, however, that many successful companies have gone through periods when they came very close to their "fume date." Many have also had to change their business plans dramatically as new information was revealed. These realities often make the staged capital commitment process not only valuable to entrepreneur and venture capitalist alike, but also a very trying experience for anyone involved.

THE OPTION TO REVALUE A PROJECT

In the preceding section, the focus was on achieving some understanding of the option to abandon a given project. There are also steps short of abandonment that warrant consideration. The process of staged capital

---

5. The reader should also keep in mind the tension that exists in such situations between the entrepreneur and the venture capitalist. For the venture capitalist, a single venture is but one of many. For the entrepreneur, the venture is all there is. Abstract discussions of the option to abandon should be tempered with knowledge that people's careers and egos are at stake.

commitment involves periodically evaluating whether to continue funding an investment and, if so, on what terms. The right to revalue a given project has value when compared to an alternative situation in which the future financing terms are decided irrevocably at the start of the venture.

Suppose a venture starts with a 50/50 split in equity ownership between the entrepreneur and the venture capitalist. One year after the venture starts, the company needs more capital. The question is: At what price will the new capital come in? If the original deal awarded the venture capitalist the right to invest in future rounds at a price to be negotiated later, the answer will depend on the progress the company has made since its last funding as well as the state of the economy and capital markets at the time. If the prospects are good, then the value will be relatively high; if not, value will be low. In the former case, the entrepreneur will suffer minor dilution; in the event of poor performance, the dilution factor will be much larger.

Now, suppose that instead of flexible pricing on the second round of financing, the venture capitalist was granted a fixed price option at the beginning to buy one million shares at a price of $10.00 per share at any point within two years. If the justifiable per share price at the end of two years is above $10.00, then the venture capitalist will exercise the option. If the price is below $10.00, the venture capitalist will walk away from the option, thereby truncating the lower side of the return distribution.

But if the company really needs the $10 million, and the justifiable price is below $10.00 per share, then the money will not necessarily be forthcoming. Moreover, another outside investor might find the existence of the call option (actually warrants in this case) problematic in terms of investing because of the potential for future dilution if the company does succeed in increasing value above $10.00 per share. If the money cannot be raised, then the venture will suffer and may even fail.

Flexibility in future pricing can make the difference between a venture succeeding and failing when performance is not as favorable as expected. The reader might argue that no venture capitalist will walk away from a venture with value simply because of some inflexible deal provisions. But the situation described above has occurred many times and a complex game of "chicken" develops between the entrepreneurial team and the venture capitalists, in which each tries to obtain the best deal. The result of such a game can be very detrimental to the economic vitality of the enterprise. Moreover, it should also be remembered that the venture capital fund has many companies in its portfolio, and the venture capitalist may well decide to walk away from one investment that is not performing up to expectations even if doing so seems not to make sense.

THE OPTION TO INCREASE CAPITAL COMMITTED

Another option to be considered is the right to increase funding to a company, particularly if the company is doing well. Consider a start-up venture in the specialty retailing area. The company's business plan calls for having 20 stores in the Northeast by the end of two years. Suppose after the first year, the company has 6 stores, each of which is performing well above expectations. It might make sense for the entrepreneur and venture capitalist to accelerate the rate at which new stores are introduced. To do so will entail raising additional capital. The venture capitalist will welcome the opportunity to invest more heavily in such a successful venture and would like to lock in the right to do so. The entrepreneur, however, would want to ensure that the price at which additional capital is raised reflects the superior past performance and prospects of the company.

In this example, the right to increase capital invested at some intermediate point is very valuable. One unresolved issue, however, is who should "own" the right to invest more money. To whom does the benefit of superior performance belong?

One way in which venture capitalists gain the right to invest more, while still allowing the entrepreneur to benefit from success, is by asking for rights of first refusal on all subsequent financings. By doing so, they buy the option to invest later, but only on whatever terms are deemed appropriate by the capital market.

In sum, there are a variety of financing options—options to abandon, to re-value, and to increase capital committed—built into the financing contracts fashioned by the professional venture capital community. Over the life of any venture capital portfolio, there are likely to be some losers, some winners, and some intermediate performers. Successful funds generate high rates of return by cutting their losses early, not investing great amounts in early rounds, and letting their winners run by investing larger amounts of money in multiple rounds of financing. Phrased differently, they frequently exercise their options to abandon and their options to participate in later rounds of financing. You will also discover that some of the most successful companies in their portfolios had a distress round of financing in which the ability to re-value the investment was the difference between continued financing and bankruptcy. Prominent examples are Federal Express and MCI Communications.

—— ANTICIPATING THE CONSEQUENCES OF FINANCING DECISIONS

Managers and capital suppliers are making extraordinarily complex decisions in environments characterized by great uncertainty. More important, they must live with the consequences of those decisions. One way to approach the task of decision making is to ask three questions before making a decision:

· What can go wrong?
· What can go right?

· What decisions can be made today and in the future that will maximize the reward-to-risk ratio?

These simple questions are designed to force the decision maker to confront uncertainty directly and to manage the uncertainty.

One of the most critical issues in venture capital financing, as we have seen, is the decision whether to raise capital in excess of expected requirements. A risk common to virtually every venture ever started is that all will not go as planned and that the introduction of a product or the sales response will fail to meet expectations. It is also often the case that the company will have to change the focus of its efforts dramatically as it gathers more information about the opportunity.

To raise capital in excess of anticipated needs is equivalent to buying an option to change strategy as required or to keep the company on sound financial footing until results do match expectations. Of course, in gaining that option, the venture capitalist is denied valuable options to re-value or to abandon. One compromise is not to raise excess capital, but nevertheless to retain the option to call on the investors for additional capital if needed, in return for which the current equity round would have to be sold at a lower price.

Maximizing the reward-to-risk ratio also requires examining the other side of the spectrum—what can go right—and ensuring that in the event of the venture's success, the value created can be fruitfully harvested. One means of harvest is for the venture to be acquired after a period of years. The question is: what decisions can management make that will increase the likelihood that such a rewarding end to the venture will take place? In this regard, management must carefully avoid introducing any form of "poison pill" into its capital structure that will preclude a buyout offer.

To illustrate, some start-up companies raise capital from a major participant in the industry. Although doing so may provide necessary capital and some expertise or marketing, it may also mean that no other large competitor of the original funder will even consider an offer later on. A start-up can thus lose the option to market the company to the highest bidder in the industry. In this situation, as when any option is being given up, this route should be pursued only if there are sufficient offsetting benefits.

Venture capitalists often ensure that they will profit in the event of success by gaining the right to force the company to go public or the right to sell stock jointly with the company's public offering. By structuring an investment in the form of preferred stock, a venture capitalist can also profit from a success that is too modest to permit a public offering—that is, by recovering capital through the redemption of preferred stock and the payout of accumulated dividends. Such a structure also permits the venture capitalist to receive some payout in the form of dividends in the event of a "sideways" scenario.

The process of anticipating good or bad news and making decisions that maximize the chance that the good will outweigh the bad is a critical element of good decision making. Moreover, it is not all that difficult to decide what events, good or bad, are likely to occur in any venture over time. These events will occur with respect to:

- The people (e.g., death, motivation);
- The individual company (e.g., production or marketing issues);
- The industry in question (e.g., competition, substitutes);
- The sociological environment (social rules/legal system); and,
- The state of the economy and capital markets (e.g., boom, recession, lower or higher stock prices).

Sensible deals will preserve options to react to and receive maximum benefit from good news and will also protect the company from going under when bad news arises. Sensible deals will also provide strong incentives to all parties to skew the outcome toward the good news side of the ledger.

AN EXAMPLE OF A BAD DEAL

Anyone familiar with start-up companies recognizes that a common problem is that the company consumes more cash than was projected when it raised capital. Frequently, the primary cause is a shortfall in revenues which may occur for many different reasons. And because running out of cash is not an uncommon occurrence, any deal terms that govern the relationship between the company and the suppliers of capital must reflect the likelihood that the company will require more capital.

Unfortunately, deals are very often designed that make it extremely difficult to raise capital when the company needs to. For example, in one case, the original capital suppliers to a start-up demanded the option to acquire up to 51% of the common stock that would be outstanding at any time in the following three years. The option could be exercised at a fixed price equal to the price paid in the first round of financing. The same group also got the right of first refusal on all subsequent financings, for a period lasting 60 days.

There were several problems that arose as time passed. First the company's progress was disappointing when compared against the business plan projections. The result was that the company needed a significant infusion of capital long before anticipated. The logical supplier of the new capital was the group owning the option. But, there was a problem: the financing group had very little incentive to exercise their option early. Doing so would sacrifice the value of being able to wait to learn more about the company. And that value was considerable because of the length of time left on the option and the high risk involved in the venture.

On the other hand, potential new capital suppliers were confronted with the problem that they might be diluted immediately after they invested because the original financing group could then acquire up to 51% of the *then outstanding* shares at a fixed price. Moreover, because the group had a 60-day right of first refusal, the new potential investors also faced the possibility that the investment of time and energy required to evaluate the deal might go for naught if the original investors exercised their right of first refusal. This was entirely possible because the very fact that the new investors were interested would signal that the company's prospects were attractive to a third party. A final problem was that the original financing group did not really have sufficient resources to exercise their options when the money was needed.

This example demonstrates precisely where the thought process described above is critical in designing deals. Neither management *nor* the investors should have signed this deal. Doing so was essentially a bet that everything would transpire exactly as outlined in the business plan, an outcome that probably has only a 10 percent chance of happening. The financial structure almost drove this company into bankruptcy, and only very intense negotiations to modify the deal saved the company.

Having stated boldly that this deal should never have been signed, we now ask if a different deal could have been structured to accomplish the same basic objectives. First, the investors were clearly interested in preserving three options: (1) the right to control the company (the "51%" option); (2) the right to invest more money at a fixed price for an extended period of time; and (3) the right to maintain their ownership position in the event a subsequent financing round was about to take place at an unfairly low valuation. Management was interested in raising enough capital to get the company off the ground. At the same time, however, it wanted to minimize the dilution from selling shares at a low valuation relative to that possible on future rounds if the company did well.

If both parties had anticipated the future by asking questions detailed at the beginning of this section, the deal they struck could have been quite different while still satisfying the implicit objectives of each party. To illustrate, both the investors and the management would probably have been far better off to raise additional capital in the first place. The company was already far behind the plan when this deal was made, and there was not sufficient new (positive) information on which to base a new capital infusion. The investors and management had raised too little capital for the company to get to the point where a new-better-informed decision about whether or not to proceed could be made.

Second, the investor group could have structured a deal in which they simply paid a lower initial price per share for the company, rather than acquiring the right to invest more money at a fixed price later. The investors purchased a package consisting of some common stock and some rights. On the surface, it would appear that they paid a relatively high price per share of stock. But when a portion of the original investment capital is attributed appropriately to these "ancillary" rights, then the actual economic price paid for the common stock turns out to be far lower. If the investor group had structured a simpler deal in which they paid the lower price, they would have been confronted with far less trouble later.

With respect to the right to invest more money later, this goal could have been accomplished by gaining proportional rights of first refusal, which would allow the investor to participate in later rounds of financing in proportion to the equity already held. Such rights, however, should not be structured so as to discourage another outside group from investing the time and resources required to decide whether or not to invest.

Also, the deal could have been structured with a "ratchet," enabling the original investors to be protected against subsequent financing rounds at lower prices. With a ratchet in place, the shares owned by the original investor would be retroactively adjusted so that the effective price per share paid would be no higher than the price paid by the subsequent round.

Finally, with respect to the control issue, the investor group was deluded into believing that 51% was a magical figure, and the only way to retain control in the situation. In reality, control vests in the hands of those who have capital when capital is needed. Control can also be attained by having a majority representation on the board of directors or through employment contracts with rigid performance specifications. The particular mechanisms by which this investor group sought to retain control—the rolling 51% option—almost brought the company to its knees.

——— CONCLUSION

We began this reading on venture capital by introducing a relatively simple example of a deal, one in which the entrepreneur sought capital from a venture capitalist. We saw that the terms negotiated affected the split of cash and the split of risk, and hence the split of value between the supplier and the user of capital. We then pointed out that alternative structures would affect the incentives of the entrepreneur such that the total amount of value at stake was affected by the terms negotiated.

We then took the relatively simple single-investment-type deal and expanded the terms to include the more realistic possibility that the investment would be made in several distinct stages over time. In so doing, we discovered that certain options provided venture capitalists, both explicit and implicit, are valuable to venture capitalist and entrepreneur alike, and thus improve the terms on which the entrepreneur is able to raise capital. Staging capital infusions into ventures, for example, enables the venture capitalist to retain the option to abandon a project if that makes sense. We also observed that the entrepreneur enters into such contracts willingly, though there are obvious possible scenarios in which having structured the deal that way will not have been in the best interests of the entrepreneur.

Similarly, both parties can gain from providing the other party the option to re-value a project or from the venture capitalist's option to increase capital committed if the project proves unexpectedly successful. Building such options into venture capital contracts also helps overcome initial differences of opinion between venture capitalist and entrepreneur as to, say, the probability of different outcomes. Such options also provide a signaling mechanism, if you will, by which entrepreneur can credibly communicate to investors their confidence in the project and in their own abilities.

These options not only add to the total project value as of a first financing round, but also provide a structure for avoiding a financing impasse should things not work out as planned. The terms of financing must allow the company to obtain the capital necessary for survival in (temporary) bad-news scenarios, as well as providing for the exploitation of good-news scenarios. If the deal is structured such that it is almost impossible to raise additional capital (for example, there is an implicit "poison pill" built into the contract), then the financial structure of the deal will reduce instead of adding to the value of the project.

The message that seems to emerge most clearly, then, from this look at venture capital is this: The total value of an investment opportunity may depend critically on the financing terms governing the deal. By restructuring terms, the size of the total economic pie can be dramatically changed—for better or worse. The extent to which these insights into venture capital markets have a bearing on the financial practices of public corporations remains an open question, but one that surely merits further attention.

—— DISCUSSION QUESTIONS

1. Apply the author's approach to decision making to a significant decision in your life—where and what to study, changing jobs, leaving a job to return to school, for example. What risks and rewards are involved? What actions could you take at the time of the decision to promote the best possible outcome in the long run?

2. The author describes a scenario in which a skeptical venture capitalist shifts risk from himself to the entrepreneur by investing in convertible preferred stock. Would you agree to the arrangement, try to negotiate it, or reject it? Explain your reasoning.

3. A staged capital commitment is a mixed blessing for the entrepreneur. By seeking as much capital as possible up front, what signals is the entrepreneur sending to the venture capitalist? Alternatively, by agreeing to incremental infusions of cash, what is the entrepreneur communicating?

4. A "fume date," the author says, "may create incentives to aim for short-term success rather than long-term value creation." Suppose after a third round of financing, you are building a manufacturing facility and undertaking a marketing campaign; cash is being

consumed much more rapidly than you had anticipated. What actions would you take to protect the long-term interests of your company?

5. Do you think venture capitalists and entrepreneurs are more like allies or more like adversaries? Is their relationship a zero-sum game—the bargains struck between the two parties represent victory for one and defeat for the other? What do you think are the hallmarks of a good deal?

17 The Legal Protection of Intellectual Property

MICHAEL J. ROBERTS

As technology-based businesses have grown in importance, intellectual property has emerged as a powerful source of competitive advantage. Yet, the legal context that surrounds patents, trademarks, trade secrets, and copyrights is complex.

Roberts articulates the legal underpinnings of the classes of protection afforded intellectual property. In addition, the enterprise's right to protect the intellectual property it has created must be balanced against the employees' right to earn a living from his or her knowledge and skills. This creates further challenges for the entrepreneur seeking to protect what may be a critical resource.

INTELLECTUAL PROPERTY

The area of intellectual property has challenged the legal system for hundreds of years, and continues to do so. Common law has historically protected property rights of individuals and corporations. But the area of intellectual property presents challenges to the legal system. If someone stole a piece of physical property—like your wedding band—it would be fairly easy to prove: that individual would have the ring, and you would be without it.

Yet, how can you tell when someone has taken an idea or a concept? A copy of a software program does not diminish the physical attributes of the original, only the economic interests of the owner. Intellectual property issues are particularly complex in situations where an individual is working on some state-of-the-art process for his employer. During the course of developing the design, the employee has some "inspiration" which was outside the scope of

---

This note was prepared by Lecturer Michael J. Roberts as the basis for class discussion. It is based upon an earlier note, HBS No. 384-188, prepared by Michael J. Roberts under the supervision of Professor Howard H. Stevenson. Copyright © 1998 by the President and Fellows of Harvard College. Harvard Business School case 898-230.

the project's original bounds. Does this idea belong to the employer or the employee? Does it matter whether the inspiration occurred on the company's premises or while the employee was at home in the shower? Could the employee continue to work for the employer, but set up an independent business to exploit the idea?

A special system of patent law and patent court system was developed to deal specifically with these questions. Recently, however, intellectual property issues have arisen outside the bounds of traditional patent and trade secret law. The legal system is currently in the midst of grappling with these problems, and recent (1995) legislation has attempted to clarify certain issues.

—— INTELLECTUAL PROPERTY AND THE LAW

Historically, it has been a specific goal of U.S. public policy to create the incentives required for the progress of technology. One of the means to this end has been through the system of patents and copyrights. These classes of intellectual property have arisen out of the statutes of the United States government, which are, quite literally, the laws of the United States as passed by Congress.

They include "titles" such as: Title 11-Bankruptcy; Title 23-Highways; Title 39-Postal Service; and Title 50-War and National Defense.

Each of the "Titles" lays down the law relating to the subject at hand, as well as the administrative systems the U.S. government will put in place to support each of the areas. There are two titles specifically relating to intellectual property: Title 17-Copyrights; and Title 35-Patents.

Patents and copyrights receive protection directly under this statutory framework, but the law in these areas is not governed exclusively by the language of the U.S. Code itself. Through their application and interpretation of the statutes in individual cases, judges define (and, indeed create) relevant legal standards. Such "common law," or judge-made law, adapts the patent and copyright laws to modern circumstances (short of constitutional amendments to the statutes themselves).

Out of common law principles have grown other areas of law which address intellectual property issues. These areas include trademarks, trade secrets, and confidential business information. Each of these topics will be explored in detail.

—— PATENTS

Patents are issued by the U.S. Patent and Trademark Office. There are three specific types of patents:

- Utility Patents: for new articles, processes, machines, etc;
- Design Patents: for new and original ornamental designs for articles of manufacture; and
- Plant Patents: for new varieties of plant life.

It is important to understand the concept of a patent. A patent *does not* grant an individual exclusive rights to an invention. The inventor *already* has that exclusive right by dint of having invented the device in the first place; he/she can merely keep the invention a secret and enjoy its exclusive use. Rather, the government grants the inventor the "negative right" to exclude others from making or using the invention. This right is granted in exchange for placing the information in the public domain.[1]

For instance, let's assume that the electronic calculator was a patentable invention, and that Mr. Sharp was issued a patent on the device. Now, let us further assume that the idea of a checkbook holder containing an electronic calculator was also patented, and that Mr. Chex was issued a patent on this invention. Mr. Chex would have the right to prevent others including Mr. Sharp from manufacturing this device. However, Mr. Chex *could not* produce his article without the consent of Mr. Sharp. In the event that patent infringement does occur, the patent holder can sue in civil court for damages. Should the patent holder become aware of potential infringement before the actual infringement occurs, he/she can sue for an injunction to prevent the infringement from actually occurring.

As mentioned, these kinds of legal battles occur in the civil courts. The purpose of the patent court system is to mediate patent claims. For example, when a patent claim is published in the *Patent Gazette*, others could come forward and challenge the patentability of the invention in the patent court system. One basis of challenge is for another inventor to claim that he/she was actually the first inventor. For this reason, it is recommended that inventors keep a daily record of their progress in a notebook. These notes should record the inventor's progress, and be signed and witnessed on a daily basis. In the event of a challenge, such a record will prove invaluable.

The three types of patents each cover different kinds of intellectual property, and are governed by different regulations.

Utility Patents   A utility patent is issued to protect new, useful processes, devices or inventions. Utility patents are issued for a term of 20 years from date of application. First, what constitutes a patentable "invention"? The invention must meet several requirements:[2]

---

1. David A. Burge, *Patent and Trademark Tactics and Practice* (New York: John Wiley & Sons, 1980), p. 25.

2. Illinois Institute for Continuing Legal Education, *Intellectual Property Law for the General Business Counselor* (Illinois: Illinois Bar Center, 1973), pp. 1–16 through 1–24.

- It must fall within one of the statutory categories of subject matter. There are four broad classes of subject matter: machines, manufacture, composition of matter, and processes.
- Only the actual, original inventor may apply for patent protection. In the case of corporations, for instance, the patent, when issued, is always granted to the individual and then *assigned* to the corporation.
- The invention must be new. That is, it will be considered novel if it is:
  - not known or used by others in the U.S.;
  - not patented or described by others in a printed publication in this or a foreign country;
  - not patented in this country;
  - not made in this country by another who had not abandoned, suppressed, or concealed it.

- The invention must be useful, even if only in some minimal way.
- The invention must be nonobvious. If the invention has been obvious to anyone skilled in the art, then it is not patentable.

Finally, even if an invention meets all of these requirements, a patent can be denied if the application was not filed in a timely fashion. Specifically, if you used, sold, described in print, or attempted to secure a foreign patent application *more than one year prior* to your U.S. application, the patent will be denied.

The process of obtaining a patent is quite laborious. Patent attorneys, who specialize in the area, will draft the patent application which includes specific claims for the patentability of the invention. After several iterations of discussions with the patent office, some or all of the claims may be approved. This process frequently takes two years or longer.

Following acceptance of the patent by the Patent Office, a general description of the invention is published in the *Patent Gazette*. Interested parties may request the full patent from the Patent Office for a very nominal fee.

During the time between application for a patent and its issue, the invention has "patent pending" status. In some ways, this offers more protection than the actual patent. The invention will not be revealed by the government during this time, and others may be afraid to copy the invention for fear of infringing on the forthcoming patent.

Design Patents A design patent protects the nonfunctional features of useful objects. Design patents are issued for 14 years. In order to obtain a design patent, the following requirements must be met:[3]

---

3. Burge, pp. 137, 138.

- Ornamentality—the design must be aesthetically appealing and must not be dictated solely by functional or utilitarian considerations.
- Novelty—the design must be new. The same criteria used for a utility patent will be applied here.
- Nonobvious—the design must not be obvious to anyone skilled in the art. This is a difficult standard to apply to a design, and is quite subjective.
- Embodied in an article of manufacture—the design must be an inseparable part of a manufactured article.

Plant Patents   A plant patent is attainable on any new variety of plant which that individual is able to reproduce asexually. The new plant must be nonobvious. A plant patent is issued for a term of 20 years.

COPYRIGHTS

Copyright protection is afforded to artists and authors, giving them the sole right to print, copy, sell, and distribute the work. Books, musical and dramatic compositions, maps, paintings, sculptures, motion pictures and sound recordings can all be copyrighted.

To obtain copyright protection, the work must simply bear a copyright notice which includes the symbol © or the word "copyright," the date of first publication, and the name of the owner of the copyright.

Copyrighted works are protected for a term of 50 years beyond the death of the author.

TRADEMARKS, SERVICE MARKS, AND TRADE DRESS

A trademark is any name, symbol, or configuration which an individual or organization uses to distinguish its products from others. A service mark is such a name which is used to distinguish a service, rather than a tangible product.

Trademark law is *not* derived from statutes of the Constitution, but is an outgrowth of the common law and service dealing with unfair competition. Unfair competition is deemed to exist when the activities of a competitor result in confusion in the mind of the buying public.

There are several regulations which govern the proper use and protection of service- and trademarks.[4] The scope of protection under the law is a function of the nature of the mark itself.

---

4. Burge, p. 114.

- Coined marks—a newly coined, previously unknown mark is afforded the broadest protection, e.g., Xerox as a brand of copier, Charmin as a brand of toilet tissue.
- Arbitrary marks—a name already in use, and applied to a certain product by a firm, but without suggesting any of the product's attributes, e.g., Apple Computer, Milky Way candy bars.
- Suggestive marks—a name in use, but suggesting some desirable attribute of the product, e.g., Sweet-n-Low as a low-calorie sweetener, White-Out correction fluid.
- Descriptive marks—a name which describes the purpose or function of the product. Descriptive marks cannot be registered until, over time, they have proven to be distinctive terms, e.g., "sticky" would probably not be approved as a trademarked brand name for glue.
- Unprotectable terms—generic names, which refer to the general class of product. Escalator, for instance, once a trade name, is now a generic term for moving staircases. One could not introduce a new brand of orange juice and call it "O.J."

In order to maintain a trademark, an owner must continue to use it and protect it. In this vein, some consumer product companies routinely produce and sell a few hundred items of several brand names which they have trademarked and wish to protect, but are not in normal production. Similarly, Coca-Cola has a crew of agents who routinely order "a coke" in establishments which do not serve Coca-Cola. If they are served a soda, they prosecute. In this way, they can maintain that they have attempted to keep their brand name from becoming a generic. Aspirin, Cellophane, Zipper and Escalator, are all names which lost their trademark status due to failure of their owners to protect the usage of the term.

Until a trademark is registered with the Patents and Trademark Office, it is desirable to use the ™ symbol after the name of a product, SM for services. After registration, the legend ® should be used.

Trade dress is a term that refers to the look and feel of a retail establishment. Just as the courts have sought to protect the value businesses have built up in a brand name, they have been asked to protect the distinctive "look and feel" of certain retail concepts. In a recent example, for instance, one Mexican restaurant chain successfully sued a "knock-off" of the concept, arguing that the imitator had copied the unique trade dress of the original concept, unfairly trading on the value created by the concept's originator.

TRADE SECRETS

A trade secret is typically defined as any formula, device, process or information which gives a business an advantage over its competitors. To be classified as a trade secret, the information must not be generally known in the trade.

One cannot, by definition, patent a trade secret, because the patent laws require that the invention be fully disclosed.

One advantage of a trade secret is that the protection will not expire after the 20-year term of the patent. Coke, for instance, maintains its recipe as a trade secret rather than patent it. Yet, should the information become public knowledge, their advantage could disappear quickly, and the inventor would have no claim on the process because it had not been patented.

Finally, should a firm decide to maintain a patentable advantage as a trade secret, and should another firm independently discover and patent that invention, this "second" inventor will have the right to collect royalties or force the "first" inventor to cease patent infringement. For this reason, many corporations routinely "defensively patent" and publish inventions so that others cannot.

In order for a company to maintain trade secret status for advantageous information, the company must keep the information secret and take precautions to keep it secret. These precautions include:

- Having certain policies relating to secret information.
- Making employees sign confidentiality and noncompete agreements.
- Marking documents "confidential" or "secret."

CONFIDENTIAL BUSINESS INFORMATION

The courts have also seen fit to protect a class of information less "secret" than a trade secret, but which is nonetheless confidential. The key here is that the information is disclosed in confidence, with the clear understanding that the information was confidential. A contractual obligation is established in which the receiver of the information agrees to treat it as confidential, and to use it only in furtherance of the objectives deemed appropriate by the owner. Even if the information is in the public domain, if the recipient derives some value from the confidential disclosure, he/she can be held liable for claims of unjust enrichment. There are several cases, for instance, where an inventor disclosed an idea, the recipient searched out the idea in *existing* U.S. patents, found the idea was already the subject of a patent, and bought that patent from the holder. The courts held that he had to give the patent to the submitter of the disclosure because of the confidential nature of their relationship.[5] One class of information that is commonly treated in this way, for instance, is a company's customer list.

---

5. Illinois Institute for Continuing Legal Education, pp. 6–9, 10.

EMPLOYEES' RIGHTS

Much of the law in this arena has evolved in an attempt to protect the rights of the enterprise. This has always been balanced, however, by the employee's right to earn a livelihood in the *best* potential source of livelihood. For instance, as an atomic engineer, the courts would protect my right to make a living *as an atomic engineer*, not merely earn a wage as a waiter or a bartender.

When a relationship between an employee and employer is severed, it is often the content of the written documents that will govern who has rights to what. Employment contracts, confidentiality, nondisclosure and noncompete agreements all come into play. For this reason, prospective employees are well advised to read these documents carefully, and negotiate, rather than merely signing all of the papers which are typically associated with the first day on the job.

An employee can bargain away some of his/her rights in this area by signing inventions agreements, noncompete contracts or employment agreements. However, the courts will not let an employee bargain away his/her fundamental right to earn a living from the best potential source.

If an employee signed an agreement which the courts found to be overly restrictive, the entire agreement would be thrown out. It is this fact which gives rise to the lawyer's advice that "It is better to sign an unreasonable employment agreement than a reasonable one."

There are three dimensions to the reasonableness test that the courts apply to employment agreements:

- time horizon;
- geographic scope;
- nature of employment.

For instance, an employment contract which required an employee not to compete for 6 months, in the state of New York, as a designer of petroleum process facilities might be viewed as reasonable. While an agreement which specified a time horizon of one year and a geographic area of the United States would probably be viewed as unreasonable.

SUMMARY

In summary, it is clear that the body of legal knowledge in the intellectual property area is evolving rapidly. Yet, the processes which the law prescribes remain vitally important; in this area in particular, dotting the "i's" and crossing the "t's" is key. Whether it be keeping notebooks and records, filing patent claims or reading the fine print on an employment contract, it is hard to overemphasize the importance of understanding the detail.

In order to gain sufficient command of the relevant body of law, specialized legal counsel is called for. In an area which is changing so rapidly, one cannot rely on prior practices and "industry standard policies" for protection.

——— BIBLIOGRAPHY

American Bar Association. *Sorting Out the Ownership Rights in Intellectual Property: A Guide to Practical Counseling and Legal Representation.* American Bar Association, 1980.

Burge, David A. *Patent and Trademark Tactics and Practice.* John Wiley & Sons, 1980.

Gallafent, R.J., N.A. Eastway, and V.A.F. Dauppe. *Intellectual Property Law and Taxation.* Oyez Publishing Ltd., 1981.

Illinois Institute for Continuing Legal Education. *Intellectual Property Law for the General Business Counselor.* Illinois Bar Center, 1973.

Johnston, Donald F. *Copyright Handbook.* R.R. Bowker Company, 1978.

Lietman, Alan. *Howell's Copyright Law.* BNA Incorporated, 1962.

White, Herbert S. *The Copyright Dilemma.* American Library Association, 1977.

——— DISCUSSION QUESTIONS

1. What tests must an invention meet in order to be eligible for patent protection?
2. When might a company choose to allow an invention to remain a trade secret rather than attempting to patent it?
3. How have the courts attempted to balance the rights of the business to protect its intellectual property with the employee's rights to earn a living?

The Horse Race Between Capital and Opportunity

18

WILLIAM A. SAHLMAN

People investing their money always try to earn high rates of return with the lowest possible risk. They scan the opportunity set for sensible places to invest. When one sector of the economy becomes particularly attractive—whether it is venture capital, real estate, or any other asset class—money flows in. Inevitably, the influx of money drives down prospective rates of return, perhaps even to levels that are unacceptably low.

This reading focuses on the private equity markets. During the mid- to late-1970s, a large amount of capital was allocated to venture capital and management buyouts. With the benefit of hindsight, it is clear that rates of return on this capital were very low. There was too much money invested relative to the opportunity set. The low realized rates of return caused investors to pull back from the sector. As investors decreased their allocations to private equity, however, prospective rates of return actually increased. During the mid- to late-1980s, rates of return on venture capital and buyouts were very high. As the night follows the day, investors came back, pouring unprecedented amounts of money into the sector.

It is impossible to predict what the consequences of the new high level of capital being committed in this sector will be. It is safe to say, however, that there has never been a time in recorded history when the supply of capital did not ultimately outstrip the supply of opportunity.

——— INTRODUCTION

The venture capital business is booming. The amount of capital in the industry is at an all-time high, as is the level of investment activity. In 1997, over $10 billion was raised and disbursed by professional venture capital firms. Reported rates of return in the past few years have been very high, in some cases approaching 50% per year. These high returns have been driven by attractive harvesting markets, notably the market for initial public offerings, but also extending to the acquisition market.

The current ebullience in the venture capital market stands in sharp contrast to the situation at the beginning of the decade. At that time, the amount of new capital coming into the industry was dropping, rates of return were anemic, at best, and industry pundits were bemoaning the demise of the industry.

The purpose of this article is to take a somewhat broader perspective on the venture capital industry. I assert that the industry is cyclical: few who have been in the industry for more than a few years will find this assertion objectionable, but it seems that many behave as though the industry is now invulnerable to cyclical forces. The real question is: what causes swings in the level of activity in the industry? And, what are the implications of so much capital flowing into the industry at the current time?

THE 1980S BOOM AND BUST

To begin the discussion, it is useful to turn back the clock to the early 1980s, the last major boom in the industry. From a healthy but modest level of less than $1 billion in 1980, the total annual capital coming into the industry soared to over $3 billion per year by 1983. That amount remained relatively high until the post-1987 period, when new capital commitments dropped each year. *Exhibit 1,* based on data from Venture Economics, depicts the movements in capital committed during the relevant time frame.

It is not hard to understand why venture capital was an attractive

EXHIBIT 1
Venture Capital Commitments

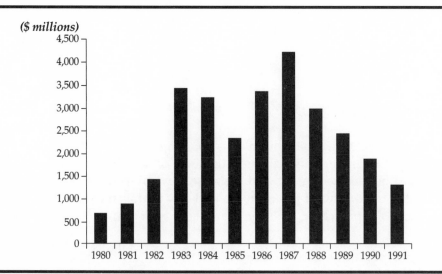

asset class during the early 1980s. First, reported rates of return on venture capital were relatively high. At that time, the median rate of return on professionally managed funds was estimated to be 25%. No fund had lost money during the life of the fund.

If you were an institutional investor at this time, you were eager to find investment opportunities that offered the prospect of high returns and low risk: venture capital seemed to fit both requirements perfectly. Liberalization of pension fund rules in the late 1970s, combined with a decrease in tax rates on capital gains, made increased commitments to venture capital feasible and attractive. Most of the new capital came from institutional sources. At the beginning of the 1980s, the total assets of insurance companies and pension funds was approximately $1.4 trillion: a small reallocation of capital to the venture capital sector resulted in a veritable torrent of new money going into the industry.[1]

At the same time, the nature of the opportunity set in the American economy seemed to shift. The advent of microprocessors, the birth and rapid growth of the microcomputer industry (in all dimensions), and the tectonic shift brought on by biotechnology resulted in new company formation potential that was virtually without precedent. Moreover, it was newly formed companies, not the entrenched competitors, that seized upon these technological changes to exploit opportunity. Prominent examples include Genentech, Amgen, Apple Computer, Compaq, Seagate, and Microsoft.

Any time a significant shift in asset allocation occurs in the economy, a question naturally follows: What are the future consequences of this shift? Does the shift make sense? In the late 1980s, I developed a simple economic model to explore the consequences of the increase in venture capital commitments. Specifically, I asked: How much value has to be created for venture capital investors to achieve some rate of return?

——— A SIMPLE MODEL

The model works as follows: assume a target rate of return on capital of 35% gross (i.e., before management fees and carried interest), which would translate into about 25% per year net to the limited partners. Then, assume that the capital committed to the industry each year is invested for 7 years at that rate of return. At any given point in time, the total value of the venture capital portfolio consistent with investors having earned their target return in the preceding periods can be calculated. To illustrate the calculation for 1990, the capital committed to the industry in 1983 is assumed to have earned

---

1. If an institution decides to increase the percentage of its assets in a particular class of investment like venture capital or real estate, then it must invest a higher percentage of each year's cash flow in order to reach the new target. The nature of the capital allocation process inevitably results in large swings in investing activity.

35% per year for 7 years; the capital committed in 1984 earned 35% per year for 6 years; and so on. The final stage of the model entails calculating the total value of the companies in the aggregate venture capital industry portfolio. Assuming that the venture capitalists own 30% of each portfolio company's stock, then the total value of the companies equals the total value of the portfolio divided by 30%.[2]

If this model is applied to total industry commitments for the years 1983 to 1989, then the implied value of the companies backed by venture capitalists in 1990 is $291 billion. Stated a different way, in order for the venture capital community to have earned a gross 35% per year on funds invested in the preceding 7 years, they would have had to help create companies with a combined market capitalization of $292 billion.

The next logical question is: Does this number make sense? To address this issue, I compared the required venture company value with the total value of all 4,100 companies listed on NASDAQ, which, at the end of 1990, was $311 billion. Using the logic of the model, the venture capital community would effectively have had to create another NASDAQ's worth of company, given the assumptions. This seems, as Mr. Spock of Star Trek fame would say, illogical—or, at least, highly implausible.

There are two possible interpretations at this point: the model is wrong *or* it is not possible to earn such high rates of return on such large amounts of capital over such extended periods of time. Addressing the first issue, there are several possibilities. First, I may have used the wrong capital base in the calculations. It might be more sensible, for example, to use the actual level of disbursements rather than commitments. In response, there is no doubt that I have used the wrong figures; however, whatever one puts in the capital investment calculation is likely to be highly correlated with the figures I have used—almost every data series related to venture capital has the same peaks and valleys. Moreover, the reported figures for professional venture capital commitments understate the amount of capital being invested in high potential earlier-stage companies. Particularly in recent years, but certainly during the 1980s, angel investors were also seeking high rate of return private company opportunities. Hence, though the numbers used as a capital base are not accurate, they are likely to be a lower bound rather than an upper bound.

With respect to the specific assumptions, it is possible to vary them without changing the basic conclusion. For example, it may well be that the appropriate time horizon to consider is not 7 years, but something less. The

---

2. No doubt, readers are already questioning the individual assumptions. For example, is the right return to use 35%? Is the right term to use 7 years? Should the model be based on commitments or disbursements? Each assumption has some relationship to historical data in the industry. Slight modifications to the model to not materially change the implications, as will be demonstrated shortly.

EXHIBIT 2
Simple Model: Logical Implications—1983 to 1990

Total Required 1990 Value ($ BILLIONS)		YEARS OF COMPOUNDING			
		4	5	6	7
APPRECIATION RATE	15%	$ 63	$ 78	$103	$133
	25%	$ 80	$103	$144	$198
	35%	$100	$134	$199	$291
	50%	$137	$196	$317	$511
% of NASDAQ Market Value (1990—$311b)		YEARS OF COMPOUNDING			
		4	5	6	7
APPRECIATION RATE	15%	20%	25%	33%	43%
	25%	26%	33%	46%	64%
	35%	32%	43%	64%	93%
	50%	44%	63%	102%	164%

very nature of compounding means that there is a considerable difference between assuming 5 or 6 years of compounding at 35% rather than 7 years. In *Exhibit 2*, I show the sensitivity of the calculations to changes in the assumptions about duration and compound rate of return.

This sensitivity analysis suggests that the interpretation of the model is fairly robust. No matter how you cut it, it would be hard for venture capitalists to earn high rates of return for long periods of time, given the relative level of other values in risk capital markets and the high levels of capital flowing into the industry in the 7 years preceding 1990. Parenthetically, if one goes back to the mid 1970s, when venture capital commitments were small (under $1 billion per year), it was entirely possible to earn high rates of return for long periods without running into a logical barrier.

I and a colleague, Howard Stevenson, first presented this model to a group of distinguished venture capitalists in 1988 and to the annual meeting of the National Venture Capital Association in May of 1989. In each case, we ended with a prediction that rates of return had to disappoint, and that the supply of capital would decrease. In the age-old race between the level of opportunity in the economy and the supply of capital, capital had won out. There was too much capital in the industry to earn high rates.

When we delivered the punch line to the venture community, there was general agreement that we were wrong, or, even if we were right, that it was someone else's problem. When we asked venture capitalists at the time to predict the IRR on their funds and on the industry, everyone boldly predicted that they would do better than average—for a subset of 25 senior venture capitalists the average difference between their expected rate of return and their prediction for the industry was 8% per year.

With hindsight, of course, the period in the late 1980s was disappointing for general and limited partner alike (see *Exhibit 3* below).[3] There were many reasons. One was simple: high perceived rates of return (and low perceived risk) encouraged entry into the venture capital business. From 1975 to 1987, the number of venture capital firms effectively tripled. Many new firms were formed by younger venture capitalists in existing firms, while others were formed by new entrants with modest levels of experience. Moreover, there was a significant increase in the relative size of the firms, partly driven by the realization that the business model of a venture capital management company typically improves with size (i.e., there are economies of scale in running a venture capital management company). Unfortunately, there may be diseconomies of scale in venture capital investing for limited partners, as opposed to general partners.

Entry into the industry also changed the nature of the rivalry between venture capital firms. My favorite illustration of this shift is the Winchester

EXHIBIT 3
Venture Capital Annual Returns, 1980 to 1990

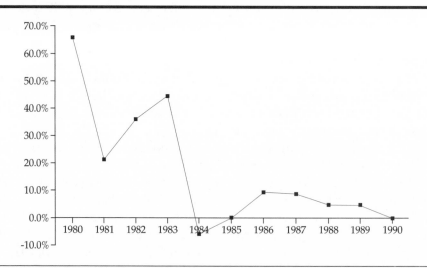

Estimated from data supplied by Venture Economics

---

3. Academics are skilled at predicting the past—by the time we were making our predictions, evidence was mounting about just how bad returns in the period from the mid-1980s to the early 1990s would be. Also, the reader should be aware that the data portrayed in *Exhibit 3* are by no means exact, but the pattern is accurate.

disk drive business.[4] From the late 1970s to the mid-1980s, professional venture capital firms invested over $400 million in 43 separate manufacturers of Winchester disk drives. Each of the new companies being formed had competent managements and aggressive financial projections. Each player only needed 10% of the potentially huge market to thrive. Unfortunately, no market ever sustains 43 entrants, let alone the over-100 domestic and foreign players active in the market at the time. The inevitable result was competitive mayhem and a high mortality rate.

The story of the disk drive business is instructive for several reasons. First, the venture capital industry did make money investing in disk drive companies. They were generally able to distribute shares in the companies at reasonably high values, which reflected the euphoric state of the capital markets in the early and mid-1980s. It was typically the public that ended up holding the bag as competitive pressures resulted in major disappointments for post-IPO investors.

The disk drive business is also interesting because the intense competitive environment ultimately led to the emergence of a few very strong, globally competitive companies like Quantum or Seagate. The U.S. has the world lead in disk drives. Consumers all over the world have benefited from the intense competition: they have high quality, high capacity products at astonishingly low prices. The story of the disk drive business illustrates how important the venture capital industry is in a global economy: intense, well-funded competition creates strong companies, high rates of innovation and job formation, and enhances the global competitiveness of the domestic economy.

——— A STRUCTURAL ANALYSIS OF THE VENTURE CAPITAL INDUSTRY

To summarize, the venture capital industry is like any industry—high perceived rates of return and modest perceived risk attract new capital from existing players and from new entrants. Entry increases rivalry among competitors. More deals get done in any industry, often at higher prices (i.e., less favorable terms for the investor). As the disk drive story illustrates, the problem was not too much capital chasing too few deals; it was too many deals being funded in each industry.

Moreover, the presence of high rates of return makes the threat of substitutes greater; entrepreneurs were able to raise money from a broad range of non-venture capital sources, including angels and corporations. *Exhibit* 4 depicts the factors affecting venture capital returns in the 1980s.

---

4. An analysis of the disk drive industry can be found in Chapter 3, "Capital Market Myopia," by William A. Sahlman and Howard H. Stevenson.

EXHIBIT 4
Determinants of Venture Capital Industry Profitability

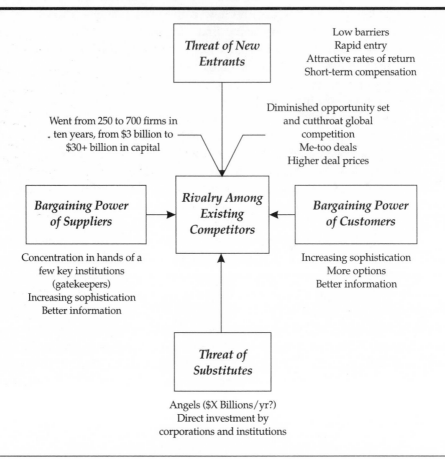

Source: Porter, Sahlman and Stevenson

——— THE POST-1991 PERIOD

When rates of return fell in the venture businesses, the process that created the initial boom reversed itself. Institutional asset managers pulled back on their commitment to the industry, diverting capital to other more promising sectors. In 1991, the amount of new capital flowing into the industry reached a cyclical low of slightly over $1 billion (see *Exhibit 1*). A number of venture firms exited the business.

The capital exodus began to change the competitive dynamics of the industry. There was subdued rivalry for deals, with pricing dropping to more reasonable levels.

The picture of declining capital must be juxtaposed with a sense of the changing opportunity set for ventures at this time. Hidden in the fog of the 1990–1991 recession was a massive improvement in the opportunities for a new technology company formation. This was the formative period for the Internet and the communications infrastructure building boom. Moreover, the previously hot industries—microcomputers, software, medical devices and biotechnology—continued to grow.

As is almost always the case, the pension funds and insurance companies were decreasing their commitments to venture capital firms just as the opportunity set was improving. At the same time, venture capital returns were disappointing, returns on a wide range of public investment vehicles were very high, notably large and small capitalization stocks (31% and 45% respectively in 1991). Money managers had no choice but to reallocate.

The assertion that the opportunity set was increasing is of course, primarily visible only in hindsight. We now know that venture capital investments in the late 1980s and early 1990s yielded high rates of returns. Among the many pronounced examples were Cisco, Ascend, UUNet and Shiva. A $2 million venture investment in Cisco in late 1987 was worth over $6 billion by 1997, assuming none of the shares were sold. Cisco's 1988 sales were less than $10 million: fiscal 1997 sales were $6.4 billion. By late 1997, the market capitalization of Cisco was a staggering $60 billion.

In the world of the Internet, value creation was similarly striking. Modest capital commitments to companies like Netscape, Yahoo! and Lycos became immodestly valued in the ebullient capital markets of the 1990's. Netscape was incorporated in April of 1994. When the company went public in August of 1995, the total market value assigned at the IPO was in excess of $1 billion. Shortly, thereafter, in early 1996, the market cap of Netscape was over $6 billion. A $6 million investment by Kleiner Perkins in Netscape in 1994 was worth well over $600 million by early 1996, a point in time at which Rule 144 holding period restrictions still applied.

The acceleration in technology investment opportunities is also illustrated by studying the post-1990 performance of four companies: America Online, Microsoft, Intel, and Compaq. *Exhibit 5* provides data on the operating and financial performance of these companies during the period from 1990 to 1997. A striking aspect of *Exhibit 5* is the dramatic appreciation in value

EXHIBIT 5

COMPANY	1990 SALES	1990 MARKET VALUE	1997 SALES	1997 MARKET VALUE
America Online	$ .01	$ .04	$ 1.7	$ 9.0
Compaq	$3.6	$ 4.9	$24.6	$ 86.0
Intel	$3.9	$ 7.6	$25.1	$116.0
Microsoft	$1.2	$ 8.2	$11.4	$146.0
TOTAL	$8.7	$20.7	$62.8	$357.0

Source: Bloomberg Financial company reports. Data are measured in billions.

EXHIBIT 6

YEAR	S&P 500	SMALL CAP STOCKS	VENTURE CAPITAL
1990	–3%	–22%	3%
1991	31%	45%	22%
1992	8%	23%	12%
1993	10%	21%	19%
1994	1%	3%	14%
1995	38%	37%	49%
1996	23%	18%	40%
1997	34%	21%	37%

Sources: *SBBI–1996 Yearbook*, Ibbotson Associates; *The Private Equity Analyst*, January 1998, page 12 (underlying data are from Cambridge Associates).

relative to sales. Between 1990 and 1997, total market value for these four companies increased by a factor of over 17 while sales increased by a factor of 7: both figures are remarkable by any standard.

The venture capital investors who persevered in the dark days of the mid to late-1980s were handsomely rewarded in the 1990s. Many companies went public, often at hard-to-imagine valuations. Many portfolio companies were also acquired by existing players. Companies like Cisco became very aggressive in consolidating their industry. A watershed event, at least in my view, was the 1995 acquisition of Tivoli Systems by IBM for almost $800 million. At the time, Tivoli's sales were approximately $50 million.

The returns that venture capitalists reported beginning in 1991 rose dramatically from the anemic levels that characterized the period from 1984 to 1990. It was not until 1994, however, that estimated annual returns in the venture business exceeded those available in the public markets, as is illustrated in *Exhibit 6*.

The outstanding performance of the venture capital industry in 1993 to 1997 did not escape the notice of institutional investors. This group, now confronted with even more capital to deploy, began in 1992 to increase the capital committed to venture investing. From a cyclical low in 1991 of $1.3 billion, total capital committed rose to a record $10.3 billion in 1997. The shift is depicted in *Exhibit 7*.

A SIMPLE MODEL—REVISITED

The logical question arises: is the dramatic increase in venture capital going to lead inexorably to a period of poor returns? Is it "illogical" to assume that venture capitalists can continue to earn high rates of return, given the

EXHIBIT 7
Venture Capital Commitments

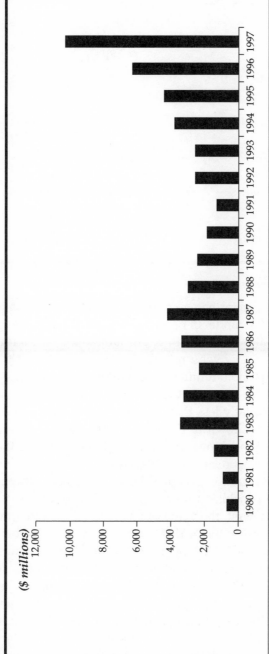

Source: Venture Capital Journal

EXHIBIT 8
Simple Model: Logical Implications, 1993 to 2000

Total Required 2000 Value		YEARS OF COMPOUNDING			
		4	5	6	7
APPRECIATION RATE	15%	$174	$203	$232	$255
	25%	$214	$260	$308	$348
	35%	$263	$329	$405	$474
	50%	$351	$462	$605	$750
% of NASDAQ Market Value		YEARS OF COMPOUNDING			
		4	5	6	7
APPRECIATION RATE	15%	6%	7%	8%	9%
	25%	8%	9%	11%	13%
	35%	9%	12%	15%	17%
	50%	13%	17%	22%	27%

large amounts of capital being committed? To address this issue, I updated the simple economic model in order to simulate the possible consequences of the most recent pattern of investing. The tables in *Exhibit 8* focus on the value that has to be created by venture capitalists as of the year 2000, assuming that the amount of capital committed to the industry stays at approximately the $10 billion annual level and that the NASDAQ total market value appreciates at 15% per year, slightly less than the historical rate.

The pattern shown in *Exhibit 8* is very different from that presented earlier: using this model, one cannot reject the hypothesis that venture capitalists can indeed earn relatively high rates of return in the next few years in spite of the large increase in capital being invested in the industry. Several factors cause the conclusion today to be different from that reached in the mid- to late 1980s. First, the value of all assets in the economy has increased at unprecedented rates: the NASDAQ, to illustrate, has grown in value from $311 billion in 1990 to $1.8 trillion in 1997. Other market values have increased as well: the estimated total market value of all equities grew from $3.3 trillion in 1990 to almost $12 trillion in 1997. Second, valuation metrics have increased—investors are willing to pay more for any given level of cash flow or income. The price-to-operating-earnings for the S&P 500 has increased from 14 in 1980 to almost 20 in 1997. Third, it seems likely that the time horizon of venture investments has decreased in the past few years—we all now operate in Web-years, an accelerated version of the real world in which markets

develop faster than ever before. Finally, the market for liquidating investments has expanded rapidly. The dollar volume of merger and acquisition
transactions last year was an astonishing $1 trillion, a five-fold increase from
the level in 1990. Similarly, almost $50 billion was raised in initial public
offerings in 1997, up from $5 billion at the beginning of the decade.

Exhibit 9 provides a different perspective from which to view the issue.
The graph depicts the total required company value (left axis—columns) for
venture capitalists to achieve a 35% per year gross return for five years and
the implied percentage of the total value of all 5,400 companies on NASDAQ
(right axis—line).

CONCLUSION

We live in a wonderful period in history. Inflation is low, interest rates
are low, unemployment is low, real growth is high. It is hard not to be
optimistic about the domestic economy. Our venture capital industry has
played a vital role in creating these favorable conditions. During the past two
decades, the *Fortune* 500 has shed something like 5 million jobs—imagine
where the U.S. economy would be had it not been for venture capital–backed
companies like Intel, Compaq, Microsoft, Genentech, Sun Microsystems,
Cisco, and Netscape. Or, imagine what the inflation picture might be were it
not for the competitive pressures brought to bear by innovation in these kinds
of companies.

In every boom in the economy, however, are the seeds of destruction
sown. There are many early warning signs that suggest the horse race between capital and opportunity is getting too close for comfort. My own list
of red flags is provided below:

- Too many deals in the same industries are being done—not
  every team can gain a ten percent market share. The mortality rate
  of new venture investments will be very high, which has implications for how partners will allocate their scarcest resource—
  time.
- Pricing discipline is crumbling—as one venture capitalist stated:
  "Good deals go quickly at high prices." Sometimes, so too do bad
  deals. . . . Often lost in the race to do deals is basic due diligence
  about the team, the opportunity, or both.
- There are many signs of labor shortages, the most problematic of
  which concern senior managers—the number of CEO searches is
  undoubtedly high relative to the supply of capable people. The
  risk is that there are too many weak teams being funded at the
  same time in the same industries, all at high valuations and with
  minimal due diligence.
- The stock market defies gravity—it shrugs off a meltdown in

EXHIBIT 9
Venture Capital Implications Model

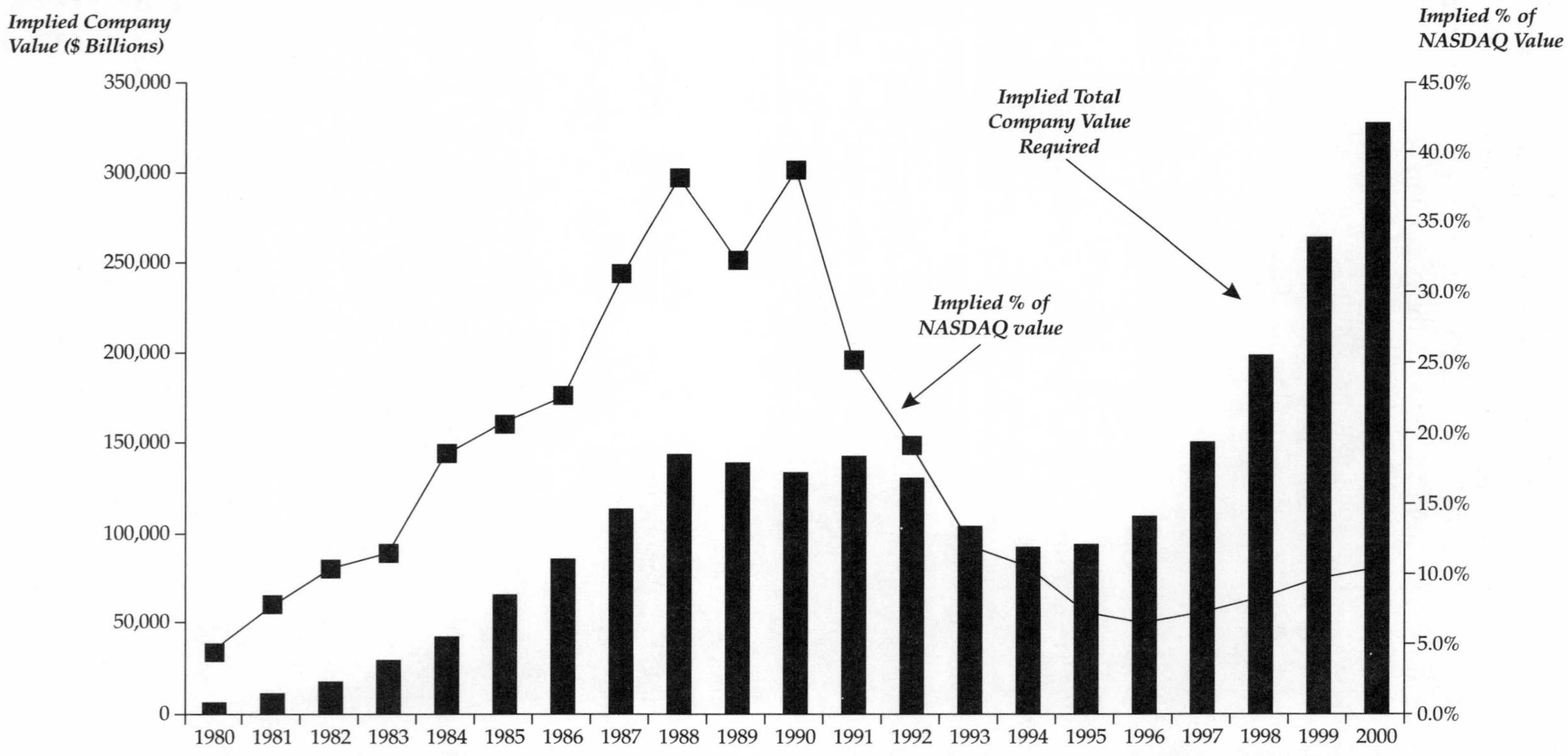

foreign markets, domestic scandals, and almost any form of disturbance. Perhaps this will continue, perhaps not. A significant stock market correction would change dramatically the economics of the venture investing process.

· Business is getting tougher—large companies are far more competent and competitive than they were in the 1980s. They are leaner and meaner, and, in some important cases, very fierce competitors pursuing many of the niches previously left to entrepreneurs and their venture capital funders.

· Angels have become a major force in the world of entrepreneurship. Angels play a vital role in the process, particularly with early stage deals. They are, however, a player whose actions are not always professional (e.g., in pricing, deal structuring, due diligence) or predictable (e.g., in value-added or participation in follow-on financing); and they certainly must be taken into account by the professional venture capital community.

· At business schools across the nation, enrollment in courses in entrepreneurial finance and venture capital is at an all-time high—vast numbers of students are eager to enter the private equity industry, start a new venture, or launch a roll-up/consolidation play. This concentration of interest has historically foretold a crash with uncanny accuracy—the real estate industry in 1973 and investment banking in 1986–1987 come immediately to mind.

One final comment seems in order. There is a tremendous amount of capital seeking opportunity in the U.S. and abroad. Last year, over $50 billion in new capital was committed to buyouts and venture capital. More interesting is the total level of financial assets seeking high returns and modest risk. Total pension and insurance assets at the end of 1997 are on the order of $6 trillion. Total mutual fund assets are approaching $5 trillion. The rise in these pools of capital helps explain why stock prices are high to be sure, but also suggests that money will move in large quantities and velocities in search of returns. If confidence in a sector weakens, the money will pour out quickly and conversely. We will, I suspect, be shocked when it happens, particularly if the sector being drained is venture capital. On the other hand, whenever the large pools of capital withdraw, that is almost always the time when prospective returns are the highest. Cycles are inevitable, and they are not all bad in the scheme of things, as long as the players anticipate that they will occur and do not behave as if they are a relic of ancient history. Remember,

> *There has never been a time in recorded history when the supply of capital did not outstrip the supply of opportunity.*

—— DISCUSSION QUESTIONS

1. What causes a cycle to begin and end?
2. What strategies should people raising money employ if they believe risk capital markets are cyclical? What should investors do?
3. What happens to the competitive situation in a market when many competitors are well-financed?

Strategy vs. Tactics from a Venture Capitalist

19

ARTHUR ROCK

The following reading looks at the entrepreneurial start-up from the venture capitalist's perspective. With more than 30 years' experience in evaluating new ventures, Arthur Rock has learned to pay more attention to the people who conceive and develop the company than to the details of the business plan. In this reading, he offers a range of insights on the personal qualities he looks for when deciding whether to back an aspiring entrepreneur: an ability to benefit from constructive criticism and perspective despite bad news and setbacks; skill in knowing when to take charge and when to delegate; an appreciation of the importance of sound and solid management; and above all, a desire to build a great company.

As a venture capitalist, I am often asked for my views on why some entrepreneurs succeed and others fail. Obviously, there are no cut-and-dried answers to that question. Still, a few general observations about how I evaluate new businesses should shed some light on what I think it takes to make an entrepreneurial venture thrive and grow.

Over the past 30 years, I estimate that I've looked at an average of one business plan per day, or about 300 a year, in addition to the large numbers of phone calls and business plans that simply are not appropriate. Of the 300 likely plans, I may invest in only one or two a year; and even among those carefully chosen few, I'd say that a good half fail to perform up to expectations. The problem with those companies (and with the ventures I choose *not* to take part in) is rarely one of strategy. Good ideas and good products are a dime a dozen. Good execution and good management—in a word, good *people*—are rare.

To put it another way, strategy is easy, but tactics—the day-to-day and month-to-month decisions required to manage a business—are hard. That's why I generally pay more attention to the people who prepare a business plan than to the proposal itself.

Another venture capitalist I know says, somewhat in jest, that the first thing he looks at in a business plan is the financial projections. Frankly, how anyone can figure out what sales and earnings and returns are going to be five years from now is beyond me. The first place I look is the résumés, usually found at the back. To me, they are the essence of any plan. (Maybe no one reads the middle section!)

I see the plan as really an opportunity to evaluate the people. If I like what I see in there, I try to find out more by sitting down and talking with the would-be entrepreneurs. I usually spend a long time on this. (Unless their first question is "How much money am I going to get?" Then the interview is very short.) I don't talk much during these meetings; I'm there to listen. I want to hear what they've got to say and see how they think.

Some of the questions I ask have little to do directly with the particular business under discussion: Whom do they know, and whom do they admire? What's their track record? What mistakes have they made in the past, and what have they learned from them? What is their attitude toward me as a potential investor—do they view me as a partner or as a necessary evil? I also ask specific questions about the kind of company they want to develop—say, whom do they plan to recruit, and how are they going to do it?

I am especially interested in what kind of financial people they intend to recruit. So many entrepreneurial companies make mistakes in the accounting end of the business. Many start shipping products before confirming that the orders are good, or that the customers will take the product, or that the accounts are collectible. Such endeavors are more concerned about making a short-term sales quota than about maximizing the long-term revenue stream.

Granted, the pressure on new businesses to make sales quotas is strong. And that's precisely why the company needs a very, very tough accounting department. Otherwise, it will get into trouble. I always ask what kind of chief financial officer the entrepreneurs plan to bring on board. If they understand the need for someone who will scrutinize the operation closely and impose appropriate controls, they are more likely to be able to translate their strategy into a going concern.

This may go without saying, but I also look at a person's motivation, commitment, and energy. Hard work alone doesn't bring success, of course, but all the effective entrepreneurs I've known have worked long, hard hours. And there's something more than the number of hours: the intensity of the hours. I think of two software entrepreneurs I know who are going at 110 miles per hour, 18 hours per day, 7 days a week. And they have instilled their intensity and their belief in the business in all the people who work for them.

Belief in the business, clearly, is critical. If you're going to succeed, you must have a burning desire to develop your idea; you must believe so firmly in the idea that everything else pales in comparison. I usually can tell the difference between people who have that fire in their stomachs and those who see their ideas primarily as a way to get rich. Far too many people are interested in building a financial empire instead of a great company.

I want to build great companies. That's how I get my kicks. I look for people who want the same thing.

At a presentation I gave recently, the audience's questions were all along the same lines: "What are the secrets to writing a business plan?" "How do I get in touch with venture capitalists?" "What percentage of the equity do I have to give to them?" No one asked me how to build a business! And here's a question that both amused me and bothered me: "How do I get rid of the venture capitalists after they've made their investment?"

I'm looking for entrepreneurs who ask, "How can I make this business a success?"—not "How do I make a fortune?" And I prefer someone who wants me to play a role in the enterprise's decision making. Obviously, when they come to me entrepreneurs are interested in getting my money. Many have the attitude, "Uh oh, is this guy going to want to come to staff meetings and open his big mouth?" But they should realize that I can be a resource for them in more ways than one. I've been around for a long time; there just aren't many business problems that I haven't seen before. And most entrepreneurs can use all the help they can get in developing and implementing the tactics that will make them successful in the long run.

When I talk to entrepreneurs, I'm evaluating not only their motivation but also their character, fiber. And the issue I set the most store by is whether they are honest with themselves. It's essential to be totally, brutally honest about how well—or how badly—things are going. It's also very difficult.

Too many businesspeople delude themselves. They want so much to believe that they listen only to what they want to hear and see only what they want to see. A good example is a top executive in the parallel-processing industry; he believed his engineering people when they told him the product would be ready on time, and he believed his marketing people when they told him how much they could sell. So he developed a sales staff and doubled the size of the plant and built up inventories before he had a product to sell. The computer was late because of some last-minute bugs, and he was stuck with it all. The first 98% of designing a computer is easy; the bugs always come up in the last 2%. Fixing the problems took time, which ate up all kinds of overhead. And when he was finally ready, he couldn't meet the company's forecasts—which had been unrealistic from the beginning.

This story illustrates well my thesis that strategy is easy, execution is hard. The company's product was two years ahead of its competition. Execution of the idea, however, was terrible. That the strategy was good is obvious now; several other manufacturers have entered the field and are doing very well. But the company has lost the competitive advantage it would have enjoyed if its management had been better.

I can cite a similar example, also from the computer industry. The three people who started the company were the president, the manager of the software division, and the manager of the hardware division. The two managers kept telling the president that things were going swimmingly, and he wanted to believe what they said. Then one day, faced with an order the company couldn't fill, the software division manager called the president, who was out of town, and let forth a blast that in essence said, "We've been making a lot of mistakes we haven't told you about. We're at least a year behind."

Now, that's a ridiculous situation; the president should have known the status of product development. He had enough background in the field, and he knew the managers well enough that he shouldn't have been caught by surprise. But he didn't look closely enough, and he didn't ask the right questions. In the meantime, the business had a rather large marketing and sales force. Then the question became whether to keep the sales force (which by this time was fully trained but doing nothing) or to let everyone go and wait for the software to be finished. If the latter, they'd have to hire and train a new sales force—a no-win situation either way.

Failure to be honest with yourself is a problem in any business, but it is especially disastrous in an entrepreneurial company, where the risk-reward stakes are so high. As an entrepreneur, you can't afford to make mistakes because you don't have the time and resources needed to recover. Big corporations can live with setbacks and delays in their "skunk works"; in a start-up situation, you'd better be right the first time.

After being honest with yourself, the next most essential characteristic for the entrepreneur is to know whom to listen to and when to listen, and then which questions to ask. Sometimes CEOs listen only to what they want to hear because of fear of the truth; in other cases, it's because they are arrogant or have surrounded themselves with yes-men/women. A lot of managers simply will not accept criticism or suggestions from other people; they demand absolute loyalty from their subordinates and call disloyal anybody who tries to tell them something they don't want to hear.

It's usually easy to spot this trait by the way someone talks with outsiders about the organization. If an entrepreneur says, "This guy's lousy and that one doesn't know what she's doing, but I saved the company"—or if he or she explains how brilliantly he or she performed at his last job, in spite of being fired—I get wary. That kind of attitude is a red flag, like the statement, "I'll be honest with you": you know you're not getting the whole story.

To be sure, there's a thin line between refusing to accept criticism and sticking to your guns. Good entrepreneurs are committed to their ideas. In fact, I knew one company was in trouble when the CEO accepted almost everything I told him without argument or question. But some people have an almost perverse desire to prove to the world that their way is the right way—and the only way. I remember one CEO who had a great strategy—an idea for a unique computer architecture—but who refused to accept any advice on anything from anyone, including potential customers. He ended up with a product that had to be totally re-engineered and a weak staff. The company is now under new management and may be able to make something out of what is still a good idea, but the CEO's tunnel vision sure stalled it at the starting gate.

Another important quality—one that also has to do with taking a hard look at oneself and one's situation—is to know when to bring in skills from outside and what kind of skills.

As I see it, a company's growth has three stages. During the start-up, the entrepreneur does everything himself: he or she is involved in engineering the product, making sales calls, and so on. After a while, the company grows and others are hired to do these things—a vice president of sales, a vice president of engineering—but they report directly to him, and he or she still knows everything that's going on.

The company reaches the third stage when it hits, say $100 million to $200 million in sales. At that point, it's just too large for the president to be involved in all the doings. More management layers are in place and a fleet of executive vice presidents, and it now calls for entirely different skills to run the company than it did during its infancy. The president has to get work done by delegating it to other people and get information through two or more organizational layers.

The ideal would be a president who could manage a company at all three stages, starting the business from scratch and staying involved until retirement. Alfred Sloan at General Motors and Tom Watson at IBM were able to do just that, and the leaders of Teledyne and Intel have done it more recently.

But not all entrepreneurs can manage a large company. And many do not want to. Some people who relish business start-ups are simply not interested in running a formal, multi-tier organization. After Cray Computer grew to a fairly good size, for example, Seymour Cray wanted to get back to designing computers. Similarly, Apple Computer's Steve Wozniak and Steve Jobs (at least in the early stages) recognized that their genius was technical and promotional, not managerial, and that they needed experienced, professional managers to oversee their company's growth.

Other entrepreneurs have been less aware of their own limitations. Consider the experience of Diasonics and Daisy. Both flourished when they were small enough that their founders were able to control all aspects of the business. But they grew too fast, and the managers didn't realize that they now needed a different style of management and control. In both cases, a resounding initial success turned into an ignominious mess. As a result, both enterprises were reorganized.

Sometimes problems arise because the entrepreneur doesn't grasp the importance of strong management. I know of one young company that has already gone through two CEOs and is looking for a third. On the plus side, the men who founded the business acknowledged that they were engineers, not managers, and they went out and looked for a CEO. They considered their strategy so brilliant, though, that they figured anyone could carry if off. The first man they hired talked a good game but had been a disaster at two other corporations; eventually they had to let him go. He just couldn't manage the company. Then the directors hired another CEO who lasted only a few months. The company's product is still a good one, but without equally good leadership it may die in infancy.

The point of these examples is simple. If entrepreneurs do not have the skills required to manage the company, they should bring in an experienced professional. And they should never settle for someone mediocre by telling themselves that the business is such a winner that it doesn't need the management and controls that other companies do.

A great idea won't make it without great management. I am sometimes asked whether there is an "entrepreneurial personality." I suppose there are certain common qualities—a high energy level, strong commitment, and so on—but there are as many different personal styles as there are entrepreneurs. Henry Singleton of Teledyne, for example, reminds me of Charles de Gaulle. He has a singleness of purpose, a tenacity that is just overpowering. He gives you absolute confidence in his ability to accomplish whatever he says he is going to do. Yet he's rather aloof, operating more or less by himself and dreaming up ideas in his corner office.

Max Palevsky, formerly at Scientific Data Systems (SDS), is, by contrast, a very warm person. At SDS he'd joke around with his employees and cajole them into doing what needed to be done. His very informal style was evidenced by his open shirt and feet up on the desk.

The CEO's personality is extremely important because it permeates the company, but there's no one style that seems to work better than another. What *is* important is to *have* a style. An "average Joe" won't inspire others and lead a business to success.

I look for an entrepreneur who can manage. A conventional manager isn't risk oriented enough to succeed with a new venture, while an entrepreneur without managerial savvy is just another promoter.

Good entrepreneurs are tough-minded, with themselves and with their teams. They can make hard decisions. They have to be able to say, "No, that won't work" to colleagues who come to them with ideas, or to say, "That's a good idea but we can't do it because we have other priorities." To make such professional judgments, managers should ideally be well versed in the technology on which the company is based.

There are exceptions, of course. John Sculley at Apple Computer comes immediately to mind. When Apple was looking for someone to fill the top slot, it instructed the executive recruiter to find a CEO with a technical computer background. But the recruiter asked Apple to consider someone from left field (from the soft-drink industry), and I need not point out that the results were excellent. It was a lucky fit. In fact, as far as the "secrets of entrepreneurial success" go, it's important to recognize that a little bit of luck helps and a lot of luck is even better.

Another company I know, formed by two young, inexperienced men, benefited from a lucky break. Though very knowledgeable, they seriously underestimated how long it would take to write the 1,500,000 lines of software code they needed to launch their product. Consequently, they were two years late in bringing the product to market. But the market was also slow in developing. If the product had been ready on time, the company probably would have gone bankrupt trying to sell something for which the market wasn't ready. As it turned out, the market and the product were ready at the same time, and the company could exploit the product without competition. Many business success stories are due at least in part to simple good luck.

I emphasize people rather than products, and for good reason. The biggest problem in starting high-tech businesses is the shortage of superior managers. There is too much money chasing too few good managers.

I have always preferred to wait and have entrepreneurs come to me, to approach me because they have a great desire to build a business. Now with all the megafunds available, it's often the venture capitalist who goes out to start a company and looks for people who can head it up.

Those who call us "vulture capitalists" do have a point; some venture capitalists lure away a company's best people, thus hampering its growth. How can an enterprise develop and thrive when its top executives are always being pursued to start new companies? Unfortunately, in the high-tech industries, more and more businesses are being formed simply to make a buck. As for myself, though, I will continue to look for the best people, not the largest untapped market or the highest projected returns or the cleverest business strategy.

After all, a good idea, unless it's executed, remains only a good idea. Good managers, on the other hand, can't lose. If their strategy doesn't work, they can develop another one. If a competitor comes along, they can turn to something else. Great people make great companies, and that's the kind of company I want to be a part of.

——— DISCUSSION QUESTIONS

1. "Strategy is easy," the author says, "but tactics are hard." What are the qualities of a good strategist and a good tactician? What can go wrong if an entrepreneur performs well in only one of these roles?

2. Rock distinguishes between a financial empire and a great company. What else, besides high sales and profits, makes a company great in your view?

3. Rock places great importance on the entrepreneur's character and describes the qualities that he thinks matter most. Are these qualities innate or can they be cultivated? What qualities would you add to the list?

4. "I prefer someone who wants me to play a role in the enterprise's decision making. . . . most entrepreneurs can use all the help they

can get in developing and implementing the tactics that will make them successful in the long run." Would you welcome or be wary of this attitude in a venture capitalist? What questions would you ask to ascertain in more detail how Rock conceives his roles and responsibilities?

5. "Belief in the business," Rock says, "is critical." How does having strong conviction serve the entrepreneur's interest? What dangers can it pose?

SECTION C

MANAGING THE GROWING ENTERPRISE

The Challenge of Growth 20

MICHAEL J. ROBERTS

In this piece, Roberts describes the forces that underlie the growth process and why they create managerial challenges. In particular, growth drives a tremendous increase in the amount of mangerial work. To accomplish this work, the entrepreneur must develop new tools for accomplishing the key managerial tasks.

The author argues that at their core, most of these approaches rely on replacing real-time decision making with tools that utilize either anticipation of future action or review of past activity. In this way, the entrepreneur frees himself from the intimate connection with the day-to-day activity of the firm and can use his time more efficiently.

Managing *any* company is a tough job. Managing a rapidly growing enterprise, however, presents a particular challenge because the essential nature of the manager's job changes with growth. As the number of employees increases, and as the volume and complexity of work expands, executives must change their fundamental approach to managing. There are many phrases that attempt to capture this challenge: "making the transition from entrepreneurial to professional management"; "moving from quarterback to coach"; "going from visual flight rules to instrument flying." However it's characterized, it remains a difficult transition for the manager.

The focus of this chapter and the next is 1) to better understand the nature of the challenges that growth presents, and 2) to explore the nature of the changes managers must make in order to respond to these challenges.

This chapter focuses on the first of these objectives, and Chapter 21, "Managing Transitions in the Growing Enterprise," will focus on the second.

The challenge of managing a growing enterprise has its roots in several sets of changes that are transpiring at the firm:

- The scope and volume of operating activity is increasing: In order to grow, the firm must serve new customers in new markets with

Professor Michael J. Roberts prepared this note as the basis for class discussion rather than to illustrate either effective or ineffective handling of an administrative situation. Copyright © 1993 by the President and Fellows of Harvard College. Harvard Business School case 393-106.

new products. New production facilities and distribution channels are required.

- The range and complexity of tasks is increasing: As the firm's operating activities expand, this creates a multiplicity of tasks that need to be defined, organized and completed. New products and new geographic markets require organizing production and supply lines. More customers and competitors must be analyzed, more prices set, more products marketed.
- The number and variety of people is increasing: As the enterprise expands its activities, new people are required to perform these tasks. As the volume of work grows, it can be standardized, so lower-skilled employees can perform it. And, the firm has a sufficient volume of specialized work so that highly skilled specialists can be hired. Employees are stationed in far-flung markets to serve customers there.

In order to meet these challenges, managers of growing enterprises must have a special set of skills. Before we can talk about managing the *growing* enterprise, however, we must address the issue of what it means to simply *manage*. Only after developing a well-grounded frame of reference can we analyze the impact of growth on the manager's job.

——— THE MANAGER'S JOB

The manager's job needs to be defined in a way such that—when we add the dynamic of rapid growth to the equation—we can analyze the critical pressures that are being added to the system, the changes that are transpiring as a result, and the responses available to the manager.

DEFINING THE MANAGER'S JOB

In order to frame the management task in a way that permits one to predict and understand the challenges that growth creates, we need to develop a model of the manager's job. Many such models already exist, and it is reasonable to ask why we need to develop a new one.

The General Management course at the Harvard Business School, for instance, defines the general manager's job in terms of 6 basic tasks: crafting strategy, marshaling and allocating resources, shaping the work environment, developing people, building the organization, and managing operations.

For several reasons, we will use a somewhat different perspective:

- Our interest will revolve around operating and administrative, rather than strategic and financial issues.
- We will have a particular focus on the impact of growth, and will want to use a framework that highlights this.

- Because growth makes such pressing demands for change on the manager herself, we will want to explicitly capture these forces and the resulting changes.

This framework will make use of terms that others have defined for their purposes. Undoubtedly, the ways others have defined these words suited their ends, but they don't necessarily suit ours. In order to facilitate our discussion, please pay careful attention to the way in which the terms below are defined.

There are three key elements that are part of the manager's responsibilities:

- Strategy and operations: The firm's activities are driven by its goals and its strategy. The strategy is the rationale for a set of operating activities, and as such, the goal-setting and strategic planning processes are a key piece of the operation. Where strategy is an idea or an objective, however, the firm's *operations* are that idea made real. Thus, the firm's strategy and operations are the set of tasks and activities that the firm is required to execute.
- Organization: This aspect of the manager's responsibilities includes all of the choices about *how* to accomplish the strategy and operating activities: how the broad set of activities will be broken down into specific responsibilities, how these responsibilities are assigned to organizational units, how they are broken down into specific tasks within units, how these tasks are grouped to comprise a job, how those jobs are defined according to performance standards and procedures, tied together with systems, and coordinated to achieve the desired objectives.
- Staff: This element includes the people who actually fill the jobs and do the work, as well as their background, training, selection, development and compensation.

These three sets of responsibilities constitute three elements of the manager's job. Yet they can't be managed in isolation. One can't simply craft a "clever" strategy, organize "effectively" and hire "good" people. We all recognize that there must be some "fit" between operation and structure,

EXHIBIT 1

RESPONSIBILITY	
Strategy & operations	*WHAT* is the enterprise's strategy and *WHAT* operating activities are required in order to achieve it?
Organization	*HOW* can these broad objectives be broken down into specific tasks, and *HOW* should these tasks be structured and coordinated?
Staff	*WHO* should do the work?

EXHIBIT 2

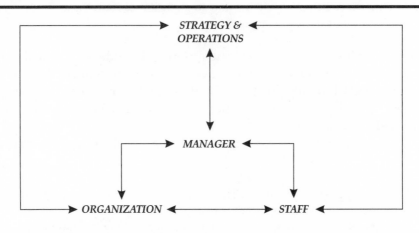

between implementation and the skills and capabilities of the people in the organization. Indeed, the art of management lies in crafting these fits.

CRAFTING A FIT AMONG THE ELEMENTS

One way to conceptualize the challenge of creating fits is to look at the elements we have been discussing and their relationship to one another, as shown in *Exhibit 2*. Note that the manager herself is a key piece of this picture. That is, the manager does not manage these elements in a way that is separate from the interdependent system they create. The manager is a key part *of* this system. The manager is a critical *link* among these components of the business. The manager creates a fit between these elements not solely by making them fit with *each other*; they must fit with the *manager* as well. In order to be effective, managers must develop a theory of action for acting as part *of* the system, not a theory for understanding the system *from* a perspective that is outside it.

Given that the manager's job is to create a fit between these elements, how should she go about it? What does it mean for these elements to be aligned? Essentially, it means that the strategy and operating activities have been determined, the organization has been defined, and the staff selected, in such a way as to maximize the performance of the enterprise.

The following section of the note will discuss the key dimensions of each element that one must understand in order to align them in an effective way.

Strategy & Operations   Strategy & operations differ along a number of dimensions that have important implications on the other elements.

- Product choices: these choices determine the difficulty of the manager's task:
  - The number and range of product-markets in which the firm competes: This determines not only the range of production and marketing issues the firm must confront, but also the range of competitors and markets with which it must be familiar.
  - The complexity of products and production: This determines the difficulty of the production, distribution and sales tasks, and increases the level of knowledge required to manage these functions. The degree of vertical integration, the degree to which custom vs. standard equipment can be used and the extent to which suppliers and subcontractors can be utilized, all have implications for the degree of difficulty of managing these tasks.
  - The complexity and range of distribution channels: This determines the difficulty of actually getting products to consumers.
- Market factors: these market-related factors make managing more difficult:
  - The geographic dispersion of markets: This determines both the complexity of logistical issues as well as the practicality of on-site involvement.
  - The pace of change in the product markets in which the firm competes: This has implications for the speed at which the firm must innovate and adapt its own product line to remain competitive.
  - The degree of competitiveness in these product markets: This has implications for the amount of "slack" that a firm will have as it competes for customers and revenues.
  - The level of uncertainty in the environment: To the extent that the firm is dependent upon resources or conditions that it cannot control, this will introduce uncertainty. This, in turn, will require the firm to expend resources and energy to try to master this uncertainty to the extent possible. It will also limit the length of the planning cycle, and serve as an incentive to make as many decisions as possible on a last-minute basis.
- Finally, the rate at which growth occurs affects the difficulty of managing the enterprise. The more rapid the rate of growth, the more rapid the series of changes that will have to occur if the firm is to remain a high performing one.

Given these characteristics of an operation, how do they affect the job of creating a fit among the remaining aspects of the manager's responsibilities?

- All of these factors serve to create demands on the manager for time and attention. Operations cannot simply be programmed and left to run on "auto pilot." The manager must be involved frequently in order to adapt the firm's activities to its evolving operation. Thus, all other things being equal, the higher the "score" on the factors described above, the more the manager will need to be involved.

- A strategy and set of operating activities that has a high score on many of these dimensions will, by definition, create tasks that are complex and more difficult to manage. (See more on this below.)
- An operation that is high on many of these factors will also create the need for a staff that is, by definition, higher in terms of sheer numbers and more varied in skill level.

The Organization   There are several attributes of the organization that are relevant:

- Differentiation: The extent to which activities and responsibilities have been parceled out to varied and distinct subunits of the organization.
- Interdependence: The degree to which the activities in one unit are interdependent with those in another unit for which the manager serves as the coordinating mechanism; and,
- Task attributes: The way in which responsibilities are divided into specific tasks will have a significant bearing on how they are managed. The task attributes that are relevant include:
  - Need for real-time input: The degree to which it is difficult to specify objectives in a measurable way and then measure them on a real time basis;
  - Importance: The potential impact of good task performance on the company's overall strategy;
  - Risk: The potential downside due to poor task performance;
  - Difficulty: The perceived difficulty of the task;

Given these organization characteristics, how do they impact the way in which a fit is created between the organization and the remaining elements?

- The higher these factors, the greater the need for the manager to be involved in the operation (all other things being equal).
- The higher these factors, the higher the level of skill and ability that will be demanded of the staff (all other things being equal).

The Staff   There are several factors relating to the staff that are relevant:

- Ability: The staff's knowledge, skills, experience and ability relative to the tasks that have been defined;
- Autonomy needs: The staff's own style and needs for autonomy vs. direction, input vs. independence; and,
- Trust: The manager's confidence in the staff's ability to ask for help or direction if needed.

How do these factors impact the fit between the staff and the other elements?

- The higher these factors the less involved the manager should need to be in the operation (all other things being equal).
- The higher these factors, the more complex, difficult and interdependent the task and organization can be.

The Manager   The elements of the manager and the managerial approach that are relevant include:

- The manager's need or desire for control: A great deal of psychological research has confirmed that individuals vary in their need for control. In a managerial setting, this typically translates into extensive involvement in the activities of subordinates: not only setting objectives, but also becoming involved in how the tasks leading to those objectives are carried out.
- The manager's capacity for work: Individuals vary in their energy and ability, and this translates into a varying capacity for managerial work.

How do these factors impact the way in which a fit is created between the manager's approach and the remaining elements?

- The higher these factors, the more involved the manager will want to be in the operation, and the less capable the staff will need to be. Indeed, skilled employees may be put off by such a style.
- When a manager has a high score on the above factors, the organization she is managing will have a lower requirement for systems, structure, and formal process. That is, these organizational elements—which make a unit more self-sustaining and self-regulating—will be less necessary. The time, energy, and involvement of the manager will be able to substitute for systems, structure, and formal process.

ALIGNING THE ELEMENTS

We've discussed how these elements relate to one another and the need to align them. However, we have not said much about how to choose which element to change and in relation to what. If the strategy and operation need to fit with the staff, do you change the operation *or* the staff? If strategy and operation need to fit the manager, do you change the person or the operation? Aligning these elements involves a complex set of choices around what to hold constant and what to change.

If we want to hold any three of these elements constant, we can try to change the one remaining element to create this fit. Of course, we can't always hold things constant. This is the very problem that growth presents.

The challenge of managing these varied components of the job requires some particular tools.

━━━ THE MANAGER'S TOOLS

We've talked about some of the principles that affect the choices a manager makes about the various elements of his responsibilities, but we haven't discussed the specific tools and techniques available to help craft a fit among them. If we think hard about what managers actually do on a day-to-day basis, it is clear that one aspect of the way that managers execute their responsibilities is time-related. That is, there are three ways of getting involved in something: before, during, and after. These correspond to three specific techniques:

- *Anticipating* the situation and doing as much as possible to prepare to deal with it. This approach includes sales and financial forecasts, marketing and operating plans, policies and procedures, and job descriptions.
- *Acting* to carry out our plans, and at the same time dealing with all of the unanticipated issues, problems and situations that could not possibly be planned for. In addition, many decisions are put off until the situation actually arises in recognition of the fact that there will be more information and experience to use as a guide once the situation is upon us.
- Finally, *reviewing* the situation, both to learn everything possible in order to apply it to the next round of events, as well as to reward (or punish) individuals who were part of the effort.

We can look at these techniques as they are applied to each of the responsibilities described earlier, and see that they define a 3 × 3 matrix, as shown in *Exhibit 3*. Note that, while the anticipating-acting-reviewing cycle makes some intuitive sense, once a business is more than one day old, it is difficult to anticipate without first reviewing. That is, in a going concern, the cycle is more likely to begin with a review of past performance, a recasting of plans and objectives in light of this review, and a new round of action.

The label "acting" is also somewhat misleading because, of course, we

EXHIBIT 3

| | *Technique* | | |
Responsibility	*Anticipating*	*Acting*	*Reviewing*
Strategy & Operating			
Organizing			
Staffing			

are always "acting"; our behavior always takes place in the present. Yet, it is the time-orientation of the thought processes and behavior that is important. Some actions do have as their focus planning for the future, others on understanding the past. And, naturally, every present action casts a shadow on the future.

Finally, it is also fair to point out that this cycle is not going on uniformly for all domains of activity. A manager may be anticipating bringing a new plant on stream and doing the action planning for it; acting with respect to a new marketing and promotion effort; and, reviewing the financial performance of the entire business, all simultaneously.

TOOLS

If we consider some common management tools, we can see that they are means of carrying out the responsibilities described above, and that they rely on the techniques of anticipating, acting, and reviewing. Budgets and plans, organization structures, salary, and performance reviews, and the manager's actions and input—all fit into the framework described above.

EXHIBIT 4

	Technique		
Issues	*Anticipating*	*Acting*	*Reviewing*
Strategy & Operating	• Strategic plans • Business plans • Contingency plans • Financial plans • Budgets • Action plans • Policies	• Exceptions • Decisions • Input • Revisions	• Plan versus actual • Follow-up audits • Budget versus actual • Variance report
Organizing	• Liaisons and links • Job definitions • Standard operating procedures • Performance standards • Unit structure • Organization structure	• Delegating • Coordinating	• Organization audit • Job review • Standards and procedures evaluation • Work flow analysis
Staffing	• Job requirements, description • Staffing plans • HR strategy	• Motivating • Teaching • Recruitment • Selection • Training • Acculturation	• Performance review • Salary/bonus review • Reward/punish

To amplify on *Exhibit 4,* we can explain the particular management tools that can be applied to operating, organizing and staffing issues.

Tools for Strategy and Operating Issues   In order to deal with operations, the manager has a number of tools available:

- Tools that help with *anticipating* include analyzing the market and the threats and opportunities it represents; developing a strategy; allocating resources to the project commensurate with its scope and attractiveness; developing business plans, action plans and financial plans (budgets) that present a view of the objectives that will be worked for, the specific actions that will be taken to help achieve those objectives, and the financial results that are expected to accrue as a result. In addition, policies represent standing decisions on anticipated issues (e.g., a shipping charge on all orders over ___, no changes in delivery date less than 10 days before anticipated ship date, etc.).
- Techniques that are required in the course of *acting* on these plans include: dealing with exceptions, crises, unanticipated events, providing input and information to others, as well as making decisions.
- Tools that help in *reviewing* operating activities include: reviewing budget vs. actual performance and variance reports, following up on action plans, operating reviews, inspection tours, etc.

Tools for Organizing Issues   Various tools are available to help the manager in organizing:

- Tools that help in *anticipating* organizing issues include: defining jobs, responsibilities and performance standards, grouping positions into units; developing standardized procedures for how work will be completed; grouping units into an overall organizational structure; creating liaisons, links and coordinating mechanisms.
- Tools that are required in the course of actually *acting* include delegating unanticipated tasks and responsibilities, motivating staffs, and coordinating activities.
- Tools that aid in *reviewing* organizational performance include audits of organizational units, job and position reviews, as well as the evaluation of standards and procedures.

Tools for Staffing Issues   In order to deal with staffing, there are a variety of tools available:

- Tools that aid with *anticipating* staffing issues include position descriptions, staffing plans, human resource strategies, workflow analysis.
- Tools that help with *acting* phase of staffing issues include recruit-

ing, selection, training, motivating, teaching, and coaching/devel-
opment.
- Tools that assist in the *reviewing* phase of staffing issues include
performance review, salary and bonus review, reward, and punishment.

All of these tools are used by the manager to create fits between the
various elements of her responsibilities.

Job definitions and performance standards help define an organization that's capable of executing the strategy; people are hired with the skills
and aptitude to perform these jobs at the required level; new markets and
opportunities are pursued to leverage the base of skills the firm has developed.

——— THE IMPACT OF GROWTH

The fit model that we examined above was relatively static. That is,
we looked at the organization of creating fits by holding several elements
constant and changing one element so that it was in alignment with the
remaining ones.

THE IMPACT OF GROWTH

Growth, however, has a dramatic effect on this assumption: Everything is changing at once! The system is always moving in the direction of
greater entropy—more complex operations, more decisions to make, more
people to manage.

If we go back to the set of tools discussed above, it is easy to conceive
of a cycle of anticipation, action and review, even in a relatively static enterprise. Customers, competitors and markets change, and the firm must adapt.
However, if we add the dynamic of growth to the equation, we can see that
the situation gets more complicated. In addition to all of the adaptation that
transpires with respect to the external environment, there is now a need to
adapt the enterprise to internal challenges: there is simply *more* work to do,
and new ways of accomplishing it must be found.

One approach to getting more done would be an organic or replicative
approach—to build new, stand-alone organizations. Gore Associates, for instance, basically starts a new business every time it launches a new product.
This is an uncommon approach for two reasons:

- Growth is an opportunity to generate economies of scale and
scope by performing larger amounts of work with proportionately
less people. These opportunities are decreased when work is not
kept under a common managerial structure.

- Chief executives—and managers in general—are generally interested in expanding their scope of responsibility, not contracting it. It is generally their preference to "keep control." This, in turn, is a further pressure to keep this new work under a common managerial structure.

What this means for the manager is that—assuming she was busy at one level of work volume—as work expands, a new way must be found to accomplish that work in *less* time, so that new work can be accommodated. If we look at our framework, we can see that there is a certain substitutability between anticipate/review and action. That is, we can substitute one for the other:

- If you can devote time and energy—on a real-time basis—to a task, it is less necessary to plan for it. Consider the task of building a new production facility. If you had an unlimited amount of time to devote to the project, you could live on-site, look at progress each day, make decisions about next steps and priorities.
- However, as time becomes a scarce resource, planning is a critical tool that allows objectives, procedures, and decisions to be specified in advance. Thus, as situations arise, you need not be there to deal with them. By planning—and then reviewing actual performance against plan—you can effectively influence an outcome with less real-time input.

What this means is that—as organizations grow and as the responsibilities on individuals increase—managers begin to look for ways in which to substitute planning and review for real-time action and decision-making. In addition to the factors outlined above, which will place increasing time requirements on the manager, there are other ways in which growth will tend to push managers toward less involved modes of management.

- The increased learning, growth, and development of the staff raises their ability to act independently. As employees become more expert in their roles, and as a manager develops more trust in their abilities, it is simply natural to delegate increased responsibility to them. Moreover, personal growth and development will push them to seek increased responsibility.
- The increased complexity of issues and scope and depth of information required to address them. This, in turn, leads to a decreased ability on the part of the manager to "know" the right answer and therefore specify behavior or even specific results. Thus, the manager will be forced to delegate more responsibility for selecting both means and ends.
- The increased ability of the organization to develop systems that diminish the need for the manager to serve as a coordinating mechanism. As managers learn about the work and activities of the organization, they can develop systems that will serve as

coordinating mechanisms, and diminish their need to act in this capacity.

· The decreased risk of catastrophic failure from a single bad decision on the part of a staff. As the organization expands and succeeds, it acquires a base of resources that can serve to insulate it from the risk of failure associated with one individual's actions.

THE EFFECT OF GROWTH ON FIT

If we go back to our fit model, we can see that every element of the model is likely to be changing:

· At the operating level, the firm is growing by adding new products, serving new customers, becoming active in new geographic markets, etc.

· At the organization level, new operating tasks are creating more work and more tasks to be managed.

· At the staff level, there are many new people to be managed.

· All of this adds up to pressure on the manager to change his approach to his responsibilities.

We can see how growth increases dramatically the demands on a manager's time. She must be involved in more activities, and many of growing complexity. There are, however, several approaches to reconfiguring the elements we've been discussing to reduce the level of involvement required. They are discussed below.

Changing the Strategy & Operations One approach to maintaining equilibrium in the system is to constrain the growth of the operation. To limit the range of products and markets to a number that can be managed with the existing organization and staff. It's worth considering how a fit is generally created in the classic, more mature firm. We often talk about strategy as the process of analyzing threats and opportunities in the market, skills and capabilities in the firm, and crafting a fit between the two sets of factors. Yet, the issue arises of *which* to fit to *what*? That is, if you see opportunities where you don't have capabilities and resources, do you build the capabilities to pursue the opportunity, or do you constrain the operation? Growing entrepreneurial firms build their organizational capabilities to pursue opportunity. But, what this means is that the task of creating fit is much more difficult. Think how easy it would be to create fit by always constraining the operation to fit the organization. As a manager, this would make your job a piece of cake (at least until the company went bankrupt). It is the job of creating new strategies, new structures and systems, new people with new capabilities, that is so difficult. This is why so many firms fail to change—it's hard work.

Changing the Organization   As we have discussed, organizations create tasks that have certain essential characteristics: their difficulty, importance, need for real time input, etc. Yet, one can reconfigure and redefine organizations to change at least some of their essential characteristics. One essential characteristic is the degree to which an organization is amenable to the planning and review, as opposed to requiring real-time involvement.

Consider an example dealing with a telemarketing organization. Let's suppose the organization markets a complex product, requiring, on average, three calls to close a sale. The company decides to organize the organization in the following way:

- Hire people with varying levels of expertise.
- Have low-level people make the first call to qualify candidates. If a candidate looks as though she is interested, code the account with a positive response, and send a brochure.
- One week later, accounts coded with a positive response are brought up on the computer and distributed randomly to higher-level employees with more technical knowledge to explain the product.
- If the customer is still interested, the account is coded as very serious, and two days later, the customer is called by a third employee who is a trained "closer."

Now, if the organization was structured this way, how would you organize it? It would be difficult to manage results for anyone but the "closer." For the other two classes of employees, if they were measured on the percentage of potential customers coded to the next level then they would have an incentive to simply be very "optimistic" in their assessments.

The only way to manage the people handling the first two "steps" in the process, is a process or "behavior" approach. You specify the kinds of behavior you believe will *lead* to results, since you can't measure results directly. You specify the number of calls per hour, average length of time per call, etc. Perhaps you monitor twenty minutes of calls per person per day as a check on "quality."

Think of how much more effort you need to spend managing *these* people than you do on the last link in the chain—people who are producing *real* results. You can simply measure the actual number of signed contracts produced by each person each day, week or month. You can develop a compensation system that pays people directly on a per-contract basis.

Now, consider the option of restructuring the organization. Eliminate the distinctions among types of callers. Hire people with a higher than average skill level. Train everyone in both "technical" and "closing" skills. Simply distribute lists of potential customers on a random basis, and collect completed contracts at the end of every day. As this example shows, we can change the way that organizations are structured and organized in order to make them more amenable to the application of different management tools.

Changing the Staff   Finally, managers may reduce the requirement for involvement on their part by hiring people with new, or more advanced levels, of skill and ability. Indeed, we all recognize that it is a common symptom of growth for managers to replace people who "haven't grown with their jobs." It's also common to expend a good deal of energy and effort training people so that they can do their best to keep up with the growing demands of their position.

Summary   Unfortunately, there is a limit to the ability of a manager to succeed with these approaches. It is difficult to hire and fire people; one constrains one's operation at a cost. And, not all organizations can be re-configured. Ultimately, managers have to fundamentally change *their own management approach*. While this may be difficult, it is the one thing that *you do have control over.*

What all of this means is that the manager must find ways of reducing the time required for his involvement *while reducing his influence over key issues as little as possible.* That is, the essence of managing is to influence outcomes in a positive manner. One simply cannot become less involved by abdicating. This raises the key challenge for the manager—how to learn new patterns of involvement and how to use new tools—to achieve the appropriate level of influence.

The specific choices that are available will be the subject of Chapter 21, "Managing Transitions in the Growing Enterprise."

———— CONCLUSION

Managing a growing enterprise is a challenging job for any executive. To the normal difficulties of the job, growth adds the imperative of constant change—not only in terms of *what* is done, but *how* it is done. Early on in the evolution of the enterprise, the entrepreneur can actually *do* much of the required work: making decisions about product features and pricing, writing marketing and promotional materials, hiring new employees.

But at some point, the demands on the entrepreneur's time become sufficiently great that he must begin to accomplish these tasks through others, rather than through the more direct means of simply "doing it." This requires the entrepreneur to learn to use the tools of management. As students of management, this phenomena provides us with a particularly interesting window on the manager's job. We can learn a great deal about managing by looking at situations where the need for the tools of formal management are first emerging. The growing enterprise provides a rich store of such situations.

——— DISCUSSION QUESTIONS

1. Why does growth stimulate an increase in the amount of managerial work required?
2. If you accept the notion that a manager needs to "fit" with the other three elements of the enterprise, what does this imply for the manager as these other three elements change?
3. Does the "tools" matrix seem to capture most of the techniques utilized by businesses to organize and manage their activities? What would you add?

Managing Transitions in the Growing Enterprise

21

MICHAEL J. ROBERTS

In a further examination of the challenges of growth, this chapter looks at how managers make the transition between different modes of management. Using the tools and techniques articulated in the previous chapter, managers craft an approach to the task at hand. Yet, as the firm grows, growth changes the fundamental nature of that task and the approach the manager has developed. The search for a new solution generates a new mode of management, and requires a transition from the old to the new.

In the previous chapter, "The Challenge of Growth," we discussed the management task in general, and the way in which growth makes that task more difficult. We concluded that growth made the manager's job more complex by introducing a dynamic element into the process of trying to align four key elements of responsibility: strategy and operations, organization, staff, and the manager himself. And, while we talked generally about the tools that a manager can use to create a fit among these elements, we didn't directly address the issue of *how* to use these tools to deal with the particular issue of growth. That's the topic of this note.

MODES OF MANAGEMENT

As we've discussed, growth exerts a powerful force on the enterprise because it expands dramatically the demands made on the manager's time and energy; yet, that critical resource remains fixed. Because a manager is generally unwilling—or unable, in the case of a chief executive—to restrict the domain of activities over which he has influence, he must find new *means* of influence. Specifically, he must find management approaches that are less time-consuming.

Professor Michael J. Roberts wrote this note as the basis for class discussion rather than to illustrate either effective or ineffective handling of an administrative situation. Copyright © 1993 by the President and Fellows of Harvard College. Harvard Business School case 393-107.

If we examine the options managers have regarding the means of influence available to them, we see that there are several possible choices:

- Creating the organizational context, in terms of the individuals who comprise it and the values that guide them, the culture that surrounds them and the mission they are pursuing.
- Specifying the business objectives and results desired.
- Deciding upon the particular tasks and behavior that will lead to these results.
- Actually doing the work.

There are four corresponding "Modes of Management" that differ in terms of which of these elements are taken as the prerogative of the manager, and which are viewed as the responsibility of the subordinate(s).

If we think of these elements as arrayed in a hierarchy, then if a manager assumes responsibility for one element, she implicitly assumes responsibility for those above it. For instance, if a manager tells someone how to behave, she's implicitly assuming responsibility for the results of that behavior. Thus, a mode is defined not according to the *one* means of influence that is being used, but according to the *most specific means* (see *Exhibit 1*).

There is a relationship between these modes and growth. As a manager moves to the right on the spectrum shown in *Exhibit 1*, he is using a less time-intensive set of tools. Specifying results demands less of an investment of time than does actually doing the work. So, as growth multiplies the time demands, there will be a natural pressure to move to the right. This, in turn, will require that the manager make a transition in terms of not only the tools he uses, but in the entire conception of his job.

Each of these modes can be named according to the primary means of influence being employed. (Note: the word appearing in brackets is the shorthand label according to which we will refer to each mode.)

1. **Real-time management of content [content]** One approach to getting something done is simply to be intimately involved in *doing it*. For example, if the task to be managed is redesigning the product features in a software package, if the CEO, simply attends all of the meetings with the software designers and product/market managers, then—by virtue of being present when

EXHIBIT 1

	Content	Behavior	Results	Context
Creating the organization	√	√	√	√
Specifying results	√	√	√	
Determining behavior	√	√		
Doing the work	√			

critical decisions are being made, providing input, and exerting authority—the CEO has had a large measure of influence over the outcome.

2. **Management of behavior [behavior]** An alternative approach to intimate involvement on a real-time basis is to prescribe *behavior.* Thus, to take another example, one might manage a sales force by directing them to call on five different accounts each day, sending them a weekly schedule of accounts to call on, the products to be pushed, the prices to be offered. Here, one's means of influence is the prescription of behavior that is designed to lead to the desired results.

3. **Management of results [results]** With this approach the manager directs a subordinate or group to achieve a particular result, without specifying the particular behavior that leads to that result. Thus, one might set a quota for a sales force, or specify design parameters for a software development group. Here, one attempts to influence the outcome by prescribing the results desired.

4. **Managment of context [context]** A final means of influence is to manage context—the people, the mission, values and culture of the firm. Thus, with this approach, one would hire people with particular abilities and values, give them broad objectives, create the right environment, and depend on them to figure out what needs to be done and how to do it.

Another way of thinking about these different modes is by looking at how they apply to each of the key responsibilities and issues identified earlier: operating, organizing, and staffing. *Exhibit 2* provides a description of how a manager might fulfill each of these responsibilities, depending on the mode in which she was operating.

One way of conceiving of this framework is that it describes the management task in terms of how *deeply* the manager is involved in the work of her subordinates. Thus, for a hypothetical relationship between a general manager and a VP of manufacturing, we could envision the range of alternatives shown in *Exhibit 3.*

Note that we have moved from discussing the management of "organization" and "staff," to analyzing the management of specific individuals in specific tasks. In fact, the framework elaborated in Chapter 20, "The Challenge of Growth," can be made more specific. Instead of talking about operations, organization and staff, we can look at tasks, jobs and subordinates. Indeed, there is a wide range in the level of analysis we can use when looking at a manager's actions and responsibilities. At one end there are "macro" or "enterprise-wide" responsibilities and actions: the strategy, compensation systems, the company's role in the community, etc. At the other end of the spectrum, there are micro or individual-specific responsibilities and actions: determining one person's bonus, assigning tasks to a subordinate, obtaining information on one individual's performance. And, between these two ends of the spectrum, there are all sorts of subunits and groups: a functional

EXHIBIT 2

| Responsibility | Mode | | | |
	Content	Behavior	Results	Context
Strategy & Operating	Do analysis, develop strategy, make plans and budgets.	Prescribe analysis to be done, criteria to be used, assumptions.	Define desired results along financial, competitive, and market dimensions.	Define mission.
Organizing	Group tasks. Define jobs, units, structure and performance standards. Oversees and coordinates day-to-day activities.	Prescribe actions and behavior.	Define results required of specific organizational units.	Create culture.
Staffing	Recruit, select and train.	Prescribe approach, process criteria for selection.	Define performance standards personnel will be held to, as well as reward and punishment system.	Instill values.

EXHIBIT 3

(1) Managing Context	(2) Managing Results	(3) Managing Behavior	(4) Managing Content
"You know the products, you know the plants, work with sales and marketing to determine the appropriate quality level, and then make these products as cost effectively as you can."	"I've developed this budget—in terms of quality, quantity, and cost. Figure out how to make it happen."	As described in 2 plus ". . . To achieve these results, you'll have to close plants A, B, and C, and consolidate manufacturing, start sourcing raw materials from the Far East, and get rid of the existing purchasing manager and engineering director."	As described in 3 plus ". . . I'll come with you to plants A, B, and C to tell them what's going on. I want to be in on the interviewing for a new purchasing manager and engineering director."

EXHIBIT 4

Responsibility	Level of Analysis		
	Macro	Mid	Micro
Strategy & operating	Enterprise-wide strategy and operations	Business or function	Task
Organizing	Entire operation	Subunit	Job
Staffing	All staff	Group	Subordinate

grouping, such as manufacturing or sales; a business unit grouping, such as consumer or industrial product divisions; groups related to responsibility level, such as middle managers or first-line supervisors; and, geographic groups, such as international operations or European sales (see *Exhibit 4*).

As we talk more about particular modes of management, it is important to recognize that the tools and approaches these modes represent can be applied at the micro or macro level, or any level in between. Indeed, the choice of an appropriate level at which to manage is another critical issue a manager must confront.

SELECTING AND IMPLEMENTING A MODE OF MANAGEMENT

Given this variety of generic approaches to managing, the issue of which mode is appropriate and how exactly one should execute that mode remain. These questions will be addressed below.

MANAGING CONTENT

Managing in a Content mode requires an expenditure of what are the manager's scarcest resources—time, energy and effort. Because involvement is intense and real-time in nature, relatively little in the way of formal tools is required. It's almost axiomatic—since the tools are things that save you time, if you are willing to devote sufficient energy to a project, you don't need much in the way of formal tools. For instance, formal job designs define the set of tasks that each individual is responsible for. But, if you are present to instruct subordinates what to do every minute of the day, they don't need a formal job description. Policies and procedures tell people how to behave, but again, if you're there to do it, they aren't necessary.

Entrepreneurs often manage in the Content mode early in the life of the enterprise for several sound reasons:

- The firm is small enough—in terms of people and volume of work—to make it physically *possible* to manage in this mode. There are so few people that a manager can interact with them all in a highly involved manner. In addition, the scope of decisions required is sufficiently narrow that the entrepreneur can be involved in them all.
- The team of employees is inexperienced, both because it is unclear what expertise is required, and because the firm can't afford the expense of experienced people.
- The risk of not being intimately involved in every activity and decision seems particularly high. Because the young firm is often resource-constrained, its very existence could easily be threatened by a few missteps. Thus, the entrepreneur feels a strong desire to influence as much activity as possible.
- The firm is so young that it has not yet learned a sufficient amount about how to accomplish its work to permit formalization or routinization. For instance, one needs to know what particular information is critical to design an information system; similarly, one needs to know what performance standards *should* be in order to design an incentive system. The manager of a young firm has simply not learned enough about these and other critical areas to apply a formal process. Real-time involvement and judgement is still required.
- The pace of change is sufficiently rapid that many attempts at formalization and routinization will only work for a short time. If, for instance, there are only a few people in the telemarketing department, there is a practical limit to the extent to which their jobs can become specialized. When the volume of work and number of people expands, it will open up new options for the organization of work. Thus, it may not pay to invest time and energy in formalizing the organization, when it is clear that it will soon change.

In a context mode, the key tools are primarily those related to acting: making decisions, assigning tasks, hiring people (see *Exhibit 5*). Other tools can be used as well, but in a way in which the manager is heavily involved. Thus, he may develop a business plan and financial plans, look at budgets, etc., but these are primarily ways in which to coordinate his own activities, rather than manage the work of others.

Managing in the Content mode requires several critical abilities. First among these is analytical skill. If one person is making virtually all of the key decisions, she had better be right about them. The nature of new activities in new enterprises is that they are *new*. There are no existing rules of thumb or conventions to tell a manager what to do. Thus, the entrepreneur must approach these situations with an open mind, and use analytical skill to determine the correct approach. Indeed, it is often the entrepreneur's willingness to look at situations with a fresh perspective—and develop innovative solutions—that is key to creating a competitive advantage.

EXHIBIT 5
Key Tools for Managing Content

Responsibility	Technique		
	Anticipating	*Acting*	*Reviewing*
Strategy & operating	Broad scope business and financial plans	Making decisions in real time	Observing outcomes
Organizing	Simple functional structure	Assigning tasks	Observing efficiency and effectiveness
Staffing	Headcount plans	Hiring people	Observing subordinates

MANAGING BEHAVIOR

Managing Behavior involves specifying *how* people should behave, rather than *what* the results of that behavior should be. The difference between managing Content and Behavior is that influence in the Content mode is achieved via real-time involvement, where influence in the Behavior mode is achieved more with formal tools. For instance, the Content approach to managing an order fulfillment function would be to come in each morning, look at the invoices specifying the orders to be shipped, prioritize them based on some sense of customer importance, assign people to "pick and pack," and review each completed order prior to shipping. A Behavior mode would entail specifying rules and procedures for each of these steps, and performing an occasional audit to ensure that they're being followed (see *Exhibit 6*).

Managing Behavior is appropriate when:

- It is difficult to specify the desired result. If, for instance, you are still in the process of perfecting a manufacturing operation, it will be difficult to know what yields, labor, and material content should be. So, it is easier to specify how people should behave—work from this time to this time, work at this pace, do this at a particular time, etc.
- The results cannot be measured easily on a real-time basis. Consider, for instance, the development of a pricing strategy. One cannot simply tell from looking at the outcome of the decision process—a set of prices—whether those prices are correct or not. The results—increased profits, market share, whatever—won't be apparent for months or even years. Thus, one approach to this kind of work to is to manage behavior: force people to consider the appropriate information—like competitive pricing and margin objectives—and manage the *process* of decision-making.

- Results can only be measured on a group level. As a manager, one is driven to evaluate and distinguish among the performance of individuals. Sometimes, however, results can only be measured at the group level. In such circumstances, it is often appropriate to evaluate individual behavior. Consider for instance, a team of cashiers at a McDonald's. One key result of their efforts should be customer satisfaction, therefore loyalty, therefore increased sales for the restaurant. But, computing sales on an individual cashier basis is fairly meaningless—customers come in and pick the shortest line or the nearest cashier. Thus, the only thing that is "auditable" is behavior—whether the employee smiles, says "please" and "thank you," etc. It is this type of behavior that is frequently audited by a "mystery shopper." It is interesting to compare these "customer service" type of results with the more immediately measurable result of incremental selling—say of dessert items. One could make a strong argument that it is less important to audit suggestive selling behavior since this is a result that is easily discernable by comparing the average sales per customer or average volume of dessert items sold for each cashier.

Given that you have decided to manage Behavior, the key tools are as follows:

- Job design: With a job design and position description, one can prescribe both the tasks and the behavior. For instance, a job description for a telemarketer may prescribe "making 30 calls per hour to the list of prospects generated and distributed weekly."
- Policies and procedures: Policies and procedures that specify how tasks are to be completed serve as valuable tools for prescribing behavior. For a telemarketer, for instance, the policies and procedures may specify that the individual should recite a prepared script, regardless of what the potential customer says.
- Review and audit systems: Systems that audit behavior, like the "mystery shopper" program described in the McDonald's example above, or a "monitoring" program in which supervisors listen to the conversations of customer service agents during an unannounced 10 minute period each day, serve as a good check on desired behavior.

MANAGING RESULTS

Managing Results is one of the most widely used modes of management. Indeed, the term "management by objective" describes exactly this approach. One reason for its popularity is its time efficiency: It takes far less involvement to specify a result than it does to detail all of the behavior that should lead to that result. For many positions, it is also the only feasible approach; it would simply be impossible to audit the behavior of field salespeople, for instance. In addition, by giving individuals discretion over how

EXHIBIT 6
Key Tools for Managing Behavior

	Technique		
Responsibility	*Anticipating*	*Acting*	*Reviewing*
Operating	Action plans	Prescribing action steps, behavior	Audit and review systems that focus on behavior
Organizing	Standard operating procedures, policies	Visual inspection of behavior	Compliance audit
Staffing	Job description in behavioral terms	Training	

to achieve results, a manager can unlock a host of knowledge and skills that he may not possess. Finally, it is widely believed that the increased degrees of freedom given to a subordinate in this mode are a powerful motivational force (see *Exhibit 7*).

The Results mode is appropriate when:

- Desired results can be specified in advance: You can only manage results when you can specify the desired results in advance. Consider the production of a new microchip on a new fabrication line. Should the yield (percentage of components that work) be 30% or 80%? It is difficult to manage in this mode unless there is a base of experience upon which to develop reasonable expectations and standards.
- Desired results can be measured on a real-time basis: If results cannot be measured on a real-time basis, then results as objectives become almost meaningless. Compare the management of manufacturing task with that of an advertising campaign devoted to increasing brand awareness. A manager can tell at the end of every day and every week how many widgets have been produced. It is more difficult, however, to judge the result of an advertising campaign until a great deal of money has been invested, and the program is well underway.

The key tools used to manage in a Results mode include:

- Plans and budgets: These are one of the most widely used tools in business because they are essential to managing in a results mode. A plan represents an agreement on what will be achieved, and the budget is the financial representation of those results.
- Reward and punishment: Incentive compensation programs, and other reward and punishment systems, are also key. A critical

EXHIBIT 7
Key Tools for Managing Results

	Technique		
Responsibility	*Anticipating*	*Acting*	*Reviewing*
Strategy & operating	Business plans Strategic plans Financial plans Budgets	Exceptions Revisions Input	Plan vs. actual Variance reports
Organizing	Performance standards Organization structure	Delegating Coordinating	Organization audit Reorganization
Staffing	Staffing plans HR strategy	Motivating Teaching Recruiting, selecting Hiring	Performance review

element of managing in a results mode is to give people an incentive to achieve those results.

- Information systems: Information systems are critical for two reasons. First, they report results so that feedback is available on the very thing that one is trying to manage. Second, an early warning system is required in order to know if things are off track. The risk of managing results is that if one does *only* this, you don't know until *after* the fact that you have a problem. Thus, the early warning system provided by an information system is essential.

- Coordinating mechanisms: precisely because the results mode is a less involved approach, there is potential for poor coordination between units. If, for example, manufacturing and sales need to coordinate in order to have enough goods on hand for a promotional event, a mechanism is required to communicate this. With a highly involved approach, the general manager would simply know what was transpiring, and could relate it to the affected parties. In a results mode, however, he may not know. Information and planning systems need to fill this coordinating role.

MANAGING CONTEXT

In the Context mode, the manager simply charts a broad set of objectives, and worries more about the type and quality of individual who becomes part of the organization, the values of the organization, and the environment it provides for its members (see *Exhibit 8*). This approach is appropriate when:

- It is difficult to specify or measure desired results. The R&D division of a pharmaceutical company, for instance, develops new drugs. But it is difficult to set out realistic timetables and mile-stones for development.

- The work has a high "custom" component: Consider a hospital, for instance. It is difficult to set out specific results and measures for each patient because most problems are of a highly custom or individualized nature, and require complex tradeoffs. Someone with a heart problem and diabetes may well have a different expected outcome than someone with just a heart problem, who differs still from someone with a heart problem and alcoholism.
- The people in the organizational unit are predominantly trained professionals. As professionals, they are assumed to possess the knowledge and skills required to do the right thing. They are also assumed to have a particular—and strongly held—set of values, which serve as a powerful external control. Thus, a college faculty is assumed to share the objectives of teaching and research, and it is difficult to hold people accountable for particular results on a regular basis.

The key tools for executing a Context mode include:

- Selection: The recruitment and selection of people are key ele-ments of managing in a Context mode.
- Review: The review, promotion, and development of employees not only gives more responsibility to particular people, but also sends powerful messages about the organization's values.
- Communication: The communication and reinforcement of mis-sion and values is a critical component of a Context approach.
- Organization Structure and Systems: These choices determine the kind of conflicts and interactions that will occur, and the mecha-nisms for dealing with them.

EXHIBIT 8
Key Tools for Managing Context

	Technique		
Responsibility	*Anticipating*	*Acting*	*Reviewing*
Strategy & operating	Mission statement Strategic objectives	Communicating mission, goals and strategy	Financial, strategy review
Organizing	Defining basis of organizational structure, performance standards	Assigning key tasks Setting standards Setting example	Organization "renewal"
Staffing	Key hires Value "screen"	Promotion decisions Motivating	Reward/punishment system

—— TRANSITIONS BETWEEN MODES

Transitions between modes are critical. By magnifying the volume and scope of work, growth forces the manager to evolve from a particular mode to one that requires less hands-on, real-time involvement. This means moving along the content-behavior-results-context spectrum.

While these transitions may happen across a time span of years, there are other transitions that happen daily. Good managers do not use only *one* mode. On any given day, there may be certain groups or subordinates, engaged in certain tasks, that require management in the content mode, while others require management in the behavior, results or even context modes. The best managers have a full repertoire of skills and tools, and can discern the specifics of the situation that make one mode more appropriate than another.

—— MANAGING YOURSELF: KNOWING WHEN TO CHANGE

One of the most difficult aspects of managing a growing enterprise is the constant pressure to change your management mode. Most of us have firmly held beliefs and strong habits that shape the way we approach situations and the way we behave. It's tempting to use "style" as the term to describe this personal inclination. We often use the concept of management style as a catch-all into which we can put all the behavior that seems personal and idiosyncratic. Yet, the very word "style" seems to suggest that—while the surface packaging or appearance may be different—the underlying principles at work are the same. The reality, however, is that differences in style often reflect dramatically different views of the world and great variation in beliefs regarding the core principles according to which one should manage the others. Thus, while the word "style" captures behavior, it is also a signal about what lies beneath behavior: principles, beliefs, values, and assumptions. The word "style" does not begin to capture the dramatic impact that this more personal set of beliefs and principles can have on an organization. For this reason, I have used the term "Modes of Management" to refer to this broader set of dimensions that describes an individual's approach to the management task.

Another common misconception that is fostered by the use of the word "style" to refer to behavior patterns is the idea that there is little choice involved. Somehow, "style" is just the way we are. Indeed it is true that many managers have one style that they don't even recognize as a "style"—there is no sense that there is a choice to be made about how to behave. There's a saying that "The fish was the last creature to discover water." This gets at the fundamental fact that we are far more likely to recognize that something exists when it changes. Because the fish is constantly surrounded by water, it assumes that this is simply "the way things are." Similarly, a manager who only behaves in one way may not recognize that there are other ways to behave.

If we think about it for even a moment, it should be clear that one style is rarely flexible enough to accommodate all circumstances. The right approach to most management tasks is contingent upon both the particular person being managed, the task at hand, and our own skills and preferences. Thus, to cite one extreme example, few of us could imagine managing a shift at McDonald's and a team of McKinsey consultants with the same "style."

By using the term "mode of management," I've tried to convey the idea of a more conscious choice over what kind of "style" to use. But I don't mean to suggest that it's easy. It is possible to change modes of management, but it is *a lot* of work. Why go through it? The fact is that changing one's own management mode is one of the *most powerful tools* a manager has, for several reasons:

- First, you can't always change the nature of the organization. Some jobs and organizations are simply not amenable to restructuring. They remain ideally suited to one particular approach.
- Second, it is difficult and time-consuming—if not sometimes impossible—to replace subordinates. Even if it were not the case, certain jobs have a mix of tasks that will require different management approaches.
- Finally, if you don't change your mode of management, you will constrain the strategy and operations of the enterprise to one that fits within your limits rather than the more expansive opportunity offered by the marketplace.

Thus, the more flexible you are as a manager, the wider the variety of people and tasks you'll be able to manage well.

We've described four common modes of management, the tools that can be used to execute these modes, and the situations in which these modes are appropriate. We haven't yet discussed the type of behavior and attitude that's required of a manager to work in each of these modes.

As *Exhibit 9* shows, each of the modes requires very different behavior on the part of the manager.

One of the reasons why it's so difficult to change modes is because *behavior* has to change. And, because behavior is so often the product of deep-seated drives, assumptions, and beliefs, it's difficult to change.

The only way to become adept at the change process is to adopt *new* habits that force you to change. If you get in the habit of thinking about each situation before you act, and can reflect on your own behavior, this is a good start. Always ask yourself what you're *really* trying to accomplish, and exactly what your role in that process should be. It also helps to have advisors and colleagues who can observe you in action, and who aren't afraid to criticize you. This is one of the easiest traps for a chief executive to fall into: there are very few people around who will actually criticize you. Finally, it

EXHIBIT 9

	Mode			
	Content	*Behavior*	*Results*	*Context*
Situation	Young, small simple enterprise	Somewhat larger, more involved enterprise	Large complex organization	Very large, very complex mature organization
Driving assumptions	Insufficient knowledge, experience to plan Subordinates not capable of independent action or decisions	Too little time to do everything Subordinates can act independently but in accordance with managerial prescription	Too little time Subordinates can achieve better outcomes with their own means	Too little time and knowledge Right people in the right environment with right mission will succeed
Behavior	On the front lines Barking orders Pitching in to help out	Developing process and procedure Observing	Attending meetings, reviews Studying plans, papers, reports Writing memos	Lots of time on key hires and promotion Tone-setting events
Key skills, tools	Action Decisions	Policies Procedures Behavior audit	Plans Budgets Organizing structure and systems	Communication Leadership by example

helps to have peers and friends with whom you can share experiences. Others will often have remarkably different perspectives on situations and your actions.

——— SUMMARY

Growth can be a very positive force, and one that is complementary to other changes going on in the organization. Just as it creates the need for a manager to delegate increasing responsibility, it feeds the desire of subordinates for that increased responsibility. The trick lies in matching the rate of one with the other.

In Chapter 20, "The Challenge of Growth," we discussed how the dynamic of growth increases the volume and scope of the manager's work. As a consequence, the manager must learn to use new tools—and use old tools in new ways—in order to get this work done.

But, successfully managing growth requires more than an intellectual understanding of what to do. It demands that the manager develop a new conception of his role, as well as the new skills and abilities required to fulfill that role.

═══ DISCUSSION QUESTIONS

1. Which modes of management seem most natural to you, and which would be most difficult to emulate?
2. Why is a transition between modes difficult, and what do you believe would improve the odds of success?
3. What advantages might a manager achieve by utilizing more than one mode?

22   Building the Self-Sustaining Firm

AMAR BHIDÉ

George Bernard Shaw said that "any fool can start a love affair, but it takes a genius to end one successfully." In a similar vein, many have observed that it is far harder to build an enterprise that endures than to merely start a new business.

Bhidé argues that existing models of growth fail to capture the variety of business development patterns that we observe. In fact, the path to sustainability must integrate the founder's vision and the internal capabilities of the organization with a realistic assessment of the external environment in which the firm operates.

Turning a fledgling enterprise into a self-sustaining business poses a difficult challenge for entrepreneurs. Of the hundreds of thousands of new businesses launched in the United States every year, many fail to attain a basic operational sustainability—they cannot function without the day-to-day intervention of their owners. Others show great early promise but then cannot cope with the problems of growth or the maturation of their markets. Few attain what one entrepreneur calls the "escape velocity to go into stable orbit after launch." And only the most exceptional ventures evolve into resilient institutions which can survive revolutionary external changes.

The failure to attain sustainability matters. Stress, burnout, or sickness can jeopardize the livelihoods of the many entrepreneurs whose businesses require their daily toil. The inability to sustain a promising start also represents an unhappy outcome. Conversely, success in building a self-sustaining business provides handsome rewards. An enterprise that is perceived to be self-sustaining can enter a virtuous cycle: expectations of longevity attract customers and other resources that further consolidate its position and open new opportunities. Entrepreneurs realize higher prices from the sale of busi-

Professor Amar V. Bhidé wrote this note as the basis for class discussion rather than to illustrate either effective or ineffective handling of an administrative situation. Copyright © 1995 by the President and Fellows of Harvard College. Harvard Business School case 395-200.

nesses thought to be self-sustaining as well as the satisfaction of leaving a more permanent mark on the world.

The challenges of building sustainability also offer attractive opportunities for individuals with managerial skills and training. Often, ventures are launched by innovative or technically proficient individuals whose limited managerial capacities threaten the survival of the enterprise. Professional managers who can subsequently bring order to the chaos and help define sustainable strategies can enjoy considerable financial and other rewards.

Building sustainability is also closely related to the problem of "managing growth." An enterprise has to grow in order to support the organizational infrastructure it needs to function without the day to day intervention of its founders. Growth may also be needed to attain sustainable advantages of market share and scale. And, attracting and retaining employees, customers, and other critical resources often requires the enterprise to keep expanding: Talented prospects are more likely to join (and key employees to stay) if they believe the firm has the growth potential to provide increasing responsibility and financial reward.[1]

The problem, however we frame it, is complex. Building sustainability (or managing growth) requires progress along an "external" (or "market") front as well as an "internal" (or "organizational") front. The external dimension pertains to the sustainability of the firm's competitive position vis-à-vis rivals and substitutes as well its access to capital and other resource markets. It derives from "structural" advantages such as patents, brand names, and customer switching costs and from the goodwill and trust the firm has established with its external constituencies. The internal dimension relates to the organization's (as opposed to the entrepreneur's) ability to serve customers profitably and to adapt to changing circumstances. It derives from the talents and training of the firm's members, its structures and systems, and its values and character (the "corporate culture").

Furthermore, the internal and external challenges are at least partially related. For example, an entrepreneur cannot delegate to poorly qualified or trained employees; but, attracting and integrating quality personnel into the organization requires a profitable market franchise or easy access to capital. Conversely, long-run external sustainability depends on internal strengths. Patents expire, consumer tastes and wants change; renewing competitive strengths requires a fresh burst of organizational creativity and will.

Confronting these interconnected problems requires the principals of the enterprise deal with high-level, some what abstract questions as well as nitty gritty tasks. Thus on the one hand the principals must decide what business they are (or aspire to be) in, how they will compete, and the long-term "purpose" of the organization; on the other hand, they must also engage

---

1. Whether to emphasize sustainability or growth is therefore a matter of taste. I prefer to put sustainability first because it is more closely linked to the rewards and objectives entrepreneurs typically seek.

themselves in the minutiae of control systems and compensation. And all this must often be accomplished under changing, uncertain market conditions and serious constraints of time and cash. This is challenging managerial territory indeed!

——— MANY DESTINATIONS AND PATHS

Some experts have proposed "stages of growth" or "life-cycle" models to describe the evolution of businesses. Just as humans pass through similar stages of physiological and psychological development from infancy to adulthood, these models posit that businesses evolve in predictable ways and encounter similar problems in their growth. And, managers of firms at different "stages of growth" have different tasks and priorities, just as parents of children of different ages face different challenges.

Their resonance with the biological world gives these models intuitive appeal. They also give entrepreneurs the comfort that an authoritative child-rearing book can provide parents by, for example, telling them what to do and expect during their child's "terrible twos." Unfortunately, however, these models fail to adequately account for the great variety in the manner in which businesses grow and what they can grow into. For example, the evolution of a Sun Microsystems has little in common with its venture capital firm, Kleiner Perkins. Sun's installed base of workstations provides a sustainable competitive advantage. Organizationally, Sun has many talented employees and is not dependent on a few individuals for its success. Kleiner Perkins, although a preeminent venture capital firm, doesn't have the same external franchise or organizational capability. Its reputation may give Kleiner Perkins somewhat better access to new opportunities; but its returns largely depend on the quality of its new investments. And, this quality depends on the skill of a handful of partners whose abilities represent about all the organizational capability the firm has. Thus successful firms in different industries can grow up to be very different creatures.

We see differences not only in destinations, but also in the paths taken. Consider, for example, the leading micro-computer software firms in the 1980s. We cannot easily map the histories of Microsoft, Lotus, Word Perfect, or Intuit into a common evolutionary story. Rather, we see great differences in how these firms, competing in the same industry, developed their strategies and organization, and in the role of their founders. And, if we look at successful firms across a range of industries, the case for a one-size-fits-all model becomes even weaker.

Some successful businesses, we find, have an ambitious blue-print for establishing sustainable advantages when they are launched which they execute for a decade or more thereafter. For example, the basic elements of Federal Express's strategy—guaranteed overnight service, hub and spoke logistics, advertising to build a brand name—have been in place for over 20 years since the company was launched. Such an early "go-for-broke" commitment to a long-term competitive strategy, however, is rare. Entrepreneurs rarely start with the breakthrough concepts that can sustain an enterprise for so long or the credibility to muster the necessary resources if they do. More commonly, entrepreneurs start with a marginal niche business, ride a popular wave, or exploit their personal, technical, or professional skills. But, these more modest start-up approaches usually cannot sustain a long-lived business. A small niche player is vulnerable to attack from mainstream competitors who enjoy lower costs and better access to resources. Jumping on to a wave may be profitable and easy, but waves do eventually crest. And, selling one's personal services does not constitute a business. Therefore, such enterprises have to change their initial strategies to survive.

And, we observe great variance in how they do so. In some cases changes are planned in advance. The entrepreneur has a long-term strategic vision at the time of launch but, lacking the resources to execute it, starts with something else—perhaps a short-term trade or consulting project—to generate cash. Then, as soon as the resources can be mustered, the entrepreneur reverts to the original blue-print. In other cases, the entrepreneur does not have a viable long-term strategy in mind at the time of launch. Subsequently, the entrepreneur makes a deliberate effort to formulate one or, more likely, a strategy emerges from chance events—a core business grows out of a customer asking for an add-on product or a new employee suggests a new market.

Competitive forces help determine how quickly firms must adopt new strategies. In a mature, low overhead business, such as consulting, an entrepreneur may bob along, seemingly forever, without a strategy for building a sustainable franchise. But an entrepreneur who has jumped on to a wave, taking advantage of temporary market imbalances, must more urgently find a viable strategy. Luck matters as well—some ventures chance upon an attractive long-term formula quickly, while others encounter several false leads first.

We also see that strategic change can be more or less radical. In some cases we see a complete change in direction—completely new markets, products, and sources of competitive advantage. In other cases we find refinements and extensions—for example, geographic expansion, adding related products or services, or forward or backward integration.

Patterns of organizational or internal development display the same variety as the patterns in strategic or external evolution. In some ventures— typically those exceptional, well-funded startups with a clear strategy to achieve competitive advantage—organizational development follows a systematic plan. An experienced founding team provides the nucleus. The founders then quickly delegate many of their responsibilities to talented employees who are recruited for specific, well-defined positions. Formal control and other systems are established well before they are necessary—investment in organizational infrastructure is made before it's needed.

Such orderly development however is unusual. Often the founders lack the experience, interest or resources to build their organizations in a systematic way. For a considerable period after launch they provide most of the crucial skills and make all the critical decisions. They do not, or cannot, hire talented employees into specific organizational slots. Rather, they recruit whoever they can for tasks they are too stretched to perform themselves. Ad hoc judgments and informal systems rather than formal procedures and policies are pervasive and investment in organizational overhead and infrastructure is minimal. The purpose of the organization is primarily to survive. To attain sustainability, the capabilities of the firm (as opposed to those of the entrepreneur) have to be somehow broadened and deepened. More qualified personnel have to be added, the specialization of functions increased, decision making decentralized, systems to cope with a larger and more complex organization instituted, and the employees oriented towards a common long-term purpose.

But, it is just as difficult to find a single process for successful organizational development as it is for strategy reformulation. If the principal impediment is the lack of resources, organizational transformations are likely to be executed after the firm acquires the financial wherewithal to upgrade its personnel and systems. But where the barrier lies in the founders' lack of interest in matters organizational, a crisis may be required to galvanize change.

We see differences in the extent of personnel change. Some organizations hire a few top managers who so change the structures and systems that all the old employees are transformed. Other firms give up on the warm bodies that they had initially hired off the street and replace them with new cadre of professionally trained employees. The rate of change, too, varies—in some cases, particularly where there is a crisis, the organization has to be reshaped quickly. In other cases changes have to be more gradual because the old order still generates the cash that the firm needs in its period of transition.

Some firms develop strong cultures and values which distinguish their employees' attitudes and behavior, right from the beginning. Other firms develop their characters and personalities more slowly, while some never establish much distinctiveness. In some cases, the founders actively seek to build a certain culture by, for example, articulating norms and values, hiring individuals who they expect will adhere to the norms and terminating those who don't. More often, however, culture-building does not represent a priority in the early days. Consequently, employees are hired for their technical skills and qualifications more than for their values. And subsequently, the mix of personalities that happens to gain the most influence shapes whatever organizational culture that eventually emerges.

Founders play quite different roles in the organizational and strategic development of their firms. Most start with broad responsibilities. Thereafter, some change but little—the founding partner of a venture capital firm may perform many of the same tasks ten years after starting the business. Others quickly put in place an extensive organizational infrastructure and involve themselves mainly in broad policy making. And yet others, like Bill Gates of Microsoft, establish the organizational infrastructure but continue to play an important day-to-day role, monitoring, for example, the progress of programming and product management teams. Some founders lead organizational transformation themselves; others have such attachments to the initial employees and approaches that they bring in a strong outsider to clean house.

IMPLICATIONS OF IDIOSYNCRATIC DEVELOPMENT

The observation that successful firms develop external and internal strengths following their own unique circumstances rather than some standard growth model has several implications for entrepreneurs (and managers brought into a fledgling enterprise).

UNDERSTANDING THE FULL SITUATION

Any actions entrepreneurs contemplate should be informed by the opportunities offered and constraints posed by the overall situation rather than by the firm's "stage of growth."

Evaluating the firm's external sustainability represents an important component of the situation analysis: What's the magnitude of the firm's cost or price advantages? Can the advantages be scaled up to larger or different markets or are they limited to a small niche? Are they controlled by the firm or by a few of its employees? Does the firm have a large, diversified base of customers? How likely are they to switch easily? Could the firm's advantages be undermined by changes in upstream or downstream technologies, standards, channels, or regulations? How likely are such changes? How confident are investors and other resource providers about the firm's prospects? Under what terms, if any, are they prepared to back the firm?

Entrepreneurs should also evaluate their firms' internal or organizational sustainability: Does the firm depend on a few individuals or do its capabilities derive from the skills and knowledge of a large number of its staff? Do most decisions and conflicts flow to the top for resolution or just the most important ones? Is the firm a collection of independent agents or do many employees cooperate to get the job done? Do employees have a shared understanding of the firm's goals and do they identify with these goals? Does the organization have the confidence and the resourcefulness to overcome unexpected adversities and crises?

And, entrepreneurs should examine their personal goals. For some entrepreneurs building a self-sustaining firm is important because they wish to build an institution that will live beyond them or because they wish to sell out. For some others, however, the desire for self-sustainability may be tempered by the satisfaction they derive from doing the day-to-day work, lack of interest in selling out, or an unwillingness to share control. To the extent that it involves extra effort and risk, the entrepreneur should really want to build an independent, on-going firm rather than sell out to someone else who does or engage in a series of lucrative deals. Entrepreneurs should also examine their personal capabilities and contributions: in what roles do they represent an asset to the firm and where do they constitute a liability?

Wishful thinking about the situation—which entrepreneurs are often prone to—may be avoided by examining objective facts. Price competition and deteriorating gross margins, for instance, provide evidence of a weakening competitive position. Onerous terms for equity demanded by investors suggest a deteriorating confidence in the firm's management or prospects. Uncollected receivables, cash shortages, executive fatigue, protracted conflicts, and personnel turnover point to a potentially malfunctioning organization.

An honest analysis can help decision makers identify the main obstacles to the realization of their goals for longevity and growth. In some cases, the analysis may show that the bottlenecks lie in its competitive strategy. Or, the firm may have a sound strategy but cannot fund the investments it needs to achieve competitive advantage because it lacks the confidence of the capital markets. The firm may also fail to realize the full benefits of its competitive strategy because of weaknesses in the organization or the unwillingness of the principals to let go.

Besides identifying the areas of vulnerability, the analysis may also reveal new opportunities. For example, the decision makers may determine that the organization has matured and that it could in fact support a more aggressive strategy to gain market share. Or, that a record of profitability through a difficult initial period has gained the firm the credibility needed to fund a new technology. Or, that the technology has gained the reputation to attract new talent to the organization.

——— MULTIDIMENSIONAL OPTIONS

Just as entrepreneurs should understand the whole situation, they should also consider a broad menu of alternatives, not just a progressive decentralization or "letting go."

To address external issues and opportunities, the decision maker should consider changes ranging from minor modification in tactics to a fundamental redefinition of goals and strategies. For example, on the incremental end of the scale, changes might cover pricing, product features, the elimination of undesirable customers, or the conversion of a line of credit into a term loan. More extensive changes could include geographic expansion, forward or backward integration, continuous flow instead of job shop production, the introduction of related products, entering new channels of distribution, building a sales force, forming alliances or joint ventures, acquiring rivals, issuing new equity or going public. And, as an extreme measure, the principals may consider serving entirely new markets with entirely new products or even selling the firm.

On the internal or organizational front, incremental or radical changes may be contemplated in firm personnel or staff, structures and reporting relationships, incentive and control systems, and in the culture of the firm. Staff changes may entail changes in the qualifications of entry level personnel, bringing in outsiders at senior positions instead of promoting from within, or eliminating the old-timers who cannot perform. Structural changes may involve adding (or reducing) levels of hierarchy, the establishment of staff functions, decentralization or changing the locus of decision making, or adopting a divisional or matrix form of organization instead of a functional form. Incentive and control systems may be made more or less formal, applied to different units and levels of the organization, or used to track or reward different variables. And, the firm's culture may be changed by articulating and promoting certain norms (say of cooperation rather than conflict), hiring employees who believe in these norms and punishing violators.

Potential external and internal changes should also force reconsideration of the principals' roles. A change in role does not necessarily entail doing less or making fewer decisions. Rather, it may involve an emphasis on different tasks and issues—for example, focusing more effort on formulating marketing strategies and less on personal selling; negotiating and reviewing budgets rather than the direct supervision of day-to-day work; designing incentive plans rather than making judgments about the compensation of individual employees; negotiating acquisitions of companies rather than of office supplies; or, developing a common purpose and norms rather than getting the product out of the door.

The consideration of a wide-ranging change does not imply that the principals must turn everything upside down. If the firm merely faces normal growing pains, the situation may call for little more than a tightening of the operations by, for instance, installing better inventory or cash management systems. Moreover, even if desirable, implementing new policies on every front may be unrealistic. But, decision makers in a fledgling enterprise must be more *willing* to consider radical changes than their counterparts in large and stable organizations.

Compared to mature firms, the fledgling enterprise often faces a more dynamic and uncertain environment—indeed external change typically creates the opportunity for start-ups. And, unlike established companies with market power, the young enterprise cannot easily shape its markets; it must adapt its competitive strategies to its changing environment. Attention to seemingly innocuous organizational routines is more important in a firm's formative years as well because ad-hoc practices can easily harden into long-term policies. At the same time, young firms have more room to maneuver and change. They don't have to cope with vast fixed assets committed to a specialized use; consequently, a fledgling firm can more easily redefine its core business than say a General Motors. The number of employees who have to be turned around and the implicit and explicit contracts redrawn is also relatively small.

━━━ MAKING IT HAPPEN

Compared to the start-up phase, when many entrepreneurs seize opportunities without great aforethought, building a sustainable business does require greater deliberation and planning. Even so, good analysis of the situation or alternatives isn't enough. Given a reasonable concept, competitive advantages are typically determined by the quality of execution. As often as not, several entrepreneurs start the same kind of business at about the same time; the successful survivors have more audacity and imagination and the right balance of vision and pragmatism, not superior analytical abilities.

AUDACITY

When they launch a venture, entrepreneurs are often quite willing to step off the beaten track. They believe they have little to lose because they bootstrap the start-up or rely mainly on other peoples' money. After the enterprise has achieved some success, however, entrepreneurs can become nervous about undertaking new investments and changes in strategy which they fear will put their now valuable stake at risk. But maintaining the status quo, especially when competitors and customers aren't standing still, can increase the risks of eventual failure. Long-term success may require the entrepreneur to apparently "bet the company." For example, to build a brand name an enterprise that has relied on word of mouth awareness may have to invest in an advertising campaign. A company that tailored products for a specialized niche may have to adopt strategies to gain cost advantages. Or, an assembler of purchased components may have to build an integrated plant. And, these investments may require the entrepreneur to risk their wealth by plowing back cash-flows, taking on new equity partners, or signing personal guarantees for debt.

Organizational development, too, entails risky investment. Building systems and staff functions and other types of administrative infrastructure requires incurring expenses for intangible long-term payoffs. To improve the skills and confidence of subordinates, the entrepreneur must be willing to let others make mistakes and tolerate suboptimal decisions. Similarly, employees who impair organizational growth may have to be let go, even if they are contributing to current profits.

IMAGINATION

Envisioning and communicating what the future will look like is another critical skill. For example, there are a myriad ways to design the structure, systems, and culture of a new organization and there is no proven method for picking the best combination. At the same time, ad hoc or incremental approaches often lead to dysfunctional and difficult-to-reverse policies. Entrepreneurs who develop a consistent long-term view of organizational design can more easily provide the predictability that attracts people to the organization and minimize traumatic changes in direction.

Similarly, entrepreneurs who can convincingly describe the evolution of a new market enhance their prospects of building competitive advantages therein. The future of a new market—the technologies that will succeed, the key factors for success, the size and nature of customer demand, and so on—cannot be predicted by extrapolating the past or applying first principles. And, in this uncertain climate, the skepticism of customers, investors, and potential employees represents a difficult hurdle for start-ups. The entrepreneurs who succeed are the ones who can tell a compelling story about how the market will evolve and why their strategy will win. Expressions of agnosticism or uncertainty, however well-founded from an objective point of view, rarely will turn skeptics into believers.

Lacking reliable deductive methods to model the future of their organizations or industries, successful entrepreneurs often imaginatively adapt examples from other fields and periods. For example, the Cleveland law firm of Jones, Day served as the organizational model for Marvin Bower's efforts to build the consulting firm of McKinsey & Company. Bill Gates reportedly has studied Alfred Sloan's tenure as CEO of General Motors from 1923 to 1946, when General Motors came to dominate the automobile industry, to inform his long-term vision for Microsoft. But, because a law firm cannot serve as the perfect model for a consulting firm nor an automobile company for a software empire, entrepreneurs have to use intuition and imagination to select what elements of a model should be adopted and sometimes have to mix and match different models.

VISIONARY *AND* PRAGMATIC LEADERSHIP

Making it happen is not, however, exclusively about boldness and drawing imaginative pictures of the future. Building a long-lived enterprise requires balancing between what might be termed as visionary and pragmatic roles. For example:

As visionaries, entrepreneurs have to break free of the constraints imposed by others' perceptions. The strategic and organizational options available to a fledgling enterprise often depend on the beliefs of potential customers, investors, and other providers of resources: if they expect the enterprise to succeed, they provide the support that allows the enterprise to meet their expectations. But if they are skeptical and withhold support, the enterprise will have difficulty in rising above their expectations. Therefore, entrepreneurs must strive to change the perceptions that determine their reality by sketching a vision of the success that their enterprise is bound to enjoy. At the same time, however, entrepreneurs must, as pragmatists, live with what is feasible. As they seek to raise serious capital and make the sale to a strategic customer, they have to keep their expenses below their meager cash inflows. While they try to project the image of a well established company, they have to manage as if they were on the verge of going under.

As visionaries, entrepreneurs set long-term goals and help shape the underlying values of the firm. They have to formulate disciplined strategies, defining what business the firm will compete in and forgoing opportunities that don't build sustainable competitive advantages. As pragmatists, the same entrepreneurs must demand immediate bottom line results and monitor day to day operating performance. And, their dedication to disciplined strategies must be tempered by an appreciation for the cash that short-term opportunities can generate and the risks of premature focus or commitment—the best long-term strategy often isn't the one initially deemed the most attractive.

As visionaries, entrepreneurs take a holistic view. For example, they base the feasibility and attractiveness of their competitive strategies not just on an industry analysis but also take into account their organization's capacity for execution, access to capital, their own management styles and goals, and so on. As pragmatists, entrepreneurs must also pay close attention to tactics and sequence. Even if a holistic analysis suggests the need for comprehensive change, they focus their attention on a few critical areas. Similarly, while they may regard the coordinated development of external strategy and organizational development to be a worthwhile long-term goal, they may push ahead aggressively into new products or technologies without waiting to put in the right organizational structures or systems.

Visionaries try to recruit subordinates more capable than themselves. They coach others, tolerate mistakes, and prefer to develop consensus rather than impose their own views. As pragmatists, entrepreneurs have to prune their organizations, terminating employees who don't fit and reducing the responsibilities of those who can't handle them. They must be prepared to do as well as delegate and make decisions that others aren't prepared to.

As with the other tasks involved in sustaining a business, balancing vision and pragmatism is difficult. There is no formula—entrepreneurs must develop, through practice and observation, a somewhat crude personal theory to guide their actions. And, the emotional drain of playing complex, fluid roles leads many to not even try. These very difficulties, however, allow the few who can build a lasting business exceptional satisfaction and financial reward.

—— DISCUSSION QUESTIONS

1. What is your own sense of the capacities an enterprise must develop in order to outlive its founder?
2. Why do so many businesses fail to develop these capacities?
3. In what ways are the characteristics that make for a successful creator of a business at odds with those required to build an enduring organization?

23 Going Public

CONSTANCE BAGLEY and CRAIG DAUCHY

An IPO, the initial public offering of a company's stock, is often the entrepreneur's dream, signaling success, wealth, and validation from the market. In this piece, Bagley and Dauchy articulate the reasons for going public, as well as the arguments against it. They then describe the process of going public, explaining the key issues and decisions that must be made along the way. Finally, Bagley and Dauchy articulate the legal context in which a public company operates, including the regulations governing public securities and the legal obligations of a public board.

For many entrepreneurs, the company's *initial public offering (IPO)* is the realization of a dream. This first offering of the company's securities to the public represents recognition of the entrepreneur's vision as well as access to the capital required for the company to achieve its potential. It also can create substantial wealth for the entrepreneur, at least on paper.

This chapter first explores the reasons to consider going public, identifies certain disadvantages of being a public company, discusses matters to consider in deciding whether to sell the company, and outlines several factors to consider in determining whether a company is a good candidate for an IPO. The chapter then presents an overview of the public offering process, summarizes the contents of the prospectus, and describes what is usually done to prepare for an IPO. It continues with a discussion of contractual and securities law restrictions on the sale of shares not being sold in the IPO. The chapter concludes with a brief summary of the ongoing responsibilities of a public company and its board of directors.

—— WHY GO PUBLIC?

Initially, an entrepreneur finances the company's operations through private financing transactions, often involving the sale of preferred stock to venture funds and sophisticated individual investors, or alliances with corporate partners. Although the timing varies by industry, most companies decide to go public when (1) the company has reached the point at which initial investors have invested the total amount of capital that they are willing to provide and are focused on *liquidity* (a return on their investment) and (2) the company has made sufficient progress to make a public offering viable. The company may need significant additional capital for research and development or product launches, or working capital to expand operations. However, as the company's value increases, the company may encounter difficulty in attracting new investors, who would rather target earlier-stage companies with a lower valuation.

A public offering of securities provides a company access to broader financial markets to fund capital requirements. Once the company goes public, it can use its stock instead of cash to acquire strategic pieces of technology or other businesses. The company will also have the benefit of public visibility, and, so long as the company is performing well and the market is receptive, the company can return to the public market to raise additional capital. Finally, the IPO will value the company's shares at many (if not hundreds of) times the price paid by the founders and will afford them access to the public market for sale of their shares.

However, there is also a significant number of disadvantages to going public. As explained in more detail below, a public company must meet a host of legal obligations that are inapplicable to private companies, including disclosure obligations and fiduciary duties owed to hundreds of shareholders whom the entrepreneur and the board have never, and will never, meet. The company will forever be in the fishbowl of public scrutiny. Disclosure requirements will apply not only to the company but also to officers and directors, who must inform the marketplace of the amount of the company's stock they and their family own and of any sales, gifts, purchases, or other changes in ownership of that stock, including stock option grants and exercises.

In addition, the going-public process is expensive, often costing more than $1,000,000 in SEC filing fees, state securities filing fees, stock exchange or over-the-counter registration fees, legal fees, accounting fees, printing costs, and increased premiums for director and officer liability insurance. Also, the process consumes an enormous amount of management time. Once public, the company will spend significantly more in legal, accounting, and printing fees than in the past.

In addition, an entrepreneur contemplating a public offering because of the desire for liquidity for his or her stock should be aware of the restrictions on the sale of that stock, even if it is fully vested. As discussed below, the first impediment to sale is that the investment banks that manage the public offering will require the entrepreneurs and all other significant shareholders to agree to not to sell their stock for at least six months after the offering. Second, after the lock-up period has expired, rules against insider trading will severely limit when the stock can be sold without risk. Third,

---

From the Trenches

A well-known maker of athletic equipment began the IPO process. The investment banks had advised the company that the public marketplace would value the outstanding shares at $125 million. Because of the disadvantages of being a public company, including the many restrictions on selling their own stock in the public marketplace after the offering, the founders seriously considered a third-party offer to buy the company for $95 million in cash, which was made after the offeror learned the public offering process had begun. The founders ultimately decided to go forward with the public offering, and after three years the public market valuation of the company was more than $800 million.

---

because the entrepreneur likely is an *affiliate* (an officer, director, or owner of more than 5% to 10% of the outstanding shares), the amount of the stock that can be sold during any three-month period is limited by rule 144 under the federal securities laws to, in most circumstances, 1% of the company's outstanding stock.

IPO VERSUS SALE OF THE COMPANY

Because of the disadvantages of going public, an entrepreneur considering a public offering may wish to think about selling the company instead. Indeed, the sale alternative is a far more common path to liquidity for the entrepreneur, particularly one with a company experiencing slow but steady growth, or in an industry not currently favored by investment bankers.

Often a larger corporation in the same general line of business will be interested in the purchase. For example, Boston Scientific, an integrated manufacturer of medical products, has purchased or offered to purchase several companies (including Cardiovascular Imaging Systems, EP Technologies, and Vesica) during the past few years, either as the companies were contemplating public offerings or soon after their IPOs. The purpose was to expand Boston Scientific's product line. A buyout by an acquisition firm such as McCown De Leeuw & Company or Genstar Capital is often an option for companies with assets against which the purchaser can borrow. Finally, direct competitors of the company may have an interest.

Potential buyers often surface about the time a company is ready to go public because they are well aware that once a company is public, they will have to pay a 15% to 30% premium over the public market price to induce the target company's board to approve the sale. In any event, there are many professionals available to help the interested entrepreneur find an appropriate buyer, including business brokers and corporate finance personnel at investment banks.

The sale of the company can offer several advantages compared to a public offering. In a cash sale, the shareholders of the target corporation can lock in their gains and have immediate liquidity, although they will have to pay taxes on their gain. The target shareholders will not be subject to the risk that stock market conditions will change and the IPO will be called off, or to market risk on their shares if the IPO does proceed.

If the sale is to be for stock of the acquiring company, the sellers will face certain restrictions on disposition of the stock, particularly if the transaction is to be tax free. A significant amount of the stock received must continue to be held by the target's shareholders to satisfy the tax-free reorganization requirements (the so-called *continuity of interest rule*). If the shares issued to shareholders of the target are registered, rule 145 (the analog to rule 144 [discussed below] for stock acquired in a merger or acquisition transaction) will prohibit affiliates of the target from selling in any three-month period more than the greater of 1% of the acquirer's outstanding shares and its average weekly trading volume in the past four weeks. If the shares are not registered, then all shareholders of the target must hold the shares for at least one year. If the acquisition is structured as a *pooling of interests* under financial accounting rules, additional limitations on disposition of the acquired stock may apply.

Although market risk remains in a stock-for-stock deal because the entrepreneur now holds stock of a public company, the market price of a more established company is usually less volatile than that of a newly public company whose price can be depressed for years if early quarterly earnings do not meet the expectations of the market. In addition, the entrepreneur acquiring stock in a merger or acquisition can engage in certain hedging activities against market risk that would be precluded by a lockup agreement with investment banks. But perhaps most important, the sale of the business enables the entrepreneur to avoid having to deal with the myriad pressures of being a public company, including meeting or exceeding revenue and earnings estimates quarter after quarter, dealing with stock analysts who are constantly seeking information and assurances, and communicating with and owing duties to shareholders the entrepreneur has never met.

Arguing against the sale of the business is the limitation on return. First, the price paid per share by a buyer will usually be less than the company could obtain in a public offering. Second, the entrepreneur's *upside* (potential profit) is capped at the purchase price if the consideration is cash, or is determined by the stock market performance of the acquiring company if the consideration is stock. Many entrepreneurs do not want to let control of their upside slip from their own hands.

—— IS THE COMPANY AN IPO CANDIDATE?

The entrepreneur and the board must determine whether the company should pursue an immediate IPO or an alternative strategy, such as waiting until the company has made additional progress so that it can command a higher valuation in an IPO or pursuing a merger with a private or public company. Factors to consider include the nature of the company's existing products and product pipeline; the strength and depth of the company's research, development, and management teams; the competitive landscape; and the company's anticipated capital requirements.

The timing of an IPO is often dependent on conditions outside of the company's control, such as general market receptivity to IPOs at the time; whether the relevant industry is "hot"; whether major institutional investors have exceeded the proportion of their portfolios reserved for investment in the relevant industry; and whether there has been an announcement of disappointing financial or regulatory results by a competitor in the industry that causes the market to be wary of the industry as a whole. When faced with less than ideal conditions, some companies elect to seek bridge financing from existing investors or mezzanine (later stage) financing from new investors to raise enough capital to permit the company to wait until market conditions improve or product milestones are achieved. If bridge financing is not available on acceptable terms and the IPO window closes, making it very difficult to get deals done (as happened in July and August 1996 after a very active IPO market in 1995 and the first six months of 1996), the company may want to reevaluate its decision to go public and instead try to find a buyer for the company.

THE IPO PROCESS

OVERVIEW

The first four weeks of the IPO process are typically spent in a series of intensive drafting sessions to prepare the registration statement for filing with the Securities and Exchange Commission (SEC). The registration statement includes a detailed selling document called a *prospectus,* which describes the company and its business and management. *Due diligence,* which is a review of the company's business and legal affairs that is done to ensure the accuracy of the prospectus, is also conducted during this period. After the registration statement is filed, 20,000 or more copies of the *preliminary prospectus* are printed, then distributed by members of the underwriting syndicate to potential buyers. The preliminary prospectus, which is preliminary because the SEC's comments have not yet been incorporated, is also known as the *red herring* because it contains a red legend mandated by the SEC on its front cover, warning of its preliminary nature.

Once the registration statement has been filed, the company will work with the underwriters to prepare a presentation about the company for the road show. The *road show* is arranged by the underwriters and consists of a series of meetings, large and small, with potential investors in a number of major cities during a two- to three-week period. Approximately thirty days after the registration statement has been filed, the SEC staff will send a letter with its comments on the registration statement to the company. Meanwhile, the road show will have commenced. The goal of this part of the process is to complete the road show at about the same time as the company's and underwriters' counsel have satisfied the SEC by filing a series of *pre-effective amendments* to the registration statement. These amendments are pre-effective because the registration statement has not yet been *declared effective* by the SEC, which is the point at which the SEC gives permission for trading in the company's stock to commence. These pre-effective amendments typically revise the registration statement and the prospectus contained therein.

Once the SEC has declared the registration statement effective, the underwriters and the company, having completed the road show, agree on a final price and the final number of shares for the offering. Trading in the stock generally commences the next day.

The closing of the purchase and sale of the shares occurs three business days after trading commences. Following effectiveness, between 10,000 and 12,000 copies of the *final prospectus* will be printed and, as required by law, distributed to purchasers of the stock in the offering. The final prospectus includes the final price and number of shares offered and reflects changes to the preliminary prospectus suggested by the SEC or necessitated by events occurring subsequent to the date of the preliminary prospectus.

SELECTING THE MANAGING UNDERWRITERS

If the company is a suitable public offering candidate and the market is generally receptive, the first step is to establish a relationship with a financial institution that will assist the company with the offering. Virtually all public offerings are managed by investment banks that arrange for the purchase of the company's stock by institutions and individual investors in exchange for a commission. (In contrast, commercial or merchant banks lend their capital in exchange for interest.) A relationship with an investment bank also provides analysts to publish ongoing research reports on the company's progress, which can foster investor interest after the offering.

Typically, the company will select two or even three investment banks to act as managing underwriters. One bank is usually designated the *lead underwriter.* If there are to be other managing underwriters, they are known as *co-managers.* The company should seek underwriters that are willing to underwrite the offering on a firm commitment (as opposed to a best-efforts) basis. In a *firm commitment offering,* the underwriters actually purchase the shares from the company for resale to investors, thereby assuming some (albeit minimal) market risk in the transaction. In contrast, investment banks conducting a *best-efforts offering* are required only to use their best efforts to sell the securities.

The role of the managing underwriters is to position the company in the public market and to form a *syndicate* (a group of investment banks) to participate in the offering. The primary purposes for syndication of an offering are risk sharing and marketing. The syndicate will be composed of multiple underwriters that share liability under the securities laws and share in the underwriting component of the gross spread. In an IPO, the underwriters buy stock from the company at a discount (usually 6% to 7% of the public offering price), then sell it to the public at the full price. The *gross spread* is an amount equal to the difference between the offering price to the public and the proceeds to the company. The syndicate may also include selling group members or dealers who do not share liability with the underwriters. Selling group members or dealers agree only to purchase a specific number of shares at the public offering price less a selling commission (typically 55% to 60% of the gross spread). Unless otherwise indicated, references in this chapter to underwriters mean the managing underwriters.

To be effective, a managing underwriter must be familiar with the company's industry and be able to differentiate the company and its products or services from others in its industry. The company should consider the reputation and experience of the underwriter in the relevant industry, its level of commitment to the deal, its ability to staff the offering appropriately with experienced and knowledgeable personnel, its marketing strength, and the quality of postpublic offering support (e.g., research analysts, market-making capabilities, and experience in mergers and acquisitions). The managing underwriters should have complementary strengths. For example, one might be stronger in making sales to institutional buyers and another might have stronger retail distribution or a better-known analyst.

A company will often hold what has come to be called a *beauty contest*

From the Trenches

A Silicon Valley company invited six prestigious investment banks to engage in a beauty contest for the IPO. Although all the firms made impressive presentations, the company was attracted to the winner for two principal reasons. First, the bank had the industry's best analyst, which the company felt was important both for completing the IPO successfully and for providing ongoing research writing about the company. Second, the bank had completed many deals as a co-manager but only recently had begun to be selected as a lead underwriter in the particular industry. The company felt that the bank, intent on building its reputation, would give them excellent service during the offering and make certain their deal attracted significant attention in an overcrowded market. The offering was wildly successful as the preliminary orders exceeded the shares available in the offering by ten times.

or *bake-off* among four or five investment banks before selecting the managing underwriters. In this process, each investment bank brings a team of three to five people to make a presentation to the board of directors. The investment bankers prepare and distribute elaborate bound materials (referred to as *books*). The books detail the strengths of the investment banking firm, its recent relevant IPOs, the post-IPO price performance of the companies it has taken public, and, perhaps most importantly, its preliminary views on how the market will value the company. These valuations are typically based on past and projected future earnings (initially supplied by the company but massaged by the bankers before the presentation), the *price/earnings ratio* (market price per share divided by earnings per share) of comparable public companies, and the strengths and weaknesses of the company compared with its competitors. Despite the similarity of approach, the valuations among investment banks can vary tremendously. Following the presentations, the company will select the lead underwriter and one or more co-managers.

TIMING

IPOs typically take ten to fourteen weeks from start to finish, although it is sometimes possible to accelerate the schedule. The underwriters typically prepare a time and responsibilities schedule setting out who does what and when those tasks must be completed. This schedule will be handed out at the first *all-hands* or *organizational meeting,* which is attended by all of the key participants. Companies well prepared to move quickly will be in the best position to control the IPO timing and minimize market risk. For example, well-organized company counsel frequently will distribute a first draft of the registration statement before the organizational meeting. *Exhibit 1* sets forth a sample timetable. *Exhibit 2* is a sample agenda for the organizational meeting.

REGISTRATION STATEMENT

The rules and regulations of the SEC require that an offering of securities to the public be made pursuant to a form of registration statement filed with and reviewed by the SEC. In the case of an initial public offering by the company of its stock, the prescribed form will be form S-1, which is filed with the SEC in Washington, D.C. Smaller companies may qualify for filing on form SB-2, which requires somewhat less disclosure. The SEC staff reviews the registration statement for compliance with SEC rules, and reviews the substance of the disclosure in the prospectus, which is the part of the registration statement that will be printed and distributed to the public.

EXHIBIT 1
Sample Timetable

Sample Initial Public Offering Timetable

April							May							June							July						
S	M	T	W	T	F	S	S	M	T	W	T	F	S	S	M	T	W	T	F	S	S	M	T	W	T	F	S
	1	2	3	4	5	6				1	2	3	4							1		1	2	3	4	5	6
7	8	9	10	11	12	13	5	6	7	8	9	10	11	2	3	4	5	6	7	8	7	8	9	10	11	12	13
14	15	16	17	18	19	20	12	13	14	15	16	17	18	9	10	11	12	13	14	15	14	15	16	17	18	19	20
21	22	23	24	25	26	27	19	20	21	22	23	24	25	16	17	18	19	20	21	22	21	22	23	24	25	26	27
28	29	30					26	27	28	29	30	31		23	24	25	26	27	28	29	28	29	30	31			
														30													

WebRunner, Inc. . . . . Company
Representatives of the Underwriters . . . . UW
Company Counsel CC
Underwriter's Counsel . . . . UC
Auditors . . . . AU

SUMMARY

April 18 and 19	Organizational meeting and due diligence sessions
April 26	First draft of Registration Statement distributed
April 29	All hands drafting sessions at CC at 8:00 a.m.
May 2 and 3	All hands drafting sessions at CC at 8:00 a.m.
May 6 and 7	All hands drafting sessions at CC at 8:00 a.m.
Week of May 13	All hands drafting sessions at the printer
May 16	File Registration Statement with SEC
Week of May 27	Preparation of road show
Week of June 3	Road show presentation finalized
Weeks of June 10 and 17	Domestic and international road shows
June 20	Registration Statement effective; pricing
June 21	Commence trading
June 26	Closing

PARTICIPANTS IN THE IPO PROCESS

The management of the company plays a central role in the offering, guided by the underwriters, counsel, and the auditors. As discussed above, the major task of this *working group* is the preparation of the prospectus.

The managing underwriters actively participate in the drafting of the prospectus and are responsible for the selling effort. They put together the syndicate of investment banks that will participate in the offering, organize the road show and marketing meetings, and coordinate other matters relating to the marketing and sale of the securities.

EXHIBIT 2
Sample Agenda

Sample Agenda for Organizational Meeting

I. **Review and Complete Working Group List**
II. **Review Time Schedule**
   A. SEC review period
   B. Drafting sessions and due diligence
   C. Shareholder communications
      1. Piggyback rights
      2. Proposed lockup
   D. Board of Directors meetings
   E. Filing/offering timing
   F. Road show
   G. Other lead-time items
III. **Discuss Proposed Offering**
   A. Size of offering
   B. Primary and secondary components
   C. General discussion of use of proceeds
   D. Green Shoe option
   E. Review existing shareholder list
      1. Registration rights
      2. Rule 144 stock
   F. Number of shares authorized
   G. Lockup agreement with principal shareholders
   H. Distribution objectives
   I. Directed shares
   J. Possibility of confidential treatment being requested
IV. **Review Legal Issues**
   A. Outstanding claims
   B. Loan agreement restrictions or other consents needed to offer the shares
   C. Blue Sky issues
      1. Shareholder notes
      2. Cheap stock
      3. Stock options
      4. Employment agreements
   D. Board Meetings
      1. Preparation of resolutions and appropriate board authorizations
      2. Filing registration statement
      3. Officers' and directors' questionnaires
      4. Pricing committee
   E. Disclosure of confidential agreements
   F. Related party and certain transactions disclosures
   G. Required shareholder approvals
   H. Expert opinions
V. **Discuss Financial and Accounting Matters**
   A. Audited financials
   B. Availability of quarterly financials
   C. Comfort letter
   D. Management letters
   E. Any special accounting issues
VI. **Discuss Publicity Policy**
   A. Pre-filing, post-filing/pre-effective, post-offering periods
   B. Pending newspaper/magazine articles to be published

EXHIBIT 2
Sample Agenda (continued)

Sample Agenda for Organizational Meeting (continued)

      C. Other corporate announcements
      D. Filing press release(s)
  VII. **Discuss Printing of Documents**
      A. Selection of printer and bank note company
      B. Use of color, pictures
      C. Volume requirements
  VII. **Due Diligence Review**
      A. Management interviews
      B. References for customer/supplier due diligence
      C. Detailed competitive analysis
      D. Projected financials (revenues, earnings, backlog)
      E. Methodology and models for financial planning
      F. Product brochures, trade press, other public relations materials
  IX. **Discuss Form and Contents of Registration Statement**
   X. **Discuss Road Show Presentation**
  XI. **Legal Due Diligence/Review of Corporate Records**

Company counsel, in addition to advising the company on compliance issues, coordinates the drafting of the registration statement and shepherds it through the SEC review process. He or she also helps the company select and coordinate with other participants in the process, such as stock exchange representatives, the printer, the transfer agent, and the bank note company. Company counsel participates in the negotiation of the *underwriting agreement* between the company and the managing underwriters, which covers all aspects of the offering, including the amount of the gross spread. Typically, company counsel will review the company's charter documents and legal records to determine what actions the company should take prior to becoming a public company. Company counsel also conducts a detailed review of the business, addressing any legal problems that may emerge and identifying items that require disclosure in the prospectus. If the company has separate patent counsel or regulatory counsel, such counsel may be asked to participate in discussions with the working group and to review, and, in many cases, render an opinion to the underwriters regarding, sections of the prospectus in their area of legal expertise.

Underwriters' counsel participates on behalf of the underwriters in the drafting process and the due diligence effort, advises the underwriters on legal issues that arise, and prepares the underwriting agreement. Underwriters' counsel also coordinates the review of the underwriting arrangements by the National Association of Securities Dealers (NASD) and the review of the offering by state securities authorities.

The company's auditors provide accounting advice in connection with the offering and work closely with the company's chief financial officer in the preparation of the prospectus as it relates to accounting issues and financial disclosure. The auditors also address SEC comments related to accounting issues and prepare comfort letters. A *comfort letter* summarizes the procedures the auditors used to verify certain financial information in the prospectus and describes the scope of their review of the prospectus. It is delivered to the underwriters when the offering becomes effective and again at the closing.

Generally, the prospectuses are printed by a financial printer. The printer must be experienced; able to produce a high-quality, timely, and accurate product; and cost-effective in responding to revisions prepared by the working group. A company should expect to spend more than $100,000 to print approximately 20,000 preliminary prospectuses and 10,000 final prospectuses, and should obtain quotes from two or three reputable financial printers with extensive IPO experience.

In addition, the company will need a transfer agent, which is typically a specialized stock transfer company or a commercial bank, to issue and effect transfers of the company's shares and to coordinate mailings to shareholders. The company will also need to select a bank note company to help design and then print the new stock certificates that will be issued to the shareholders after the public offering.

DUE DILIGENCE

The company, the underwriters, and their respective counsel assemble and review the information about the company in the registration statement, thereby conducting a legal audit of the company and its business. This time-consuming process, along with the data and backup materials used by the company, its underwriters, and their counsel to verify the accuracy of this information, is called *due diligence*. Due diligence is also used to determine what additional information should be disclosed and to uncover any problems or risks that need to be addressed or disclosed in connection with the public offering. The company must make sure that all participants are aware of the importance of complete candor in the due diligence process to ensure that the information in the prospectus is complete and accurate.

The underwriters, their counsel, and company counsel ask numerous questions of the company's officers and key employees in order to understand thoroughly the company's business, its products and markets or potential markets, and their inherent risks. The due diligence review often includes discussions with key customers and suppliers; a review of environmental issues; analysis of projections, business plans, and product strategy; a review of industry publications; and consultations with patent counsel, technology advisors, and regulatory counsel. It also includes a legal audit of company

---

From the Trenches

Due diligence in a recent offering revealed a situation that the investment bankers concluded had to be changed before they were willing to proceed. It turned out that the two founders had transferred patents to the company in exchange for future royalties. If the company met its sales projections, the royalties would amount to several million dollars a year, commencing in three years. These royalties would have significantly reduced the company's earnings per share. The underwriters refused to try to market the company unless these royalties were eliminated. The company reached a settlement with the founders, and the offering proceeded.

---

records, including minutes of board and shareholder meetings, charter documents, qualifications to do business, and all material contracts.

The company must be prepared to back up the claims it makes in the prospectus. Even if stated as opinion, such as its belief that it is becoming the industry leader, the company must be able to demonstrate the reasonableness of this belief. Industry publications and market surveys are common forms of support for statements regarding market size and the company's position in the market. The information collected in the due diligence process is useful in responding to the SEC if it asks for support for the company's assertions, which is common.

A company should expect the unexpected during the due diligence process. Matters of personal and professional character can become significant issues. The entrepreneur should discuss with counsel any and all issues, both real or perceived, that could affect the offering.

DETERMINATION OF STOCK PRICE AND OFFERING SIZE

Although underwriters generally like the company's offering price to be more than $10 and less than $20 per share, the offering price and the size of the offering will be determined by negotiations between the company and its underwriters. The company often will need to effect a stock split of the outstanding stock prior to the offering to bring the expected price per share into this range.

The valuation of the company takes into account market conditions, comparable companies in the industry, past and projected financial performance, product and technology position, the management team, the potential for growth, and new products in development. As noted above, the valuation of the company will have been preliminarily proposed by the managing underwriter at the outset of the IPO process. Additional due diligence by the underwriters' financial analysts and revisions to the company's financial models will take place before the registration statement is filed. This may result

---

From the Trenches

For one company's officers, the prospect of personal liability for misstatements prompted the disclosure of unorthodox accounting practices by the chief financial officer and patterns of sexual harassment on the part of the chief executive officer. The revelations slowed the offering process and proved highly embarrassing when they were disclosed. The issues should have been discussed with company counsel before the offering process commenced so that counsel could have framed them for the bankers at the outset of the IPO process.

---

in a valuation in the red herring different from that initially proposed. This valuation is still preliminary, and is reflected in a *price range* set forth on the cover of the red herring, such as $14–$16 per share.

The final offering price is usually set after the SEC review process is completed and just before the commencement of the offering. The determination of the final price is based on the market and the reaction of potential purchasers to the offering, which is reflected in nonbinding indications to the underwriters of potential investors' intent to purchase shares (commonly referred to as the *underwriters' book*). Typically, underwriters would like a book equal to at least seven times the offering size. The underwriters generally will try to price the shares slightly below the price at which the underwriters predict the stock will trade in secondary trading after the initial sale by the underwriters (the *target price*) to give the stock room to move up in the aftermarket. This *IPO discount* is typically 15% of the target price.

The size of the offering is based on the company's capital needs, dilution to existing shareholders, the level of *public float* (shares held by investors other than officers, directors, and 10% shareholders) desirable to achieve an active trading market and to provide liquidity for existing shareholders, market receptivity, and the proposed price per share. The underwriters are typically granted an overallotment option, called the *green shoe*, to purchase additional shares at the IPO price. The option typically gives the underwriters the right to purchase an amount of additional shares equal to 15% of the amount originally offered, within a set period after the offering commences, usually thirty days. The option may be exercised only to cover overallotments, that is, to cover the underwriters' short positions when the offering has been oversold.

If the underwriters want to sell more shares than the company is willing to sell, the underwriters may invite certain shareholders to offer shares they own for resale as part of the initial offering. Moreover, some shareholders may have registration rights entitling them to sell shares in the offering pursuant to agreements entered into with the company at the time of their initial investment. These registration rights can usually be limited if the underwriters do not want to include selling shareholders because they believe

---

From the Trenches

The relationship between the IPO price and subsequent trading prices is anything but predictable. Amgen, perhaps the most successful biotechnology company in history, remained at (and even below) its IPO price for several years, before going on to give investors extraordinary returns. By contrast, Netscape Communications, originally priced at $13 per share, was raised to $28 on the eve of the IPO as demand continued to grow. On the first day of trading, the stock soared to $75 before coming to rest at $52 a few days later.

---

that an offering limited to company shares is optimal or that management or significant investors may be perceived as bailing out if they make substantial sales.

CONFIDENTIAL TREATMENT OF MATERIAL AGREEMENTS

Generally, all of the company's material contracts must be filed as exhibits to the registration statement. These filings are public documents, and copies can be obtained by anyone. However, when documents contain information that could harm the company's legitimate business interests if disclosed, the company can seek to protect such information from public disclosure. In response to a narrowly framed request, the SEC may grant confidential treatment, for a limited number of years, of select portions of the agreements, such as royalty rates, payment amounts, volume discount rates, proprietary technical data or chemical compounds, and fields of research. A copy of the exhibit with the confidential portions carefully excised will then be available to the public. Requests for confidential treatment must be cleared with the SEC prior to effectiveness of the IPO. Prolonged negotiations with the SEC, or a third party who might be affected by such disclosure, may delay this clearance and thus delay the offering.

EXCHANGES, NASDAQ, AND BLUE SKY LAWS

Each exchange has its own listing requirements, which must be satisfied for a company, upon application, to be listed on that exchange. Underwriters will typically recommend that companies list their shares for trading on the Nasdaq Stock Market National Market System (*Nasdaq/NMS*) concurrently with the public offering. When stock is traded on the Nasdaq/NMS, brokers and traders are able to obtain real-time trading information. Listing on the Nasdaq/NMS is generally viewed as preferable to the Nasdaq Small Cap Market because of the greater information available for Nasdaq/NMS companies, the larger following by analysts and shareholders, and the availability of broad state securities law exemptions and corporate governance benefits.

To list its stock on the Nasdaq/NMS, the company must file an application and satisfy specified criteria. It is important to begin the application process as early as possible in the offering. The requirements for being listed on the Nasdaq/NMS are generally more stringent than those for the Nasdaq Small Cap Market, and include financial as well as corporate governance requirements. As part of its Nasdaq/NMS listing application, the company must select a unique four-letter trading symbol.

Alternatively, if the company satisfies the more stringent listing requirements of the New York Stock Exchange or the different requirements of the American Stock Exchange, the company may file a listing application and become approved for listing.

Early-stage companies may have difficulty meeting the Nasdaq/NMS listing requirements. A special appeal process is available to permit the company to present additional facts to support its application. For example, one company, unable to satisfy the three-year operating history requirement, was able to demonstrate that the period of preincorporation research and development conducted by the company's founder should be taken into account.

Trading on the Nasdaq/NMS or an exchange requires the company to register under the Securities Exchange Act of 1934 (the *1934 Act*), which subjects the company and its officers and directors to certain additional securities law requirements. Company counsel usually files to register the company under the 1934 Act at the time of the initial filing of the IPO registration statement with the SEC. Registration under the 1934 Act takes effect simultaneously with the commencement of trading on the Nasdaq/NMS or an exchange. Such registration would typically not otherwise be required for a number of months after a company's IPO.

The company must also comply with the securities or Blue Sky laws of each state in which shares are offered or sold except to the extent that such state laws are preempted by federal law. Underwriters typically ask a company to qualify in each state in which the underwriters may offer the shares, as well as in Guam and Puerto Rico. Blue Sky qualification is usually handled by underwriters' counsel. The fees and expenses incurred in this process are typically paid by the company, subject to a cap on attorneys' fees. However, designation for trading on the Nasdaq/NMS or certain exchanges allows the company to avoid time-consuming merit review by state regulators (whereby regulators evaluate the fairness of the terms of the offering) and eliminates the need for any pre-offering state filings.

THE ROAD SHOW

After the registration statement is filed, the underwriters organize a series of informational meetings at which company management makes presentations to institutional investors and other prospective investors about the company, its business, and its strategy. This is called the *road show.* The underwriters typically time the road show to take place in the last weeks of the SEC review period. The meetings are set up for large audiences at select cities throughout the United States and sometimes Europe and Asia, and are often followed up by one-on-one meetings with certain potential investors. The road show can take two or three weeks and generally ends just prior to the expected effective date of the offering. The material presented in the road show must be consistent with, and cannot go beyond, the information contained in the prospectus, and no written materials other than the preliminary prospectus should be distributed to the potential investors.

SEC COMMENTS

The SEC's internal policies provide that comments to the prospectus be delivered within thirty days after filing; however, during extremely busy periods, the comments may be delayed. The company responds to the SEC's staff comments by filing a pre-effective amendment to the registration statement, usually within a week after receiving the comments. The amendment is typically reviewed by the SEC examiner within a few days after receipt. If there are no additional comments, the examiner will indicate that an acceleration request to declare the registration statement immediately effective will be accepted from the company and the managing underwriters. It is not unusual to file more than one pre-effective amendment, particularly if the initial comments are numerous or broad in nature. As the company is filing its amendments, the underwriters are finishing the road show and finalizing their book of nonbinding commitments.

PRICING AND COMMENCEMENT OF TRADING

After the SEC review process is completed, the company and its underwriters each request that the SEC declare the registration statement effective by submitting a request for acceleration. The underwriters and a subcommittee appointed by the board of directors to act as a pricing committee negotiate the final price, usually after the stock market has closed on the day before the offering is to commence. This actual price is usually, but not necessarily, within the price range set out on the cover page of the preliminary prospectus. The company may reject the price proposed by the underwriters and elect not to proceed with the offering, although this rarely happens. Once the registration statement has been declared effective, the deal priced, and the underwriting agreement between the company and the underwriters signed, trading the stock will commence, usually on the Nasdaq/NMS or an ex-

---

From the Trenches

The delicate timing of effectiveness can be unsettled by external events. In one case, a company was threatened with litigation a week prior to the proposed effective date. The working group was warned by company counsel that if the threat were disclosed in a pre-effective amendment to the registration statement, the SEC might delay the offering and require the company to recirculate a new preliminary prospectus with the additional disclosure. (*Recirculation* involves circulating the revised version of the preliminary prospectus to all persons who received a copy of the old version; it is often called for if material changes are made to the preliminary prospectus.) This risk could be avoided if no SEC filing were made and the lawsuit never materialized. On the other hand, if the lawsuit were filed on the eve of effectiveness, the offering most certainly would have to be delayed and the preliminary prospectus recirculated. The working group decided to fully disclose the risk in a pre-effective amendment to the registration statement; if the lawsuit were filed thereafter, the risk would have been fully disclosed. To the company's delight, no recirculation was required as a result of the amendment. The lawsuit was never filed, and the offering came to market as planned.

---

change, depending on where the stock is listed. Trading typically commences the morning after the pricing.

THE CLOSING

The offering is not *closed* (consummated) until the stock certificates are delivered and the funds are received. The closing usually takes place on the third business day after trading has commenced.

RESTRICTIONS ON SALES OF SHARES

LOCKUP AGREEMENTS

The possibility of having additional shares of the company's stock come onto the market creates a very significant risk for the underwriters, the company, and the investors. Referred to as the *overhang,* an excess supply of shares in the marketplace can substantially depress stock prices. As a condition to the offering, underwriters typically require most shareholders, including all employees of the company, to sign *lockup agreements,* restricting their ability to sell any shares for a specified period of time, generally 180 days from the effective date of the IPO. In many cases investors agree in advance to such a lockup at the time of their initial investment.

From the Trenches

The CEO of Eagle Computer was killed in a car crash during the period between effectiveness and closing. This dramatic event caused the underwriters to exercise their rights under the underwriting agreement not to close the offering. This meant that all trades since effectiveness had to be reversed. The offering was completed a week later (at $1 less per share), after the investment community could evaluate the impact of the CEO's death on the company's prospects.

Most underwriters believe that unless the company secures lockups for at least 90% of the shares, an IPO could be jeopardized. Because of the risk, the underwriters may be reluctant to file the registration statement until sufficient lockup agreements have been obtained.

TRADING OF STOCK NOT ISSUED IN OFFERING AND THE IMPACT OF RULE 144

In addition to the lockup agreement provisions, trading of company stock acquired prior to the IPO is restricted under the federal securities laws. Consequently, common stock issued to employees and common stock issued when preferred stock is converted may not be sold in the open market unless certain conditions are satisfied. Employee shares issued prior to the IPO under written compensatory plans may be sold, pursuant to rule 701 of the 1933 Act, ninety days after the IPO by employees who are not affiliates of the company and are not otherwise locked up. Employee shares held by affiliates, such as directors, executive officers, and significant shareholders of the company, may also be sold ninety days after the IPO pursuant to rule 701, subject to the volume limitations described below. After the IPO, stock issued pursuant to employee plans is often registered with the SEC on form S-8.

Restricted stock (i.e., stock not sold in a public offering) that was not issued under employee plans or for compensatory purposes must generally be resold in compliance with rule 144 under the 1933 Act. Rule 144 generally requires that the securities be held for at least one year after purchase and be sold in limited quantities (*dribbled out*) through brokers or market makers. Rule 144 limits the amount that may be sold in a three-month period to the greater of 1% of the outstanding shares and the average weekly trading volume in the preceding four weeks. A form 144 notice must be filed with the SEC when the order to sell is placed. However, non-affiliates who have held their restricted stock for more than two years may sell their shares pursuant to rule 144(k) without complying with any of these requirements.

Sales by affiliates must generally be made pursuant to rule 144 even if they are selling stock acquired on the open market that was previously registered. However, sales by affiliates of stock acquired pursuant to employee plans under an S-8 registration statement or pursuant to rule 701 are not subject to the one-year holding period requirement of rule 144.

CONTENTS OF THE PROSPECTUS

The prospectus begins with a one-page summary of the offering, referred to as the *Box Summary,* which summarizes the key elements of the company's business and financial statements. Following the Box Summary is an extremely important section entitled *Risk Factors,* which alerts investors to the key risks and challenges faced by the company. It is important that risks specific to the company be identified. Additionally, some of the risks that are universally addressed in an IPO prospectus include the absence of an ex-tended operating history or profitable operations; the fact that the nature of the business is inherently risky; the dependence on a sole supplier or particu-lar customers; the uncertainties regarding technology or regulatory approvals; the uncertainty of proprietary rights; intense competition from more mature companies; and the lack of manufacturing or marketing experience, all of which make the stock particularly speculative. The Risk Factors section is not intended to produce a balanced view of the company; rather, it highlights potential risks and serves as important protection in the event of shareholder litigation.

The *Use of Proceeds* section describes how the company intends to use the proceeds of the offering in its business. The company should be able to support, by projections or otherwise, the proposed uses. The SEC staff has recently been insisting on fairly detailed discussions of the proposed uses of the funds, despite resistance by companies that want to avoid specific com-mitments to the extent possible or that might not have specific uses planned.

The *Management's Discussion and Analysis of Financial Condition and Results of Operations (MD&A)* section contains an analysis of the financial statements for at least the three most recent fiscal years and any applicable

---

From the Trenches

The underwriter and its counsel often must exert great effort to convince the company's chief executive officer to make the risk factors in a prospectus as strong as possible. The CEO may believe that strong risk factors will have a negative effect on the offering; the CEO also may disagree with what he or she perceives as trashing the company's business in a public document. The underwriter, of course, wants to make certain that all possible risks are disclosed. In a recent offering, the CEO initially refused to permit certain risk factors to be included. It was only after the managing underwriter offered to write him a letter to the effect that the inclusion of the factors would not have a negative impact on the IPO that the CEO relented.

From the Trenches

One way to persuade the SEC that a cheap stock charge is inappropriate (or to reduce the amount of such a charge) is to obtain a valuation report from an independent expert concluding that the stock was issued at fair market value. In a recent deal, several hundred thousand shares of stock were issued seven months before the IPO at a price of $1 per share. The proposed public offering price was $15 per share. Knowing that the SEC might argue that the company should recognize $11 per share of compensation expense (based on 80% of $15), amounting to several million dollars of charges over time, the company hired a valuation expert after the IPO process commenced to value the company's stock as of the issuance seven months before. The expert concluded, based on the company's precarious financial condition at that time, that a value of $3 per share was appropriate. The company took a charge based on this amount and filed the report with the SEC. No additional earning charges were required.

interim periods (unless the company has been in business for a shorter period of time). The analysis provides a year-to-year and period-to-period comparison, focusing on material changes and the reasons for those changes, as well as unusual or nonrecurring events that could cause the historical results to be a misleading indicator of future performance. This section has been the subject of heightened SEC scrutiny. Although projections per se are not required, the MD&A section does require a forward-looking analysis of the effect of known trends, events, or uncertainties, including information that may not be evident on the face of financial statements. As part of the MD&A, the company's historical and projected sources of funds for the business must be discussed.

The *Business* section provides a narrative description of the company, its strategies and goals, products or products in development, technology, manufacturing, and marketing. Within certain limits, this section can be customized both in terms of presentation and substance. Potential risks, such as technological uncertainties, shortages of raw materials, timing of new product introductions, or reliance on sole suppliers, are highlighted throughout. This section will reflect the tension between the need to provide complete risk disclosure of the investment and the desire to describe the company in a manner that is attractive to investors and does not reveal sensitive or competitive information.

The *Management* section provides biographical information about officers, directors, and key employees, and describes executive compensation, employee benefit plans, and insider transactions. Disclosure of executive compensation is quite comprehensive and must follow certain prescribed tabular formats designed to facilitate comparisons among companies.

Audited Financial Statements are also required, including balance sheets as of the end of the last two fiscal years and income statements for the three most recent fiscal years. Unaudited interim financial statements are required for offerings that become effective 135 or more days after the end of the most recent fiscal year. All financial statements must conform to generally accepted accounting principles (GAAP) and to SEC accounting requirements.

If the company has recently (i.e., within twelve months prior to effectiveness) granted stock options or otherwise issued stock at a price significantly below the IPO price, a charge to earnings to reflect the issuance of this so-called *cheap stock* may be required. The theory is that cheap stock is actually additional compensation to the employee and should be accounted for as such. Cheap stock is often the subject of SEC comment on the prospectus, and, if the proposed charge is significant, can jeopardize the offering. It is important to discuss this issue with the company's auditors prior to the organizational meeting.

The company need not but often does include photographs, illustrations, and graphs in the prospectus. Although color photographs or illustrations add to the cost of printing and require additional lead time, many companies and underwriters believe that they assist readers who lack a technical background to understand the company's business and products. The SEC staff has commented negatively on the use of professional models rather than employees in product photographs. Photos of prototype products, fully disclosed as such, may be used in the prospectus.

——— LIABILITY FOR MISSTATEMENTS IN THE PROSPECTUS

Securities laws regulating IPOs and other registered public offerings of securities are geared, in large part, toward ensuring that sufficient disclosure of relevant facts is made to permit potential investors to make informed investment decisions. To further this goal, section 11 of the 1933 Act makes certain persons associated with a registered offering of securities (including the company, its officers who sign the registration statement, the directors, the named nominees for director, and the underwriters) civilly liable to the purchasers of the shares for any untrue statement of a material fact contained in a registration statement and for any failure to state a material fact necessary to make the other statements not misleading. The auditors are liable for any material misrepresentation or omission in the financial statements.

The company is absolutely liable for any material misrepresentation or omission, regardless of the degree of care that was used in preparing the prospectus. A director or an underwriter may avoid liability by establishing that he, she, or it exercised due diligence; that is, that, after undertaking a reasonable investigation, such person reasonably believed the statement at issue to be accurate. This *due diligence defense* is technically available to officers as well, but it is much more difficult for officers to demonstrate that they would not have been aware of the inaccuracy or omission if they had exercised due diligence. Underwriters, directors, and officers are often named as defendants in section 11 lawsuits, and even a successful defense is expensive, time-consuming, and unpleasant.

PREPARING FOR AN IPO

PREFILING PUBLICITY

Any publication of information or publicity effort made in advance of a proposed public offering that has the effect of conditioning the public mind or arousing public interest in the issuer or its securities may constitute an impermissible offer to sell securities under federal securities laws. This type of impermissible activity during the *prefiling period* (the period before the registration statement is filed) is referred to as *gun jumping*. Disclosures that may run afoul of the securities laws include marketing letters, press releases, speeches, presentations at seminars or conferences, articles in the financial press, and other forms of advertising. Gun-jumping violations, in addition to embarrassing the issuer and its underwriters, may delay the marketing of the securities, because the SEC may refuse to declare a public offering registration statement effective until the effect of the violations has dissipated. Such violations may also result in criminal and civil actions against the issuer and underwriters.

Companies in the registration process must be careful to avoid inappropriate publicity. During the prefiling period, it is illegal for the company to offer to sell any securities pending registration. Therefore, during this period, the company's communications are most significantly restricted. For example, the company may not issue forecasts, projections, or predictions about its expected future performance. The only communication about the offering permitted during this period is a notice of proposed offering, the

---

From the Trenches

After years of unsuccessful attempts to attract press coverage, Amgen and its founder and then CEO, George Rathman, were unexpectedly featured in a prominent article published by *Business Week*. The article appeared on the day that the SEC received the company's registration statement. Counsel for the company spent a long weekend drafting a letter of explanation to the SEC, emphasizing that the interview was granted well before the offering process began, explaining that the company had no notice of publication, and requesting that the offering not be delayed. Fortunately, the request was granted.

---

contents of which are narrowly prescribed by regulation. These notices are rarely used in connection with IPOs.

However, the company need not completely discontinue its normal public relations activities. It is permitted to continue advertising that is consistent with past practices, to send out its customary reports to shareholders, and to make routine press announcements with regard to factual business developments, so long as such activities can be conducted without having an impact on the offering. The company should remember that newspaper and magazine articles often have a long lead time. Thus, an article currently being researched and written may not be published until many months later, when the public offering process is in full swing.

The company should consider setting up an internal control procedure to ensure that all public disclosures are properly reviewed and coordinated in advance. Counsel for the company and the underwriters should review all press releases and publicity, including product announcements, to be released for publication, broadcast, or distribution during the registration period. In addition, the company should establish a policy prohibiting employees, officers, and directors from recommending the company's securities, offering their opinions or forecasts regarding the company or, without the advice of counsel, providing any information regarding the IPO.

POSTFILING PUBLICITY

After the registration statement is filed but before it is declared effective by the SEC, the company is in the period called the *registration period* or *waiting period,* during which the company can offer its securities for sale but cannot actually sell them. The offer of securities must be made by means of the preliminary prospectus or through oral communications. During this time, the company and the underwriters will conduct the road show. Antifraud provisions and the securities laws still apply, and selective disclosure of material not included in the prospectus is problematic. Members of the press are typically excluded from the meetings with potential investors during the road show.

Industry conferences are extremely important opportunities for the company to meet the investment community. These conferences are planned long in advance, and invitations to present at them are intensely sought after. After discussion with counsel and the underwriters, a company may go forward with previously arranged conference presentations provided that the red-herring prospectus is available at the conference (and no other written materials are given out because they would be considered offering materials not included in the prospectus). The presentation should be the same as the road show presentation; the company will typically not participate in one-on-one or breakout sessions.

POSTEFFECTIVE QUIET PERIOD

The 25-day period after effectiveness of the registration statement and commencement of the IPO is called the *quiet period.* During this period, sales of the securities can begin and the final prospectus is delivered. Distribution of other written literature is permitted, provided that it is accompanied or preceded by a prospectus. It is also traditional for the underwriters to issue a tombstone advertisement in the financial press to announce the commencement of the sale of the securities. This tombstone advertisement is governed by both regulation and custom.

Even though the offering may be complete from the company's perspective once the closing has occurred, publicizing the offering may be considered by the SEC as an inappropriate attempt by the company to encourage the public to purchase shares from dealers who are still required to deliver a prospectus during this quiet period. As a result, issuers are generally careful to remain quiet, releasing information only as necessary in bare factual form. If, during this period, material developments do occur, it may be necessary to supplement, or sticker, the prospectus to reflect the new developments or, in some cases, to file a posteffective amendment with the SEC.

BOARD COMPOSITION

The company should review the composition of its board of directors prior to the offering. Public investors occasionally will have a concern if there are not enough *outside* or *independent directors* on the board, that is, persons who are not officers or employees of the company or its subsidiaries or who do not otherwise have a relationship to the company that would interfere with the exercise of independent judgment in carrying out the director's responsibilities. To be listed on the Nasdaq/NMS, a company must have at least two independent directors.

Board committees, such as audit and compensation committees, be-

---

From the Trenches

In a recent proposed IPO involving a Salt Lake City company, a significant shareholder (who owned 25% of the stock) had the contractual right to elect a majority of the company's board of directors. The shareholder wanted to maintain this right even after the IPO to protect its investment. The underwriters felt that board control by a single investor would adversely affect the marketability of the IPO. After extensive discussions, the investor agreed that it would retain only the right to elect one-third of the board. The offering proceeded.

---

come much more important once a company goes public. A company listed on the Nasdaq/NMS or the New York Stock Exchange must have an audit committee composed solely of independent directors. The audit committee, which reviews the company's independent auditors and evaluates the company's accounting system and internal controls, is perceived as having a critical oversight role in preventing and detecting fraudulent financial reporting. The SEC's proxy rules require a report from the compensation committee (or the full board if there is no such committee) on how the compensation of the company's executive officers was set. Additionally, a committee composed of at least two non-employee directors generally must administer most of the company's employee stock plans if the company intends to take advantage of the favorable treatment afforded those plans by certain exemptions from liability under section 16 of the 1934 Act, discussed later in this chapter.

REINCORPORATION IN DELAWARE

There are a number of reasons companies choose to incorporate in Delaware. Delaware law generally provides broader powers and flexibility to companies to indemnify their directors, officers, employees, and agents, and there is more extensive case law in Delaware regarding the interpretation of indemnification provisions than in other states. For example, Delaware permits companies to eliminate monetary liability even for gross negligence, while California law requires directors to remain liable under certain circumstances for acts or omissions that constitute an unexcused pattern of inattention or reckless disregard of their duties. In addition, Delaware law is often viewed as more receptive to shareholder protection measures designed to reduce a corporation's vulnerability to hostile takeover attempts than other states, which either do not permit such measures or restrict their use.

Accordingly, companies not already incorporated in Delaware frequently reincorporate there as part of the IPO process. Shareholder protection measures available in Delaware are often adopted at the same time.

─── RESPONSIBILITIES OF A PUBLIC COMPANY AND ITS BOARD OF DIRECTORS

The realities of being a public company include heightened public scrutiny and disclosure obligations which a private company does not face. Once public, a company must file a number of periodic reports and other documents with the SEC disclosing information about its business, management, and financial results and condition. The company's officers, directors, and principal shareholders must file documents with the SEC that disclose their ownership of and transactions in the company's securities. The company, as well as its directors and officers, also face increased potential liability as a result of their fiduciary responsibilities to public shareholders and their disclosure obligations.

The periodic reporting requirements, together with the practice of issuing press releases and managing the expectations of securities analysts and public shareholders, add significant pressure to achieve short-term results at the expense of long-term goals, and may limit the flexibility of management and the board of directors in making strategic corporate decisions. Finally, the periodic reporting requirements bring additional costs to a public company in the way of increased legal, accounting, and printing expenses. The company may also need to hire additional management personnel to handle its expanded reporting and other obligations.

PERIODIC REPORTS

Public company status increases a company's responsibilities to its shareholders and to the trading market. In addition to describing in the prospectus how the company plans to use the net proceeds from the offering, the company must file with the SEC an initial report on form SR within ten days after the end of the first three-month period following the effective date of the offering. Form SR must specify how the proceeds have been used and explain any material deviation from the plan of use described in the prospectus. Subsequent periodic reports on form SR must be filed until all of the offering proceeds have been fully applied, with the final report on form SR filed within ten days after all of the offering proceeds have been used.

The company will also be required to file certain periodic reports with the SEC (e.g., annual reports on form 10-K, quarterly reports on form 10-Q, current reports on form 8-K, and reports by Nasdaq/NMS issuers on form 10-C). In addition, companies that trade on the Nasdaq/NMS must file with Nasdaq copies of documents filed with the SEC, and companies that trade on the New York and American Stock Exchanges must file copies with the applicable exchange. Additionally, public companies must comply with the SEC's proxy regulations when soliciting a vote of consent shareholders.

Form 10-K   The report on form 10-K is an annual report filed with the SEC that provides a continuing update of information about the company and its management substantially similar to that contained in the company prospectus. It will include a description of the company's business for the preceding fiscal year, audited financial statements, and an MD&A section relating to the periods covered by those financial statements.

Form 10-Q   The report on form 10-Q is a quarterly report filed with the SEC and includes summary unaudited quarterly financial statements, an MD&A section covering those results, and certain other specified disclosures, such as information concerning new developments in legal proceedings or shareholders' actions taken within the quarter.

Form 8-K A report on form 8-K is intended to supplement the normal recurring filing requirements (e.g., form 10-K and form 10-Q) when material events occur that should be brought to the prompt attention of the investing public, such as a merger, change in control, sale of significant assets, bankruptcy, or a change in accountants.

Form 10-C If the company's shares will be quoted on the Nasdaq/NMS, the company must file form 10-C with the SEC within ten days after (1) an aggregate increase or decrease of 5% or greater in the amount of its outstanding shares as last reported, or (2) a change of corporate name.

EFFECT OF PROXY RULES

A company registered under the 1934 Act must comply with the SEC proxy rules when soliciting a shareholder vote or consent. Generally, these rules require that a proxy statement be mailed to each shareholder of record in advance of every shareholders' meeting. The proxy statement must set forth detailed information regarding the company's management and the matters to be voted on. For example, a proxy statement relating to the election of directors must include a report of the compensation committee (or the full board, if there is no such committee) explaining how executive compensation was determined and the relationship between pay and performance; it also must include a graph comparing performance of the company's stock against a broad-based index and an industry-group index. In some cases, such as a shareholder vote on a merger, the proxy statement and form of proxy must first be submitted to the SEC for review and comment. Because of the filing and other procedural requirements applicable to proxy solicitations, the company should plan all meetings of shareholders well in advance.

INSIDER TRADING

Definition Insider trading liability may arise as a result of trading by someone who has material nonpublic information about a company and owes a duty to that company, its shareholders, or others, either by reason of employment by the company or some other fiduciary relationship. Directors, officers, employees, accountants, attorneys, and consultants are considered insiders with a fiduciary duty to the company. An insider in possession of material nonpublic information must either disclose it before trading in the company's securities (which is often impossible for a variety of reasons) or refrain from trading. Failure to observe these restrictions may subject the individual (and perhaps the company) to both civil and criminal liability, including treble damages, fines of up to $1 million, and prison sentences. In past court cases involving insider trading, what the insider thought or knew, or later claimed he or she thought or knew, has not necessarily provided a successful defense if, in hindsight, the insider's personal securities transaction created the impression that the insider was in fact taking advantage of undisclosed information about the issuer. Thus, it is important that insiders avoid even the appearance of impropriety.

Insiders are also prohibited from disclosing material inside information to others who might use the information to their advantage in trading in the company's securities. Both the person who discloses the information (the *tipper*) and the person who receives it (the *tippee*) may be liable under the insider trading laws. Assume, for instance, that a director is also a partner in a venture capital partnership and knows of a significant unannounced contract the company has won. Although the director-partner has not communicated this information to anyone, one of his or her partners, based entirely on public information, purchases securities of that company. Shortly thereafter, the company's securities increase substantially in value. Because it would be possible for an objective fact finder to find, based on appearances, that the director-partner had tipped the nondirector-partner, the partners and the fund could have significant exposure to litigation and potential liability, despite not having actually violated the law. Accordingly, persons with special relationships with insiders of a company are well advised to check with the insider before trading in the company's stock to make certain the insider is not in possession of material nonpublic information about the company.

Company Liability   Legislation adopted in 1988 extends potential liability for insider trading violations to employers under certain circumstances. The Insider Trading and Securities Fraud Enforcement Act of 1988 (ITSFEA) provides that any controlling person who knew or recklessly disregarded the fact that a controlled person was likely to engage in acts constituting an insider trading violation and failed to take appropriate steps to prevent such acts before they occurred may independently be liable for a civil penalty of up to the greater of $1 million or treble the profits resulting from the violation. This penalty provision theoretically would permit a court to assess a company a penalty of $1 million even if the insider trading by the employee involved only a few thousand dollars.

Adopting a written policy prohibiting insider trading can reduce the company's exposure for controlling-person liability. A well-drafted policy educates employees on the law of insider trading and establishes internal procedures to safeguard against both intentional and unintentional illegal trading. In the event that an employee does violate the law, the policy and related procedures reduce the risk that the company itself will be liable under the ITSFEA.

Some companies go beyond a simple insider trading policy applicable

From the Trenches

In a recent SEC insider trading investigation, the son of the president of MCA Corporation overheard his father discussing the pending sale of MCA to Matsushita. The son heeded his father's warning not to trade on the information, but passed on the information to his ex-wife and her boyfriend. They traded for their own account and passed the information on to others who also traded. Following public announcement of the sale, MCA's stock rose sharply, and the SEC launched an investigation. Those who traded as a result of the son's tip settled with the SEC by disgorging their profits, plus penalties; the son settled by paying the SEC $418,000 in penalties, even though he hadn't traded and had not made a dime on the information he passed on.

---

to all employees and adopt an additional policy limiting the times when directors, officers, and principal shareholders can sell or purchase stock. These so-called *window period policies* typically prohibit the person from trading in the company's stock during a period commencing four weeks before the end of a quarter and extending through a point seventy-two hours after the company has released its earnings report for that quarter (typically three weeks after the quarter has ended). The company usually retains the right to close the trading window early or not open it at all if there exists undisclosed information that would make trades by insiders inappropriate. The theory of these policies is that the company does not want to be sued because an officer or director traded stock at a time when the insider might have known how the quarter was going to turn out and the market did not. It takes management time and company resources to defend such lawsuits, and they can bring ill repute to the company. A window period policy lessens the possibility of such a lawsuit.

Liability for Short-Swing Profits   Section 16 of the 1934 Act provides for the automatic recovery by the company of any profits made by executive officers, directors, and greater-than-10% shareholders on securities purchased and sold, or sold and purchased, within a six-month period (i.e., on *short-swing trading*). Section 16(b) is mechanically applied and liability is imposed regardless of the trader's intent to use, or actual use of, inside information. Furthermore, the reports filed by executive officers, directors, and greater-than-10% shareholders pursuant to section 16(a) are monitored by professional plaintiffs' attorneys for indications of short-swing trading violations. Thus, even if a company might choose to ignore the short-swing trading of its insiders, insiders who have violated the strictures of section 16(b) will still be pursued by plaintiffs' attorneys in shareholder derivative suits. Complex rules exist for the attribution to insiders of purchases and sales by persons and entities related to insiders for the purposes of section 16(b).

Insider Reports   Executive officers and directors of public companies are subject to a number of reporting requirements designed, among other things, to provide to the investing public information regarding their holdings and trading activity in the securities of the companies by which they are employed or on whose boards they serve. Section 16(a), for instance, requires that each executive officer and director of a company involved in an IPO file a form 3 detailing his or her beneficial ownership of the securities of that company. The form 3 is typically filed at the same time as the public offering becomes effective. (A public company must also file a form within ten days of the election of any new director or officer of the company.) A form 4 must be filed within ten days after the end of any month in which a change in beneficial ownership occurs, including gifts and transfers to trusts. Finally, a form 5 must be filed annually to report certain transactions that were not otherwise reportable or reported. It should be noted that, for purposes of these reporting requirements, complex rules exist regarding what constitutes beneficial ownership of securities.

The SEC has the power to seek monetary fines from individuals for violation of the securities laws up to the following limits: (1) up to $5,000 ($50,000 for entities) per violation for plain vanilla violations, such as a late filing or a nonfiling of a required form under section 16; (2) up to $50,000 ($250,000 for entities) per violation for violations involving fraud, deceit, manipulation, or deliberate or reckless disregard of the law; and (3) up to $100,000 ($500,000 for entities) per violation for violations that not only involve fraud or reckless disregard of the law, but also result in, or create a substantial risk of, substantial losses to others or a substantial gain to the individual involved. According to the SEC, a new violation may occur for each day a filing is made late or not corrected. The SEC recently announced that it is increasing its scrutiny for late filing or nonfiling of section 16 forms.

POST-IPO DISCLOSURE AND COMMUNICATIONS WITH ANALYSTS

A public company should establish and follow the practice of prompt and complete disclosure through the press of all material developments, both favorable and unfavorable, that, if known, might reasonably be expected to influence the market price of the company's shares. However, disclosure may sometimes be delayed for valid business reasons or if it is otherwise premature.

Disclosure Obligation   The duty to disclose material information imposed by securities laws will arise as a result of a number of events or circumstances. Some examples are (1) when necessary to satisfy a company's SEC reporting requirements or obligations under listing agreements with Nasdaq or an exchange; (2) when the company or its insiders are trading in the company's own securities; (3) when necessary to correct a prior statement that the company learns was materially untrue or misleading at the time it was made; (4) when a company is otherwise making public disclosure and the omission of material information could be misleading; or (5) when necessary to correct rumors in the marketplace that are attributable to the company. A company may incur liability under the antifraud rules adopted by the SEC pursuant to the 1934 act to any person who purchases or sells the company's securities in the market after issuance of a misleading proxy statement, report, press release, or other communication.

Information is considered *material* if its dissemination would be likely to affect the market price of that company's stock or would likely be considered important by a reasonable investor who is considering trading in the company's securities. In the event of nondisclosure for any reason, officers, directors, and other insiders should be advised against trading in the company's securities until the information has been adequately disseminated. Otherwise, a plaintiff's attorney will use the fact that insiders were trading as evidence of intent to deceive the market. For example, if a company expects its earnings to be less than the analysts have projected and insiders are selling, then when the earnings are announced and the market price drops, it may appear that insiders misled the market so they could sell their stock at an artificially high price.

Communications with Analysts Discussions with market analysts, who write reports following the progress of the company and generally keep the public informed of business developments, are inherently risky.[1] No information given to an analyst is ever off the record. Casual or ill-considered disclosure to an analyst of material inside information can lead to shareholder lawsuits and SEC investigations for securities fraud and insider trading. Although it is important to maintain good relations with the press and analysts, it is also critical to avoid selective disclosure of material information. *Selective disclosure* is simply the release of material information on an individual basis without its simultaneous release to the public generally.

In most cases, however, it is permissible in dealing with analysts and the press to provide general background information or to fill in incremental details regarding a matter that has been disclosed in all material respects. In an attempt to avoid selective or premature disclosure problems, many companies observe a consistent no-comment policy with respect to certain material undisclosed corporate developments, such as acquisitions. The company should always consult with counsel to determine whether a press release is appropriate when material developments occur that may require disclosure

---

1. For a general discussion of legal issues associated with dealing with analysts, *see* Dale E. Barnes, Jr. and Constance E. Bagley, "Great Expectations: Risk Management Through Risk Disclosure," 1 *Stanford Journal of Law, Business & Finance* 155 (1994). *See also* Dale E. Barnes, Jr. and Karen L. Kennard, "Greater Expectations: Risk Disclosure Under the Private Securities Litigation Reform Act of 1995—An Update," 2 *Stanford Journal of Law, Business & Finance* 331 (1996).

through formal mechanisms or when the company becomes aware of rumors circulating in the marketplace.

Caution also should be taken in informal meetings with members of the business community not to make inadvertent disclosure of nonpublic information that might be considered material. The SEC has stated that the antifraud provisions of the federal securities laws apply to all company statements that can be expected to reach investors and trading markets, not just to SEC filings or press releases.

Liability for an Analyst's Report   If an analyst provides an inaccurate projection regarding the company, it is generally considered to be the analyst's assessment and not the company's unless the company confirms the information or otherwise becomes entangled in the analyst's report. Companies should always consult carefully with counsel whenever they are tempted to comment on an analyst's report. Disclaimers, warnings, and generalities can reduce risk if a decision is made to comment. However, any spokesperson talking to analysts must understand that, if he or she comments on projections and forecasts, the company may be held liable if the projections prove incorrect or if the analyst uses the information to engage in trading before the information is released to the public. Generally, the safest course is for the company not to comment.

Safe Harbor for Forward-Looking Statements   Federal legislation adopted in December 1995 increased the opportunity for companies to protect themselves from litigation concerning certain disclosures made after an IPO. In passing the legislation, Congress established a safe harbor for certain oral and written forward-looking statements, such as projections, forecasts, and other statements about future operations, plans, or possible results. For a company to be protected, a statement must disclose that it is forward-looking and that the company's actual results may differ materially. In addition, the company must, in the case of a written statement, provide a detailed discussion of the factors that could result in a discrepancy and, in the case of an oral statement, refer the audience to a readily available written statement that contains such a discussion. The scope of the safe harbor's protection has yet to be tested in the courts. Disclosure issues continue to be sensitive and should be discussed thoroughly with counsel.

DIRECTORS' RESPONSIBILITIES IN A PUBLIC COMPANY

Because directors have a fiduciary relationship to both the company and its shareholders, they are bound by the duties of loyalty and care imposed by the law of the state where the company is incorporated. These duties are applicable to directors of all companies, whether public or private.

Director Liability for Securities Claims   Companies and their officers and directors are subject to damage claims for securities fraud under the antifraud rules if their regular quarterly and annual disclosures to the SEC and the public are inaccurate in any material way. Similarly, the securities laws make it unlawful for any person to solicit proxies in contravention of the rules and regulations of the SEC. In this context, directors may be held liable if they knew, or in the exercise of due diligence should have known, that a proxy solicitation issued on their behalf contained material false or misleading statements or omissions. Beyond required disclosures, it is possible to incur liability for securities fraud in connection with the issuance of misleading press releases, reports to shareholders, or other communications that could be expected to reach investors and trading markets.

Indemnification and Liability Insurance for Directors   Under the law of most states, companies are given broad and flexible powers to indemnify directors who are made parties to proceedings and incur liability by reason of their status as directors. A sample indemnity agreement is provided in "Getting It in Writing" at the end of chapter 15. In addition, companies can acquire directors' and officers' (D&O) liability insurance. Most companies secure D&O liability insurance prior to completion of an IPO or consider increasing the company's current coverage while still a private company.

From the Trenches

Not long ago, a company facing a disappointing earnings announcement decided that it might be able to soften the impact on the market by disclosing the news to two analysts who followed the company several days before the issuance of a press release. One of the analysts decided to tell his firm's favored clients the news, and the company's stock began to fall rapidly. Not only did the company have to issue a press release quickly to respond to calls from panicky investors, it also had to defend itself in an SEC insider trading investigation.

Putting It into Practice

Soon after the successful product launch of IRRS, Alexandra met with the other WebRunner directors to decide whether to proceed with an initial public offering or to sell the company. They knew that additional funds were needed for WebRunner to accelerate its growth and continue to leapfrog over its competitors. Alexandra and her board felt it would be relatively easy to find a buyer for the company, given the enormous interest in the Internet area. In fact, two customers had already made unofficial overtures. But the directors also felt that WebRunner had a huge potential for growth that would not be reflected even in the IPO price, much less the price they would be able to command as a prepublic company. In the end, they were unwilling to cap this upside by selling for cash or by taking stock in a larger company whose stock price would be determined in large part by the performances of businesses other than WebRunner. They also were excited by the challenge of taking WebRunner to the next level of growth as an independent company. They decided to proceed with an IPO.

Once Alexandra and her board reached this decision, Alexandra assembled a team of investment bankers, lawyers, and accountants. The first step in picking an investment banking firm was to update and assemble a corporate profile to present to potential underwriters. This consisted of a business plan, marketing literature, and audited yearly and unaudited quarterly financial statements for the three years WebRunner had been in existence. Next, Alexandra compiled a list of suitable and likely candidates for underwriters. She wanted to consider firms with expertise in and commitment to companies involved in the Internet, firms that employed respected analysts who were likely to support the company by providing research reports to the investment community in the future, and firms that would not have any conflicts of interest. The list of potential underwriters included firms that had expressed interests in the company in the past and others that were likely to be receptive to the company. Michael Woo and other experienced securities counsel at his firm were helpful in providing leads and introductions.

Prior to the first organizational meeting, Alexandra met with Michael and the company's auditors to determine whether there were any corporate or financial cleanup items that could affect the timing or success of the offering. At the organizational meeting, attended by Alexandra, Paul, and Sheryl on behalf of WebRunner, Michael as company counsel, the underwriters, underwriters' counsel, and the auditors, all such issues were fully aired and thoroughly discussed. By discussing these issues up front, the group was able to develop a realistic time line.

In addition to disclosure and timing issues, the WebRunner working group also discussed a number of other important issues at the organizational meeting, including the size of the offering, the price range, a required stock split, the length of lockup agreements and who would be required to execute them, reincorporation in Delaware, and other corporate matters. Finally, the various executive officers and key employees of WebRunner introduced themselves and each gave a short (thirty-minute) presentation on his or her respective area of responsibility. Alexandra had reviewed the content of the presentations with the officers in advance. At a minimum, she wanted them to include an overview of the business, a review of the intellectual property portfolio, a description of significant corporate partners and strategic relationships, and a review of the company's current financial condition and projections.

After the organizational meeting, company counsel produced the first draft of the registration statement with significant input from Alexandra and her partners. Alexandra had prepared the first draft of the Business section. Because all prospectuses have a particular tone and set of language conventions with which Alexandra and her partners were unfamiliar, Michael substantially revised the Business section to reflect standard prospectus language. Once the first draft was completed and distributed, the working group met for a series of all-hands meetings. The dates for these meetings had been confirmed at the organizational meeting and took place at the offices of Michael's firm.

Once the draft had progressed sufficiently, a smaller group met at the financial printer to finalize the document and file it with the SEC. Alexandra chose a printer early in the process based on competitive bids and recommendations of the under-writers and counsel. Given the SEC requirement that all documents be transmitted to the SEC electronically (through a system referred to as EDGAR), it was important that Alexandra retain an experienced financial printer that could meet the company's proposed schedule.

After the registration statement was filed with the SEC, Alexandra and her partners turned their attention to corporate matters that required completion prior to the closing of the offering. For example, the company needed to undertake a shareholder mailing to obtain written shareholder consents to amend charter documents, reincor-porate in Delaware, and effect a stock split. In addition, the underwriters worked with Alexandra and her partners to develop the road show presentation and also recom-mended a consultant to assist in that process. The road show was timed so that the first set of SEC staff comments would be received approximately halfway through the road show. If all went well, this would put the parties in a position to complete the road show and price the offering very soon thereafter. Alexandra planned to spend at least two or three weeks on the road show, making her presentation twenty to thirty times in as many as fifteen different U.S. cities. (The road show would have been even longer if Europe had been included.)

After approximately thirty days, the SEC staff provided comments on the registra-tion statement. At this point, the working group reassembled at the printer to prepare the first amendment to the registration statement to respond to the comments. The group believed that certain of the SEC's comments were not clear or reflected a misunderstanding on the part of the SEC staff. In those cases, the company explained supplementally in a letter to the SEC why the company believed that the registration statement should not be revised in response to those comments. In addition, the SEC requested certain supplemental information to determine whether other comments were appropriate. A number of the comments related to accounting matters. Alexandra obtained from the auditors a realistic estimate of the time they needed to revise any numbers, draft additional disclosures, and prepare any required supplemental re-sponse.

After filing the amended registration statement, Alexandra expected one or more additional sets of oral or written comments from the SEC, each of which generally would require another amendment to the registration statement. These comments were delivered within a few days after the filing. Each amendment was signed on behalf of the company and included an executed consent of the auditors. Once the SEC had no further comment, the company requested that the SEC declare the registration statement effective. This was done by means of a letter filed electronically with the SEC. The underwriters joined in the request with their own letter.

The underwriters set up a telephonic conference call on the day the offering was declared effective, after the close of the market. The underwriters first congratulated Alexandra on a successful road show, and then proposed the final size of the offering, the offering price, and the underwriters' gross spread (commission). Alexandra wanted to try to negotiate with the underwriters about the gross spread and the price, so she came to the meeting armed with the latest information about WebRunner's competitors, particularly recent trends in their stock prices and price/earnings ratios. Because WebRunner was considered "hot," she was able to negotiate a slightly higher price, although the underwriters would not budge from a 7% gross spread. Once the deal was struck, the underwriting agreement was executed that same day. Trading commenced the following morning. The final prospectus was then prepared based on the final price information, and the offering closed three business days following the commencement of trading.

After the offering closed, Alexandra invited Michael to visit the company to meet with her and the other executive officers to set up procedures to implement the company's insider trading and window period policies, the SEC and Nasdaq/NMS compliance procedures, and the investor relations strategy. Michael then spoke to the employees about the implications for them of owning stock in a public company and applicable restrictions on trading.

After Michael finished, Alexandra addressed the employees. She thanked them for their long nights and weekends of toil to get the IRRS ready for the product launch. She also reminded the longtimers of the dark days before venture financing, when WebRunner's creditors were hounding the company and it almost failed. Finally, she spoke of the future. WebRunner had made remarkable progress from the time when it was merely a dream of Alexandra, Paul, and Sheryl, but it was now time for the next stage. The challenges of entrepreneurship had been met, and now the challenges of becoming a successful public company lay ahead. "But first," she declared, "break out the champagne—it's time to party!"

───── DISCUSSION QUESTIONS

1. What factors would make an IPO an attractive alternative to the sale or private financing of a company?
2. How is the value of a share set in the IPO process?
3. What restrictions influence how public securities may be bought and sold?
4. Would you serve on the board of a public company? What concerns would you have?

Why Sane People Shouldn't   24
Serve on Public Boards

WILLIAM A. SAHLMAN

When asked to be on the board of directors of a publicly held corporation, the author of this article was flattered, but certain he would decline the offer. He follows a simple rule: Never join the board of a public company. He recommends that others follow that rule too, since the economics of serving on a board are fundamentally off balance.

The fees directors are paid sound attractive, but meeting the "duty of care" responsibilities can be tremendously time consuming. And no matter how conscientious directors are, shareholders can easily file lawsuits against them. Suits are aimed at the whole board and don't distinguish between good directors and bad. Resolving a lawsuit takes time and money; settling one appears to be an admission of guilt and is a black mark on a director's reputation.

The existing corporate governance system must change if public companies hope to attract strong, competent, motivated directors. The boards of public companies should be more like those in LBO and venture capital situations. There the directors have the wherewithal and the incentive to contribute actively to making the company run better, and the owners trust that the directors have a big stake in the company's success.

The other day I was asked to be on the board of directors of a company listed on the New York Stock Exchange. I was flattered to be considered for such an important position, but I knew right away I would turn it down. I have a simple rule: Never join the board of directors of a publicly traded company.

I realize that it would be bad for society if everyone invited to sit on the board of a public company followed my rule—but I think everyone should. Talented, intelligent people shouldn't make economically stupid decisions. And the fact is, the economics of being a director are fundamentally off balance. For a fixed amount of money in the near term, directors expose their time, reputations, and finances to great risk.

I don't take my rule lightly. I teach a course on entrepreneurial finance and am a director of several private companies, so I understand something about fiduciary responsibility and know what it means to be a director. U.S. industry needs strong, competent, motivated directors. But the corporate governance system makes being the director of a public company an unattractive if not outright dangerous proposition.

Two things have to change: the risk and the reward. We must eliminate the incentive for shareholders to file frivolous lawsuits, which sap valuable time from directors and companies and damage reputations regardless of blame. At the same time, we must boost the incentive for directors to spend time with the company to add to its long-term value. Considering the risk directors face, giving them the incentive to get involved operationally probably means both raising the amount of compensation and skewing rewards to the long term by paying directors mostly in stock rather than in cash. In venture capital situations, for instance, directors are paid in equity; lawsuits are rare because shareholders know that directors' interests are aligned with theirs.

Let me explain how I see the role of a director—and how the law and shareholders see it. Then I'll demonstrate the logic of my rule by analyzing the specific invitation I received.

THE EXPECTATION

I believe a director's main responsibility is to help management maximize distributable value for the company's equity holders. I also believe that directors have a fiduciary responsibility to protect investors' interests and to make the company perceptibly better than it would have been in their absence.

This is not a direct translation of the legal requirements. Legally, directors are held accountable to two standards: the "duty of care" and the "duty of loyalty." Under the law, directors can meet the duty of care requirement by acting "in good faith and with the care of an ordinary, prudent person in like position under similar circumstances." They are expected to attend directors' meetings, to demand and receive adequate information, to review that information, and to monitor the decisions management makes. Directors can meet the duty of loyalty requirement by avoiding direct conflicts of interest.[1]

Note that these two duties have nothing to do with value maximiza-

---

1. See Edward Brodsky and M. Patricia Adamski, *Law of Corporate Officers and Directors: Rights, Duties, and Liabilities* (Wilmette, Ill.: Callaghan & Company, 1984).

tion or even fiduciary responsibility. The law establishes no goal or metric. Directors aren't charged with acting on behalf of anyone—shareholders, employees, or society. And they're not required to "maximize" anything. The law also leaves directors with a lot of decision-making latitude. As long as they study the issues carefully and avoid flagrant self-dealing, directors can make decisions that are not in the best interests of shareholders and still not be held liable.

In short, what the law demands may differ widely from what directors demand of themselves or from what external groups expect of them. Often, the law demands less.

But while the legal standards are loose, many decisions boards make are subject to second-guessing in court. Lawsuits are in fact frequent. Directors often settle—even when the suits are unfounded—to avoid the chance of a large award or the hassle of legal procedures, with consequences I'll expand on later.

——— THE INVITATION

On with the specifics. The letter of invitation stated that "we have four meetings a year" and that "our current board compensation is $4,000 per year and $750 per meeting." Being clever at mathematics, I determined that in return for a minimum commitment of four days, I would receive $7,000, or about $1,750 per day. Not bad for an academic.

But for each day actually spent in meetings, my duty of care and responsibility would require at least one day spent talking on the phone, traveling, reading, evaluating. My commitment would likely be upwards of eight days. That $1,750 per day was already shrinking.

The letter of invitation had included an inch-thick package of materials describing the business and its 22 profit centers. As I leafed through the reports and summaries, I wondered how long it would take to get up to speed on the industry and the company. What would I need to know to be confident that I could make decisions in the shareholders' interests (a responsibility I thought harder to fulfill than the legal obligations)? This question was but the first of many that began to occur to me:

- Who are the real leaders in management and on the board?
- What have they accomplished?
- Do they have integrity?
- What kinds of relationships does management have with the board, shareholders, employees, and regulatory authorities?
- Are there any skeletons in management's or the board's closet?
- How much industry-specific knowledge do I need to spot problems before they become actionable?
- What scenarios are plausible for the industry and the company?

I estimated that answering these questions—which is the least I would do before even considering joining the board—would take a week of gathering information. Then I assumed that I would accept the position. A different set of questions came to mind:

- How much control would I have over the business and the competitive environment?
- How could I verify the information I would receive from the company?
- Would I be able to control how much time I gave to the company?
- What financial risks would I expose myself and my family to?
- Would I be able to continue to fulfill my obligations to my family and my employer?

So far, most of my questions were aimed at figuring the tangible and intangible costs of joining the board. I also needed to consider the potential rewards, beyond the fees:

- Would it be a learning experience?
- Would new opportunities result?
- Would I develop lasting friendships and contacts?
- Would the position reflect well on the institution I work for?
- Would my work benefit society?
- How did these potential benefits compare with those from pursuing other options?

Having filled my mind and half a note pad with questions, I started thinking about the answers. I contemplated whether the potential benefits— the opportunity to learn, professional contacts, and so on—were unique to this offer. That one was easy. I have many opportunities to learn, to find attractive projects, to make friends, to help my institution and my family. The intangible benefits of joining this board would be no greater than those of any number of activities I might pursue.

If the incremental intangible benefits were modest, the real question became one of weighing the direct economic benefits against the risk. Assessing the risk was particularly important because the company didn't have insurance to protect directors and officers. Insurance was too expensive. Instead, the company suggested that it had ample capital to indemnify directors for actions taken on its behalf.

I looked at several categories of risk. I wondered, for instance, what might happen to the industry and the company. While the industry had done extremely well in recent years, competition—including the dreaded Japanese variety—was intensifying. And while the company had prospered during this period, I wasn't sure whether it was because of good strategy, good execution, or a favorable environment.

I also thought about the people. The person who asked me to join the board was a terrific fellow with a sterling reputation. Were others in the organization as competent and ethical? Would top management know of any past illegal conduct?

How might outside factors, like macroeconomic performance and the capital markets, affect the company? What would happen to the business if the economy soured or if stock prices dropped precipitately? How would these business and industry issues relate to me personally? Suppose, for example, that the stock market crashed after I joined the board. Would I be in trouble even though the circumstances were beyond my control? If the stock became undervalued and management proposed a leveraged buy-out, who would protect shareholders' interests? Would the event lead to litigation against me as a director?

A takeover attempt also would be sticky. On the one hand, the tender price would probably be higher than the prevailing market price; on the other, the price might be less than the company's true value. Regardless of my opinions, management would undoubtedly oppose the takeover and might strap the company with debt to deter a raider. That too could lead to litigation against me.

Or suppose that someone in the company had committed fraud. Even if I joined the board after the illegal act, might I be held responsible?

In imagining these different scenarios, I could see that three things were in jeopardy: reputation, money, and time. To try to protect them, I would have to invest a tremendous amount of time on investigation and analysis. But even if I were the most perspicacious director ever, I would not be immune to a tarnished reputation or to lawsuits. When a board gets in trouble, the whole board comes under fire. Litigants and the business press don't distinguish between good and bad directors or between new ones and those with long tenures.

Moreover, the law doesn't always protect those who are right. Frivolous lawsuits, all too common, require the same, reasoned response as legitimate claims. At the very least, directors lose control over their time. To protect that precious resource and to save legal fees, directors often settle their lawsuits out of court, even when they stand a good chance of winning. But settling a case is like pleading the Fifth Amendment. It implies culpability, whether or not there is any. The pragmatic resolution of frivolous lawsuits can therefore damage a director's reputation.

Lawsuits are proliferating in part because of a fundamental bias in the U.S. legal system. It is relatively easy to file a suit but difficult to get rid of one. If allegations are "proved" correct, the payoffs to the plaintiff are high. If allegations have no merit, the costs are modest since the plaintiff is not required to bear any costs of the successful defense.

Some people might think I'm being paranoid. They might argue that the law protects those who are diligent, that accountants and lawyers can ferret out fraud, and that regulatory agencies like the FCC, FSLIC, and SEC protect would-be directors. I say to those who would rely on the law or on the efforts of others: don't be naive. Newspapers are replete with examples of competent and conscientious directors being sued. Accountants have a mediocre record of detecting fraud before much damage is done. Outside and inside counsel have an equally dismal record, and regulators are often the last to know of a problem.

The layperson might also point to changes in statutes that have greatly reduced the risk for directors. True, statutes adopted first by Delaware and later by other states allow companies to amend the certificate of incorporation to eliminate or limit a director's personal financial liability—unless he or she has failed to act in good faith, violated the law, or derived an "improper" personal benefit. But the statutes address only the monetary risk. Shareholders who merely perceive a breach of faith or improper benefit can bring suit, costing the director control of his or her time and possibly his or her reputation in the business community.

The fact that the company inviting me to be on its board didn't have any insurance and relied instead on its pool of capital was not pivotal. Even if I were protected by the most comprehensive policy possible, which I would welcome, I would still feel vulnerable. In my view, insurance is most valuable when you never have a claim. When something does happen, it's likely the insurance company will tell you you're not protected against exactly that—and again, you end up in litigation.

If the insurance company agrees that you are covered, you now have a new set of problems. Though you're protected monetarily, the insurer can make demands on you to help its own legal case. And it can agree to settle frivolous suits and ruin your reputation in the process.

THE ANSWER

Having gone through this analysis, I come to the only conclusion that makes sense: don't join the board. To do so would be to abandon my responsibility to my family, the institution I work for, and myself.

Don't assume I wear a seat belt in the car and have a portfolio of short-term Treasury bills and detest risk per se. Although I don't seek out risk, I am not risk averse. I am deeply involved—and heavily invested—in a number of venture capital situations. I just prefer a better balance between risk and reward. Indeed, if the rewards are sufficiently high, I will bear more risk than many people.

But there is something fundamentally wrong with the equation in the situation I've described. The financial reward for serving on the board of a public company is strictly limited. The most I could hope for is several thousand dollars a year. True, I would learn through the experience and would make potentially important contacts, but these benefits would accrue in other situations as well. And the offer was not an opportunity to contribute to some broad, societal goal.

Accepting the position would mean I was flying naked with no insurance protection and little help from other sources. The risk was high that I would suffer a large monetary loss, a damaged reputation, or loss of control over my time. And I would have few options for managing those risks.

It's important to explain that my involvement with private company boards is quite different. While there may be risk in those situations, I can manage it. Because I get involved early in a company's life, I help shape operating and financial strategy. I work hard to maintain intimate knowledge of virtually every facet of the business (which, given the relatively small scale of the enterprises, is possible to do). I even go on sales calls. If I help a company raise money, I know the providers of capital, and they know me. Communication with everyone—from the receptionist to the accountants and lawyers—is thorough and frequent.

Not only can I control some kinds of risk, but the reward side isn't limited to a few thousand dollars a year. In fact, I won't get involved in a company unless I can make a sizable cash investment that gives me the chance to earn a substantial return over five to ten years.

When things don't work out, the investors don't question my integrity. For one thing, they know that because my compensation is largely in the form of equity, I will make money only if they do. Investors know too that I'm motivated to help companies thrive because my livelihood depends on my reputation for doing so. They believe that my interests are aligned with theirs.

THE LOSS

Managers and directors face a different and tougher set of challenges than they once did. Domestic and global competition has intensified, uncertainty has grown, and the pace of change is accelerating. The nature of corporate governance also has changed dramatically. Being a director of a public company used to be a relatively calm and rewarding position. Now it's a hot seat. Tough issues concerning management-board conflicts (like hostile takeovers and management-led LBO proposals) and the business environment (like investments in South Africa and oil spills in Alaska) arise in quick succession. At the same time, lawsuits are more frequent; the increased incidence of suits raises the risk to directors' time and reputations.

The potential rewards have not grown in proportion to the risks. I disagree with those who argue that the asymmetry in risk and reward is essential to our corporate governance system. I don't think greed is the primary motivating force in the world, but for most people, economics is and should be part of the analysis. And the economics of the current system make no sense.

If the goal is to attract the best directors, defined by their ability to make a company more valuable than it would have been in their absence, then we must choose directors who have something to offer and encourage them to get involved operationally. To create the incentive for them to get involved, we must increase the rewards and reduce certain kinds of risk.

As long as fees are fixed, we probably can't raise them high enough. Let's say the company that solicited me had proposed to pay me $50,000 a year for the same number of meetings. Would it have made a difference? Frankly, no. However attractive the upside, it was effectively capped, while the risk to my finances, reputation, and time was beyond my control.

The best way to reward directors is to give them significant stakes in the company. That creates the potential for large rewards relative to their personal wealth and the incentive to see that the company performs well. LBOs and venture capital are interesting models in this regard; the incentives for management and directors to add value and make the business flourish are huge.

In an LBO, two important changes take place: management ends up with a big equity holding, and the board of directors is revamped to include only people with big stakes. Similarly, in venture capital, management typically has a lot of equity. Venture capitalists, who are often chosen partly because of what they bring to the business besides money, dominate the board and benefit only if value is created. When outside directors are recruited, they receive equity, not cash.

At the same time that we increase the rewards, we must mitigate the risks of being a director. Although punishment for malfeasance and gross negligence should be stiff, groundless lawsuits should be discouraged. This can be done by making those who file such suits responsible for the direct and indirect costs to the defendants and by limiting awards paid in successful suits.

The fact that I am unwilling to become a director of a publicly traded company may not have a big impact on national competitiveness. But if enough talented men and women engage in the same thought process and reach the same conclusion, U.S. industry could be in trouble.

We can't let that happen. To compete effectively in the current environment, every aspect of the management system must work right. I don't have all the answers, but I do have the conviction that U.S. corporations will continue to underperform until we change our corporate governance system.

We have every right to demand a lot of our directors, but not to subject them to unjustified claims on their time and reputations. We should choose them for what they can add to the business and then give them the incentive to work hard and spend a lot of time on the company's operations. Paying directors more gives them an incentive to contribute what they can, and skewing the rewards to the long term ensures that they will focus, like owners, on the long-term value of the business.

—— DISCUSSION QUESTIONS

1. Would you join a board of directors? If so, under what circumstances?
2. What due diligence is appropriate for a new director?
3. What public policy decisions are appropriate with regard to corporate boards of directors?
4. As an entrepreneur or CEO, how would you recruit a good board of directors?

25 How Small Companies Should Handle Advisers

HOWARD H. STEVENSON and WILLIAM A. SAHLMAN

Gone are the days when small business owners or managers could get all the advice they needed from just a couple of old and trusted advisers. More than likely, the old and trusted advisers are gone too. In their place is an advising world in a whirlwind of change. Mergers and reorganizations have reshaped professional service companies; higher operating costs now entice such organizations to pursue more profitable, short-term consulting roles and forsake smaller clients. And a stream of new laws and regulations has made it impossible for advisers to know the full range of concerns faced by most small businesses today.

At the same time, operating a small business is more complex than it was even a decade ago. Problems like toxic waste disposal or choosing the right computer system increase both the chance for and the cost of error. So getting good advice is more important than ever.

But where can you turn for timely, accurate advice in the midst of so much change? Authors Howard Stevenson and William Sahlman recommend that you build a new kind of relationship with your advisers: you must manage them, not the other way around. Becoming an activist manager of the advice-giving process means doing two seemingly contradictory things: seeking out the best advisers—specialists, if necessary—and involving them more thoroughly, and at an earlier stage, than you might have done before. At the same time, you need to be more skeptical of their credentials and advice.

Your knowledge and attitude as a manager of your advisers will be your best tools for getting the best advice amid the tumult.

Managing your outside advisers and service providers—the accountants, lawyers, bankers, ad agencies, and others who help you compete—has become a new ball game.

Once upon a time, Japan, South Korea, Taiwan, and Hong Kong were still exporting junk; the Clean Air Act, ERISA, 401(k) plans, and OSHA didn't exist yet; and computers were just for the biggest of companies. The stuff the accountants, bankers, and lawyers worried about didn't affect the bottom line much. So you'd call a CPA when you needed the taxes done, but not before. And when you wanted the legal effect of a contract explained (maybe even after it was signed), you'd get your lawyer. Back then, the pace of change in products and the financial markets was slow enough that even the most lackadaisical professional could keep up with it.

All of that is no longer true. The environment for small business is more competitive and confusing than it was even a decade ago. The chance of error is higher while the results of error are more damaging. That piece of real estate you bought for a new distribution center could trap you in a $50 million lawsuit if your lawyer didn't warn you beforehand to have it tested for toxic waste. A consultant's bad advice on a computer system could throw your entire business into turmoil and threaten your ability to compete.

The problem is that as your world is changing, so is the world of the adviser and service provider, and getting timely accurate advice—always tough for the small company with limited resources—is more difficult than it used to be. (See *Exhibit 1*, "The Changing World of Advisers.")

Competition has led once-staid professions like accounting and law into waves of mergers and reorganizations in a search for efficiency and resources; higher operating costs have enticed firms into pursuing more profitable short-term consulting roles, which are sometimes in conflict with long-term relationships; complex laws and regulations (as well as a myriad of new marketplace niches) have made it impossible for any adviser to know deeply the broad range of concerns that a business faces today.

In that environment, the notion that a company can have one all-knowing accountant or one all-knowing banker over the life of a business seems about as quaint as a Norman Rockwell painting. Experience has taught us that these days, the "all-knowing" adviser doesn't know enough to really help you and has probably been asked too late anyway to keep your company from bearing unnecessary risk.

We recommend creating a new relationship with your outside advisers. Become an activist manager of the advice-giving process by doing two seemingly contradictory things: seek out the best advisers—specialists if you have to—and involve them more thoroughly, and at an earlier stage, than you have in the past. At the same time, be more skeptical of their credentials and their advice. The link in the process is your knowledge and attitude, as well as the resources you're willing to use. You will have to work harder and probably spend more money, but you'll save time and money at the other end.

EXHIBIT 1
The Changing World of Advisers

Because the world of professional service firms is in tumult, many firms are redefining how they want to do business—often at the expense of their established clients. Mergers and corporate restructurings are disrupting the traditional relationships between advisers and their clients. Today a small ad agency may consider you their big client; tomorrow that small agency is part of a giant multinational advertising corporation, and you're considered a small client. Even without a merger, people frequently get redeployed via internal reorganizations, or they simply move on to other jobs. A friend of ours recently looked at the Rolodex card for his lead bank and discovered that, in an 18-month period, he had been assigned nine different "personal" bankers.

Keen competition, huge expenses, and the fast pace of change are putting professional service firms under extreme pressure to look short term. "What have you done for the firm lately?" is a driving question at head offices, even after associates become partners. Accumulated wisdom doesn't count for very much when the game is to develop new products and gather new accounts. Once-staid firms act like hard-driving consultants in aggressively marketing lucrative short-term services. Everyone is hustling for money, and those who don't produce can soon find themselves out on the street regardless of seniority.

Moreover, as junior partners move up to senior partner level, they tend to focus on the big clients, even if they've served you for eight years. Small companies tend to get relegated to the junior associates. Some giant consulting firms are going against the grain, saying their strategy remains to build lifetime relationships with important clients. But they are not in the majority, nor are their pricing strategies aimed at the small-company market.

All of these developments have helped forge a more transaction-oriented professional today, who is inclined toward the quick hit and disinclined to think about the long-term implications of decisions made today. One business executive told us, "I get the feeling my accountant is always selling, selling, selling, and I'm always buying."

Even the axiom "what's good for the customer is good for me" may not apply. The social pressure that used to militate against screwing the customer has weakened. We know of one Wall Street investment bank that arranged to advise a target company in a hostile takeover bid at a specific fee if it prevented the takeover, but if the company was sold, its fee would be a percentage of the price increase. The bank had an obvious conflict: it would come out ahead by forgetting the company's real goal and going for top dollar. Not surprisingly, the company was sold and the fee was increased threefold.

Another investment bank was on a modest retainer to advise a small company that was the target of a takeover attempt. In the midst of the battle, a bigger takeover came along, and the partner who had been retained strayed to the more lucrative deal, leaving a fresh-faced MBA to pick up the pieces of the strategy. For the company it was a life-or-death struggle, but from the partner's viewpoint there was a big-money fish that he couldn't let get away.

Two decades ago, such behavior would have been unthinkable. Today, it's commonplace. It's therefore crucial for the operator of a small business to be aware of the changes in the advising environment and understand what the changes will mean.

——— A NETWORK OF SPECIALISTS

Operating a business always means managing risk. Successful entrepreneurs endlessly educate themselves about opportunities and dangers to help narrow the odds in a changing environment.

It goes without saying that you should read voraciously and have a wide network of friends inside and outside your industry whom you can call and ask how they handled particular problems, what experts they used, and what their successes and failures were. By doing so, you broaden your base of experience before the fact—and you can weed out many a bad service provider.

Getting the best advice today, however, means more than networking with friends and associates or relying on your old standby adviser. It also means specialists. In medicine you'd go to your general practitioner for a cold, but if you've got a kidney problem you go to a urologist and to a neurosurgeon if you have a brain tumor.

The same principle applies to the business adviser. You no longer can rely on the GP to give you the sophisticated advice you may need on handling taxes or financing—not to mention toxic waste. Sometimes you may need a securities lawyer, at other times a tort lawyer, a contracts lawyer, or an intellectual property lawyer. You may not need an accounting firm but a consulting firm specializing in high-tech startups, which has contacts and intimate knowledge of the problems facing new businesses.

In the new world, you need multiple relationships to diversify your sources (just as you do for capital and other resources) to get the best advice. You'll also need that diversity in case something happens, as when your accountant fails to keep up with a changing world, or her firm is acquired and she is transferred.

The general practitioner has not lost importance. Far from it. The GP remains the most important link in the information chain, usually being more familiar with the business over a longer period of time. But you have to find one whose ego isn't threatened by an occasional request to see a specialist.

In some cases, hooking up with the vast resources of a large law firm or Big Eight accounting firm may be the best course, but we don't necessarily advise that strategy. You can usually get reasonable tax or estate planning advice from a big law firm merely by picking up a telephone. The trade-off is that, if you're a small company and they've got a dozen General Electrics as clients, you may get short shrift. One- or two-person firms can have an excellent network of specialists to refer to for problems outside their bailiwick. The point is, you'd better use the specialists when you have to.

——— MANAGING ADVICE SUPPLIERS

Big companies can afford to have many of their experts on the inside. Little companies can't do that. And specialists are temporary help; they're called on in limited circumstances, and it's difficult to make them part of a permanent team. But you can manage your outside experts as you do the other parts of your business. You're simply managing people you don't control hierarchically.

You've got parts suppliers, inventory suppliers, and money suppliers. Consider your outside advisers as advice suppliers, and deal with them accordingly. You wouldn't order a part without knowing its cost, whether it will meet your requirements, or whether the supplier can produce it. The same rules apply to your advice suppliers. That implies a more tough-minded attitude than many people bring to their relationships with professionals.

So it's important to be up front with an accountant or lawyer and ask directly about fees and other essential matters: "How much is this going to cost me? Who is actually going to perform the work? What are that person's credentials? What if I don't like her?" Demand interim, itemized bills that will show who performed what task.

But this line of questioning is just a small part of the new relationship. The product of advice suppliers is not worth much if it is set in stone by the time you see it. Managing the advice suppliers means you work with the experts as they develop their recommendations. To do this you have to find out the skills and weaknesses of the people making the product. What are their incentives? How do they make money? What helps them with their employer, and what gets them into trouble? Does the loan officer at your bank get rewarded when a loan is placed—if you default does it count against him?

Ask yourself, does the professional see you as a hockey ticket—a one-shot event—or a meal ticket, an important repeat client? The system of compensation sets up a tug on the service provider as it does on anyone else (when you grab advisers by the wallet, their hearts and minds will follow). Knowing the direction of the pushes and pulls, you'll be in a better position to judge the value or reliability of the advice or service and act accordingly. If your bank has just lost a bundle in your industry, the lending officer may be overly negative in assessing your company's financial needs. Perhaps you should switch to a firm that hasn't been burned, at least not recently.

You may prefer to seek a big hunk of your financing from a local bank—it will be more likely to see you as a meal ticket rather than as a hockey ticket. Storage Technology Corporation, a Colorado computer equipment supplier, borrowed hundreds of millions of dollars, all from New York bankers. When Storage ran into financial problems, the New York banks, rather than work to solve the problems, pulled the plug and forced the company into Chapter 11 and a costly, complex reorganization.

A large West Coast bank pulled a similar strategic reversal only a few months after advertising heavily that it was a bank that welcomed long-term relationships with high-tech startups on the East Coast. It abandoned all non-California, small and medium-size high-technology companies in its new $150 million loan portfolio, even those at a fragile stage of growth. The companies summarily were told to find a new bank. You may want help from a heavyweight financial institution, but a local bank has a strong incentive not to harm the local economy, its reputation, and its own balance sheet, and will think twice about the impact before it pulls the plug.

QUESTION THE LOGIC

With expert advisers, you must be skeptical in other ways. Question their advice; find out the reasons behind it, the logic they relied on to reach it. Don't be afraid to sound dumb. If you fail to understand, take it as a sign of your adviser's incompetence, not your own. Even when you've found a so-called expert, be careful. Specialists themselves quickly become obsolete if they don't spend hours assimilating the latest developments in their field. You're entitled to find out what they know.

Be like the vice president who thought his small company's annual payment to the union pension fund was much too high. He kept questioning the charge, but the insurance company funding the plan kept saying he was wrong. He even spoke to a pension consultant who said the calculation was made according to the "best methods."

The VP finally called on the insurance company's chief actuary, who said the insurer used the particular methodology because it was traditional for such companies. But the VP also learned that the methodology incorporated incorrect assumptions based on another industry—for example, that employees remained many years on the job and as a group were older. The VP's company actually had a high turnover, and the workers' average age was 26. Eventually the actuary changed the assumption and the methodology. The company recaptured 80% of its pension fund contributions for the previous nine years.

That vice president (who incidentally was not an accountant) showed the necessary attributes in today's climate: skepticism and persistence. Belief in experts' infallibility is one of the least likely-to-succeed strategies in the new world of business. You have to test continually to be sure the expert is providing you adequate service or advice. Don't assume anything.

Here's an example of a service buyer who didn't ask the right questions up front. He allowed himself to be snowed by a sophisticated selling job. As the owner of a small company that wanted to sell out, he hired a big investment bank after one glitzy presentation at which top executives displayed reams of charts and statistics to prove the investment bank's competence. After the contract was signed, the owner discovered that the team leader assigned to the project was four years out of business school and the other team members were either one year out of business school or one year out of college. As low-level as the team was, moreover, it was quite busy and devoted little time to the deal. The investment bankers seemed to think they had spent enough time and money just getting the contract—which was too small to justify further effort.

The owner should have insisted that the contract call for the assignment of a partner to the sale, to the extent of a minimum percentage of the time required. If the bank had balked, the owner would have learned its level of commitment before signing. He learned, however, that in investment banking circles, what is done cannot be easily undone. He was told by other bankers that he had better stick with his choice of investment banker or he'd look like a flake to potential investors. Maybe that advice was sound. But we think it's axiomatic to dump a bad adviser if the potential damage from bad advice or inattention will be higher than the added cost of getting someone else.

GET THEM IN EARLY

Your goal is to get the best advice or service early enough to do you some good. You can't do that by telling the experts, "I know where you fit, and you should stay in your little box." You can't treat them like fire fighters whom you call in only to put out your little conflagrations or (more to the point) like janitors to clean up your messes. By then, it's too late. You've lost your most valuable commodities: time and the control of your own destiny.

So another important part of managing the experts is to anticipate the events—positive and negative—that may affect your organization. This isn't new advice. The good business manager has always been someone who increases the odds in his or her favor. Today, however, planning and anticipating are absolutely mandatory if you want to control your adviser instead of your adviser controlling you.

You've got to ask what can go right and what can go wrong in a given situation—not all the things in the world that can go wrong or right, but which are likely to do so. What are the consequences across your business if you switch to foreign parts suppliers? What if your product has a defect—what kinds of liabilities do you face, and can you prepare for them now? What if your earnings take off—what steps do you take now to minimize taxes later? If your business might generate a healthy cash flow, should you set up a Subchapter-S corporation so you can funnel money through without paying double taxes? If you hope to expand your business into other states someday, do you want to register your business name and logo there now?

If you sat down and took half an hour each day to think about them, you might think of hundreds of questions about your business. Many you'll be able to answer yourself with more thought or through reading or by asking your network of friends; but some questions take experts to answer. You should seek their help especially in ascertaining the consequences of a given strategy. To provide such advice, they must first understand the business aspects of a decision, not just the legal or accounting aspects. They need to see the whole picture and the context in which the activity is taking place.

You want your important suppliers to think of themselves not as mere sellers of a product but as an integral part of your business. That way they'll recognize that it's in their interests to keep product quality high, costs down, and delivery on time. So too for the professional adviser. Using the adviser to help anticipate not only keeps you in the driver's seat, it helps you forge the bond needed to generate sound, timely advice under the right constraints. The head designer at an ad agency producing your catalog might not worry about the indirect costs of any design decision unless warned that cost is important. The lawyer negotiating an agreement might be so zealous in protecting your interests as to lose the deal, unless you spell out how important the deal is and how far you're willing to go to make it.

Unless they understand your path of evolution, the experts may build in their own constraints. You have expansion plans, say, and you're dealing with architects. It makes sense to let them know your long-term needs. By letting the architects understand where you may be in five years, they can build in the essentials that allow you to connect to the next phase—like raceways for new cables, or knockout doors. You may spend a little more money now, but you save a lot in terms of flexibility of the building.

That's true of advice in general. Going to a variety of experts in the beginning will likely cost you more money up front. Getting the right advice is rarely cheap. But staying out of trouble is vastly more cost efficient than trying to get back out once you've stepped in. The negative side of excluding the adviser is needless risk.

You may think you're saving money by not consulting a lawyer before expanding the sales of your chemical product to the West Coast. But how much have you saved if you're ordered to pay an injured California worker $500,000 in damages because you failed to supply warning labels in Spanish as required by California law? If you've set up a Sub-S corporation to get favorable tax status, you may jeopardize that status by making what seem like trivial changes—moving from 75% to 80% ownership of a subsidiary, for example, or having 36 shareholders instead of 35.

So you should be up front with your accountant and lawyer, saying that next year you're going to be 20% larger, or you're going to have 20 more employees, or be selling in 15 states. Or you're changing your production process and using new materials. And you ask whether there are any things you should know or be thinking about—like agencies to notify, tests to run, documents to distribute. In other words, you must communicate the nature of the future that you're planning for.

THE HUMAN TOUCH

We're saying the obvious: your advisers are, after all, people. People you don't control hierarchically you must manage in other ways.

In dealing with service providers, you want every advantage you can get. So take those little steps that will bring added dimensions to their services. Closer involvement with your company gives advisers practical rather than abstract knowledge of your needs.

Sincere flattery is another way to make your relationship more human and helpful. Obviously you don't want to puff the firm, but if it does a good job, recommend other clients. Tell the senior partner how well the junior associate has handled your problem—it ratifies the senior partner's choice of the associate and the associate will think of you as a friend. It's simple psychology. They'll think better of you, and you'll have better access to them on the next go-round.

There's another psychological benefit from greater involvement: an implication of future interaction that may motivate the experts to do a particularly good job on this assignment. You're saying that if they help you on this one, the future is bright for them as well as for you, that you'll work with them as long as you work well together.

In today's world, you have to manage your advisers—lead your guides. But first you've got to manage yourself, and that implies a much larger set of analytical responses to the environment than you've probably been making. You must know what path you're on and anticipate its twists and turns. You've got to know a lot simply to ask the right questions. Feel free to ask enough questions to understand your advisers' motives. Find out what's in it for them. Be cautious, more inquisitive, more persistent, more independent. Be willing to switch horses in midstream—better that then drown halfway across.

At the same time, involve the expert more directly at an early stage. Explain up front your expectations and requirements. Be at once distant and reliant. In a sense you've got to become an expert on using experts. That's a tall order, but your company can only benefit if you do.

——— DISCUSSION QUESTIONS

1. What is the definition of a good advisor? How can you find out if an individual or group is qualified?
2. What steps can managers take to make it more likely that they will recruit and manage their outside resources more effectively?
3. How can you educate your management team to deal with outside resources?
4. How should you evaluate the performance of your existing advisors?

Bankruptcy: A Debtor's Perspective   26

HOWARD H. STEVENSON and MICHAEL J. ROBERTS

While an IPO or sale of the business can be the pot of gold at the end of the entrepreneurial rainbow, not every story has such a happy ending. When the debts of a business exceed its ability to satisfy these obligations, bankruptcy is an option that must be considered. The various chapters of the bankruptcy code are an attempt to balance the creditors' rights to collect what is owed, while giving the owners of the business some breathing room to sort out the issues at hand.

In this chapter, Stevenson and Roberts lay out the legal principles that underlie the U.S. bankruptcy system, as well as the practical realities that business owners and creditors face.

The Bankruptcy Code is a federal statute intended to alter the legal rights and remedies of debtors and creditors to provide a solution to the circumstances which arise when a debtor's financial affairs have reached such a state of disarray that the usual rules no longer work in an orderly and efficient manner. From the perspective of individual debtors, bankruptcy law provides freedom from lawsuits, the discharge of past due obligations and an opportunity for a fresh start. For business debtors, the Bankruptcy Code provides an opportunity for the debtor to restructure its business, create enhanced value for its creditors (and maybe its stockholders) and provides an opportunity to maintain employment that otherwise would be lost. From the perspective of creditors, bankruptcy provides an orderly and equitable distribution scheme which replaces a race to the courthouse by each creditor seeking to enforce its own rights. Further, in a reorganization, creditors can hope to benefit from the enhanced value of an ongoing enterprise, rather than accepting a pro rata share of a liquidation.

Bankruptcy is by no means the only option in times of financial

This note was prepared by Professor Howard H. Stevenson and Lecturer Michael J. Roberts, with the assistance of Richard E. Mikels, Esq. (member) and Kevin J. Walsh, Esq. (associate) of Mintz, Levin, Cohn, Ferris, Glovsky and Popeo, P.C., as the basis for class discussion rather than to illustrate either effective or ineffective handling of an administrative situation. It is based upon an earlier note of the same name, HBS No. 384-119, prepared by Martha Gershun under the supervision of Howard H. Stevenson. Copyright © 1998 by the President and Fellows of Harvard College. Harvard Business School case 898-278.

trouble. There are many types of financial adversity and many solutions other than resorting to bankruptcy proceedings. An individual or a firm which becomes insolvent, without cash to pay the bills, may simply stall creditors until the situation improves. They may also default on loan payments, negotiate reduced schedules, or liquidate inventory to generate funds. Further, options such as trust mortgages to restructure debt, assignments for the benefit of creditors which allow an orderly liquidation in a less formal setting than bankruptcy, and state court receiverships are alternatives to bankruptcy. For a bankruptcy case to be commenced, someone, either debtors or creditors, decides that the individual or firm should not continue in its present financial incarnation. Then, bankruptcy becomes an option under which either the debtors or creditors seek to utilize the bankruptcy law and the courts to resolve the situation.

This note will discuss bankruptcy from the point of view of the individual or corporate debtor. First, it will provide a brief overview of existing bankruptcy law. Then, it will examine bankruptcy in general and three forms of bankruptcy in particular: liquidation, reorganization, and the adjustment of debts of an individual with a regular income. Municipal bankruptcies and family farmer bankruptcies will not be covered in detail in this note. Finally, it will talk about some of the ways debtors can protect themselves before taking this significant step and discuss what actions are prohibited under bankruptcy law.

——— OVERVIEW

The genesis of our bankruptcy laws can be traced back to the United States Constitution which empowers Congress "to establish . . . uniform laws on the subject of bankruptcies throughout the United States." Until it was repealed by the Bankruptcy Reform Act of 1978, the prevailing law for bankruptcy in the United States was the Bankruptcy Act of 1898. In 1938, through the Chandler Act, Congress amended the Bankruptcy Act to give the debtor the option of rehabilitation. The Bankruptcy Reform Act of 1978 was a total overhaul of the existing bankruptcy system, and its provisions are reflected in the Bankruptcy Code. The Bankruptcy Code has eight substantive chapters. All of the chapters have odd numbers except Chapter 12 which was added in 1986 as an experiment to assist with the adjustment of debts of the family farmer with regular annual income. The first three chapters are administrative provisions which are applicable in all bankruptcy proceedings; the remaining chapters deal with specific types of bankruptcies. The provisions of the operative chapters, Chapters 7, 9, 11, 12 and 13 apply specifically and only to cases filed under those chapters. In other words, the provisions of Chapter 11 do not apply to a bankruptcy case filed under Chapter 13, but the provisions of Chapters 1, 3 and 5 apply to all types of bankruptcy cases. Specifically, the Bankruptcy Code consists of the following chapters:

- Chapter 1 sets forth general definitions and provisions.
- Chapter 3 deals with case administration.
- Chapter 5 deals with creditors, the debtor and the estate.
- Chapter 7 deals with liquidation.
- Chapter 9 deals with the adjustment of debts of a municipality.
- Chapter 11 deals with reorganization (includes businesses, individuals and railroads).
- Chapter 12 deals with adjustment of debts of a family farm or with regular annual income.
- Chapter 13 deals with adjustment of debts of an individual with regular income.

The Bankruptcy Code was amended significantly in 1984, 1986 and 1994. The primary purpose of the 1984 amendment was to cure the problem created by the Supreme Court's decision in what is known as the *Marathon* case in which the jurisdictional grant to bankruptcy judges was declared unconstitutional. The 1986 amendments were primarily concerned with establishing Chapter 12 for the rehabilitation of the family farmer. The 1994 amendments were an attempt to address issues concerning case administration and certain substantive issues in commercial, consumer and municipal bankruptcy cases. The 1994 amendments also established the National Bankruptcy Review Commission which was charged with investigating and evaluating the Bankruptcy Code. The Commission has recently submitted a report to Congress which may lead to significant changes to the Bankruptcy Code.

The Bankruptcy Code is designed to achieve the competing goals of maximizing creditor recovery and providing forgiveness to an honest debtor for its financial failures by providing relief from its debts. Regardless of which chapter a debtor falls under, the filing of any bankruptcy proceeding gives the debtor an initial "breathing spell" through an automatic stay which stops, among other things, all lawsuits against the debtor and all foreclosures of the debtor's assets. A creditor, however, can request that the bankruptcy court lift the automatic stay to allow the creditor to proceed against the debtor's assets in which the creditor holds a pre-petition lien. Debtors, particularly in reorganization cases, will often contest such a request by a creditor, particularly when the asset is essential to the proposed reorganization.

It should be noted that not all companies are eligible to file for bankruptcy protection. Under the Bankruptcy Code, banks, savings and loans, insurance companies and all foreign companies are prohibited from doing so.

——— GETTING INTO TROUBLE

For an individual, the path to bankruptcy is often clearly discernible in retrospect; it is easy to see where a person made a bad decision, when they became overextended, how they misjudged their financial situation. There are at least two ways individuals accumulate sufficient unpaid debts to contemplate bankruptcy. The first common experience is painfully simple: they purchase more on credit than they can afford to buy. This happens because they underestimate the amount of money they will have to pay for their accumulated credit purchases or because they overestimate the amount of income they will earn. Thus, the incidence of individual bankruptcies has increased with rises of easy consumer credit and in periods of unemployment, when people may lose their jobs unexpectedly or be unable to find new work if they are laid off. For example, the 1990s has witnessed a tremendous growth in consumer credit card debt, followed by an increase in bankruptcy cases. From 1996 to 1997, consumer bankruptcies rose 20% and represented 96% of all bankruptcy filings in 1997.[1] It is interesting that during that period, unemployment has been low, unlike typical periods of high bankruptcy filings. However, consumer credit has also reached unprecedented highs. Therefore it appears that an extended period of easy consumer credit coupled with the abundance of confidence arising in response to an economy which can generate extremely high employment levels is a recipe for abnormally high levels of personal bankruptcy filings. This explains why consumer bankruptcies have increased while corporate bankruptcies have significantly diminished in numbers. Over the past few years however the market for business debt has evolved from an extremely tight market where loans were often simply unavailable, to a period of easy business credit. The easing of business credit developed later in the economic cycle than did the easing of consumer credit and replaced an environment of far tighter business credit than existed on the consumer side. The question arising from the combination of easy credit and the confidence generated by an economy that can result in stock valuations as high as they presently are, is whether the same factors which have led to such high levels of consumer bankruptcy will also eventually lead to high levels of business bankruptcy.

Another interesting trend is the tendency of consumers to liquidate under Chapter 7 rather than rehabilitate under Chapter 13. In a Chapter 7, an individual will give up all assets except those assets set aside by state or federal law as exempt, but will retain the unfettered use of all future income. In a Chapter 13, the individual debtor will retain his assets but must utilize some future income to pay old debt. This trend for consumers to simply shed their debt is under consideration in Congress and it is possible that amendments to the Bankruptcy Code will require a relatively high earning debtor to utilize some portion of future income to satisfy creditors.

The second common road to individual bankruptcy is more complex. It occurs when an individual's personal finances are in order; but he or she chooses to act as guarantor for a business or for another individual whose situation may not be as fortunate. When an individual agrees to accept the burden of another's debts (either for an individual or a corporation), then that

---

1. *ABI Journal,* "Bankruptcy Filings Top 1.4 Million in 1997 with 20 Percent Increase in Consumer Filings" (April 1998).

person becomes legally responsible if the first entity defaults on payments. Sometimes, this additional financial requirement is more than the individual's personal budget can accommodate. Bankruptcy then becomes a way of resolving these added debts, leaving the individual free to begin again.

For corporations, the path to bankruptcy is considerably more complicated. Ray Barrickman, in a somewhat dated but nevertheless compelling publication, outlines 20 potential causes of business failure:[2] excessive competition, the general business cycle, changes in public demand, governmental acts, adverse acts of labor, acts of God, poor overall management, unwise promotion, unwise expansion, inefficient selling, overextension of inventories, poor financial management, excessive fixed charges, excessive funded debt, excessive floating debt, overextension of credit, unwise dividend policies, and inadequate maintenance and depreciation.

John Argenti, studying corporate failures in Great Britain, posits a chain of events, beginning with poor management, which usually precipitates a firm's slide into bankruptcy:

> If the management of a company is poor then two things will be neglected: the system of accountancy information will be deficient and the company will not respond to change. (Some companies, even well-managed ones, may be damaged because powerful constraints prevent the managers making the responses they wish to make.) Poor managers will also make at least one of three other mistakes: they will overtrade; or they will launch a big project that goes wrong; or they will allow the company's gearing to rise so that even normal business hazards become constant threats. These are the chief causes, neither fraud nor bad luck deserve more than a passing mention. The following symptoms will appear: certain financial ratios will deteriorate but, as soon as they do, the managers will start creative accounting which reduces the predictive value of these ratios and so lends greater importance to non-financial symptoms. Finally the company enters a characteristic period in its last few months.[3]

These are not all of the root causes of bankruptcy. Each situation contains its own causes and circumstances for financial distress. However, the direct catalyst for bankruptcy proceedings is usually a person or company's inability to pay their debts on time. When this situation occurs, the individual or company may begin voluntary bankruptcy proceedings or their creditors may try to force them into involuntary bankruptcy. With certain exceptions provided in the Bankruptcy Code, any person, partnership, or corporation can file for voluntary relief under the Bankruptcy Code. Even solvent entities

2. Ray E. Barrickman, *Business Failure, Causes, Remedies, and Cures* (Washington: University Press of America, 1979), p. 28.

3. John Argenti, *Corporate Collapse: The Causes and Symptoms* (London: McGraw-Hill, 1976), p. 108.

can file for bankruptcy (most likely under the reorganization provisions of the Bankruptcy Code) as long as there is no intent to defraud creditors.

For example, Manville Corporation filed for bankruptcy in late 1982, even though the company had a book net worth of nearly $1.2 billion. The asbestos manufacturer was seeking protection from an anticipated 34,000 lawsuits relating to the injury or death of workers who used Manville's asbestos products. Assuming an average settlement of $40,000 per lawsuit, Manville calculated that it could not afford to stay in business and sought bankruptcy relief from these "creditors." Other companies have been forced into Chapter 11 because of potential tort liability. For example, A.H. Robbins Co. filed because of potential liability related to the Dalkon Shield, Dow Corning Corp. filed because of potential liability related to breast implants, and Piper Aircraft filed bankruptcy because of potential product liability obligations. In fact, because a number of asbestos manufacturers in addition to Manville, like UNR Industries, Inc. and Eagle-Picher Industries, Inc., were forced to file for reorganization, the Bankruptcy Code was amended in 1994 to codify certain of the procedures used in such asbestos cases for dealing with "future claims."

———— FILING FOR BANKRUPTCY

In order to seek relief from their debts, a person or corporation must file in the office of the Clerk of the United States District Court in which the domicile, residence, principal place of business or principal assets of the entity have been located for the preceding 180 days. The filing fee is $130 for parties commencing a bankruptcy case under Chapter 7 (liquidation) or Chapter 13 (adjustment of debts or an individual with regular income). The filing fee for debtors seeking relief under Chapter 11 (reorganizations) is $800; railroads must pay a filing fee of $1,000. The filing fee for Chapter 12 (family farmer rehabilitation) is $200. Somewhat ironically, there is no *in forma pauperis* in bankruptcy; if the debtor cannot afford the filing fee the debtor cannot file a bankruptcy petition.

In certain situations, creditors can force debtors to go bankrupt. An involuntary bankruptcy case can be commenced by:

- Three or more creditors whose aggregate claims amount to more than $10,775 over the value of any assets securing those claims; or
- One or more such creditors if there are less than 12 claim holders;
- Fewer than all the general partners in a limited partnership; or
- A foreign representative of the estate in a foreign proceeding concerning such person.

Creditors do not have to prove that the debtor has insufficient assets to pay his or her debts; mere failure to generally pay debts on time, regardless of ability to pay, is sufficient grounds for creditors to seek involuntary bankruptcy. However, in an involuntary bankruptcy proceeding, if the creditors cannot meet the burden for even this simple standard, the petition will be dismissed and the creditors will be assessed costs and reasonable attorneys' fees. Furthermore, if the creditors are found to have filed the petition in bad faith, the court may award the debtor any damages caused by the proceedings, including punitive damages. In fact, the court may require the petitioners to post a bond to compensate the debtor for costs incurred in defending the involuntary petition. In practice, however, involuntary bankruptcy is uncommon. In a recent year, for instance fewer than 0.5% of personal bankruptcy cases and 1.5% of Chapter 11 cases were involuntary. It appears that the reasons why there are comparatively few involuntary filings are the possible, but unlikely, significant damages which can be awarded if the debtor successfully defeats an involuntary petition, the lack of available reliable information about the debtor's affairs, and the fact that an aggressive creditor will often pursue remedies designed to benefit itself rather than the entire creditor body. When involuntary cases are filed, it is often to avoid a dissipation of the debtor's assets or to allow for asset recoveries available under the preference and fraudulent conveyance sections of the Bankruptcy Code.

CHOOSING YOUR POISON: WHICH CHAPTER?

There are five distinct chapters of the bankruptcy code which can shape the outcome of the bankruptcy proceedings: Chapter 7 (liquidation), Chapter 11 (reorganization), Chapter 9 (municipalities),[4] Chapter 12 (family farmer) and Chapter 13 (adjustment of an individual's debts).

In theory, bankruptcy proceedings can be concluded very quickly. In practice, however, they are often long, drawn-out affairs. Corporate reorganizations, in particular, can take many months or even years to reach completion. The average Chapter 11 case in the 1980s lasted just under 18 months.[5]

In a Chapter 7 bankruptcy the assets of the individual or corporation are liquidated and distributed to creditors. By filing for Chapter 11 or Chapter 13 bankruptcy, the debtors typically seek to keep their assets with some arrangement to pay off their debts over time. Since the outcomes of these types of bankruptcies are radically different, affecting the amount of the assets which the debtor keeps as well as the timing and amount of payments which the creditors receive, both groups have some ability to influence the outcome of cases under the prevailing chapters.

When the creditor files for an involuntary bankruptcy case under Chapters 7 or 11, the debtor can convert the case to a bankruptcy under any

---

4. Given the relatively few number of Chapter 9 and Chapter 12 cases filed, this note will not discuss these chapters in detail.

5. New Generation Research, *The 1992 Bankruptcy Yearbook Almanac* (1992).

of the other chapters. When a debtor files for voluntary bankruptcy under any chapter, the creditors can request that the court convert the case to a Chapter 7 or a Chapter 11 bankruptcy case. Only a Chapter 13 bankruptcy case cannot be commenced without the debtor's consent. Before choosing a chapter for bankruptcy, debtors should carefully consider whether they would prefer to liquidate their assets or continue their business or personal finances, attempting with reorganization or adjustment to pay off their debts over time.

CHAPTER 7: LIQUIDATION

Chapter 7 of the Bankruptcy Code provides for either voluntary or involuntary liquidation of the assets of the debtor for distribution to the creditors. When a petition is filed under Chapter 7 it constitutes an Order for Relief. After the entry of the Order for relief, the debtor has a legal obligation to:

- File a list of creditors, assets and liabilities and a statement of financial affairs.
- Cooperate with the trustee appointed to the case.
- Give the trustee all property of the estate and all records relating to the property.
- Appear at any hearing dealing with a discharge.
- Attend all official meetings of creditors.

As soon as possible after the entry of the Order for Relief, the Office of the United States Trustee (the branch of the Department of Justice charged with being the watchdog over bankruptcy proceedings) will appoint a disinterested person to serve as the interim Chapter 7 trustee. Creditors holding at least 20% of specified unsecured claims may elect a successor Chapter 7 trustee. A Chapter 7 trustee will be elected if the candidate receives a majority in amount of specified unsecured claims. If no trustee is elected in this manner, the interim trustee will continue to serve. The duties of the trustee include:

- Reducing the property of the debtor's estate to cash and closing up the estate as expeditiously as possible.
- Accounting for all property received.
- Investigating the financial affairs of the debtor and examining all claims for validity.
- Providing information about the estate to any interested party, furnishing reports on the debtor's business if it is authorized to be operated, and filing a final report of the disposition of the estate with the court.

Certain of an individual debtor's assets will be exempt from liquidation; that is, they may not be distributed to the creditors, but rather will be retained by the debtor. In many states, the debtor can choose between the federal exemptions provided by the terms of the Bankruptcy Code or the relevant state and federal exemptions which are available to debtors absent bankruptcy. However, states can require their residents to adhere only to the non-bankruptcy exemptions. The following states have enacted legislation prohibiting the election of the bankruptcy exemptions: Alabama, Arizona, California, Colorado, Delaware, Florida, Georgia, Idaho, Illinois, Indiana, Iowa, Kansas, Louisiana, Maine, Maryland, Mississippi, Missouri, Montana, Nebraska, Nevada, New York, North Dakota, North Carolina, North Dakota, Ohio, Oklahoma, Oregon, South Carolina, South Dakota, Tennessee, Utah, Virginia, West Virginia, and Wyoming. In those states, the debtor must rely on the non-bankruptcy exemptions and has no opportunity to choose the exemptions provided by the Bankruptcy Code. As of April 1, 1998, under the current bankruptcy exemptions, a debtor gets to keep:

- The debtor's interest, not to exceed $16,150, in the debtor's (or a dependent's) residence; in a cooperative that owns property used by the debtor (or a dependent) as a residence; and in a burial plot for the debtor or a dependent (so called homestead exemption);
- The debtor's interest, not to exceed $2,575, in a motor vehicle;
- The debtor's interest, not to exceed $425 in value for any particular item or $8,625 in aggregate value, in household furnishings, clothing, appliances, books, animals, crops, or musical instruments, that are kept for the personal, family or household use for the debtor or a dependent;
- The debtor's interest, not to exceed $1,075, in jewelry held for personal, family or household use of the debtor or a dependent;
- The debtor's interest in any property, not to exceed $800 (so called wild card exemption) plus up to $8,075 of any unused amount of the homestead exemption;
- The debtor's interest, not to exceed $1,625, in any implements, professional books, or tools of the trade of the debtor or a dependent;
- Any unmatured life insurance contract owned by the debtor, other than a credit life insurance contract;
- The debtor's interest, not to exceed $8,625 less any amount transferred to prevent forfeiture of a life insurance contract entered into prior to the bankruptcy case, in any accrued dividends or interest or loan value or any nonmature life insurance contract under which the debtor or a dependent is insured;
- Prescribed health aids for the debtor or a dependent;
- The debtor's right to receive social security benefits, unemployment compensation benefits, local public assistance benefits, veterans' benefits, illness or disability benefits, receive alimony, support, or separate maintenance, a payment under a (subject to certain exceptions) stock bonus, pension, profit sharing annuity, or similar plan on account of illness, disability, death, age, or length of service; and
- The debtor's right to receive an award under a crime victim's reparation law; a payment on account of a wrongful death of an

individual of whom the debtor was a dependent; a payment under a life insurance contract that insured the life of an individual of whom the debtor was a dependent; a payment not to exceed $16,150 on account of personal bodily injury, not including pain and suffering or compensation for actual pecuniary loss, of the debtor or an individual of whom the debtor is a dependent; or a payment in compensation of loss of future earnings of the debtor or an individual of whom the debtor is or was a dependent.

In those states where the option exists, the Bankruptcy Code exemptions are available in all cases involving individuals. The 1994 amendments provided for an automatic adjustment of certain dollar amounts found in the Bankruptcy Code, including the exemptions. The adjustments, rounded to the nearest $25, are made every three years (the next adjustment will occur on April 1, 2001) and are tied to the Consumer Price Index for All Urban Consumers.

The rest of the debtor's estate is liquidated by the trustee and distributed first to secured creditors. These secured creditors receive payment up to the amount which can be obtained from the disposition of the asset which constituted the security. Any amount remaining unsatisfied following the disposition of these assets goes into the unsecured creditors pool.

Following the payment of secured creditors with the proceeds from specific assets, the next class of claimants consists of "priority claimants." Priority claims include, in order: administrative expenses and filing fees assessed against the debtor's estate; certain unsecured claims arising from the time of the filing of an involuntary petition and the appointment of a trustee or the entry of an Order for Relief (gap creditors); wages, salaries or commissions, including vacation severance, and sick leave pay to the extent of $4,300 per individual earned within 90 days of the date of filing or the date of cessation of business, whichever occurred first; contributions to employee benefit plans up to $4,300 per employee earned within 180 days; claims of individuals, up to $1,950 each, arising from the deposit of money in connection with purchases of property or services that are not delivered; claims of governmental units for taxes and custom duties.

Next come the general unsecured creditors. In the rare case where the general unsecured claims are satisfied in full, late filed claims may be paid. If funds are still available, fines and penalties and multiple or punitive damages may be paid. Interest may then be paid on the principal amount of the general unsecured claims. Finally, if there is any surplus, it is paid to the debtor. It is rare for distributions to be made beyond distributions to unsecured creditors. If there aren't enough funds to pay a class in full, claims within the class are paid pro rata.

When the debtor is an individual, the court will usually grant a discharge. This means the debtor is discharged from all debts which arose prior to the commencement of the bankruptcy case, except certain debts explicitly excepted from discharge by the Bankruptcy Code, including debts arising from alimony, child support, certain taxes, student loans, drunk driving injuries, willful and malicious torts or debts that were not listed on the debtor's financial statements when bankruptcy was filed. A debtor who has received a discharge in a case commenced within six years before the date of the filing of a subsequent petition is not eligible to receive a discharge in the subsequent case. A debtor may repay any debt voluntarily, even a debt that has been discharged. A creditor, however, may not enforce any discharged debt.

CHAPTER 11: REORGANIZATION

The purpose of Chapter 11 of the Bankruptcy Code is to provide a mechanism for reorganizing a firm's finances so it can continue to operate, pay a dividend to its creditors, provide jobs, and hopefully even produce a return to its investors. Usually debtors and creditors will opt for this form of bankruptcy if they think a business has more value as a going concern than would the proceeds of liquidated assets. The objective of the reorganization is to develop a plan which determines how much creditors will be paid and in what form the business will continue. An individual may file a Chapter 11 petition, although Chapter 11 is typically used by businesses. Stockbrokers and commodity brokers are not eligible for Chapter 11 relief. Furthermore, railroads can proceed under Chapter 11, while they are prohibited from seeking liquidation under Chapter 7.

Like Chapter 7, a reorganization case can be either voluntary or involuntary. After the entry of the Order for Relief, the United States Trustee will appoint a committee of general unsecured creditors. This committee is often comprised of those creditors holding the seven largest claims; however the United States Trustee has great latitude in composing the committee to make it representative of the different kinds of interests in the case. As such the committee may vary in size and may include creditors that are not among the largest, and, maybe more significantly, exclude creditors that are among the largest. The committee, acting as a fiduciary for all like creditors, is primarily responsible for working with the debtor on the administration of the case, investigating the debtor's business and claims against the estate and negotiating and formulating a plan. The committee may hire professionals which can seek reimbursement for their expenses from the estate. The United States Trustee may appoint, or the bankruptcy court may order the appointment of, additional committees if necessary to assure the adequate representation of other constituencies in the case. For example, if the debtor appears to be solvent, the United States Trustee may consider the appointment of an equity holders committee.

The debtor keeps possession of its assets and may operate its business unless a party in interest can show the debtor is guilty of fraud, dishonesty, incompetence, or gross mismanagement or otherwise proves such an arrangement is not in the interests of the creditors. If the court finds that either of these conditions exist, a trustee will be appointed, although the instances of such appointments are the exception rather than the rule. The duties of a Chapter 11 trustee include being accountable for all of the information and records necessary to formulate the reorganization plan and filing the plan with the court or recommending conversion to a Chapter 7 or a Chapter 13 case, as may be appropriate, or recommending the dismissal of the case altogether.

If a trustee is not appointed, the debtor, as a debtor in possession of its assets, possesses the duties and the powers of a trustee. No court order is necessary for the debtor to continue to run the firm; rather the business is to remain in operation in the ordinary course unless the court orders otherwise. Activities that are not in the ordinary course of the debtor's business must receive prior court approval.

The debtor has a 120-day exclusivity period in which only the debtor may file a reorganization plan and 60 more days to obtain acceptances of the plan, unless the court, for cause, shortens or lengthens these time periods. The exclusivity period terminates automatically upon the appointment of a trustee. After the exclusivity period expires, any creditor or party in interest can file a plan. The debtor's right of exclusivity is of critical importance to the debtor. Once exclusivity is lost, other plans can be filed which could force the debtor to negotiate additional consideration to creditors or could call for the transfer of the debtor's business to a third party at the expense of the debtor's stockholders.

A plan must designate the various classes of creditors and show how they will be treated. Classes will normally include creditors with similar legal rights. Secured creditors (those with lien rights in certain assets of the debtor) are normally separately classified and in typical circumstances, general un-secured creditors will be classified together. The plan can be a liquidating plan. Thus, a business could be liquidated under Chapter 11 rather than Chapter 7. In order for the plan to be confirmed, if the legal rights of the creditors in a class are altered, the class must accept the plan by more than one half in number and at least two-third in amount of these creditors voting on the plan. In the event that a particular class of creditors rejects the plan, the plan proponent may seek to "cramdown" the plan over the objection of that class. The Bankruptcy Code contains extensive criteria establishing when a plan is "fair and equitable" to a dissenting class and may be confirmed over the objection of the class.

Notwithstanding the vote of the creditors, the bankruptcy court may confirm a plan only if the court makes certain findings which are required by the Bankruptcy Code. These findings are required to ensure protection of creditors, the integrity of the bankruptcy system and the policies of the Bankruptcy Code. For example, the court must find that the plan has been proposed in good faith and that if future operations are contemplated by the debtor, they are likely to succeed and will not be followed by a liquidation or further reorganization. Further, with respect to each class that does not accept the plan by a unanimous vote, the plan must provide that each creditor in such class will receive at least as much from the plan as the creditor would have received in a Chapter 7 liquidation. The purpose of this rule (the so called best interest of creditors test) is to ensure that a minority member of a class is not forced to accept the results of a plan if the majority of the class is motivated by factors other than the amount of the dividend. For example, if most creditors in the class continue to do business with the debtor, they are likely to be more concerned with the debtor's continued existence rather than the amount of the dividend. The rule, therefore, protects the minority claim-holder by setting a floor on what may be paid to the class.

If the court confirms a reorganization plan, the individual debtor is discharged from any past debts except as they are handled under the plan. A corporate debtor receives a discharge unless the plan contemplates liquidation. The provisions of the confirmed plan bind the debtor, any entity issuing securities under the plan, any entity acquiring property under the plan, and any creditor, equity security holder, or general partner of the debtor, whether or not they have accepted the plan.

The 1994 amendments to the Bankruptcy Code included provisions designed to streamline "single asset real estate" cases and "small business" Chapter 11 cases. The Bankruptcy Code defines a single asset real estate debtor as one having real property, other than residential property with fewer that 4 residential units, on which the debtor conducts no business other than operating the real estate and from which the debtor generates substantially all of its gross income, where such real estate has secured debt of no more than $4 million. There is a perceived problem that a single asset real estate debtor files for bankruptcy protection only to stall, in bad faith, a foreclosing creditor. To alleviate this problem, the automatic stay was amended to allow a secured creditor relief from the stay 90 days after the commencement of a bankruptcy case, unless the debtor has made a certain level of progress in the case.

A small business is a commercial venture with aggregate secured and unsecured debt not exceeding $2 million. A small business can elect to be treated on an expedited basis, which puts the burden on the debtor to file a plan in a shorter time than allowed in a normal Chapter 11 case. There is little benefit to a small business in making the election and therefore such elections are rare. Congress is presently considering proposals that would alter both the definition of small business and the procedures to be used in their reorganization cases.

CHAPTER 13: ADJUSTMENT OF DEBTS OF AN INDIVIDUAL WITH REGULAR INCOME

Chapter 13 of the new Bankruptcy Code covers individuals with regular income whose unsecured debts are less than $269,250 and whose secured debts are less than $807,750. This includes individuals who own or operate businesses. It does not include partnerships or corporations. Note that there cannot be an involuntary bankruptcy case under Chapter 13.

The purpose of Chapter 13 is to allow an individual to pay off debts with future earnings while the Bankruptcy Code protects him or her from harassment by creditors and allows the debtor to retain its assets. Furthermore, it allows the debtor to continue to own and operate a business while the Chapter 13 case is pending. A debtor's obligations under a plan pursuant to Chapter 13 is typically payable over three years, with up to a two-year extension allowed for cause. Chapter 13 is popular with debtors who own homes and want to keep them notwithstanding the bankruptcy. Chapter 13 allows a debtor to reinstate a defaulted mortgage, pay it current on a going forward basis and pay any past due amount in the plan.

In a Chapter 13 case the property of the estate includes property and earnings acquired after the commencement of the case but before it is closed. The standing Chapter 13 trustee administers the case by collecting and disbursing payments made by the debtor under its plan.

Chapter 13 has several major advantages for the debtor:

- Once the case is filed, all of the debtor's property and future income are under the court's jurisdiction. The automatic stay protects the debtor, and any codebtor on an obligation, against litigation and collection efforts.
- Unlike Chapter 7, the trustee does not take possession of the debtor's property. The debtor can increase the value of his or her estate while in Chapter 13.
- Chapter 13 can help preserve the debtor's credit rating since a Chapter 13 contemplates some effort to repay old debts.
- Only the debtor can file a plan, there are no competing proposals allowed.

The debtor must file a plan within fifteen days after he or she filed the petition. The court will hold a confirmation hearing on the plan and any party in interest may object to confirmation. The court will confirm the plan only after making certain findings. Some of these findings are similar to the findings a court must make before it will confirm a Chapter 11 plan. For example, a Chapter 13 plan must be proposed in good faith and the plan must satisfy the best interest of creditors test.

In addition, unless the holder of each secured claim has accepted the plan, each such holder must either i) retain the lien securing such claim and receive property of a value not less than the amount of such claim; or ii) receive the property securing such claims.

If a creditor holding an unsecured claim (or the Chapter 13 trustee) objects to confirmation of the plan, the court cannot approve the plan unless the plan provides either i) the value of the property to be distributed on account of such claim is not less than the amount of such claim; or ii) that all of the debtor's projected disposable income to be received over the three-year period commencing on the date of the first payment under the plan is used to fund the plan.

The court will grant the debtor a discharge only after all payments under the plan are completed. A Chapter 13 discharge is broader that the Chapter 7 discharge in that certain debts that would not be discharged under Chapter 7 are discharged under Chapter 13. For example, debts discharged under Chapter 13 include debts for willful and malicious torts and for fines and penalties. In addition, certain tax claims that are nondischargable in a Chapter 7 case may be discharged in a Chapter 13 case. This explains why some debtors file Chapter 13 cases even though Chapter 7 cases would be fiscally more advantageous.

——— POWERS OF A TRUSTEE

In addition to the responsibilities enumerated in Chapters 7 and 11, the trustee in a bankruptcy case has a great deal of power which can determine how assets are allocated and debt restructured. Chapters 3 and 5 of the Bankruptcy Code set forth such powers as the ability to employ professionals to help carry out the duties of trustee; the power to use, sell, or lease property; the power to obtain credits secured by priority claims and new liens; the power to reject or assume contracts and unexpired leases; and the power to avoid preferences and fraudulent transfers, known as the avoiding powers. These powers can change the status of certain classes of creditors, depending on how they are applied. For instance, by rejecting an unexpired lease, the trustee can convert a long-term leaseholder into just another unsecured creditor. If a trustee is not appointed, then the debtor in possession of the estate assumes the trustee's duties and powers.

——— NEGOTIATIONS AND SETTLEMENTS

While they may feel persecuted and helpless, debtors actually have a great deal of power to negotiate with their creditors for arrangements that will leave the firm intact, either before or after bankruptcy is declared. This power stems from several sources, including without limitation:

- the incentive for creditors to reach a speedy and workable solution to the debtor's financial problems that could yield earlier payments to creditors.
- the differing interests of various classes of creditors. A creditor for whom speed of settlement is more important than full payment might negotiate with another creditor whose interest lies in full payment rather than a quick solution. In such an instance, both groups of creditors can be satisfied if the first pays the second's claims in order to expedite a settlement. Trade creditors and

money creditors might have varying interests, too, with trade creditors preferring a settlement that leaves the firm intact to do business in the future and money creditors preferring a liquidation that provides as much cash as possible. Debtors can use this dichotomy to their advantage, using available cash to pay off money creditors while asking trade creditors to forbear in the hope of putting the firm back on solid financial ground rather than driving it into bankruptcy.

- the automatic stay which can cause substantial delay in a creditor's ability to recover on its debt.
- the debtor's exclusive right to file a plan. As long as the debtor retains this right, the creditor's two choices are to accept the plan or accept liquidation value.
- the debtor's threat to cease operations which would impair the value of the assets as a going concern.
- the cost of litigation or extended reorganization proceedings.
- creditors may be willing to negotiate terms favorable to a debtor if the debtor is an important customer and the continued operations are more valuable to the creditor than an enhanced dividend that is large enough to impair the debtor's operations.
- the debtor's knowledge of its business operations. The debtor will usually have a better grasp of its business and prospects than will the creditors. The debtor, therefore, will have the benefits in negotiations derived from this greater knowledge.

Creditors also have certain leverage in negotiating with debtors. A creditor may derive negotiating strength from the following factors, among others:

- the debtor's exclusive right to file a plan is not perpetual. Once exclusivity is terminates, creditors may file competing plans on terms more favorable to the creditors and less favorable to the debtor and its stockholders.
- Some creditors may hold the personal guarantees of the debtor's principals. This significantly enhances the creditor's leverage to influence the operations of the debtor and the terms of the plan.
- Tremendous negotiating leverage can be gained by developing alternatives to the debtor's plan. For example, if a third party buyer for the debtor's business can be located, the debtor may have to increase its price in order to maintain its business.
- If the creditors can discover fraudulent conveyances or preferences between the debtor and its principals, substantial leverage can be gained.

The Bankruptcy Code was designed to provide debtors and creditors motivation for seeking a solution that will maximize the settlement for all parties. While the cases do not always succeed in meeting this objective, and the rights of the debtor or creditors may not be protected to the fullest extent, the Bankruptcy Code does provide a framework whereby the value of the debtor's assets can be enhanced to the benefit of some or all of the parties in interest.

———— DEBTOR'S OPTIONS

While the Bankruptcy Code deals generously with debtors, providing a chance to discharge debts and begin again, no debtor wants to be thrown into bankruptcy proceedings against his will. There are several steps a debtor can take to insure against involuntary bankruptcy. These include being sure that the number of creditors exceeds 12 and that no 3 creditors' claims amount to more the $10,775. Sometimes, this could mean paying off some creditors in full while not paying others all that they are due. If there are more than 12 creditors in a case, 1 or 2 claimants cannot force an individual or a corporation into involuntary bankruptcy.

Further there are many steps a debtor can take to maximize the amount of exempt assets that can be retained in a bankruptcy case. In contemplating bankruptcy, the debtor should examine exemptions closely, and arrange his affairs in such a way as to give the best possible start following discharge. The legal cases on this point are inconsistent and do not draw a clear line as to when a debtor is simply taking advantage of available exemptions and when a debtor is engaging in fraudulent conveyances by transferring assets that would have otherwise be available for creditors. This uncertainty makes bankruptcy planning extremely difficult. In some cases, a transfer of general assets to exempt assets may be viewed as intelligent planning; in other cases, the same transfer may be viewed by the judge as having civil or criminal implications. There are also many actions debtors cannot take under the law without risking their discharge. For example, hiding assets or liabilities and embezzling from the estate.

One of the most important creditor protections existing under bankruptcy law is the trustee's right to avoid and recover preferential payments made to creditors prior to the bankruptcy case. The trustee has the power to disallow certain payments to a creditor which enables that creditor to receive more than others in the same class. A preferential payment is one made 90 days prior to the bankruptcy filing. If the creditor had an "insider" of the debtor, the 90-day period is extended to one year. This provision ensures the bankruptcy policy of equality of distribution among creditors. Any creditor who manages to receive a larger share than others of the same class during the preference period is forced to return it to the general pot for equitable allocation. The possibility of having to turnover a preference limits the debtor's ability to play one creditor off against others in an attempt to avoid bankruptcy, since creditors know such settlements could be disallowed if bankruptcy is declared within three month. There are defenses available to creditors facing a preference lawsuit. For example, payments received by the creditor in the ordinary course of business and payments received at the same time the creditor is providing additional value to the estate cannot be recovered by the trustee.

There are many avenues available for the savvy debtor to pursue, either before filing for bankruptcy or after such proceedings have been initiated. Debtors in financial trouble would be wise to seek competent legal counsel early so as to carve the best path through their predicament.

──── BIBLIOGRAPHY

"A Brief Note on Arrangements, Bankruptcy, and Reorganization in Bankruptcy," Harvard Business School Case 9-272-148, Rev. 7/75, written by Jasper H. Arnold, Research Assistant, under the supervision of Associate Professor Michael L. Tennican.

"Asbestosis: Manville Seeks Chapter 11," *Fortune*, September 20, 1982.

"A $2.5 Billion Tale of Woe," by Paul Bluestein, *Forbes*, October 30, 1978, p. 51.

"Bankruptcy," Harvard Business School Case 9-376-221, prepared by Laurence H. Stone, copyright 1976.

Bankruptcy Reform, American Enterprise Institute for Public Policy Research, Washington, D.C., 1978.

Business Failure: Causes, Remedies, and Cures, Ray E. Barrickman, University Press of America, Washington, D.C., 1979.

Corporate Collapse: The Causes and Symptoms, John Argenti, McGraw-Hill: London, 1976.

Corporations in Crisis: Behavioral Observations for Bankruptcy Policy, by Philip B. Nelson, Praeger: New York, 1981.

Current Developments in Bankruptcy and Reorganization: 1980, Arnold M. Quittner, Chairman, Practicing Law Institute, 1980.

"Manville's Costs Could Exceed $5 Billion in Asbestos Suits, Study it Ordered Shows," *Wall Street Journal*, September 15, 1982, p. 7.

Table of Bankruptcy Statistics with reference to bankruptcy cases commenced and terminated in the United States District Courts during the period July 1, 1978 through June 30, 1979, Administrative Office of the United States Courts.

Ibid., July 1, 1976 through June 30, 1977.

The New Bankruptcy Law: A Professional's Handbook, Jeff A. Schnepper (Addison-Wesley Publishing Co., Philippines, 1981).

Bankruptcy Law Letter, Vol. 18, No. 5, p. 2–3 (May 1995).

"Bankruptcy Overview: Issues, Law and Policy," American Bankruptcy Institute (April 1996).

Laurence P. King, et al., Eds., *Collier on Bankruptcy* (3 ed. 1998).

James F. Queenan, Jr., Philip J. Hendel and Ingrid M. Hillinger, Editors, *Chapter 11*

Theory and Practice: A Guide to Reorganization (Horsham, Pennsylvania: LRP Publications, 1994).

"Bankruptcy Filings Top 1.4 Million in 1997 with 20 Percent Increase in Consumer Filings," *ABI Journal* 1 (April 1998).

Harlan D. Platt, *Principles of Corporate Renewal* 55–57 (Advance printing 1997).

—— DISCUSSION QUESTIONS

1. What specific circumstances lead to a voluntary corporate bankruptcy? An involuntary one?
2. What conditions lead to personal bankruptcy?
3. What factors influence the choice between a Chapter 7 and a Chapter 11 filing?

PART THREE

INNOVATION AND ENTREPRENEURSHIP IN THE LARGER COMPANY

Tough-Minded Ways   27
to Get Innovative

ANDRALL E. PEARSON

Andrall Pearson was president of PepsiCo and a managing director of McKinsey & Company prior to joining the faculty at Harvard Business School. In this piece, Pearson articulates a performance-oriented approach to innovation.

Arguing that innovation is a systematic process, the author highlights the specific strategies and behaviors that drive successful innovation. A key element of this perspective is the ability to see the connection between innovation and the value drivers of the business at hand, rather than viewing innovation as an activity to be undertaken for its own sake. Pearson clearly believes that innovation should be grounded in a company's attempts to improve its operating performance.

Most chief executives fervently want their companies to be more competitive, not just on one or two dimensions but across the board. Yet outstanding competitive performance remains an elusive goal. A few companies achieve it. Most do not.

What distinguishes outstanding competitors from the rest? Two basic principles. First, they understand that consistent innovation is the key to a company's survival. Being innovative some of the time, in one or two areas, just won't work. Second, they know that the most powerful changes they can make are those that create value for their customers and potential customers. The result? Competitive companies constantly look for ways to change every aspect of their businesses. Then, when they've found them, they make sure that they translate those changes into advantages customers will appreciate and act on.

Lincoln Electric has understood and applied these principles for years. That's why it has been able to offer its customers better products at lower cost year after year. Yet many people see only Lincoln's success in cutting costs. They miss the fact that the company is a great innovator too because they

Harvard Business Review, May–June 1988. Copyright © 1988 by the President and Fellows of Harvard College, all rights reserved.

481

think about innovation too narrowly—in terms of home runs only and not all the hits players make, inning after inning, game after game.

Lincoln Electric and other outstanding performers look at innovation systematically. They know that their competitive success is built on a steady stream of improvements in production, finance, distribution, and every other function, not just a big hit in sales or marketing or R&D. So they make sure they've got players who can deliver consistently. And they create organizations that give those players all the backup they need. That means:

- Creating and sustaining a corporate environment that values better performance above everything else.
- Structuring the organization to permit innovative ideas to rise above the demands of running the business.
- Clearly defining a strategic focus that lets the company channel its innovative efforts realistically, in ways that will pay off in the market.
- Knowing where to look for good ideas and how to leverage them once they're found.
- Going after good ideas at full speed, with all the company's resources brought to bear.

Individually, none of these activities may be very complicated or hard to do. But keeping a company focused on all five, all the time, takes tremendous discipline and persistence. That systematic effort to institutionalize innovation is what gives market leaders their competitive edges. And it's what other companies can learn from them.

——— BEGIN WITH THE RIGHT MIND-SET

To convert a solid performer into an aggressive competitor, you have to create an organization that not only values better performance but also sustains the commitment year after year. That means a major shift in values, not a slight step-up in the number of new ideas for next year.

Even a brief exposure to companies that are consistently successful innovators shows their constant dedication to changing things for the better. Everyone in the business thinks and acts that way, not just a few people at the top. Just picture what it was like to work at Apple Computer or Cray Research or Nike in their early years. Or the way things are today at innovative leaders like Wal-Mart Stores or Toys "R" Us or Progressive Mutual Insurance. Or ask anyone at Heinz about the pressure on innovation since Tony O'Reilly introduced risk taking into that once sleepy outfit. Change is a way of life in companies like these.

To sharpen an organization's receptivity to change, several ingredients are essential. First and foremost, top management must be deeply and personally involved in the process.

Innovative companies are led by innovative leaders. It's that simple. Leaders who set demanding goals for themselves and for others, the kinds of goals that force organizations to innovate to meet them. Specific, measurable goals that constitute outstanding relative performance—like becoming number one in a particular market. Not vague, easily reached objectives.

Innovative leaders aren't necessarily creative, idea-driven people themselves (though obviously many are). But they welcome change because they're convinced that their competitive survival depends on innovation. That's a mind-set most executives can develop—if their conviction is based on a specific understanding of a particular competitive environment, not just a bromidic generality.

Look at what Cummins Engine has done to stay alive and gain market share in a truck engine market that's dramatically off. As any key Cummins executive will tell you, the company cut its costs and prices per engine by close to 40% and materially improved its products for one simple reason: to prevent the Japanese from repeating their auto triumph in the truck engine business. To accomplish all this Cummins had to overhaul nearly everything that, historically, had made it the industry leader: products, processes, prices, distribution methods—the works.

People throughout Cummins found the grit to make these changes by looking at their business through the eyes of a Japanese competitor. Other innovative companies do the same thing. They get their people to focus on beating a particular competitor, not just on doing better. One-on-one competition pushes the entire organization to be bolder, to take more risks, and to change faster than companies that have no particular target for their innovative efforts. It also makes a company a tighter, more effective competitor because its innovative efforts are designed to cut away at a particular opponent's current competitive advantages.

For instance, in the 1960s and early 1970s, Pepsi was a much more aggressive and innovative company than Coca-Cola. It had to outflank Coke to survive. When Coke finally woke up—after losing its market leadership—it did a terrific job of innovating too. Why? Coke's new management began to focus on beating Pepsi, not just on doing better. And when Pepsi's managers responded by revving up their already aggressive culture, the result made history. There has been more innovation in soft drinks in the past 5 years than there had been in the previous 20. Industry growth has doubled, and both companies' market shares are the highest ever.

The same thing happened in the beer business when Miller began to take market share from Anheuser-Busch. Suddenly Busch became a much more aggressive, innovative competitor because it was focused on Miller. In contrast, I believe IBM paid a huge price in the 1970s and early 1980s because the company wasn't focused on a number of specialized competitors who were eroding its leadership, segment by segment.

If you don't have any major competitors you can't focus on them, of course. But targeting smaller local competitors is just as effective and invigorating. It's also a good way to ward off the complacency that undoes a lot of winners. At one time, for example, Frito-Lay thought that it didn't have to pay attention to its regional competitors since its market share was more than 50%. Then, collectively, the little guys cut the company's growth rate in half. Frito became very focused very fast.

Finally, innovative companies have lots of experiments going on all the time. This encourages more risk taking since people don't expect every experiment to succeed. It contains the cost since tests and trials don't get expanded until they show real promise. And it improves the odds of success because you're betting on a portfolio, not on one or two big, long-odds projects.

Sometimes, however, the work environment is so risk-averse that management has to bring in outsiders who haven't been intimidated by the sins of the past. That was what happened when PepsiCo acquired Taco Bell, which had been run by an ultraconservative management that regarded all new ideas with suspicion. It took an infusion of three or four outsiders to create a critical mass and get the company moving again.

Unfortunately, it's very easy for managers to convey the wrong messages about risk taking. Appearing to be short-term oriented, giving the impression that only winners get promoted, searching for people to blame, second-guessing managers who take risks (often before they even have time to work out the bugs)—actions like these send a much clearer signal than all the speeches about innovation a chief executive may make. We learned that at PepsiCo when we surveyed our middle managers and found out that many of them thought we were saying one thing and doing another. We had to correct signals and practices like these before they'd credit what we said.

All three of these ingredients—commitment, a specific villain, and risk taking—are soft requirements. Not tangible things like structure and process. But just because they're soft doesn't mean they're unimportant. In fact, unless all three are in place, I question whether you'll ever emerge as a leader.

─── UNSETTLE THE ORGANIZATION

Most big organizations are designed mainly to operate the business: to get the work done, control performance, spot problems, and bring in this year's results. And for the most part, that's as it should be.

But the structures, processes, and people that keep things ticking smoothly can also cut off the generation of good ideas and block their movement through the business system. Excessive layering, for example, kills ideas before they ever get considered by senior managers. Barriers fencing off R&D, marketing, production, and finance bottle up functional problems until it's too late for effective solutions. Elaborate approval systems grind promising innovations to a halt. Staff nitpick ideas or put financial yardsticks on them long before they are mature enough to stand rigorous scrutiny.

To get around organizational roadblocks like these you have to differentiate between what's needed to run the business and what's needed to foster creative activity. Most successful innovations require four key inputs:

- A champion who believes that the new idea is really critical and who will keep pushing ahead, no matter what the roadblocks.
- A sponsor who is high up enough in the organization to marshal its resources—people, money, and time.
- A mix of bright, creative minds (to get ideas) and experienced operators (to keep things practical).
- A process that moves ideas through the system quickly so that they get top-level endorsement, resources, and perspective early in the game—not at the bottom of the ninth inning.

There are, of course, lots of ways to organize your company to bring these four elements together. One is to use task forces on either a full- or part-time basis. Even Procter & Gamble (the ultimate product-manager company) has begun to superimpose multifunctional project teams, often headed by senior managers, onto its old structure. Other companies use full-time task forces to achieve similar goals. They've found their old structures didn't allow enough cross-functional interaction early on. Or enough top-level involvement and support.

Still other companies, like Hasbro, rely on frequent, consistent, and freewheeling meetings with top management to achieve their integration goals. They work within the existing structure but install a process to prevent rigidity and delay. Johnson & Johnson, on the other hand, has thrived largely by spinning off operations into small divisions to encourage its general managers to act more like free-standing entrepreneurs. In all these cases, the companies are striving to create the freedom needed to cross lines, get a variety of inputs, and take risks. They've tried to organize the creative parts of the company differently from the operational ones.

These efforts aren't cost free, of course. When you're trying to change and run the business at the same time, there's bound to be some competition and conflict. But bright people can live with that, and sooner or later the bumps get smoothed out. The risk I'd worry about is leaving one of the critical bases uncovered—by trying to make a champion out of someone who isn't committed to a project, say, or neglecting to temper your whiz kids with some seasoned people who'll be able to tell them whether the product they envision can actually be made. Because if you announce you're going to innovate more aggressively, yet consistently come up short, people will get discouraged and turn off.

——— BE HARDHEADED ABOUT YOUR STRATEGY

Once the entire organization is committed to stepping up the pace of innovation, you have to decide where to direct your efforts. One way, of course, is to put smart and talented people to work and pray that they'll come up with something great. But more often than not, an unfocused approach like that produces lots of small ideas that don't lead anywhere, big costs and embarrassing write-offs, and a great deal of frustration and stop-and-go activity.

In contrast, successful innovators usually have a pretty clear idea of the kind of competitive edges they're seeking. They've thought long and hard about what's practical in their particular businesses. And just as hard about what's not.

Frequently, you'll hear CEOs say that their companies are committed to becoming the low-cost producer, or the industry leader in new products and production processes, or the best service provider. All are worthy visions or concepts—provided they apply to that particular business and company. But in many cases, the vision and the reality don't match up.

For much of smokestack America, for example, the concept of becoming the low-cost producer is simply a cruel fantasy. The Japanese already occupy that position, in many cases permanently. So the best that U.S. manufacturers can possibly hope for is to close the gap, which isn't likely to bring them back to being number one.

Likewise, leading the way in new products has turned out to be a fool's mission for most companies in mature industries like packaged goods. The reason? Fewer than ten new products a year are successful, despite expenditures of literally tens of millions of dollars by the major companies.

Finally, superior service can be an illusory and impractical goal for many large retailers. It simply takes more management and discipline than they can muster to bring so many outlets up to a higher-than-average level of service and keep them there.

The moral here is that your strategic vision has to be grounded in a deep understanding of the competitive dynamics of your business. You have to know the industry and your competitors cold. You have to know how you stack up on every performance dimension. (The way Ford did before it was able to close the gap on some 300 product features on which it lagged Japanese competitors.) And you have to be hardheaded about using this knowledge to position your company to gain a competitive edge. Are you big enough? Technically strong enough? Good enough at marketing? In short, you must be practical—not go after a pie in the sky.

Hasbro, a $1.5 billion (and growing) toy company, has a strategic vision that works. Unlike most of its competitors, Hasbro doesn't focus on inventing new blockbuster toys. Its management will take blockbusters if they come along, of course. But the company doesn't spend the bulk of its product development dollars on such long-odds bets. Instead, it centers its efforts on staples—toy lines like G.I. Joe, Transformers, games, and preschool basics that can be extended and renewed each year.

Another fine example is Crown Cork & Seal, one of America's best-performing companies for more than 30 years despite its five-star terrible business—tin cans. How did Crown do it, especially when it was number four in a mature business dominated by two giants (American Can and Continental Can), where size and scale appear to be essential? Simple. Crown focused its efforts on growth segments (beverages), on being the lowest-cost producer in each local area (instead of nationally), on growing in lesser developed countries (too small for the biggies to worry about), and on taking over the profitable, residual business left open as Continental and American diversified out of cans.

Both Hasbro and Crown Cork & Seal are tightly focused; they don't try to be all things to all customers. And because their directions are so clearly set, their creative people can channel their efforts toward things that will work against competitors in their particular businesses. Strategic focus works—in real life, not just in articles about strategy.

——— LOOK HARD AT WHAT'S ALREADY GOING ON

How do you find good, concrete ideas? Brainstorming is one approach, but I've never found that very helpful except when nobody in the group knows much and nobody cares whether the output is realistic. No, I firmly believe the best backdrop for spurring innovation is knowledge—knowing your business cold. Good ideas most often flow from the process of taking a hard look at your customers, your competitors, and your business all at once. So in looking for ways to innovate, I'd concentrate on:

- What's already working in the marketplace that you can improve on and expand.
- How you can segment your markets differently and gain a competitive advantage in the process.
- How your business system compares with your competitor's.

Looking hard at what's already working in the marketplace is the tactic that's likely to produce the quickest results. I call this robbing a few gas stations so that you don't starve to death while you're planning the perfect crime.

Lots of companies think that the only good innovations are the ones they develop themselves, not the ideas they get from smaller competitors—the familiar not-invented-here syndrome. In my experience, the opposite is usually true. Normally, outside ideas are useful simply because your competitors are already doing your market research for you. They're proving what customers want in the marketplace, where it counts.

I've found that good ideas come from all over—conventional competitors, regionals, small companies, even international competitors in Europe and Japan. So it may not surprise you to learn that most of PepsiCo's major strategic successes are ideas we borrowed from the marketplace—often from small regional or local competitors.

For example, Doritos, Tostitos, and Sabritos (whose combined sales total roughly $1 billion) were products developed by three small chippers on the West Coast. The idea for pan pizza (a $500 million business for Wichita-based Pizza Hut) originated with several local pizzerias in Chicago. And the pattern for Wilson 1200 golf clubs (the most successful new club line ever) came from a small golf clubber in Arizona.

In each case, PepsiCo spotted a promising new idea, improved on it, and then out-executed the competition. To some people this sounds like copycatting. To me it amounts to finding out what's already working with consumers, improving on the idea, and then getting more out of it. You can decide how much this idea appeals to you. But in PepsiCo it led to $2 billion to $3 billion worth of successful innovations without which the company's growth would have been a lot less dynamic.

Next, I'd look at how to create new segments or markets for the kinds of products you can produce. It sounds simple, but, believe me, it takes a lot of creativity and skill to: segment a market beyond simple demographics (which rarely ever produce meaningful edges); ferret out what each group of consumers really wants (as opposed to what it says it wants); and actually create distinctive product performance features (despite the technological and operational problems you usually encounter).

Several examples will illustrate what I have in mind. At Taco Bell, the biggest Mexican fast-food restaurant chain in the United States, top management found that working women were avoiding its outlets like the plague. Women felt Taco Bell's food was "too heavy," "too spicy." So the company developed a taco salad served in a light flour tortilla and seasoned very mildly. That salad increased per-store sales more than 20%, with 70% of the sales coming from women—mostly new customers. It also added about $100 million to Taco Bell's sales in its first full year.

It sounds simple, I'm sure: pick out a big segment you're not reaching, find out what consumers don't like about existing products, and develop a product to serve them better. But it took Taco Bell nearly two years to get the idea, develop it in R&D, test market several versions of the salad, and finally launch the winner nationally.

Another example, much more familiar, is what the Japanese have done in the camera business. They decided there was a segment of camera users who couldn't afford German top-of-the-line models but wanted vastly better pictures than those they could get from their existing Kodaks or Polaroids. Camera technology has been around for a long time, and the Japanese just hammered away at improving it until they succeeded in making superior 35mm cameras at a price people could afford. In the process, they created and now dominate a new (and huge) segment that no one else had seen.

Finally, there's Budget Gourmet, a four-year-old company you may never have heard of. Its management developed a very profitable $300 million business from scratch in a field—frozen foods—characterized by enormous price pressures, undistinguished products, little innovation, and low returns. Its founder's strategic vision was to offer working families high-quality-recipe products intended for microwave ovens and aimed at the low end of the market. So the company started out by developing a process to make and sell a line of entrees for $1.69, which gave it a good price advantage. But unlike other low-priced lines, Budget Gourmet's products were comparable to the over-$2 competition. And it backed up the product with first-class packaging, promotion, and advertising (the kind its low-end competitors didn't think of investing in). The result—a remarkable success in an extremely competitive field previously dominated by three of America's largest, most successful food companies. It's a terrific example of how segmentation and strategic focus interact. And like most good ideas it looks obvious—once you see how it works.

As these examples show, successful segmentors are very clear about what they're trying to do: offer their customers better value than their competitors do. This usually takes one of three forms: lower prices, better performing products, or better features for certain uses (a niche). Unless you can beat your competitors on one of these three dimensions, your innovation probably won't be a big success. The key idea, of course, is that you're trying to outperform the competition on a specific performance dimension and scale, not with vague platitudes. And successful innovators don't give up until customers reassure them that they've done just that.

The third place to look for good innovative ideas is in your business system. Beyond its products, every company has a business system by which it goes to market. That system is the whole flow of activities starting with product design and working its way through purchasing, production, MIS, distribution, customer sales, and product service. It will come as no surprise that these systems differ from one competitor to another, even in the same industry. And in almost every case, each competitor's system has particular strengths and vulnerabilities that can provide a fruitful focus for your innovative energies.

The underlying concept here is that a distinctive system can give you a big competitive edge for all your products because it will help you leverage their inherent consumer appeals in ways your competitors find hard to match. And once you understand how your business's system works at each step—both in terms of the marketplace and comparative system costs—it's surprising how often you'll uncover weak spots in a competitor's system or potential strengths in your own.

The number of Pizza Hut outlets (4,500), for example, dwarfs that of its nearest competitor (about 500). Scale like that is no guarantee of success. But it means that only the Pizza Hut system can market pizza products on a national basis virtually overnight—and thereby preempt local competition.

At one time, the biggest marketing problem Pizza Hut faced was lunch. Compared with McDonald's, its restaurants had virtually no lunchtime sales, and neither did any of its pizza competitors. The reason, of course, is that it takes 20 minutes to cook a pizza from scratch in a traditional pizza oven, and most people won't spend that long at lunchtime waiting to be served. By using a new, continuous-broiling technology adapted from the burger business, Pizza Hut developed a personal pan pizza that could be served in less than five minutes. It was quick, tasty, and moderately priced. And Pizza Hut rolled it out to all 4,500 stores and locked up the pizza-lunch business almost everywhere, almost overnight.

A good example of using a business system to maintain a competitive edge comes from the cookie business. P&G decided it could produce better cookies than Nabisco, the current leader. So the company came out with a great new cookie that tasted and looked better than Nabisco's Chips Ahoy!, the market leader. Duncan Hines cookies were the kind of superior product P&G has used to become the market leader in scores of products.

But its managers didn't count on the retaliatory strength of Nabisco's store-door distribution system and its intense desire to protect that big, profitable base system. Nabisco quickly matched P&G's cookie, in addition to expanding and improving its entire cookie line, and it used the leverage of its bigger system to get trade support and consumer impact. Despite the inherent superiority of P&G's single-product entry, it stood no chance against Nabisco's system strengths.

Virtually any part of your business system can be the basis for building competitive edges. Product technology has been a fruitful source of systemic advantages for Cray Research. Lincoln Electric's decades-long leadership is based largely on a systemic edge in production. Truly superior marketing and service have made Fidelity Investments' Fidelity Funds the dominant player in a business in which it was once an also-ran.

Naturally, in analyzing your business system and your competitors', you have to look at them dynamically since structural changes are usually at work altering what's required for success. When Philip Morris bought 7-Up, for example, its management knew they were entering an industry that historically had allowed smaller brands to prosper nicely. In fact, many Coke and Pepsi bottlers also handled 7-Up. But the battle between Coke and Pepsi was heating up, and as it became more intense, those cola competitors put tremendous pressure on their bottlers to launch new products, promote more often, and scramble for supermarket space. Both 7-Up and its new cola brand were left out in the cold. A one-time forgiving industry had become downright hostile.

───── GO FOR BROKE

Even the best concepts or strategies tend to develop incrementally. They rarely ever work the first time out or unfold just as they were planned.

In fact, the original concept or its execution usually gets changed considerably before it's ready to be implemented broadly. Pizza Hut's pan pizza, for instance, went through four or five different iterations. So even after you spot a promising segment and develop a product to serve it, you've usually still got at least one major hurdle to jump before you can capitalize on your new idea.

Tab initially flopped as a diet cola because consumers couldn't tell the difference between Tab with 1 calorie and Diet Pepsi, which then had 100. Then Coke figured out that it could dramatize the difference by surrounding a bathing beauty with 100 empty Tab bottles. Armed with that insight, it flooded the TV screen with ads and backed them up in stores with displays, signs, and samples. It was frightening to see how quickly that one idea, which sounds pretty small, changed the competitive dynamics.

To take another example, the Wilson Sting was developed to sell for half the price of the Prince graphite tennis racket. But very few high-end consumers believed they could get the same quality for $125 as Prince provided for $250, even though it was true. Fortunately, an alert marketing person at Wilson then uncovered a new segment for the Sting—people who were buying metal rackets because they couldn't afford graphite. Sting's pitch became "a graphite racket for the same price as steel," and that positioning made it a major success.

Once an idea or concept is properly developed, it seems logical to assume that any sensible company would throw the book at it to make it a success. Yet I've found that reality is often quite different. Looking back, most of the new-product mistakes I've seen grew from the company's failure to back up the innovation with enough resources—not from overspending.

Several factors explain this phenomenon. First and most important, many people fail to recognize that their competitors will retaliate—especially if their innovation takes customers away. People get so captivated by their own product that they plan new launches implicitly assuming there will be no significant competitive response. Almost inevitably, that turns out to be a poor assumption.

Second, people try to stretch their resources to finance too many projects at once because the prospect of four or five successes instead of one or two is so attractive. But new products generally involve considerable front-end investment and lots of management attention. So in a world in which money, people, and programs are necessarily limited, this usually means that none of the projects gets enough sustained support and effort to ensure its success. The only way around it is to be disciplined enough to say "next year" to most of the good ideas available.

Finally, people are often in such a hurry to get into the market with a new product that they neglect to think through all the things needed to launch it properly. These include programs to get adequate retailer support, advertising to generate high customer awareness, and above all, trial-inducing devices to entice consumers to pick the new product instead of the one they're already using. One or more of these essentials often goes by the boards.

In contrast, the big winners make careful plans to throw everything needed at new products to ensure their success—money, people, programs in every functional area. They don't just allocate resources, they marshal them, and then they execute like the Russian hockey team or the Boston Celtics. They've learned that doing it right the first time is lots more effective (and usually far less costly) than doing the job on a shoestring and then scrambling to fix things when what happens doesn't meet expectations. They also know they're never going to have the first-blood advantage again, and that the best way to preempt or block out competition is to do it right the first time.

I'm a firm believer in developing innovations as fast as you can do each one properly, which includes stopping to be sure you've got everything needed to generate a big success and then going to war to make the idea a winner. Sounds so obvious, you wonder why so many companies fail to do either of these pieces properly.

To sum up quickly, I believe there are five steps you can take to make your company more dynamic and innovative. Create a corporate environment that puts constant pressure on everyone to beat your specific competitors at innovation. Structure your organization so that you promote innovation instead of thwarting it. Develop a realistic strategic focus to channel your innovative efforts. Know where to look for good ideas and how to use your business system to leverage them once they're found. Throw the book at good ideas once you've developed them fully.

It all sounds simple because, of course, it is. Simple but not easy, since each innovation is a constant challenge from beginning to end. Yet innovation is a challenge you have to meet because that's what builds market leadership and competitive momentum. That's the bottom line. And that's why it's worth the extra effort to become an innovative company.

──── DISCUSSION QUESTIONS

1. Why is it so difficult to be consistently innovative?
2. What aspects of an organization are most important for promoting successful innovation?
3. Which models of innovation articulated by the author seem easiest to execute, and which seem most difficult?

Discovery-Driven Planning   28

RITA GUNTHER MCGRATH and IAN C. MACMILLAN

Established companies frequently stumble when they step outside the boundaries of their existing business. The assumptions and standard operating procedures that allow them to operate efficiently on their "home turf" can become liabilities in a new undertaking.

The authors describe a process for unearthing the implicit assumptions and testing them in a series of "experiments" before freezing a strategy that may prove to be fatally flawed.

Business lore is full of stories about smart companies that incur huge losses when they enter unknown territory—new alliances, new markets, new products, new technologies. The Walt Disney Company's 1992 foray into Europe with its theme park had accumulated losses of more than $1 billion by 1994. Zapmail, a fax product, cost Federal Express Corporation $600 million before it was dropped. Polaroid lost $200 million when it ventured into instant movies. Why do such efforts often defeat even experienced, smart companies? One obvious answer is that strategic ventures are inherently risky: The probability of failure simply comes with the territory. But many failures could be prevented or their cost contained if senior managers approached innovative ventures with the right planning and control tools.

Discovery-driven planning is a practical tool that acknowledges the difference between planning for a new venture and planning for a more conventional line of business. Conventional planning operates on the premise that managers can extrapolate future results from a well-understood and predictable platform of past experience. One expects predictions to be accurate because they are based on solid knowledge rather than on assumptions. In platform-based planning, a venture's deviations from plan are a bad thing.

The platform-based approach may make sense for ongoing businesses, but it is sheer folly when applied to new ventures. By definition, new

Harvard Business Review, July–August 1995. Copyright © 1995 by the President and Fellows of Harvard College, all rights reserved.

The authors wish to thank Shiuchi Matsuda of Waseda University's Entrepreneurial Research Unit for providing case material on Kao's floppy disk venture.

ventures call for a company to envision what is unknown, uncertain, and not yet obvious to the competition. The safe, reliable, predictable knowledge of the well-understood business has not yet emerged. Instead, managers must make do with assumptions about the possible futures on which new businesses are based. New ventures are undertaken with a high ratio of assumption to knowledge. With ongoing businesses, one expects the ratio to be the exact opposite. Because assumptions about the unknown generally turn out to be wrong, new ventures inevitably experience deviations—often huge ones—from their original planned targets. Indeed, new ventures frequently require fundamental redirection.

Rather than trying to force start-ups into the planning methodologies for existing predictable and well-understood businesses, discovery-driven planning acknowledges that at the start of a new venture, little is known and much is assumed. When platform-based planning is used, assumptions underlying a plan are treated as facts—givens to be baked into the plan—rather than as best-guess estimates to be tested and questioned. Companies then forge ahead on the basis of those buried assumptions. In contrast, discovery-driven planning systematically converts assumptions into knowledge as a strategic venture unfolds. When new data are uncovered, they are incorporated into the evolving plan. The real potential of the venture is discovered as it develops—hence the term discovery-driven planning. The approach imposes disciplines different from, but no less precise than, the disciplines used in conventional planning.

——— EURO DISNEY AND THE PLATFORM-BASED APPROACH

Even the best companies can run into serious trouble if they don't recognize the assumptions buried in their plans. The Walt Disney Company, a 49% owner of Euro Disney (now called Disneyland Paris), is known as an astute manager of theme parks. Its success has not been confined to the United States: Tokyo Disneyland has been a financial and public relations success almost from its opening in 1983. Euro Disney is another story, however. By 1993, attendance approached 1 million visitors each month, making the park Europe's most popular paid tourist destination. Then why did it lose so much money?

In planning Euro Disney in 1986, Disney made projections that drew on its experience from its other parks. The company expected half of the revenue to come from admissions, the other half from hotels, food, and merchandise. Although by 1993, Euro Disney had succeeded in reaching its target of 11 million admissions, to do so it had been forced to drop adult ticket prices drastically. The average spending per visit was far below plan and added to the red ink.

The point is not to play Monday-morning quarterback with Disney's experience but to demonstrate an approach that could have revealed flawed assumptions and mitigated the resulting losses. The discipline of systematically identifying key assumptions would have highlighted the business plan's vulnerabilities. Let us look at each source of revenue in turn.

Admissions Price In Japan and the United States, Disney found its price by raising it over time, letting early visitors go back home and talk up the park to their neighbors. But the planners of Euro Disney assumed that they could hit their target number of visitors even if they started out with an admission price of more than $40 per adult. A major recession in Europe and the determination of the French government to keep the franc strong exacerbated the problem and led to low attendance. Although companies cannot control macroeconomic events, they can highlight and test their pricing assumptions. Euro Disney's prices were very high compared with those of other theme attractions in Europe, such as the aqua palaces, which charged low entry fees and allowed visitors to build their own menus by paying for each attraction individually. By 1993, Euro Disney not only had been forced to make a sharp price reduction to secure its target visitors, it had also lost the benefits of early-stage word of mouth. The talking-up phenomenon is especially important in Europe, as Disney could have gauged from the way word of mouth had benefited Club Med.

Hotel Accommodations Based on its experience in other markets, Disney assumed that people would stay an average of four days in the park's five hotels. The average stay in 1993 was only two days. Had the assumption been highlighted, it might have been challenged: Since Euro Disney opened with only 15 rides, compared with 45 at Disney World, people could do them all in a single day.

Food Park visitors in the United States and Japan "graze" all day. At Euro Disney, the buried assumption was that Europeans would do the same. Euro Disney's restaurants, therefore, were designed for all-day streams of grazers. When floods of visitors tried to follow the European custom of dining at noon, Disney was unable to seat them. Angry visitors left the park to eat, and they conveyed their anger to their friends and neighbors back home.

Merchandise Although Disney did forecast lower sales per visitor in Europe than in the United States and Japan, the company assumed that Europeans would buy a similar mix of cloth goods and print items. Instead, Euro Disney fell short of plan when visitors bought a far smaller proportion of high-margin items such as T-shirts and hats than expected. Disney could have tested the buried assumption before forecasting sales: Disney's retail stores in European cities sell many fewer of the high-margin cloth items and far more of the low-margin print items.

Disney is not alone. Other companies have paid a significant price for pursuing platform-based ventures built on implicit assumptions that turn out to be faulty. Such ventures are usually undertaken without careful up-front identification and validation of those assumptions, which often are unconscious. We have repeatedly observed that the following four planning errors are characteristic of this approach:

- *Companies don't have hard data but, once a few key decisions are made, proceed as though their assumptions were facts.* Euro Disney's implicit assumptions regarding the way visitors would use hotels and restaurants are good examples.
- *Companies have all the hard data they need to check assumptions but fail to see the implications.* After making assumptions based on a subset of the available data, they proceed without ever testing those assumptions. Federal Express based Zapmail on the assumption that there would be a substantial demand for four-hour delivery of documents faxed from FedEx center to FedEx center. What went unchallenged was the implicit assumption that customers would not be able to afford their own fax machines before long. If that assumption had been unearthed, FedEx would have been more likely to take into account the plunging prices and increasing sales of fax machines for the office and, later, for the home.
- *Companies possess all the data necessary to determine that a real opportunity exists but make implicit and inappropriate assumptions about their ability to implement their plan.* Exxon lost $200 million on its office automation business by implicitly assuming that it could build a direct sales and service support capability to compete head-to-head with IBM and Xerox.
- *Companies start off with the right data, but they implicitly assume a static environment and thus fail to notice until too late that a key variable has changed.* Polaroid lost $200 million from Polavision instant movies by assuming that a three-minute cassette costing $7 would compete effectively against a half-hour videotape costing $20. Polaroid implicitly assumed that the high cost of equipment for videotaping and playback would remain prohibitive for most consumers. Meanwhile, companies pursuing those technologies steadily drove down costs. (See *Exhibit 1*, "Some Dangerous Implicit Assumptions.")

—— DISCOVERY-DRIVEN PLANNING: AN ILLUSTRATIVE CASE

Discovery-driven planning offers a systematic way to uncover the dangerous implicit assumptions that would otherwise slip unnoticed and thus unchallenged into the plan. The process imposes a strict discipline that is captured in four related documents: a *reverse income statement*, which models the basic economics of the business; *pro forma operations specs*, which lay out

EXHIBIT 1
Some Dangerous Implicit Assumptions

1. Customers will buy our product because we think it's a good product.
2. Customers will buy our product because it's technically superior.
3. Customers will agree with our perception that the product is "great."
4. Customers run no risk in buying from us instead of continuing to buy from their past suppliers.
5. The product will sell itself.
6. Distributors are desperate to stock and service the product.
7. We can develop the product on time and on budget.
8. We will have no trouble attracting the right staff.
9. Competitors will respond rationally.
10. We can insulate our product from competition.
11. We will be able to hold down prices while gaining share rapidly.
12. The rest of our company will gladly support our strategy and provide help as needed.

the operations needed to run the business; a *key assumptions checklist*, which is used to ensure that assumptions are checked; and a *milestone planning chart*, which specifies the assumptions to be tested at each project milestone. As the venture unfolds and new data are uncovered, each of the documents is updated.

To demonstrate how this tool works, we will apply it retrospectively to Kao Corporation's highly successful entry into the floppy disk business in 1988. We deliberately draw on no inside information about Kao or its planning process but instead use the kind of limited public knowledge that often is all that any company would have at the start of a new venture.

The Company   Japan's Kao Corporation was a successful supplier of surfactants to the magnetic-media (floppy disk) industry. In 1981, the company began to study the potential for becoming a player in floppy disks by leveraging the surfactant technology it had developed in its core businesses, soap and cosmetics. Kao's managers realized that they had learned enough process knowledge from their floppy disk customers to supplement their own skills in surface chemistry. They believed they could produce floppy disks at a much lower cost and higher quality than other companies offered at that time. Kao's surfactant competencies were particularly valuable because the quality of the floppy disk's surface is crucial for its reliability. For a company in a mature industry, the opportunity to move current product into a growth industry was highly attractive.

The Market   By the end of 1986, the demand for floppy disks was 500 million in the United States, 100 million in Europe, and 50 million in Japan, with growth estimated at 40% per year, compounded. This meant that by 1993, the global market would be approaching 3 billion disks, of which about a third would be in the original equipment manufacturer (OEM) market, namely such big-volume purchasers of disks as IBM, Apple, and Microsoft, which use disks to distribute their software. OEM industry prices were expected to be about 180 yen per disk by 1993. Quality and reliability have always been important product characteristics for OEMs such as software houses because defective disks have a devastating impact on customers' perceptions of the company's overall quality.

The Reverse Income Statement   Discovery-driven planning starts with the bottom line. For Kao, back when it began to consider its options, the question was whether the floppy disk venture had the potential to enhance the company's competitive position and financial performance significantly. If not, why should Kao incur the risk and uncertainty of a major strategic venture?

Here, we impose the first discipline, which is to plan the venture using a reverse income statement, which runs from the bottom line up. (See *Exhibit 2*, "First, Start with a Reverse Income Statement.") Instead of starting with estimates of revenues and working down the income statement to derive profits, we start with *required profits*. We then work our way up the profit and loss to determine how much revenue it will take to deliver the level of profits we require and how much cost can be allowed. The underlying philosophy is to impose revenue and cost disciplines by baking profitability into the plan at the outset: Required profits equal necessary revenues minus allowable costs.

At Kao in 1988, management might have started with these figures: net sales, about 500 billion yen; income before taxes, about 40 billion yen; and return on sales (ROS), 7.5%. Given such figures, how big must the floppy disk opportunity be to justify Kao's attention? Every company will set its own hurdles. We believe that a strategic venture should have the potential to enhance total profits by at least 10%. Moreover, to compensate for the increased risk, it should deliver greater profitability than reinvesting in the existing businesses would. Again, for purposes of illustration, assume that Kao demands a risk premium of 33% greater profitability. Since Kao's return on sales is 7.5%, it will require 10%.

If we use the Kao data, we find that the required profit for the floppy disk venture would be 4 billion yen (10% × 40 billion). To deliver 4 billion yen in profit with a 10% return on sales implies a business with 40 billion yen in sales.

Assuming that, despite its superior quality, Kao will have to price competitively to gain share as a new entrant, it should set a target price of 160 yen per disk. That translates into unit sales of 250 million disks (40 billion yen in sales divided by 160 yen per disk). By imposing these simple performance measures at the start (1988), we quickly establish both the scale and scope of the venture: Kao would need to capture 25% of the total world OEM market (25% of 1 billion disks) by 1993. Given what is known about the size

EXHIBIT 2
How Kao Might Have Tackled Its New Venture:
First, Start with a Reverse Income Statement*

Total Figures

Required profits to add 10% to total profits = 4 billion yen
Necessary revenues to deliver 10% sales margin = 40 billion yen
Allowable costs to deliver 10% sales margin = 36 billion yen

Per Unit Figures

Required unit sales at 160 yen per unit = 250 million units
Necessary percentage of world market share of OEM unit sales = 25%
Allowable costs per unit for 10% sales margin = 144 yen

* The goal here is to determine the value of success quickly. If the venture can't deliver significant returns, it may not be worth the risk.

of the market, Kao clearly must be prepared to compete globally from the outset, making major commitments not only to manufacturing but also to selling.

Continuing up the profit and loss, we next calculate allowable costs: If Kao is to capture 10% margin on a price of 160 yen per disk, the total cost to manufacture, sell, and distribute the disks worldwide cannot exceed 144 yen per disk. The reverse income statement makes clear immediately that the challenge for the floppy disk venture will be to keep a lid on expenses.

The Pro Forma Operations Specs and the Assumptions Checklist The second discipline in the process is to construct pro forma operations specs laying out the activities required to produce, sell, service, and deliver the product or service to the customer. Together, those activities comprise the venture's allowable costs. At first, the operations specs can be modeled on a simple spreadsheet without investing in more than a few telephone calls or on-line searches to get basic data. If an idea holds together, it is possible to identify and test underlying assumptions, constantly fleshing out and correcting the model in light of new information. When a company uses this cumulative approach, major flaws in the business concept soon become obvious, and poor concepts can be abandoned long before significant investments are made.

We believe it is essential to use industry standards for building a realistic picture of what the business has to look like to be competitive. Every industry has its own pressures—which determine normal rates of return in that industry—as well as standard performance measures such as asset-to-sales ratios, industry profit margins, plant utilization, and so on. In a globally competitive environment, no sane manager should expect to escape the competitive discipline that is captured and measured in industry standards. These standards are readily available from investment analysts and business information services. In countries with information sources that are less well developed than those in the United States, key industry parameters are still used by investment bankers and, more specifically, by those commercial bankers who specialize in loans to the particular industry. For those getting into a new industry, the best approach is to adapt standards from similar industries.

Note that we do not begin with an elaborate analysis of product or service attributes or an in-depth market study. That comes later. Initially, we are simply trying to capture the venture's embedded assumptions. The basic discipline is to spell out clearly and realistically where the venture will have to match existing industry standards and in what one or two places managers expect to excel and how they expect to do so.

Kao's managers in 1988 might have considered performance standards for the floppy disk industry. Because there would be no reason to believe that Kao could use standard production equipment any better than established competitors could, it would want to plan to match industry performance on measures relating to equipment use. Kao would ascertain, for example, that the effective production capacity per line was 25 disks per minute in the industry; and the effective life of production equipment was three years. Kao's advantage was in surface chemistry and surface physics, which could improve quality and reduce the cost of materials, thus improving margins. When Kao planned its materials cost, it would want to turn that advantage into a specific challenge for manufacturing: Beat the industry standard for materials cost by 25%. The formal framing of operational challenges is an important step in discovery-driven planning. In our experience, people who are good in design and operations can be galvanized by clearly articulated challenges. That was the case at Canon, for example, when Keizo Yamaji challenged the engineers to develop a personal copier that required minimal service and cost less than $1,000, and the Canon engineers rose to the occasion.

A company can test the initial assumptions against experience with similar situations, the advice of experts in the industry, or published information sources. The point is not to demand the highest degree of accuracy but to build a reasonable model of the economics and logistics of the venture and to assess the order of magnitude of the challenges. Later, the company can analyze where the plan is most sensitive to wrong assumptions and do more formal checks. Consultants to the industry—bankers, suppliers, potential customers, and distributors—often can provide low-cost and surprisingly accurate information.

The company must build a picture of the activities that are needed to carry out the business and the costs. Hence in the pro forma operations specs, we ask how many orders are needed to deliver 250 million units in sales; then how many sales calls it will take to secure those orders; then how many salespeople it will take to make the sales calls, given the fact that they are selling to a global OEM market; then how much it will cost in sales-force compensation. (See *Exhibit 3*, "Second, Lay Out All the Activities Needed to Run the Venture.") Each assumption can be checked, at first somewhat

EXHIBIT 3
How Kao Might Have Tackled Its New Venture:
Second, Lay Out All the Activities Needed to Run the Venture

Pro Forma Operations Specs

1. Sales

Required disk sales = 250 million disks
Average order size (Assumption 8) = 10,000 disks
Orders required (250 million/10,000) = 25,000

Number of calls to make a sale (Assumption 9) = 4
Sales calls required (4 × 25,000) = 100,000 per year

Calls per day per salesperson (Assumption 10) = 2
Annual salesperson days (100,000/2) = 50,000
Sales force for 250 days per year (Assumption 11)
  50,000 salesperson days/250 = 200 people

Salary per salesperson = 10 million yen (Assumption 12)
  Total sales-force salary cost (10 million yen × 200) = 2 billion yen

2. Manufacturing

Quality specification of disk surface: 50% fewer flaws than best competitor (Assumption 15)

Annual production capacity per line = 25 per minute
  × 1440 minutes per day × 348 days (Assumption 16) = 12.5 million disks
Production lines needed (250 million disks/12.5 million disks per line) = 20 lines

Production staffing (30 per line [Assumption 17] × 20 lines) = 600 workers

Salary per worker = 5 million yen (Assumption 18)
Total production salaries (600 × 5 million yen) = 3 billion yen

Materials costs per disk = 20 yen (Assumption 19)
Total materials cost (20 × 250 million disks) = 5 billion yen
Packaging per 10 disks = 40 yen (Assumption 20)
Total packaging costs (40 × 25 million packages) = 1 billion yen

3. Shipping

Containers needed per order of 10,000 disks = 1 (Assumption 13)
Shipping cost per container = 100,000 yen (Assumption 14)
Total shipping costs (25,000 orders × 100,000 yen) = 2.5 billion yen

4. Equipment and Depreciation

Fixed asset investment to sales = 1:1 (Assumption 5) = 40 billion yen
Equipoment life = 3 years (Assumption 7)
Annual depreciation (40 billion yen/3 years) = 13.3 billion yen

---

roughly and then with increasing precision. Readers might disagree with our first-cut estimates. That is fine—so might Kao Corporation. Reasonable disagreement triggers discussion and, perhaps, adjustments to the spreadsheet. The evolving document is doing its job if it becomes the catalyst for such discussion.

The third discipline of discovery-driven planning is to compile an assumption checklist to ensure that each assumption is flagged, discussed, and checked as the venture unfolds. (See *Exhibit 4*, "Third, Track All Assumptions.")

The entire process is looped back into a revised reverse income statement, in which one can see if the entire business proposition hangs together.

EXHIBIT 4
How Kao Might Have Tackled Its New Venture:
Third, Track All Assumptions

Assumption	Measurement
1. Profit margin	10% of sales
2. Revenues	40 billion yen
3. Unit selling price	160 yen
4. 1993 world OEM market	1 billion disks
5. Fixed asset investment to sales	1:1
6. Effective production capacity per line	25 disks per minute
7. Effective life of equipment	3 years
8. Average OEM order size	10,000 disks
9. Sales calls per OEM order	4 calls per order
10. Sales calls per salesperson per day	2 calls per day
11. Selling days per year	250 days
12. Annual salesperson's salary	10 million yen
13. Containers required per order	1 container
14. Shipping cost per container	100,000 yen
15. Quality level needed to get customers to switch: % fewer flaws per disk than top competitor	50%
16. Production days per year	348 days
17. Workers per production line per day (10 per line for 3 shifts)	30 per line
18. Annual manufacturing worker's salary	5 million yen
19. Materials costs per disk	20 yen
20. Packaging costs per 10 disks	40 yen
21. Allowable administration costs (See revised reverse income statement in *Exhibit 5*)	9.2 billion yen

(See *Exhibit 5*, "Fourth, Revise the Reverse Income Statement.") If it doesn't, the process must be repeated until the performance requirements and industry standards can be met; otherwise, the venture should be scrapped.

Milestone Planning   Conventional planning approaches tend to focus managers on meeting plan, usually an impossible goal for a venture rife with assumptions. It is also counterproductive—insistence on meeting plan actually prevents learning. Managers can formally plan to learn by using milestone events to test assumptions.

Milestone planning is by now a familiar technique for monitoring the progress of new ventures. The basic idea, as described by Zenas Block and Ian C. MacMillan in the book *Corporate Venturing* (Harvard Business School Press, 1993), is to postpone major commitments of resources until the evidence from the previous milestone event signals that the risk of taking the next step

EXHIBIT 5
How Kao Might Have Tackled Its New Venture:
Fourth, Revise the Reverse Income Statement*

Required margin	10% return on sales
Required profit	4 billion yen
Necessary revenues	40 billion yen
Allowable costs	36 billion yen
Sales-force salaries	2.0 billion yen
Manufacturing salaries	3.0 billion yen
Disk materials	5.0 billion yen
Packaging	1.0 billion yen
Shipping	2.5 billion yen
Depreciation	13.3 billion yen
Allowable administration and overhead costs	9.2 billion yen (Assumption 21)
Per-unit figures	
Selling price	160 yen
Total costs	144 yen
Disk materials costs	20 yen

* Now, with better data, one can see if the entire business proposition hangs together.

is justified. What we are proposing here is an expanded use of the tool to support the discipline of transforming assumptions into knowledge.

Going back to what Kao might have been thinking in 1988, recall that the floppy disk venture would require a 40-billion-yen investment in fixed assets alone. Before investing such a large sum, Kao would certainly have wanted to find ways to test the most critical assumptions underlying the three major challenges of the venture:

- capturing 25% global market share with a 20-yen-per-disk discount and superior quality;
- maintaining at least the same asset productivity as the average competitor and producing a floppy disk at 90% of the estimated total costs of existing competitors; and
- using superior raw materials and applied surface technology to produce superior-quality disks for 20 yen per unit instead of the industry standard of 27 yen per unit.

For serious challenges like those, it may be worth spending resources to create specific milestone events to test the assumptions before launching a 40-billion-yen venture. For instance, Kao might subcontract prototype production so that sophisticated OEM customers could conduct technical tests on the proposed disk. If the prototypes survive the tests, then, rather than rest on the assumption that it can capture significant business at the target price, Kao might subcontract production of a large batch of floppy disks for resale to customers. It could thus test the appetite of the OEM market for price discounting from a newcomer.

Similarly, for testing its ability to cope with the second and third

EXHIBIT 6
How Kao Might Have Tackled Its New Venture:
Finally, Plan to Test Assumptions at Milestones

Milestone Event—Namely, the Completion of:	*Assumptions to Be Tested*
1. Initial data search and preliminary feasibility analysis	4: 1993 world OEM market 8: Average OEM order size 9: Sales calls per OEM order 10: Sales calls per salesperson per day 11: Salespeople needed for 250 selling days per year 12: Annual salesperson's salary 13: Containers required per order 14: Shipping cost per container 16: Production days per year 18: Annual manufacturing worker's salary
2. Prototype batches produced	15: Quality to get customers to switch 19: Materials costs per disk
3. Technical testing by customers	3: Unit selling price 15: Quality to get customers to switch
4. Subcontracted production	19: Materials costs per disk
5. Sales of subcontracted production	1: Profit margin 2: Revenues 3: Unit selling price 8: Average OEM order size 9: Sales calls per OEM order 10: Sales calls per salesperson per day 12: Annual salesperson's salary 15: Quality to get customers to switch
6. Purchase of an existing plant	5: Fixed asset investment to sales 7: Effective life of equipment
7. Pilot production at purchased plant	6: Effective production capacity per line 16: Production days per year 17: Workers per production line per day 18: Annual manufacturing worker's salary 19: Materials costs per disk 20: Packaging costs per 10 disks
8. Competitor reaction	1: Profit margin 2: Revenues 3: Unit selling price
9. Product redesign	19: Materials costs per disk 20: Packaging costs per 10 disks
10. Major repricing analysis	1: Profit margin 2: Revenues 3: Unit selling price 4: 1993 world OEM market
11. Plant redesign	5: Fixed asset investment to sales 6: Effective production capacity per line 19: Materials costs per disk

challenges once the Kao prototype has been developed, it might be worth-while to buy out a small existing floppy disk manufacturer and apply the technology in an established plant rather than try to start up a greenfield operation. Once Kao can demonstrate its ability to produce disks at the required quality and cost in the small plant, it can move ahead with its own full-scale plants.

Deliberate assumption-testing milestones are depicted in *Exhibit 6,* "Finally, Plan to Test Assumptions at Milestones," which also shows some of the other typical milestones that occur in most major ventures. The assumptions that should be tested at each milestone are listed with appropriate numbers from the assumption checklist.

In practice, it is wise to designate a *keeper of the assumptions*—someone whose formal task is to ensure that assumptions are checked and updated as each milestone is reached and that the revised assumptions are incorporated into successive iterations of the four discovery-driven planning documents. Without a specific person dedicated to following up, it is highly unlikely that individuals, up to their armpits in project pressures, will be able to coordinate the updating independently.

Discovery-driven planning is a powerful tool for any significant strategic undertaking that is fraught with uncertainty—new-product or market ventures, technology development, joint ventures, strategic alliances, even major systems redevelopment. Unlike platform-based planning, in which much is known, discovery-driven planning forces managers to articulate what they don't know, and it forces a discipline for learning. As a planning tool, it thus raises the visibility of the make-or-break uncertainties common to new ventures and helps managers address them at the lowest possible cost.

▬▬ DISCUSSION QUESTIONS

1. What is the role of what the authors term a "reverse income statement"?
2. How would you actually track reality against the assumptions that are surfaced?
3. How do you integrate "discoveries" into the planning process?

29 Disruptive Technologies: Catching the Wave

JOSEPH L. BOWER and CLAYTON M. CHRISTENSEN

History is replete with examples of companies that were unable to make their core technologies shift with the market, and lost sales revenues and market share as a result. The authors argue that this fate derives from staying too close to customers, and listening to their current needs, which are in turn, based on current market conditions.

Disruptive technologies—by definition—produce a different package of customer benefits, and may well be valued more by new customers in different markets. This can lead established companies to ignore these opportunities, relinquishing the market to upstart new entrants, who use the market as a toehold, and go on to become powerful, across the board competitors.

One of the most consistent patterns in business is the failure of leading companies to stay at the top of their industries when technologies or markets change. Goodyear and Firestone entered the radial-tire market quite late. Xerox let Canon create the small-copier market. Bucyrus-Erie allowed Caterpillar and Deere to take over the mechanical excavator market. Sears gave way to Wal-Mart.

The pattern of failure has been especially striking in the computer industry. IBM dominated the mainframe market but missed by years the emergence of minicomputers, which were technologically much simpler than mainframes. Digital Equipment dominated the minicomputer market with innovations like its VAX architecture but missed the personal-computer market almost completely. Apple Computer led the world of personal computing and established the standard for user-friendly computing but lagged five years behind the leaders in bringing its portable computer to market.

Why is it that companies like these invest aggressively—and successfully—in the technologies necessary to retain their current customers but then fail to make certain other technological investments that customers of the

Harvard Business Review, January–February 1995. Copyright © 1994 by the President and Fellows of Harvard College, all rights reserved.

future will demand? Undoubtedly, bureaucracy, arrogance, tired executive blood, poor planning, and short-term investment horizons have all played a role. But a more fundamental reason lies at the heart of the paradox: leading companies succumb to one of the most popular, and valuable, management dogmas. They stay close to their customers.

Although most managers like to think they are in control, customers wield extraordinary power in directing a company's investments. Before managers decide to launch a technology, develop a product, build a plant, or establish new channels of distribution, they must look to their customers first: Do their customers want it? How big will the market be? Will the investment be profitable? The more astutely managers ask and answer these questions, the more completely their investments will be aligned with the needs of their customers.

This is the way a well-managed company should operate. Right? But what happens when customers reject a new technology, product concept, or way of doing business because it does *not* address their needs as effectively as a company's current approach? The large photocopying centers that represented the core of Xerox's customer base at first had no use for small, slow tabletop copiers. The excavation contractors that had relied on Bucyrus-Erie's big-bucket steam- and diesel-powered cable shovels didn't want hydraulic excavators because initially they were small and weak. IBM's large commercial, government, and industrial customers saw no immediate use for minicomputers. In each instance, companies listened to their customers, gave them the product performance they were looking for, and, in the end, were hurt by the very technologies their customers led them to ignore.

We have seen this pattern repeatedly in an ongoing study of leading companies in a variety of industries that have confronted technological change. The research shows that most well-managed, established companies are consistently ahead of their industries in developing and commercializing new technologies—from incremental improvements to radically new approaches—as long as those technologies address the next-generation performance needs of their customers. However, these same companies are rarely in the forefront of commercializing new technologies that don't initially meet the needs of mainstream customers and appeal only to small or emerging markets.

Using the rational, analytical investment processes that most well-managed companies have developed, it is nearly impossible to build a cogent case for diverting resources from known customer needs in established markets to markets and customers that seem insignificant or do not yet exist. After all, meeting the needs of established customers and fending off competitors takes all the resources a company has, and then some. In well-managed companies, the processes used to identify customers' needs, forecast technological trends, assess profitability, allocate resources across competing proposals for investment, and take new products to market are focused—for all the

right reasons—on current customers and markets. These processes are designed to weed out proposed products and technologies that do *not* address
customers' needs.

In fact, the processes and incentives that companies use to keep
focused on their main customers work so well that they blind those companies
to important new technologies in emerging markets. Many companies have
learned the hard way the perils of ignoring new technologies that do not
initially meet the needs of mainstream customers. For example, although
personal computers did not meet the requirements of mainstream minicomputer users in the early 1980s, the computing power of the desktop machines
improved at a much faster rate than minicomputer users' *demands* for computing power did. As a result, personal computers caught up with the computing needs of many of the customers of Wang, Prime, Nixdorf, Data General, and Digital Equipment. Today they are performance-competitive with
minicomputers in many applications. For the minicomputer makers, keeping
close to mainstream customers and ignoring what were initially low-perfor-
mance desktop technologies used by seemingly insignificant customers in
emerging markets was a rational decision—but one that proved disastrous.

The technological changes that damage established companies are
usually not radically new or difficult from a *technological* point of view. They
do, however, have two important characteristics: First, they typically present
a different package of performance attributes—ones that, at least at the outset,
are not valued by existing customers. Second, the performance attributes that
existing customers do value improve at such a rapid rate that the new technology can later invade those established markets. Only at this point will
mainstream customers want the technology. Unfortunately for the established
suppliers, by then it is often too late: the pioneers of the new technology
dominate the market.

It follows, then, that senior executives must first be able to spot the
technologies that seem to fall into this category. Next, to commercialize and
develop the new technologies, managers must protect them from the processes and incentives that are geared to serving established customers. And
the only way to protect them is to create organizations that are completely
independent from the mainstream business.

No industry demonstrates the danger of staying too close to customers
more dramatically than the hard-disk-drive industry. Between 1976 and 1992,
disk-drive performance improved at a stunning rate: the physical size of a
100-megabyte (MB) system shrank from 5,400 to 8 cubic inches, and the cost
per MB fell from $560 to $5. Technological change, of course, drove these
breathtaking achievements. About half of the improvement came from a host
of radical advances that were critical to continued improvements in disk-drive
performance; the other half came from incremental advances.

The pattern in the disk-drive industry has been repeated in many other industries: the leading, established companies have consistently led the industry in developing and adopting new technologies that their customers demanded—even when those technologies required completely different technological competencies and manufacturing capabilities from the ones the companies had. In spite of this aggressive technological posture, no single disk-drive manufacturer has been able to dominate the industry for more than a few years. A series of companies have entered the business and risen to prominence, only to be toppled by newcomers who pursued technologies that at first did not meet the needs of mainstream customers. As a result, not one of the independent disk-drive companies that existed in 1976 survives today.

To explain the differences in the impact of certain kinds of technological innovations on a given industry, the concept of *performance trajectories*—the rate at which the performance of a product has improved, and is expected to improve, over time—can be helpful. Almost every industry has a critical performance trajectory. In mechanical excavators, the critical trajectory is the annual improvement in cubic yards of earth moved per minute. In photocopiers, an important performance trajectory is improvement in number of copies per minute. In disk drives, one crucial measure of performance is storage capacity, which has advanced 50% each year on average for a given size of drive.

Different types of technological innovations affect performance trajectories in different ways. On the one hand, *sustaining* technologies tend to maintain a rate of improvement; that is, they give customers something more or better in the attributes they already value. For example, thin-film components in disk drives, which replaced conventional ferrite heads and oxide disks between 1982 and 1990, enabled information to be recorded more densely on disks. Engineers had been pushing the limits of the performance they could wring from ferrite heads and oxide disks, but the drives employing these technologies seemed to have reached the natural limits of an S curve. At that point, new thin-film technologies emerged that restored—or sustained—the historical trajectory of performance improvement.

On the other hand, *disruptive* technologies introduce a very different package of attributes from the one mainstream customers historically value, and they often perform far worse along one or two dimensions that are particularly important to those customers. As a rule, mainstream customers are unwilling to use a disruptive product in applications they know and understand. At first, then, disruptive technologies tend to be used and valued only in new markets or new applications; in fact, they generally make possible the emergence of new markets. For example, Sony's early transistor radios sacrificed sound fidelity but created a market for portable radios by offering a new and different package of attributes—small size, light weight, and portability.

In the history of the hard-disk-drive industry, the leaders stumbled at each point of disruptive technological change: when the diameter of disk drives shrank from the original 14 inches to 8 inches, then to 5.25 inches, and finally to 3.5 inches. Each of these new architectures initially offered the market substantially less storage capacity than the typical user in the established market required. For example, the 8-inch drive offered 20 MB when it was introduced, while the primary market for disk drives at that time—mainframes—required 200 MB on average. Not surprisingly, the leading computer manufacturers rejected the 8-inch architecture at first. As a result, their suppliers, whose mainstream products consisted of 14-inch drives with more than 200 MB of capacity, did not pursue the disruptive products aggressively. The pattern was repeated when the 5.25-inch and 3.5-inch drives emerged: established computer makers rejected the drives as inadequate, and, in turn, their disk-drive suppliers ignored them as well.

But while they offered less storage capacity, the disruptive architectures created other important attributes—internal power supplies and smaller size (8-inch drives); still smaller size and low-cost stepper motors (5.25-inch drives); and ruggedness, light weight, and low-power consumption (3.5-inch drives). From the late 1970s to the mid-1980s, the availability of the three drives made possible the development of new markets for minicomputers, desktop PCs, and portable computers, respectively.

Although the smaller drives represented disruptive technological change, each was technologically straightforward. In fact, there were engineers at many leading companies who championed the new technologies and built working prototypes with bootlegged resources before management gave a formal go-ahead. Still, the leading companies could not move the products through their organizations and into the market in a timely way. Each time a disruptive technology emerged, between one-half and two-thirds of the established manufacturers failed to introduce models employing the new architecture—in stark contrast to their timely launches of critical sustaining technologies. Those companies that finally did launch new models typically lagged behind entrant companies by two years—eons in an industry whose products' life cycles are often two years. Three waves of entrant companies led these revolutions; they first captured the new markets and then dethroned the leading companies in the mainstream markets.

How could technologies that were initially inferior and useful only to new markets eventually threaten leading companies in established markets? Once the disruptive architectures became established in their new markets, sustaining innovations raised each architecture's performance along steep trajectories—so steep that the performance available from each architecture soon satisfied the needs of customers in the established markets. For example, the 5.25-inch drive, whose initial 5 MB of capacity in 1980 was only a fraction of the capacity that the minicomputer market needed, became fully performance-competitive in the minicomputer market by 1986 and in the mainframe market by 1991. (See *Exhibit 1*, "How Disk-Drive Performance Met Market Needs.")

A company's revenue and cost structures play a critical role in the way it evaluates proposed technological innovations. Generally, disruptive tech-

EXHIBIT 1
How Disk-Drive Performance Met Market Needs

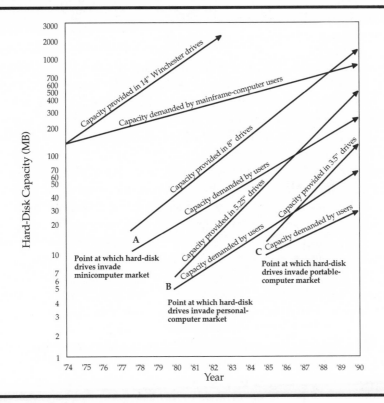

nologies look financially unattractive to established companies. The potential revenues from the discernible markets are small, and it is often difficult to project how big the markets for the technology will be over the long term. As a result, managers typically conclude that the technology cannot make a meaningful contribution to corporate growth and, therefore, that it is not worth the management effort required to develop it. In addition, established companies have often installed higher cost structures to serve sustaining technologies than those required by disruptive technologies. As a result, managers typically see themselves as having two choices when deciding whether to pursue disruptive technologies. One is to go *downmarket* and accept the lower profit margins of the emerging markets that the disruptive technologies will initially serve. The other is to go *upmarket* with sustaining technologies and enter market segments whose profit margins are alluringly high. (For example, the margins of IBM's mainframes are still higher than those of PCs). Any rational resource-allocation process in companies serving established markets will choose going upmarket rather than going down.

Managers of companies that have championed disruptive technologies in emerging markets look at the world quite differently. Without the high cost structures of their established counterparts, these companies find the emerging markets appealing. Once the companies have secured a foothold in the markets and improved the performance of their technologies, the established markets above them, served by high-cost suppliers, look appetizing. When they do attack, the entrant companies find the established players to be easy and unprepared opponents because the opponents have been looking upmarket themselves, discounting the threat from below.

It is tempting to stop at this point and conclude that a valuable lesson has been learned: managers can avoid missing the next wave by paying careful attention to potentially disruptive technologies that do *not* meet current customers' needs. But recognizing the pattern and figuring out how to break it are two different things. Although entrants invaded established markets with new technologies three times in succession, none of the established leaders in the disk-drive industry seemed to learn from the experiences of those that fell before them. Management myopia or lack of foresight cannot explain these failures. The problem is that managers keep doing what has worked in the past: serving the rapidly growing needs of their current customers. The processes that successful, well-managed companies have developed to allocate resources among proposed investments are *incapable* of funneling resources into programs that current customers explicitly don't want and whose profit margins seem unattractive.

Managing the development of new technology is tightly linked to a company's investment processes. Most strategic proposals—to add capacity or to develop new products or processes—take shape at the lower levels of organizations in engineering groups or project teams. Companies then use analytical planning and budgeting systems to select from among the candidates competing for funds. Proposals to create new businesses in emerging markets are particularly challenging to assess because they depend on notoriously unreliable estimates of market size. Because managers are evaluated on their ability to place the right bets, it is not surprising that in well-managed companies, mid- and top-level managers back projects in which the market seems assured. By staying close to lead customers, as they have been trained to do, managers focus resources on fulfilling the requirements of those reliable customers that can be served profitably. Risk is reduced—and careers are safeguarded—by giving known customers what they want.

Seagate Technology's experience illustrates the consequences of relying on such resource-allocation processes to evaluate disruptive technologies. By almost any measure, Seagate, based in Scotts Valley, California, was one of the most successful and aggressively managed companies in the history of the microelectronics industry: from its inception in 1980, Seagate's revenues had grown to more than $700 million by 1986. It had pioneered 5.25-inch hard-disk drives and was the main supplier of them to IBM and IBM-compatible personal-computer manufacturers. The company was the leading manufacturer of 5.25-inch drives at the time the disruptive 3.5-inch drives emerged in the mid-1980s.

Engineers at Seagate were the second in the industry to develop working prototypes of 3.5-inch drives. By early 1985, they had made more than 80 such models with a low level of company funding. The engineers forwarded the new models to key marketing executives, and the trade press reported that Seagate was actively developing 3.5-inch drives. But Seagate's principal customers—IBM and other manufacturers of AT-class personal computers—showed no interest in the new drives. They wanted to incorporate 40-MB and 60-MB drives in their next-generation models, and Seagate's early 3.5-inch prototypes packed only 10 MB. In response, Seagate's marketing executives lowered their sales forecasts for the new disk drives.

Manufacturing and financial executives at the company pointed out another drawback to the 3.5-inch drives. According to their analysis, the new drives would never be competitive with the 5.25-inch architecture on a cost-per-megabyte basis—an important metric that Seagate's customers used to evaluate disk drives. Given Seagate's cost structure, margins on the higher-capacity 5.25-inch models therefore promised to be much higher than those on the smaller products.

Senior managers quite rationally decided that the 3.5-inch drive would not provide the sales volume and profit margins that Seagate needed from a new product. A former Seagate marketing executive recalled, "We needed a new model that could become the next ST412 [a 5.25-inch drive generating more than $300 million in annual sales, which was nearing the end of its life cycle]. At the time, the entire market for 3.5-inch drives was less than $50 million. The 3.5-inch drive just didn't fit the bill—for sales or profits."

The shelving of the 3.5-inch drive was *not* a signal that Seagate was complacent about innovation. Seagate subsequently introduced new models of 5.25-inch drives at an accelerated rate and, in so doing, introduced an impressive array of sustaining technological improvements, even though introducing them rendered a significant portion of its manufacturing capacity obsolete.

While Seagate's attention was glued to the personal-computer market, former employees of Seagate and other 5.25-inch drive makers, who had become frustrated by their employers' delays in launching 3.5-inch drives, founded a new company, Conner Peripherals. Conner focused on selling its 3.5-inch drives to companies in emerging markets for portable computers and small-footprint desktop products (PCs that take up a smaller amount of space on a desk). Conner's primary customer was Compaq Computer, a customer that Seagate had never served. Seagate's own prosperity, coupled with Conner's focus on customers who valued different disk-drive attributes (ruggedness, physical volume, and weight), minimized the threat Seagate saw in Conner and its 3.5-inch drives.

From its beachhead in the emerging market for portable computers, however, Conner improved the storage capacity of its drives by 50% per year.

By the end of 1987, 3.5-inch drives packed the capacity demanded in the mainstream personal-computer market. At this point, Seagate executives took their company's 3.5-inch drive off the shelf, introducing it to the market as a *defensive* response to the attack of entrant companies like Conner and Quantum Corporation, the other pioneer of 3.5-inch drives. But it was too late.

By then, Seagate faced strong competition. For a while, the company was able to defend its existing market by selling 3.5-inch drives to its established customer base—manufacturers and resellers of full-size personal computers. In fact, a large proportion of its 3.5-inch products continued to be shipped in frames that enabled its customers to mount the drives in computers designed to accommodate 5.25-inch drives. But, in the end, Seagate could only struggle to become a second-tier supplier in the new portable-computer market.

In contrast, Conner and Quantum built a dominant position in the new portable-computer market and then used their scale and experience base in designing and manufacturing 3.5-inch products to drive Seagate from the personal-computer market. In their 1994 fiscal years, the combined revenues of Conner and Quantum exceeded $5 billion.

Seagate's poor timing typifies the responses of many established companies to the emergence of disruptive technologies. Seagate was willing to enter the market for 3.5-inch drives only when it had become large enough to satisfy the company's financial requirements—that is, only when existing customers wanted the new technology. Seagate has survived through its savvy acquisition of Control Data Corporation's disk-drive business in 1990. With CDC's technology base and Seagate's volume-manufacturing expertise, the company has become a powerful player in the business of supplying large-capacity drives for high-end computers. Nonetheless, Seagate has been reduced to a shadow of its former self in the personal-computer market.

It should come as no surprise that few companies, when confronted with disruptive technologies, have been able to overcome the handicaps of size or success. But it can be done. There is a method to spotting and cultivating disruptive technologies.

Determine Whether the Technology Is Disruptive or Sustaining. The first step is to decide which of the myriad technologies on the horizon are disruptive and, of those, which are real threats. Most companies have well-conceived processes for identifying and tracking the progress of potentially sustaining technologies, because they are important to serving and protecting current customers. But few have systematic processes in place to identify and track potentially disruptive technologies.

One approach to identifying disruptive technologies is to examine internal disagreements over the development of new products or technologies. Who supports the project and who doesn't? Marketing and financial managers, because of their managerial and financial incentives, will rarely support a disruptive technology. On the other hand, technical personnel with outstanding track records will often persist in arguing that a new market for the technology will emerge—even in the face of opposition from key customers and marketing and financial staff. Disagreement between the two groups often signals a disruptive technology that top-level managers should explore.

Define the Strategic Significance of the Disruptive Technology.   The next step is to ask the right people the right questions about the strategic importance of the disruptive technology. Disruptive technologies tend to stall early in strategic reviews because managers either ask the wrong questions or ask the wrong people the right questions. For example, established companies have regular procedures for asking mainstream customers—especially the important accounts where new ideas are actually tested—to assess the value of innovative products. Generally, these customers are selected because they are the ones striving the hardest to stay ahead of *their* competitors in pushing the performance of *their* products. Hence these customers are most likely to demand the highest performance from their suppliers. For this reason, lead customers are reliably accurate when it comes to assessing the potential of sustaining technologies, but they are reliably *in*accurate when it comes to assessing the potential of disruptive technologies. They are the wrong people to ask.

A simple graph plotting product performance as it is defined in mainstream markets on the vertical axis and time on the horizontal axis can help managers identify both the right questions and the right people to ask. First, draw a line depicting the level of performance and the trajectory of performance improvement that customers have historically enjoyed and are likely to expect in the future. Then locate the estimated initial performance level of the new technology. If the technology is disruptive, the point will lie far below the performance demanded by current customers. (See *Exhibit 2*, "How to Assess Disruptive Technologies.")

What is the likely slope of performance improvement of the disruptive technology compared with the slope of performance improvement demanded by existing markets? If knowledgeable technologists believe the new technology might progress faster than the market's demand for performance improvement, then that technology, which does not meet customers' needs today, may very well address them tomorrow. The new technology, therefore, is strategically critical.

Instead of taking this approach, most managers ask the wrong questions. They compare the anticipated rate of performance improvement of the new technology with that of the established technology. If the new technology has the potential to surpass the established one, the reasoning goes, they should get busy developing it.

Pretty simple. But this sort of comparison, while valid for sustaining technologies, misses the central strategic issue in assessing potentially disrup-

EXHIBIT 2
How to Assess Disruptive Technologies

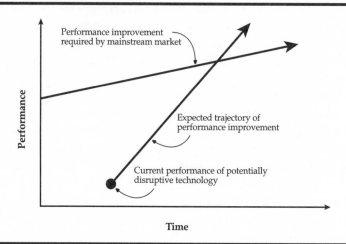

tive technologies. Many of the disruptive technologies we studied *never* surpassed the capability of the old technology. It is the trajectory of the disruptive technology compared with that of the *market* that is significant. For example, the reason the mainframe-computer market is shrinking is not that personal computers outperform mainframes but because personal computers networked with a file server meet the computing and data-storage needs of many organizations effectively. Mainframe-computer makers are reeling not because the performance of personal-computing technology surpassed the performance of mainframe *technology* but because it intersected with the performance demanded by the established *market*.

Consider the graph again. If technologists believe that the new technology will progress at the same rate as the market's demand for performance improvement, the disruptive technology may be slower to invade established markets. Recall that Seagate had targeted personal computing, where demand for hard-disk capacity per computer was growing at 30% per year. Because the capacity of 3.5-inch drives improved at a much faster rate, leading 3.5-inch-drive makers were able to force Seagate out of the market. However, two other 5.25-inch-drive makers, Maxtor and Micropolis, had targeted the engineering-workstation market, in which demand for hard-disk capacity was insatiable. In that market, the trajectory of capacity demanded was essentially parallel to the trajectory of capacity improvement that technologists could supply in the 3.5-inch architecture. As a result, entering the 3.5-inch-drive business was strategically less critical for those companies than it was for Seagate.

Locate the Initial Market for the Disruptive Technology.   Once managers have determined that a new technology is disruptive and strategically critical, the next step is to locate the initial markets for that technology. Market research, the tool that managers have traditionally relied on, is seldom helpful: at the point a company needs to make a strategic commitment to a disruptive technology, no concrete market exists. When Edwin Land asked Polaroid's market researchers to assess the potential sales of his new camera, they concluded that Polaroid would sell a mere 100,000 cameras over the product's lifetime; few people they interviewed could imagine the uses of instant photography.

Because disruptive technologies frequently signal the emergence of new markets or market segments, managers must *create* information about such markets—who the customers will be, which dimensions of product performance will matter most to which customers, what the right price points will be. Managers can create this kind of information only by experimenting rapidly, iteratively, and inexpensively with both the product and the market.

For established companies to undertake such experiments is very difficult. The resource-allocation processes that are critical to profitability and competitiveness will not—and should not—direct resources to markets in which sales will be relatively small. How, then, can an established company probe a market for a disruptive technology? Let start-ups—either ones the company funds or others with no connection to the company—conduct the experiments. Small, hungry organizations are good at placing economical bets, rolling with the punches, and agilely changing product and market strategies in response to feedback from initial forays into the market.

Consider Apple Computer in its start-up days. The company's original product, the Apple I, was a flop when it was launched in 1977. But Apple had not placed a huge bet on the product and had gotten at least *something* into the hands of early users quickly. The company learned a lot from the Apple I about the new technology and about what customers wanted and did not want. Just as important, a group of customers learned about what they did and did not want from personal computers. Armed with this information, Apple launched the Apple II quite successfully.

Many companies could have learned the same valuable lessons by watching Apple closely. In fact, some companies pursue an explicit strategy of being *second to invent*—allowing small pioneers to lead the way into uncharted market territory. For instance, IBM let Apple, Commodore, and Tandy define the personal computer. It then aggressively entered the market and built a considerable personal-computer business.

But IBM's relative success in entering a new market late is the exception, not the rule. All too often, successful companies hold the performance of small-market pioneers to the financial standards they apply to their own performance. In an attempt to ensure that they are using their resources well, companies explicitly or implicitly set relatively high thresholds for the size of the markets they should consider entering. This approach sentences them to making late entries into markets already filled with powerful players.

For example, when the 3.5-inch drive emerged, Seagate needed a $300-million-a-year product to replace its mature flagship 5.25-inch model, the ST412, and the 3.5-inch market wasn't large enough. Over the next two years, when the trade press asked when Seagate would introduce its 3.5-inch drive, company executives consistently responded that there was no market yet. There actually *was* a market, and it was growing rapidly. The signals that Seagate was picking up about the market, influenced as they were by customers who didn't want 3.5-inch drives, were misleading. When Seagate finally introduced its 3.5-inch drive in 1987, more than $750 million in 3.5-inch drives had already been sold. Information about the market's size had been widely available throughout the industry. But it wasn't compelling enough to shift the focus of Seagate's managers. They continued to look at the new market through the eyes of their current customers and in the context of their current financial structure.

The posture of today's leading disk-drive makers toward the newest disruptive technology, 1.8-inch drives, is eerily familiar. Each of the industry leaders has designed one or more models of the tiny drives, and the models are sitting on shelves. Their capacity is too low to be used in notebook computers, and no one yet knows where the initial market for 1.8-inch drives will be. Fax machines, printers, and automobile dashboard mapping systems are all candidates. "There just isn't a market," complained one industry executive. "We've got the product, and the sales force can take orders for it. But there are no orders because nobody needs it. It just sits there." This executive has not considered the fact that his sales force has no incentive to sell the 1.8-inch drives instead of the higher-margin products it sells to higher-volume customers. And while the 1.8-inch drive is sitting on the shelf at his company and others, last year more than $50 million worth of 1.8-inch drives were sold, almost all by start-ups. This year, the market will be an estimated $150 million.

To avoid allowing small, pioneering companies to dominate new markets, executives must personally monitor the available intelligence on the progress of pioneering companies through monthly meetings with technologists, academics, venture capitalists, and other nontraditional sources of information. They *cannot* rely on the company's traditional channels for gauging markets because those channels were not designed for that purpose.

Place Responsibility for Building a Disruptive-Technology Business in an Independent Organization.   The strategy of forming small teams into skunkworks projects to isolate them from the stifling demands of mainstream organizations is widely known but poorly understood. For example, isolating a team of engineers so that it can develop a radically new sustaining technology just because that technology is radically different is a fundamental misapplication of the skunk-works approach. Managing out of context is also unnecessary in the unusual event that a disruptive technology is more financially attractive than existing products. Consider Intel's transition from dynamic random access memory (DRAM) chips to microprocessors. Intel's early microprocessor business had a higher gross margin than that of its DRAM business; in other words, Intel's normal resource-allocation process naturally provided the new business with the resources it needed.[1]

Creating a separate organization is necessary only when the disruptive technology has a lower profit margin than the mainstream business and must serve the unique needs of a new set of customers. CDC, for example, successfully created a remote organization to commercialize its 5.25-inch drive. Through 1980, CDC was the dominant independent disk-drive supplier due to its expertise in making 14-inch drives for mainframe-computer makers. When the 8-inch drive emerged, CDC launched a late development effort, but its engineers were repeatedly pulled off the project to solve problems for the more profitable, higher-priority 14-inch projects targeted at the company's most important customers. As a result, CDC was three years late in launching its first 8-inch product and never captured more than 5% of that market.

When the 5.25-inch generation arrived, CDC decided that it would face the new challenge more strategically. The company assigned a small group of engineers and marketers in Oklahoma City, Oklahoma, far from the mainstream organization's customers, the task of developing and commercializing a competitive 5.25-inch product. "We needed to launch it in an environment in which everybody got excited about a $50,000 order," one executive recalled. "In Minneapolis, you needed a $1 million order to turn anyone's head." CDC never regained the 70% share it had once enjoyed in the market for mainframe disk drives, but its Oklahoma City operation secured a profitable 20% of the high-performance 5.25-inch market.

Had Apple created a similar organization to develop its Newton personal digital assistant (PDA), those who have pronounced it a flop might have deemed it a success. In launching the product, Apple made the mistake of acting as if it were dealing with an established market. Apple managers went into the PDA project assuming that it had to make a significant contribution to corporate growth. Accordingly, they researched customer desires exhaustively and then bet huge sums launching the Newton. Had Apple made a more modest technological and financial bet and entrusted the Newton to an organization the size that Apple itself was when it launched the Apple I, the outcome might have been different. The Newton might have been seen more broadly as a solid step forward in the quest to discover what customers really want. In fact, many more Newtons than Apple I models were sold within a year of their introduction.

Keep the Disruptive Organization Independent.   Established companies can only dominate emerging markets by creating small organizations of the sort CDC created in Oklahoma City. But what should they do when the emerging market becomes large and established?

---

1. Robert A. Burgelman, "Fading Memories: A Process Theory of Strategic Business Exit in Dynamic Environments," *Administrative Science Quarterly 39* (1994), pp. 24–56.

Most managers assume that once a spin-off has become commercially viable in a new market, it should be integrated into the mainstream organization. They reason that the fixed costs associated with engineering, manufacturing, sales, and distribution activities can be shared across a broader group of customers and products.

This approach might work with sustaining technologies; however, with disruptive technologies, folding the spin-off into the mainstream organization can be disastrous. When the independent and mainstream organizations are folded together in order to share resources, debilitating arguments inevitably arise over which groups get what resources and whether or when to cannibalize established products. In the history of the disk-drive industry, *every* company that has tried to manage mainstream and disruptive businesses within a single organization failed.

No matter the industry, a corporation consists of business units with finite life spans: the technological and market bases of any business will eventually disappear. Disruptive technologies are part of that cycle. Companies that understand this process can create new businesses to replace the ones that must inevitably die. To do so, companies must give managers of disruptive innovation free rein to realize the technology's full potential—even if it means ultimately killing the mainstream business. For the corporation to live, it must be willing to see business units die. If the corporation doesn't kill them off itself, competitors will.

The key to prospering at points of disruptive change is not simply to take more risks, invest for the long term, or fight bureaucracy. The key is to manage strategically important disruptive technologies in an organizational context where small orders create energy, where fast low-cost forays into ill-defined markets are possible, and where overhead is low enough to permit profit even in emerging markets.

Managers of established companies can master disruptive technologies with extraordinary success. But when they seek to develop and launch a disruptive technology that is rejected by important customers within the context of the mainstream business's financial demands, they fail—not because they make the wrong decisions, but because they make the right decisions for circumstances that are about to become history.

—— DISCUSSION QUESTIONS

1. What is the difference between a sustaining and a disruptive technology? As a manager, how do you tell the difference?
2. Why do companies often miss the opportunities presented by disruptive technologies?
3. How can companies improve the odds of successfully making the correct technology bets?

Managing for Creativity 30

TERESA M. AMABILE

Amabile reports on a large body of research focusing on the organizational stimulants and obstacles to creativity. She describes the settings most conducive to creativity, and the means available to managers to influence this environment in positive ways. In particular, certain extrinsic factors—such as time pressure and critical evaluation—seem to hamper the creative process. Others—such as freedom, diversity, and a challenging work environment—seem to positively promote creative thinking and results.

Management did not believe that there was a solution to the problem. That's why they assigned me. I was new in the field, and since they didn't believe the problem could be solved, they didn't want to waste their senior experience. As a consequence, I was left alone more than is normal. And, since I didn't know that the problem couldn't be solved, with this kind of freedom, I just went ahead and solved it.[1]

$\mathbf{A}$ll innovation begins with creative ideas. Successful implementation of new programs, new product introductions, or new services depends on a person or a team having a good idea—and developing that idea beyond its initial ill-formed state. In contrast to the popular view that creativity is an immutable personality characteristic, exhibited only in geniuses and immune to the situational surroundings, recent research has discovered that the social environment can influence both the level and the frequency of creative behavior. Because managers can exert a strong influence over the work environ-

---

Professor Teresa M. Amabile prepared this note for the second-year elective MBA course "Entrepreneurship, Creativity, and Organization." It is adapted from several articles written by Teresa M. Amabile (especially Amabile [1994a], Amabile [1994b], Amabile [in press] and Amabile, Conti, Coon, Lazenby, & Herron [in press]; see References section at the end of this note). This note should be used in conjunction with the notes, "Creativity and Innovation in Organizations," and "The Motivation for Creativity in Organizations." Copyright © 1996 by the President and Fellows of Harvard College. Harvard Business School case 396-271.

1. Quote from an interview reported in Amabile, T.M. & Gryskiewicz, S.S. (1988). Creative human resources in the R&D laboratory: How environment and personality impact innovation. In R.L. Kuhn (Ed.), *Handbook for creative and innovative managers*. New York: McGraw-Hill.

ment in an organization, it is particularly important to understand the role that the environment can play.

Of case studies describing business creativity, one of the most interesting is the report of Data General Corporation's invention of the Eagle super-mini computer in the late 1970s (Kidder, 1981). In that relatively small, entrepreneurial, high-tech company, an elite band of scientists and engineers was chosen to work in a highly protected environment under the management of a "maverick" engineer. This description of the reward system driving the team emphasizes the intrinsic value of the work itself:

> They didn't have to name the bigger game. Everyone who had been on the team for a while knew what it was called. It didn't involve stock options. Rasala and Alving and many of the team had long since decided that they would never see more than token rewards of a material sort. The bigger game was "pinball." . . . You win one game, you get to play another. You win with this machine, you get to build the next. Pinball was what counted.[2]

It is perhaps not surprising that one of the engineers on the Eagle project described their environment as "an atmosphere of pure work." This may very well describe the optimal environment for all forms of creativity.[3]

Academic studies in firms, utilizing a variety of methods, have specified some particularly important aspects of the work environment. For example, in their ground-breaking studies, Andrews and his colleagues (Andrews & Farris, 1967; Pelz & Andrews, 1966) used questionnaire instruments to assess influences on the creativity of R&D scientists. They discovered that, as illustrated in the opening quote, creativity seemed to be enhanced when supervisors allowed a good degree of autonomy in the day-to-day conduct of the work. This finding has been replicated in work by other researchers using different questionnaire and interview methods (e.g., Amabile & S. Gryskiewicz, 1987; Bailyn, 1985).

On the basis of her case studies of innovative companies, Kanter (1983) concluded that organizational innovation is supported by top management strategies oriented toward rational risk-taking, by participative, collaborative management, by open communication systems and constructive feedback, by recognition of creative work, and by access to resources for innovative problem-solving. Similarly, a critical-incident interview study focusing on both innovative and non-innovative situations highlighted the importance of organizational encouragement to innovate, sufficient resources, and managerial support (Delbecq & Mills, 1985). In a comparative study, a small engineering firm that is known to be highly innovative had a higher level of perceived management support for innovation than did a less innovative firm (Orpen, 1990). A search for possible mechanisms to explain this

2. Kidder, T. (1981). *The soul of a new machine.* Boston: Atlantic-Little, Brown.
3. See the HBS note, "The Motivation for Creativity in Organizations."

difference found that job satisfaction, work motivation and job involvement were higher among employees of the more innovative firm.

Effective, frequent and comfortable communication within the organization has also been shown to boost creativity. Two studies conducted to explore the impact of work relationships on the development of new ideas and innovations found that friendships among coworkers that were rated as important, credible, supportive and work-compatible were conducive to creating a climate for innovation (Albrecht & Hall, 1991). Other research has found that both communication among coworkers and free sharing of information by management are positively related to innovation (Monge & Cozzens, 1992).

Research has also revealed that innovation within organizations has additional benefits aside from the creation of new products, services, and processes. In a study of 288 bank employees, higher degrees of innovation within a group were associated with lower levels of turn-over among employees in the group (McFadden & Demetriou, 1993). In a similar study of 314 nurses, job satisfaction was strongly related to innovation (Robinson, Roth, & Brown, 1993).

ENVIRONMENTAL STIMULANTS AND OBSTACLES TO CREATIVITY

Recent research has attempted to comprehensively identify all work-environment factors that may have an impact on creativity. To this end, an exploratory interview study uncovered a broad set of influences on creativity and innovation in organizations (Amabile & Gryskiewicz, 1987). The participants in the study, 120 R&D scientists from over 20 corporations, were asked to describe an example of high creativity and an example of low creativity from their own work experiences (defining creativity as they saw fit, and considering only projects where creativity was possible and desirable). The researchers asked them to mention anything about the events that stood out in their minds—anything about the person or persons involved, and anything about the work environment. This critical incident technique, focusing the interviewees on factually reporting specific events, was designed to avoid the interjection of personal beliefs about creativity that might surface if the interviewees were simply asked what they thought was important for supporting or undermining creativity in research organizations.

A detailed analysis of the transcripts of these interviews revealed four major categories of projects. In decreasing order of frequency, they are: The development of a new product, the development of a new process, the improvement of an existing product, and the improvement of an existing process. The prominent features of these events also fell into four major categories. Rank-ordered by frequency, they are: qualities of environments that promote creativity, qualities of environments that inhibit creativity, qualities of problem-solvers that promote creativity, and qualities of problem-solvers that inhibit creativity. "Qualities of environments" are any factors outside of the people working on the project (including other people) that appeared to consistently influence creativity positively, as in the high creativity stories, or negatively, as in the low creativity stories. "Qualities of problem-solvers" are any factors of ability, personality, or mood within the people working on the project that seemed to consistently influence creativity either positively or negatively.

Two findings on personal qualities are particularly noteworthy. Among the unfavorable personal qualities that appeared in the low creativity stories, the most frequently mentioned was "unmotivated," and the fourth most frequently mentioned was "externally motivated." Among the favorable personal qualities that appeared in the high creativity stories, the second most frequently mentioned was "self-motivation." These results attest to the crucial role of intrinsic motivation in creativity—the motivation that people feel when they seek enjoyment, interest, satisfaction of curiosity, self-expression, or personal challenge in their work.[4]

Interestingly, environmental factors were mentioned much more frequently than personal qualities. This finding appeared in both the high and the low creativity stories, and did not depend on whether the interviewee was a central character (a "problem-solver") in the project. The prominence of the work environment in these interviews is an important finding. This does not mean that, in an absolute sense, environmental factors account for more of the variance in creative output than do the skills and characteristics of the people involved. Certainly, at a macroscopic level, personal factors such as general intelligence, experience in the field, and ability to think creatively are the major influences on output of creative ideas by R&D scientists. But, assuming that hiring practices at major corporations select scientists who exhibit relatively high levels of these personal qualities, the variance above this baseline may well be accounted for primarily by factors in the work environment.

In other words, social factors may be responsible for only a small part of the total variance in creative behavior, but they may account for the lion's share of the variance that managers can do anything about. It is almost always easier to change the social environment (or people's perception of it) than it is to change traits and abilities.

The content analyses of the interview transcripts revealed nine qualities of environments that promote creativity (termed "Environmental Stimulants"), and nine qualities of environments that inhibit creativity (termed "Environmental Obstacles"). They appear below, rank-ordered by the percentage of R&D scientists who mentioned them in their event descriptions. The

---

4. See the HBS note, "The Motivation for Creativity in Organizations."

same factors were found in later samples of bank and railroad employees, although there was some re-ordering in the rankings.

ENVIRONMENTAL STIMULANTS TO CREATIVITY

1. *Freedom:* freedom in deciding what to do or how to accomplish the task; a sense of control over one's own work and ideas.
2. *Good Project Management:* a manager who serves as a good role model, is enthusiastic, has good communication skills, protects the project team from outside distractions and interference, matches tasks to workers' skills and interests, and sets a clear direction without managing too tightly.
3. *Sufficient Resources:* access to necessary resources, including facilities, equipment, information, funds, and people.
4. *Encouragement:* management enthusiasm for new ideas, creating an atmosphere free of threatening evaluation.
5. *Various Organizational Characteristics:* a mechanism for considering new ideas, a corporate climate marked by cooperation and collaboration across levels and divisions, an atmosphere where innovation is prized and failure is not fatal.
6. *Recognition:* a general sense that creative work will receive appropriate feedback, recognition, and reward.
7. *Sufficient Time:* time to think creatively about the problem, to explore different perspectives rather than having to impose an already-determined approach.
8. *Challenge:* a sense of challenge arising from the intriguing nature of the problem itself or its importance to the organization (internalized by the individual as a personal sense of challenge).
9. *Pressure:* a sense of urgency that is internally generated from competition with outside organizations, or from a general desire to accomplish something important.

ENVIRONMENTAL OBSTACLES TO CREATIVITY

1. *Various Organizational Characteristics:* inappropriate reward systems in the organization; excessive red tape; a corporate climate marked by a lack of cooperation across divisions and levels; little regard for innovation in general.
2. *Constraint:* lack of freedom in deciding what to do or how to accomplish the task; a lack of a sense of control over one's own work and ideas.
3. *Organizational Disinterest:* a lack of organizational support, interest, or faith in a project; a perceived apathy toward any accomplishments coming from the project.
4. *Poor Project Management:* a manager who is unable to set clear direction, who has poor technical or communication skills, who

controls too tightly, or who allows distractions and fragmentation of the team's efforts.

5. *Evaluation:* inappropriate or inequitable evaluation and feedback systems; unrealistic expectations; an environment focused on criticism and external evaluation.
6. *Insufficient Resources:* a lack of appropriate facilities, equipment, materials, funds, or people.
7. *Time Pressure:* insufficient time to think creatively about the problem; too great a workload within a realistic time-frame; high frequency of "fire-fighting."
8. *Overemphasis on the Status Quo:* reluctance of managers or co-workers to change their way of doing things; an unwillingness to take risks.
9. *Competition:* interpersonal or intergroup competition within the organization, fostering a self-defensive attitude.

THE COMPONENTS OF ORGANIZATIONAL CREATIVITY AND INNOVATION

Current findings on managerial and work environment influences on creativity are summarized in a theoretical framework that includes three primary organizational components (Amabile, 1988a, 1988b).[5] These components contain several positive elements that can support creativity, and negative elements that can undermine creativity. Within normal ranges, higher degrees of the positive elements and lower degrees of the negative elements should be associated with greater levels of creativity.

ORGANIZATIONAL MOTIVATION TO INNOVATE

This component is made up of the basic orientation of the organization toward innovation, as well as supports for creativity and innovation throughout the organization. The orientation toward innovation must come, primarily, from the highest levels of management, but lower levels can also be important in communicating and interpreting that vision. On the basis of existing information (Amabile & S. Gryskiewicz, 1987; Cummings, 1965; Delbecq & Mills, 1985; Hage & Dewar, 1973; Havelock, 1970; Kimberley, 1981; Kanter, 1983; Orpen, 1990; Russell & Russell, 1992; Siegel & Kaemmerer, 1978), it appears that the most important elements of the innovation orientation are:

- a value placed on creativity and innovation in general
- an orientation toward risk (versus an orientation toward maintaining the status quo)

5. See the HBS note, "Creativity and Innovation in Organizations."

- a sense of pride in the organization's members and enthusiasm about what they are capable of doing
- an offensive strategy of taking the lead toward the future (versus a defensive strategy of simply wanting to protect the organization's past position).

Several researchers have investigated the primary organization-wide supports for innovation (Amabile & S. Gryskiewicz, 1987; Ashford & Cummings, 1985; Cummings, 1965; Ettlie, 1983; Kanter, 1983; Monge & Cozzens, 1992; Paolillo & Brown, 1978). These supports include:

- mechanisms for developing new ideas
- open, active communication of information and ideas
- reward and recognition for creative work
- fair evaluation of work—including work that might be perceived as a "failure."

Notably, the organizational motivation toward innovation includes the *absence* of several elements that can undermine creativity (Amabile & S. Gryskiewicz, 1987):

- political problems and "turf battles"
- destructive criticism and competition within the organization
- strict control by upper management
- an excess of formal structures and procedures.

RESOURCES

This component includes everything that the organization has available to aid work in the domain targeted for innovation. These resources include a wide array of elements (Amabile & S. Gryskiewicz, 1987; Delbecq & Mills, 1985):

- sufficient time for producing novel work in the domain
- people with necessary expertise
- funds allocated to this work domain
- material resources
- systems and processes for work in the domain
- relevant information
- the availability of training.

MANAGEMENT PRACTICES

This component includes management at both the level of the organization as a whole and the level of individual departments and projects. This component has received the most attention from researchers and theorists (e.g., Abbey & Dickson, 1983; Albrecht & Hall, 1991; Amabile & S. Gryskiewicz, 1987; Andrews & Farris, 1967; Bailyn, 1985; Ekvall, 1983; King & West, 1985; Monge & Cozzens, 1992; Pelz & Andrews, 1966; Paolillo & Brown, 1978; Siegel & Kaemmerer, 1978; West, 1986). This work suggests that creativity and innovation are fostered by:

- a considerable degree of freedom or autonomy in the conduct of one's work (as illustrated in the opening quote)
- a sense of positive challenge in the work, which can be fostered by appropriately matching individuals to work assignments, on the basis of both skills and interests (as illustrated by the Data General case)
- project supervision that is marked by:
  - an ability to clearly set overall project goals while allowing procedural autonomy
  - clear planning and feedback
  - good communication between the supervisor and the work group
  - enthusiastic support for the work of individuals as well as the entire group
- establishing effective work groups whose members:
  - represent a diversity of skills
  - trust and communicate well with each other
  - challenge each other's ideas in constructive ways
  - are mutually supportive
  - are committed to the work they are doing.

Although some of the elements in these three organizational components operate at very high levels in organizations (such as top management's orientation toward innovation), it is likely that, even within the same firm, different divisions, departments, and teams will perceive these high-level elements somewhat differently. In a large organization especially, each unit, department, or local work group can perceive "the company" through its own perceptual filters. These filters likely depend on complex interactions between characteristics and behaviors of the team, team members, or team supervisors, and actual differences in the ways higher-level managers and the organization at large view and treat the particular project.

──── ASSESSING THE CLIMATE FOR CREATIVITY

A questionnaire instrument called "KEYS: Assessing the Climate for Creativity" was created as a tool for providing managers with standardized, quantitative measures of work environment factors that might influence creativity positively or negatively within their firms, divisions, departments, or work teams (Amabile, 1987; 1990; 1995; formerly called "The Work Environment Inventory). This 78-item questionnaire asks employees to rate their perceptions of their current work environment. The 78 items are scored according to 10 scales; these scales are combinations of the Environmental Stimulants and Environmental Obstacles to Creativity identified in the critical-incidents interview study, as well as environmental influences on creativity identified in earlier empirical and theoretical research. Of the ten scales, six assess Environmental Stimulants, two assess Environmental Obstacles, and two assess work outcomes—Creativity and Productivity:

KEYS SCALES FOR ASSESSING ENVIRONMENTAL STIMULANTS TO CREATIVITY

1. *Organizational Encouragement* (15 items): an organizational culture that encourages creativity through the fair, constructive judgment of ideas, reward and recognition for creative work, mechanisms for developing new ideas, an active flow of ideas, and a shared vision of what the organization is trying to do. Sample item: "People are encouraged to solve problems creatively in this organization."
2. *Supervisory Encouragement* (11 items): a supervisor who serves as a good work model, sets goals appropriately, supports the work group, values individual contributions, and shows confidence in the work group. Sample item: "My supervisor serves as a good work model."
3. *Work Group Supports* (8 items): a diversely skilled work group in which people communicate well, are open to new ideas, constructively challenge each other's work, trust and help each other, and feel committed to the work they are doing. Sample item: "There is free and open communication within my work group."
4. *Freedom* (4 items): freedom in deciding what work to do or how to do it; a sense of control over one's work. Sample item: "I have the freedom to decide how I am going to carry out my projects."
5. *Sufficient Resources* (6 items): access to appropriate resources, including funds, materials, facilities, and information. Sample item: "Generally, I can get the resources I need for my work."
6. *Challenging Work* (5 items): a sense of having to work hard on challenging tasks and important projects. Sample item: "I feel challenged by the work I am currently doing."

KEYS SCALES FOR ASSESSING ENVIRONMENTAL OBSTACLES TO CREATIVITY

1. *Organizational Impediments* (12 items): an organizational culture that impedes creativity through internal political problems, harsh criticism of new ideas, destructive internal competition, an avoid-

ance of risk, and an overemphasis on the status quo. Sample item: "There are many political problems in this organization."
2. *Workload Pressure* (5 items): extreme time pressures, unrealistic expectations for productivity, and distractions from creative work. Sample item: "I have too much work to do in too little time."

KEYS SCALES FOR ASSESSING WORK OUTCOMES

- *Creativity* (6 items): a creative organization or unit, where a great deal of creativity is called for and where people believe they actually produce creative work. Sample item: "My area of this organization is innovative."
- *Productivity* (6 items): an efficient, effective, and productive organization or unit. Sample item: "My area of this organization is effective."

Two of the KEYS environment scales fit within the first component of organizational innovation, Organizational Motivation: Organizational Encouragement, which includes those elements that should ideally be present, and Organizational Impediments, which includes those elements that should be minimized if an organization's leaders are motivated toward innovation. KEYS contains two scales that capture elements of the second component, Resources: Workload Pressure (or time pressure), which should not be present in excess, and Sufficient Resources, which should be available for project work. Four KEYS environment scales tap various aspects of the third component, Management Practices: Freedom, Challenging Work, Supervisory Encouragement, and Work Group Supports.

The KEYS instrument has been used to address the central question concerning the work environment and creativity: Are there demonstrated differences in the creativity of the work that is produced in different work environments? A study addressing this question compared the work environments of projects rated as high in creativity by experts, with the work environments of projects rated as low in creativity by experts (Amabile, Conti, Coon, Lazenby, & Herron, in press). (For all projects, creativity was both possible and desirable.) Members of the project teams of both types of projects filled out KEYS to describe the work environment surrounding that project. The high creativity projects scored higher on the KEYS "Stimulant" scales, and the low creativity projects scored higher on the KEYS "Obstacle" scales. Moreover, as might be expected, the high-creativity projects were rated higher on both of the outcome scales, Creativity and Productivity.

Although all of the work environment dimensions did differ between the high and the low creativity projects, some dimensions appear to carry more weight than others. In this study, the most important environmental aspects for creativity and innovation (in terms of effect sizes) appeared to be Challenging Work, Organizational Encouragement of Creativity, Work Group

Supports, and Organizational Impediments to Creativity. The aspects that appeared to carry the least weight were Sufficient Resources and Workload Pressure. Moderate effect sizes were obtained by Freedom and Supervisory Encouragement of Creativity. It is important to emphasize that, although some aspects of the work environment appear to be more important in relationship to creativity, they all do play a role.

Another recent study demonstrated how the environment for creativity and innovation might change in an organization that is undergoing rapid transition (Amabile & Conti, 1995). As part of another study at this high-tech electronics company, KEYS data had previously been gathered on the work environment. Several months later, a major (30%) downsizing was announced by the chairman. In order to investigate possible changes in the work environment, additional KEYS data were collected at three points in time: half-way through the downsizing, just as the downsizing had ended, and four months after the end of the downsizing. The results showed a striking pattern. All of the Environmental Stimulants to Creativity declined during the downsizing, but appeared to rebound as the downsizing came to an end. Although Workload Pressure remained unchanged during the downsizing, the Environmental Obstacle of Organizational Impediments increased significantly and then declined as the downsizing ended. Importantly, both Creativity and Productivity (as assessed by KEYS) declined during the downsizing. However, only Productivity had rebounded to a significant degree by four months after the downsizing. Potentially longer-term effects on creativity were suggested by a decline in the per-capita invention disclosures logged by the company's engineers during the downsizing.

Additional questionnaire and interview data collected as part of the downsizing study allow some insight into mechanisms by which these negative effects might have occurred. Although the degree of actual downsizing experienced in an individual's department did not relate strongly to perceptions of the work environment or reported work behaviors, the degree of *anticipated* downsizing did strongly relate to such perceptions and behaviors. The most important aspects in determining perceptions and behaviors appeared to be the trustworthiness and frequency of the communication experienced, and the degree of stability in one's own work group.

——— THE DELICATE BALANCE IN MANAGING FOR CREATIVITY

In the study analyzing high-creativity stories and low-creativity stories from R&D managers (Amabile & Gryskiewicz, 1987), *intrinsic motivators* (such as challenging work and a sense of autonomy) were much more common in the high-creativity events than in the low creativity events. In fact, intrinsic motivators were notably absent in the low-creativity events, while certain *extrinsic motivators* (such as threatening evaluation or competition or extreme time pressure) were abundantly present.

Interestingly, however, certain other types of extrinsic motivators appeared frequently in the *high*-creativity stories; in fact, they were more common in those events. These motivators included reward and recognition for creative work, informative work evaluation, and a sense of urgency. These motivators, and the overall patterns of work environments that support or inhibit creativity, suggest four *balance factors* that appear to be important in the management of creativity in organizations. Striking the appropriate balance can contribute to the creativity of individuals and teams and, ultimately, to successful innovation across the organization. As used here, the term *balance* does not simply mean a moderate or medium level of a particular management tool; rather, it suggests a combination of different forms of the management tool.

GOAL-SETTING

As illustrated by the opening quote, goal-setting can be important to project creativity. It seems that creativity suffers when goals are too tight at the level of day-to-day operations, or too loose at the overall strategic level. Ideally, project managers will be able to find the balance point between these two extremes by blending loose control with tight control: Setting a clear overall strategic vision for the project, articulating the overall goal at the outset, but allowing the project team members relative autonomy in deciding how to meet that overall goal.

EVALUATION

The low creativity stories often had an abundance of evaluation pressure; people were concerned about overly critical reactions to their ideas. As one interviewee described it, "Part of the problem was that everyone was looking for a breakthrough. Expectations were too high. Upper management was very involved in the work and would constantly ask for results." On the other hand, there was an *absence* of evaluation and feedback in many of the low creativity stories. In these situations, the project team members believed that no one knew what they were doing, or cared. The crucial balance seems to involve a great deal of frequent, work-focused evaluation and feedback that is truly informative and constructive. Ideally, these evaluation sessions should involve peers (as well as supervisors) discussing the work. This pattern appeared frequently in the high-creativity stories: "We had a mutual respect for each other's abilities and a willingness to listen but not hang on someone's idea—to say, 'Well, that's a good idea, but here are some problems . . . '"

REWARD

In some of the low creativity stories, the interviewees felt that they material rewards were being dangled before them like carrots on a stick. This led them to feel externally controlled and, quite likely, led to lower levels of creativity. Interestingly, however, many other low creativity stories were marked by an *absence* of reward or recognition for good work. By contrast, in many of the high creativity stories, project team members felt that the rewards would be there if they did well—although the rewards rarely took the form of large monetary payments. "Part of the reward is having your manager listen to what you have done. Having access to your supervisors increases internal motivation, so managers should be available on an informal basis." "It was good to hear management say, 'You made a good discovery this month, and we are going to show it to top management, and you are going to be there to make the presentation.' The pat on the back, the recognition, felt good."

Apparently, creativity will be fostered most strongly when employees know that rewards and recognition will follow from good, creative efforts—without being told constantly about exactly which rewards will follow from which outcomes. Moreover, it is important that the rewards either provide important information about the employees' competence and the value of their work, or enable them to do something important that they really want to do—or both (Amabile, 1993).

PRESSURE

Various forms of external pressure appeared in the low creativity stories, primarily time pressure and competitive pressure. "There was pressure to get the product produced quickly. It was a long-range product, but this is a short-range company." "We had two groups trying to achieve the same thing. This fostered competition. It became a win-lose situation, and we all ended up losing." Surprisingly, however, such pressures also appeared in the high-creativity stories; and a complete absence of urgency sometimes marked the low creativity stories. The seeming paradox is intriguing.

It seems that both the meaning (or source) of the pressure and the level of pressure make a difference. Most often, time pressure and competitive pressure in the low creativity stories were perceived as arbitrary; no one knew of any particular reason why this project had to be completed in only two months, or of any purpose to having three teams in direct win-lose competition with each other on the same project. In the high creativity stories, the pressure usually arose from a realistic sense of urgency; the organization or the society at large desperately needed a solution to the problem.

Regardless of the meaning of the pressure, however, creativity will be impossible if the pressure is extreme. Beyond some limit, there will simply be no time to try any new, unusual approaches.

───── MANAGING THE UNMANAGEABLE

Because, by its very nature, creativity is something different from what has been done before, managers cannot direct creativity by telling employees exactly what they should do to produce a novel and useful result. In this sense, creativity is unmanageable. However, although it may not be possible to directly manage creativity, research has shown that it is possible to *manage for* creativity. Leaders and firms of the future that are able to successfully maintain continuous innovation will be those that can foster work environments that stimulate creativity, eliminate work environment elements that undermine creativity, and dynamically achieve the optimal balance of work environment factors for each unit, each team, and each individual.

None of this is simple or straightforward. Although research has revealed much, managing for creativity will, for the foreseeable future, remain as much an art as a science.

───── BIBLIOGRAPHY

Abbey, A. & Dickson, J. W. (1983). R&D work climate and innovation in semiconductors. *Academy of Management Journal, 26,* pp. 362–368.

Albrecht, T. L. & Hall, (1991). Facilitating talk about new ideas: The role of personal relationships in organizational innovation. *Communication Monographs, 58,* pp. 273–288.

Amabile, T.M. (1987). *The Work Environment Inventory, version 3.* Unpublished instrument, Center for Creative Leadership, Greensboro, NC.

Amabile, T.M. (1988a). A model of creativity and innovation in organizations. In B. M. Staw and L. L. Cummings (Eds.), *Research in organizational behavior* (Vol. 10), pp. 123–167. Greenwich, CT: JAI Press.

Amabile, T.M. (1988b). From individual creativity to organizational innovation. In K. Gronhaug & G. Kaufmann (Eds.), *Innovation: A crossdisciplinary perspective.* Oslo: Norwegian University Press.

Amabile, T. M. (1990). *The Work Environment Inventory, version 4.* Unpublished instrument, Center for Creative Leadership, Greensboro, NC.

Amabile, T. M. (1993). Motivational synergy: Toward new conceptualizations of intrinsic and extrinsic motivation in the workplace. *Human Resource Management Review,* 3, pp. 185–201.

Amabile, T. M. (1994a). The "atmosphere of pure work": Creativity in R&D. Chapter in W. R. Shadish & S. Fuller (Eds.), *The social psychology of science.* New York: Guilford Press.

Amabile, T. M. (1994b). The delicate balance in managing for creativity. *R&D Innovator*, August 1994.

Amabile, T. M. (1995). *KEYS: Assessing the Climate for Creativity*. Greensboro, NC: Center for Creative Leadership.

Amabile, T. M. (in press). Creativity in context: Update to the social psychology of creativity. Boulder, CO: Westview Press.

Amabile, T. M., Conti, R., Coon, H., Lazenby, J. & Herron, M. (in press). Assessing the work environment for creativity. *Academy of Management Journal*.

Amabile, T.M. & Gryskiewicz, S.S. (1987). *Creativity in the R&D laboratory*. Technical report number 30. Greensboro, N.C.: Center for creative leadership.

Amabile, T. M., & Gryskiewicz, S. S. (1988). Creative human resources in the R&D laboratory: How environment and personality impact innovation. In R. L. Kuhn (Ed.), *Handbook for creative and innovative managers*. New York: McGraw-Hill.

Andrews, F. M. & Farris, G. F. (1967). Supervisory practices and innovation in scientific teams. *Personnel Psychology*.

Ashford, S. J. & Cummings, L. L. (1985). Proactive feedback seeking: The instrumental use of the information environment. *Journal of Occupational Psychology*, 58, pp. 67–80.

Bailyn, L. (1985). Autonomy in the industrial R&D laboratory. *Human Resource Management*, 24, pp. 129–146.

Cummings, L. L. (1965). Organizational climates for creativity. *Journal of the Academy of Management*, 3, pp. 220–227.

Delbecq, A. L., & Mills, P. K. (1985). Managerial practices that enhance innovation. *Organizational Dynamics*, 14, pp. 24–34.

Ekvall, G. (1983). Climate, structure, and innovativeness of organizations: A theoretical framework and an experiment. Report 1, The Swedish Council for Management and Organizational Behaviour.

Ettlie, J. E. (1993). Organizational policy and innovation among suppliers to the food processing sector. *Academy of Management Journal*, 26, pp. 27–44.

Hage, J. & Dewar, R. (1973). Elite values versus organizational structure in predicting innovation. *Administrative Science*, 18, pp. 279–290.

Havelock, R. G. (1970). *Planning for innovation*. Ann Arbor: Center for Research on Utilization of Scientific Knowledge, University of Michigan.

Kanter, R. M. (1983). *The change masters*. New York: Simon and Schuster.

Kidder, T. (1981). *The soul of a new machine*. Boston: Atlantic-Little, Brown.

Kimberly, J. R. (1981). Managerial innovation. In P. C. Nystrom & W. H. Starbuck (Eds.), *Handbook of organizational design*. Oxford: Oxford University Press.

King, N. & West, M. A. (1985). *Experiences of innovation at work*. SAPU Memo No. 772, University of Sheffield, Sheffield, England.

McFadden, M. & Demetriou, E. (1993). The role of immediate work environment factors in the turnover process: A systemic intervention. *Applied Psychology: An International Review*, 42, pp. 97–115.

Monge, P. R., Cozzens, M. D., & Contractor, N. S. (1992). Communication and motivational predictors of the dynamics of organizational innovation. *Organizational Science*, 3, pp. 250–274.

Orpen, C. (1990). Measuring support for organizational innovation: A validity study. *Psychological Reports, 67*, pp. 417–418.

Paolillo, J. G., & Brown, W. B. (1978). How organizational factors affect R&D innovation. *Research Management, 21*, pp. 12–15.

Pelz, D. C., & Andrews, F. M. (1966). *Scientists in organizations.* New York: Wiley.

Robinson, S. E., Roth, S. L., & Brown, L. L. (1993). Morale and job satisfaction among nurses: What can hospitals do? *Journal of Applied Social Psychology, 23*, pp. 244–251.

Russell, R. D. & Russell, C. J. (1992). An examination of the effects of organizational norms, organizational structure, and environmental uncertainty on entrepreneurial strategy. *Journal of Management, 18*, pp. 839–856.

Siegel, S. M., & Kaemmerer, W. F. (1978). Measuring the perceived support for innovation in organizations. *Journal of Applied Psychology, 63*, pp. 553–562.

West, M. A. (1986). *Role innovation in the world of work.* Memo no. 670, MRC/ESRC Social and Applied Psychology Unit. University of Sheffield, Sheffield, England.

—— DISCUSSION QUESTIONS

1. What factors stimulate creativity?
2. What factors inhibit it?
3. What resources and management practices seem most conducive to the creative process?

The Business of Innovation: 31
An Interview with Paul Cook

WILLIAM TAYLOR

Economist Joseph Schumpeter described the entrepreneur as a person who "carries out new combinations"—a definition that gives the entrepreneur a wide arena in which to develop and implement new ideas. Paul Cook, founder and chief executive officer of Raychem Corporation, heads an organization consisting of 30 plants in 12 countries; it supplies technical products to industrial customers in fields ranging from aerospace to telecommunications. Since its founding in 1957, the company has created numerous propriety products based on core technologies.

As both pioneer and executive, Cook has had to translate his vision into action and to keep it fresh and alive. In this reading, Cook offers valuable lessons on corporate innovations: how to overcome such obstacles as creativity, size, the inevitable drudgery of new-product development, and even success itself; how to motivate people so that they will continue to innovate; and how to investigate markets and look at new products from the customer's point of view.

$\mathbf{P}$*aul M. Cook, founder and CEO of Raychem Corporation, is in the business of supplying technology-intensive products to industrial customers in sectors such as aerospace, automobiles, construction, telecommunications, and utilities. Raychem builds products that connect, seal, and protect signal-carrying cables for telephone networks and cable television systems. It manufactures much of the high-performance wire and cable that runs through military and commercial aircraft. Self-regulating heaters based on conductive polymers ensure the smooth flow of oil through pipelines in harsh environments and deice rails for mass transit systems.*

On a more basic level, though, Paul Cook is in the business of innovation. Since its founding in 1957, Raychem has pursued a consistent and ambitious strategy: to master a set of core technologies and create thousands of proprietary products based on those technologies. Today Raychem generates annual revenues of more than $1 billion through the sale of some 50,000 products. For most of those products, it is the

---

world's leading supplier; for many, it is the only supplier. Its products have found receptive customers around the world. Raychem generates more than 60% of its revenues outside the United States and has extensive manufacturing and research facilities in Western Europe and Asia. The company has more than 900 U.S. patents with some 300 pending, as well as some 3,000 foreign patents with another 9,000 pending.

Raychem's powerful market position has contributed to outstanding financial performance. It consistently earns gross margins of more than 50%, unrivaled in the industries in which it operates. The company has no net bank borrowings. Its price-earnings multiple of 30 is well above market averages.

Innovation at Raychem goes beyond products. Indeed, the company is in the process of reinventing itself. For its first 25 years, Raychem recorded explosive growth (averaging 25% per year) as it tapped the global potential of its products. Since the early 1980s, as growth slowed, Raychem has worked to develop new core technologies and to position itself in new markets. Its recently developed expertise in thin-film and liquid-crystal displays has created a role for the company in burgeoning markets for computer touchscreens and "switchable windows." A ten-year initiative in fiber optics has made Raychem, through its Raynet subsidiary, a leading contender to bring fiber optics to the home—a vast global market worth billions of dollars.

Mr. Cook, 65, is a graduate of the Massachusetts Institute of Technology and a former head of the Radiation Laboratory at the Stanford Research Institute. He will step down as Raychem's CEO on April 1 but will remain chairman. The interview was conducted in Boston and at Raychem's Menlo Park, California headquarters by HBR associate editor William Taylor.

HBR: What's the secret to being an innovative company?

Paul Cook: There is no secret. To be an innovative company, you have to ask for innovation. You assemble a group of talented people who are eager to do new things and put them in an environment where innovation is expected. It's that simple—and that hard. There are, after all, a limited number of things management can ask for. We get innovation at Raychem because our corporate strategy is premised on it. Without innovation we die.

And I don't mean just from the engineers. Innovation is as much about sales or service or information systems as it is about products. We spend twice as much on selling as we do on research and development, so creativity from our sales force is just as important as creativity from the labs. How do you sell a product no one has seen before? How do you persuade a customer to accept us as a sole source for an important component? There's no one in any organization who can't be clever and imaginative about doing his or her job more effectively. We expect innovation from our secretaries and the people on the loading docks as well as from the scientists.

Still, few American companies are as innovative as they could be—or must be—to survive intense global competition. What's missing?

You won't get innovation without pressure. Most companies put pressure on their sales force to go out and get orders. They put pressure on manufacturing to cut costs, increase yields, improve quality. But they forget the importance of pressure when it comes to new products and processes. We want to grow this company from $1 billion a year to $5 billion, and we don't do big acquisitions. The only way to get that kind of growth is to get more and better products out the door faster.

I'm convinced that's a big reason Raychem grew so explosively in the early days. When we started the company, we didn't know what products we were going to make. We knew the first electron-beam machines were coming to market from General Electric, and we knew there were potential industrial applications for the technology. So we bought a machine. And pretty soon we started running out of money. We were under enormous pressure to find successful products—and we did. We came up with lots of good ideas because we had to. People need a fair amount of pressure to have creative ideas.

How do you maintain pressure in a successful global company?

Everyone has heard the cliché, "management by walking around." Well, you can't walk around 30 plants in 12 countries, which is what Raychem has right now, without dropping from exhaustion. But you can practice what I refer to as "management by calling about." Almost every day I use the telephone to contact Raychem people somewhere in the world. "How did your experiment go last night? What results do you have this morning? What are your ideas for a new approach? Why don't you fax me your product plan?" If you keep the pressure on in a constructive way, if you demonstrate genuine curiosity about what's happening in the labs, it stimulates people to keep the creative process going.

Why do organizations need such pressure and prodding? Isn't innovation the most exhilarating part of being in business?

What separates the winners and losers in innovation is who masters the drudgery. The creative process usually starts with a brilliant idea. Next you determine whether, if the brilliant idea worked, it would be worth doing from a business standpoint. That's the exhilarating part. It may be the most stimulating intellectually, but it's also the easiest.

Then comes the real work—reducing the idea to practice. That's the drudgery part of innovation, and that's where people need the most pressure and encouragement. You can draw a chart of how the original excitement of a new idea creates all kinds of energy, but then people go into the pits for a long time as they try to turn that idea into products that are reproducibly manufacturable. That's when you use the phone and the fax machine. That's when you have review meetings between the technical people and senior management. That's when, as CEO, you show the entire organization that you are just as interested in new product and process development as you are in manufacturing costs, sales, or quality.

We don't often hear the words "innovation" and "drudgery" together.

Too many people still think innovation is about one brilliant technologist coming up with one breakthrough idea. It's not. When we started Raychem, we began to learn what radiation chemistry could do. Within three or four years, we had generated virtually every idea behind the products we're selling today, and we're still working on that original inventory of ideas. Ten years ago, after we began work on conductive polymers, we identified a market for all the manifestations of the technology that totaled $747 million a year. We made our "747 list" and began working through it. At the time, it was a $5 or $10 million business. Today we're up to $150 million a year. So we still have a long way to go.

Or think about semiconductors. I can make a case that the semiconductor world hasn't had a really new idea for 15 or 20 years. Those companies have essentially been practicing the same technology. They've learned more about it, they've penetrated it throughout the economy, but the core technologies haven't changed that much. The pioneers of the semiconductor industry could recite within the first few years all that could be done with the technology. The winners have been the companies that reduced the technology to practice most quickly.

Does that explain some of our competitive slide against the Japanese?

This is where the Japanese are eating us alive. They're making us look like amateurs in product development. American technologists are still without peer in terms of the imagination they bring to problems. No one can question our technical brilliance. The Japanese don't pioneer the brilliant solutions, but they find the brilliant solutions. Then they bring them over to Japan and master the drudgery to reduce them to practice. Japan may not have the Nobel laureates yet, but I'm not sure it needs them to flourish. And if it wants them, all it has to do is create the right environment and that will happen too.

What's frightening to me is the thoroughness with which the Japanese scan the world for important technologies, learn them, know the patent literature, know the technical literature, and turn over every stone. We've been working on shape-memory alloys for almost 25 years. The Japanese keep knocking on our doors; they want a license from us. They are the only companies in the world besides Raychem that see the potential for this technology. In fact, whenever we find technologies that we consider powerful, for which we have great expectations, it isn't long before the Japanese show up and say, "How about a license?" or "How about a joint venture?" We seldom get chased by American or European companies.

Can a company teach its people to be innovative?

No. Innovation is an emotional experience. You can train people technically, but you can't teach them curiosity. The desire to innovate comes partly from the genes; you're born with it. It also comes from your early life, your education, the kind of encouragement you got to be creative and original. Innovative people come in all shapes and sizes and in all personality types. Some people are happiest when they're wrestling with a problem; I'm one of those. Others go into a green funk. They're miserable and depressed until they have the answer. But you can't have a good technologist who's not emotionally involved in the work. You can't have a good technologist who doesn't wake up in the middle of the night searching for answers. You can't have a good technologist who doesn't come into the lab eager to see the results of last night's experiment.

So before you hire people, you ask about their childhood?

You bet. One of my most important jobs is finding the right people to add to the Raychem environment—people who genuinely want to serve the customer, who want to build new products that are superior to anything that's come before, who are willing to stick their necks out to do new things. That means learning how their minds work, what they think about, what excites them, how they approach problems.

The top management of this company spends a huge amount of time—I probably spend 20% of my time—recruiting, interviewing, and training. It's not unusual for a technologist candidate to go through ten in-depth interviews. Now some people do better in interviews than others. But by keeping the evaluation process broad, we usually get broad agreement on candidates. I can't think of anyone who's been a great success at Raychem who wasn't a big success in the interviews.

How do you motivate people over the long haul to keep them focused on innovation?

The most important factor is individual recognition—more important than salaries, bonuses, or promotions. Most people, whether they're engineers, business managers, or machine operators, want to be creative. They want to identify with the success of their profession and their organization. They want to contribute to giving society more comfort, better health, more excitement. And their greatest reward is receiving acknowledgment that they did contribute to making something meaningful happen. So the most important thing we do is build an organization—a culture, if you'll pardon the word—that encourages teamwork, that encourages fun and excitement, that encourages everyone to do things differently and better—and that acknowledges and rewards people who excel.

Of course, people do use financial yardsticks to measure how they're doing. So you have to pay well. We pay our people above average, but only slightly above average—sixtieth percentile or so. Bonuses give them an opportunity to move up a fair amount based on overall corporate results and individual performance. Every person in the company earns a cash bonus each quarter based on after-tax profits as a percentage of sales. Ten percent of our people are in a second bonus pool. The size of a pool reflects the performance of the group or division; the distribution of the pool reflects individual performance.

Some companies spread bonuses quite evenly among group members. We have a different approach. Typically within a division there are significant differentials based on performance. Having a big spread causes some unhappiness. But it also creates drive, because I think people respect how we evaluate their contribution. We don't just reward success; we reward intelligent effort. We've paid sizable bonuses to people who have worked day and night, with remarkable proficiency, on a year-long project—only to find the market had disappeared.

We must be doing something right, by the way. Our attrition rate is very low, and the number of people who have left to start businesses to compete with us is virtually nil. That's pretty unusual when you consider what happens in the rest of Silicon Valley.

Let's talk about technology. Increasingly, companies are trying to close the innovation gap by working with other companies—often their competitors—in strategic alliances, joint ventures, and research partnerships. Does this worry you?

Yes. No company can do everything, and we use partnerships on a selective basis. We're working with Nippon Sheet Glass on switchable windows and with Furukawa Electric in shape-memory alloys. But those and a few other alliances are the exceptions. I've always believed that truly innovative companies must build an intellectual and technical infrastructure around core technologies. At Raychem, those core technologies are radiation chemistry, conductive polymers, shape-memory alloys, cross-linked gels, liquid-crystal displays, and a few others. Companies need a single-minded commitment to their core technologies, a commitment to knowing more about them than anyone else in the world. No partnership or joint venture can substitute for technology leadership.

You also have to make sure your company has the very brightest people in your core technologies. Some who know the analytical part of the technology, some who know the molecular part, some who know the physics, some who know the chemistry. You make sure those people talk to each other, that there is regular and intensive interchange between all those disciplines. They have to work together, communicate, sweat, swear, and do whatever it takes to extract from the core technology every product possibility. The fax machine has been absolutely magnificent in that regard. Our technologists are using it to share sketches and plans, annotate them, and feed them back. The fax machine is much more important than videoconferencing as a tool for technical interaction.

Still, effective communication doesn't come easy. One of the problems with people at the cutting edge of their field is that they don't think anyone can teach them anything. That's why we recently started a "Not Invented Here" award at Raychem. We celebrate people who steal ideas from other parts of the company and apply them to their work. We give the person who adopts a new idea a trophy and a certificate that says, "I stole somebody else's idea, and I'm using it." The person on the other side, the person who had the idea, also gets an award. His certificate says, "I had a great idea, and so and so is using it." We hope to give out hundreds of these awards.

How does being committed to core technologies differ from how most companies manage technology?

Too many American companies are only immersed in their markets. They bring along whatever technology they think is necessary to satisfy a market need. Then they fall flat on their faces because the technology they deliver isn't sophisticated enough or because they don't know what alternatives the competition can deliver.

We think about our business differently. Raychem's mission is to creatively interpret our core technologies to serve the marketplace. That means we don't want to be innovators in all technologies. We restrict our charter to the world of material science, and within material science, to niches that can sponsor huge growth over a long period of time and in which we can be pioneers, the first and best in the world. And I mean *the* first. That means we can't just go to universities and find trained people; we have to train them ourselves. We usually can't use technologies from university and government labs, although we stay abreast of what's happening. After all, if we're a pioneer in a technology, how can we go to a university and learn about it?

Then we draw on those core technologies to proliferate thousands of products in which we have a powerful competitive advantage and for which our customers are willing to pay lots of money relative to what it costs us to make them. Think about that. If you can pioneer a technology, use it to make thousands of products, sell those products at high price-to-cost relationships to tens of thousands of customers around the world, none of which individually is that important to you, you wind up with an incredibly strong market position. That philosophy hasn't changed for 33 years. Our challenge has been to apply it to a bigger and bigger organization.

Why don't more companies follow this model?

Because it's a harder way to do business. Most companies say, "Let's pick markets in which we can be big players and move as fast as we can to do the simple things." More companies today want to be dominant players in big markets—you know, number one or number two in the world—or they get out. Jack Welch, General Electric's chairman, has followed that strategy very successfully for years. That's not our strategy at all.

A different, and I think more powerful, way to compete is to avoid competition altogether. The best way to avoid competition is to sell products that rivals can't touch. When we started Raychem, the last thing we wanted to do was make products that giants like GE or Du Pont would also be interested in making. We made sure to select products that would not be of interest to large companies. We selected products that could be customized, that we could make in many varieties—different sizes, different thicknesses, different colors. We wanted products that were more, not less, complicated to design and build. We wanted products with small potential annual revenues compared with the total size of the company, and we wanted lots of them.

After 33 successful years, I still have trouble pushing that vision inside Raychem; people struggle against it all the time. It takes a lot of confidence to believe that you can go out and master a technology, stay ahead of everybody else in the world, capture markets based on that technology, obtain broad patent coverage, and then end up with a strong gross profit margin in a protected business. People argue that it would be much easier, that we would grow more quickly, if we put less inventive content in our products and went for bigger markets. That's not my idea of a smart way to grow a business.

So innovation is primarily about pushing technology out the door?

Not quite. What we're really talking about is economically disciplined innovation. Sure, you have to know your core technologies better than anyone else. But you also have to know your marketplace better than anyone else. You have to understand your customers' needs. You have to understand whether or not your product is reproducibly manufacturable, which isn't easy when you're pioneering new technologies. You have to understand the competition's ability to respond to your innovation. You have to understand whether the product can generate a gross profit margin big enough to fund the new investments you need to keep pioneering and to allow for some mistakes along the way. For us, that means a gross profit margin of at least 50%. Unless you can figure ways to save your customers lots of money, to be economically important to them, and to beat the hell out of the competition with products for which they have no alternatives, and to do all that cost-effectively enough to earn big margins, you won't have economically successful innovation.

Don't all companies try to understand their markets and their customers?

But how do they do it? They go out and ask customers what they want. That's not nearly enough. I'm not talking about lip service. There are a whole series of questions that we have to answer before launching a new product. Will it save customers a little money or a lot of money? Will it make marginal improvements in the performance or efficiency of the customers' products or will it make major advances? What does it cost customers to use this new product beyond what we charge them? What are their overhead rates? What are the hourly rates for the people doing the installation? I could go on. That's why Raychem probably has more MBAs per capita than any other technology company in the United States. We have to know our customers' business problems and economics as well as we know our technology.

We also have to ask one last question: Will the customer accept a sole-source relationship with us? After all, we're in the business of delivering pioneering, proprietary products. An oil company can't decide to use one of our couplings for a pipeline in the desert and then bring in two other suppliers for the same product. We're the only supplier in the world. So we have to understand the customer deeply enough—and the customer has to know we understand him—that he has the confidence to establish a sole-source relationship with us for a new and novel product.

So companies aren't just selling innovation, they're selling confidence that they will stand behind the innovation?

Absolutely. Many customers have stuck their necks out to buy products from us that they have never seen before. That means we get into trouble from time to time. But I can't remember one case where this organization didn't rally day and night, as long as it took, to solve the problem. In fact, when you have those experiences, customers always wind up more friendly, more favorably disposed toward the next innovation. That's not the way we intend to do business, but it's part of the territory.

Customer responsiveness and trust can also lead to tremendous business opportunities. Cross-linked gels are now one of our core technologies. That business grew out of a very specific problem we had to solve for a customer. A hurricane hit Corpus Christi, Texas, and knocked out a bunch of telephones. We sent down a task force at the request of Southwestern Bell and discovered that most of the shorting out occurred in certain terminal boxes. At the time we had a tiny research effort in the area of cross-linked gels, and we thought we could use the technology to solve the problem. It worked, even though we didn't understand all the principles behind it. So we plugged gels into research to explore what fundamental technologies were involved. We discovered all kinds of fascinating things and expanded the research effort. Today we probably have 100 people throughout the company working on gels. It's a profitable, fast-growing business.

How do you develop an in-depth understanding of markets?

You can't understand the market unless you get your technologists to the customer in a deep and sustained way. Your sales force, the traditional link to the customer, only gets you part of the way. It can open doors and find opportunities, but it can't really solve the customer's problems. And you can't pass the details of what the customer needs through the filter of the salesperson. You can't expect salespeople to have the imagination and expertise to know what can be accomplished through manipulating the technology.

We have technologists at Raychem who are superb in the labs. We have salespeople and marketers, most with technical training, who are superb at understanding customer needs. The person who can combine deep knowledge of the technology with deep knowledge of the customer is the rarest person of all—and the most important person in the process of innovation. We don't have very many of those people at Raychem, but those we do have are all technologists. We have never come up with an important product that hasn't been primarily the work of a technologist. That's because doing something truly important in our field requires knowing all the things that have gone before. You have to have the technology in your bones.

It's easier to teach a technologist economics than it is to teach an economist technology. And our technologists enjoy learning about the business. Whenever they go out to visit customers, they absolutely love it. It stimulates them. It excites them. It teaches them all kinds of things they wouldn't know if they stayed in the labs. It's a very important part of the innovation process here. That doesn't mean we do enough of it; nobody does.

What are the biggest obstacles to innovation?

For an organization to remain innovative, it has to be willing—even eager—to "obsolete" itself as fast as it can. So one of the biggest obstacles to successful innovation is success itself. All too often a company will develop an important new product and spend years asking itself the same questions—how can we make it a little better, a little cheaper, a little more sophisticated? Those are all important questions; there's always room for incremental improvement. But you can't let the entire innovative thrust revolve around making products faster, better, cheaper. A truly innovative company never stops asking more fundamental questions about its most successful products. Are there whole new ways to solve the problem—ways that might cut costs in half or double or triple performance?

So Raychem is working to "obsolete" its own products?

Every day. Right now we are in the process of "obsoleting" one of our best products, a system for sealing splices in telephone cables. That product generates $125 million of revenue per year, more than 10% of our total sales. We introduced the original splice closure, which was based on our heat-shrinkable technology, about 20 years ago. It absolutely took over the market. Our customers, the operating telephone companies of the world, have been thrilled with it. We also do pretty well on it financially—gross profits are well above average.

Now we could have kept on improving that product for years to come. Instead, we've developed a radically new splice-closure technology that improves performance tremendously, and we're working very hard to cannibalize the earlier generation. We introduced this new technology, which we call SuperSleeve, in the last few years. Today we're about halfway through the conversion process; 50% of our splice-closure revenues this year will be from the new technology, 50% from the old. By the end of next year, we want virtually 100% of these revenues to be from the SuperSleeve technology. In fact, we recently closed our only U.S. manufacturing line for the old technology.

> *How's that different from what any good company does—
> once an old product runs out of steam, you introduce a new
> product?*

That's precisely my point—our old product *wasn't* running out of steam. Our customers had virtually no complaints about it. But because we knew the product and its applications even better than our customers did, we were able to upgrade its performance significantly by using a new technology. Our margins on the new technology, at least until we get manufacturing costs down, are lower than our margins on the old product. We had to do an aggressive selling job and take a short-term financial hit—to persuade customers to adopt the new product.

Why are we doing it? Because we understand that if we don't "obsolete" ourselves, the world will become more competitive. We'd spend most of our time and energy reducing costs and outmaneuvering the competition that springs up. And for all that, we'd wind up with products that are only incrementally better, not fundamentally better.

Remember, we want products for which there is no competition. Even if we could have maintained our margins on the old product—and we probably could have by reducing manufacturing costs to keep pace with declining prices—we don't want to play that game. So today we're capable of delivering a demonstrably better product at the same price. And we're trying to persuade our telecommunications customers to write new specifications that require performance as good as what SuperSleeve can deliver. That's the game we want to play. And it's one of the hardest games any organization can play.

> *Are there other obstacles?*

Size is the enemy of innovation. You can't get effective innovation in environments of more than a few hundred people. That's why as we continue to grow, we want Raychem to feel and function less like a giant corporation than a collection of small groups, each of which has its own technical people, marketing people, engineering people, manufacturing people. Sure we want to get big. But we must stay innovative.

Innovation happens in pockets, and the location of those pockets changes over time. So we play musical chairs with people and make extensive use of skunk works and project teams. Using small groups also allows us to make sure that a technologist is at the head of the group making the decisions. I prefer to put development decisions on the backs of technologists rather than on businesspeople. I don't want our new product teams automatically going after the biggest markets. I want them going after the best way to develop the technology along proprietary lines so long as growing and profitable markets exist. Once the product succeeds and your problems become cost, quality, and efficiency, then you can think about putting different managers in charge.

I'm surprised you haven't mentioned money as an obstacle.

Innovation takes patient capital. American companies just aren't spending enough on R&D. If companies increased their R&D spending by 2% of sales, and therefore lowered profits by 2% of sales, they'd be much better off in the long run—and so would the United States. Normally, we spend 6% or 7% of sales on R&D. This year we'll spend more than 11% of sales on R&D, even though revenues are flat and margins down a bit, because we're working on several technologies that are going to materialize into really good businesses. That's an extraordinary commitment for us to make during a disappointing period, but it's the kind of commitment more companies are going to have to start making.

Let me give you a specific example. About 25 years ago, we learned that the Naval Ordnance Laboratories were experimenting with metals that shrunk with incredibly high force when heated. We were in heat-shrinkable plastics, so we thought this was something we should know about. We started some research. We developed a metal coupling to join hydraulic lines for the F-14 fighter, and the Navy bought it in the second year we had the technology. So we continued the research and made major investments. We kept pushing to get manufacturing costs down. We searched for markets in which these shape-memory alloys could have explosive growth.

Last year, for the first time, we made money on that technology. We stayed with it for more than two decades. We are without question the world's pioneer. We have patents coming out of our ears. After 25 years, shape-memory alloys are on the verge of becoming a big and profitable business. And believe me, we are going to stick with that technology.

But you know the corporate lament: Wall Street won't let us make the investments we know we have to make to stay competitive.

Wall Street does apply pressure; Raychem's market value dropped by 10% in one day last year when we reported disappointing quarterly results. But the analysts aren't totally unreasonable. Our fiber-optics subsidiary, which is one of the most exciting new ventures in the company, is a good example. We started exploring the fiber-optics area more than ten years ago. After we worked with the technology for a few years and made some technical discoveries, we began to see what was possible. We concluded it would take several hundred million dollars to bring the technology to market and make it profitable. So far it's taken $150 million to get Raynet on its feet, and we haven't made the first sale yet. (See *Exhibit 1,* "Innovation at Raychem: The Raynet Story.") Wall Street was shocked when we told the analysts about Raynet. We had been secretly working on the technology for years so the competition couldn't find out. Wall Street is still nervous. But the more it learns about our system and the potential markets, the more comfortable it gets. We've also tried to be smart about the financing. We brought in BellSouth as a partner to share some of the costs. And we break out Raynet's financials so the analysts can evaluate our existing businesses on a stand-alone basis.

Sure, it takes some courage to tell Wall Street, "Dammit, I'm going to spend a couple more percentage points of revenues on R&D and let my profits go down. But I'm going to show you how over a period of time that investment is going to pay off." That's not an easy story to sell. But it is sellable—especially if you have a track record of effective technology innovation.

Based on our conversation, we might identify the following principles of innovation: necessity is the mother of invention. Invention is 1% inspiration and 99% perspiration. Possession is nine-tenths of the law. Is the secret to innovation redis-covering old truths we somehow forgot?

Not quite. There are at least three new forces today. First, intellectual property is absolutely key. We are always driving for an ironclad proprietary position in all our products around the world. The ability of companies from other countries to copy important developments has increased so much that there's no way for this society, with our high standard of living, to compete against societies with lower standards of living unless we have protected, proprietary positions. So we make aggressive use of intellectual property laws and work as hard as we can to get the rest of the world to adopt effective protections.

Second, technology is becoming more complex and interdependent. To practice pioneering innovation, you must develop a critical mass of many different skills. If you're a small company, you better restrict yourself to one core technology in which you can do this. If you're a big company, you better take advantage of your technology scale and scope. You can't make that assumption anymore. You have to use your leadership position to push the frontiers of the technology, or you won't be a leader for long.

What's the third difference?

Innovation is a global game—both on the supply side and on the demand side. Raychem's most innovative lab is our telecommunications lab in Belgium. It's a relatively small facility, but it's a melting pot of scientists and engineers from Belgium, America, England, France, and Germany. I can predict with a good deal of accuracy how a technologist brought up in the Flemish region of Belgium will approach a particular problem. I can tell you how a French engineer might approach that same problem. You have to create an organization that can mix and match all of its skills around the globe.

EXHIBIT 1
Innovation at Raychem: The Raynet Story

Early this year, in neighborhoods outside Boston, Massachusetts and Cologne, West Germany, Raynet technicians began field trials of a telecommunications system that may usher in the next stage of the digital revolution. The development of that system is a case study in Paul Cook's approach to innovation.

Rapid advances in optics and electronics are moving us quickly toward a world in which optical fiber can be delivered to the home as cheaply as copper wire—an economic watershed for the creation of all-digital, fiber-based telecommunications networks. Fiber-optic highways between homes, offices, and factories will allow for the proliferation of two-way entertainment, information, and electronic distribution systems that are only hypothetical glimmers today. Raynet, Raychem's fiber-optics subsidiary, has developed a Loop Optical Carrier (LOC) system that delivers fiber from telephone-company central offices to the home—the last leg of the U.S. telecommunications network still dominated by analog transmission over copper wire.

AT&T has developed a competing system and is also starting field trials. Telecommunications analysts debate the merits of each system, although many argue that Raynet's proprietary non-invasive coupler, the heart of its LOC technology, makes its system easier and cheaper to install than AT&T's "star" architecture. What most everyone agrees on is that the global market for fiber optics runs into the hundreds of billions of dollars and that both Raychem and AT&T are well positioned to become major players.

Raynet's LOC system grows out of a ten-year initiative in fiber optics that shares many qualities with past Raychem successes. First, the project began with management's recognition that it needed to obsolete a thriving product. Second, although it represented a move into unfamiliar technologies, Raychem's early effort drew on its core R&D capabilities. Third, the company was prepared to make a big financial bet: Cook and his colleagues estimated they might have to spend several hundred million dollars. Finally, Raychem's research into the new technology revolved around a search for innovative technical solutions that would yield proprietary products.

In the late 1970s, Raychem was fabulously successful in the telecommunications industry—in particular, as a supplier of products designed to protect splices and terminations in the copper cables running from telephone-company central offices to homes. These splice closures were the fastest growing part of Raychem, which quickly became the world's largest cable-accessory company—a status it still enjoys.

But even during the years of rapid growth, management understood the powerful technical and economic logic behind optical fiber. So the company began experimenting in this field. At first, management had virtually no idea in what product directions their efforts would point.

So Raychem began in optical fiber where it left off in copper-developing products to make and protect splices. It hired a handful of scientists and engineers and acquired a small company in Phoenix that made plastic-clad silica, a form of optical fiber. Drawing on the company's expertise in radiation chemistry, engineers developed a splicing device (a clear plastic tube filled with a clear liquid monomer) that could be irradiated with ultraviolet light to form a strong connection. That intriguing advance still left a thorny problem: finding a microscopically precise technique to align the ends of two fibers (each only 250 microns in diameter, about five times the width of a human hair) that was easy enough to use that field technicians working in rain or snow could do the installation.

Two fibers are optimally aligned when the maximum possible light flows through their splice point. Determining the alignment requires transmitting light through the fibers, typically between two points each several miles from the splice. Raychem engineers saw that the splicing process would be much more efficient if the technician making the splice could measure locally rather than over miles how much light was going through the potential splice point. It was in wrestling with this problem that Raychem engineers developed the technical breakthrough at the heart of the LOC system.

Raychem's clever solution draws on the fact that light can enter or escape an optical fiber when it is bent. Company engineers reasoned that by bending one of the fibers to be spliced and shining light in, and then bending the second fiber and measuring the light escaping, the technician making the splice could determine when the maximum amount of light was getting through—and could thus identify when the fibers were properly aligned. That insight lay behind the creation of the non-invasive coupler. Later, company engineers realized that since light could be injected into or extracted from fibers through this technique, splicing itself was unnecessary in many applications. Light could be passed from one fiber to another without physically breaking either one.

This idea led to a 12-person task force to develop local area networks (LANs) for computers. The project showed technical promise, but it soon became clear it had a limited market. So Raychem turned its attention away from LANs to the local telephone network. It was at this point that senior management launched the major research initiative. The goal was to use the non-invasive coupler to develop a distribution system through which hundreds of residential telephone subscribers could share optics and electronics resources—a system that would create radical economies of scale and drastically lower the costs of delivering fiber to the home.

In effect, this ambitious goal meant Raychem was embarking on the development of an entirely new core technology. So Cook and his colleagues set about hiring some of the best people in the field—electrical engineers from MIT, optics physicists from major companies, bright scientists from Silicon Valley startups. The number of employees on the fiber project went from 10 to 350 in three years. And Raychem was creative about how the venture was organized. It established a subsidiary, Raynet, whose structure resembled that of a typical Silicon Valley startup. Raynet employees enjoyed not only a separate identity but also stock options in the new enterprise and the freedom to establish their own procedures.

Cook also was creative about Raynet's financing. He formed an alliance with BellSouth, the regional operating company most aggressively pursuing fiber optics, and financed part of the research under contract to the company. He allowed BellSouth to buy convertible preferred shares in Raynet for $25 million, injecting still more capital. Finally, after disclosing the fiberoptics project to a skeptical Wall Street, Cook segregated Raynet's financials from Raychem operating statements—making both companies easier for the analysts to understand.

Three years after Raynet was formed and ten years after the invention of the non-invasive coupler, Paul Cook and his colleagues are on the verge of entering a vast new market that may mean billions of dollars in additional revenues. Raychem products may change. But its business—the business of innovation—remains the same.

William Taylor

On the demand side, you can't leave a technology window open in another geographical marketplace. You have to fight foreign competition before it starts. Twenty years ago, MITI [Japan's Ministry of International Trade and Industry] targeted radiation chemistry as one of its industries of the future. MITI supported a lab in Osaka and tried to get the technology off the ground. Today there are 30 Japanese companies with radiation-processing technology, but together they probably have only 20% of our business. Why? Because we took the threat seriously; we refused to license our technology. We also built a business in Japan so that Japanese companies couldn't get a safe haven in which to charge high prices, grow their businesses, and then give us trouble around the world. If you want to lead with a new technology, you have to lead everywhere.

Can any company be innovative?

Every company *is* innovative or else it isn't successful. It's just a question of degree. The essence of innovation is discovering what your organization is uniquely good at—what special capabilities you possess—and taking advantage of those capabilities to build products or deliver services that are better than anyone else's. Every company has unique strengths. Success comes from leveraging those strengths in the market.

—— DISCUSSION QUESTIONS

1. "The Japanese don't pioneer brilliant solutions," states Paul Cook, "but they find the brilliant solutions." Based on what you have read about Raychem's strategies and practices, how would you distinguish between pioneering and innovating? What conditions in U.S. companies tend to encourage pioneering at the expense of innovation?

2. Cook calls size "the enemy of innovation." Do you agree? Or are there ways that size can contribute toward innovation? Cite examples from the interview and your own experience to support your view.

3. Aspiring entrepreneurs are constantly advised to "know what the customer wants." Many companies rely on their sales force to relay customer preferences to line managers and product development teams. What, in Cook's view, are the weaknesses of this approach? How does the approach to understanding the market differ?

4. How do Raychem's hiring and compensation practices promote an innovative company culture?

5. "I prefer to put development decisions on the backs of technologists rather than the businesspeople," Cook states, thereby blurring the traditional distinctions between line and staff. What are the benefits and risks of placing decision-making power in the hands of technologists?

PART FOUR

ENTREPRENEURSHIP IN THE NONPROFIT SECTOR

Virtuous Capital: What Foundations Can Learn from Venture Capitalists

32

CHRISTINE W. LETTS, WILLIAM RYAN, and ALLEN GROSSMAN

The for-profit world has a highly evolved and sophisticated network of venture capital firms to finance early-stage ventures. In the nonprofit world, foundations play a similar role of funding early efforts to build new programs. The authors make a case for applying the venture capital model to the nonprofit context as a means of improving the focus on performance and results.

For decades, foundations have been making large grants to nonprofit organizations in the hope of meeting a wide range of society's most pressing and vital needs. In 1995 alone, foundations invested more than $10 billion in programs dealing with, for example, poverty, homelessness, the environment, education, and the arts. Even as these large sums of money are put to work, however, many people in the nonprofit field are reporting a growing frustration that their programs' goals, although valuable and praiseworthy, are not being achieved. Many social programs begin with high hopes and great promise, only to end up with limited impact and uncertain prospects.

Forces beyond the control of either foundations or nonprofit organizations account for some of the problems. For one thing, the federal government has scaled back funding for social services, leaving the foundations and nonprofits without an ally they had come to rely on. Furthermore, many leaders of nonprofits are finding that, despite their best efforts, social problems persist and may even be worsening. But part of the difficulty needs to be traced back to the relationship between the foundations and the nonprofits.

Traditionally, foundations make grants based on their assessment of the potential efficacy of a program. Although that approach creates an incentive for nonprofits to devise innovative programs, it does not encourage them to spend time assessing the strengths, goals, and needs of their own organizations. Thus they often lack the organizational resources to carry out the programs they have so carefully designed and tested. Foundations need to find new ways to make grants that not only fund programs but also build up the organizational capabilities that nonprofit groups need for delivering and sustaining quality.

Many foundations are well aware of the problem and are trying new approaches. In particular, some foundations have been studying venture capital firms and their techniques for guiding their portfolio companies through the early stages of organizational development. The idea makes sense. Clearly, foundations and venture capitalists face similar challenges: selecting the most worthy recipients of funding, relying on young organizations to implement ideas, and being accountable to the third party whose funds they are investing.

To gain a better understanding of just which venture capital practices could be put to use in the nonprofit sector, we brought together a number of leaders of foundations, nonprofit groups, and venture capital firms. Their insights helped clarify for us what foundations can learn from venture capitalists. As Edward Skloot, executive director of New York's Surdna Foundation, puts it, a closer study of venture capital practices can inspire foundations "to make a new set of rules to play by."

——— THE STATE OF FOUNDATION FUNDING

In the words of former Ford Foundation president Franklin Thomas, philanthropy has seen itself as "the research and development arm of society." In the 1960s, for example, there was a tacit division of labor between foundations and the public sector. Foundations focused on research and development. If new ideas proved successful, the federal government would embrace them and assume responsibility for their widespread implementation through government agencies. Several of the signature programs of President Lyndon B. Johnson's War on Poverty, for example, were developed and tested in demonstrations funded by foundations.

To carry out their R&D role, foundations organize around program development. Grants are given primarily to develop and test new ideas. The grant funds the program demonstration, the evaluation of the early results, and, occasionally, the promotion of the findings to create interest in the program elsewhere. Although this R&D approach has been quite successful in stimulating innovative program ideas, it is clearly not suited to building the organizational strength necessary for the widespread and sustained implementation of those ideas. In the process of making a grant, foundations often overlook the organizational issues that could make or break the nonprofit. Instead, they fold organizational requirements into the category of routine overhead costs—costs that divert precious resources from the real work of delivering programs. Foundations' attitudes have long encouraged nonprofit organizations to focus on mission and to regard organizational capacity as worthwhile in principle but a distracting burden in practice. Hence a serious problem for the nonprofit sector: no one is investing in nonprofit organizational capacity.

The lack of support has meant that a number of specific needs at the nonprofits are routinely underfunded. The urgent and neglected requisites of organization building include funds to track the needs of the nonprofits' clients and how those needs are changing; time for nonprofit staff to plan new programs and processes; training and development for managers; and sound operating systems in the areas of finance, quality, and human resource development. Until those needs are addressed, the impact of programs will be limited.

IDENTIFYING RELEVANT VENTURE-CAPITAL PRACTICES

It is helpful to compare some of the differences in how venture capitalists interact with their start-up companies and how foundations work with nonprofit organizations. These differences can be the starting point for a process of reflection and change in the nonprofit sector.

RISK MANAGEMENT

Perhaps the most striking difference between venture capital firms and foundations is in how they manage risk. Many venture-capital investors believe that out of a portfolio of ten investments, only two will be "moon rockets"—ventures that produce a big payoff with a successful initial public offering. The rest may be projects that have a chance of going public someday, projects that will survive but probably won't issue stock, or projects that will fail outright. If a firm has too many project failures, future investors may be scared off and the venture capital fund itself may fail. It is in response to those risks that venture capital firms have developed many of their organization-building skills.

Foundations generally face little risk when making grants. Far from worrying about losing money, foundations are more likely to worry about not spending *enough*. (Failing to meet the IRS mandate that they pay out 5% of their assets annually means steep financial sanctions.) Because their funds are not at risk, foundations have not had to implement the kinds of controls that venture capitalists use. They rarely tie the compensation and career prospects of their program officers to the performance of grantees. Hence the program officers feel little pressure to learn and apply organizational lessons on the next round of grants. Unlike a venture capital firm, a foundation can prosper—and even bask in the glow of good works—with little risk of being tarnished by the weak performance of grantees.

PERFORMANCE MEASURES

The venture capital firm and the start-up begin building their relationship around financial and organizational projections, which then act as a set of performance measures. The measures, which can include cash flow, sales, profits, or market share, are continually updated to reflect the start-up company's progress and the market conditions. Clear objectives give the investors and the start-up managers a focus for their working relationship.

Like venture capitalists and start-ups, foundations and nonprofits share a goal: theirs is to improve conditions in the social sectors in which they operate. Although it can be difficult to quantify such goals—for example, when the program is targeting inner-city development—the foundation and the nonprofit usually agree that the problem needs attention. However, foundations do *not* share one important goal of nonprofits. The nonprofit has a very explicit need to keep its organization healthy in terms of staff, revenue, and basic operating systems; the foundation, with its focus on program efficacy and its practice of making one-, two-, or three-year grants, does little to support those long-term goals. The sad irony is that although the nonprofit may serve its clients well in the short term, it may end up lacking the organizational strength it needs to continue its work.

CLOSENESS OF THE RELATIONSHIP

To enhance the prospects for growth and sustainability, the venture capitalist offers a range of noncash, value-added assistance. For example, investors will often take one or more seats on the company's board to help shape strategy. To supplement formal governance, the venture firm's officers engage in extensive coaching and mentoring of the start-up's senior managers. Furthermore, the venture capitalist gets involved in critical hiring decisions, such as the succession that takes place when some of the early founders are replaced with professional managers. The quality of the venture capitalist's input can be critical to success: *whose* money the start-up gets can be as important as how much the company gets or how *much* it pays for that money.

The bulk of a foundation's work comes even before a grant is made—in screening applications or seeking out new ideas. Once a grant has been made, the foundation assumes an *oversight* role to uncover poor management rather than a *partnering* role to develop capable management and adaptive strategies. Many program officers are reluctant to get involved with their grantees' organizational problems. For example, foundations require periodic financial reports but are unlikely to contribute the services of an expert to work with the nonprofit on financial planning. Most foundations never take a seat on a nonprofit board or act as mentors or partners: in fact, they believe that such involvement would be intrusive.

Even foundations that do commit to the capacity building of nonprofit organizations often do so at arm's length. They hire third-party consultants who work on the nonprofit's particular organizational needs, such as back-office systems or professional development. However, because of the foundation's sensitivity about interference, the third-party consultant usually reports back only to the nonprofit. Hence the foundation loses the opportunity to learn about organizational needs or to respond effectively to them in the future. To be fair, the arm's-length relationship between a foundation and a nonprofit is partly due to the large workloads carried by foundation officers. The typical foundation officer handles hundreds of grant requests and scores of actual grants each year, as opposed to the venture capitalist officer, who manages maybe five or six companies at a time. Clearly, this oversize load of grants is something that foundations need to attend to if good organization building is going to take place.

AMOUNT OF FUNDING

As an industry, venture capitalist firms fund a very small percentage of the businesses that are started each year, but the impact that venture capitalists have on their start-up companies is quite significant. That is because the venture firm, once it has made the commitment, can help the start-up get the funding it needs to grow. Although the CEO is involved to a degree in fund-raising, he or she can count on venture investors to help raise money for the next stage of growth—and hence can concentrate on managing the growth.

Foundations, too, fund only a small percentage of the thousands of needy nonprofit organizations because there is only a limited amount of funding dollars. However, the common practice for foundations is to parcel out those limited dollars to a much higher number of recipients than a venture business would. The result is that a foundation grant covers only a small proportion of a nonprofit's costs. One foundation officer we spoke with put it this way: "We undercapitalize virtually everything we do." Even when a number of grants are combined, most nonprofit organizations are still starved for general operating support. Nonprofit executives, therefore, are forced to spend a large part of their time raising money year after year; some report spending more than half of their time on fund-raising. Under the circumstances, it is not surprising that many nonprofits are not managed well or that good managers may not be attracted to or willing to stay in nonprofit organizations.

LENGTH OF THE RELATIONSHIP

Venture capitalists usually are engaged with a start-up for five to seven years, and some relationships last even longer. That longevity gives them the time to become intimate with the start-up's organizational needs and to find ways to fill them.

Foundations' grant-making time horizons are much shorter and leave little time for nonprofits to develop products, processes, or marketing plans to exploit a new idea. Of the more than 35,000 grants made in 1995 in the five states with the highest number of foundations, only 5.2% were for more than one year. On average, the multiyear grants were only 2.5 years in length. Many foundations simply state that they will not fund any program for more than two or three years. Most of them believe that to offer support for a longer period would make the recipients overly dependent and that nonprofits should become self-sustaining in that time. That line of reasoning has led to foundations' time horizons being out of sync with those of their grantees, which are trying to build organizations that can sustain programs.

THE EXIT

Venture capitalists invest with the understanding that, ultimately, they will sell their stake to a takeout investor. The sale of the venture capitalist's stake effectively ends the formal relationship; it also provides the start-up with an infusion of capital to continue its growth. And, of course, there can be no sale unless the start-up seems to have a strong organization and a viable future.

The nonprofit world has no such mechanism for passing the baton. Few national foundations want to be takeouts for their peers; because of their devotion to innovation, most want to be in on the ground floor. In some instances, foundations are able to structure a series of milestones to govern the release of installments over the life of a large grant. The nonprofit has to demonstrate a new level of performance—operating in a certain number of sites, for example, or serving a certain number of people. But there is often no logical process for one foundation to step back and the next one to step in.

In other instances, foundations will challenge nonprofit organizations to demonstrate that they can sustain a program after a grant terminates. But unlike businesses, nonprofits cannot expect to have investment bankers and their clients waiting to step in with another infusion of capital. Thus when the grant runs out, nonprofit organizations are left to mount a time-consuming search for funds to cover ongoing operation and expansion of programs.

—— THE NEXT STEP: VENTURE CAPITAL IDEAS AT WORK

Comparing venture capitalists and foundations can be a useful starting point for a reassessment of foundation practices. Such an assessment may yield a new set of practices that foundations can use to build stronger nonprofits. We would like to suggest preliminary queries for foundations and nonprofits to ponder.

QUESTIONS FOR FOUNDATIONS

Foundations can begin the self-assessment by answering the following:

Will our grants give nonprofits the organizational support necessary to achieve program goals?   If foundations and nonprofits agree in advance on organizational requirements in addition to desired program results, the grant has a much greater chance of having a sustained impact. Hopes for sweeping social change will need to be converted into a series of clear interim results that the grantee and the funder can work toward together.

The GE Fund's College Bound initiative provides a good example. The GE Fund established a clear goal for its education improvement program: to double the number of college-bound students at selected public schools in towns with General Electric Company facilities. It indicated that it would be willing to support local schools over the long term—up to five years in one case—if the schools met certain milestones along the way. As long as the principal is leading the school in new efforts and there are signs of improvement, the GE Fund will stay with the school. GE employees are closely involved in mentoring of students and thus add additional value to the grant. Although the work takes longer and involves more foundation effort, the results have been gratifying, with one school boosting the percentage of college-bound students from 25% to 75%.

What internal capacity do we need to build organizational strength at the nonprofit?   Foundation managers and boards will need to reassess their own capacity for a hands-on, organization-centered approach. Many will need additional staff with more experience in organization building to ensure that intelligent bets are made and sound strategies are developed. Foundations can consider recruiting officers with varied backgrounds—in business, institution building, and consulting. The Robin Hood Foundation, for example, has included former management consultants on its staff to help make grants and to deliver management assistance.

In addition to developing in-house managerial expertise, foundations also can give their program officers the authority and the time to respond to the organizational needs of nonprofits. Currently, program officers' workloads are driven by preparation for the next meeting of the board of directors; as a result, program officers have less time to respond to nonprofits. If program officers get more latitude, a closer and more productive bond can be forged between granter and grantee.

Is our grant portfolio too heavy on program innovation at the expense of organization building?   According to the Foundation Grants Index, general support grants, which can be used for organization building, represented only about 15% of total grants in 1993—down from nearly 25% in 1980. Program grants, meanwhile, grew from just over 30% of all grants made in 1980 to 45% in 1993. Foundations need to determine whether they are invested too heavily in program support to the detriment of organizational capacity.

A group of Philadelphia-based consultants to nonprofits, the Conservation Company, has recommended that funders begin making a new kind of grant—an *organization grant*. The grants would be something between totally unrestricted general support and highly targeted program funds. They could, for example, specify organizational growth targets, as venture capitalists do with private sector start-ups.

In Boston, several foundations have joined with the United Way of Massachusetts Bay and the Massachusetts Department of Public Health to try a new approach to organization building. They have funded the Common Ground project—an intensive three-year program for 17 multiservice, community-based organizations. The funders consider these organizations essential to improving the prospects of several distressed neighborhoods and have therefore moved beyond the traditional quick fix of an organizational assessment and short consultation. Instead, Common Ground will offer the funded organizations ongoing training and professional development plus longer-term consulting resources to help them implement and sustain new approaches. The funders recognize that it is organizational strength that will ultimately determine how successful the programs are.

Foundations might also consider whether they are too wedded to early-stage funding of programs. Many could give support at later stages, when a program or organization is at a critical juncture and other foundations have already invested and left. Later-stage funding, combined with a focus on building organizational capacity, could help nonprofits sharpen their impact.

Are we close enough to nonprofits to help them build organizational strength?   Just as foundations' program officers are working more closely with nonprofits on program design, so they should be getting closer to nonprofits on organizational issues. The more that funders understand the organizational complexity of nonprofits' work—and shoulder some of the burden and risk—the better positioned they will be to enhance program impact. Hiring a third-party consultant is a step in the right direction but does not enable foundations to understand and fund the appropriate organizational enhancements.

One promising approach is for foundations to create a separate intermediary organization dedicated to specialized, long-term work with grantees. A good example is the New American Schools, based in Arlington, Virginia. NAS, which is funded with grants from corporations, foundations, and philanthropists, was established to give young school-reform programs what most foundations cannot: large grants over a long period in conjunction with formal and informal assistance to expand. Led by a former IBM executive and a board of corporate CEOs and leading educators, NAS staff members are close enough to their grantees to offer effective consulting support—such as developing a quality assurance program—and to define clear goals for which the grantees can be held accountable. The capacity building is explicitly understood as a powerful way to deliver and expand programs. The depth of the relationship (NAS works with only seven programs) enables NAS to act more like a venture capitalist than like a foundation.

Are there ways for us to experiment with some new types of grants? Foundations can consider experimenting with alternative approaches to grant making by earmarking a share of their annual outlays for new approaches. For example, foundations could make an unusually long-term grant and see if it results in organizational enhancements and improved programs. Another approach would be to give a few program officers a radically lower caseload to see what they can accomplish with grantees who are eager for a real partnership. Third, foundations might consider partnering with third-party consultants, bringing their capability in-house, and delivering their services along with the grant money.

QUESTIONS FOR NONPROFIT ORGANIZATIONS

Like the foundations that support them, nonprofit organizations need to reconsider their approach to building capacity. Many have been conditioned by the existing grant-seeking process to camouflage their organizational expenses and needs. Nonprofits need to begin articulating compelling organizational strategies and asking foundations to invest in those strategies. Like the foundations, they need to ask themselves a few key questions.

Are we defining our organizational needs for funders? To get more support for organizational needs, a nonprofit will have to articulate a disciplined plan for using the nonprogram money and show how that money will enhance the impact of programs. Instead of worrying about exposing their organizational weaknesses, nonprofits will have to "sell" those weaknesses by explaining that they know where to strengthen their organizations and how to deploy resources efficiently and strategically to get the job done.

When Family Service America, a Milwaukee-based nonprofit, mounted a fund-raising campaign to help the 250 nonprofits in its membership adopt new community-centered approaches, it didn't pitch a new model program. Instead, it laid out an analysis of the members' organizational needs—from training and change management to staff recruiting and benchmarking—and got foundations to invest in organization-strengthening programs as a way of driving program outcomes.

Are we selective about which foundations we want as partners? Although the tendency in fund-raising is to go after any possible grant, getting into an intensive partnership with the wrong venture-type funder is likely to mean wasted effort and considerable angst. Even cash-starved business start-ups are selective about whose venture capital they seek. Nonprofits looking for value-added funding need to communicate clearly where they are trying to take the organization, establish expectations that the funder will share risk and burdens, and create a plan that demands value-added support from a funder. Nonprofits should be wary of foundations that have repositioned themselves under a venture capital banner but lack the capacity, willingness, and patience to do the gritty work.

Are we showing foundations a clear plan that justifies longer-term support? In order to sustain organizational growth, nonprofits need to look beyond the current round of funding. They should propose that early funders stay with them until they are ready for the next stage of funding. One organization that used that approach is Cooperative Home Care Associates (CHCA), a worker-owned cooperative in the New York City borough of the Bronx that provides health care to the elderly in their homes. The cooperative has proved quite successful: it offers home health aides attractive pay, working hours, and benefits, and it offers the community high-quality services. Because of its success, CHCA wanted to expand its operations and launch a training institute to create new cooperatives. When it approached a previous funder—the Charles Stewart Mott Foundation in Flint, Michigan—CHCA presented a long-term plan for building self-sustaining cooperatives. The Mott Foundation subsequently made a series of renewable grants over a seven year period. Programs such as CHCA's provide a clear incentive for funders to move away from traditional terms of one or two years toward the longer-term grants that can have sustained impact.

The venture capital model emerged from years of practice and competition. It is now a comprehensive investment approach that sets clear performance objectives, manages risk through close monitoring and frequent assistance, and plans the next stage of funding well in advance. Foundations, although they excel in supporting R&D, have yet to find ways to support their grantees in longer-term, sustainable ways. Because organizational underpinnings were not in place, many innovative programs have not lived up to their initial promise. The venture capital model can act as a starting point for foundations that want to help nonprofits develop the organizational capacity to sustain and expand successful programs.

——— DISCUSSION QUESTIONS

1. What are the similarities and differences between the roles played by VCs in funding new ventures and foundations in funding new nonprofit programs?
2. What explains the principles that create the status quo in foundation funding practices?
3. Which aspects of the VC funding model would be most useful in the nonprofit context?
4. What difficulties would you expect to face in implementing the VC model in nonprofits?

33   Starting a Nonprofit Venture

ALICE OBERFIELD and J. GREGORY DEES

The spirit of innovation and entrepreneurship that pervades the business world is alive and well in the nonprofit sector. In this piece, Alice Oberfield and Greg Dees articulate the defining characteristics of a nonprofit enterprise, as well as explain the particular tax status and compliance burden under which these ventures operate.

In addition, the managerial challenges of starting a new nonprofit and of operating in this unique environment are described. It should be noted that—while the nonprofit sector has its own challenges and issues—it also has a host of advantages to leverage, such as the commitment of employees and volunteers, as well as the satisfaction derived from meeting important social goals.

Despite the popular image that entrepreneurs are driven by the desire for wealth, the creation of innovative new ventures has not been limited to the for-profit sector of the economy. The entrepreneurial spirit is reflected each year in the creation of thousands of new nonprofit organizations.

The decision to start a nonprofit venture may be determined by the personal values of the founders or by the economics of the opportunity. On the personal side, a common element seems to be the entrepreneur's desire to make a contribution to society, coupled with the belief that this contribution cannot be made (at least, not as well) through a traditional business venture. On the economic side, some opportunities cannot be effectively pursued or financed on a for-profit basis. Usually, this situation arises most clearly when it is not feasible to charge an adequate fee for the product or service delivered or when the profit motive would hamper the organization's effectiveness by undermining the trust that must be established between the organization and its many stakeholders.[1]

Research Associate Alice Oberfield and Professor J. Gregory Dees prepared this note as the basis for class discussion. Copyright © 1991 by the President and Fellows of Harvard College. Harvard Business School case 391-096.
    1. For a discussion of the economic justifications of nonprofit enterprise, see Henry Hansmann, "Economic Theories of Nonprofit Organization," *The Nonprofit Sector: A Research Handbook,* edited by Walter W. Powell (New Haven: Yale University Press, 1987).

The purpose of this note is to provide a basic understanding of the nature of nonprofit status, tax and regulatory treatment of nonprofit organizations in the United States, and the distinctive management challenges associated with a nonprofit start-up.

——— WHAT IS A "NONPROFIT"?

"Nonprofit" is a misleading label. Contrary to popular perception, nonprofit organizations are permitted to generate profit (a surplus of revenues over expenses). However, unlike for-profit organizations, nonprofit organizations *may not distribute* this surplus to those parties who have a controlling interest in the organization (i.e., officers, directors, or employees). Thus, nonprofit organizations have no "owners." No individual or group of individuals has a right to the economic residuals that might be created by a nonprofit organization. This constraint is the central defining characteristic of nonprofit organizations. The purpose of this "nondistribution constraint" is to prevent individuals in nonprofit organizations from personally profiting at the expense of donors, members, volunteers, or intended beneficiaries, not to mention the U.S. Internal Revenue Service. Any economic surplus must be used to further the approved nonprofit mission of the organization.

The nonprofit sector is sizable, dynamic, and diverse. The number of nonprofit organizations registered in the United States is fast approaching one million. In recent decades, that number has been increasing steadily, such that the rate of growth in the number of nonprofit organizations registered in the United States between the mid-1960s and the mid-1980s exceeded that of the for-profit sector.[2] Prior to the 1960s, nonprofits largely provided charitable services.[3] Social service, health care, religious, cultural, scientific, and educational organizations still comprise a sizable portion of the nonprofit economy. As of 1985, they made up only 40% of the nonprofits registered with U.S. Internal Revenue Service.[4] In addition to traditional charitable nonprofits, the tax code allows a wide range of non-charitable groups to organize as nonprofits. The non-charitable nonprofit categories include, for example, civic groups, social and recreation clubs, credit unions, farmer's cooperatives, cemeteries, mutual insurance companies, labor unions, industry associations, and political advocacy groups.

The richness and diversity of the nonprofit sector, defined in this broad sense, may best be illustrated by a brief list of prominent nonprofits:

Children's Television Workshop (*Sesame Street*)
Consumer Union (*Consumer Reports*)
Outward Bound

---

2. Burton A. Weisbrod, *The Nonprofit Economy* (Cambridge, MA: Harvard University Press, 1988), p. 62.

3. Hansmann, p. 27.

4. Weisbrod, p. 69.

Educational Testing Service
National Geographic Society
Harvard Community Health Care Plan
National Organization for Women
American Cancer Society
Wang Performing Arts Center
Harvard Business School
Blue Cross and Blue Shield
Habitat for Humanity
Planned Parenthood
Nature Conservancy
National Rifle Association

A fairly large number of service industries involve a mix of nonprofit and for-profit players. The kinds of organizations that could take either form include, among others, insurance companies, non-commercial banks, day care centers, hospitals, health maintenance organizations, nursing homes, environmental services companies, performing arts centers, fitness clubs, social clubs, housing developers, education and training centers, drug rehabilitation centers, research groups, psychological counseling services, publishing concerns, broadcast stations, and media production companies. In recent years, the diversity of the nonprofit sector has been increasing. Only the imagination and the tax code limit the range of organizations which can be fit into the nonprofit form.

——— TAX TREATMENT AND GOVERNMENT REGULATION

In return for abiding by the nondistribution constraint, nonprofit organizations are largely exempt from federal income taxes, under the Internal Revenue Code (IRC sections 501 to 528). Moreover, they normally get relief from various state and local taxes, as well. This favored tax status is accompanied by a number of regulations devised to monitor the economic and political activity of the organizations. The specific nature of the tax relief and the degree of government regulation vary, depending on the type of nonprofit organization in question.

VARIATIONS IN TREATMENT

The tax code concerning the varieties of nonprofit organizations is too complex to be covered in detail in this note. We can only highlight the major distinctions and differences in treatment.[5] Readers who have in mind a spe-

---

5. This discussion is based on John Simon's "The Tax Treatment of Nonprofit Organizations: A Review of Federal and State Policies," *The Nonprofit Sector: A Research Handbook,* edited by Walter W. Powell (New Haven: Yale University Press, 1987), especially pp. 67–73.

cific form of nonprofit organization should consult the tax code for relevant details.

Charitable   Organizations which satisfy the conditions stated in section 501(c)(3) of the IRC are usually described as *"charitable."* Relative to other nonprofits, these organizations receive the most favorable tax treatment and bear the greatest regulatory burden. Qualification for this status is determined primarily by the purpose for which the organization was created. The purpose must be:

> Religious, Educational, Charitable, Scientific, Literary, Testing for Public Safety, to Foster National or International Amateur Sports Competition, or Prevention of Cruelty to Children or Animals.

To label these organizations "charitable" is not to imply that they serve the needy, nor that they give their services away. Harvard University, for instance, falls into this category. This designation is more closely related to the fact that donations to such organizations are, within limits, deductible to the donor, and are exempt from gift and estate taxes.

Because of this additional tax benefit, charitable nonprofits are exposed to greater government regulation. They are audited more frequently and more intensely than their non-charitable counter parts. The audits are concerned with whether the organization is being operated exclusively for its approved purpose and whether there is any self-dealing by controlling parties. Charitable nonprofits are prohibited from electoral campaigning and severely limited with regard to lobbying activity.

Within the category of charitable nonprofits, there are some important differences in treatment. Three general groups can be distinguished. *Public foundations*[6] include organizations that have a particularly public character. Specifically, schools, hospitals, and churches are included in this class, along with organizations that pass certain complicated tests of public status. In principle, the tests focus on whether the organization receives a substantial portion of its support from a broad public (as opposed to a few private donors) and whether it has a governing board that is reflective of broad public participation (not donor controlled). Usually, these organizations engage directly in the delivery of services, rather than in grant-making. *Private foundations*, on the other hand, fall into two categories: operating and nonoperating. *Operating private foundations* are actively engaged in delivering a service. They must spend at least 85% of their income on actively carrying out charitable programs. Many of them operate in the same manner as public foundations. They simply fail the test for "public" status. The remaining charitable nonprofits fall into the category of *nonoperating private foundations*. These are

---

6. Note that all charitable nonprofits are referred to as "foundations" in the tax code. This term is not limited to grant-making organizations, but also covers organizations primarily involved in delivering services.

generally grant-making organizations. They fund the activities of other charitable nonprofits.

Of these three groups, the public foundations and operating private foundations receive the greatest tax benefit. For instance, the cap on deductibility of individual donations to these organizations is 50% of adjusted gross income, compared with a 30% cap for nonoperating private foundations. As for regulation, private foundations of both types face more frequent audits than do public foundations, with strict rules governing self-dealing, speculative investing, and corporate control. The private foundations also face stricter limits on lobbying than their public counterparts.

Non-Charitable   We have lumped all other nonprofits into the category of *non-charitable* nonprofit organizations. These organizations are described in IRC sections 501 (c) (4)–(23). Some of the diversity was mentioned earlier in this note. Non-charitable nonprofits are exempt from income tax, but donations to them are (with rare exceptions) not tax deductible. They are generally not eligible for foundation grants. Non-charitable nonprofits are in most cases privately controlled and funded organizations that engage in provision of services for the benefit of their members. They are commonly referred to as "mutual benefit organizations." These organizations face far fewer regulatory constraints than do charitable nonprofits. They are less frequently audited, and they have more freedom to engage actively in politics. Some organizations whose purposes would qualify them for charitable status choose to take a non-charitable form in order to be free to engage in the political process.

THE LIMITS OF TAX EXEMPTION

For-profit businesses which operate in the same markets as nonprofits have been pressuring the legislature to abolish or to curtail nonprofit tax exemptions, claiming that these exemptions promote unfair competition. This pressure has intensified as nonprofit organizations explore creative and sustainable sources of revenue. For now, the exemptions stand, although some alterations occurred after the 1986 tax reforms (e.g., charitable donations no longer are deductible for individuals unless they itemize their deductions).

There are, however, some constraints on the kinds of income generating activities nonprofit organizations can operate. Many nonprofits have been trying to decrease their dependence on donations by establishing other sources of revenue. For example, a nature club might sell hiking guides, or a museum might distribute a mail-order gift catalog. Revenue generating activities may expose the organization to an unrelated business income tax (UBIT). If income from unrelated business activities becomes a significant portion of the organization's revenue stream, it will jeopardize the organization's tax-exempt status. Unrelated business income is considered to be income derived from any activities that are:[7]

- unrelated to the exempt purpose of the organization,
- considered a trade or business, and
- regularly carried on by the organization.

In order to be considered "substantially related," the activity may not be undertaken simply to raise money. Even if all profit from the activity is used to support the organization's tax-exempt mission, the activity itself must still contribute in an "important way" to the accomplishment of the mission of the organization in order for it to be considered "related." The easiest test of whether something is a trade or business is whether individuals, or for-profit businesses, engage in the same activity as a source of income. "Regularly carried on" means that the venture is a frequent or continuous activity, not just something which happens once or twice a year (e.g., an occasional bake sale or car wash). All three conditions must generally be present to raise the issue of tax liability.

Even when the three criteria are met, a nonprofit organization may be able to avoid taxation provided that one or more of the following conditions hold:[8]

- the activity is conducted primarily by volunteers,
- the merchandise being sold was donated,
- the activity is carried on for the convenience of the members, or
- the activity produces "passive income" such as interest payments, royalties, dividends, or rents on property that is not mortgaged.

MANAGEMENT CHALLENGES OF NONPROFIT ENTREPRENEURSHIP

In addition to attending to tax and regulatory compliance, the nonprofit entrepreneur is likely to face a different set of management challenges than a for-profit entrepreneur. The rest of this note highlights some of these distinctive challenges. They go beyond the generic liabilities of newness and smallness, associated with all new ventures, to reflect the special character of nonprofit organizations. It would be an oversimplification to suggest that all new nonprofit ventures face exactly the same problems. Nonetheless, certain issues are sufficiently widespread in the nonprofit sector to merit attention.

---

7. See IRC 512 and 513 for a further explanation of UBIT.
8. Edward Skloot, "Enterprise and Commerce in Nonprofit Organizations," *The Nonprofit Sector: A Research Handbook,* edited by Walter W. Powell (New Haven: Yale University Press, 1987), pp. 390–1.

DEFINING AND MEASURING SUCCESS

In a world of scarce resources, the ultimate justification for any new organization is that it creates more value than it consumes. Frequently, if this is true, the organization will be able to collect sufficiently large fees from the beneficiaries (its customers) to pay for the production of its goods or services, including providing a fair wage for the labor used and a fair return on the capital employed. In this way, the market provides a reality check, albeit an imperfect one, on whether sufficient value is being created to justify the commitment of resources to a venture. When potential investors and other high-commitment stakeholders assess the attractiveness of an opportunity in the for-profit sector, they tend to focus on the economic gauges of profitability and growth.

For most nonprofit organizations, this simple market test is inappropriate. Economic stability and growth is certainly one of the goals of a nonprofit venture, but it is usually a subsidiary goal. Success is defined in terms of creating social value that may be difficult to measure and particularly resistant to conversion into dollar terms. The social benefits created by the venture may be intangible, widely dispersed, or have a long latency period. Determining the organization's degree of success, its relative efficiency and effectiveness is generally a complicated task.[9]

The challenge for the nonprofit entrepreneur centers on how to assess whether the proposed venture is likely to be a net value creator, or even whether it is a particularly good use of the resources that it requires. Even if the entrepreneur believes in the value of the venture, how might the value be conveyed convincingly to potential donors, board members, volunteers, and other high-commitment stakeholders? Once the venture is up and running, how does the entrepreneur judge success and justify further commitment of time and resources? These challenges underscore the importance of articulating clear goals and finding tangible measures of success in achieving these goals.

ATTRACTING AND MOTIVATING PEOPLE

The nondistribution constraint, in effect, serves as a cap on the financial rewards that a nonprofit venture can offer its founders and its employees. Though the organization is legally free to pay "market rate" wages, informal norms in many nonprofit fields seem to hold wages below those for comparable for-profit jobs. This tendency is especially true in organizations that

---

9. For a discussion of nonprofit performance measurement, see Rosabeth Kanter and David Summers, "Doing Well While Doing Good: Dilemmas of Performance Measurement in Nonprofit Organizations and the Need for a Multiple-Constituency Approach," *The Nonprofit Sector: A Research Handbook,* edited by Walter W. Powell (New Haven: Yale University Press, 1987).

serve the needy, rely heavily on donations, or are subsidized by the use of voluntary labor. Supporting constituencies may perceive market salaries, particularly in the management ranks, to be an illegitimate expense, a sign that either the organization's staff is not sufficiently altruistic, or that the organization does not really need as much outside support. To make things worse, joining a nonprofit organization may hamper job mobility. It is believed by some that the lower salaries in nonprofits attract only less qualified individuals who could not compete in the more demanding world of business. Nonprofit workers and managers may have difficulty trying to enter the for-profit work force at a comparable level.

The compensation issue[10] raises a host of questions for nonprofit entrepreneurs. The first question is personal. The entrepreneur has to ask, "Will I be happy accepting the risks of nonprofit entrepreneurship with a limited financial reward for taking those risks?" This is a question that each individual must sort out personally. Even for-profit entrepreneurs must often sacrifice cash compensation during the early years of their ventures, but if they are successful, the ultimate pay-off can be quite handsome. This pot of gold does not exist for the nonprofit entrepreneur. The pay-off has to come in non-economic terms.

Another set of questions has to do with the entrepreneur's ability to attract individuals with the requisite skills and the commitment. Attracting talented individuals to a risky new venture is difficult enough. Without an offer of ownership, a share of the profits, or perhaps without a fully competitive market wage, it is likely to be even more problematic. The entrepreneur must ask whether the organization should pay market rate wages, in the face of contrary industry norms. If the answer is yes, this decision must be sold to the supporting constituencies. If the answer is no, the entrepreneur must address the recruiting challenge. Fortunately, financial incentives are not the only incentives that might be offered. In some fields (e.g., health care and education), many of the professionals who would staff the organization may prefer to work in a nonprofit setting, allowing them to pursue professional goals without having to worry about the profitability of their activities. They may believe that the nonprofit setting provides more opportunity for professional autonomy. Others might be drawn in by a strong identification with the organization's mission. Mature nonprofits may offer prestige, job security, and a collegial, less intense working environment. These will be rarely available to the new nonprofit. In order to attract key staff, the nonprofit entrepreneur must rely on the appeal of their mission and the excitement found in being part of something new.

Once talented individuals are attracted, the questions shift to how the organization will retain and properly motivate them. Compensation systems

---

10. For a general discussion of nonprofit personnel management, see "Executive Leadership in Nonprofit Organizations," *The Nonprofit Sector: A Research Handbook*, edited by Walter W. Powell (New Haven: Yale University Press, 1987), especially pp. 172–7.

have become an important management tool. Yet, in a nonprofit organization, profit-based incentives are out of the question. They would bump up against the nondistribution constraint. Profit-based incentives might well be dysfunctional, making economic profit more salient to managers than the social goals for which the organization was created. Nonprofits seem to display a strong resistance to any "pay for performance" systems. This resistance may exist partly because the relevant performance is often difficult to measure with any degree of confidence. In any case, the use of the compensation system as an on-going management tool is limited in the nonprofit environment.

RAISING FUNDS

Raising funds poses a different challenge for nonprofit entrepreneurs than it does for their for-profit counterparts. By definition, nonprofit organizations lack access to equity markets. They must rely instead on donations and loans. Loans are difficult for any new venture to secure. Finding donors whose interests are congruent with the goals of the new venture is no easy task. The markets for major donations are complex and highly competitive. Furthermore, many nonprofits are in need of continuing operating subsidies. They must raise funds year in and year out regardless of capital investment or expansion plans. Consequently, fund raising is likely to be a major part of the nonprofit entrepreneur's job, even after the venture is underway.

The inability to raise equity funds may constrain capital investment and growth. Some argue further that the absence of equity investors may increase operating inefficiencies. The ability to attract risk capital is one test of the economic viability of an enterprise. Once invested, equity investors have an incentive to see that the organization operates in an effective and efficient manner. Investor scrutiny can serve as a check on management's judgment.

Risk capital for a new for-profit venture generally comes at a high cost. Though equity investors typically forego cash payout early on, they expect a high return at some point. In contrast, donations to nonprofits are essentially "no cost" capital. The nonprofit organization never worries about paying dividends or buying back stock. The use of donations by nonprofits not only relieves them of the burden of generating cash for investors, it allows them to pursue projects with longer time horizons and noncash payoffs. Any economic surplus can be used to further the organization's goals. The challenge is finding donors whose special interests match those of the new nonprofit venture and who also have the expertise and commitment to provide an independent check on management judgment.

Raising start-up funds is difficult for any new venture. The challenge of fund-raising seems to be compounded in the nonprofit sector. The nonprofit entrepreneur needs an ample measure of creativity and perseverance to be successful. Proposals and business plans must be tailored to donor values, which vary widely from one donor to another. If foundations are intended to be an important source of funds, the entrepreneur will have to operate in a manner consistent with foundation procedures. Some foundations work on strict funding cycles. Most take a fair amount of time to review grant applications and to make funding decisions. The nonprofit entrepreneur needs to craft and to execute a fund-raising strategy that targets appropriate donors and that is consistent with the goals of the planned venture.

MANAGERIAL CONTROL AND AUTONOMY

Founding and managing a nonprofit venture differs in another way from founding and managing a for-profit organization. For-profit entrepreneurs seem to place a high value on autonomy and independence. The desire for autonomy is not as easy to satisfy in a nonprofit setting. Founders of nonprofit organizations cannot be controlling owners. Consequently, they have less direct control over the organization. They certainly have a different basis of authority than their for-profit counterparts.

The founder who becomes the chief executive officer of a nonprofit organization serves at the discretion of the board. Though founders usually control the composition of the board, they have significant incentives to appoint strong, independent board members. This is frequently a prerequisite for attracting significant outside funding. An independent board may be a great asset, but it can seriously constrain (even dismiss) a founding manager.[11]

Authority and control issues also arise with regard to workforce management. It is common for a nonprofit organization to employ a significant number of professionals and volunteers. It is not unusual for these kinds of employees to question the authority of management. Successful management of professionals and volunteers presents a special challenge. Professionals play a prominent role in many nonprofits, especially in health care, education, and social work. These individuals are characteristically committed to professional goals and standards. If the management does not have impressive professional credentials, managerial authority is likely to carry less weight in their eyes.

Volunteers are widely used in nonprofits. One out of every two American adults volunteers in some sort of nonprofit organization, providing enough labor power to equal 5% of GNP if they were paid at the minimum wage.[12] Though volunteers are unpaid, they are not costless to an organiza-

---

11. For a discussion of the potential tensions between nonprofit boards and managers, see Melissa Middleton, "Nonprofit Boards of Directors: Beyond the Governance Function," *The Nonprofit Sector: A Research Handbook,* edited by Walter W. Powell (New Haven: Yale University Press, 1987), especially pp. 149–52.

12. Peter F. Drucker, "What Business Can Learn from Nonprofits," *Harvard Business Review,* July–August 1989.

tion. They must be trained, managed, inspired, and supported. Volunteer absenteeism or turnover can create serious problems. While volunteers are generally dedicated and enthusiastic workers, a command-and-control leadership style may not work well with them. They may feel free to challenge management, because unlike paid staff, volunteers face few barriers to leaving.

Nonprofit entrepreneurs must reflect on their management style and personal values to determine whether they can accept the control and authority challenges inherent in nonprofit organizations. Depending on their staffing plans, nonprofit entrepreneurs must ask whether they have the ability to motivate and lead volunteers, the credibility to command the respect of professionals, and the skills to build and maintain a consensus between the different constituencies who are essential to the organization's success. If the entrepreneur does not possess these skills, a senior manager may need to be added to the founding team in order to provide them.

MISSION AND STRATEGIC FLEXIBILITY

In many cases, what draws key stakeholders (donors, board members, volunteers, and professional staff) to a nonprofit organization is its distinctive mission. The commitment of these individuals to the mission can be a tremendous asset, motivating them in a way that mere financial rewards could not. The mission is the centerpiece of the nonprofit organization. However, the centrality of the mission can create a problem. All ventures, especially new ventures, face risk and uncertainty. When new information comes to light suggesting a change in direction, it is useful to be able to redirect the organization's energies. This shift in focus can be difficult if the mission commits the organization to a specific direction.[13] How do you change the mission or deviate from it without undercutting the intangible asset of stakeholder commitment?

The nonprofit entrepreneur would be well advised to create a mission statement that is specific enough to inspire commitment while being sufficiently open to allow strategic redirection as is necessary. This is not a trivial task. The entrepreneur may want to establish a mechanism for revisiting and perhaps revising the mission statement as needed.

———— ALTERNATIVES TO NONPROFIT STATUS

Facing these challenges, the would-be nonprofit entrepreneur might want to consider whether a for-profit venture could better serve his or her

---

13. For a balanced discussion of nonprofit flexibility, see "Organizational Change in Nonprofit Organizations," *The Nonprofit Sector: A Research Handbook*, edited by Walter W. Powell (New Haven: Yale University Press, 1987).

objectives. Debate abounds regarding the effectiveness and efficiency of non-profit organizations relative to their for-profit counterparts.[14] In some cases, the only feasible way to achieve a specific goal is through a nonprofit organization. However, in a surprising number of instances, the entrepreneur may have a meaningful choice. We have already noted a number of industries (from health care to education and television production) that straddle these two sectors of the economy. Many of the nonprofits in these industries would (in principle) be able to fund themselves on a fee-for-service, for-profit basis. This shift in orientation would probably alter the values, focus, and orientation of these organizations, but it is feasible.

It might even be possible to convert some traditional, charitable non-profits into for-profit businesses. One of the primary reasons for establishing a charitable nonprofit is that the intended beneficiaries lack resources to pay the full cost of the services they receive, at least at the time the service is delivered. In these cases, mechanisms may be available either to reduce the immediate financial burden on beneficiaries, or to eliminate it completely. It might be feasible to finance the service purchase on a pre-payment (insurance) basis, to institute a deferred payment (credit) program, or to find a willing and able third-party payor. Insurance mechanisms make health care afford-able for many who might be devastated on a pay-as-you-go basis. Student loans help private educational organizations to serve disadvantaged popula-tions. A popular third party payor is the government. With increasing priva-tization, government contracts allow social service providers, such as job training programs, to operate on a for-profit basis. This has opened the door for a number of for-profit service providers to enter markets once economi-cally closed to them.

Any method of converting a traditional nonprofit organization into a for-profit business will raise questions that deserve careful investigation. The use of pre-payment and deferred payment schemes face their own set of practical and strategic problems. Pre-payment for a social service can be a hard sell in the open market. How many inner city parents would buy drug rehabilitation insurance for their children? Deferred payments may be hard to collect, as student loan default rates indicate. Having government agencies as the sole paying customer can have practical and strategic disadvantages. The service provider must often work through cumbersome, bureaucratic government contracting processes. Because of rigid bidding procedures, it may have to compete on price alone. In times of fiscal restraint, the service provider is vulnerable to funding cuts and political battles. The profitability of the venture, if it becomes known, may raise political questions. Many will ask whether the firm is profiting at the expense of the taxpayers or its disadvantaged clientele. In some cities, government contracts for major social

---

14. For further information on this debate, see Richard Steinberg, "Nonprofit Organizations and the Market," *The Nonprofit Sector: a Research Handbook,* edited by Walter W. Powell (New Haven, CT: Yale University Press, 1987).

projects, such as the construction of affordable housing, go only to nonprofit organizations, to avoid this problem.

Even when the practical problems can be overcome, it may not be sensible to restructure the nonprofit venture along for-profit lines. The profit motive can have advantages, but it carries some risks. Once in place, it is a powerful motivator. Focus on profits could pull an organization away from pursuing its initial social objectives and change the culture and work climate of the organization in unproductive ways.

───── THE VALUE OF NONPROFITS

The availability of nonprofit status and its associated tax benefits enables individuals to tackle social problems that cannot be easily solved by standard market mechanisms. In this way, nonprofits fill a niche in an economy that relies heavily on market-based organizations, and in a society that prefers private responses to expanding the role of government.

At the heart of nonprofit organizational status lies a valuable economic and social asset, namely trust. Nonprofit status can create a sense of trust that is essential to achieving certain organizational objectives. Trust is largely a function of the nondistribution constraint, which limits the opportunity for someone to make excess profits at the expense of the needy or the organization's supporters. This sense of trust in nonprofit organizations encourages the public to make donations, volunteers to give their time, workers to accept lower-than-market wages, and customers to buy the organization's products or services. Of course, this trust is sometimes abused and it comes at a cost, but it has significant economic and social value.

───── SOME USEFUL RESOURCES

The following sources were helpful in providing background information for this note. They may serve as a useful source for readers interested in learning more about nonprofit organizations.

Connors, Tracy D. (ed.), *The Nonprofit Organization Handbook,* Second Edition (New York: McGraw-Hill Book Company, 1988).

Drucker, Peter, *Managing the Nonprofit Organization: Principles and Practices* (New York: Harper Collins Publishers, 1990).

Hodgkinson, Virginia A. and Lyman, Richard W. (eds.), *The Future of the Nonprofit Sector: Challenges, Changes, and Policy Considerations* (San Francisco: Jossey-Bass, 1989).

Powell, Walter W. (ed.), *The Nonprofit Sector: A Research Handbook* (New Haven: Yale University Press, 1987).

Weisbrod, Burton A. *The Nonprofit Economy* (Cambridge, Mass.: Harvard University Press, 1988).

——— DISCUSSION QUESTIONS

1. What factors determine whether an enterprise can operate with nonprofit status?
2. What considerations would drive you to choose nonprofit status if it was an option?
3. What managerial challenges are presented by operating in the nonprofit environment? What unique advantages does it offer?

34 Surviving Success: An Interview with the Nature Conservancy's John Sawhill

ALICE HOWARD and JOAN MAGRETTA

In this interview with the Harvard Business Review, *the Nature Conservancy's John Sawhill articulates the conservation principles that have underpinned his organization's efforts. Under Sawhill's leadership, the Nature Conservancy underwent a change in strategy as it expanded the scope of its activities and breadth of its missions.*

Not only does Sawhill address the key challenges in today's environment, he also highlights important lessons for organizational change.

C*an an organization with a four-decade track record of growth avoid becoming the victim of its own success? Since the Nature Conservancy was founded in 1951, it has worked to save threatened habitats and species by buying and setting aside land. Year by year, the number of acres under its protection has increased, membership has risen, and donations have grown.*

Today the Conservancy manages some 1,600 separate preserves—the largest private system of nature sanctuaries in the world—from more than 200 offices spread from Maine to Micronesia. With an estimated $1 billion in assets, it has become one of the largest conservation organizations in the world. Among its peers, the Conservancy has had the fastest growth rate during the 1990s.

The leader of any nonprofit company might justifiably envy the Conservancy's performance, but its president and CEO, John Sawhill, isn't satisfied. Since taking the job in 1990, the 59-year-old Sawhill has led a major shift in strategy with far-reaching implications for the day-to-day activities of the organization's 2,000 employees. He believes that the Conservancy must change now to achieve its mission over the long term—and that the organization's mission holds the key to guiding that change.

Sawhill's career has spanned the social, public, and private sectors. He was president of New York University from 1975 to 1979, deputy secretary of the Depart-

Harvard Business Review, September–October 1995. Copyright © 1995 by the President and Fellows of Harvard College, all rights reserved.

ment of Energy during the Carter administration, and a director at McKinsey & Company from 1981 to 1990.

In this interview with HBR editors Alice Howard and Joan Magretta, Sawhill discusses the challenges inherent in refocusing a large, successful, mission-driven organization.

HBR: *In 1990, Peter Drucker referred to the Nature Conservancy as "the best example of a winning strategy in a nonprofit institution." Yet you are leading the organization through significant change. Was Drucker wrong?*

John Sawhill: Sometimes an organization is slow to accept change because it's doing so well. Peter Drucker was a teacher of mine, and one of the things he said to me was that the worst thing that could happen to any organization is 40 years of unbroken success.

The Conservancy has always had a very clear mission: to preserve plants and animals and special habitats that represent the diversity of life. We are completely focused on that mission; it drives everything we do. We had to change, though, because while we were doing a lot of good conservation work, there were more and more signs that we were not making significant progress toward accomplishing our mission.

Your mission wasn't conservation?

Our mission hasn't changed; our approach has. You might call our original approach a Noah's Ark strategy. For four decades, the Conservancy focused almost exclusively on setting aside critical habitats for endangered species. In practice, that meant buying the specific piece of wetlands, forest, or prairie that supported a particular species or natural community. Like Noah, the Conservancy was intent on building an ark—or, more accurately, building a lot of little arks.

That approach was easily measurable. In the past, whenever we wanted to know how we were doing, we could simply count the acres we'd protected and check our membership figures. By those traditional measures of success, we were doing just fine. But we started to realize that those measures weren't giving us the right information. We had a terrific collection of preserves, but there was growing concern about the lasting effectiveness of our conservation strategy. The more we looked at the scientific data, the more we became concerned that our arks were springing leaks. In other words, places we thought were protected really weren't. That wasn't a sudden revelation. People in the field were talking about it, but nobody knew whether it was true or false or what we should do about it.

How did you come to believe that you might have a problem?

Our experience with Schenob Brook in Massachusetts, for example, helped to alert us. A number of years after we had acquired that property, we were alarmed to find that the bog turtle population was declining. It turned

EXHIBIT 1
The Nature Conservancy at a Glance

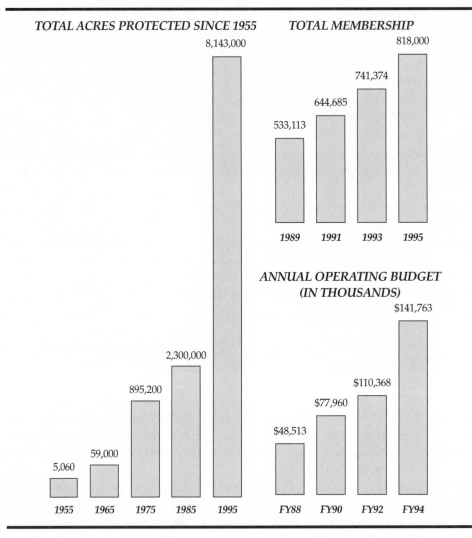

out that activities outside our preserve were affecting the water that the turtles ultimately depended on. Here was the problem: We thought we could buy a piece of land, fence it off, and thereby protect whatever was in that preserve. But that thinking proved mistaken, which meant that our old performance measures—such as how much land we had acquired for conservation— weren't valid indicators of institutional progress.

We simply couldn't go on with business as usual. For-profit companies can look at their financial statements every day to see how they're doing: They're either making money or not. Without the discipline of the bottom line, it's easier for nonprofit organizations to get off track. For the Conservancy, science is really our bottom line.

And science led us to our new strategy. It became clear that we needed to influence land use in larger areas surrounding the kinds of core preserves that we had traditionally acquired. Now we focus on much larger landscapes, areas we call Last Great Places. That way we can work to ensure that the economic and recreational activities going on outside the preserves don't undermine the balance of life inside them.

How did you arrive at this new approach?

When I joined the Conservancy in 1990, the first thing I did was to initiate a review of our strategy. Like most other environmental organizations, we had grown rapidly in the 1980s. Some of the basic systems we were using to run the enterprise hadn't kept up with that growth: Our financial system was not producing reports on time, our marketing system was not giving us accurate, up-to-date information on our members, and our personnel systems were antiquated. In addition, the board of governors was concerned that the organization was becoming fragmented. It needed leadership, it needed to be pulled together, it needed to have a clear vision of where it was going. But it was our strategic planning process itself that brought the fundamental need for a new strategy to the surface.

Can you describe that process?

I asked our senior managers to identify the most capable of the up-and-coming managers in the organization—its future leaders—and I picked four of them for the strategy task force. Those four are still with the organization, and they're all in leadership roles today. I tried to have some balance in expertise and in geography: We had two scientists, one fund-raiser, and one person who was involved in land acquisition; they came from Florida, Hawaii, North Carolina, and from our international program. The head of the group was someone I'd recruited from outside who brought planning expertise but lacked conservation experience. For four months, these people left their jobs and came together to work on the strategic plan.

I spent about 25% of my time on this effort, meeting frequently with the planning team and with the different groups that make up the Nature Conservancy: our state directors, chapter trustees, and national board. We conducted a series of meetings and informational sessions around the country for volunteers and staff. That was important. When you rely on people's love for the organization's mission, rather than on their career ambitions or financial incentives, it is absolutely critical to have a highly participative decision-making process. Many companies limit real participation in strategic decision making to senior managers. Their top-level managers get the most powerful people in the company together, convince them of something, and then assume that everyone else will follow. The best companies, in contrast, make an effort to get more people involved.

Our task force conducted about 75 interviews all over the organization, which helped bring to the surface many of the ideas and concerns that had been floating around. It also interviewed outsiders, including scientists and people in other conservation organizations. After five months of discussion, the organization coalesced around the new strategy of larger landscapes as well as a variety of new challenges. We were going to have to build our science capability and develop new, riskier conservation strategies.

What was risky about your new conservation strategies?

We're concentrating more on strategies that address what I consider to be *the* conservation issue of the 1990s: integrating economic growth with environmental protection. How do you protect a species when the chief threat to that species comes from 100 miles away? We have to broaden our scope.

The risk comes from our getting deeply involved in places where people live and work, because people are as much a part of the landscape as the plants and animals we're trying to protect. So we have to find ways to work with communities and businesses as partners, and that won't happen if conservation means throwing people out of work or driving companies out of business. Promoting compatible economic development has therefore become a strategic imperative for us.

What do you mean by compatible development?

It means that when we're trying to do a project to protect a landscape or one of our Last Great Places, we have to be concerned with both economic and environmental issues. We have to be sure that there are jobs for people, even as we are trying to protect natural areas. This dual concern has gotten us involved in a number of economic ventures that may seem a bit removed from traditional land conservation measures.

The Virginia Coast Reserve is probably our most ambitious undertaking in this area. That project began in 1969 in traditional Conservancy fashion. We bought a chain of barrier islands on Virginia's eastern shore—about 40,000 acres in all—to protect both migratory birds and shorebirds as well as the islands' natural communities. But by the mid-1980s, we realized that the islands were part of a much larger ecological system. The birds on the islands were dependent on the health of the coastal waters, and the waters were dependent on how land was used on the mainland. All of a sudden, we were looking at much larger and more complex conservation initiatives.

Science drove our new approach. We knew that the birds depended on salt marshes and mudflats behind the islands, but we were not sure how to protect those marine resources. You see, the Conservancy had never worked on the water. We bought the *land.* You can't buy water, except for maybe an inland lake and Western water rights; navigable waters are all part of the public domain. At the same time, the waters around those islands were the heart of the ecological system. How were we going to protect the salt marshes and mudflats? We just stared at the blackboard until eventually we realized, to put it simply, that water runs downhill. In short, what happens on the mainland is what governs the health of the water surrounding it.

So we started to address mainland uses of the watershed. We put together a team—they were called Four Scientists and an M.B.A.—to develop a strategic plan and think through how we would go about conserving this area. We spent more than a year identifying and analyzing the activities that pose the greatest threats to the whole system. We concluded that permanent residential and resort development on the mainland was far worse for the watershed than the traditional use of the land, which was farming. If you have too many septic systems, wastewater overloads the coastal waters with nutrients, which in turn produce too much algae, which kills the marine life. Once those relationships became clear, we had our answer. We had to find a way to encourage and promote low-density development on the waterfront.

In typical Conservancy fashion, our first move was to buy more land. We started acquiring key mainland properties on the seaside waterfront—not to manage them as nature preserves but rather to resell them with permanent restrictions prohibiting environmentally incompatible uses. As a result, we succeeded in keeping more of the land maintained for farming. We also felt that unless we could do something about the area's weak economy, there would be too much pressure for development in ways inconsistent with our conservation objectives. And so we're trying to find new, low-impact businesses to come into the area, profit from the eastern shore's comparative advantages, and provide jobs for people.

If your core capabilities as an organization are in science and real estate, what you're describing sounds like a real departure. Do you have to go outside the organization for people?

Yes, for two new skills. First, we need community-development organizing skills. We typically hire someone who will live in the area, be rooted in the community, and will work with other local people to build and strengthen a conservation ethic. Second, we need business-development and marketing skills. For the Virginia project, we recruited the former vice president and chief business officer of Colonial Williamsburg to help manage a new for-profit company called the Virginia Eastern Shore Sustainable Development Corporation, which has three goals: profitability, job creation, and environmental protection. We felt that the enterprise had to be for-profit in order to succeed. On the other hand, we and our investors realized that we couldn't expect to make venture capital returns.

The trick to economic development anywhere is to identify what is special about the place—its comparative advantages—and to build on that. Also, there is strength in diversity, so our strategy is not to look for 2 different 50% solutions but 50 different 2% solutions. Specifically, our goal with the Virginia shore project is to create 50 small businesses that will generate 250 jobs over the next five years. The company will initially focus on developing and marketing nature-tourism programs and related services, which are a natural fit given the region's beauty and proximity to major population centers. In addition, it will try to take advantage of the area's strong agricultural base to develop and market high-quality, high-margin specialty foods and organic produce. Today the farmers are growing commodity crops and losing money.

If we're as successful as we hope to be, the project will become a model we'll use elsewhere. We're very excited about this venture—the spark is lit.

Our mission leads us to this kind of activity because once you say you're going to work on the scale of an entire landscape to protect biological resources, you've touched the tar baby whether you like it or not. You're in the community-development business and the conservation business; the two are inextricably linked.

As you learn more about sustainable development, do you find areas where a species' survival and economic activity clash irreconcilably? What about the battle in the Pacific North-west between environmentalists and the logging industry over the spotted owl?

Obviously, there are no easy answers to conflicts like those, but such clashes are not inevitable. The controversies surrounding the Endangered Species Act show that people on all sides are not doing a good job in planning and prevention. The lesson to be learned is this: The best way to avoid divisive conflicts over endangered species is to get out in front of the issue, to address the problem before it becomes a crisis. It's just plain bad policy to wait until a plant or animal is on the brink of extinction before taking action. Too often, we wait until we have to send in the cavalry when a little diplomacy before-hand could have avoided the whole mess.

If we get to the point where a species is nearing extinction, we've let things go too far. Whether it's an owl or a gnatcatcher or a salmon—these creatures are not responsible for the decline of industries. Their near extinction is usually symptomatic of a larger problem. The plight of the spotted owl in the Pacific Northwest, for instance, suggests that a once-plentiful resource, the old-growth forest, is in trouble. And we depend on that resource for future, sustainable economic development.

On my desk, I have a little sign that says, "If you're not the lead dog, the view never changes." Businesses and communities that get out in front on environmental issues will have an enormous competitive advantage over those that stall, file lawsuits, or simply bury their heads in the sand.

How are business leaders doing on environmental issues today?

Some of the most innovative and competitive companies I know have been in the forefront of energy conservation and the search for less-polluting methods of operation. Perhaps the bigger problem is the perception that environmental protection and economic vitality are at odds with each other. An unfortunate legacy of the 1980s seems to be that many in the business community still perceive *environmentalism* as a dirty word. At the same time, many environmentalists seem to have nothing good to say about the corporate world.

You might call the result of these hostile perceptions the "spotted owl syndrome": a kind of economic-environmental gridlock. The symptoms are easy enough to detect. Endless litigation. Stubborn, entrenched interests. All-or-nothing thinking and either-or choices. And on the sidelines, lots of lawyers cheering the combatants on.

How do your new strategies break the gridlock?

We try to help companies find a constructive approach to what they want to do. If an oil company wants to drill in an environmentally sensitive area, we won't say, Don't drill. Instead we ask, Is there any way you can drill and not harm the area's ecological integrity? Let's try to develop a drilling plan that won't disturb the wildlife habitat. We believe in partnerships. Consequently, we seek to work with a broad variety of people and organizations: individuals, businesses, government, other nonprofits, universities, you name it. We'll work with anyone—from gigantic multinational companies to an individual farmer or fisherman—who will help us achieve our mission.

In recent years, for example, we've become quite active in mitigation; that is, in helping to find solutions that offset environmental damage. In 1992, the Walt Disney Company wanted to expand its operations in Orlando, Florida, to build its wild animal theme park. The state, however, was concerned about damage to wetlands. A solution was jointly engineered by Disney, the Nature Conservancy, and local, state, and federal agencies: In exchange for permission to develop the Orlando site, which will affect about 340 acres of wetlands over a 20-year period, Disney agreed to purchase, protect, and restore 8,500 acres of wetlands and wilderness in central Florida. Disney will donate this land in phases to the Conservancy and provide an endowment to make sure that we can continue to operate it. By the way, these kinds of mitigation agreements will become more and more popular in the future. They offer creative, nonregulatory solutions that help the environment without hurting the ability of businesses to develop their valuable assets.

Another way we help break the gridlock is by using our expertise to help companies with site planning and land management. Information from our species inventory can be invaluable in helping planners site power lines, pipelines, construction projects, or roads. A little biological homework beforehand can avert costly delays, lawsuits, and negative public opinion.

A recent example is instructive. The Georgia-Pacific Corporation wanted to consider how it might contribute to conservation but not give up all its rights to harvest timber in perpetuity on a particular piece of property. The company called in the Nature Conservancy and said, "Let's think about this together. Which parts of this area should be permanently set aside, and which might be selectively logged or logged at some future time using our normal methods?" We talked about it and ultimately signed a contract that gives the two organizations equal rights in determining future timber harvests on the property. The Conservancy and Georgia-Pacific each have one vote, and questions of future harvests must be resolved unanimously. Instead of getting into a situation where it might have incurred opposition from environmental groups, Georgia-Pacific worked out a plan that they found very satisfactory, and it also got a lot of good publicity for having taken that approach.

What major challenges do you face as you work more in various partnership arrangements?

We have a strong results-oriented culture. One former director of the U.S. Fish and Wildlife Service described the Conservancy as "all action and no talk." We like to get things done and, as we all know, the best way to get things done is to do it yourself. What we have to realize is that in a partnership it's *not* our job to get things done on our own. Our job is to help our partners by giving them the tools they need.

One of the fundamental challenges that every manager faces—how to measure success—has become even more difficult for us because of the complex objectives of our partnerships. As I said earlier, it was a lot easier when we measured our success by the number of acres we bought or the number of dollars we raised. But the compatible development initiatives that are critical to our mission don't fit neatly into those categories, and it may take years to tell how effective our projects have been.

At the same time, an organization has to set goals and objectives annually to make sure that people understand clearly what is expected of them. One of the problems common in nonprofits is that people don't have specific, measurable goals and objectives. So, for instance, we'll set fundraising goals for a program such as the Oklahoma Tallgrass Prairie Preserve, in which our aim was to raise the $15 million we needed to buy the land. With a project such as the Virginia shore, the goals might include the number of jobs to be created.

Some of the objectives critical to our mission are difficult to quantify, but we can still use them as goals. For instance, if we are to succeed, we have to establish programs that can serve as models for future conservation work. Our state program in Hawaii set a standard in rain forest protection, but we measured its success not just by what we accomplished in Hawaii but also by our ability to apply what we learned there about island ecology to other areas in the Pacific. Today we are successfully extending the Hawaiian model to Indonesia, Papua New Guinea, and Micronesia. We're always trying to build on our strengths. In that way, the "transportability" of programs is an important measure of success for us.

You alluded earlier to changes in your science organization. What changes did you make?

We set priorities for conservation—our operating strategy, in a sense—based on objective, scientific data about species and habitats. Although we appreciate the value of beautiful landscapes as much as anyone else, we won't try to save a place unless it harbors a rare species or an important habitat. To put it another way, we have always been in the science business, not the pretty business.

But even though we have always thought of ourselves as a science-driven organization, we have long needed to integrate science more effectively into our conservation planning. After undertaking the strategic review, we discovered that we were actually in two separate businesses. On the one hand, we maintain the world's best databases on species and their habitats, and our science business provided information on threatened areas both for the Conservancy and for outsiders such as government agencies and corporations. On the other hand, we were in the business of buying land and protecting it. It wasn't always clear that we were successfully integrating our scientific information with our conservation work. We had to use science to understand better the ecological processes at work on the land that interested us.

We also needed new capabilities in the area of stewardship; that is, in managing properties once we acquire them. To bring about that major change, we hired specialists in such fields as fire ecology, weed control, and bio-hydrology—a subspecialty of water management. People with skills in those areas help us understand how to manage properties to best protect their native plants and animals.

Were there any changes in your donor strategy as a result of the strategic review?

I wouldn't say that our strategy has changed, but we did learn some things that have helped keep us on course. We have always had a clear donor strategy that fit our mission. Some people at the Conservancy think our customers are the plants and animals we're trying to save, but our real customers are the donors who buy our product, and that product is protected landscapes. Because fund-raising takes place locally, we have organized around local chapters in every state. Our target market is the broad and growing segment of people who love the outdoors and want to preserve it—and who are looking for groups that are achieving tangible results. They like the fact that we use private-sector techniques to achieve our objectives, that we protect the environment the old-fashioned way: We buy it.

We have made a conscious, strategic decision to rely on individual donors and not to become too heavily dependent on government, because we want to be clearly identified as a private organization, one that is financed privately and uses free-market techniques. We think of ourselves as Adam Smith with a green thumb.

Our nonconfrontational strategy gives us a very broad and stable base of support that runs the whole political spectrum—George Bush and Bill

EXHIBIT 2
From Good Intentions to Good Performance

Performance measures are the vehicle for converting a mission statement into specific goals. One of the things I found when I first looked at the Conservancy's plans was that they never defined success. The plans detailed a whole series of activities that we were going to conduct, but they never suggested how we would know when we had achieved our goals. Today we require a clear definition of success for every Last Great Place project we undertake. We developed a planning format that defined the *system* we were trying to protect, the *stresses* to that ecological system, the *source* of the stresses, the *strategy* for dealing with those stresses, and how we would measure our *success*.

This plan became known as the 5-S format, but it was just a way of communicating to the organization what a good protection plan would contain. Take our Fish Creek Project in northeastern Indiana; we're trying to protect a system of freshwater mussels there. The stress comes from excessive silt in the water, and the sources of the silt are two agricultural practices: tillage up to the water's edge and fall plowing. Farmers can't practice no-till agriculture without expensive special equipment. Our strategy is to lower that barrier by subsidizing 15% of the equipment's cost if a farmer agrees to

practice no-till agriculture on a minimum of 250 acres for at least three years. We have three key measures of success: the number of acres under the no-till method, the silt levels in the water, and the size of the mussel population in Fish Creek.

In contrast, earlier strategic plans had been created more for fund-raising purposes than for setting a clear direction for the organization. I knew we needed concrete goals, objectives, and action plans. The old plans were full of good intentions, not performance measures. They were characterized by phrases like "We need to work more effectively with the local community" or "We should try to influence public land managers to do a better job."

Ultimately, we have to measure our success by the species we save. But in the short term, to find out if we're on the right track, we have to learn what we should be monitoring. As we build our scientific capabilities in the area of stewardship, we learn what measures to take and how to take them. Are the eco-systems we're trying to protect maintaining their functions, for example, in purifying water and maintaining soil? We're trying to develop measures that can answer such questions.
John Sawhill

Clinton are both financial supporters—and you know, we like it that way. I would guess that the only thing all our members could agree on is the importance of the work we do.

In the strategic review, we identified two fundamental strengths that we never want to tamper with. First, our success in fund-raising really stems from the decentralized nature of our organization. Every single one of our operating units has fund-raising responsibility. We have a culture that says if you want to do something, then you have to go out and find the money for it. You can't turn to the development department and say, "Gee, I'd really like to do this great thing—you guys go find the money for me." Being decentralized is also important because people give to people they know. Donors want to get to know members of their community, to build relationships with them, to help them understand what the organization is really about. That's the most powerful fund-raising tool we have.

Second, our market research has shown that people appreciate the Conservancy's positive message. Much environmental activism is based on bad news, which spurs people to action by forcing them to confront unpleasant realities. Our strategy lets us tell people good news. We buy a place or we take some other action that yields positive results. No matter how our strategy changes, those two aspects of our work are the bedrock on which we build.

We're asked to deviate from our mission all the time. Donors say they'll give us more money if we get involved in, for example, population. A few years ago, one of the big foundations offered us several hundred thousand dollars to start a program on population. But that's not what we're good at; it's not an area in which we have expertise. So we said no.

Whenever someone comes to me with a proposal for an exciting new Nature Conservancy project, I ask myself the same question: Given our limited resources and the enormous challenges we face, how will this advance our mission of protecting biodiversity? We often have to say no to projects that, however tantalizing, are tangential to our goals.

Have any organizational changes flowed from the new strategy?

Yes. For years we had the kind of management committee you'd find in almost every organization: a war council composed of the heads of the major units. Its members spent all their time talking about day-to-day operations, and conservation strategy was relegated to the secondary spot. I became dissatisfied with that way of operating; it just didn't give us the right focus on our mission. It is a common problem in organizations that the mundane triumphs over the strategic.

One of the amazing consequences of our strategy shift was that about a year ago the management group voted to disband itself. We were searching for a way to focus on the most advanced thinking in conservation, a way to propel the organization forward on conservation issues. In place of the old structure, we have established a conservation committee, which discusses and debates issues affecting our mission, and an operations committee, which handles administrative issues. We've also made significant changes in the faces around the table. Instead of the old war council, the traditional horizontal slice at the top, we took a vertical slice of the organization for both groups. We now have a mixture of people from throughout the organization, including practitioners from the field, people with dirt under their fingernails. Finally, we created a third entity, a management council, comprising roughly 150 managers from all parts of the organization. That group will meet once a year to review the work done by the conservation and operations committees.

The new structure replaces a tighter management team that had consisted only of senior staff, and it represents a real shift in management philosophy. The early returns are positive. We have been able to hone further our conservation agenda and eliminate layers of bureaucratic review for day-to-day decision making.

Our new conservation strategy demands a high level of creativity from people throughout the organization, and any organization that has grown as we have must guard against bureaucratic tendencies. I don't think you can get people to be more entrepreneurial unless you make them responsible for a piece of the organization and give them control of their own destinies. We can give people in the field a lot of autonomy as long as we have absolute clarity about our mission and our core values.

Usually when we have a successful program it's because the person running it is entrepreneurial and knows how to take advantage of opportunities, mobilize resources, and attract a good board. The success of any program often comes down to the skills, energy, and leadership of the individual heading it. The difference in results between two programs is generally not that we did it one way here and one way there, and that the first way was much better than the second. Usually the difference is that in one case an individual figured out what the community's needs were and developed a program that met those needs.

In our organization, the state director is usually the prime mover. The team obviously plays an important role, but if you don't have a strong leader, it's hard for the team to operate effectively. So we spend a lot of time and care recruiting our state directors. I personally interview all of them before they're hired. What I most want to know about them is how entrepreneurial they are, how creative they are, what new things they're doing.

Has there been much resistance within your organization to the changes you've set in motion?

People in this organization are deeply committed to its mission. They care about it; they think about it all the time. Fundamentally, it's what drives them. There is something about a nonprofit's mission that motivates people by closely aligning personal values with professional values. Maybe there's a lesson here for corporations. When mission comes first, people are more open to change: They accept changes that would probably cause a lot of anxiety if they weren't committed to the larger purpose. We invested an enormous amount of time and energy in the strategy process, and once we got it done, our people generally accepted the changes. They were convinced that the new strategy was the right way to achieve our mission.

What is the most satisfying part of your job?

I tell people I have the best job in America. First, I work with committed, energetic, bright people. Second, I do something that I regard as extremely important. Protecting natural areas and leaving them for future generations is one of the most important things we could possibly do; it's leaving the world a better place than it would otherwise be. So I'm motivated by the significance of the task. A lot of businesspeople think that someday they'll do a stint in government to make their contribution to society. They ought to think about working in a nonprofit instead. Not only will they get a lot more done, but nonprofit work is also much more rewarding than government service. I can say that because I've done both.

—— DISCUSSION QUESTIONS

1. What factors precipitated a change in The Nature Conservancy's strategy?
2. Does the new strategy seem to you to be well-grounded in the reality of the environment?
3. What lessons seem most transferable to any organizational change effort?

INDEX

A. C. Nielson, 150
Abacus Direct, 150–151
Abbey, A., 528
Academic Press
  electronic-content delivery, 107
  selling countrywide license, 107–108
Administrative behavior, pressures for,
  10–18, 20–21
Advent Software, 234
Advisers. *See* Management of advisers
  by small companies
A.H. Robbins, bankruptcy, 464
Albrecht, T. L., 523, 528
Alger, Horatio
  his notion of success, 24, 25
  Ragged Dick, or Street Life in New York,
  23
Allen, Paul, 227
Alsop, Joseph, 69
Altra Energy Technologies, Internet-
  based, 114
Amabile, Teresa M., 521–536
Amazon.com, 101, 103–106, 112, 115
America Online, 343
Amgen, 418, 426
Anderson, Warren, 233
Anderson Soft-Teach, 233
Andrews, F. M., 522, 528

Angel investors, 338, 341, 349
Anheuser-Busch, competing with
  Miller, 483
Apple Computer, 215, 232, 355, 356
  development of the Newton, 519
  late entry of portable computer,
  506
  lessons learned from Apple I, 517
"Arbitrage" businesses, 152
Argenti, John, 463
Ashford, S. J., 527
ASK Computer Systems, 147
AST Research, 234
Automotive Caliper Exchange, 235, 236

Bagley, Connie, 262–303, 404–440
Bailyn, L., 522, 528
Bain Capital, investment in Staples,
  171–172
Bankruptcy
  alternatives to, 459–460
  asbestos cases, 464
  Bankruptcy Code, 459–475
  bankruptcy law, an overview, 460–461
  bibliography, 476–477
  business bankruptcy, causes, 463–464
  Chapter 11: reorganization, 469–471
  Chapter 7: liquidation, 466–469

Bankruptcy (*continued*)
  Chapter 13: for individuals with regular income, 471–473
  choosing a chapter, 465–466
  debtor's options, 475–476
  filing for bankruptcy, 464–465
  getting into trouble, 461–464
  individual bankruptcy, causes, 461–463
  involuntary bankruptcy, 464–465, 475
  National Bankruptcy Review Commission, 461
  negotiations and settlements, 473–475
  powers of a trustee, 473
Barnes & Noble, 105, 112
Barrickman, Ray, 463
Beauty contest, in an IPO, 410–411
Behavioral theory of entrepreneurship. *See* Entrepreneurial behavior
BellSouth, 31
Bhidé, Amar, 65–79, 80–93, 94–100, 121–137, 211–222, 223–237, 392–403
Biotechnology industry, 145
Block, Zenas and Ian C. MacMillan, *Corporate Venturing*, 502
Blockbuster Video, 75, 78
Blue Sky laws, 419
Board of directors. *See also* Serving on public boards
  responsibilities in a public company, 436–437, 442
  seats for venture capitalists, 286–287
Bohdan Associates, 232
Bookman, Phil, 235
Bootstrap finance. *See also* Start-up strategies
  abandoning the rules, 236–237
  bank relationship, 235
  finding quick break-even projects, 230–231
  flying on empty, 229–235
  focus on cash, 234–235
  getting operational, 229–230
  hidden costs of others' money, 227–229
  hiring employees, 232–233
  interviews from *Inc.* "500" list, 224, 225
  keeping growth in check, 233–234
  overcoming customer inertia, 231–232
  poor fit between entrepreneur and investor, 226–227
  use of direct personal selling, 231–232
Borland International, 81, 83, 84, 86–87
Boston Scientific, 406
Bower, Joseph L., 150, 506–520
Bower, Marvin, 78, 401
Brostoff, George, 227, 232
Brown, L. L., 523
Brown, W. B., 527–528
Bucyrus-Erie, loss of mechanical-excavator market, 506–507, 509
Budget Gourmet, 489
Buffet, Warren, 151
Business plans
  addressing investors' needs, 182–185
  attributes of great businesses, 141–142
  case of Internet Wicked Ale, 138–139, 143
  cash flow implications, 148, 153–157
  common pitfalls, 267
  contextual factors, 140, 159–160
  the deal, 140, 160–166. *See also* Entrepreneurial process and deals
  the development stage, 184
  discovering the market's interest, 179–181
  documenting claims: marketing research, 181–182
  due diligence, 171–172, 268
  dynamic fit management, 141–142, 175
  emphasizing the market, 178–182
  exit options, 168
  financial projections, 169–171
  importance of packaging, 186
  integration, or fit, 140, 174
  issues to be addressed, 147
  issue of cashing out, 183
  making sound projections, 183–184
  the opportunity, 140, 144–158. *See also* Opportunity in a venture
  the people, 140, 142–144, 267
  personalizing the effort, 173
  price and projected worth, 185
  proformas in, 169–171

questions the plan must answer, 142, 172
risk/reward management, 166–169, 172–173
showing the user's benefit, 179
translation glossary for, 176

Canion, Rod, 229
Canon, the personal copier, 500, 506
Cantillion, Richard, 2, 8
Carnegie, Andrew, 25
Cash flow, 148, 153–157, 242–243, 305–306
    accounting income *vs.* free cash flow, 239
    allocation of, 307
    cash and growth, 240–241
Cash flow analysis, 205
Cashing out, 183
Charles Stewart Mott Foundation, 564
Christensen, Clayton, 150, 506–520
Chrysler Corporation, 252
Cisco Systems, 104, 146, 343–344
CNET, 107
Coastal Corporation, 85
Coca-Cola
    competing with Pepsi, 483
    idea for pushing Tab, 491
    protection of recipe as trade secret, 332
    protection of trademark, 331
Collective entrepreneurship, 23–34
    and changing organizational structure, 30–31
    dangers of the hero myth, 27–28
    heroes and drones, 24–27
    implications for managers and workers, 33
    and new economic paradigm, 28–31
    the team as hero, 31–33
    working relationships in, 29–31
Commercialization skills, importance of, 151–152
Common Ground project, 562
Compaq, 104–105, 234, 343
    formation of, 146, 229
Competition, 152–153
    avoidance of, 544–545, 549

considered in business plan, 153
    in disk drive business, 54–55, 145
CompUSA, 106
Computer Media Technology, 232
Conner Peripherals, 3.5-inch drives, 513–514
Conservation Company, 562
Conti, R., 530, 531
Contingent claims analysis, 315
Continuity of interest rule, 407
Control Data Corporation (CDC), 46
    acquisition by Seagate, 514
    skunk-works development of 5.25-inch drive, 519
Conversion price, 279
Cook, Paul M., 537–552. *See also* Raychem Corporation
Coon, H., 530
Cooperative Home Care Associates (CHCA), 564
Cornish, Brian, 235
Cozzens, M. D., 523, 527–528
Cray, Seymour, 355
Cray Computer, 355, 490
Creativity. *See* Managing for creativity
Crown Cork & Seal, 487
Culture, organizational, 75, 77, 393, 395–397
Cummings, L. L., 526–527
Cummins Engine, and the need to innovate, 483

Daisy, 355
Data General Corporation, Eagle supermini computer, 522
Dauchy, Craig, 262–303, 404–440
Da Vinci Systems Corporation, 78
Davis, Tom, 227, 231
Dees, J. Gregory, 566–579
Delbecq, A. L., 522, 526–527
Dell, Michael, 72, 227
Dell Computer, 72, 104–105, 234
Demetriou, E., 523
Dewar, R., 526
Diasonics, 355
Dickerson, Thomas, 77
Dickson, J. W., 528
DiMarco, Stephanie, 233–234

Discounted cash flow (DCF), 123
Discount rate, calculation of, 245–246
Discovery-driven planning, 493–505
    designating a keeper of assumptions,
        505
    as a discipline for learning, 505
    an illustrative case: Kao Corporation,
        496–505. *See also* Kao Corporation
    key assumptions checklist, 497,
        501–502
    milestone planning, 497, 502–505
    vs. platform-based planning,
        493–494
    pro forma operations specs, 496,
        499–501
    reverse income statement, 496,
        498–499
Disk drive industry, 133, 149. *See also*
    Seagate Technology; Winchester
    disk drives
    disruptive technologies in, 508–514,
        516, 518, 520
    effects of shrinking drive diameters,
        509–510, 518
    intense competition, 54–55, 145
    opportunity traps, 151
    performance *vs.* market needs, graph,
        511
    as "wave" industry, 155–156
Doerr, John, 161
Doriot, Georges F., 146
Dow Corning Corp., bankruptcy, 464
Down-priced financing, 283
Drucker, Peter, 581
Due diligence, 272
    in an IPO, 415–416
    and business plans, 171–172, 268
Dynamic analysis, of start-ups, 122
Dysan Corporation, 48

Eaglebrook Plastics, 229–230
Eagle-Picher Industries, bankruptcy, 464
Ekvall, G., 528
Entrepreneur, the
    profile of, 95, 126
    reputation as gambler, 12
    as risk-taker, 94
    stereotype of, 15–17

Entrepreneurial behavior, 9–19
    vs. administrative behavior, 10–18,
        20–21
    and commitment to opportunity,
        12–13
    and commitment of resources, 13–15
    and control of resources, 15–17
    and management structure, 17
    pressures for, 10–18, 20–21
    and reward philosophy, 18
    and strategic orientation, 10–12
Entrepreneurial career, the, 94–100
    vs. the alternative, 95–96
    as an available option, 94–95
    constraints of low initial capital,
        97–98
    knowing one's goals, 99–100
    learning to sell, the challenges, 98–99
    and low personal overhead, 98
    making major changes, 99
    the rewards, 95
    rules for evaluating opportunities,
        96–97
    to wait or not to wait, 96
Entrepreneurial hero, the myth, 24–25
    vs. collective entrepreneurship, 28, 32
    dangers of, 27–28, 32
Entrepreneurial process and deals
    amount of capital to be raised, 162
    characteristics of sensible deals,
        165
    choosing a venture capitalist, 160–161
    deal structure: valuation and terms,
        163–166
    staging of capital commitment,
        162–164
Entrepreneurship, 7–22
    as a behavioral phenomenon. *See*
        Entrepreneurial behavior
    defined, 1, 2, 8–9, 10
    increasing interest in, 1, 7–8
    and innovation. *See* Innovation
    in nonprofit sector, 553–593
    and risk. *See* Risk
Environmental protection. *See* Nature
    Conservancy, The
Ethics. *See* Honesty
Ettlie, J. E., 527

Euro Disney (Disneyland Paris)
    miscalculations about revenue
        sources, 494–495
    platform-based planning at, 494–496
Excite, 112
Exit strategies, 72, 168, 207
Exxon, *Valdez* disaster, 81

Family Service America, 563
Farris, G. F., 522, 528
Federal Express, 126, 132, 164, 394
    losses with Zapmail, 493
FemRx, 265
Ferguson, Bruce, 173
Fidelity Funds, 490
Fields, Randy and Debbi, 76
Financial contracting in venture capital,
        304–325
    allocating cash flow, 307
    allocating risks: common *vs.* pre-
        ferred stock, 307–310
    anticipating consequences of financ-
        ing decisions, 319–323
    application to dealmaking, 316–317
    dealmaking in real world, 306–307
    example of a bad deal, 321–323
    first principles, 304–319
    option to increase capital committed,
        318–319
    option to revalue a project, 317–318
    a simple example, 305–306
    staged capital commitment, 311–313,
        316–317, 323. *See also* Staged capital
        commitment
    value of option to abandon, 313–317
Financial flexibility, value of, 259–260
Financial performance evaluation, 240
Financial projections, 169–171, 183–184
Financing decisions and value creation,
        252–254
First Main Capital Corp., 195
Flexible pricing, 318
Floppy disks. *See* Kao Corporation
Ford, Henry, 25
Ford, Henry, II, 26
Foundation Grants Index, 562
Foundations learning from venture capi-
        talists, 555–565

Free cash flow, defined, 239
Fruhan, Bill, 304
Fuel Tech, 152
Full ratchet antidilution protection,
        281–283

Gammalink, 224, 226, 228
Gates, Bill, 78, 131, 173, 227, 397, 401
Gateway Design Automation, 232
GE Fund's College Bound initiative, 561
General Electric, buying via Internet,
        104–105
General Motors, and United Auto Work-
        ers, 33
General Motors–Toyota joint venture,
        31
Geneva Business Services, 194–195
Genstar Capital, 406
Georgia-Pacific Corporation, work with
        the Nature Conservancy, 587–588
Ghosh, Shikhar, 101–115
Gilder, George, 27
Gillette, 151
Goel, Prabhu, 231
Going public, 404–440
    board composition, 428–429
    the closing, 421
    confidential treatment of material
        agreements, 418
    determining stock price and offering
        size, 416–418
    disadvantages of, 405–406
    due diligence, 415–416
    exchanges, Nasdaq, Blue Sky laws,
        418–419
    insider trading, 431–434
    the IPO process, 408–421
    IPO *vs.* sale of company, 406–407
    the prospectus, 408–409, 423–426
    publicity, 426–427
    reasons for, 404–405
    registration statement, 408, 411
    responsibilities of public company
        and board, 429–437
    restricted stock and rule 144, 422–423
    restrictions on sales of shares, 421–423
    the road show, 288, 408–409, 419–420,
        427

Going public (*continued*)
  role of company counsel, 413–414,
    419, 427
  role of SEC, 408–409, 411, 415–440
  sample case study, 437–440
  SEC comments, 420
  selecting the managing underwriters,
    409–411
  timing, 411, 412
Gore Associates, 371
Greenwood, John, 233
Grosshandler, Robert, 230
Grossman, Allen, 555–565
Growing enterprise, the, managing tran-
    sitions in, 377–391. *See also* Growth,
    the challenges
  applying management modes to re-
    sponsibilities, 379–381
  issues of time, 377–378, 384
  managing behavior, 383–384, 385
  managing content, 381–383
  managing context, 386–387
  managing oneself: when to change,
    388–390
  managing results, 384–386
  modes of management, 377–381
  transitions between modes of manage-
    ment, 388
Growth, the challenges, 361–376. *See
    also* Growing enterprise, the, man-
    aging transitions in
  the anticipating-acting-reviewing
    cycle, 368–371
  changes happening at the firm,
    361–362
  defining the manager's job, 362–364
  effect of growth on fit, 373–375
  the fit among manager's responsibili-
    ties, 364–367
  the impact of growth, 371–373
  the issue of time, 372, 375
  the manager's tools, 368–371
Gryskiewicz, S., 522–523, 526–528, 531
Gumpert, David E., 177–188

Hage, J., 526
Hall, 523, 528

Ham and egging, 219
Haney, William, 152
Harriman, Edward, 25
Harris, Jim, 229
Hart, Myra, 143–144
Harvesting, of value created, 167–168,
    320
Hasbro, 485, 486–487
Havelock, R. G., 526
Heinz, risk taking at, 483
Herron, M., 530
Hewlett, William, 79
Hinton, Kevin, 225
Honesty, 80–93
  case of department stores, 83–84, 89
  case of Philippe Kahn and *BYTE*
    magazine, 81–83
  case of Rick Pitino, 82–85
  and cognitive inertia, 84–85, 87
  economic value of trustworthiness,
    90–91
  limits of retaliation, 87–88
  moral and social motives, 90–91
  overlooking past lapses, 86–87, 92
  power as substitute for trust, 83–84, 87
  the protection of trustworthiness,
    88–89
  reliance on ambiguity, 85–86
  taking people at face value, 86
  tolerance and risk taking, 92
  trust in the marketplace, 80–81, 89–90
Howard, Alice, 580–593
Huizenga, H. Wayne, 78
Hutton, E.F., 81

Iacocca, Lido, 26, 31
IBM, 483
  acquisition of Tivoli Systems, 344
  Infomart, 108
  loss of minicomputer market, 506–507
  success as "second" in PC market, 517
  as tough buyer, 54
  Winchester disk drives, 46, 145
  World Avenue, 108
Immulogic, 223
Inc. magazine, 81, 149, 196
  the *Inc.* "500" interviews, 95, 99, 224

Ingram Micro, 106
Innovation
  avoiding competition, proprietary
    products, 544–545, 549
  commitment to core technologies,
    542–543
  comparing business system with com-
    petitor's, 489–490
  critical mass of different skills, 549
  deep understanding of customers'
    needs, 544–546
  defining a strategic focus, 486–487
  discovering unique strengths, 552
  in entrepreneurship, 8, 125
  expecting, 538
  finding and leveraging good ideas,
    487–490
  finding the right people, 541
  focusing on a particular competitor,
    483–484
  "go for broke" with new ideas,
    490–492
  inborn nature of creativity, 541
  individual recognition as motivator,
    541–542
  innovation as global game, 549, 552
  innovative leaders, 482–483
  key elements for innovation, 485
  and major shift in values, 482–484
  mastering the drudgery, 539–540
  need to "obsolete" successful prod-
    ucts, 546–547, 550
  need for patient capital, 548–549
  Paul Cook on, 537–552
  pressure as stimulant for creativity,
    539
  risk taking, 482, 484
  segmenting markets differently,
    488–489
  size as enemy of, 546–547, 551
  unsettling the organization, 484–485
Insider Trading and Securities Fraud En-
    forcement Act of 1988, 432
InsWeb, as industry magnet, 113–114
Intel, 343, 355
  transition from DRAM to microproc-
    essors, 518–519

Intellectual property, legal protection of,
    145, 326–334
  "common law" principles, 327
  complexity and evolution of, 326–327
  confidential business information, 332
  copyrights, 330
  employees' rights: reasonableness
    test, 333
  patents, 327–330. See also Patent
  at Raychem Corporation, 549
  Title 17-Copyrights, 327
  Title 35-Patents, 327
  trademarks, service marks, trade
    dress, 330–331
  trade secrets, 331–332
International Memories, 47
Internet, business opportunities,
    101–115
  advantages of moving first, 104–105
  building direct links to customers,
    102–105
  business model magnets, 114–115
  creating a customer magnet, 110–115
  customer segment magnets, 113
  digital value creation, 108–110
  industry magnets, 113–114
  inexpensive service, 103–104
  level of service, 102
  need to develop new skills, 108
  personalizing the service, 102–103
  pirating the value chain, 105–108
  product magnets, 112
  protecting existing value chains,
    105
  service magnets, 112–113
Internet Profiles, 150
Intrepreneurship, 8
Intuit, 394
  investment in technical support, 74
  Quicken, 72, 74, 149
Inventions agreements, 301
Iomega, Zip Drives, 151
IPO (initial public offering). See Going
    public

Jobs, Steven, 26, 91, 130, 211, 232, 355
Johnson & Johnson, 485

Kaemmerer, W. F., 526, 528
Kahn, Philippe, 81, 87
Kakacek, Keith, 235
Kanter, R. M., 522, 526–527
Kao Corporation
  the company, 497
  discovery-driven planning at,
    496–505
  key assumptions checklist, 497,
    501–502
  the market for floppy disks, 497–498
  milestone planning, 502–505
  pro forma operations specs, 496,
    499–501
  reverse income statement, 496,
    498–499
  revised reverse income statement,
    501, 503
Kapor, Mitch, 224, 227
Kent, 9
Khosla, Vinod, 70
Kidder, Tracy, *The Soul of a New
  Machine*, 24, 522
Kimberley, J. R., 526
King, N., 528
Kleiner Perkins, 343, 394
Kresch, Arnold, 265
Kroc, Ray, 92
Kurtzig, Sandra, 147–148

Land, Edwin, 517
Lazenby, J., 530
Letts, Christine W., 555–565
Lincoln Electric, as great innovator,
  481–482, 490
Liquidation
  in bankruptcy, 466–469
  preference, as right of preferred
    stock, 274–276, 289, 295
Liquidity, and going public, 405
Lotus, 224, 227, 394
Lutz, Michael, 224, 226, 228
Lycos, 112
Lynch, Peter, 146

McCown DeLeeuw & Company, 406
McFadden, M., 523

McGrath, Rita Gunther, 493–505
McKinsey & Company, 78, 401
MacMillan, Ian C., 493–505
Magazine publishing business
  cash flow in, 148–149, 154
  economic drivers in, 170
Magretta, Joan, 580–593
Management of advisers by small com-
    panies, 450–458
  the changing world of advisers, 452
  getting advice early enough, 456–457
  the human touch, 457–458
  managing outside advice suppliers,
    453–458
  need for skepticism, 455–456
  a network of specialists, 453
Management by objective, 384
Managing for creativity, 521–536. *See
    also* Innovation
  assessing the climate for creativity:
    KEYS questionnaire, 528–531
  assessing work outcomes, 530
  bibliography, 534
  components of organizational creativ-
    ity and innovation, 526–528
  critical-incident technique: research
    tool, 523
  the delicate balance in, 531–534
  environmental obstacles to creativity,
    523–526, 529–530
  environmental stimulants to creativ-
    ity, 523–525, 529
  evaluation, 532
  goal setting, 532
  influence of social environment,
    521–522
  intrinsic and extrinsic motivators,
    531–532
  managing the unmanageable, 534
  during period of rapid transition, 531
  personal qualities and motivation, 524
  rewards, 533
  role of communication, 523, 531
  and source or level of pressure,
    533–534
  strategies that promote innovation,
    522

Managing transitions in the growing enterprise. *See* Growing enterprise, the, managing transitions in
Manville Corporation, bankruptcy, 464
Marshall Industries, 102
Matthias, Rebecca, 71
MCI Communications, 152
Memorex, 46–47
Mezzanine stage, round, 266, 283
MicroAge, 106
Micron Separations, 233
Microsoft, 78, 227, 343, 394, 397, 401
Milestones
  in discovery-driven planning, 497, 502–505
  as a right of preferred stock, 287–288
Miller, competing with Anheuser-Busch, 483
Mills, P. K., 522, 526–527
Mineck, John, 231, 236
Miniscribe, 47, 55
MIT Enterprise Forum, 178–181, 183–184, 187
Modular Instruments, 227, 231
Molten Metals, 152
Monge, P. R., 523, 527–528
Mothers Work, 71
Mrs. Fields Cookies, 76
Multiples analysis, 205
Murto, Bill, 229

Nabisco, 490
NAC, 230
National Association of Securities Dealers (NASD), 414
National Communications Sales Promotion, 236
National Federation of Independent Business, study of start-ups, 122–123
National Venture Capital Association, 339
Nation-List Network of Business Brokers, 195
Nature Conservancy, The, 580–593
  bog turtles at Schenob Brook, 581–582

Endangered Species Act, 586
  interview with John Sawhill, 580–593
  Last Great Places, 583, 584
  role in mitigation agreements, 587–588
  surviving success, 581–582
  Virginia Coast Reserve project, 584–585
NECX, 114
Netscape Communications, 109, 343, 418
New American Schools (NAS), 562–563
NeXT, 232
Nonprofit entrepreneurship, 566–579
  alternatives to nonprofit status, 576–578
  attracting and motivating people, 572–574
  bibliography, 578
  charitable *vs.* non-charitable nonprofits, 567, 569–570
  compensation issues, 573–574
  dealing with volunteers, 575–576
  defining and measuring success, 572
  defining a "nonprofit," 567–568
  growth and diversity of, 567–568
  management challenges of, 571–576
  managerial control and autonomy, 575–576
  mission and strategic flexibility, 575–576
  the nondistribution constraint, 567–568
  personal and economic sides of, 566
  raising funds, 574–575
  tax treatment and government regulation, 568–571
  the value of nonprofits, 578
Nonprofit sector, 553–593. *See also* Nature Conservancy, The
Norris, Ron, 235
Nussey, Bill, 78

Oberfield, Alice, 566–579
Onsale, 114
Opportunity in a venture, 140, 144–158
  and "arbitrage" businesses, 152

Opportunity in a venture (*continued*)
  assessing market potential, 144
  and competition, 152–153
  entrepreneur's commitment to, 12–13
  graphical analysis tools for assessment of, 153–158
  opportunity traps, 151
  rules for evaluation of, 96–97
Options
  incentive stock options (ISOs), 291–292
  option to abandon, 313–317
  option to increase capital committed, 318–319
  option pricing theory, 315
  option to revalue a project, 317–318
  options and values, 256–259
Orbital Sciences Corporation, 173
O'Reilly, Tony, 483
Organizational infrastructure, investing in, 76
  hard and soft infrastructure, 75
Orpen, C, 522, 526
Oscor Medical Corporation, 235

Packard, David, 79
Palevsky, Max, 356
Paolillo, J. G., 527–528
Patel, Raju, 230
Patent
  the concept of, 328
  design patents, requirements, 329–330
  patent court system, 328
  Patent Gazette, 328, 329
  plant patents, 330
  types of, 327–330
  U.S. Patent and Trademark Office, 327
  utility patents, requirements, 328–329
Pay-to-play provision, 285
Pearson, Andrall E., 481–492
Pelz, D. C., 522, 528
Pemberton, Robert, 231
Pepsi, PepsiCo
  acquisition of Taco Bell, 484
  competing with Coke, 483
  menu changes at Taco Bell, 488
  successes with borrowed ideas, 488
Performance trajectories, 509

Perot, Ross, 224
Personal computers
  catching up with minicomputers, 508
  sales via Internet, 106
Philip Morris, acquisition of 7-Up, 490
Physician Sales & Service (PSS), 77
Pipeline model, 149–150
Piper Aircraft, bankruptcy, 464
Pitino, Rick, 82–85
Pizza Hut, innovation for lunch, 489–490, 491
Platform-based planning
  common planning errors of, 496
  vs. discovery-driven planning, 493–494
  at Euro Disney, 494–496
Pochop, Laura, 225
Polaroid, 493, 517
Porter, Jim, 46, 60
Post-money valuation, 269, 277, 311
Practice Management Systems, 231, 236
Pratt's Guide to Venture Capital, 266
Preemptive right, 280–281
Preferred stock, rights of, 272–290, 308–310
  conversion rights, 279–280, 295
  co-sale rights, 290, 301–302
  information rights, 289–290, 297–298
  redemption rights, 277–279, 296
  registration rights, 280, 288–289, 298–300
  voting rights, 285–287, 296
Pre-money valuation, 269
Priam Corporation, 46–47
Princeton Review, 236
Procter & Gamble, 485, 490
Progress Software Corporation, 69
Projection discount factor, 184–185
Promoter, the, 10–18, 20–21
Protective provisions, 285–286
Public float, 288
Purchase agreement, 301
Purchasing a business, 189–208
  adding value, 207
  business screening analyses, 200–202
  caution on recast financial statements, 205–206
  deal criteria, 192–193

the deal process, 199–204
deal sources, 193–197
defining target company profile, 192
the evaluation process, 204–206
financing structure, 206
negotiating the deal, 206–207
the preliminary meeting, 202
resources: cash, credibility, contacts,
  197–199
selecting a business lawyer, 198–199,
  204
self-assessment, as tactical process,
  191–192
timing issues, 199
understanding "seller's psychology,"
  203–204
using business brokers, 194–195

Quantum, 341, 514

Ratchet, 281–283, 323
Rathman, George, 426
Raychem Corporation
  the company, 537–538
  the products, 537–538
  Raynet fiber-optics subsidiary, 548–551
  selective partnerships, 542
  SuperSleeve splice-closure technol-
    ogy, 546–547
  work on shape-memory alloys, 540,
    548
"Razors and razor blades" strategy, 151
Redemption price, 279
The Red Herring, 266
Red herring, in an IPO, 408, 417
Registration rights, 280, 288–289,
  298–300
Reich, Robert B., 23–34
Resources
  commitment of, in a venture, 13–15
  control of, in a venture, 15–17
  required for purchasing a business,
    197–199
Rich, Stanley R., 177–188
Right of first refusal, 280–281, 300
Risk, 2, 9, 12, 211, 243–249
  allocation: common vs. preferred
    stock, 307–310

and commitment of resources, 13–15
definitions of, 244
discout rates, benchmarks, and,
  245–246
as factor in performance evaluation,
  248
investment in risk reduction, 247
level of risk at each stage, 312
measurement of, 244–245
and need for diversification, 244–245,
  247
risk management, 247, 259, 557
and rules of the game, 248–249
systematic risk, defined, 245
and time, 247
Risk/reward ratio, 141–142
  in analysis of opportunity, 153
  in financial contracting, 320
  graphical analysis of, 156–158
  risk/reward management, 166–169
Rizzo, William, 237
Rizzo Associates, 237
The road show, in an IPO, 288, 408–409,
  419–420, 427
Roberts, Michael J., 78, 189–208,
  326–334, 361–376, 377–391, 459–477
Robin Hood Foundation, 561
Robinson, S. E., 523
Rock, Arthur, 144, 147, 161, 216, 226,
  351–358
Rockefeller, John D., 25
Rodriguez, 236
Rosen, Ben, 146, 229
Rosen, Edward, 72
Roth, S. L., 523
RoweCom, Internet subscription agent,
  107
Rule 144, 343, 422–423
Russel, Carol, 232
Russell, C. J., 526
Russell, R. D., 526
Russel Personnel Services, 232
Ryan, William, 555–565

Sahlman, William A., 35–64, 138–176,
  238–261, 304–325, 335–350,
  441–449, 450–458
Savage, T. George, 265

Sawhill, John, 580–593
Say, Jean Baptiste, 8
Schroeder, William, 46
Schumpeter, Joseph, 2, 8, 537
Science Technology, 162
Sculley, John, 356
Seagate Technology, 37, 47–48, 52, 106, 341
  acquisition of Control Data, 514
  facing "disruptive" 3.5-inch drives, 512–514, 516, 518
  staying too close to customers, 513, 518
Securities and Exchange Commission (SEC)
  role in an IPO, 408–409, 411, 415–440
Securities Exchange Act of 1934 (the 1934 Act), 419, 431, 433, 435
Self-sustaining firm, the
  and audacity of entrepreneurs, 400
  balance of vision and pragmatism, 401
  building, 392–403
  the external dimension and structural advantages, 393, 395–399
  goals and capabilities of founders, 397–398
  and imagination of entrepreneurs, 401
  implications of idiosyncratic development, 397–398
  the internal dimension and corporate culture, 393, 395–397, 399
  and managing growth, 393
  many destinations and paths, 394–397
  multidimensional options, 398
  the rewards, 392
  the roles of founders, 396–397, 399
Sensitivity analysis, 250–251, 339
Serving on public boards, 441–449
  assessing the risks, 444–446
  changes needed to attract good directors, 446–448
  the decision not to serve, 446–447
  negative economics of, 441–442
  the potential rewards, 444
  questions raised by the invitation, 443–444
  responsibility and legal requirements, 442–443
  risks of frivolous law suits, 442, 443, 445–448
  vs. serving on private boards, 447
Sevin, L. J., 146, 161
Shugart, Alan, 47–48
Sideways deal, 277
Siegel, S. M., 526, 528
Silton-Bookman, 235
Singleton, Henry, 356
SIR Lloyds, 235
Skloot, Edward, 556
Sloan, Alfred, 355
Small business, defined, 471
"Smart money" vs. "dumb money," 264
Smith, Fred, 126
Snap-on Tools, 109
Softa, 230
Software 2000, 231
Sprout Capital, 265
Staged capital commitment, 311–313
  and "burn rate," "fume date," 316–317
  and retaining option to abandon, 313, 316–317
  and right to revalue a project, 313, 317–318
  valuation at each stage, 311–312
Stages of company development, 266, 355
Stakeholders
  attracting, 211–222
  the challenge of attracting, 211–212
  convincing, 218–221
  cultivating risk seekers, 218
  customer investment, 213–214
  diversification and risk tolerance, 215–216
  experienced and specialized, 216–217
  ham and egging, 219
  minimizing stakeholder exposure, 213–215
  necessary entrepreneurial attributes, 218–219
  offering trade-offs, 214–215
  reducing risks, 213–214, 217
  and sales closing skills, 219–221
  selecting, 215–218
  with excess capacity, 217
  value of "bell cows," 216–217, 219

Standard & Poor's Corporation, 109
Staples
    Bain Capital investment in, 171–172
    customized catalogs on Internet, 103
    founding of, 146
Start-up strategies, 121–137. *See also*
        Bootstrap finance
    assessing viability and attractiveness,
        122–124
    and capacity for execution, 125–128,
        130
    and creativity of basic concept, 125
    evangelical investigation, 136
    flexible perseverance, 136–137
    integrating action and analysis, 121,
        134–137
    for niche businesses, 126–127, 129, 133
    parsimonious planning and analysis,
        131–134
    and personal preferences, 128–130
    pitfalls avoided, 130–131
    plugging holes quickly, 136
    for propagators of emerging prod-
        ucts, 127, 129, 133
    for revolutionary ventures, 126,
        128–129, 132–133
    screening out losers, 124–131
    for speculative ventures, 128,
        129–130, 134
    staging analytical tasks, 135
    for ventures based on hustle,
        127–128, 129, 134
Stemberg, Tom, 146, 171–172
Stephens, Andrew, 229
Stevenson, Howard H., 7–22, 35–64,
        80–93, 161, 167, 211–222, 225, 339,
        450–458, 459–477
Storage Technology Corporation, 46, 454
S-3 rights, 288, 299
Sun Microsystems, 70, 131, 133, 394
Surdna Foundation, 556
"Sweat equity," 276
Symplex Communications, 227, 232

Tandon, 47–48
Taylor, William, 537–552
Team, as hero. *See* Collective en-
    trepreneurship

Technologies, disruptive, 506–520
    being "second to invent," 517
    case of disk-drive industry, 508–514.
        See also Disk drive industry; Sea-
        gate Technology
    characteristics of, 508
    and company's investment processes,
        512
    defining strategic significance of,
        515–516
    and emergence of new markets,
        509–512
    evaluating technological innovation,
        510–511, 512
    identification and cultivation of,
        514–520
    keeping the disruptive organization
        separate, 519–520
    locating initial market for, 516–518
    and performance trajectories, 509
    peril of staying close to current cus-
        tomers, 506–508, 512
    a skunk-works approach to, 518–519
    vs. sustaining technologies, 514–515
Teledyne, 355–356
Teramo, Clay, 232
Thomas, Franklin, 556
Thompson, Andrew, 265
Thompson, Bob, 229
Thompson, David, 173
Time Warner, Pathfinder Internet site, 103
Tripod, 113
Trust, in the marketplace, 80–81, 89–90.
        See also Honesty
Trustee, the, 10–18, 20–21, 134

Ueberroth, Peter, 26
United Parcel Service, Internet service
        for virtual merchants, 106–107
UNR Industries, bankruptcy, 464
Upside, 266
U.S. Army, emphasis on teams, 31
U.S. Venture Partners, 265

Valentine, Don, 146
Valuation of a venture, 165–166, 269–272
    case of purchasing a business, 204–206
    at each stage, 311–313

Value
  and the financial perspective,
    249–260
  and financial transactions, 304–305
  and financing terms of a deal, 305, 324
  and interaction of cash and risk, 249,
    304
Venture, 196
Venture capital industry
  competitive dynamics of, 340,
    342–343
  cyclical nature of, 336, 344–345
  decline of available funds, 1984, 55
  factors making funds available, 48,
    337
  recent boom in, 335–336, 344
  structural analysis of, 341–342
Venture capital (VC), 262–303
  board of directors, 286–287, 297
  and the business plan, 266–267. *See
    also* Business plans
  a case study, 292–293
  current level of investment, 262
  determining the valuation, 269–272
  and foundations, 555–565
  and future stock issuances, 271
  and key-person insurance, 302
  and options, 291–292
  other protective arrangements,
    290–292
  pros and cons of using VC, 263–264
  and rights of preferred stock,
    272–290, 308–310. *See also* Preferred
    stock, rights of
  sample term sheet for, 294–302
  selecting a venture capitalist, 266–269
  strategies for finding VC, 264–266
  and vesting schedule, 290–291, 301
Venture capitalist, 351–358
  and desire to build a great company,
    352–353, 357
  and entrepreneur's ability to delegate,
    355
  and entrepreneur's acceptance of ad-
    vice, 354–355
  and entrepreneur's appreciation of
    strong management, 355–356

  evaluating people in a venture,
    351–353
  need for tough accounting depart-
    ment, 352
  strategy *vs.* tactics, 351–358
Venture Economics, 59, 226, 336
Venture Graphics, 234
VentureOne, 262
Vertex Peripherals, 48
Vesting schedule, 290–291, 301
VR Business Brokers, 194
Vydec, 72

Wal-Mart Stores, 79
Walt Disney Company
  losses at European theme park, 493.
    See also Euro Disney
  work with the Nature Conservancy
    in Florida, 587
Walton, Ennis J., 189–208
Walton, Sam, 79
Waste Management, 78
Watson, Thomas, 91, 355
Webster, Scott, 173
Weighted average antidilution, 283–285
Welch, Jack, 544
West, M. A., 528
West Coast Venture Capital, 266
Wilson, Al, 46
Wilson Sting, marketing idea for, 491
Winchester disk drives
  investment by public capital markets,
    35, 48–49, 52
  investment by venture capital firms,
    35–36, 47–49, 52, 341
  and the IPO market, 48–51, 53
  period of explosive growth, 37, 47,
    52–53
  research and development, 58–59
  rising industry forecasts, 1978–1987,
    42–43, 46
  sales, profits, and margins data, 44–45
  and shake-out in computer industry,
    54, 57
  stock prices and valuation levels,
    38–39, 52, 60
  technological issues, 53, 56

WordPerfect, 234, 394
Wozniak, Steve, 216, 355
W.T. Grimm & Co., 195
Wyatt, Oscar, 85

Xerox, loss of small-copier market to
    Canon, 506–507

Yahoo!, 101, 107, 112–113, 115
Yamaji, Keizo, 500

Zacharkiw, Peter, 233
Zak, Fred, 234
Zaleznik, Abraham, 78